Evaluation Guide for *Focus*

Focus on Physical Science presents the most m
ical science. Recent developments and basic ideas
order to make your students' study of physical sci
Many features have been included to strengthen the presentation of the textual material with the intent of increasing your students' understanding and interest in physical science.

To examine the features of ***Focus on Physical Science*** please turn to the following pages:

(pp. 2-3)	A two-page **unit opening** collage provides a visual and textual introduction to each of the seven units.
(p. 23)	A **color photo** and **thought-provoking paragraph** introduce each chapter.
(p. 45)	A **Goal** statement at the beginning of each chapter lets the students know what they are expected to learn from the chapter.
(pp. 90-91)	**Diagrams,** along with **photographs** and **line drawings,** help students visualize ideas presented in the text.
(pp. 106-107)	**Student questions** printed in the margins guide students' thinking while reading and reviewing.
(p. 144)	**Activities** immediately reinforce scientific principles. Drawings accompany most of the activities to help students prepare laboratory materials.
(p. 107)	**New terms** are presented in boldfaced type, defined in context, and often spelled phonetically.
(pp.208, 270, 322)	**Focus Pages, People • Careers • Frontiers** present new developments and current information in physical science.
(p. 384)	**Focus on Skills** pages present additional aids geared toward reading comprehension.
(pp. 404-407)	Photo essays, **In Focus,** present additional relevant information concerning physical science and technology.
(p. 422)	**Tables** appear within the context of related material.
(p. 423)	**Example problems** are presented to guide students through the mathematical concepts needed for physical science calculations.
(p. 427)	**Making Sure** questions and problems are presented at the end of sections to reinforce the preceding material.
(pp. 447-449)	A summary of **Points to Remember,** a variety of **Questions for Review,** suggestions for **More Ideas to Explore** and **Readings to Discover** appear at the end of each chapter.
(pp. 496-509)	The **Appendices** include supplementary information on SI measurement, laboratory techniques, and laboratory safety.
(pp. 512-521)	The **Glossary** includes all important terms used throughout the text.
(pp. 524-530)	The **Index.**

Focus on Physical Science

Charles H. Heimler
California State University
Northridge, California

Jack Price
Superintendent, Vista Unified School District
Vista, California

Charles E. Merrill Publishing Co.
A Bell & Howell Company
Columbus, Ohio
Toronto •London •Sidney

Teaching Specialist:

Annette M. Saturnelli
Marlboro Schools
Marlboro, New York

ISBN 0-675-02818-3
Published by
Charles E. Merrill Publishing Co.
A Bell & Howell Company
Columbus, Ohio 43216

Contents

Introduction

Philosophy

Focus on Physical Science is a study of matter, energy, and their relationship.

The approach of this text emphasizes the everyday applications of physical laws. As students progress from chapter-to-chapter, they soon realize that most of the technological advances they have taken for granted are merely applications of basic physical science principles. For example, the importance of machines is stressed in Chapter 2. The students see that complex machines are merely combinations of one or more simple machines.

Unit 1 concerns basic principles of measurement. Motion is placed here as it is more concrete in nature. Thus, students begin the year with easier and more familiar topics.

Unit 2 begins the nine chapter study of matter. At this time, the student must begin to conceptualize abstract information through the use of models. Unit 3 contains descriptive material concerning the elements which provides a breather before the applied chemistry in Unit 4.

Unit 5 has been enhanced to give students a better visual approach to the study of light. Practical topics of high interest have been added to emphasize the everyday use of physical science principles.

Unit 6 gives students a practical approach to the study of heat. Students look at the efficiency of heating systems, engines, and insulation. As consumers of electricity, students are given a basic background in circuitry. They see that topics such as heat and electricity need not be sophisticated in nature. Units 5 and 6 integrate some lifetime consumer skills. In looking at the parts of a camera or a type of heating system, students may be able to make better informed decisions in the future.

Making decisions is an underlying theme for Unit 7. Nuclear energy is discussed in detail. As future voters, students will be called upon to make decisions concerning our energy future. They should be aware of the advantages, disadvantages, and trade offs to be made in order to decrease our dependence on fossil fuels. We are responsible for the changes which influence our environment. Students will be better prepared to make decisions in these areas using the skills gained from the study of physical science.

Readability

Readability plays a major role in determining the success of a textbook in the classroom. A text which can be comprehended by the majority of students in a given class promotes student interest and involvement in the subject area. This feature, in turn, promotes teachability of the text and helps facilitate classroom management. ***Focus on Physical Science*** was revised with these ideas in mind.

In controlling the reading level, careful attention has been given to vocabulary, sentence construction, paragraph structure, sequence, illustrations, and format.

The vocabulary in the text is consistent with the developmental level of the students for whom the text is designed. Important science terms are printed in boldface type. Many of these are respelled phonetically for the student. Once a new science word is introduced, it is used over and over so that it becomes familiar to the student. This technique enhances readability. However, since many science terms are multisyllable words, a formula such as the Fry test does not accurately measure the readability of this text. For additional information concerning *Reading Science* see page 34T.

Samples of the many text features are shown on the next six pages.

A large **photograph** introduces each chapter. The accompanying paragraph relates the photo to the text topics in the chapter.

A **Goal statement** is found at the beginning of each chapter. This statement identifies for the student the main objective of the chapter. The Performance Objectives in this Teacher's Guide are an expansion of the Goal statement.

The gourds in the picture are all in the same family. Yet they can be broken down into smaller groups by size, shape, or color. At this time there are over 104 elements. This large number can also be broken down or classified into smaller groups or families. How are the elements classified?

Frank Psante

Elements and the Periodic Table 6

Chapter 6 begins with a discussion of the elements and the arrangement of the periodic table. Atomic models are introduced to further reinforce the logic behind the periodic table. See the Teacher's Guide at the front of this book for additional teaching strategies for this chapter.

6:1 Elements

All matter is made up of basic substances called elements. Carbon, iron, and aluminum are common elements. An **element** cannot be broken down into simpler substances by a chemical change. Eighty-eight elements have been found on the earth. At least fifteen more have been produced in the laboratory. The air we breathe is mostly the elements, oxygen and nitrogen.

GOAL: *You will learn how the elements are classified using a model for the atom.*

What is an element?

There is a shorthand way to write the names of elements. Table 6-1 gives the names of some of the common elements and the symbols used to represent them. Note that some elements have one letter for their symbol. This letter is always uppercase. *If the symbol for an element is two letters, the second letter is always lowercase.* Some of the symbols of the elements are quite different from their English names. The symbol for iron, Fe, is taken from the Latin word for iron, *ferrum.*

Name five elements.

Write the symbols for five elements.

Table 6-1

Names and Symbols for Some Common Elements

Element	Symbol	Element	Symbol	Element	Symbol
aluminum	Al	hydrogen	H	nitrogen	N
carbon	C	iron	Fe	oxygen	O
chlorine	Cl	magnesium	Mg	silver	Ag
copper	Cu	mercury	Hg	sodium	Na
				sulfur	S

101

Each of the 23 chapters is divided into **short numbered sections** to facilitate planning lessons and assigning reading.

Phrases and sentences to be emphasized are printed in italic type.

Tables are included wherever appropriate to summarize and organize text material. Many tables contain photos to help students visualize tabular data.

Overprinted on the student's text are **red annotations.** These appear in the Teacher's Edition only. These annotations include answers to questions and problems as well as teaching suggestions. The red tint blocks highlight the answers to the student margin questions.

Questions are printed **in the margin** in blue. Answering these questions will highlight for the student the important points in the text.

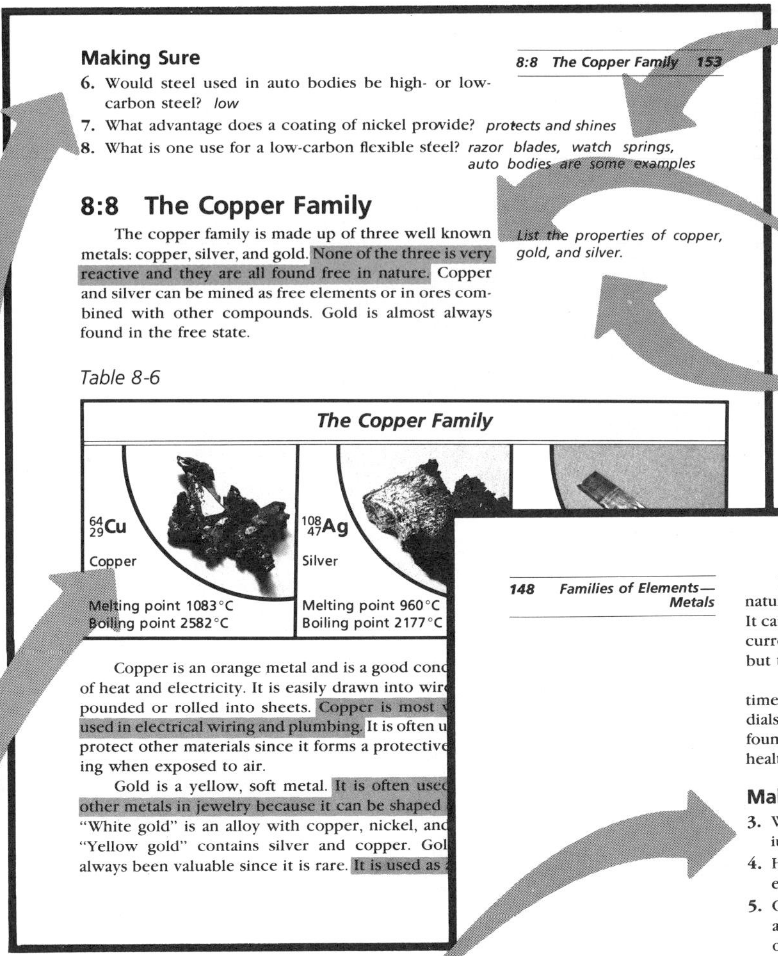

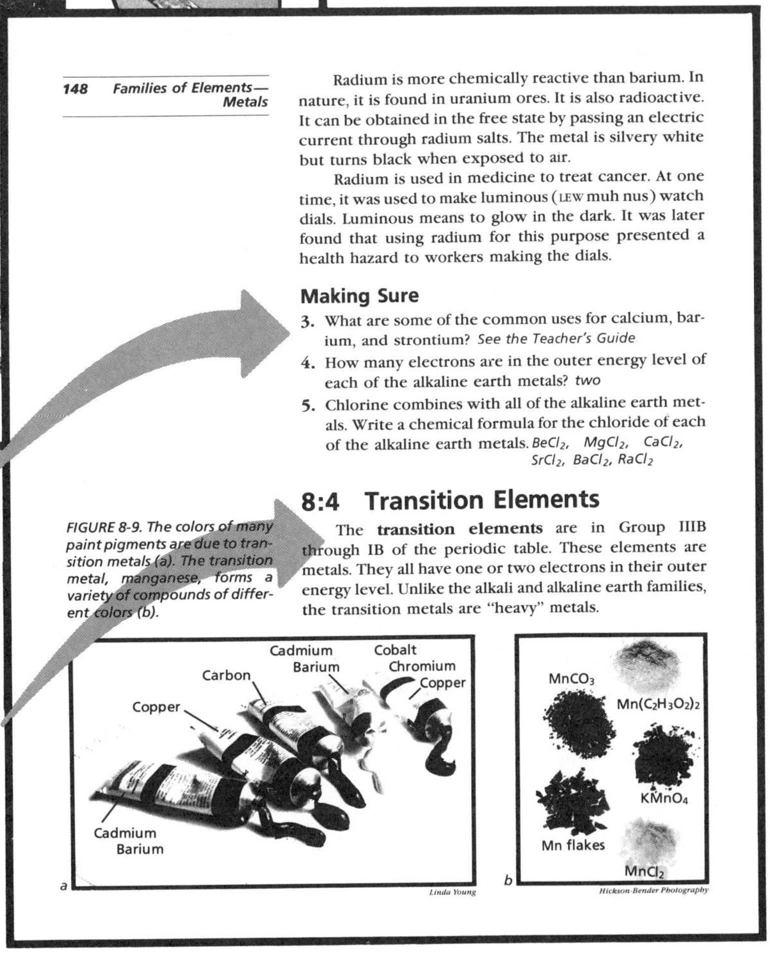

Groups of **questions** and **problems** are located throughout each chapter under the heading **Making Sure.** They can be used for immediate review of the material just studied.

New terms are printed in boldface type where they are first defined. Many of these terms are respelled phonetically for the student. Once a new term is introduced it is used repeatedly throughout the text for reinforcement.

Throughout the text, there are **over 700 photographs and illustrations.** Each is positioned close to the appropriate text material. The captions relate the photos and illustrations to the text and provide additional relevant information.

Example problems are used when it is necessary to integrate math skills with science content. These problems follow a clear, logical format to help students apply their mathematical skills to physical science calculations.

38

How can you increase the efficiency of a machine? Efficiency is increased by reducing friction. Sanding or waxing smooths a surface and reduces friction. Oil and grease are used in many machines to reduce friction. Ball bearings in bicycle wheels and other machines reduce friction.

Increasing the efficiency of machines is an important step in conserving natural resources. Many machines are run by electricity or fuels such as gasoline. When efficiency is increased, less fuel or electricity is needed to do a given amount of work. Thus, resources are conserved. For example, steps are being taken to improve the gasoline engine. Moving parts are made so there is less friction between them. These parts will last longer.

Example

The box in Figure 2-8 weighs 200 newtons. An inclined plane that is 2 meters long is used to lift the box 1 meter. A force of 140 newtons is required (including ion). Calculate the efficiency of the inclined plane.

tion:

The work input is the force needed to move the box multiplied by the distance the box is moved.

$$140\ \text{N} \times 2\ \text{m} = 280\ \text{J}$$

The work output is the weight of the box multiplied by the distance it is moved without using the inclined plane.

$$200\ \text{N} \times 1\ \text{m} = 200\ \text{J}$$

Write the equation for the percent efficiency of the machine.

$$\textit{percent efficiency} = \frac{\textit{work output}}{\textit{work input}} \times 100$$

$$= \frac{200\ \text{J}}{280\ \text{J}} \times 100 = 71.4\%$$

nor glass conducts heat well. The air spaces are too small for convection to occur. Insulating the walls and roof will reduce the heat loss in a house.

In addition to the walls and roof, doors and windows need to be insulated. One way to insulate them is to use weather stripping. Weather stripping closes gaps that allow convection with the air outside. Double paned windows also help by putting a space between the glass panes. Since the panes are not touching, conduction cannot occur. The space is small enough to prevent convection. Recall that heat can move in three ways. Insulation must be designed to control more than one of these ways.

393

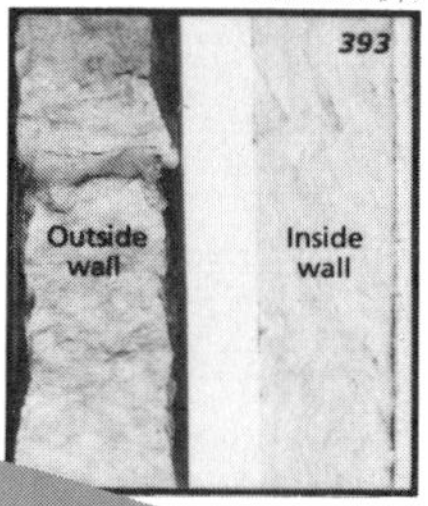

FIGURE 19-7. The cross section of this wall is stone, foam, fiberglass, and drywall.

Activity *Which bottle has the best insulation?*

Setting Up

3 clear glass bottles
vacuum bottle
2 sheets of aluminum foil
sauce pan
hot plate
4 thermometers

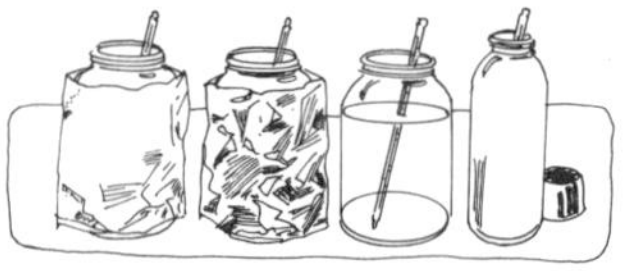

FIGURE 19-8.

Getting Started

1. *Cover one bottle with aluminum foil, shiny side in, as in Figure 19-8.*
2. *Cover a second bottle with aluminum foil, shiny side out.*
3. *Leave the third bottle uncovered.*
4. *Using the sauce pan, heat water to boiling. Make sure you have enough to fill each bottle 2/3 full with hot water.*
5. *Carefully fill the vacuum bottle and each glass bottle 2/3 full with the hot water.*
6. *Place a thermometer in each bottle and record the temperatures.*
7. *Allow each to stand for 20 minutes. Observe and record the temperatures in the four bottles every five minutes.*

Keeping Track

bottle 1	bottle 2	bottle 3	vacuum bottle

Summing Up

1. *In which bottle does the water cool fastest?*
2. *Which way does heat travel in the bottles?*
3. *Which of the bottles is insulated the most?*
4. *How does the aluminum foil affect the movement of heat?*
5. *What could you do to improve the insulation of the bottles?*

Activities are included throughout the text to reinforce scientific principles and teach scientific inquiry. Refer to page 13T for additional information on the structure and types of Activities found in this text.

Points to Remember—a listing of major points presented in the chapter. Section references, printed in blue, key each point to the numbered section where it is discussed.

Questions for Review—this section contains *True or False, Multiple Choice,* and *Completion* questions. These three parts check recall of the chapter contents. The *How and Why* questions enable students to apply their knowledge of the chapter.

Points to Remember

1. Acids have a sour taste and react with metals. *13:1*
2. Bases have a bitter taste and feel slippery. *13:2*
3. Acids increase the hydronium ion concentration of a solution. *13:3*
4. Bases increase the hydroxide ion concentration of a solution. *13:3*
5. The acidity of a solution is rated on the pH scale. *13:4*
6. Indicators turn different colors in acidic and basic solutions. *13:5*
7. A salt and water are the products of a neutralization reaction. *13:6*
8. Anhydrides form acids or bases when added to water. *13:7*

Words to Use

Write a sentence in which you correctly use each of the following words or terms.

acid	hydroxide ion	pH
anhydride	indicator	phenolphthalein
base	litmus paper	salt
hydronium ion	neutralization	

Questions for Review

Do not write in this book.

A. True or False *Have the students rewrite the fals*

Determine whether each of the following sentenc

T 1. The formula for nitric acid is HNO_3.

T 2. Vinegar contains an acid.

F 3. Ammonia is a ~~strong~~ base. *weak*

T 4. The strength of an acid in solution is measur

F 5. A solution which has a pH of 4 is ~~a base~~. *an*

T 6. A neutralization reaction is a reaction betw base.

T 7. OH is the formula for a hydroxide ion.

T 8. An indicator may be used to determine whet acid or a base.

T 9. Strong acids produce more ions than weak a

F 10. An acid anhydride contains a ~~metal~~. *nonmeta*

Words to Use—a vocabulary list of important science terms presented in the chapter.

More Ideas to Explore—questions and activities which take the students beyond the material presented in the chapter. These include experiments, reports, and projects.

Readings to Discover—suggested references for further or more in-depth study of the chapter material or related topics.

D. How and Why *Detailed answers to these questions are given in the Teacher's Guide at the front of this book.*

1. What kind of reaction is shown by the following equation?

$$HCl(aq) + NaOH(aq) \longrightarrow NaCl(aq) + H_2O(l)$$

2. What are the "parent" acids and bases for these salts?
   a. Na_2SO_4 **b.** NaCl **c.** $NaNO_3$
3. How are acids and bases detected?
4. List three important industrial acids. What are the primary uses of each?
5. Classify each substance as an acid, a base, or a salt:
   a. HNO_2 **c.** KOH **e.** $Ca(OH)_2$
   b. HCOOH **d.** CaI_2 **f.** $Fe(NO_3)_3$
6. Name two common household bases. Give their uses.

More Ideas to Discover

1. Check the labels on many household products such as medicines, kitchen aids, and foods. See how many involve acids or bases.
2. Prepare solutions of different liquid synthetic detergents. Use the same number of drops of each in the same volume of water. Use a Universal Indicator to determine the pH of each.
3. Boil some natural and synthetic fibers for about 5 minutes in a weak solution of sodium hydroxide. Test the same type of fibers in dilute sulfuric acid. What do you conclude?
4. Certain gases in the air form acids when dissolved in water. What gases are they? Where do they come from? How do the acids they form affect the environment?
5. Using information from garden books, farm publications, your local garden store, or florists make a list of plants that require acid soil and those that require basic soil. Find out what methods can be used to make soil basic or acidic.

Readings to Discover

Cecil, George, *Salt.* NY: F. Watts, 1976.

La Bastille, Anne, "The Deadly Toll of Acid Rain: All of Nature Is Suffering." *Science Digest,* October 1979, pp. 61-66.

Salisbury, David F., "Salt: An Untapped Source of Abundant Energy." *Science Digest,* December 1978, pp. 45-47.

Focus on Careers • People • Frontiers are magazine like pages scattered throughout the text. These pages feature articles on current science topics.

Focus on Skills pages feature activities designed to reinforce study skills.

The two **In Focus** features give students additional insights into the practicality of physics and chemistry. These features stress the relevance of science and the impact of new research on everyday life.

Appendix A—additional background information of the International System of Measurement (SI).

Appendix A

Units of Measurement and the International System (SI)

You will make a great number of measurements in physical science and throughout your life. The common measurements made are those of mass, volume, length, time and temperature. The International System (SI) of measurement is accepted as the standard for measurement throughout most of the world. SI was selected for two reasons: (1) its simplicity; and (2) most countries of the world already use it as their standard. The International System consists of seven base units, Table A-1.

Table A-1

SI Base Units		
Measurement	**Unit**	**Symbol**
length	*meter*	*m*
mass	*kilogram*	*kg*
time	*second*	*s*
electric current	*ampere*	*A*
temperature	*kelvin*	*K*
amount of substanc		
intensity of light		

Larger and small
obtained by multiply
some multiple of ten.
prefix to the name of t
meter is a decimeter.

Table A-2

Common SI Prefix			
Prefix	**Symbol**	**Multiplier**	**Prefix**
	Greater than 1		
Mega-	*M*	*1 000 000*	*deci-*
kilo-	*k*	*1 000*	*centi-*
hecto-	*h*	*100*	*milli-*
deka-	*da*	*10*	*micro-*

496

504 *Appendix B*

B:5 Using Chemicals and Reagents

Craig Kramer

FIGURE 14.
When smelling a substance use a fanning motion to direct the vapor toward you. Never smell a substance in a test tube directly.

Craig Kramer

FIGURE 15.
Use a spatula to remove solids from bottles. Always clean the spatula before inserting it into a bottle containing another chemical.

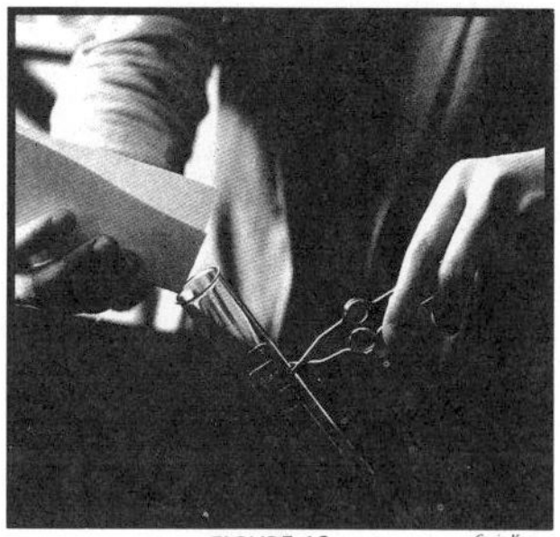

FIGURE 16. Craig Kramer
A solid is easily transferred to a test tube using folded paper.

Appendix B—laboratory techniques a student will need throughout the year in performing the Activities in the text. The last section contains important safety information.

Appendix C—two tables of useful reference data concerning the elements.

A **Glossary** of important terms is included to provide students with a quick reference for the vocabulary of physical science.

Using Focus on Physical Science

Sequence

Focus on Physical Science is designed for maximum flexibility in teaching. The text is divided into seven units which are further subdivided into 23 chapters. A chapter is divided into numbered sections, each being a specific topic of study. The listing of topics in the Table of Contents can be used as a unit outline for the student. These subdivisions will aid you in planning your lessons and giving assignments. The *Planning Guide,* on page 16T, will further assist you in planning and organizing your lessons to meet the needs of your students.

This text provides an adequate balance between basic physics and chemistry principles. Several unifying themes pervade ***Focus on Physical Science.*** These themes serve as a conceptual framework for a physical science course.

1. Physical laws explain the relationship between matter and energy. Studies of everyday occurrences lead to a knowledge about the physical laws of the universe. Observation and experimentation are the bases of scientific inquiry and reasoning.
2. Physical science concerns an in-depth study of matter. Matter can be classified in a number of ways—by structure, by patterns in physical properties, and by chemical behavior.
3. All matter has definite structure. Elements have predictable physical and chemical properties which are related to their structure.
4. Many technological developments utilize the properties of light and sound.
5. The effective use of energy now and in the future is linked directly to human resourcefulness.

Unit Overview and Teaching Tips

The overview gives you background information concerning the relationship of the chapters in the unit. A collage of photographs was selected for each unit opening in the student's text. The opening paragraph relates the photographs to the upcoming text. You can use these pages to preview the topics they will be studying or start class discussions on how the photographs relate to the unit title.

The Teaching Tips listed below each unit overview provide you with insights on how you can present the unit. Ideas for long term projects, such as bulletin boards, or letter writing activities, may be found here.

Chapter Overview

A brief summary of the topics presented in the chapter is given. Teaching strategies are given to help you start the chapter.

Performance Objectives

The main Goal of each chapter is listed with an expanded list of objectives. These objectives highlight important concepts for you. They can be used to assess class and individual student performance. Refer to the background discussion on utilizing Performance Objectives on page 29T.

Section Background

Teaching strategies for presenting each section are given. Information concerning the text's approach to a particular topic will be stated. For example, 1:5 Measurement gives you a rationale for the types of measurement units used throughout the text. Suggestions are also given as to how you can use the illustrations in that section as teaching tools.

Equipment for Activities

The equipment and chemicals you will need to carry out the activities is listed for a class size of thirty broken down into 15 groups of two. A master list of all equipment and chemicals is found on page 21T. This list can be used for ordering purposes.

Activities

Require that all students wear safety glasses when conducting activities and experiments. Demonstrate the parts and proper use of the Bunsen burner, as well as other laboratory equipment.

Specific safety precautions necessary for individual activities are given in the activity itself and in teacher annotations. Note these precautions and explain them to the students. Student laboratory work must always be supervised. Encourage students to develop serious attitudes toward laboratory methods.

In addition to these general procedures of safety, refer students to the list of safety regulations on page 506.

Each Activity in this text is numbered for you using a red annotation. Use these numbers when referring to the guide in the front of the book for background information. The Activities in this text are of two types. For example, turn to the Activity on page 7. Note that it is a different format than the Activity on pages 13-15. The short paragraph activities are usually observational in nature. The procedure and equipment are simple to set up and quick to finish. The Teacher's Guide lists the materials needed and the answers to all questions.

The longer stepwise activities require more time for data collection and interpretation. The equipment for these Activities is still relatively simple but may require more time to assemble. Potentially dangerous chemicals, such as acids and bases, are not listed in the student's materials list. For safety reasons it was felt that you would prefer to supervise the dispensation of these types of chemicals.

The tables shown under *Keeping Track* are provided to assist students in organizing experimental data.

The answers to the *Summing Up* questions require students to interpret the data they have previously collected.

You will note that all Activities are placed toward the end of a text section. This placement should not imply that the activities are to be performed after the reading. We are aware that teachers use Activities at many different points in presenting a concept. By consistently placing them toward the end of a section, you can be more flexible in introducing them at the time which best suits your purposes. The insertion of Activity copy within the text copy may distract some students and hamper readability. In reading a section, you want the student to establish the logical flow of ideas. By keeping the sections short and uninterrupted comprehension is increased.

Keeping a Science Notebook

Make it clear to students why keeping a notebook is important. Records are essential to scientific inquiry. Data is used to discover patterns and to draw conclusions. Observations about events can be recorded in many different ways such as simple drawings or complicated graphs. Scientists use records to guide the direction of future investigations. Data is recorded accurately in a notebook as soon as possible. Scientists communicate with each other through written papers reporting their work. If students are given enough practice listing and recording information, their observational skills will become sharper.

You can vary the type of record you have your students keep. The following are some ideas:

1. Labeling objects—name, where found, composition, and so on.
2. Collecting specimens and pictures
3. Making drawings, diagrams, and using symbols
4. Making graphs and charts
5. Writing short formal reports (see the example on page 8)
6. Giving oral reports

You can have students maintain a chronological table of contents as the course progresses. They can include everything in their notebooks—class notes, activities, homework, quizzes, and tests. Help students to organize those things that will aid their learning. Assist them with expressing their thoughts in writing.

Role of Teacher Demonstrations

Good teacher demonstrations are important in helping students visualize abstract concepts. Good demonstrations allow for development of observational skills and proper techniques. Safety rules and procedures can be emphasized. Demonstrations can be preceded with a clearly identified problem or silent type demos where the aim of the lesson is brought out as a result of observations. A good demo allows students to recognize and verbalize relationships as a result of their own experiences. Demos allow you to present a maximum amount of text information while providing concrete and illustrative experiences. You will find a number of demonstrations included throughout the chapter-by-chapter information in this Teacher's Guide.

Importance of the Review Lesson

Review lessons are necessary and valuable before chapter or unit exams, mid-terms or finals. The *Focus on Skills* pages help students establish models on how to summarize, gather, and eliminate unimportant information from the important material. Review lessons should give students an overall picture. Many students will finally understand how parts fit together to form the whole. The review lesson can be teacher-directed or student-directed. For example, the class can be divided into teams. Each team can prepare questions for others. The questions can be a homework assignment. Another alternative would be to have a team of "experts" (differing for each unit) be responsible for preparing questions that will be answered by the rest of the class. Students can be graded on the basis of quality and the number of questions others get right or wrong.

Scientific Models

Models are extremely valuable tools for scientists. They can be used to test hypotheses. They can predict effects and suggest precautions. However, it is important to see the limitations of models.

Students will be presented with a variety of different models in ***Focus on Physical Science.*** Sometimes they are not told outright "This is a model for. . . ." Sometimes the model will be a physical model. Other times the model will be a mental model because nothing can be drawn and nothing tangible can be constructed. Descriptive words are used from which the student is required to picture the phenomena, occurrence or thing. Linus Pauling first drew a rough outline of the structure of a protein molecule on a piece of paper. He then folded the paper "model" until he had one that satisfied the different requirements for proteins. Eventually, he moved from a paper model to a molecular model. Paper airplane models can be used to study the effects of different shapes on distance, direction, and speed. Maps are models too. Utilize the models presented throughout the text. Encourage students to always try to formulate a mental image of an abstract concept from the information given in the text. The formal discussion of models is presented in Chapter 6.

Questions in the Margins

Questions in the margins near the related text material assist the student by identifying the major principles and concepts, and by serving as a guide to reading and study. In assigning a section for study, you may wish to read these questions to the class or have students read them silently in order to clarify the nature and purpose of the assignment. Questions in the margins provide an opportunity for students to check their learning as they proceed through the assignment. Questions and problems in a given section make excellent written assignments. Oral review of the questions following each assignment makes an excellent summary and helps you to identify points which may require additional explanation.

Examples

Selected mathematics concepts from the junior high school curriculum are integrated into the text. This integration provides meaningful illustrations of practical applications of mathematics in science. It also makes mathematics more relevant and interesting for the student. Also, the use of selected mathematics concepts in science reinforces learning.

Calculations for working each kind of physical science problem are presented in step-by-step detail.

All problems dealing with chemical composition and chemical change involve the concept of ratio or proportion. This topic is covered in the upper elementary and junior high school mathematics curriculum. In teaching quantitative chemical concepts, you may wish to review ratio and proportion. Point out to students the frequency with which this type of calculation is used in chemical change problems.

Making Sure

All questions in these sections are answered in detail. Additional notes concerning the rationale behind certain questions are presented here also. These questions are placed at the end of a section for consistency. You may wish to assign them individually at different points in the reading.

You will note that many of these questions involve more than simple recall. Problems are inserted as a quick test of understanding of new concepts. Each student should solve each problem on an individual basis. Solutions should be demonstrated and discussed. This will clarify concepts and guard against vague acceptance of statements without definite application of new ideas. You may want to keep this in mind when working with students of lower ability levels.

Focus Pages

The Focus on Skills pages are designed to give students additional practice in reading, math, and study skills. The pages were placed at the end of each chapter so as not to disrupt the flow of ideas in the chapter. However, you will probably want to use them as soon as possible. For example, the Skills page in Chapter 3 concerns reading and interpreting graphs. You'll note that the material in Chapter 3 on velocity, speed, and acceleration is presented by using graphs. You may want to use the Skills page before you begin Chapter 3.

Words to Use

Boldfaced scientific terms presented within each chapter are listed alphabetically in this section. You may want to vary your approach in developing vocabulary. However, we strongly urge you to make vocabulary development an integral part of your lesson plan. The following are suggestions that can be employed as alternatives to the instructions for *Words to Use.*

1. Students should be given the opportunity to use new terms as often as possible in writing and class discussion. You may ask them to write a paragraph or short story using the words in this section.
2. You may wish to have students make an outline of the chapter using these key terms. An example of this technique is shown on page 230.
3. A number of other vocabulary development activities and techniques are found in ***Focus on Physical Science: Review and Reinforcement Guide.***

Questions for Review

As the student progresses from Parts A to D, the questions are progressively more difficult. You may want to keep this fact in mind if you are trying to individualize or gear your course to the overall ability level of your class. Some of the How and Why questions may require paragraph type answers and will involve application and interpretation of their knowledge. Parts A to C are mostly simple recall questions.

More Ideas to Explore

These questions and projects enable you to individualize or gear your course to the ability level of the students. The reports required give students practice in using the library and researching information. The experiments encourage an inquiring attitude toward science. Many times these questions show the link between science principles and everyday applications.

Planning the Course

The ***Focus on Physical Science*** program has been designed to meet both student and teacher needs. The program material will satisfy most teaching methods. For example, the teacher who uses the lecture/demonstration method or inquiry method will find the material as workable as the teacher who stresses a student-oriented/laboratory approach. Students will find clear, uncluttered explanations and the logical development of concepts. Students who require concrete examples will be satisfied. The creative thinkers who need challenges will not have their curiosity stifled but will be stimulated instead. These needs are met either through the design of the text itself or through the teaching materials presented in the *Teacher's Annotated Edition.*

The course can be adjusted for either one semester or two. If it is to be two semesters, and your needs require that all of the chemistry be taught in one semester and all of the physics be taught in the other, the following adjustment will provide the sequence that you need. Place Chapters 2, 3, and 4 of Unit I before Chapter 14 of Unit V. This sequence will provide an introductory chapter which includes measurement followed by 9 chapters (3 units) of chemistry for the first semester and 13 chapters (3 units) of physics in the second semester.

If the program is to be limited to one semester, the following sequence is suggested:

Unit I Chapter 1
Unit II Chapters 5-7
Unit III Chapters 8-9
Unit IV Chapter 11
Unit I Chapters 2-4
Unit V Chapter 15
Unit VI Chapters 18 and 20
Unit VII Chapter 23

This sequence consists of 14 chapters divided equally between fundamental chemistry and physics concepts. In a one semester course, students should read the entire chapters suggested but be held accountable for only the sections of primary importance listed on page 17T.

The time suggestions are only guidelines. They are based on a school calendar of 180 days for two semesters and 90 days for one semester.

The emphasis placed on laboratory depends on the needs and interests of your students and any requirements set forth by school district, state, and so on. If, for some reason, student laboratory work is not possible, there are numerous paper and pencil student activities and teacher demonstrations in this *Teacher's Annotated Edition,* in the ***Focus on Physical Science: Activity Centered Program Teacher's Guide,*** and in the ***Focus on Physical Science: Review and Reinforcement Guide*** which accompanies the text. If a more student oriented/laboratory approach is desired, the ***Focus on Physical Science: Activity Centered Program Teacher's Guide*** and ***Focus on Physical Science: A Learning Strategy for the Laboratory*** will provide an extensive variety of challenging problems for investigation.

Planning Guide

Chapter	Class Sessions: 1 Semester Course	Class Sessions: Full Year Course	Emphasis Level: Of Primary Importance	Emphasis Level: Of Secondary Importance	Suggested Laboratory and Activity Topics
1	10	10	all Sections		Science reading inventory Observing, graphing, and measurement
2	6	6	all Sections		Machines Mechanical advantage
3	4	4	all Sections		Forces Friction
4	5	6	4:1-4:4, 4:7	4:5-4:6	Laws of motion
5	7	7	all Sections		Physical and chemical properties Classification Physical and chemical changes
6	7	7	all Sections		Properties of elements Atomic models Periodic table
7	6	7	7:1-7:4, 7:6	7:5, 7:7	Bonding models
8	6	8	8:1-8:6, 8:8-8:9	8:7, 8:10	Qualitative analysis Properties of metals Compounds
9	6	8	9:1-9:3, 9:7-9:9, 9:11	9:4-9:6, 9:10, 9:12-9:13	Qualitative identification of selected substances
10	—	9	10:1-10:5, 10:7, 10:9	10:6, 10:8, 10:10-10:12	Soaps and detergents Food chemistry
11	7	10	all Sections		Hydrates Factors affecting solubility Effect of dissolved substances on physical properties
12	—	10	12:1-12:6	12:7	Types of chemical reactions Conservation of mass

Chapter	Class Sessions 1 Semester Course	Class Sessions Full Year Course	Emphasis Level Of Primary Importance	Emphasis Level Of Secondary Importance	Suggested Laboratory and Activity Topics
13	—	10	13:1-13:6	13:7	Chemical properties of acids and bases Indicators Neutralization
14	—	10	14:1-14:3, 14:5	14:4, 14:6-14:11	Properties of waves
15	7	8	15:1-15:5	15:6, 15:7	Mirrors Images Focal length Refraction Spectrums Spectroscope
16	—	10	16:1, 16:3, 16:4, 16:6	16:2, 16:5	Lenses Real and virtual images
17	—	9	17:1-17:5	17:6-17:8	Compressional and transverse waves
18	6	6	all Sections		Specific heat Calorimetry Effect of heat on metals and gases
19	—	6	19:1-19:5	19:6	Conduction, convection, radiation Insulation Evaporation
20	7	9	20:1-20:3, 20:6-20:7	20:4-20:5, 20:8	Static electricity Electroscopes Series and parallel circuits
21	—	7	21:1-21:4, 21:10	21:5-21:9	Current meters and generators
22	—	8	all Sections		Model for radioactive decay
23	6	6	all Sections		Alternative energy sources Conservation activities
Total Days	90	180			

Adaptability to Differences in Student Performance Abilities

Focus on Physical Science is designed for maximum flexibility. It can be utilized by teachers preferring a conventional approach with some laboratory and/or demonstration experiences, or an activity-centered approach using a discovery method of learning. The text, as well as the program supplements—***Focus on Physical Science: Review and Reinforcement Guide, Focus on Physical Science: Activity-Centered Program Teacher's Guide, Focus on Physical Science: A Learning Strategy for the Laboratory,*** and ***Physical Science Skillcards***—provide many activities for a variety of approaches.

Focus on Physical Science is adaptable to meet the needs of students with different performance abilities. There are often many levels of performance within a single class or among several classes. Many students are able to meet performance objectives easily, while there are those functioning above or below this level. To help teachers plan appropriate and meaningful learning experiences for students with a wide range of ability levels, many alternatives and aids are included within the ***Teacher's Annotated Edition.***

Specific teaching suggestions are included throughout each chapter of the ***Teacher's Annotated Edition.*** Each annotation is designed to facilitate teacher planning. The *Teacher's Guide* offers many helpful methods of organizing the course for a variety of student abilities. The *Planning Guide,* pages 17T-18T, is a tool which may be used to plan a year's course for students functioning at varied performance levels. The headings "Primary" and "Secondary Importance" identify the key sections in each chapter. The Activities in these sections should be undertaken by all students.

The supplementary materials offer many alternatives to you in planning for several ability levels. For students requiring a more advanced course of study, independent enrichment activities and exercises are recommended. Many of the activities in ***Focus on Physical Science: Activity-Centered Program Teacher's Guide*** are suitable for use as independent enrichment material. Selected materials in ***Focus on Physical Science: A Learning Strategy for the Laboratory*** and ***Physical Science Skillcards*** can also be used independently. Encouragement should be given to capable students to engage in these supplementary activities, as well as the *More Ideas to Explore* activities found at the end of each chapter in the text.

The supplementary materials may also be used by students functioning at lower performance levels. These students may require additional study in selected areas and/or reinforcement of previously introduced concepts. ***Focus on Physical Science: Review and Reinforcement Guide*** is designed to reinforce science using reading and mathematics skills exercises. With frequent evaluation of the less able student's progress, a teacher may determine the areas in which additional attention is needed. The ***Evaluation Program for Focus on Physical Science*** contains questions of varying difficulty focused on different levels of learning. You can select the evaluation mode best suited to the ability level of your class.

The activities in the supplementary materials, when used in conjunction with the text, offer many opportunities to the less able student.

Supplementary Materials

Evaluation

Focus on Physical Science Evaluation Program Spirit Duplicating Masters has been created to reinforce student learning, to evaluate student progress, and to discover areas of weakness in instruction. The program consists of a four-part test for each of the 23 chapters of ***Focus on Physical Science.*** The four sections of each chapter test include:

Understanding Concepts—students demonstrate their ability to pick out specific facts from the large body of information in the chapter.

Interpreting Concepts—students demonstrate their ability to interpret basic facts and apply these interpretations.

Using Concepts —students demonstrate their ability to apply physical science concepts to new situations.

Completing Concepts—students demonstrate their ability to use physical science terms in context.

The teacher background information lists the purpose, supplemental use, learning level, and diagnostic measures for each test section. These tests can be used not only for assessments but also as learning tools to help students improve their knowledge of physical science. Annotations are used to answer all questions on the tests.

Review and Reinforcement

Focus on Physical Science: Review and Reinforcement Guide provides additional review in areas where students are deficient. The exercises in this workbook are designed to focus on science content while reinforcing reading and math skills. Word processing skills, context processing skills, study skills, graphing, and problem-solving skills are the major areas of concentration. The ***Teacher's Annotated Edition*** provides background information to help you assist your students in studying text material and diagnosing weaknesses in the skill areas.

Laboratory Programs

Focus on Physical Science: Activity-Centered Program Teacher's Guide is designed to assist you in conducting a physical science program using a laboratory approach. This guide is correlated to the activities which appear in the text. It provides additional questions and hints for directing the student in making observations and interpretations of physical processes. The ***Activity Centered Program*** contains detailed instructions for carrying out the paragraph format *Activities* in the text, demonstrations, additional activities and probing follow-up questions. Most of the additional activities and demonstrations use inexpensive and readily available materials. Suggestions for use of alternate supplies and organizing laboratory materials in your classroom is also provided.

Focus on Physical Science: A Learning Strategy for the Laboratory is a learning-through-doing program of activities. Based on the philosophy that scientific knowledge is acquired through individual activity and experimentation, the manual consists of many varied laboratory activities designed to reinforce physical science concepts presented in ***Focus on Physical Science.*** The procedures and drawings are simple, so little interpretation is necessary. However, all activities should be carried out under your supervision. The equipment needed is inexpensive and readily available. All activities can be conducted in an ordinary classroom environment or in the schoolyard.

The ***Teacher's Annotated Edition*** contains teaching strategies, suggestions, answers, and complete lists of materials and supplies.

Physical Science Skillcards offer supplementary activities for those students needing additional reinforcement of learned concepts or independent enrichment. The Skillcards effectively supplement the material covered in ***Focus on Physical Science.*** The activities are such that they can be used at all levels. They can be used effectively in constructing an individualized physical science course. Students are encouraged to work toward logical conclusions without your assistance. Materials needed are inexpensive and can be easily procured.

Equipment and Supplies for Activities

Equipment

A complete list of equipment for the entire course is given below for your convenience in ordering equipment for the entire school year. The amounts listed are for one class of thirty students. While most activities should be done in groups of two, some require larger groups and some should be done individually. The activities are designed so that simple apparatus can be used. Use materials that are available locally whenever possible.

aluminum foil—1 roll
ammeter, 0-5 amp. D.C.—15
assorted small objects, easily recognized—30-40
balance, double pan—10
balls
- rubber—15
- iron with ring—15

balloons, round—1 pkg of 50
batteries, 6 volt—15
beakers
- 100 mL—15
- 250 mL—30
- 400 mL—30
- 600 mL—15

bottles (same size)
- glass—24
- vacuum—8

Bunsen burner—15
candles—30
cans
- #2 1/2—15
- #1—15

cardboard
- boxes with lids—15
- heavy squares 10 × 10 cm—15
- tubes—15
- white sheets—15

cards
- white index—30
- playing (optional)—15

clamps
- extension—15
- test tube—15

clock with second hand or 15 stopwatches
cloth
- miscellaneous—15
- silk—15
- wool—15

coins, assorted nickels and quarters—30
comb, plastic—15
campass, small—15
cotton, absorbent—1 pkg
cups, plastic drinking—60
curtain rod, 20 cm length—15
dowel rod, 0.5 × 20 cm—15
evaporating dish—15
filter paper—1 box
fishing line—1 spool
flashbulbs—30
flash unit—5
flask
- 250 mL—30
- 500 mL—30

- forceps—15
- funnel—15
- galvanometer—15
- glass plates—15
- glass prism, triangular—30
- glass rod
    - friction—30
    - stirring—15
- glass slides, microscope—15
- glass tube
    - 10 cm—30
    - 15 cm—15
- glass wool—2, 1 lb pkg
- goggles—30
- graduated cylinder
    - 10 mL—15
    - 25 mL—15
    - 50 mL—15
- hot plate—10
- knife—5
- knitting needle and glass rod of the same size—15 sets
- lead shot—1 lb
- lead sinkers—15
- lens, concave—15
- light bulbs and sockets, 6 volt—45
- light ray box—15
- litmus paper, red and blue—several vials
- magnet, bar—30
- magnifying glass—15
- marbles—75
- matches—15 boxes
- medicine dropper—30
- metal
    - assorted small blocks—45
    - strips of Al, Cu, Fe with the same mass—15 sets
    - washers—150
- meter sticks—15
- mirror
    - magnifying—15
    - parabolic—15
    - plane, small—15
- pan
    - sauce $1\frac{1}{2}$ to 2 qt size—15
    - shallow pie plate size—15
- paper
    - graph, thin centimeter rule—1 pkg
    - unlined art, colored—1 pkg
    - writing, white unlined—pkg
- paper clips—1 pkg.
- paper cups—45
- paper towels—several rolls
- plastic diffraction grating, 1 cm^2—15
- plastic friction rod—30
- platinum of nichrome wire—1 small roll
- polarizing filter—30
- protective clothing for each person
- resistors, 25Ω slide variable—15
- ring stand and ring—15
- rope, 4.5 m—15
- rubber bands—1 pkg
- ruler, metric—30
- scissors—15
- soda straws—30
- spring coil,
    - coil 7 to 10 cm—15
    - slinky coil—15
- spring scale
    - 5 newton—30
    - 20 newton—45
- steel wool—1 box
- stoppers
    - cork—15
    - rubber 1-hole for flasks—45
    - rubber 2-hole—15
    - rubber for flasks—30
    - rubber for test tubes—60
- string—several rolls
- switch—15
- tape, masking—several rolls
- tape measure—15
- teacup—15
- test tube
    - assorted sizes—150
    - large—15
- test tube brush—15
- test tube rack—15
- thermometer—32
- tongs—15
- tuning forks, assorted frequencies—15
- Universal indicator paper—several boxes

voltmeter, 0-10 volt D.C.—15
watch glass—15
weight, 2 newton (.2 kg mass)—15
wire, insulated bell—100 meters
wire screen—15
wood
  large blocks—15
  plank, 0.5 m smooth—15
  small blocks, assorted sizes—45
wood splints—1 box

Chemicals

The approximate amounts needed for a class of 30 for each activity are listed here. Most reagents are more economical to buy in standard lots rather than in small amounts listed.

alcohol, ethanol—400 mL
alum crystals—100 g
aluminum pieces—several
ammonium hydroxide, concentrated—200 mL
antimony(III) chloride—40 g
ascorbic acid (dilute)—150 mL
banana—several
barium chloride—30 g
bread—several slices
cadmium nitrate crystals—80 g
calcium chloride, anhydrous—15 g
carbon—several pieces
carrot—several
cobalt chloride crystals—50 g
copper(I) chloride, crystals—50 g
copper(II) chloride, crystals—70 g
copper, pieces about 50 g—15
copper(II) sulfate
  fine crystals—700 g
  technical crystals—400 g
  powder—50 g
corn, kernels—1500
detergent, liquid—150 mL
food coloring—several vials
fruit and vegetable juices, assorted
household liquids, assorted
hydrochloric acid, concentrated (12M)—1 L
hydrogen peroxide, 3%—100 mL
ice—as needed
indophenol—1 g
iodine
  crystals—50 g   tincture of—several vials
iron(II) chloride—50 g
iron(III) chloride—50 g
iron filings—150 g
iron—several pieces
iron(II) sulfate heptahydrate—200 g
iron(III) sulfate crystals—50 g
iron(II) sulfide—50 g
lard—1 liter
lead—several pieces
lemon juice—100 mL
lithium chloride—10 g
manganese dioxide—50 g
milk—100 mL
milk of magnesia—250 mL
mineral oil—250 mL
molasses—400 mL
naphtha (lighter fluid)—200 mL
nickel(II) sulfate—125 g
petroleum jelly—1 jar
phenolphthalein—1 g
potassium chloride—10 g
potassium nitrate—15 g
potato—several
Rochelle salt crystals—150 g
sand—1400 g
soap
  liquid—75 mL   solid—1 bar
soda pop—100 mL
sodium bicarbonate—30 g
sodium chloride—4600 g
sodium hydroxide—800 g
sodium nitrate—60 g
starch, liquid—250 mL
strontium chloride—20 g
sugar—100 g
sulfur—50 g
sulfuric acid, concentrated 96%—100 mL
vegetable oil—500 mL
vinegar—200 mL
water—as needed
wax (paraffin), small blocks—45
zinc
  mossy—75 pieces   strips—15
zinc sulfate—80 g

Preparation of Solutions

This list gives directions for the preparation of various reagent solutions. Solutions are prepared by diluting the solid to the volume listed. For example, in making a 0.167 molar solution of antimony(III) chloride, dilute 38 grams of the solid to 1 liter with distilled water. Use distilled water for the preparation of solutions.

Ammonium hydroxide (dilute), 3*M*: 200 milliliters of concentrated NH_4OH per liter

Antimony(III) chloride, 0.167*M*:38 grams $SbCl_3$ per liter

Barium chloride, 0.1*M*: 24.4 grams $BaCl_2 \cdot 2H_2O$ per liter

Cadmium nitrate, 0.25*M*: 77 grams $Cd(NO_3)_2 \cdot 4H_2O$ per liter

Calcium chloride, 0.1*M*: 11.1 grams of reagent grade $CaCl_2$ per liter

Copper(II) chloride, 0.1*M*: 17.05 grams $CuCl_2 \cdot 2H_2O$ per liter

Copper(II) sulfate, 0.5*M*: 124.8 grams $CuSO_4 \cdot 5H_2O$ per liter

Hydrochloric acid, 6*M*: Mix equal volumes of 12*M* (concentrated) HCl and water

Hydrochloric acid (dilute), 3*M*: 258 milliliters concentrated HCl per liter

Hydrochloric acid, 0.1*M*: 8.55 milliliters concentrated HCl per liter

Hydrogen sulfide water: Generate H_2S gas by adding dilute HCl to a few grams of FeS in a gas generation apparatus. Bubble the gas in distilled water for at least 5 minutes. Use a 250-mL widemouth jar about half-filled with distilled water.

Indophenol, 0.1% solution: Dissolve 1 gram of indophenol in 1 liter water

Iron(II) sulfate, saturated: 156.5 grams of $FeSO_4 \cdot 7H_2O$ per liter at room temperature

Lithium chloride, 0.1*M*: 4.24 grams LiCl per liter

Nickel sulfate, 0.25*M*:66 grams $NiSO_4 \cdot 6H_2O$ per liter

Phenolphthalein: 1 gram phenolphthalein (solid) per 100 mL 50% ethanol

Potassium chloride, 0.1*M*: 7.46 grams KCl per liter

Potassium nitrate, 0.1*M*: 10.1 grams KNO_3 per liter

Sodium chloride, 0.1*M*: 5.85 grams NaCl per liter

Sodium hydroxide, 20%: 250 grams NaOH per liter

Sodium hydroxide (dilute), 3*M*: 126 grams NaOH per liter

Sodium hydroxide, 0.1*M*: 4 grams NaOH per liter

Sodium nitrate, 0.1*M*: 8.5 grams $NaNO_3$ per liter

Strontium chloride, 0.1*M*: 15.85 grams $SrCl_2$ per liter

Zinc sulfate, 0.25*M*: 72 grams $ZnSO_4 \cdot 7H_2O$ per liter

Teacher References

Books

Carin, Arthur and Robert Sund. *Teaching Science through Discovery.* Columbus, Ohio: Charles E. Merrill Publishing Co., 1973.

Educators Guide to Free Films. Educators Progress Service, Inc., Randolph, WI 53956. (published yearly)

Educators Guide to Free Science Materials. Progress Service, Inc., Randolph, WI 53956. (published yearly)

Farmer, Walter A. and Margaret A. Farrell. *Systematic Instruction in Science for the Middle and High School Years.* Reading, MA: Addison-Wesley Publishing Co., 1980.

Guidelines for Self-Assessment of Secondary School Science Programs. NSTA Publication No. 471-14682, Washington, D.C.: National Science Teachers Association, 1976.

How To Do It Series. National Science Teachers Association, 1742 Connecticut Ave., NW, Washington, D.C. 20009.

Joseph, A., P.F. Brandwein, E. Morhott, H. Pollock and J.F.A. Castka. *A Sourcebook for the Physical Sciences.* New York: Harcourt Brace Jovanovich, 1961.

Kahle, Jane B., *Teaching Science in the Secondary School.* New York: D. Van Nostrand Co., 1979.

Lowery, Lawrence F. *The Everyday Science Sourcebook: Ideas for Teaching in the Elementary and Middle School.* New York: Allyn and Bacon, 1978.

Musgrave, G. Ray. *Individualized Instruction: Teaching Strategies Focusing on the Learner.* Boston: Allyn and Bacon, Inc., 1975.

Safety in the Science Classroom. National Science Teachers Association 1742 Connecticut Ave., NW, Washington, D.C. 20009, 1978.

UNESCO. *The New Unesco Sourcebook for Science Teaching.* New York: Uni Publishing, Inc., 1975.

Vivian, Eugene. *Sourcebook for Environmental Education.* St. Louis, MO: C.V. Mosby, 1973.

Periodicals

The Science Teacher. National Science Teachers Association, 1742 Connecticut Ave., NW, Washington, D.C. 20009.

School Science and Mathematics. School Science and Mathematics Association. P.O. Box 1614, Indiana University of Pennsylvania, Indiana PA 15701.

Audiovisual Materials

Unit 1

Attraction of Gravity. BFA Educational Media
Black Holes of Gravity. Time-Life Films
Dawn of the Solar Age: Wind and Water. Time-Life Films
Forces Make Forms. Film Fair Communications
Mac's Mill. Bullfrog Films
Make Mine Metric. Pyramid Films
Metrics for Measure. BFA Educational Media
Pedal Power. Bullfrog Films
Principles of Lubrication. International Film Bureau
Powers of Ten, revised. Pyramid Films
Simple Machines—Using Mechanical Advantage. Barr Films
Splash: Science and Swimming. Centron Educational Films
Thonk! Science and Hitting a Ball. Centron Educational Films

Unit 2

Atomic Structure and the Periodic Table. Encyclopedia Britannica Educational Corporation
Atom in the Hospital (2nd ed). Handel Films
The Nature of Matter. McGraw-Hill Text Films
The World of Molecules, 2nd ed. Churchill Films

Unit 3

Crystallization. Churchill Films
Energy: The Fuels and Man. National Geographic Society
Oil—From Fossil to Flame. Centron Educational Films

Unit 4

Chemistry in Nature. Centron Educational Films
Lead in Motion. Lead Industries Association, Inc., 292 Madison Ave., New York 10017.
Mars: Chemistry Looks for Life. Wards Natural Science Establishment
Oxygen—An Introduction to Chemistry. Barr Films

Unit 5

A Visit to Spectrum II. Agency for Instructional Television
Color from Light. Churchill Films
How to Make a Solar Heater. Handel Films
Learning About Sound. Encyclopedia Britannica Educational Corp.
Light and Its Relation to Color. Science Software Systems
Light Is Many Things. Barr Films
Quiet, Please! Fenwick Productions
Sunspot Mystery: Sunspots Explained. Time-Life Films
Superconductors: Tomorrow's Energy Breakthrough Is Here! ACI Films
The Light of the 21st Century. Time-Life Films

Unit 6

Electricity All About Us, 2nd ed. Coronet Instructional Media
Electricity—The Energy of Electrons. Barr Films

Unit 7

Dawn of the Solar Age: Solar Energy. Time-Life Films

Energy: The Problems and the Future. National Geographic Society

Saving Energy at Home. Ramscate Films

The Breeder. Stuart Finley, Inc.

Terraset Sun. Solarium Productions

The Sun and Its Energy, 2nd ed. Coronet Instructional Media

Film Distributors

ACI Films
34 West 45th Street
New York, NY 10036

Agency for Instructional Television
P.O. Box A
1111 West 17th Street
Bloomington, IN 47401

Barr Films
P.O. Box 5667
3490 East Foothill Blvd.
Pasadena, CA 91107

BFA Educational Media
P.O. Box 1795
2211 Michigan Ave.
Santa Monica, CA 90404

Bullfrog Films
Oley, PA 19547

Centron Educational Films
1621 West 9th Street
Lawrence, KS 66044

Churchill Films
662 West Robertson Blvd.
Los Angeles, CA 90069

Coronet Instructional Media
65 East South Water Street
Chicago, IL 60601

Encyclopedia Britannica Educational Corporation
425 North Michigan Ave.
Chicago, IL 60611

Fenwick Productions
Box 277
West Hartford, CT 06107

Handel Films
8730 Sunset Blvd.
West Hollywood, CA 90069

International Film Bureau
332 South Michigan Ave.
Chicago, IL 60604

McGraw-Hill Text Films
110 Fifteenth Street
Del Mar, CA 92014

National Geographic Society
17th and M Streets, NW
Washington, D.C. 20036

Pyramid Films
P.O. Box 1048
Santa Monica, CA 90406

Ramscate Films
704 Santa Monica Blvd.
Santa Monica, CA 90401

Science Software Systems
11890 West Pico Blvd.
Los Angeles, CA 90064

Solarium Productions
1061 31st Street, NW
Washington, D.C. 20007

Stuart Finley, Inc.
3428 Mansfield Road
Falls Church, VA 22041

Time-Life Films
100 Eisenhower Dr.
Paramus, NJ 07652

Wards Natural Science Establishment
Modern Learning Aids Division
P.O. Box 1712
Rochester, NY 14603

Student Resource Material

The following is a list of addresses to which you can write to obtain subscriptions to current magazines containing articles related to physical science. Many of these may be carried already in your school library. Having magazines such as these available in your classroom enables students to see practical applications of the principles they are learning in physical science.

Current Science
Subscription Offices
P.O. Box 10790
Des Moines, IA 50340

Popular Mechanics
P.O. Box 10064
Des Moines, IA 50350

Sci Quest
Circulation Manager
American Chemical Society
Post Office Box 2895
Washington, D.C. 20013

Popular Science
Boulder, CO 80302

Science Digest
P.O. Box 10076
Des Moines, IA 50350

Science News
Science Service, Inc.
231 W. Center St.
Marion, OH 43302

Science 80
Subscription Department
Xerox Publications
Columbus, OH 43216

National Geographic Society
1155 Sixteenth Street, NW
Washington, D.C. 20036

Careers Related to Physical Science

Career exploration must begin early in the formal education process. Young people must be exposed to the vast possibilities that are open to them. Scientific and science-related careers provide challenges, stimulation, satisfaction, and many opportunities for creativity. For students who do not seek traditional scientific careers, it is important to make them aware of the significance of physical science in other fields.

Use the *Focus on Careers • People • Frontiers* to give students an insight into science-related careers. Emphasis on career education throughout the year adds relevance and a special significance to the topics presented in your physical science course.

Field trips to nearby places such as water treatment plants, hospitals, food processing plants, industries, and police crime labs are just a few of the places available in your community for learning sites. If funds and district requirements prevent you from traveling, ask the agency of industry to send a speaker. Local sections of the *American Chemical Society* usually have a speaker's bureau. Colleges in your area probably have such a service too. If possible, document field trips with photographs, slides, or video tapes. These materials can be used for bulletin board displays, essay topics, or as a way of motivating next year's students. Your bulletin board display can be made active by placing a mirror in the middle of the display. You can title the board "Picture yourself in a science career!" Many students will come up just for curiosity, but a good number of them will read something of what is there.

The following information is included to show you the variety of careers that require some knowledge of physical science. Students should be exposed to jobs at all levels from Ph.D. chemists to technical assistants needing only a high school diploma. A short bibliography and list of addresses is included to provide you and your students with sources for more specific job descriptions and training requirements. Obtaining catalogs from colleges, technical schools, and vocational schools in your area can be excellent sources of information.

Engineering

All aspects of engineering require a knowledge of design, properties of materials, and machines. Engineers must have an extensive background in physical science since the major portion of their work involves applying scientific principles in developing new products or more efficient ways of manufacturing existing products. Most engineering positions require at least a four-year college degree in the particular field. The following list covers some branches of engineering: aerospace, agricultural, biomedical, ceramic, chemical, civil, electrical, industrial, mechanical, metallurgical, mining, and nuclear.

Pure Science

Scientific research requires an extensive knowledge of physical laws and the properties of matter and energy. Scientists are actively involved in the quest for more knowledge about life, matter, and the universe. Most scientific positions require at least a four-year degree. The following list covers some of the branches of scientific research requiring a background in physical science—chemists, physicists, geologists, geophysicists.

Technical Fields

Technical people provide support services for scientists and engineers. Their jobs involve the development and production of new products. These jobs are usually more specific and limited in scope than that of an engineer or research scientist. Since they work closely with scientists and engineers, they need an adequate background in physical science. Some technical positions require only a high school diploma. However, many technicians have associate (2 year) degrees or additional training in post secondary technical schools. Many companies will provide on-the-job training for interested applicants. Some branches of technical work outside the medical field are broadcasting, drafting, electronics, food processing, heating and cooling systems, nuclear energy, and surveying.

Health and Medicine

The jobs in the fields of medicine, dentistry, and pharmacy are many and diverse. Most all workers in these fields need some background in basic chemistry or physics. Professional fields such as physicians, dentists, optometrists, pharmacists, podiatrists, opthalmologists, and veterinarians require a college degree, post college professional training, and passing a state licensing exam.

Careers in nursing, physical and occupational therapy, dietetics, environmental health, and medical technology usually require a four-year college degree and passing a state licensing exam.

A two-year associate degree or on-the-job training is required for most assistant and technician jobs. The following are some examples: EKG and EEG technicians, medical and dental assistants, operating room technicians, optometric assistants, dental hygienists, dental laboratory technicians, X-ray technicians, practical nurses, nurses aides, and orderlies.

Graphics and Design

Careers in the field of graphics and design require a basic knowledge of physical laws and materials. An architect must have a basic knowledge of materials in order to design safe and functional buildings. Photography, art, lithography, and photoengraving require a background in materials, chemical processes, and color theory. The training for these jobs is usually acquired through apprenticeship programs or vocational school training. However, with increasing technological developments in the printing industry, many jobs now require more advanced degrees with an emphasis on mathematics and physical science.

Education

Teaching positions requiring a background in physical science exist at all levels. Teachers at the elementary and secondary level must have at least a four-year college degree. Positions at the university level require at least a master's degree.

Technical librarians and information science specialists must have an extensive background in one or more of the physical sciences as well as a master's degree in library science.

Construction and Machine Trades

Jobs in construction and machine trades require a knowledge of machines, properties of materials, mathematics, metallurgy, and electronics. Entry in these fields is usually through apprenticeship programs combining on-the-job training with classroom instruction. Examples of jobs in these fields are foundry workers, machinists, tool and die makers, millwrights, instrument makers, electroplaters, waste water treatment workers, electricians, bricklayers, welders, iron workers, painters, plasterers, plumbers, and pipefitters.

Mechanics and Service People

Service and repair occupations usually require background knowledge of electricity, electronics, properties of materials, machines, and acoustics. Jobs in these fields are usually obtained through apprenticeship programs, post secondary vocational school programs, or on-the-job training combined with classroom instruction. Some examples of jobs in these fields are business machine repair people, computer service technicians, mechanics for all forms of transportation, jewelers, piano tuners and technicians, and TV and radio repair technicians.

Additional Information

General References

Keys to Careers in Science and Technology
National Science Teachers Association
1742 Connecticut Ave., NW
Washington, D.C. 20009

Occupational Outlook Handbook
U.S. Department of Labor
Bureau of Labor Statistics
Washington, D.C. 20212

Engineering

American Society for Engineering Education
Suite 400, 1 DuPont Circle
Washington, D.C. 20036

Engineers' Council for Professional Development
345 East 47th St.
New York, NY 10017

Scientific Research and Related Fields
American Chemical Society
Department of Educational Activities
1155 Sixteenth St. NW
Washington, D.C. 20036

American Institute of Physics
335 East 45th St.
New York, NY 10017

Manufacturing Chemists Association Inc.
1825 Connecticut Ave. NW
Washington, D.C. 20009

Health and Medicine
American Dental Association
Council on Dental Education
211 East Chicago Ave.
Chicago, IL 60611

American Medical Association
Council on Medical Education
535 North Dearborn St.
Chicago, IL 60610

Design
American Institute of Architecture
1735 New York Ave.
Washington, D.C. 20036

American Institute for Design and Drafting
3119 Price Rd.
Bartlesville, OK 74003

National Art Education Association
National Education Association
1201 16th St., NW
Washington, D.C. 20036

Education
National Council of Technical Schools
1835 K St. NW, Room 907
Washington, D.C. 20006

U.S. Department of Education
Washington, D.C. 20202

Performance Objectives

Books on science education list many valid reasons for teaching the subject. These reasons may range from general goals to more specific goals. A general goal might be to help students acquire habits of critical thinking while a specific goal might be to teach these students the definition of an element and compound. Statements of what science teaching intends to accomplish are valid and justifiable. Parents, administrators, and teachers are asking or being asked to show proof of the successful achievement of these goals. Therein lies the value of performance objectives—the behaviors which you can observe and which indicate that students are achieving the goals of science education.

In many cases, several types of behaviors will indicate that the students are achieving the objectives. For example, how do you, the teacher, determine that the students are acquiring habits of critical thinking? Some behaviors which you might observe include students:

1. asking questions related to the topic being discussed.
2. gathering data or sharing evidence which supports their answers.
3. questioning or expressing doubt about the hypotheses posed by others.
4. suggesting alternate solutions to a problem.
5. rejecting their ideas when the evidence they gather does not support their hypotheses.

Performance objectives are only suggested outcomes of what students should be able to do after or during your teaching. You may also find the objectives useful in other ways. You may want to use the objectives:

1. to help decide what materials, classroom conditions, and teaching strategies you should employ.
2. to help gather and provide evidence that students in your class are learning.

3. to diagnose a student's abilities and/or weaknesses.
4. to provide students with the criteria of what they should expect from themselves in each lesson.

Performance objectives form the basis of each chapter of ***Focus on Physical Science.*** The objectives are related to four broad goals of education—the development of **Attitudes, Processes** of inquiry, **Knowledge,** and **Skills.**

1. **Attitudes:** To develop students' attitudes of curiosity, wonderment, and involvement with phenomena in their natural environment; to develop an appreciation for the contributions of science to daily living; and to develop skills toward solving problems in a scientific manner.
2. **Processes:** To develop those intellectual processes of inquiry by which scientific problems and phenomena are explained, predicted, and/or controlled.
3. **Knowledge:** To develop knowledge of facts, terminology, concepts, generalizations, and principles which help students confront and interpret their environment.
4. **Skills:** To develop students abilities to handle, construct, and manipulate materials and equipment in a productive and safe manner and to develop the ability to measure, organize, and communicate scientific information.

Performance objectives for each chapter are listed in the Teacher's Guide beginning on page 35T. Each objective is identified by one or more of the following letters: A, P, K, S. They indicate the goal(s) on which the objective is based. It is important to keep in mind that each of these four goals are of equal priority when evaluating student performance.

1. **Attitudes (A)** You will find such statements as:

Students will volunteer to perform the activity at home.

Students will volunteer to do research and report their findings in class.

2. **Processes (P)** You will find such statements as:

When presented with various objects, students will compare and contrast their similarities and differences and classify as metallic or nonmetallic.

Given data on the solubilities of various substances in water, students will predict the solubility of other compounds from the same chemical factory.

Given pictures of various types of levers, students will identify the fulcrum, effort and resistance and group them in one of three classes.

3. **Knowledge (K)** You will find such statements as:

When asked, students will define the term element correctly.

Students will explain the reason why objects fall toward the earth by using the term gravity or force of gravity.

Students will describe the water cycle and its relationship to generating hydroelectric power.

4. **Skills (S)** You will find such statements as:

Students will construct a cooling curve for water.

While performing an activity, students will record their data and observations in their notebooks.

Students will assemble the proper equipment to set up a filtration system.

How to Use the Objectives

In the Teacher's Guide that follows, a specific goal is stated for each chapter. This Goal is repeated for the student at the beginning of each chapter.

Following the Goal statement in the Teacher's Guide, specific performance objectives for each section of the chapter are listed. There may be several objectives in each section. Each objective is numbered to correspond to that section of the chapter. For example, 2:5 is Chapter 2, Section 5.

From these objectives you should be able to determine and plan for the achievement of the objectives for each section of a chapter.

Remember, these performance objectives are not meant to be all inclusive. You should supplement them with your own objectives or objectives from other sources.

You will also find that the criterion or level of performance for each objective is not included. The intent was to create guidelines and not to state levels of expectancies for you. Only you can decide if 100% or only 50% of your students should be able to accomplish each task. You will need to develop and insert these criterion levels for your own students based on your knowledge of their abilities, your materials, and your own situation.

Evaluation

There are several ways to evaluate whether or not students have achieved the science objectives. Informal observation is an excellent way to evaluate student growth and the development of a positive attitude toward science. A performance checklist is often helpful in recording your observations of student behavior. The following is an example of a simple performance checklist based on the objectives of one chapter.

Other types of checklists may help you keep track of the development of a positive attitude toward science.

Date *September 30* Topic *Force and Work*

Pages *22 - 43*

OBJECTIVE	Patty	Mike	Sue	Jeff	
1. Demonstrate the relationship between force and work.	✓	✓		✓	
2. Define the meaning of the terms effort force and resistance force.	✓	✓	✓	✓	
3. Differentiate among inclined plane, wedge, and screw.		✓	✓	✓	
4. Calculate the efficiency of a machine when given the work input and work output.	✓		✓	✓	

Student *Patricia Jedick*

Date *Sept. 28*

BEHAVIOR	Never	Sometimes	Always	Other Comments
1. Expresses a liking for science.		✓		
2. Requests to use science materials.		✓		
3. Reads science books.	✓			
4. Does activities at home.			✓	
5. Volunteers to bring in		✓		
6.				

OPINION SURVEY

Name ____________

Date ____________

1. While studying this chapter, I found it most difficult to: (Check the answer(s) which best describe your feelings.)

_____ read the text
_____ understand the photographs and diagrams
_____ follow the Activity directions
_____ remember the important facts
_____ understand the new vocabulary
_____ follow the Example problems

2. Which of the following ideas would you like to find out more about?

_____ What alternate sources of fuel are being used?
_____ What can I can do to conserve energy?
_____ How important is nuclear energy?

Chapter 5 Number of students 30
Topic Properties of Matter

Page	Date(s)	Activity	No. of students completing	Time spent
86	11/12	Determining the density of liquids.	28	30 min.
90	11/19	Determining the freezing point of water.	25	30 min.

Recording group behavior is another way of evaluating progress. It allows you to estimate the number of students who have completed each activity and the time spent on each. This information might indicate whether you should spend more time with the whole class or with individual students.

These performance checklists are merely suggestions to supplement the many other forms of evaluation with which you may be familiar. They are intended to help you answer the question: "How do you know you are achieving the goals of science education?"

Bibliography

Bloom, Benjamin, Hastings, J. Thomas, and Madaus, George, *Handbook on Formative and Summative Evaluation of Student Learning.* McGraw-Hill Book Co., New York, 1971.

Bloom, Benjamin, and others, *Taxonomy of Educational Objectives, Handbook I: Cognitive Domain.* David McKay, New York, 1956.

California State Department of Education, *Science Framework for California Public Schools.* Sacramento, Calif., 1970.

Eiss, Albert F., and Harbeck, Mary B., *Behavioral Objectives in the Affective Domain.* National Science Teachers Association, National Education Association, Washington, D.C., 1969.

Krathwohl, D. R., Bloom, Benjamin, and Masia, Bertram R., *Taxonomy of Educational Objectives, Handbook II: Affective Domain.* David McKay, New York, 1956.

Lindvall, C. M., ed., *Defining Educational Objectives.* University of Pittsburgh Press, Pittsburgh, 1964.

Mager, Robert, *Preparing Instructional Objectives.* Fearon Publishers, Inc., Palo Alto, Calif., 1962.

Picard, Anthony, and Sund, Robert, *Behavioral Objectives and Evaluational Measures for Science and Mathematics.* Charles E. Merrill Publishing Co., Columbus, Ohio, 1971.

Plowman, Paul, *Behavioral Objectives in Science.* Science Research Associates, Chicago, 1969.

Popham, W. James, *The Teacher-Empiricist.* Aegeus Publishing Co., Los Angeles, 1965.

Popham, W. James, and Baker, Eva L., *Establishing Instructional Goals.* Prentice Hall, Inc., Englewood Cliffs, N.J., 1970.

Walbesser, Henry H., *Constructing Behavioral Objectives.* Bureau of Educational Research and Field Services, University of Maryland, College Park, Md., 1970.

Reading Science

It is important to recognize that most scientific information is gathered through reading. Students should be made aware that most scientists gain their information through literature searches.

When reading science materials, students may encounter difficulties that they have not experienced before. Prior to this time students have been accustomed to reading materials of narration, not the precise language of scientific writing. Many new concepts are presented on a page and these are usually developed on an ascending scale requiring the reader to use his/her background of previous knowledge. The reader of science must sense relationships and think critically about what is already known and what is being read. Students must be able to apply study skills when interpreting charts, tables, graphs, and formulas. The technical vocabulary of science can also present problems to students.

While all these difficulties may seem insurmountable, they are not. The procedures presented in the *Focus on Skills* features in ***Focus on Physical Science*** are there to help students achieve success in science.

Efficient and effective study requires that students be able to organize scientific data into a logical structure. In order to do this successfully, students must first be shown the organizational method that the text uses and then be led to apply this method on their own. That is the rationale for the Reading Inventory and the emphasis on note taking in the *Focus on Skills* features. Notes can be organized in chart, outline, or diagram form. These models can serve as future guides for students. When the scientific reading is difficult, you might supply students with a skeletal plan.

Chapter previews serve as an effective means of introducing students to new material. The preview also serves to set the purpose for reading the specific chapter.

Early in the course students should develop skill in gaining accurate information from graphic aids such as charts, diagrams, and graphs. Some of the *Focus on Skills* pages encourage students to look critically at charts and illustrations. Make it a point to direct your students in the use of these aids until they reach a level where they see the purpose of the aids themselves and can use them independently.

It is also important that students use the built-in aids when defining and mastering vocabulary. In ***Focus on Physical Science,*** technical terms are presented in boldface type and, for the most part, defined in context. Many students read in a superficial manner. Though they may recognize a word they may not know what it means. The *Focus on Skills* features help students decipher the correct meaning from context. Students should also be encouraged to use their glossary as a regular aid to vocabulary development.

Readings to Discover at the end of each chapter can give you a start at compiling a bibliography of reference material for your students. Encourage students to be looking for pertinent articles in the local newspaper and in the national news magazines. Various industries provide booklets and pamphlets which students may find interesting. Not all scientific information at this level need come from technical journals.

It is probably wiser to start students out on familiar ground before you proceed to the more academic reading found in journals.

Bibliography

Barbe, Walter B., Levin, A. Joyce, Rehling, Charles W. and Margaret H., *Reading Skills Check List and Activities, Advanced Level.* The Center for Applied Research in Education, Inc., West Nyack, NY, 1976.

Heilman, Arthur W., *Principles and Practices of Teaching Reading,* 4th ed. Charles E. Merrill Publishing Co., Columbus, OH, 1977.

Shepherd, David L., *Comprehensive High School Reading Methods,* 2nd ed. Charles E. Merrill Publishing Co., Columbus, OH, 1978.

West, Gail B., *Teaching Reading Skills in Content Areas: A Practical Guide to the Construction of Student Exercises.* Sandpiper Press, Inc., Orlando, FL, 1974.

Unit 1 Measurement and Motion

Overview

In Chapter 1 physical science is defined and measurement skills are introduced utilizing SI units. The methods of science used to develop and test ideas are clearly established. A smooth transition is made to Chapter 2 where the relationship between force and work is developed in studying machines. The concept of balanced and unbalanced forces, introduced in Chapter 2, is further developed in Chapter 3. Emphasis is placed on the fact that all motion starts and stops through the action of forces. The final chapter of the unit deals with the effect of forces on the speed and direction of moving objects through a presentation of Newton's Laws of Motion and Galileo's work with falling objects.

Teaching Tips

- Start a "junk box." On the first day of school, ask students to bring in one or two small unwanted items from home. The "junk box" will have numerous uses throughout the year. In Chapter 1, you will use these items for the Activity on page 7.
- A bulletin board display of different systems of measurement can be very effective in emphasizing the simplicity of SI units.
- Arrange a display table or board with examples of simple and compound machines. If on a board, they can be hung using strong cord and tacks. Examples might be a screwdriver, hammer, eggbeater, scissors. You may prefer to have students bring in pictures instead of using real objects.
- Have students make a display of everyday items found at home, the grocery, or hardware store that have quantities labeled in SI units.

1 The Nature of Science

Overview

Chapter 1 introduces physical science as the study of matter and energy. It discusses the methods of science and introduces measurement and standard units. The chapter opening photo can be used to begin a discussion concerning your class' concept of a scientist. You can use this discussion to formulate a definition of science in general. At this point, focus in on the nature of physical science so students have an idea what they will be studying.

At this time, you may also want students to complete the Textbook Inventory in the front of their book. Students are usually excited about using a new text. It is important to acquaint them with its features as soon as possible. Hopefully, in using these features to their full advantage, they will be more successful in their studies.

Performance Objectives

Goal: Students will gain an understanding of the nature and methods of science. They will learn how measurements, experiments, and other scientific methods are used in physical science.

Objectives: Upon completion of the reading and activities and when asked to diagram, demonstrate, or respond either orally or on a written test, students will:

1:1	K	define physical science.
1:2-3	K	list methods used by scientists in developing and testing scientific knowledge.
1:4	K	differentiate between theory and law.
1:5-9	K/P	explain the uses of measurement standards and list the units used to measure length, volume, mass, and temperature.
	S/P	conduct activities to develop skill in measurement practices.
	S/A	demonstrate proper use of equipment and materials.
	A	attempt at least one *More Ideas to Explore.*

Equipment for Activities

The amounts listed are for a class of 30 students broken down into groups of 2.

assorted small blocks of wood or metal—45
assorted small objects, easily recognized—30 to 40
balance, double pan—5
balloons—30
beakers
250 mL—15 400 mL—15
Bunsen burner—15
cloths—15
flasks, 500 mL—30
glass tubes, 10 cm—30
graduated cylinder, 25 mL—15
lead sinkers—15
matches
paper
ring stand and ring—15
ruler, metric—15
stoppers, 1-hole—30
string
test tubes, several sizes—45
thermometers—15
trays—2
wire screens—15
Chemicals
ice
mineral oil

1:1 Physical Science

You may wish to spend time helping students develop an understanding of the term "property." The material in Units 2, 3, and 4 will be an indepth study comparing and contrasting the properties of matter.

You may wish to give an early quiz on laboratory equipment if you plan to allow students to undertake the Activities. Refer students to the Laboratory Techniques section and Safety Rules in the Appendix. Time spent now familiarizing students with laboratory procedures will pay off the rest of the year.

Page 5. Making Sure

1. The rider (you) furnishes the energy. The bicycle and rider move as a result of the movement of the feet and pedals.
2. Food supplies one's body energy.

1:2 Methods of Science

You may want to have a discussion concerning myths and legends. These are often the result of hasty conclusions. Such notions like "the world is flat" were believed for long periods of time. By contrast, scientific methods are based on separating observations from inferences, and facts from conclusions.

Activity 1-1

This Activity tests a student's memory and observational acuity.

Materials needed: Any number of objects can be used. Make certain that everyone in the class is familiar with the objects you use.

Questions: A tape recorder would help. Students could "read" the objects on the tray. A camera would record a total picture for study later. Both of these devices are becoming important tools to the scientist.

1:3 Using Experiments

You may want to spend time here showing students how you prefer they organize their Activity report sheets. A sample report is given in Figure 1-3. Emphasize the function of the control in scientific research.

Activity 1-2

The title of the Activity is the hypothesis. The procedure tests this hypothesis and makes use of a control.

Materials needed: 2-500 mL Erlenmeyer flasks, 2 one-hole stoppers, 2 pieces of glass tubing, 2 balloons, and a hot plate.

Questions: When the flask is heated, the balloon expands. When the flask is cooled, the balloon contracts. Note that flask B does not change.

Page 8. Making Sure

3. Problem: Do pigeons use the sun to find their way home?
   Procedure: Release pigeons on a sunny day. Count the number that return. Release the same pigeons on a cloudy day from the same place. Count the number that return.
   Observation: All 25 returned on the sunny day. Only 10 returned on the cloudy day.
   Conclusion: The sun has some effect on a pigeon's ability to find its way home. This conclusion may or may not be correct. Stress that replication of experiments is extremely important to scientists.
4. The group not given the drug is the control.

1:4 Theories and Laws

It is important to differentiate between theories and laws. Abandon the old idea that a law is a theory proven to be correct. A law is an observed fact. For example, Newton's second law of motion states: *Acceleration of an object increases as the amount of force causing the acceleration increases.* This statement represents an observed fact. A theory is an explanation of how or why a phenomenon occurs.

1:5 Measurement

You may want to have a discussion of old measurement standards and the limitations of each.

The International System of Units is used throughout the text. You may find some of the units to be unfamiliar, i.e. joules for work and heat energy. However, your students will be learning fewer units using this system. Only the prefixes *kilo-*, *centi-*, and *milli-* are used in the text with the exception of decibel in Chapter 17. Additional information concerning the International System is found in Appendix A. You can use this discussion to reinforce the idea that SI is really much simpler to use than English units. You can have students make a list of English units and the conversion factors which show the relationships between each. They can do the same for SI units. The SI list should be shorter and less complicated.

Note that commas are not used to group digits in long numbers. In some countries, a comma indicates a decimal point. To avoid confusion, the American National Metric Council recommends using spaces to separate groups of three digits. For example:

10 000 100 000 1 000 000
0.000 01 0.000 001

1:6 Measuring Length

You will note throughout the text that English measurement standards are not used for comparison in the text discussions. For example, the length of a meter is described as being about as long as a golf club. An attempt is being made to get students to think in terms of SI units rather than trying to convert back and forth between SI and English units. Figure 1-5 is another example of this approach. The distances are measured in SI units. Students should be able to grasp the relative magnitudes of each measurement. Making Sure questions on page 12 ask students to estimate the lengths of objects in terms of SI units. In order to answer these questions, they must develop a concept of each unit of length.

Activity 1-3

The Activity provides practice in measuring length. Students are also learning to use maps and distance scales. You may want to develop map reading further by asking students to bring in maps of their community or state. You can have them measure various distances using these maps. Map reading is a lifetime skill.

Materials needed: metric rulers

Page 12. Making Sure

5. 88 km/h This question should not involve a conversion process. Most cars now have speedometers also calibrated in kilometers. The question can be answered by reading the speedometer when traveling on a freeway.
6. golf club and bath towel are examples
7. the little fingernail, the distance between lines ~~on~~ standard notebook paper, and the width of a large paper clip are examples
8. wire diameter, book thickness, tape width, and camera film are examples

1:7 Measuring Volume

The American National Metric Association recommends the use of the liter and milliliter for fluids and dry ingredients in recipes. The unit derived from SI base units is the cubic meter. However, this unit is too large for everyday use. Emphasize the relationship between milliliters and cubic centimeters as these units are used interchangeably throughout the text.

Figure 1-7 should be used to give students a concept of the relative magnitudes of volume measurements. You will note most measuring cups for cooking now have metric equivalents listed on them. Science equipment supply houses now stock sets of all metric cups and spoons. If you can make arrangements with the school home economics department, a metric cooking activity could be fun.

In this section use Figure 1-8 to emphasize the proper way to read the liquid level in a graduate. This skill is necessary for the following Activity.

Activity 1-4

The Activity provides opportunity for practice in measuring volumes as well as recording and interpreting data. Students measure liquid volumes in Part A. The calculated volume of a regular solid is compared to the volume reading obtained by water displacement. Emphasize this relationship. In Part C, students measure volumes of irregular solids. In answering the Summing Up questions, students are expected to think in terms of which volume measuring method is most suitable for a particular situation.

Be sure students have read through the Activity and have rewritten the data tables in their notebooks. Getting ready for lab makes a good homework assignment. You might check to see that students are prepared by asking a few questions about the activity before they begin.

Summing Up

1. They should be the same. An object should displace a volume of water equal to its volume. If they were not submerged completely, the volumes might be different.
2. The volumes should be the same. Inaccurate readings could be the source of error.
3. A 4. B or C 5. A or B

Page 15. Making Sure

9. 7 mL
10. teaspoon, tablespoon, cup; measurements are defined more precisely
11. 3125 cm^3

1:8 Measuring Weight and Mass

It is important to establish the difference between weight and mass. These units are never used interchangeably in this text. Emphasize that different types of devices are used for measuring each. Figure 1-10 shows two types of spring scales used to measure weight. Both springs actually measure the amount of force exerted by the weighed object. These photos may help students see the relationship of weight and force. The grocery store in Figure 1-13 should help students conceptualize the relative magnitudes of mass measurements. In the text, common objects like a paper clip and their book are used as reference points.

Activity 1-5

Refer students to Appendix B, pages 498-499, for a background discussion on using the balance. The Activity provides practice in measuring mass.

Materials needed: balance, three objects (wood or metal blocks, sinkers, or similar objects), and a beaker

Questions: Answers will vary on the mass of water. It can be found by subtracting the mass of the beaker from the mass of the beaker and water. Find the mass of the balloon empty and full, then subtract.

1:9 Measuring Temperature

Figure 1-14a shows a temperature reading on a thermometer. You may want to spend time with students on reading a thermometer before attempting Activity 1-6. Figure 1-14b should help students conceptualize some temperatures on the Celsius scale. The SI temperature unit, the kelvin, is presented in Chapter 9 in the discussion of cryogenics. Background information concerning kelvin temperature is found in Appendix A, pages 496-497 in case you wish to present it here.

At this point you can stress the inadequacy of our senses and the need for instruments to describe length, time, mass, and especially temperature. Try the following demonstration: Prepare four pans of water. Pan 1 contains ice and water. Pans 2 and 3 contain lukewarm water at the same temperature. Pan 4 contains very warm water. Have student volunteers place their left hands in pan 1 and their right hands in pan 4. After a few minutes, have each place the left hand in pan 2 and the right hand in pan 3. Ask each student to describe the temperature of the water in pans 2 and 3. Have another student read the temperature of the water in each pan with a thermometer. The need for precise measuring tools should be apparent.

Activity 1-6

The Activity provides practice in measuring temperature. You may want to keep the results of the Activity in mind when you cover change of state in Chapter 18.

Summing Up

2. The temperature rises when all ice is melted.
3. The temperature stops rising at the boiling point.
4. It stopped because it reached the boiling point.

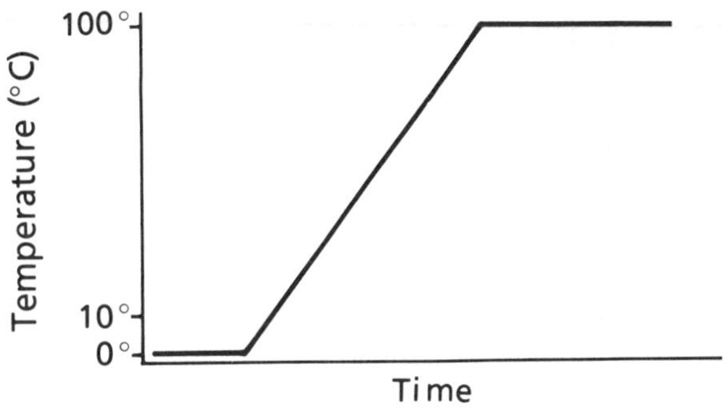

Questions for Review

A. True or False

1. True **2.** False (A hypothesis is not always true.) **3.** True **4.** False (The control in an experiment is not the same as a conclusion.) **5.** False (A scientific law can be changed.) **6.** True **7.** False (The liter is the unit of volume.) **8.** False (Mass is measured in kilograms.) **9.** False (Mass and weight are different.) **10.** True

B. Multiple Choice

1. 100 **2.** 1/100 **3.** 10 **4.** 1/1000 **5.** 1000 **6.** 1000 **7.** milliliter **8.** 1 **9.** 1000 **10.** length

C. Completion

1. 1/100 **2.** 100 **3.** volume **4.** 4 **5.** 15 **6.** 10 **7.** Celsius **8.** volume **9.** newtons (N) **10.** 1000

D. How and Why

1. Examples are rulers (centimeters), thermometer (degrees), graduated cylinder (cm^3), sextant (angles), balance (grams)
2. Physical science is the study of matter and energy.
3. Easy to calculate, worldwide use and acceptance
4. mass—balance; volume—graduated cylinder
5. 0.250 L, 0.100 L, 0.500 L
6. 1000 mL, 500 mL
7. 0.55 m, 5.50 m, 55.00 m

More Ideas to Explore

4. The scale in the doctor's office is a balance. Your bathroom scale is a spring scale.

2 Force and Work

Overview

The concepts of force and work are developed through the presentation of simple and compound machines. Mechanical advantage, friction, power, and efficiency are explored.

Performance Objectives

Goal: Students will learn how machines can change forces and do work.

Objectives: Upon completion of the reading and activities and when asked to diagram, demonstrate, or respond either orally or on a written test, students will:

2:1	P	compare and contrast force and resistance.
2:2	P	explain how work is related to force and distance.
2:3-8	K	list the six simple machines and give examples of each.
2:4-8	S	determine the mechanical advantage of each type of simple machine.
2:4-8	S/P	conduct activities to demonstrate how machines make work easier.
2:9	P	relate efficiency to work output and work input.
2:10	P	explain the relationship among power, work, watt, and joule.
	S/K	solve numerical problems related to work, mechanical advantage, power, and efficiency.
	S/A	demonstrate proper use of equipment and materials.
	A	attempt at least one *More Ideas to Explore.*

Equipment for Activities

The amounts listed are for a class of 30 students broken down into groups of 2.

cardboard sheets—15
clamps, extension—15
clock with second hand or stopwatch—15
marbles—15
metal washers—150
meter stick—15
paper clips—30
paper cups—15
pulleys—45
ring stand—15
ruler, metric—15
scissors—15
spring, coil 7 to 10 cm—15
spring scale
  5 newton—30 20 newton—15
string
weight, 2 newton (0.2 kg mass)—15
wood
  large blocks or bricks—15
  planks 0.5 m, smooth—15

2:1 Force

Stress the relationship among force, weight, and newtons. Tie the material on weight presented in Chapter 1 to force in Chapter 2. Note that the formal definition of the newton will not be presented until Chapter 4. Until the students have studied acceleration (Chapter 3), they will not be able to grasp the formal definition.

You may wish to have some students demonstrate force by moving various size objects, such as hitting different size balls with a bat on the playground.

Activity 2-1

The Activity helps students understand the concept of force (weight) and the development of a standard scale for measurement.

Materials needed: ring stand, clamp, spring, string, paper cup, paper clip, cardboard, ten washers, marble, pencil, and ruler.

You may wish to do one large demonstration but the Activity will be more effective if teams of two or more students can work on their own. When dispensing materials, be sure to provide the exact amount your class will need. Account for everything at clean-up time to prevent a marble or paper clip from becoming a projectile later in the day in someone else's class.

Questions: Washers are not used as standard units of force because they vary in size and weight.

If the spring were overloaded, it would not go back to the zero point when the load is removed. The stretched spring will cause the measurements to be inaccurate.

Page 24. Making Sure

1. The forces of muscles on bones move your body parts.
2. You can lift yourself by sitting on a chair, placing your hands on the chair, and pushing down. In order to lift yourself, the force must be greater than your weight.

2:2 Work

Before students are asked to read this section, demonstrate the following: Ask a student to push as hard as possible against the wall for at least a minute. Ask another student near you to hand you a piece of paper or a pencil. Then, ask the class which student has worked harder. Take a vote. Indicate no right or wrong answer. Have a few students define their answers. An open question such as this one will give you a great deal of information about the background of your students. After the discussion, assign the reading.

This book will continue to use SI units, using the joule rather than calories, foot-pounds, or newton-meters. Using joules cuts down on the number of different abstract units your students will have to learn throughout the year. The joule is used again in Section 2:10 on power and in the heat and energy discussions in Chapters 18 and 19.

Page 25. Making Sure

3. $W = F \times d$
   $W = 60 \text{ N} \times 0.5 \text{ m} = 30 \text{ J}$
4. $W = F \times d$
   $W = 14 \text{ N} \times 0.5 \text{ m} = 7 \text{ J}$
5. Less work is needed to push the suitcase because the force necessary to overcome friction is less than that to overcome gravity.
6. $W = F \times d$
   $W = 40 \text{ N} \times 4 \text{ m} = 160 \text{ J}$

2:3 Machines

Refer to the examples of machines you have on display. Ask students in what way they think each machine makes work easier. It may change the direction of the force, increase the force applied, or increase speed. Use the tables on page 26 if you do not have a display. Have students study Table 2-1. Ask them to list other common objects that could be classified as one of the six simple machines. You may want to refer back to Table 2-2 once students have studied each of the simple machines in Sections 2:4-8. Once again have them list familiar objects and the simple machines that comprise each.

Hand two pieces of sandpaper to a student. Ask the student to rub the papers together. Note the friction created. Have the student put some grease (petroleum jelly will do) between the pieces and rub again. The friction is reduced because the grease fills the irregularities on the surface of the paper. Applying grease to the moving parts reduces friction in the same way. This idea is presented in Section 2:9 Efficiency.

Page 28. Making Sure

7. **a.** The force used to move the pedals of a bicycle is converted into a large force of the wheel pushing on the road.
   b. The oar acts as a lever to push the boat.
   c. The needle of a sewing machine acts as a wedge with a large gain in speed over hand sewing.
   d. The elevator uses pulleys to reduce the force needed to lift objects.
8. The friction of the boat and water and the oar and oar lock increases the amount of force needed to move the boat. However, if there were no friction between the oar and the water, the boat would not move.

2:4 Levers

Use Figure 2-3 to point out the parts of a lever. There is a game on the market called *Jaws.* It is based on the leverage concept. Objects are placed in the mouth of the plastic model. The objects are removed before the jaw snaps shut. One of your students may have this game at home. There are other games which may also be used, *The Last Straw* and *Don't Spill the Beans* are examples.

Activity 2-2

The Activity gives practice with the first class lever.

Materials needed: ruler, pencil, three washers

Questions: The single washer is twice as far from the fulcrum as the double washer.

The ruler is a lever because it is free to turn about a fixed point (the pencil).

2:5 Mechanical Advantage

Reinforce the idea that the M.A. of a lever depends on the lengths of the effort arm and resistance arm. Ask students if they would prefer to use a small twig or a large branch to move a large rock. If it is easy for your class to go outdoors, take them out to try different size levers.

Page 30. Making Sure

9. $M.A. = \frac{\textit{effort arm}}{\textit{resistance arm}} \quad M.A. = \frac{45 \text{ cm}}{6 \text{ cm}} = 7.5$

10. $M.A. = \frac{\textit{effort arm}}{\textit{resistance arm}} \quad M.A. = \frac{0.8 \text{ m}}{0.2 \text{ m}} = 4$

2:6 Pulleys

Ask the students to look around the room for examples of pulleys (window shades and blinds).

Activity 2-3

The Activity gives practice in working with pulleys and in determining mechanical advantage.

Summing Up

1. The force is nearly divided by the number of supporting ropes.
2. $W = F \times d$
   $W = 2 \text{ N} \times 0.2 \text{ m} = 0.4 \text{ J}$
3. $W = F \times d$
   $W = 2 \text{ N} \times 0.2 \text{ m} = 0.4 \text{ J}$
4. $W = F \times d$
   $W = 2 \text{ N} \times 0.2 \text{ m} = 0.4 \text{ J}$

Point out to students that the amount of work done by each pulley system is the same. However, they will note from their spring scales that the force required to do the work is different.

2:7 Wheel and Axle

Remove the cover from a pencil sharpener and tie a string tightly around the end of the shaft. Tie one or two books or some other object to the end of the string and turn the handle. Note that the force needed to turn the handle is much less than the force of gravity on the object. Point out that the pencil sharpener is being used as a wheel and axle. Note that the handle is the wheel (larger radius) and that the shaft is the axle (smaller radius). They can determine the mechanical advantage by measuring. Be sure to point out that the doorknob is also a wheel and axle. If possible have a disassembled doorknob available for inspection.

Page 34. Making Sure

11. Answers will vary; automobile, lawnmower, bicycle, steering wheel, eggbeater are some examples.
12. $M.A. = \frac{\textit{radius of wheel}}{\textit{radius of axle}} \quad M.A. = \frac{1.5 \text{ cm}}{0.25 \text{ cm}} = 6$
13. $M.A. = \frac{\textit{radius of wheel}}{\textit{radius of axle}} \quad M.A. = \frac{3.5 \text{ cm}}{1.5 \text{ cm}} = 2.33$

2:8 Inclined Planes

Make sure students study Figure 2-9 to see why a screw and wedge are considered inclined planes.

Activity 2-4

The Activity demonstrates use of the inclined plane as a simple machine.

Summing Up

1. It takes less force to move the block up the plane.
2. Answers will vary. Use $W = F\text{ (N)} \times d\text{ (m)}$
3. Answers will vary. Again use force in newtons and distance in meters.
4. It takes more work to move the block.

Students should understand that even though it requires more work to move the block using the inclined plane, it takes less force.

Page 37. Making Sure

14. The stairs break the distance into smaller steps and change the direction of the force.
15. The mountain has the same effect as the stairs.
16. Can opener, scissors, knife, and ax are some examples.

17. Soap or wax is used to reduce friction.
18. The screw has the inclined plane wrapped around a shaft.

2:9 Efficiency

You might find it interesting to introduce perpetual motion machines at this time. This topic could be used as a library research project.

Page 39. Making Sure

19. The efficiency is decreased when the tires are low because the friction between the tires and the road surface is increased.
20. Cars that have a teardrop shape allow wind to flow over them. Friction is reduced.
21. An engine with a low efficiency would use more fuel.

2:10 Power

Watt is the SI unit of power. This unit is used again in Unit 6 concerning electricity. Horsepower is introduced only because it is a term that may be familiar to students. You can ask students to check appliances in their homes for the power ratings of each. It would be interesting for students to see the wide range for some appliances like stereos or vacuum cleaners.

Activity 2-5

The Activity gives a practical use of power. Students can vary the speed and compare the power.

Materials needed: meter stick, timing device

Use the following equation to convert students' weights from pounds to newtons.

$$\textit{weight in newtons} = \frac{\textit{9.8 (student weight in pounds)}}{\textit{2.2 pounds}}$$

Page 40. Making Sure

22. 1 kW = 1000 W

a. 4.5 kW	b. 0.001 kW
c. 10 kW	d. 0.00025 kW

23. $P = \frac{W}{t}$

$$P = \frac{4000 \text{ J}}{20 \text{ s}} = 200 \text{ W}$$

Questions for Review

A. True or False

1. True 2. False (A pulley is an example of a simple machine.) 3. False (The mechanical advantage of a machine is not always greater than one.) 4. True 5. False (An eggbeater is an example of a compound machine.) 6. True 7. True 8. False (One watt is one joule of work per second.) 9. True 10. False (Friction decreases the mechanical advantage of a machine.)

B. Multiple Choice

1. force 2. work 3. lever 4. two or more 5. Friction 6. Fulcrum 7. spring scale 8. first 9. wheel and axle 10. inclined plane

C. Completion

1. friction 2. 4 3. output, input 4. efficiency 5. supporting strands 6. unbalanced 7. heat 8. lever 9. two 10. low

D. How and Why

1. They are all simple machines. They use effort distance and resistance distance.
2. $W = F \times d$
   $W = 25 \text{ N} \times 10 \text{ m} = 250 \text{ J}$
3. $P = \frac{W}{t}$
   $P = \frac{21\,600 \text{ J}}{180 \text{ s}} = 120 \text{ W}$
4. Power is a measure of work in a unit of time. Since both machines put out the same amount of work, the one with the most power will do the work faster.
5. $W = F \times d$ $\quad W = 780 \text{ N} \times 5 \text{ m} = 3900 \text{ J}$

More Ideas to Explore

1. A mobile is made by balancing objects on both ends of a bar (lever) resting on a fulcrum.
2. Students might want to build a model of an early experiment.
3. Mixer, blender, washer, dryer, disposal are examples.
4. The EPA will have information on fuel economy.
5. Local dealers should be good sources of information on motorcycles.

3 Moving Objects

Overview

The chapter begins with a presentation of how the force of gravity affects the weight of objects. Concepts related to the motion of objects, such as speed, velocity, and acceleration are developed. The dependence of energy on speed, mass and position of objects is firmly established. This chapter confirms the information in Chapter 2 that all motion starts and stops through the action of forces.

Performance Objectives

Goal: Students will gain an understanding of forces, motion, energy, work, and the relationship among them.

Objectives: Upon completion of the reading and activities and when asked to diagram, demonstrate, or respond either orally or on a written test, students will:

3:1	K	differentiate between weight and mass.
3:2	K	define gravity as a property of all matter.
3:3-4	P/K	compare and contrast speed, velocity, and average speed.
3:5	P	compare acceleration and deceleration.
3:6	K	define kinetic and potential energy.
	S/K	solve problems relating to gravity and speed.

Equipment for Activities

The amounts listed are for a class of 30 students broken into groups of 2.

balance, double pan—5
graduated cylinder, 25 mL—15
lead sinkers—15
rubber bands
spring scale, 5 newton—15
string

3:1 Weight and Mass

The reading on the scale under water is not your normal weight. Your mass does not change. The water has a buoyant force which reduces the force of gravity. Thus, your weight is less.

Activity 3-1

This Activity develops experimentally the difference between weight and mass. It is suggested that students have their data tables set up before they begin the Activity. Review how to read the water level in a graduated cylinder.

Summing Up

1. The graduate gains both mass and weight as water is added.
2. The sinker loses weight when it is submerged.

3-4. Answers will vary. The weight the sinker loses equals the weight of water the graduate gains.

3:2 Gravity

Ask the students to describe what they think the earth would be like with no gravity. Try to elicit responses related to such things as the water cycle, the oceans, tides and currents.

Ask the students if they can push or pull an object without touching it. Discuss some forces that can—gravity, magnetism.

You might want to use a magnet and some paper clips to show how distance affects the attraction.

Use this section to reinforce math skills relating to fractions and squaring numbers.

Page 47. Making Sure

1. Your weight would be $^1/_4$ that on Earth.
2. 12 800 km is 3 times distance from the center of the Earth to the surface. Therefore, your weight would be $^1/_9$ that on Earth.

3:3 Speed

Show students how to manipulate the equation for speed to isolate each variable. All students should have a clear understanding of how to arrive at

$$t = d/s \text{ from } s = d/t$$

You can use proportions $\frac{s}{1} = \frac{d}{t}$. Cross multiply, then divide both sides by s. $\frac{d}{s} = \frac{st}{s}$ $t = \frac{d}{s}$.

Show students how units cancel when solving the problem.

Page 49. Making Sure

3. $s = \frac{d}{t}$

$s = \frac{100\text{m}}{50\text{ s}}$

$s = 2\text{ m/s}$

4. $d = st$

$d = (500\text{ m/s})(10\text{ min})(60\text{ s/min})$

$d = 300\,000\text{ m}$

3:4 Average Speed

Time should be spent familiarizing students with graphs. You may want to use the *Focus on Skills* (p. 53) at this point. The graphs in Figure 3-3 show students the graphic difference between a trip at constant speed and a trip with a number of starts and stops. Impress upon students that both vehicles can have the same average speed.

Ask students to recall a recent trip they have made. Have them identify the total distance traveled and the total time it took them. Help them calculate their average speed, making sure they realize that there were times when they traveled slower than the average speed and that there were times when they traveled faster than the average speed.

Page 50. Making Sure

5. 3-3a after 5 min = 400 m/min $\frac{2000\text{ m}}{5\text{ min}}$

after 10 min = 400 m/min $\frac{4000\text{ m}}{10\text{ min}}$

3-3b after 5 min = 250 m/min $\frac{1250\text{ m}}{5\text{ min}}$

after 10 min = 225 m/min $\frac{2250\text{ m}}{10\text{ min}}$

6. *average speed* $= \frac{10\text{ km}}{45\text{ min}}$

$= 0.22\text{ km/min}$

or for an answer in km/h

$(0.22\text{ km/min})(60\text{ min/h}) = 13.3\text{ km/h}$

3:5 Acceleration

The concepts behind velocity and acceleration may be very abstract to most students. Stress the difference between these two rates. Students should compare Figures 3-4 and 3-5 with the graphs in Figure 3-3. Make sure they realize that an acceleration of zero does not necessarily mean the object is at rest. Students should note that Figure 3-4a is the reverse of Figure 3-5. This graphic representation should reinforce the difference between acceleration and deceleration.

Page 51. Making Sure

7. Accelerate

   car—force produced by the engine and the tires against the road.

   bicycle—force produced by the cyclist pushing against the pedals.

   jet plane—reaction force by the jet engine similar to a released balloon.

   Decelerate

   car—brake drum against wheel and wheel against road.

   bicycle—force of foot on pedal or hands on hand brake, wheel on road.

   jet plane—force of air, reversing engines, brakes, wheels on runway.

8. 8 m/s

3:6 Energy

Have students relate their ideas of the definition of energy to the scientific definition of energy—the ability to do work. You can develop potential energy as follows:

Find the mass of a small rock. Lift it from a table top to a shelf or some higher position above the table. Measure the vertical distance through which you moved the rock. Ask if you did work to move the rock. Have students calculate how much work was done. Explain that this work (energy) has been stored in the rock and that theoretically the rock has the potential to do work equal to that which you put in to it. Let the rock fall to a position halfway to the table. Note that it still has some stored energy. Allow it to fall all the way to the table. Now ask if it still has some stored energy (yes, it can still fall closer to the center of the earth—off the table to the floor, then if you are on the second floor, it could fall to the first floor, and so on.) When falling, the stored potential energy is changed to kinetic energy.

Ask how many students have been on a roller coaster. Have students turn to pages 2 and 3. Using this photo or others you may have of roller coasters, you can ask the following discussion questions:

1. How do the designers of a roller coaster utilize changes from kinetic to potential energy? (Coaster is lifted by a power source to the top of an incline. Coaster falls and then rises to next peak using stored potential energy from when it moved to the top of the first peak.)
2. Are there any patterns in the design of the peaks or are they just a random arrangement?
3. Are the relative heights of each peak important?
4. What sort of training would a roller coaster designer need? (career emphasis)

You may wish to pursue amusement park rides and the physics applied as long as the interest is there. You might even be able to plan a field trip if you are close to an amusement park. Maybe you can get a group of students to design a bulletin board around the "Physics of an Amusement Park."

After students have read Section 3:6, ask them which could do more damage, the train or the car moving at the same speed. (The train has more energy.) Ask: Why does the train have more energy? (It has more mass.) Ask: Which of the two cars described in the section could do more damage and why? (The car traveling at 90 km/h has more energy because it is traveling faster.)

Focus on Skills

Using and Interpreting Graphs

The three types of graphs shown on this page are used in various places throughout the text. Additional reinforcement and information on graphing can be found in ***Focus on Physical Science: Review and Reinforcement Guide.***

Page numbers of in-text graphs
Bar graphs—294, 355
Line graphs—49, 50, 51, 224, 349, 378, 460, 461
Circle graphs—172, 476

Answers

1. 1930-1970 **2.** miles per gallon **3.** 1940
4a. 13.2 **b.** 15.2 **c.** 14.5 **d.** 13.8
5. 1930-1940 2 MPG's
1. 1975-1980 **2.** 1960-1965 **3a.** 14 cents
b. 36 cents **c.** $1.15 **4.** 60 cents
1. 100% **2.** automobiles—boats
3a. 481 barrels **b.** 620 barrels **c.** 1412 barrels

Focus on People

Teen Energy Saver

Nick now splits his time between attending classes at Southern Methodist University and running Parsec. His success shows that a person does not need a degree to make contributions to science and technology. All a person needs is common sense and initiative. Have your students research some famous people who made contributions at a young age without credentials. Some examples are Edison, Bell, and Einstein. Also, have your students research other young people who are making contributions. Articles may be found in magazines such as *Science News* and *Popular Science.* Another source is the annual Science Talent Search sponsored by Westinghouse Electric Corporation and Science Service. Information is available from Science Service in Washington, D.C.

Questions for Review

A. True or False

1. True **2.** True **3.** True **4.** True
5. True **6.** True **7.** True **8.** True
9. False (The kilometer is a unit of length.)
10. False (A moving object has potential energy.)

B. Multiple Choice

1. newton **2.** 30 km/h **3.** $s = \frac{d}{t}$
4. loses speed **5.** kilograms **6.** gravity
7. rates **8.** decreases **9.** speed **10.** joule

C. Completion

1. weight **2.** gravity **3.** direction **4.** time **5.** accelerates **6.** newton **7.** force **8.** deceleration **9.** negative **10.** potential

D. How and Why

1. *average speed* $= \frac{d}{t}$

$= \frac{120 \text{ km}}{2 \text{ h}} = \frac{60 \text{ km}}{\text{h}}$

$\frac{60 \text{ km}}{\text{h}} \times \frac{1 \text{ h}}{60 \text{ min}} = 1 \text{ km/min}$

2. $1 \text{ m/s}^2 \times 6 \text{ s} = 6 \text{ m/s}$

3. *average speed* $= \frac{d}{t}$

$= \frac{18 \text{ m}}{6 \text{ s}} = 3 \text{ m/s}$

4. The sledgehammer exerts more mass than the tackhammer.

5. $\frac{6 \text{ m/s}}{3 \text{ m/s}^2} = 2$ seconds

4 Laws of Motion

Overview

The effect of forces on the speed and direction of moving objects is continued in this chapter. Newton's Laws of Motion are introduced and reinforced through numerous examples, applications, and activities. The work of Galileo and falling objects is presented. Motion in two directions is covered in Sections 4:5 and 4:6. The relationship among mass, velocity, and momentum is presented in the last section.

Performance Objectives

Goal: Students will gain an understanding of Newton's laws, motion related to gravity, projectiles and curves, and momentum.

Objectives: Upon completion of the reading and activities and when asked to diagram, demonstrate, or respond either orally or on a written test, students will:

4:1-3	K	state Newton's three laws and give examples of each.
4:1-3	S/P	conduct activities to demonstrate Newton's Laws.
4:4	K	explain the effect of gravity on falling objects.
4:5	S/P	conduct an activity to demonstrate how the velocity of a projectile changes during flight.
4:6	K	define centripetal force and describe situations in which this force acts on an object.
4:7	K	indicate the relationship among mass, velocity, and momentum.
	S/A	demonstrate proper use of equipment and materials.
	A	attempt at least one *More Ideas to Explore.*

Equipment for Activities

The amounts listed are for a class of 30 students broken into groups of 2.

cards, index or playing—15
clock with second hand or stopwatches—15
coins, assorted nickels and quarters—30
fishing line, 1.5 m—15 pieces
glass, plastic drinking—15
glass tube 15 cm—15
graph paper, thin centimeter ruled—30
metal washers—135
paper clips—15
ruler, metric—15
spring scale, 20 newton—45
stoppers, 2-hole—15
string
tape, masking

4:1 First Law of Motion

You may want to use the chapter opening photo in a discussion at some time during the chapter. Some of your students may be involved in gymnastics. If possible, try to hold a class in the gym or other suitable location. Students can demonstrate some of their skills. You can discuss with the class how the demonstrators use forces in performing various moves. The student demonstrators can be your best resource as they have probably been well coached in proper techniques.

To illustrate inertia, you can use the following demonstration: Stack 4-5 checkers. Use a ruler to knock the bottom checker out of the stack. Repeat until there is only one checker left.

Call attention to inertia as the cause of injury and damage in car accidents. You can have students research new car safety devices as a topic for discussion.

You can also pick up on the amusement park discussion suggested in the last chapter (see page 46T).

Other examples other than the cases listed throughout the chapter can be used. For example, snow or dirt moved from a shovel demonstrates inertia; hitting a golfball and a baseball or softball with a bat (Newton's Second Law); standing on the floor, your weight down and the floor pushing up (Newton's Third Law).

Activity 4-1

The Activity demonstrates inertia of an object at rest.

Materials needed: drinking glass, various coins, index card, and a sheet of paper

You cannot use paper drinking cups because they are too light. Plastic or metal containers would be safer than glass. You might want to practice this activity yourself before the students try it.

Questions: Yes, the coin remains at rest. Yes, all matter possesses inertia as a property.

Page 61. Making Sure

1. slot car—wheels against track
   sailboat—wind on the sails
   girl—motion of the bus
   The speed and direction is directly proportional to the size and direction of the forces involved.
2. basketball—muscles of the players put the ball in motion
   arrow—snap of the bowstring resulting from the release of potential energy of the bent bow
3. bicycle—rider on pedals, friction of sprockets and wheels
   surfboard—wave against board, board against beach, gravity in a wipe-out
   ball—gravity, wind
4. Seatbelts protect riders from inertia effects resulting from a sudden stop.

4:2 Second Law of Thermodynamics

It is in this section that the precise definition of the newton is introduced. Stress an understanding of this definition.

If you are fortunate to have a student bring in a train set, you might want to show that increasing the number of cars (mass) affects the amount of power needed to get the cars started. You could also demonstrate this concept using a small car or truck (toy). Hook a spring scale to it, and add some weights. Compare the amount of force needed to accelerate the toy from a rest position as the mass increases.

After students have read through the section together, reread the cases on pages 62-63. Emphasize the relationship among force, mass, and acceleration in each case.

Page 63. Making Sure

5. The moving van requires more force to stop because it has greater mass.
6. Examples are bunting or hitting a ball, putting or driving a golfball, pedaling harder on a bike, exerting more pressure on an accelerator, and throwing a ball.

4:3 Third Law of Motion

There are various types of lawn sprinklers on the market other than the one shown in Figure 4-7. You can have students bring in some from home. The class can analyze each to determine how forces are used to cause each to move.

Try the following before assigning the reading: Blow up a balloon. Release it into the air. Have students observe and record independently their observations. Then as a group you can arrive at an explanation for their observations.

If there is a model rocketry club in your school have the members demonstrate their models for the class. Using rockets is a good outdoor activity.

Activity 4-2

The Activity gives an example of action and reaction forces.

Materials needed: three spring scales

Questions: Answers will vary. However, the scales should read the same if there is no motion involved.

Action = Reaction

Using the three scales, the middle scale should equal the sum of the outer two scales.

Page 64. Making Sure

7. The floor exerts an upward force on your feet.
8. The force of the floor against the force of the ball, the compression of the ball, and the release of the compression.
9. The paper reaction force pushing up equals the pencil action force pushing down.
10. Both the rocket and balloon would have the same motion. If there were no gravity, they would continue in a straight line into space.

4:4 Falling Objects

The concept of all falling objects accelerating at the same rate is extremely important: 9.8 m/s. Remind students that ideally this value holds true in a vacuum. Air resistance causes the value to differ. Point out that feathers, handkerchiefs, and pieces of paper offer too much air resistance and consequently accelerate at a slower rate. Also point out terminal velocities differ for different air resistances.

For career emphasis you can discuss how a knowledge of air resistance is important to designers, engineers, and others in the aerodynamics industry.

Page 66. Making Sure

12. $3 \text{ s} \times 9.8 \text{ m/s}^2 = 29.4 \text{ m/s}$

4:5 Motion in Two Directions

Students have a great deal of difficulty believing this section. Eventually they accept the principles more as an act of faith than understanding.

If the students have trouble visualizing and drawing the path they are asked to draw in the first paragraph, remind them that the earth is a moving object. It is therefore analagous to the jet plane described. Students know when they jump straight up on the earth, they land in the same place even though the earth has moved. When you are above the earth, you keep the forward velocity. You continue in the same path as the earth. If they want to jump forward and land ahead in a different spot, they must exert a force in that direction. They have shown motion in two directions—horizontal and vertical.

Activity 4-3

The Activity demonstrates rate of change of velocity during flight.

Materials needed: centimeter graph paper

Questions: The time between each three positions is $3 \times 1/30 = 1/10 = 0.1$ s.

The velocity is the greatest at the beginning and the end of the chart.

The percent change in velocity is greatest at the high point of the curve. The actual change in velocity each second is a constant.

4:6 Motion in Curves

In the car example, the door exerts a force against your body to keep you moving around the curve with the car.

Centrifugal force is not discussed in this text. This force does not actually exist. The effects on objects which many people interpret as centrifugal force are actually the effects of inertia.

Activity 4-4

The Activity gives a definition of centripetal force and its effect on velocity. If weather permits, try to do this Activity outdoors. Before you allow students to proceed, reinforce the following ideas as you whirl the stopper above your head: Your hands are continually pulling the apparatus inward to make it move in a circular path. This inward force is the centripetal force. It is exerted on the stopper by the string. The string causes the stopper to move in a circular path. If the speed of the stopper is increased, the string has to exert a greater force to keep the stopper in a circular path. If the string is shortened, the string again has to exert a greater force.

Summing Up

1. The greater the mass, the shorter the period.
2. The greater the velocity, the greater the centripetal force.

Page 71. Making Sure

13. Due to inertia, the car tends to keep moving in a straight line. The ice reduces friction between the wheels and the ground (centripetal force). The tendency to move in a straight line is greater than the tendency to move toward the center of the curve.
14. The inertia of the sinker pulls the rubber band. The centripetal force increases as it whirls, thus causing the rubber band to stretch.
15. Banking a curve puts more of the car's weight over the wheels increasing the centripetal force.

4:7 Momentum

Ask the following questions: Why does a pitcher windup? (The pitcher winds up to apply force to the ball.) Why does a batter follow through? (The batter keeps the bat in contact with the ball for a longer time with a follow through.) How does a bunt affect the path of the ball? (Bat and ball are in contact for a short time, the ball does not go far.)

Page 73. Making Sure

16. Billiard ball, has more mass than a tennis ball.
17. If the mass and the velocity are the same, the momentum will be the same.
18. Momentum is directly proportional to mass and velocity.
19. The bowling ball has greater mass and thus a greater momentum.
20. Since the acceleration due to gravity is the same for both, their final velocities are the same.

Focus on Frontiers

Imitating a Hip

With the hip simulator as a starting point discuss how machines can be used to help understand how a human body works. Some students may want to research prosthetic devices. To understand how prostheses work have some students construct models of joints. You may want to have a physician give a presentation on prosthetic devices and how joints function.

Questions for Review

A. True or False

1. True 2. True 3. True 4. True 5. False (Water exerts a force to make a lawn sprinkler turn.) 6. False (As the speed of a moving object increases, momentum increases.) 7. False (Speed and acceleration are not the same.) 8. False (To hit a distant target, an arrow is aimed directly above the target.) 9. True 10. True

B. Multiple Choice

1. scale 2. more 3. action-reaction 4. bowling ball 5. equal 6. does not change 7. 2 8. inertia 9. increases 10. opposite

C. Completion

1. Centripetal force 2. newton 3. gravity 4. reaction 5. vertical 6. terminal velocity 7. increases 8. acceleration 9. zero 10. forces opposing motion

D. How and Why

1. It takes more force to accelerate a bowling ball than a baseball to the same rate.
2. Time the fall of the stone. Each second, it accelerates 9.8 m/s. Thus, at the end of the first second it has gone from zero to 9.8 m/s. At the end of the second, it is falling at the rate of 19.6 m/s. Use the equation

   $$\text{distance} = (\text{rate})(\text{time})$$

   and use the average rate.
3. An automatic washer spins the clothes. The water is not held by the centripetal force of the tub (tub has holes in it), as the clothes are. The water moves out of the tub by inertia.

More Ideas to Explore

2. Reports on Dr. Robert Goddard and Dr. Werner von Braun might also be of interest to students.

Unit 2 Classification of Matter

Overview

In the first chapter of the unit, students look at the broad term "matter" through a study of properties. The study of properties is carried on in Chapter 6 where students look at the elements and their arrangement on the periodic table. Chapter 7 considers the behavioral properties of the elements when they combine to form compounds. After studying the unit, students see the importance of developing classification systems in order to study matter more logically. Students should be aware that different criteria can be used to classify matter. However, all classification systems are based on one or more properties of matter (physical state, solubility, reactivity, and so on).

Teaching Tips

- ▶ Prepare lists of items that can be used in a chemical scavenger hunt. For example, ask students to find a substance used in cooking which contains an element from Group I of the periodic table. Students can bring in such items as baking soda ($NaHCO_3$) and table salt ($NaCl$). This type of activity encourages students to note labels. The chapter opening photograph for Chapter 7 also exemplifies this idea.
- ▶ Make a large periodic table for the classroom wall. Even if you have a commercial table, prepare a blank chart. Add symbols and other pertinent information as each element is introduced. Keep the table for use in Unit 3 which is a more detailed study of the elements.

5 Properties of Matter

Overview

Chapter 5 is an introduction to matter. The states of matter are discussed to show students one way that matter can be classified. As students study physical and chemical properties and changes, they begin to look at matter in an analytical manner. Physical changes and properties are further developed in the last section on separating mixtures. There are only six major concepts in this entire chapter. However, it is important that each student understand these basics. Stress these concepts and repeat sections for review. Brief quizzes on each section may help you monitor student progress.

Performance Objectives

Goal: Students will gain an understanding of matter and some of its properties.

Objectives: Upon completion of the reading and activities and when asked to diagram, demonstrate or respond either orally or on a written test, students will:

5:1	K	define matter.
5:1	S	conduct an activity to show that no two pieces of matter can occupy the same place at the same time (one of the text criteria for determining if something is matter).
5:2	K	define the four states of matter.

5:3	K/S	distinguish physical properties of an object.
5:4	K/S/P	conduct an activity to determine the density of an object.
5:5	K/P	distinguish physical changes.
	S/P	conduct activities to determine change of state as a physical change.
5:6	K/S	distinguish chemical properties of a substance.
	P	compare physical and chemical properties.
5:7	K/S	distinguish chemical changes in a substance.
	P	compare physical and chemical changes.
5:8	K	define mixture.
	S/P	conduct an activity to separate a mixture through physical changes.
	S/A	demonstrate proper use of equipment and materials.
	A	attempt at least one *More Ideas to Explore.*

Equipment for Activities

The amounts listed are for a class of 30 students broken into groups of 2.

balance—5
beaker

100 mL—15	400 mL—30
250 mL—15	600 mL—15

clock with second hand or stopwatch—15
filter paper
funnel—15
glass, plastic drinking—45
goggles—30
graduated cylinder, 25 mL—15
hot plates—10
marbles—75
matches
protective clothes
ring stand and ring—15
stirring rod—15
test tubes—15
test tube racks—15
thermometers—30
watch glass—15
wire screens—15
wooden splints

Chemicals
vegetable oil
hydrochloric acid (dilute)—45 mL
ice
molasses
mossy zinc—15 pieces
sodium chloride—4125 grams
sand—375 grams

5:1 Matter

In this section, you want students to formulate an understanding of the characteristics of matter. The questions at the end of the first paragraph are designed to stimulate a thought process. In discussing these and other questions you may think of, students should be able to tell you why something is matter or why it is not.

The theme of the chapter opening photo shows students that matter is everything in the universe that has mass and takes up space.

Activity 5-1

The Activity demonstrates that no two pieces of matter can occupy the same space at the same time.

Materials needed: 25 mL graduated cylinder, 5 marbles, water

Use polypropylene (plastic) graduated cylinders to avoid breaking the glass type when the marbles are dropped into the cylinders. If you only have glass cylinders, have them tilt the cylinder slightly. Stress that the marbles should be rolled gently down the side of the cylinder. Be sure to collect all marbles from students at the conclusion of the Activity.

Questions: The marbles displaced the water. The space occupied by the marbles will vary with the size of the marbles.

Answers will vary ($^1/_5$ of the difference in the water levels).

The amount of air in the cylinder decreases as it is displaced by the water.

5:2 States of Matter

It is important that all students understand the characteristics of each physical state. They have probably covered solids, liquids, and gases in elementary school. The plasma state will be new to them. Many students will probably form a mental model of plasma as blood plasma. Be sure they are aware that plasma particles exist only at high temperatures. Collisions between these particles are so violent that electrons are knocked away from atoms leaving electrically charged particles.

Using the theme of Figure 5-2, have students classify all matter in their classroom by physical state.

5:3 Physical Properties

Have students read the section. Review the table on page 84 with them. Arrange a display containing the following: copper, iron, aluminum, sulfur, water, alcohol, vinegar, naphthalene, ice, ammonia water, copper(II) sulfate, sand, salt, and sugar. Select one sample and list the physical properties of the substance as an example. Then have students list the properties of the others independently. Take pairs of substances such as copper and iron, or water and alcohol. Have students identify the properties they would use to distinguish between them. This activity exemplifies the idea established in paragraphs one and two of the section. For example, physical state shows the difference among water and ice, odor (ammonia and naphthalene), color (copper(II) sulfate and sulfur), magnetic properties (iron and zinc).

Page 85. Making Sure

1. **a.** color, melting point, density
   b. color, taste
   c. odor, taste, density
   d. color, density, luster
   e. taste
   f. shape, color
2. All are colorless and odorless.
3. Solids—glass, plastic wrap
   Liquids—water
   Gases—carbon dioxide, air

5:4 Density

Use Figure 5-5 on page 85 to establish a relationship between mass and volume. It is important that all students have a firm grasp of the fact that in comparing substances greater volume does not always mean greater mass. Once you have developed density as mass per unit volume, ask some application questions. For example, which sample would have the greatest volume—5 grams of gold ($D = 19.3$ g/cm^3) or 5 grams of copper ($D = 8.9$ g/cm^3)? Do not have students calculate the actual volumes at this time. It is more important that they understand the significance of the density values listed in Table 5-1.

Density values in this text are in grams per cubic centimeter (g/cm^3) unless otherwise stated.

You can float a marble as a demonstration. Add 65 grams of potassium iodide (KI) to 75 grams of mercury(II) iodide (HgI_2) and 15 mL of water. K_2HgI_2 is produced. The resulting solution has a density of 3.2 g/cm^3, which is dense enough to float a marble. A marble has a density of about 2.6 g/cm^3. **CAUTION:** Use care when handling all mercury compounds. Do not let any of the material come in contact with the skin.

Activity 5-2

The Activity provides practice in determining the density of various liquids.

You may want to use two graduated cylinders per lab station. Washing the oil out of the cylinder will take some time.

Summing Up

1. Molasses has the greatest density.
2. Cooking oil would be on top and molasses on the bottom.
3. The low density substance is at the top of the beaker. The most dense substance is at the bottom of the beaker.

Page 87. Making Sure

4. $D = \frac{m}{V}$

$$D = \frac{10.8 \text{ g}}{10 \text{ cm}^3} = 1.08 \text{ g/cm}^3$$

5. $D = \frac{m}{V}$

$$D = \frac{23 \text{ g}}{25 \text{ cm}^3} = 0.92 \text{ g/cm}^3$$

6. $D = \frac{m}{V}$

$$D = \frac{30.3 \text{ g}}{30 \text{ cm}^3} = 1.01 \text{ g/cm}^3$$

7. Salad oil would float on the vinegar because it is less dense (0.92 g/cm^3 vs. 1.01 g/cm^3).

5:5 Physical Changes

You can use the following in a demonstration showing physical changes:

a. bend a piece of glass using a flame spreader on a burner
b. break a few wooden splints
c. stretch a rubber band
d. dissolve sugar in water
e. magnetize a nail (stroke it with a permanent magnet)
f. heat the nail to demagnetize it

Activity 5-3

The Activity shows the three states of water simultaneously as well as the associated changes of state.

Materials needed: beaker, hot water, watch glass, ice cubes

Questions: Water is changing to steam at the surface.

Steam is changing to water on the underside of the watch glass.

In both cases, the ice cubes are melting.

Activity 5-4

The Activity shows the student how to determine the freezing point of water experimentally. Students may observe the supercooling of water. However, some reference books say that it is difficult to achieve. Students may need help in setting up their graphs.

Keeping Track—The graph should go down in nearly a straight line.

Summing Up

1. Yes, the water freezes.
2. Salt is mixed with ice to lower the freezing point.
3. The freezing point of water should be approximately 0°C. The graph should flatten at this point.

5:6 Chemical Properties

Try the following demonstrations to stress that a chemical property describes the way a substance behaves in the presence of other substances: **1.** Place 50 mL of water and 50 mL of hydrogen peroxide in separate beakers. Have students describe the physical properties of each by observing the liquids only. Students should have the same physical properties listed for each. Add a solution of iron(III) chloride ($FeCl_3$) to each beaker. Students will observe a difference in chemical properties.

2. Add a piece of copper and a piece of magnesium to separate test tubes. Then add some 1*M* HCl (85.5 mL concentrated HCl diluted to 1 liter). Students will observe different chemical behavior for the two metals in the presence of the acid.

3. Place an iron nail in a 1*M* copper(II) sulfate solution (249 grams of $CuSO_4 \cdot 5H_2O$ diluted to 1 liter). Place another nail in a test tube containing water. Students should observe the test tubes after 5 minutes and after 24 hours.

You may wish to conduct the experiment on page 91. The first test tube contains dilute HCl; the second, concentrated H_2SO_4; the third, $AgNO_3$; the fourth, $CuSO_4$. The gas produced in the first test tube is H_2; the second, H_2S. Silver appears in the third and copper plates out on the nail in the fourth test tube. You may wish to use water as a control in the experiment.

Page 92. Making Sure

8. Wood, coal, paper, cloth, magnesium, and hydrogen are examples of flammable substances.
9. Burning generally depends on oxygen to occur.

10. Physical properties—white, malleable, ductile, boiling point, melting point, conductor
Chemical properties—not attacked by water or oxygen, inert to most acids, reacts with dilute HNO_3

If possible have chemical handbooks available for students to look at and use. You can give them a list of substances and have them use a handbook to research information on its properties. This type of exercise exposes students to technical material as well as providing reinforcement concerning chemical and physical properties.

5:7 Chemical Changes

Spend time here reinforcing the differences between chemical and physical changes. After reviewing the photos, demonstrations, and examples in the previous sections, students should have a firm grasp of the difference.

Activity 5-5

The Activity introduces the preparation of hydrogen from zinc and hydrochloric acid. The pop of the splint may frighten some students because they are not expecting it. Be sure students keep their test tubes in a rack when doing the splint test.

Materials needed: protective glasses, hydrochloric acid dilute (250 mL of concentrated HCl diluted to 1 liter), test tube, test tube rack, mossy zinc, wooden splints, matches

Questions: Small explosion occurs and the gas produced burns with a blue flame.

A chemical change occurred because new substances were formed; heat and light were given off.

Page 94. Making Sure

11. **a.** physical
b. chemical
c. physical
d. chemical
e. physical
f. chemical
g. physical

5:8 Mixtures

Emphasize to students that the vast majority of the clothes we wear and the foods we eat are mixtures rather than pure substances. Even clothes made exclusively of a synthetic fiber may contain dyes to give them color. Have students start checking food labels around the house to confirm your statement. Nutritional labels on foods should indicate to students that foods are also mixtures of vitamins and minerals.

Discuss the three methods of separating mixtures shown in Figure 5-19. Note that each uses a different physical property by which the substances can be separated. You might want to add where each type of equipment is used. Centrifuge—medical laboratories, Chromatography—food laboratories, Distillation—the petroleum industry.

Activity 5-6

The Activity demonstrates one method of separating a mixture using solubility, a physical property.

Materials needed: sand, salt, filter paper, funnel, beaker, ring stand, hot plate

Demonstrate the proper method of folding filter paper. Refer students to Appendix B for additional information on setting up the filtration system.

Questions: The sand remains in the funnel.

The salt is in solution in the beaker. It can be recovered by evaporating the water.

Sand and sugar could also be separated in this way as could any combination in which one of the components is soluble in water while the other is not.

Focus on Careers

The Scrap Industry

Beginning with the scrap industry, talk about the reuse of natural resources, recycling. Discuss the types of jobs needed for the recycling industry. Information is available from news magazines, conservation groups, and the Scrap Iron and Steel Institute, Inc., 1627 K Street N.W., Washington, DC 20006. Have students construct a display of items that are recycled or made of recycled material. Since almost anything can be reused, ask students to think of unusual ways to use items such as plastic milk cartons. Examples are bird feeders, scoops for sand at a beach, and piggy banks. Ask students to think of other items they could recycle in this way. Students might use this idea as a way to raise money for projects.

Questions for Review

A. True or False

1. True **2.** False (Ideas are not matter because they do not have mass.) **3.** False (Making ice cubes is a physical change.) **4.** True **5.** False (The composition of a mixture may vary.) **6.** False (Mixtures may be separated by physical means.) **7.** True **8.** True **9.** False (Density is a physical property.) **10.** True

B. Multiple Choice

1. Burning **2.** Burning **3.** solid **4.** gas **5.** Rusting **6.** solid **7.** melting **8.** condensation **9.** chemical change **10.** temperature

C. Completion

1. mixture **2.** physical **3.** chemical **4.** physical **5.** Density **6.** chemical **7.** matter **8.** chemical **9.** plasma **10.** liquid

D. How and Why

1. Physical properties—colorless, odorless, density of 1 g/cm^3, tasteless, boiling point = 100° C, melting point = 0° C.
   Chemical properties—does not react with oxygen, corrodes metals in the presence of oxygen.
2. Color, shape, and taste would be needed to describe an apple.
3. Air, soil, lemonade, tea, and fruit juices are some examples of mixtures.
4. Seat covers should be strong, resilient, colorful, and durable.
5. Evaporate some of the sample. If a residue remains, the substance is salt water.
6. Oil is less dense than water.
7. Ice is less dense than water.

More Ideas to Explore

1. A can of antifreeze or coolant will have this kind of information.
2. The Brinell test determines the hardness of metals by pushing a steel ball against the metal and measuring the diameter of the indentation.
3. The following could be used: *Lange's Handbook of Chemistry, The Handbook of Chemistry and Physics, The Merck Index.*
4. The plasma state is important because of its relationship to the development of nuclear energy (fusion).

6 Elements and the Periodic Table

Overview

Students can now recognize physical and chemical properties. This information is then applied in Chapter 6 where students are given their first introduction to the periodic table and the classification of elements according to properties. The theme of the Unit, Classification of Matter, is brought out by having students look at one small part of matter, elements. In studying the periodic table, students see how the elements can be classified in groups and periods, or as metals, nonmetals, and metalloids.

Atomic structure is fully discussed and then related to the properties and arrangements of elements on the table. The chapter concludes by defining the characteristic properties of metals, nonmetals, and metalloids.

This chapter is extremely important in understanding the remaining chemistry chapters. Proceed slowly.

Performance Objectives

Goal: Students will gain an understanding of the arrangement of elements on the periodic table and will be able to use information they derive from understanding the table.

Objectives: Upon completion of the reading and activities and when asked to diagram, demonstrate, or respond either orally or on a written test, students will:

6:1	K/P	define an element and give symbols for the common elements.
6:2	K	recognize a periodic table of the elements.
6:3-4	K/P	list and explain the basic parts of an atom.
6:4	K	relate atomic number to number of protons in the nucleus of an atom.
6:5	K/P	describe electron clouds and energy levels using a mental model.
6:6	K	describe the relationship between atomic mass and isotopes.
6:7	K/P	list various families of elements and locate them on the periodic table.
6:8	K/P	describe what happens to the metallic character of elements from left to right on the periodic table. distinguish among metals, nonmetals, and metalloids.
	S/A	recognize the usefulness and limitations of atomic models.
	A	attempt at least one *More Ideas to Explore.*

Equipment for Activities

Chemicals

Several pieces of:

aluminum, carbon, copper, iodine crystals, iron, lead, sulfur, and zinc.

6:1 Elements

Some elements have been known for thousands of years because they occur in the pure form in nature. Eleven elements have symbols which were derived from the Latin name for the element.

antimony	Sb	*stibnum*
copper	Cu	*cuprum*
gold	Au	*aurum*
iron	Fe	*ferrum*
lead	Pb	*plumbum*
mercury	Hg	*hydrargyrum*
potassium	K	*kalium*
silver	Ag	*argentium*
sodium	Na	*natrium*
tin	Sn	*stannum*
tungsten	W	*wolfrum*

Only 13 elements were known before 1700. About 26 elements were known by 1800. About 63 elements were known by 1869 (Mendeleev's time). About 81 elements were known by 1908 (the time Mendeleev died). Another 25 elements have been discovered since.

6:2 The Periodic Table

Point out that the periodic table represents a number of facts that would be very difficult to remember if they were not organized. As students move through the chapter, have them make a list of items they know about an element by looking at the periodic table. For example, the table on pages 104-5 shows the element name, symbol, atomic number, atomic mass, group number, period number, physical state, synthetics, metals, nonmetals, transition elements, noble gases, lanthanides, actinides. The table on page 115 shows more specifically a breakdown of elements into metals, nonmetals, and metalloids. The table on page 116 shows some of the characteristic properties associated with each class. You can expand this list depending on how specific you wish to be. The material in Unit 3 covers the more important elements in detail. The material in Chapter 13 covers the acid-base properties of compounds.

Page 103. Making Sure

1. **a.** Au **e.** Al
b. Sn **f.** F
c. Na **g.** U
d. Fe **h.** La

2. **a.** potassium **e.** sulfur
b. zinc **f.** copper
c. oxygen **g.** iron
d. arsenic **h.** nitrogen

3. cobalt (a), iron (d), silver (e)

6:3 Atoms

Refer to the section about scientific models on page 14T. The example of the electric fan, the photograph of the fan in an automobile engine, and the galaxy pictured on page 109 are presented to enable students to formulate a visual model for something they cannot see. Figure 6-5 can be used to start a discussion on how much more we know about the atom today. Students should note how unrefined Dalton's model is. They should also note the time in history when it was proposed. If your class is constructing the time line (Unit 1 Teaching Tips), the study of the period from 1800-1932 (discovery of the neutron) can be a fascinating addition to this chapter. It is important that students know that science is constantly growing and changing. A historical approach to the study of the atom can help accomplish this goal.

6:4 Parts of the Atom

You may wish to add the following descriptive information to your discussion concerning the parts of the atom.

The electron has a mass of 9.11×10^{-28} grams which is equivalent to 0.000549 a.m.u. and is 1/1836 the mass of a proton. The radius of an electron is about 2.82×10^{-15} meters. In small atoms, the first electron is located about 5×10^{-11} meters from the nucleus.

The proton has a mass of 1.673×10^{-24} grams which is equivalent to 1.0073 a.m.u. and is 1836 times heavier than an electron.

The neutron has a mass of 1.675×10^{-24} grams which is equivalent to 1.0087 a.m.u. and is only slightly heavier than a proton. The nucleus (protons and neutrons) of an atom occupies only about one trillionth of the total volume of the atom. Thus, we find that most of the atom consists of empty space. The radius of a nucleus can vary between 1.2×10^{-15} meters and 7.5×10^{-15} meters.

You can use the following model to help students visualize these relationships: if the nucleus is the size of a table tennis ball, an electron would be about the size of a tennis ball. The tennis ball would be about 1.35 kilometers away from the table tennis ball.

Activity 6-1

The Activity introduces a diagram as a model for the atom. Remind students that their model is only a representation and that it lacks a 3-dimensional appearance.

Before attempting the Activity, you will have to show students how to determine the number of neutrons in an atom.

atomic mass (nearest whole number)
– atomic number
number of neutrons

Materials needed: pencil and paper

Questions: The inner circle represents the nucleus.

Answers will vary—the diagram is larger, it is not 3-dimensional, the electrons are shown in orbits.

Page 108. Making Sure

4. **a.** oxygen, O **b.** magnesium, Mg **c.** calcium, Ca **d.** cobalt, Co **e.** tin, Sn **f.** gold, Au

5. **a.** 29 **b.** 26 **c.** 10 **d.** 11 **e.** 80 **f.** 92

6. **a.** 2 **b.** 6 **c.** 47 **d.** 53 **e.** 19 **f.** 30

6:5 Electron Clouds

You might add to the galaxy model by asking students to visualize the flight of a mosquito inside a basketball. Can they imagine two or more mosquitoes in there? The basketball model will help establish the atom as being 3-dimensional.

Page 110. Making Sure

7. **a.** 8 **b.** 6 **c.** 1 **d.** 17

8. **a.** 2, 6 **b.** 2, 4 **c.** 1 **d.** 2, 8, 7

6:6 Atomic Mass and Isotopes

You may want to draw models similar to those shown in Figure 6-9 for the isotopes of an atom. Students will retain a visual picture more readily. You can use the following as examples: protium, deuterium, tritium; carbon-12, carbon-14; oxygen-15, oxygen-16.

Page 113. Making Sure

9. **a.** 9 **b.** 17 **c.** 35 **d.** 53 **e.** 8 **f.** 16

10. 11 protons, 11 electrons, and 12 neutrons

11. **a.** 3, 6.939 **d.** 13, 26.9815
b. 7, 14.0067 **e.** 18, 39.948
c. 19, 39.102 **f.** 26, 55.847

6:7 Groups of Elements

Stress that the number of outer energy level electrons can be determined by looking at the Roman numerals above each A column. Each family has the same number of electrons in the outer energy level. The similarity in properties is a consequence of this electron arrangement.

Page 114. Making Sure

12. The atomic number and the mass number increase.

13. **a.** hydrogen **c.** uranium
b. vanadium **d.** sulfur

6:8 Periods of Elements

Use the tables in this section to stress the differences in properties among metals, nonmetals, and metalloids. Figure 6-14 shows the diverse ways the transition metals can be used. More detail on the transition metals will be presented in Chapter 8.

Activity 6-2

This Activity gives practice in observing physical properties.

Materials needed: aluminum, copper, carbon, iodine, iron, lead, sulfur, and zinc

You might have chemical handbooks available so students can use these for additional information.

Page 117. Making Sure

14. Atomic number increases from left to right.

15. **a.** aluminum **c.** uranium
b. oxygen **d.** argon

Focus on Skills

Using Activities

The purpose of this exercise is to get students to analyze instructional material. Though the Activity shown is relatively short, it requires the student to refer back to information previously learned and apply it to the study of metals and nonmetals.

Rewriting the procedure as a series of numbered steps is a technique which enhances readability. Note that most of the Activities which require a number of steps are shown in a stepwise format.

Posing questions such as these before each Activity enables you to evaluate your students comprehension of the instructions and purpose for doing the Activity.

Questions for Review

A. True or False

1. True **2.** False (The mass of an electron is less than that of a proton.) **3.** True **4.** True **5.** False (Atoms of the same element can have different masses.) **6.** True **7.** False (The electron occupies a cloud outside the nucleus of an atom.) **8.** False (Most of the mass of an atom is contained in the nucleus.) **9.** True **10.** True

B. Multiple Choice

1. proton **2.** 2 **3.** electron **4.** atomic number **5.** neutral **6.** 2 **7.** 12 **8.** electrons **9.** group **10.** 2

C. Completion

1. isotopes **2.** positive **3.** Mendeleev **4.** IA **5.** 3 **6.** iron, cobalt **7.** 26, 30 **8.** transition **9.** 5 **10.** 3

D. How and Why

1. The periodic table gives clues to properties of elements. Families of elements tend to have similar properties due to the same electron arrangement in their outer energy level. The table also provides such data as atomic number, atomic mass, element name, symbol, number of electrons in the outer energy level (A Groups only), total number of protons and electrons, and the number of neutrons.
2. Neutron—neutral, slightly heavier than a proton contained in the nucleus.
   Proton—positive charge, mass close to that of the neutron, over 1800 times heavier than an

electron, contained in the nucleus.

Electron—lightest of the three particles, occupies the area outside the nucleus, negative charge.

3. Metals

1-3 electrons in the outer energy level, luster, malleable or ductile, conductors of heat and electricity.

Nonmetals

5-8 electrons in the outer energy level, no metallic luster, brittle, nonconductors

4. Magnesium is a metal, chlorine is a nonmetal therefore, the differences between metals and nonmetals apply to these elements. See question 3.
5. The noble gases have complete outer energy levels of electrons.

7 Compounds and Bonding

Overview

This chapter expands upon the information presented in Chapter 6. The material deals with the combining of elements through transfer and sharing of electrons. The student also progresses further into the classification scheme for matter in studying compounds. The text material covers how compounds are formed, how formulas are written, and how compounds are named.

It is important that students learn to write and recognize formulas. Frequent quizzes can help you monitor their progress.

Performance Objectives

Goal: Students will gain an understanding of how elements combine to form compounds and will be able to name common compounds.

Objectives: Upon completion of the reading and activities and when asked to diagram, demonstrate, or respond either orally or on a written test, students will:

7:1	K	define compounds and recognize formulas for compounds.
7:2-4	K/P	explain how atoms combine and contrast the transfer and sharing processes of bonding.
7:5	K/P	use oxidation numbers to write formulas for compounds.
7:6	K/P	name binary compounds.
7:7	K	identify and write formulas for compounds containing polyatomic ions.
	S/A	demonstrate the usefulness of models to show how atoms combine.
		demonstrate the proper use of equipment and materials.
	A	attempt at least one *More Ideas to Explore*.

Equipment for Activities

The amounts listed are for a class of 30 students broken into groups of 2.

glass slides, microscope—15
magnifying glass—15
microscope—5
paper, colored—15 sheets

Chemicals

alum crystals—100 g
nickel sulfate—50 g
Rochelle salt crystals—150 g
sodium chloride—150 g
sodium nitrate—50 g

7:1 Compounds

After students have read the section, you may want to take time developing a chart which lists the properties of elements, compounds, and mixtures. This chart can serve as a mini-summary of the unit.

Elements

1. Cannot be broken down further by chemical means.
2. Each has a specific set of physical and chemical properties.
3. Similarities in properties among groups (families) of elements exist due to similarities in outer energy level electron arrangement.

4. All atoms of the same element have the same number of electrons and protons, however they may have different numbers of neutrons.

Compounds

1. A compound has chemical and physical properties which are different from its components.
2. Compounds can be broken down by chemical means only.
3. The components of a compound exist in a definite ratio.
4. Compounds are formed through chemical change.

Mixtures

1. The components of a mixture retain their physical and chemical properties.
2. The components can be separated by physical means.
3. The components can be mixed in any proportions.
4. Mixtures are formed through the mechanical process of mixing, no chemical change occurs.

You can have students check labels at home for compounds they recognize. This type of activity is important in establishing the importance of learning about chemical formulas, as they are so much a part of our lives. Stress the importance of subscripts in formulas. You can use CO and CO_2, or H_2O and H_2O_2 as examples illustrating the difference in properties.

Page 124. Making Sure

1. nitrogen and hydrogen in a ratio of 1 to 3
2. N_2O
3. sugar—carbon, hydrogen, and oxygen
baking soda—sodium, hydrogen, carbon, and oxygen
peroxide—hydrogen and oxygen
sand—silicon and oxygen
alcohol—carbon, hydrogen, and oxygen
chalk—calcium, carbon, and oxygen
tin(II) fluoride—tin and fluorine
4. a. 2 hydrogen: 2 oxygen (1:1)
b. 1:1
c. 1:2:3:2
d. 1:1:1
e. 2:1:4
f. 1:1
5. a. 4 **b.** 2 **c.** 8 **d.** 3
e. 7 **f.** 2

7:2 How Atoms Combine

It is important to establish that chemical reactivity depends on the electron arrangement in the outermost energy level. It is also important that you spend a sufficient amount of time on Sections 7:2-4 as this material may be abstract for some students.

Page 126. Making Sure

6. a. 4 b. 1 c. 2 d. 6

7:3 Electron Transfer

You can demonstrate the existence of ions using a conductivity apparatus. It can also be used to establish the existence of uncharged particles (molecules) in Section 7:4. Stress the points brought out in Figure 7-7 that compounds have a different set of physical and chemical properties than the elements from which they are made.

Activity 7-1

The Activity demonstrates electron transfer through the use of a paper and pencil model. Have students refer to the bonding model for NaCl in Figure 7-6.

Materials needed: paper and pencil

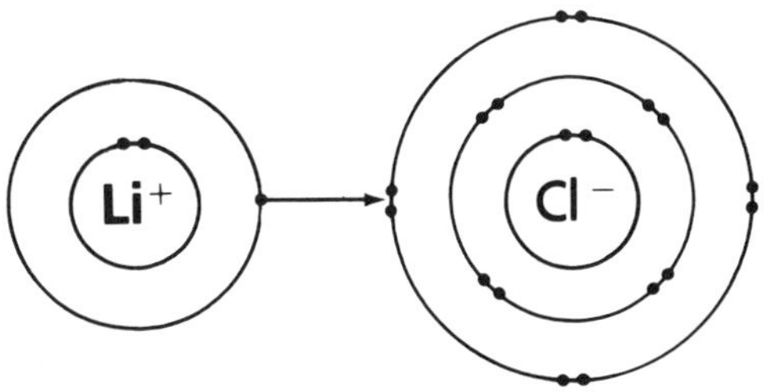

Questions: Lithium and chlorine bond ionically.

The calcium-bromine compound has the formula $CaBr_2$.

Activity 7-2

The Activity relates crystal structure to bonding.

Materials needed: table salt, Rochelle salt, alum, nickel sulfate, sodium nitrate, magnifying glass, microscope, and glass slides

Questions: The crystals are different in shape.

They have different shapes because the number of ions varies. As a result, the ions have different arrangements.

Students may have some difficulty formulating these answers. You may want to establish these ideas in a group session.

7:4 Electron Sharing

The theme of Figure 7-9 is to point out once again the difference in properties between compounds and their component elements. Figure 7-9a shows the explosion of the Hindenburg. This airship was filled with a mixture of hydrogen and air. Such airships now contain helium. Being a noble gas, helium is relatively inert and also has the desirable property of being less dense than air.

At this point you may want to have students construct a summary list showing the differences between ionic and covalent bonding.

Activity 7-3

The Activity demonstrates the use of a paper-pencil model for covalent bonding. Have students refer to Figure 7-8 as an example of how to construct their models.

Materials needed: paper and pencil

Questions:

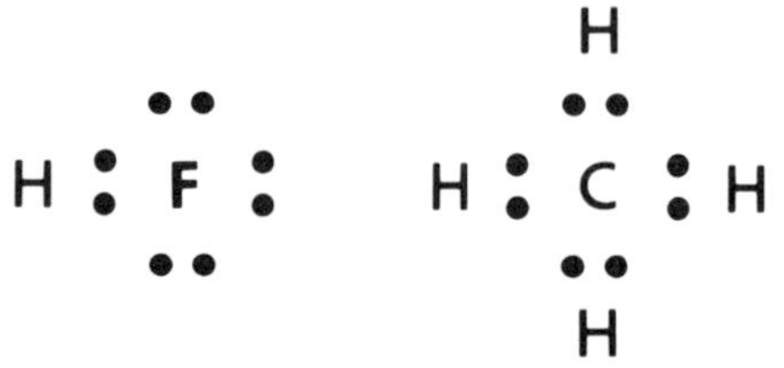

7:5 Oxidation Numbers

You may want to teach your students the criss-cross method of writing formulas. For example,

copper(II) bromide

Cu^{2+} Br^{1-}

Cu_1 Br_2

$CuBr_2$

iron(III) fluoride

Fe^{3+} F^{1-}

Fe_1 F_3

FeF_3

magnesium oxide

Mg^{2+} O^{2-}

Mg_2 O_2

correct formula is MgO

sodium bromide

Na^{1+} Br^{1-}

Na_1 Br_1

NaBr

calcium chloride

Ca^{2+} Cl^{1-}

Ca_1 Cl_2

$CaCl_2$

iron(III) oxide

Fe^{3+} O^{2-}

Fe_2 O_3

Fe_2O_3

This method may help students see that the sum of the oxidation numbers in a compound is zero.

Page 131. Making Sure

7. **a.** NaBr **e.** MgF_2
   b. KI **f.** $CaCl_2$
   c. HBr **g.** Li_2S
   d. H_2S **h.** CuS

7:6 Binary Compounds

Most students should easily grasp this material. Provide adequate drill and reinforcement so the knowledge stays with them.

Page 132. Making Sure

8. **a.** sodium chloride
   b. copper(II) bromide
   c. barium sulfide
   d. magnesium oxide
   e. potassium iodide
   f. magnesium bromide
   g. calcium sulfide
   h. copper(II) oxide
   i. iron(III) chloride
   j. iron(II) oxide
9. **a.** $CaBr_2$ **e.** Cu_2S
   b. K_2O **f.** LiF
   c. $AlCl_3$ **g.** NaBr
   d. FeI_3 **h.** $CuCl_2$

7:7 Polyatomic Ions

Stress the idea that polyatomic ions act as a single unit. Spend additional time with students on the use of parentheses in formulas to indicate multiples of a polyatomic ion. You may want to teach the criss-cross method here too.

ammonium bromide
NH_4^{1+} Br^{1-}
$(NH_4)_1$ Br_1
NH_4Br

ammonium sulfide
NH_4^{1+} S^{2-}
$(NH_4)_2$ S_1
$(NH_4)_2S$

sodium sulfate
Na^{1+} SO_4^{2-}
Na_2 $(SO_4)_1$
Na_2SO_4

magnesium sulfate
Mg^{2+} SO_4^{2-}
Mg_2 $(SO_4)_2$
correct formula is
$MgSO_4$

potassium hydroxide
K^{1+} OH^{1-}
K_1 OH_1
KOH

calcium hydroxide
Ca^{2+} OH^{1-}
Ca_1 OH_2
$Ca(OH)_2$

ammonium nitride
NH_4^{1+} N^{3-}
$(NH_4)_3$ N_1
$(NH_4)_2N$

aluminum sulfate
Al^{3+} SO_4^{2-}
Al_2 $(SO_4)_3$
$Al_2(SO_4)_3$

aluminum hydroxide
Al^{3+} OH^{1-}
Al_1 OH_3
$Al(OH)_3$

Page 133. Making Sure

10. a. $NaNO_3$ **d.** K_3PO_4
b. Ag_2SO_4 **e.** $NaHCO_3$
c. $FeCl_2$ **f.** $NaC_2H_3O_2$

11. a. sodium sulfate
b. ammonium phosphate
c. iron(II) oxide
d. silver nitrate
e. potassium bromide
f. sodium hydroxide

12. Problem 10
a. 1 sodium, 1 nitrogen, and 3 oxygen
b. 2 silver, 1 sulfur, and 4 oxygen
c. 1 iron and 2 chlorine
d. 3 potassium, 1 phosphorus, and 4 oxygen
e. 1 sodium, 1 hydrogen, 1 carbon, and 3 oxygen
f. 1 sodium, 2 carbon, 3 hydrogen, and 2 oxygen

Problem 11
a. 2 sodium, 1 sulfur, and 4 oxygen
b. 3 nitrogen, 12 hydrogen, 1 phosphorus, and 4 oxygen
c. 1 iron and 1 oxygen
d. 1 silver, 1 nitrogen, and 3 oxygen
e. 1 potassium and 1 bromine
f. 1 sodium, 1 oxygen, and 1 hydrogen

Focus on Frontiers

The Search for a Nondigestible Sweet

Using nose plugs and blindfolds, investigate the relationship between taste and smell. Discuss the role of chemistry in the production of artificial sweeteners and why people use them.

Questions for Review

A. True or False

1. True **2.** True **3.** True **4.** True **5.** True **6.** False (When atoms share electrons, molecules are formed.) **7.** False (The elements of Group VIIA have seven electrons in their outer energy level.) **8.** True **9.** True **10.** False (Some elements have more than one oxidation number.)

B. Multiple Choice

1. oxygen **2.** neutral **3.** FeS **4.** one **5.** two **6.** 12 **7.** 1− **8.** polyatomic ion **9.** subscript **10.** compound

C. Completion

1. 1+ **2.** loses **3.** 3 **4.** covalent **5.** ion **6.** 2 **7.** Ionic **8.** transferring **9.** Na_2O and **K_2S are examples** 10. **ratio**

D. How and Why

1. Covalent bonding results from the sharing of electrons by two or more atoms. Ionic bonding results from the transfer of electrons from one atom to another.

2. a. sodium chloride **b.** ammonium nitrate **c.** calcium phosphate

3. a. K_2SO_4 **b.** SO_2 **c.** Hg_2S

4. The oxidation number should be 2+. The atom has 2 available electrons to share or transfer in forming a bond and completing its outer energy level.

5. 1 magnesium, 2 nitrogen, and 4 oxygen

6. See page 60T for a table of differences.

7. Iron has two oxidation numbers 2+ and 3+. Thus it can combine with chlorine by transferring and/or sharing 2 or 3 electrons.

Unit 3 Patterns in Matter

Overview

Students now begin to appreciate the role of chemistry in their lives. In this unit, they see how knowledge of elements and bonding can be applied to produce useful products. As the families of elements are explored, the differences between metals and nonmetals are again reinforced after completing Chapters 8-9. The unit concludes with a presentation of the chemistry of carbon and its compounds. A careful study of this material will enable students to be wise consumers and scientifically literate citizens.

Teaching Tips

- ▶ You can set up a gold rush bulletin board using pictures, stories, and books about the gold rush of 1848 in California. The Gold Information Center runs advertisements in magazines such as *Time* which give information on uses of gold today. Figure 6-14 shows a fireproof suit made of gold. Thin gold foil can be used to coat windows of buildings made of glass as an insulating material.
- ▶ You can continue the scavenger hunt to include items containing elements from each family.
- ▶ Construct a bulletin board on the importance of trace elements in the body. Have students look at food labels for good sources of each important element. In this way you make your study of the elements more practical.
- ▶ You can construct a bulletin board display illustrating the uses of elements and compounds. Many of these uses are listed throughout the chapters (flashbulb, aluminum foil, paint pigments, deodorants, fireworks, medical diagnostic uses and so on).
- ▶ If possible, you can have the class set up a recycling center for aluminum cans.

8 Families of Elements—Metals

Overview

The chapter develops the trends which exist for each family of elements in the metals section of the periodic table. Common uses are given for the elements discussed. As a result, students are able to relate their study of chemistry to familiar objects. The importance of alloys is stressed through explicit examples of their uses and properties.

Performance Objectives

Goal: Students will learn the characteristics of metals and the uses of some important metals and alloys.

Objectives: Upon completion of the reading and activities and when asked to diagram, demonstrate, or respond either orally or on a written test, students will:

8:1	K	list the properties of metals.
8:2	K/P	list and describe some of the properties of alkali metals.
8:3	K/P	list and describe some of the properties of alkaline earth metals.
8:4	K/P	explain the characteristics of transition elements and list some of the common metals.
8:5	K	define alloys.
8:6	K	list some properties of the iron family.
8:7	K/P	distinguish among various alloys of steel used for specific purposes.
8:8	K	list some of the properties of the copper family.
8:9	K	list some of the properties of the zinc family.
8:10	K	list some of the properties of aluminum and boron.
	K/P	distinguish between metals and metalloids.
	S/A	demonstrate proper use of equipment and materials in performing activities where color is used to identify elements.
	A	attempt at least one *More Ideas to Explore.*

Equipment for Activities

The amounts listed are for a class of 30 students broken into groups of 2.

Bunsen burner—15
clamp, test tube—15
goggles—30
graduated cylinder, 25 mL—15
laboratory apron—30
matches
platinum or nichrome wire—15 pieces
test tube—105
test tube rack—15

Chemicals

water, distilled
ammonium hydroxide (dilute)—100 mL
cobalt chloride—50 g
copper(I) chloride—50 g
copper(II) sulfate—50 g
hydrochloric acid—100 mL
iron(II) chloride—50 g
iron(III) chloride—50 g
iron(II) sulfate—50 g
iron(III) sulfate—50 g
sodium hydroxide (dilute)—100 mL
solutions of:
barium chloride—100 mL
calcium chloride—100 mL
copper(I) chloride—100 mL
copper(II) sulfate—100 mL
lithium chloride—100 mL
nickel(II) sulfate—100 mL
potassium chloride—100 mL
sodium chloride—100 mL
strontium chloride—100 mL

8:1 Properties of Metals

You may want to have students refer back to Table 5-1 on page 84 to review physical properties. A display of various metals can enable students to visualize the properties of metals listed in the section. You can demonstrate the various properties with metals you have available.

8:2 Alkali Metals

You can demonstrate the reactivity of the alkali metals by adding sodium to water. **CAUTION:** Use only a small piece (no bigger than the size of a small pea). You should, of course, be wearing a lab apron and goggles (safety emphasis). Cover the beaker immediately with a wire gauze.

Activity 8-1

The Activity demonstrates the flame test as a method of metallic ion identification.

Before beginning the Activity, you should demonstrate the proper procedure to follow in performing the flame tests. If you do not have nichrome or platinum wire, you can place the solutions in small plastic squirt bottles. By directing a spray of the liquid at the burner flame, the color can be observed. Maintain strict control so that students don't start squirting each other with the squirt bottles.

One molar solutions of each chloride will be sufficient.

$LiCl$—42 grams per liter
KCl—65 grams per liter
$NaCl$—58 grams per liter
$CaCl_2$—110 grams per liter
$SrCl_2$—158 grams per liter
$BaCl_2$—207 grams per liter

Page 144. Making Sure

1. There is one electron in the outer energy level of each alkali metal atom.
2. These elements react with water and/or air.

8:3 Alkaline Earth Metals

You can demonstrate the reactivity of the alkaline earth metals. Burn some magnesium ribbon in a flame, or place a small piece of calcium metal in 25-50 mL of cold water.

Point out the chlorophyll structure in Figure 8-5 on page 145. Later, when students study iron, the heme structure is shown in Figure 8-12. Make sure they note the similarities between the two structures.

You may want to emphasize here the importance of calcium and other minerals and trace elements in the diet. Research indicates that some disorders such as epilepsy may be caused by trace element deficiencies.

Page 148. Making Sure

3. Calcium is used in making glass and paints and is vital to human health.
   Barium is used to trace the digestive tract.
   Strontium is used in fireworks.
4. There are two electrons in the outer energy level of each alkaline earth metal.
5. $BeCl_2$, $MgCl_2$, $CaCl_2$, $SrCl_2$, $BaCl_2$, $RaCl_2$

8:4 Transition Elements

Students will be familiar with most of these elements. You may want to explain why the text refers to the transition elements as heavy metals. You can have students look up their densities in a handbook.

Activity 8-2

In this Activity, students compare color of transition metal ions with their oxidation states.

Materials needed: solutions or crystals of $FeSO_4$, $FeCl_3$, $FeCl_2$, $Fe_2(SO_4)_3$, $CuCl$, $CuSO_4$

Questions: $Fe(NO_3)_3$—green; $Cu(NO_3)_2$—blue

8:5 Metal Alloys

Emphasize that metals are mixed to obtain materials with more desirable properties as stated in the platinum-iridium example.

8:6 Iron, Cobalt, and Nickel

You may want to discuss the magnetic properties of these three metals. At this point in time it is obvious that the students would not understand magnetism as a result of the unpaired electrons. However, they should note the positions of these three elements on the periodic table.

Emphasize the importance of iron in the diet.

Activity 8-3

In this Activity, students compare colors of some transition metal compounds.

Cobalt chloride can be used as an indicator of changes in humidity. The substance is red in the presence of high humidity and blue when the air is dry.

Use 0.1*M* solutions of $NiSO_4$—15.5 grams per liter and $NaOH$—4 grams per liter.

Summing Up

1. the addition of water
2. The composition of water is different than that of HCl. The chloride ion causes the formation of a new compound.
3. The ammonia solution replaced the chloride ions forming a new compound.

8:7 Steel

You may want to have students do a report or construct a display of the many uses of steel. This type of activity should reinforce the versatility of steel in their minds.

Page 153. Making Sure

6. low carbon steel
7. A coating of nickel protects a metal and adds luster.
8. Razor blades, watch springs, and auto bodies are some examples.

8:8 The Copper Family

Students should realize that the elements of the copper family are found free in nature because of their relative inertness.

Activity 8-4

The Activity demonstrates some of the properties of copper(II) sulfate.

Materials needed: 0.1*M* $CuSO_4 \cdot 5H_2O$ solution—25 grams per liter; $CuSO_4 \cdot 5H_2O$ crystals, 0.1*M* NaOH solution—4 grams per liter; 0.1*M* aqueous ammonia solution—6.7 mL concentrated reagent per liter of water, 3 test tubes, burner

Questions: The heat caused the water to boil off the crystals; the substance turns pale blue/white.

The additions of ammonia and sodium hydroxide cause new compounds to be formed.

Both cobalt and nickel exhibit similar reactions using HCl and aqueous ammonia.

8:9 The Zinc Family

Information concerning the toxicity of some elements such as mercury, cadmium, and lead can be found in the book, *The Poisons Around Us* by Henry Schroeder, Indiana University Press, © 1974.

Emphasize the toxicity of mercury. Many times children think mercury is fun to play with. It is a deadly poison.

8:10 Aluminum and Boron

You may want to set up a display using Figure 8-16 as a theme. Aluminum is used everywhere in the home. The Aluminum Association puts out a number of pamphlets concerning this metal. Write:

The Aluminum Association
818 Connecticut Avenue, N.W.
Washington, D.C. 20006

Focus on Skills

Taking Notes in Chart Form

Have students recopy and complete the chart shown. Setting up charts can be an excellent way of reviewing previously studied material. You will note that students should be directed to look at the photos and art as resources in completing their chart and not only the reading material.

Questions for Review

A. True or False

1. True **2.** False (Calcium is an alkaline earth metal.) **3.** True **4.** False (Solutions of transition metal compounds are usually highly colored.) **5.** False (Nickel often coats other metals to make them stronger.) **6.** False (Boron is a metalloid.) **7.** True **8.** True **9.** True **10.** False (The alkali metals are stored under oil.)

B. Multiple Choice

1. Cadmium **2.** silver **3.** iridium **4.** chromium **5.** copper **6.** cadmium **7.** Selenium **8.** 2 **9.** magnesium **10.** metalloid

C. Completion

1. flame test **2.** 2 **3.** sharing **4.** less **5.** in medicine (X-ray tracking) **6.** medicines **7.** liquid **8.** tarnish **9.** hard **10.** borax

D. How and Why

1. The alkaline earth metals have a wide variety of uses from medicines to construction. See pages 145-148 of the text.
2. The alkali metals are light metals which form compounds by ionic bonds and are never found free in nature.
   The copper family consists of heavy metals which bond covalently and are found free in nature.
3. The melting points of the heavier alkali metals decrease. The heavier atoms are larger. As a result, the force of attraction between atoms is reduced.
4. Zinc and nickel are used to coat other metals, forming a protective layer which resists corrosion.
5. **a.** ionic **c.** ionic
   b. covalent **d.** covalent
6. See the chart on page 116 of the text.

9 Families of Elements—Nonmetals

Overview

This chapter concerns the study of nonmetals, their properties and uses. The approach and intent is the same as that in Chapter 8. Each family illustrates a particular chemical concept that should be stressed: noble gases—absolute zero and kelvin temperature; halogens—diatomic molecules; oxygen—allotropes; nitrogen—law of multiple proportions.

Performance Objectives

Goal: Students will gain an understanding of the properties of nonmetals and the relationship among various members of nonmetallic families.

Objectives: Upon completion of the reading and activities and when asked to diagram, demonstrate, or respond either orally or on a written test, students will:

9:1	K	list properties of nonmetals.
9:2	K	list properties of members of the noble gas family.
9:3-6	K/S	compare and contrast the properties of the halogens.
9:7-10	K/S	compare and contrast the properties of the oxygen family.
9:11-12	K/S	compare and contrast the properties of the nitrogen family.
	S/A	demonstrate the proper use of equipment and materials.
	A	attempt at least one *More Ideas to Explore.*

Equipment for Activities

The amounts listed are for a class of 30 students broken into groups of 2.

beaker, 400 mL—15
beakers and other containers for
  food samples—45
Bunsen burner—15
clamp
  extension—15
  test tube—15
corks—15
goggles—30
graduated cylinder, 25 mL—15
laboratory apron—30
matches
medicine dropper—30
pan, deep sauce—15
ring stand and ring—15
steel wool—1 pkg
stirring rod—15
tape, masking
test tube—60
test tube, large—15
test tube rack—15
thermometer—15
wire screen—15

Chemicals

alcohol, ethanol—100 mL
banana—several
bread—several slices
carrot—several
iodine crystals—50 g
mineral oil—100 mL
potato—several
solutions of:
  antimony chloride—100 mL
  cadmium nitrate—100 mL
  copper(II) sulfate—100 mL
  hydrogen sulfide—100 mL
  iron(II) sulfate, fresh—100 mL
  sodium or potassium nitrate—100 mL
  zinc sulfate—100 mL
starch, liquid—100 mL
sulfuric acid, concentrated—50 mL
tincture of iodine—several vials
water
Wood's metal—15 pieces

9:1 Properties of Nonmetals

Allow students to examine some sulfur as it exhibits the properties listed in this section for nonmetals.

9:2 Noble Gases

Discuss the uses of the noble gases. Helium is used to fill balloons as it is lighter than air (less dense). Electric light bulbs contain argon to prevent burning of the tungsten filament. Neon and krypton are used in fog and air runway lights.

The kelvin temperature scale is introduced here because of its importance to cryogenics and as the SI unit of temperature. The degree symbol (°) is not used when expressing kelvin temperatures. You may want to prepare an overhead transparency comparing the Celsius and kelvin scales.

Page 165. Making Sure

1. Cryogenics is the study of materials at very low temperatures. Research in this area is important in the medical field.
2. Radium is used to form radon.

9:3 Halogen Family

Emphasize that these elements are highly reactive and are not found free in nature. You can sketch on the board the covalent bond between atoms of a halogen molecule. Emphasize the sharing of electrons.

9:4 Fluorine

Ask students to bring in samples of etched glass they may have at home. Point out that a number of toothpastes contain fluoride compounds.

9:5 Chlorine

If any of your students have a swimming pool, ask them to bring in the test kit and demonstrate for the class how they determine when chlorine must be added. You can set up a display of the effects of bleach on different types of fabrics.

9:6 Bromine, Iodine, and Astatine

Emphasize the unique ability of iodine to sublime. You can use dry ice as a material to demonstrate sublimation. The sublimation of iodine should be performed only under a fume hood as the fumes are poisonous.

Be sure to point out that astatine has not been found in nature but is made in the lab.

Activity 9-1

This Activity demonstrates the iodine test for starch.

Materials needed: potato, bread, banana, carrot, tincture of iodine (iodine-alcohol solution)

Questions: The presence of a dark blue color after treatment with iodine indicates the presence of starch. The bread and potato tests should be positive.

Activity 9-2

The Activity demonstrates the solubility of iodine in various solvents.

Materials needed: test tubes, water, alcohol, mineral oil, iodine crystals, liquid starch or a suspension of commercial dry starch

Questions: Iodine dissolves in alcohol and very slightly in water.

Adding a drop of starch to the original test tubes will determine the solvent reacted.

Page 170. Making Sure

3. F_2, Cl_2, Br_2, I_2

4. 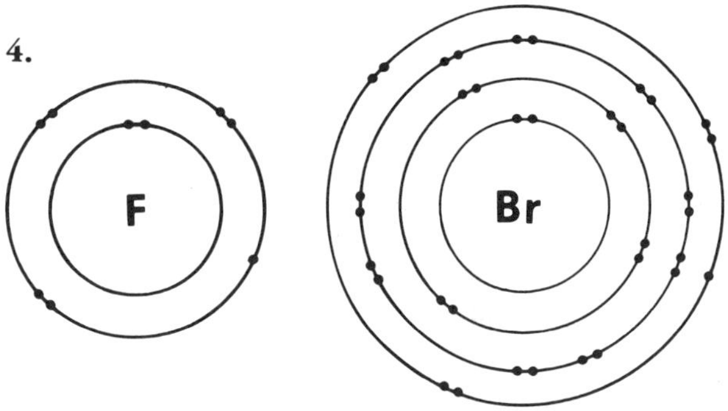

They each have seven electrons in their outer energy level.

5. Fluorine—HF is used to etch glass; chlorine—bleach; bromine—AgBr in photography; iodine—an essential component of the diet.

9:7 Oxygen Family

Be sure students understand allotropes. They will be reinforced in Chapter 10 when the allotropes of carbon are discussed and in Section 9:13—Phosphorus.

9:8 Oxygen

Use Figure 9-9 to emphasize the abundance and importance of oxygen to human life. Students should note that although we often times consider air to be oxygen (since this is the component we utilize) it is comprised mostly of nitrogen, Table 9-4, page 173.

Activity 9-3

The Activity is a simple method used to determine the approximate percent of oxygen in the air. It depends on the steel wool reacting with oxygen in air and effectively removing it.

Materials needed: shallow pan, water, steel wool, cork, ring stand and metal ring or clamp, graduated cylinder.

You could also plug the steel wool halfway up the cylinder if you do not have any corks.

Questions: The water displaces the oxygen as the outside pressure is greater as the oxygen is used. The water should rise about 4-5 mL.

$$\% \text{ oxygen} = \frac{\text{water level rise}}{25} \times 100$$

Be sure students realize that Fe_2O_3 is formed.

9:9 Sulfur

You may want to point out that more sulfur is recovered in refining natural gas than by mining using the Frasch process.

Emphasize the significance of sulfur compounds as pollutants. There is considerable controversy over acid rain which is produced in a reaction between sulfur pollutants and rain. Many of the lakes in the industrial regions of the northeastern United States have such a low pH that fish populations have died out. Figure 9-14 shows how an acid environment can affect the development of salmon.

Activity 9-4

The Activity demonstrates a qualitative test for some metal ions using the color of their sulfides.

Materials needed: test tubes, test tube rack, dropping pipet, H_2S solution—use a 5% solution of thioacetamide in water, heat gently; and 0.1*M* solutions of the following:

$CdNO_3$—17.4 grams per liter
$ZnSO_4$—16.1 grams per liter
$SbCl_3$—22.8 grams per liter
$CuSO_4 \cdot 5H_2O$—25 grams per liter

9:10 Selenium

Selenium was discovered in 1817. As shown in Figure 9-16, selenium is used in photocopy machines for its photosensitive properties. Selenium is a poison. In humans and animals, it replaces sulfur found as compounds in hair, nails, and hooves of animals. When the sulfur is replaced, these parts become brittle and break. Selenium is an essential trace element in the body but it is toxic in large amounts.

Page 177. Making Sure

6. Oxygen—component of water, necessary for breathing; sulfur—used in medicines; selenium—photocells, ruby glass.
7. six
8. All elements of the oxygen family have six electrons in their outer energy level.
9. Selenium is a solid, and conducts electricity.

9:11 Nitrogen Family

Stress the changes in physical properties as you proceed down the column from nitrogen to bismuth. Point out the outer energy level structure for these elements. Bismuth, the largest atom, has many levels of electrons. As a result, it tends to behave as a metal. The middle elements in the family, arsenic and antimony, have properties of both metals and nonmetals (metalloids). Both nitrogen and phosphorus are nonmetallic.

9:12 Nitrogen

You may want to review the fact that air is about 80% nitrogen. You may want to show students the bonding arrangement of electrons for the nitrogen molecule, N_2.

This strong triple bond makes nitrogen somewhat unreactive. It does not burn in oxygen.

Activity 9-5

The Activity demonstrates a test for the presence of the nitrate ion.

Materials needed: 0.1*M* $NaNO_3$ solution—42.5 grams per liter or 0.5*M* KNO_3 solution—50.5 grams per liter; saturated solution of $FeSO_4$—add solid $FeSO_4$ until no more will dissolve, filter to remove any undissolved solid; concentrated H_2SO_4; test tubes; ring stand; dropper pipet; clamp.

Students will use concentrated sulfuric acid in this Activity. It is suggested that you move from station to station with the supply of concentrated acid. You can then provide the acid and supervise its addition.

Questions: The water is used as a control, no brown ring forms.

9:13 Phosphorus

You might have students do some research on fertilizers—types and uses. A trip to the local hardware or garden store can be a source of information. You might ask questions such as:

1. How do vegetable fertilizers differ in composition from those used for lawns? (Answers will vary.)
2. How do organic fertilizers differ from commercial types? (The nutrients in organic fertilizers are derived from decayed plants and animals. The nutrients in chemical fertilizers come from refining minerals and synthesizing chemical compounds.)
3. What compounds are used to supply these nutrients? (nitrogen—ammonia; phosphorus—phosphate $Ca_{10}(PO_4)_6F_2$; potassium—potassium chloride)
4. What are controlled release fertilizers? (Fertilizer granules are coated with an insoluble substance such as sulfur.)

9:14 Arsenic, Antimony, and Bismuth

You might ask students to check at home for the well known antacid containing bismuth *(Pepto-Bismol).* Wood's metal:

Element	*Melting point °C*	*Percentage*
bismuth	271	50
lead	327	25
tin	232	12.5
cadmium	321	12.5

Activity 9-6

The Activity demonstrates the low melting point of Wood's metal.

Materials needed: Wood's metal, beaker, thermometer, ring stand, metal ring, wire gauze, tongs, burner

Questions: Answers will vary. Wood's metal has a low melting point and would melt when exposed to a heat situation (fire). If the valve on a sprinkler system is made of the alloy, it will melt when exposed to fire and water will be released.

Page 181. Making Sure

10. use phosphate free detergents
11. Fertilizers, medicines, water softeners, matches, and body constituents are some examples.
12. Nitrogen, the lower boiling compound, comes off first.

Focus on Frontiers

Alcohol for Cars

Have students investigate the uses of oil in the 1800's. It was used as a lubricant, a medicine, and fuel for lamps. Compare that with the use of oil today. Some uses are plastics, generation of electricity, lubricants, heating, and fuel for diesel and gasoline engines. As we discovered more uses, we increased our consumption of oil. However, oil is a fossil fuel and is not renewable. Alcohol is a renewable fuel. Discuss areas where alcohol might replace oil, such as fuel for cars and heating homes. Ask the students why alcohol will not solve the oil shortage. Try to convey a sense of the complexity of the issue. There is no simple, single solution. We have to use all of our resources in the best possible manner.

Questions for Review

A. True or False

1. True **2.** False (Under normal room temperature and pressure, all of the halogen elements form diatomic molecules.) **3.** False (Uncombined fluorine is not found free in nature.) **4.** True **5.** False (At room temperature, iodine is a grey solid.) **6.** False (All elements in the oxygen family have six electrons to share in chemical bonds.) **7.** True **8.** True **9.** True **10.** False (The low melting point of bismuth makes it suitable for use in automatic sprinkler systems used for fire prevention.)

B. Multiple Choice

1. Arsenic **2.** selenium **3.** 7 **4.** covalent and ionic **5.** ice cream **6.** nitrogen **7.** Bismuth **8.** oxygen **9.** nitrogen **10.** Helium

C. Completion

1. diatomic **2.** O_2, O_3 **3.** light **4.** oxygen **5.** air **6.** distillation **7.** ozone **8.** bismuth **9.** Selenium **10.** bones, genes

D. How and Why

1. NH_3—ammonia; HNO_3—nitric acid; $NaNO_3$—sodium nitrate

2. Binary compounds of nitrogen are formed by covalent bonding, whereas binary compounds of the alkali metals and halogens are usually formed through ionic bonds.

3. Observe their properties. Generally, the elements with higher atomic numbers will be more metallic.

4. Allotropes are different molecular forms of the same element, whereas isotopes are atoms of the same element which differ in the number of neutrons in the nucleus.

5. Answers will vary. The noble gases do not combine easily. They are found in very small quantities in air making them difficult to isolate.

6. A diatomic gas is one in which the molecular form contains two atoms. Cl_2—chlorine; O_2—oxygen; N_2—nitrogen; H_2—hydrogen; F_2—fluorine; Br_2—bromine are examples.

10 Families of Elements—Carbon and Silicon

Overview

The chapter begins with a study of the structural differences between carbon allotropes. The student is then given a fundamental introduction to organic chemistry. This introduction includes exposure to single, double, and triple-bonded carbon compounds, isomers, saturated and unsaturated hydrocarbons, and polymers. The latter part of the chapter covers body fuels and nutrients as well as the importance of organic compounds in producing energy. The chapter concludes with a small section covering silicon. The similarities between silicon and carbon should be emphasized in studying these two members of the carbon family.

Performance Objectives

Goal: Students will learn the properties of carbon and silicon, and some important uses of their compounds.

Objectives: Upon completion of the reading and activities and when asked to diagram, demonstrate, or respond either orally or on a written test, students will:

10:1	K	list the names and properties of some allotropic forms of carbon.
10:2	K	explain reasons why there are so many carbon compounds.
10:3	P/A	explain why structural formulas are important in describing and differentiating among carbon compounds.
10:4	K/P	define isomers and diagram formulas of examples.
10:5	K/P	distinguish between saturated and unsaturated hydrocarbons.
10:6-8	K	list and define various classes of compounds of carbon.
10:9	K/A	list and explain the importance of carbon compounds in living things.
10:10-12	K/P/A	distinguish among and explain the importance of various organic energy sources

		both naturally-occurring and synthetic.
10:13	K	list some of the properties of silicon.
	S/A	demonstrate the proper use of equipment and materials.
	A	attempt at least one *More Ideas to Explore.*

Equipment for Activities

The amounts listed are for a class of 30 students broken into groups of 2.

beaker, 250 mL—15
Bunsen burner—15
forceps—15
glass plate—15
goggles—30
laboratory aprons—30
matches
medicine dropper—15
paper towels
ring stand and ring—15
stirring rod—15
stopper,
  solid for test tube—30
test tube—30
wire screen—15

Chemicals

detergent,
  liquid—75 mL
lard—1000 mL
soap, liquid—75 mL
sodium chloride
  —200 g
sodium hydroxide,
  20% solution
  —2.5 liters
water, distilled

10:1 Carbon

Exhibit samples of various carbon materials listed in the first paragraph. Review the definition of an allotrope. Emphasize the difference in properties between graphite and diamond is a result of the difference in molecular structure (shown in Figure 10-1).

Graphite was discovered in Cumberland, England about 500 years ago. In 1760, it was used by the Faber family in Germany to make the first pencil. The graphite was brittle and not functional. Graphite was later mixed with clay and water to produce a more usable product. Pencils are now made exhibiting 19 different grades of hardness. You might want to set up a display showing pencils of different hardness and their uses. The more clay that is added, the harder the pencil becomes. The casing of a pencil is made of either cedar or pine. The wood is shaped in halves and grooved down the center to hold the lead. The graphite mixture is passed through a press to form a ropelike shape. It is straightened and dried in an oven. Once the lead is placed on one half of the pencil casing, the halves are glued together.

You may want to put the following on the board when discussing graphite, diamond, and Figure 10-1.

Diamond	**Graphite**
Melting point—4000°C	Boiling point— sublimes at 3850°C
Density 3.52 g/cm^3	Density—2.27 g/cm^3

Page 188. Making Sure

1. 6, 12
2. silicon, germanium, tin, and lead

10:2 Organic Compounds

It is important for students to understand that compounds have 3-dimensional structures. Make a model of a carbon atom using a commercial kit, balloons, or gumdrops and toothpicks. Emphasize the tetrahedral arrangement of atoms in the diamond structure, Figure 10-1.

You can use a handbook to point out the diversity of carbon compounds. Students should note that the section concerning the physical properties of organic compounds is far larger than that of the inorganic compounds.

10:3 Formulas for Organic Compounds

Use 3-dimensional models in this section in conjunction with the structural formulas shown in the text. The terminology may overwhelm students at first. Emphasize the differences among ethane, ethene, and ethyne. (Use a handbook to list the physical properties of each on the board.)

Page 191. Making Sure

3. The ethene structure contains one double bond between the carbon atoms and four hydrogens, C_2H_4. The ethane structure is composed of all single bonds and six hydrogen atoms, C_2H_6.
4. A carbon atom can form four single covalent bonds, two double covalent bonds, and one triple covalent bond.

10:4 Isomers

Use models whenever possible to reinforce the structural differences among isomers. After studying the butane and pentane isomers on pages 191-192, have students list the isomers for hexane, C_6H_{14}. There will be six isomers.

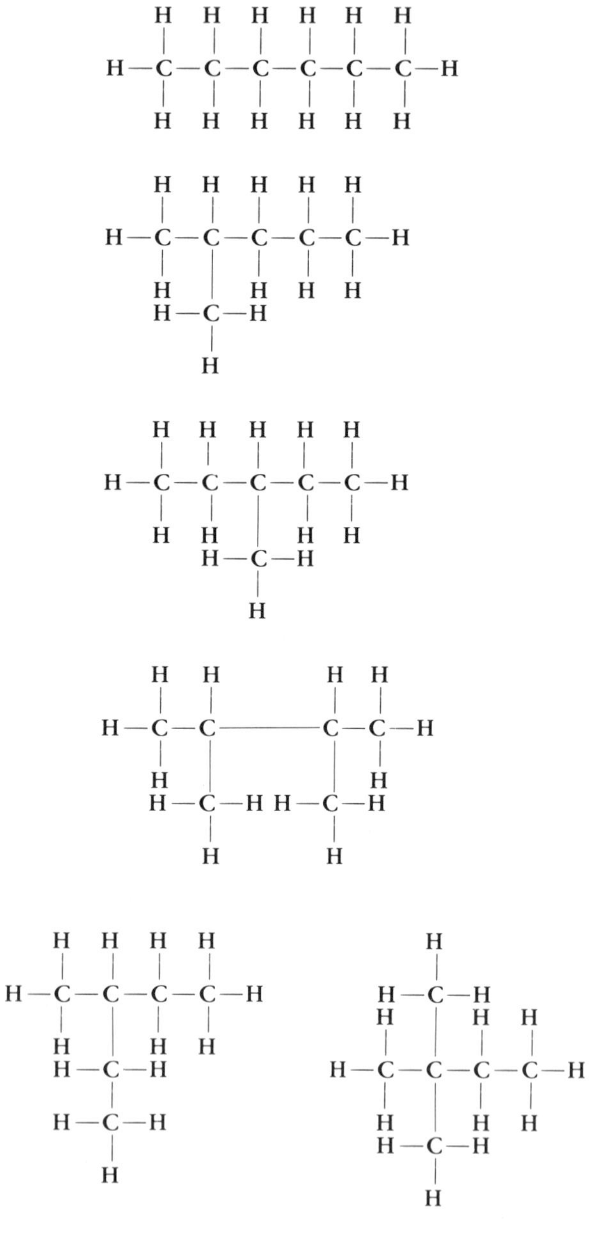

Page 192. Making Sure

5. Butane is an unbranched chain of carbon atoms. Isobutane contains a chain of three atoms and a branched chain of one carbon atom.

10:5 Hydrocarbons

This section emphasizes the distinction between saturated and unsaturated hydrocarbons. It is more important that students see the development of the hydrocarbon series than to memorize formulas. If you are using a handbook, point out that the melting and boiling points of hydrocarbons increase as the number of carbons in the chain increases. The first alkane, methane, is a gas. Unbranched chain compounds containing more than 16 carbons are waxy solids.

Be sure students realize oils are unsaturated while fats are saturated hydrocarbons. Using the theme of Figure 10-6, you might have students do further research into foods containing saturated and unsaturated fats.

10:6 Polymers

Inform students that there are both natural and synthetic polymers. Starch and proteins are natural polymers. All of the new fibers can be classed as synthetic polymers. Have students note the molecular structure shown in Figure 10-7. Emphasize that a polymer consists of many small units bonded together.

10:7 Soap and Detergent

Emphasize the chemical reasons why soap works. The nonpolar end dissolves grease while the polar end dissolves in water. The water is able to carry away the particles of grease and dirt surrounded by the soap molecules.

The equation for the soap making reaction is

fat + base $\rightarrow$ soap + glycerin

$$C_3H_5(OCC_{17}H_{35})_3 + 3NaOH \rightarrow 3C_{17}H_{35}COONa + C_3H_5(OH)_3$$

stearin + sodium hydroxide $\rightarrow$ soap + glycerol

Synthetic detergents differ from soaps in that they are made from an alcohol instead of fat. One alcohol that is used is the 12 carbon alcohol, lauryl alcohol. The product of the reaction is lauryl sulfate. Have students check the labels on shampoos and so on to find products containing this compound.

Hard water contains salts of calcium and magnesium. A scum is formed when these ions combine with soaps. When these ions react with a detergent molecule, the product formed is soluble in water and no scum forms.

Activity 10-1

The Activity demonstrates the preparation of soap, an organic compound.

Materials needed: beaker, 50 mL of lard, 150 mL of 20% NaOH solution, 10 g NaCl, paper towels, ring stand, metal ring, and burner, goggles and laboratory apron

You may use cottonseed oil instead of lard. The 20% NaOH solution is prepared by dissolving 20 grams of NaOH in 100 mL of water. Students should definitely wear aprons and goggles for this Activity. Caution them to use care in handling the NaOH solution.

Questions: The soap should make suds.

Activity 10-2

The Activity compares the action of soap and detergent on hard water.

Materials needed: 2 test tubes, liquid soap, liquid detergent, distilled water, hard water solution—dissolve some $CaSO_4$ or $MgSO_4$ in water.

Check labels on dishwashing products to determine if they are detergents or soaps. If the product does not specify dishwashing detergent but states that it is dishwashing liquid, it is probably a soap and not a detergent.

Questions: Suds should appear in all four test tubes. The detergent foams far better however. Detergent would be better to use in hard water areas since scum does not form.

10:8 Other Organic Compounds

This section emphasizes the numerous other compounds of carbon that can be formed by substituting other elements such as oxygen and the halogens.

If you have samples of acetic, butyric, and lactic acids, make solutions of these and compare their odors with vinegar, rancid butter, and sour milk.

Students are probably aware of antifreeze used in automobiles in cold climates to prevent freezing of the cooling system. Antifreeze is a solution of ethylene glycol and water.

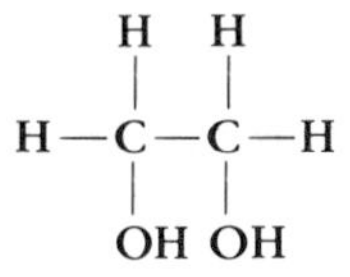

A solution containing equal parts of ethylene glycol and water can keep water from freezing until the temperature drops to about $-40°$ C. If the solution is one part antifreeze and two parts water, the freezing point is about $-20°$ C.

You can have your students write to the Exxon Company regarding the publications they have on antifreeze, motor oil, synthetic fibers, film, paint, plastics, synthetic rubber and so on. Write to:

Exxon Corporation
P.O. Box 3272
Houston, TX 77001

10:9 Organic Compounds in Living Things

Have students do some research on nutrition. They can make charts or posters using magazine pictures of food which are good sources of proteins and each of the different vitamins. Establish the fact that fats, carbohydrates, and proteins are all important to a good diet. It is refined sugar and products containing refined sugar that nutritionists object to in the carbohydrates category. There are a number of paperback books on the market with different viewpoints on nutrition. You can assign some reading and have a debate as a class project. Exposing students to nutritional information should be an essential part of their educational training.

Food products that are enriched or fortified must contain a label which states the nutritional information. You can assign students to bring in labels from home and discuss the nutritional claims of each.

Page 200. Making Sure

7. In the food chain, the sun enables plants to grow, animals eat plants, and people eat animals. As a result the energy we utilize comes ultimately from the sun.
8. Carbohydrates have a 2:1 ratio of hydrogen and oxygen. Fats supply more energy per gram than carbohydrates. Both classes of compounds contain carbon, hydrogen, and oxygen.

10:10 Petroleum

Emphasize the many types of products made from petroleum, as shown in Figure 10-18. This approach should make it clear to students why our demand for foreign oil is so great. It should also be pointed out why it is necessary that we develop new energy sources to alleviate this demand.

You might want to have students research the meaning of octane ratings for gasoline, or why unleaded gasolines are used.

Page 200. Making Sure

9. Distillation is a method of separating mixtures based on differences in boiling point of the mixture components. This process utilizes the physical change of boiling.
10. Plastics, asphalt, synthetic fibers, and the materials listed in Figure 10-18 are some examples.

10:11 Energy from Organic Compounds

Emphasize the importance of a good diet to provide our bodies with the fuel they need to perform efficiently.

More about diesel engines will be presented in Chapter 19. The function of catalysts and the catalytic converter for reducing pollution is covered in Chapter 12.

Activity 10-3

The Activity demonstrates complete and incomplete combustion.

Materials needed: burners, forceps, glass plates

This would be a good time to provide some fire safety information. The three essentials necessary to support combustion are kindling temperature, fuel, and oxygen to support combustion. Removal of any of the three puts out the fire. A candle flame goes out when you blow on it because the temperature falls below the kindling temperature. Water puts out a fire by cooling the fuel. Sand and carbon dioxide put out flames by removing the oxygen.

Questions: Carbon forms on the plate. A blue flame is hotter because the combustion reaction is complete.

Page 203. Making Sure

11. Air is mixed with gas to ensure a sufficient oxygen supply for complete combustion.
12. Answers will vary; coal, oil, gas, solar, and electricity are some examples.
13. Reduce thermostats in winter, raise thermostats in summer, turn off unnecessary devices using electricity, conserve hot water, buy energy efficient cars and appliances (see also Figure 23-15, page 490).

10:12 Synthetic Fuels

Inform students that ethanol be 100% pure in order to be used for gasohol. The fermentation process produces alcohol that is about 12% pure. In removing that water, an azeotrope is formed. An azeotrope is a mixture of alcohol and water containing 95% alcohol that will not separate. As a result, methods other than distillation are being investigated. This processing makes the gasohol conversion process very expensive at this point in time. At Purdue University, a method is being explored which utilizes a glass column packed with starch. Vapors from an alcohol-gas fermentation mixture are passed through the column. The water is absorbed by the starch. However this method is still in the experimental stage. A high school student in New York entered a science project in the state science fair which improved the yield of the process used at Purdue.

You might have students research alternative fuels other than gasohol.

Page 205. Making Sure

14. Use of synthetic fuels will decrease our demand for nonrenewable fossil fuels.
15. The energy required to produce the fuel may equal or be greater than the energy obtained from the fuel.

10:13 Silicon

Emphasize the location of silicon on the periodic table. The following lists some of the physical properties of silicon which can be used in a comparison with carbon.

Silicon
Melting point—1415°C
Boiling point—2680°C
Density—2.33 g/cm^3

Silicon also forms long chain compounds analogous to carbon. The structures of many silicon compounds are similar to carbon which accounts for its versatility.

Focus on Frontiers

Composites, Lighter Than Steel

Discuss with students the relationship between the mass of an object and the energy needed to move it. Talk about the advantages in using composites in cars. How can they save fuel? Ask students to suggest some other areas where composites could be helpful. Some areas are farm machines, boats, and bicycles. In the case of a bicycle, reducing the weight allows more energy to be used for speed. The frame for a good racing bicycle weighs about 12 to 16 newtons. Some of the companies involved in the manufacture of carbon-fiber composites are GRAFTEK/Division of Exxon Enterprises Inc., Monsanto Company, Union Carbide Corp., and E. I. du Pont de Nemours & Company Inc.

Questions for Review

A. True or False

1. True **2.** False (Carbon combines with hydrogren.) **3.** True **4.** True **5.** True **6.** False (Butane and isobutane have different properties.) **7.** False (Methane is an example of an alkane.) **8.** True **9.** True **10.** False (The boiling point of gasoline is lower than the boiling point of kerosene.)

B. Multiple Choice

1. Diamond **2.** C_2H_6 **3.** C_2H_2 **4.** isomers **5.** Octane **6.** organic compounds **7.** benzene **8.** organic compounds **9.** carbohydrate **10.** silicon

C. Completion

1. Diamond **2.** Natural gas **3.** Ethanol **4.** CCl_4 **5.** hydrocarbons **6.** CO (carbon monoxide) **7.** Coal, oil, gas **8.** corn **9.** oxygen **10.** sand

D. How and Why

1. Graphite and diamond are both pure carbon. They differ in bonding structure which results in a difference in hardness, strength, color, and use.
2. Carbon forms many organic compounds because it forms single, double, or triple bonds with itself and many other elements. Other elements can bond at various points on the carbon chain, with each resulting in a different compound.
3. 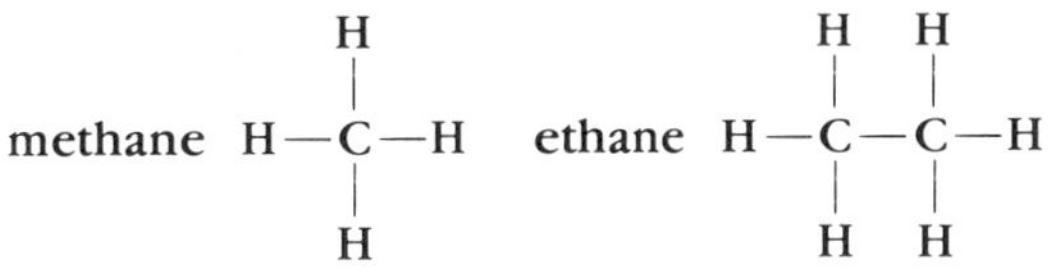

4. 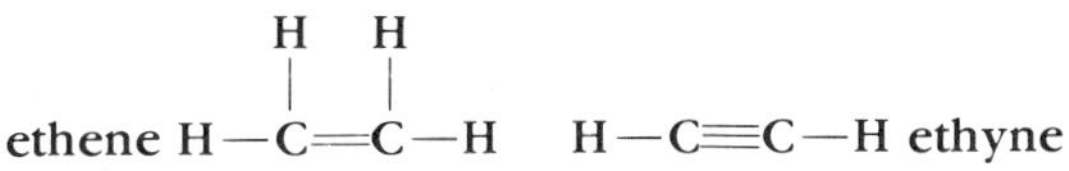

5. Rubber, nylon, orlon, dacron, polyester, and latex in paint are some examples.
6. Carbon is the major constituent of organic compounds. These compounds include fats, carbohydrates, proteins, and vitamins which are all essential to living things.
7. Energy can be obtained from organic compounds through eating food. Coal, oil, and gasoline can be burned to provide energy. They are external fuels.
8. The use of synthetic fuels will decrease our demand for fossil fuels.
9. Gasoline is obtained from petroleum through fractional distillation in large towers (Figure 10-18). In this process various components boil off at different temperatures.
10. Silicon is similar to carbon in the ways in which it bonds and in uses such as lubricants and abrasives. It is different in color and physical properties and found as inorganic compounds rather than organic.

Unit 4 Changes in Matter

Overview

The study of chemistry continues as students look at the properties of dissolved substances. Since most chemical reactions occur in solution, the following chapter covers equation writing and types of chemical reactions. The unit concludes with a chapter covering the behavior of acids and bases in solution and the formation of salts through neutralization reactions. The material in Chapter 13 is merely an extension of the concepts learned in Chapters 11 and 12.

Teaching Tips

- Use the theme of the unit opening photos to start a discussion concerning the changes a raw material undergoes in the manufacture of a useful product. Students can refer back to the uses of petroleum distillates in Chapter 10 as a starting point. You could also set up a bulletin board titled *Changes in Matter* showing the sequence of events in the steel-making process or the refining of important metals such as aluminum and copper.
- In studying Chapter 12, you can set up a bulletin board titled *Types of Reactions.* Place each of the following materials in plastic bags, label, arrange in groups and tack them to the board:

Group 1— seashell, baking soda, chalk, marble chips, eggshells
Caption: How are these materials alike?
(They all react with acids to release carbon dioxide—reaction of a carbonate with an acid.)

Group 2— copper(II) sulfate, copper(II) chloride, copper(II) nitrate, iron nail
Caption: How are these materials related?
(An iron nail will displace copper from solutions of the three copper compounds—single displacement.)

Group 3— iron filings, copper pieces, zinc pieces, sulfur
Caption: How are these materials related?
(The three metals will all react with sulfur to produce a sulfide—synthesis reaction.)

- Put a knowledge of chemical reactions to work using a discussion on fire extinguishers. Mix vinegar with baking soda. The carbon dioxide gas produced is heavier than air. It can be poured on a candle flame to extinguish it. You might consider inviting a firefighter to talk to the class concerning the methods used to handle chemical fires, types of equipment used, and the construction of a firefighter's clothing. Ask the speaker to share with the students the importance of science in a career like firefighting.

11 Solutions

Overview

Chapter 11 covers one part of those materials which are classified as mixtures. The behavior of solute and solvent is emphasized through many examples throughout the chapter. Types of solutions, the factors which aid or inhibit the solution process, and methods of classifying solutions are discussed.

Performance Objectives

Goal: Students will gain an understanding of the properties of solutions and the terms used to describe them.

Objectives: Upon completion of the reading and activities and when asked to diagram, demonstrate, or respond either orally or on a written test, students will:

11:1	K/P	distinguish among the three types of solutions.
11:2	P	describe the solution process.
11:3	K/P	list and explain the factors which assist the solution process.
11:4	K/P	contrast organic and inorganic solvents.
11:5-6	K/P	describe why some solutions conduct electricity and others do not.
11:7	K/P	use the solubility rules to determine whether certain compounds are soluble in water.
11:8	K/P	list and explain various methods for describing the concentration of a solution.
11:9	K	describe the effect of a solute on the boiling point and freezing point of a solvent.
	S/A	demonstrate the proper use of equipment and materials.

Equipment for Activities

The amounts listed are for a class of 30 students broken into groups of 2.

balance—5
beaker, 250 mL—30
Bunsen burner—15
clamp, test tube—15
evaporating dish—15
filter paper
flask, 250 mL—30
funnel—15
goggles—30
graduated cylinder
  25 mL—15
  50 mL—15
laboratory apron—30
matches
medicine dropper—30
ring stand and ring—15
soda straw—15
stoppers
  for flasks—30
  for test tubes—60
tape, masking
test tube—60
test tube rack—15
thermometer—15
wire screen—15

Chemicals

copper(II) sulfate
  fine crystals—300 g
  technical crystals—300 g
detergent, liquid—75 mL
ethanol—75 mL
ice
mineral oil—75 mL
naphtha (lighter fluid)—200 mL
soap—1 bar
sugar—100 g
vegetable oil—75 mL

11:1 Types of Solutions

Stress the difference between the meaning of the words *liquid* and *solution.* Liquid refers to the physical state in which the substance exists. Solution means you have a mixture of at least two substances, which may or may not be liquids. Discuss those substances not commonly thought of as solutions: coins, soda water, shaving foam or whipped cream, smoke, and fog.

Plaster of Paris comes from the mineral gypsum a natural hydrate, $CaSO_4 \bullet 2H_2O$. Plaster is made by driving off some of the water of crystallization. When this substance is mixed with water, it absorbs the water and produces heat as it hardens.

Activity 11-1

The Activity demonstrates the relationship between hydrated and anhydrous crystals.

Materials needed: test tube, copper(II) sulfate crystals, burner, test tube holder, goggles and laboratory apron

Questions: The blue crystals turn to a white powder. Water forms at the mouth of the test tube.

When water is added to the powder, a blue solution is formed. The addition of water causes the blue color.

11:2 The Solution Process

You can demonstrate solvation by placing a crystal of potassium permanganate in a beaker of warm water. Place the beaker on the overhead while you go over the material in the first paragraph of the text.

You can demonstrate the absorption of energy as a solid dissolves, by adding ammonium nitrate to a beaker containing 50 mL of water. You can set the beaker on a wet block of wood. After a time, the beaker should freeze to the block of wood as energy is absorbed in dissolving the ammonium nitrate.

You can demonstrate the release of energy as a solid dissolves by carefully pouring 20 mL of concentrated sulfuric acid into a beaker containing 100 mL of water. **CAUTION:** Wear eye and clothing protection. Place a test tube containing 5 mL of ethanol in the beaker. The heat released from the solvation of the acid should cause the ethanol to boil.

You can have students observe the differences in bubbling when opening warm and cold bottles of soda.

Activity 11-2

The Activity demonstrates the behavior of substances in the presence of polar and nonpolar solvents.

Materials needed: four test tubes, salt, sugar, ethanol, mineral oil, stoppers for each test tube, graduated cylinder, dropper pipet

Caution students about using the same dropper in the mineral oil and ethanol.

Questions: Salt, sugar, and ethanol dissolve in water. Mineral oil and water dissolve in ethanol.

11:3 Rate of Solution

Students may need some help in understanding the area values listed in Figure 11-6. Take time to review this diagram with them.

You might ask students what other appliances are used to speed the solution process—mixer, food processor, heating element on a stove or any other heating device used in dissolving substances.

Activity 11-3

The Activity demonstrates one method used to increase the rate of solution.

Materials needed: copper(II) sulfate crystals—both large and crushed, two 250 mL flasks, stoppers to fit the flasks, balance

Be sure students use the same amount of water in both flasks.

Page 219. Making Sure

1. The tiny crystals dissolve faster because there is more surface area exposed to the solvent. For example, consider a cube 4 cm on a side. The total surface area is 96 cm^2 (4 cm x 4 cm x 6 sides). If the cube is cut in the middle of each edge, eight cubes—2 cm on a side—are formed. The surface area is now 192 cm^2 (2 cm x 2 cm x 6 sides x 8 cubes). If each cube is cut again in the same manner, there would be 64 cubes—1 cm on a side. The total area is 384 cm^2 (1 cm x 1 cm x 6 sides x 64 cubes). Every cut doubles the area. Using this explanation and having the students count the blocks in Figure 11-6 should help them understand surface area.
2. Carbon dioxide gas escapes from solution leaving "flat" soda.
3. Dirt and grease dissolve better in hot water.

11:4 Solvents

Have students check at home for products used as dry cleaning agents. Emphasize that "dry cleaning" means without water.

Though the terms polar and nonpolar are not used in the discussion, this section attempts to cover the behavior of substances in polar and nonpolar solvents. Since most organic solvents are nonpolar in nature, this approach was used to pick up on the organic chemistry in Chapter 10. Having a limited background in chemical bonding, students may have difficulty understanding polarity.

Activity 11-4

The Activity demonstrates the solubility of an organic compound in various solvents.

Materials needed: four test tubes, vegetable oil, soap, detergent, naphtha, dropping pipet, stoppers to fit the test tubes

You may want to review the section on soap and detergents from Chapter 10.

Questions: The oil does not dissolve in water; it dissolves slightly in soap; more so in detergent, and completely in naphtha.

Oil, soap, detergent, and naphtha are organic compounds. Water is inorganic.

Page 221. Making Sure

4. Water is an inorganic compound.
5. Latex paint dissolves in water. It is only oil-base paints which will not dissolve in water.

6. Latex paint should dissolve even better in soapy water. (Review the structure of the soap molecule, Figure 10-9, page 195.)
7. Oil base paints require turpentine or other organic solvent in order to dissolve.

11:5 Particles in Solution

The section is a good opportunity to review covalent and ionic bonding in compounds. Emphasize the behavior of HCl in solution, Figure 11-11. Students will be utilizing this information again in Chapter 13.

11:6 Solutions as Conductors

You can do the demonstrations shown in Figure 11-12 if you have a conductivity apparatus. Point out to students that the conductivity of some solutions is a bit of evidence used in formulating our theories concerning ionic and covalent bonding.

Page 222. Making Sure

8. Distilled water does not conduct. There are no free ions to complete the circuit.
9. Any electric appliance should be handled with dry hands. Care should be taken not to stand in water that can conduct electric current.

11:7 Solubility

Demonstrate the solubility of some of the compounds listed in Table 11-1. Mix solutions of barium chloride and dilute sulfuric acid in a beaker to illustrate the insolubility of barium sulfate.

Students are again asked to derive information from graphs. Check to see that they fully understand the values obtained from the graph.

Activity 11-5

The Activity demonstrates how to determine the solubility of a salt.

You may want to have students cover the evaporating dish with a watch glass to avoid loss of product from splattering.

Summing Up

1. Answers will vary.
2. To determine the mass of the salt subtract the mass of the dish from the mass of the dish and residue.
3. Heating the water would increase the solubility of the salt.

Page 225. Making Sure

10. a. 80 g/100 g H_2O
    b. 170 g/100 g H_2O
    c. 108 g/100 g H_2O
    d. 40 g/100 g H_2O

11:8 Concentration

Discuss the meaning of the word *percent* (per hundred). Write the symbol % and show its resemblance to the fixed denominator of the fraction—5% = 5/100.

You may want to relate specific gravity to density (discussed in Chapter 5) by reviewing the density equation.

Activity 11-6

The Activity demonstrates the use of a hydrometer to determine specific gravity.

To save time you may want to make the homemade hydrometers yourself. Use 50 mL graduates.

Summing Up

1. The soda straw floats higher in the salt water.
2. The salt water is more dense than fresh water.
3. Your body would float higher in salt water than in fresh water.

11:9 Using Solutions

Use the models shown in Figures 11-18 and 11-19 to help students visualize why the change in boiling and freezing points occurs when solute is added.

Activity 11-7

The Activity demonstrates the effect of a solute on the boiling and freezing points of a solvent.

Materials needed: beaker, thermometer, salt, ice, burner or hot plate

Do not be surprised if the thermometer readings do not register exactly 0°C and 100°C for the boiling and freezing points of water. Tap water may contain many dissolved minerals, the pressure in your area is probably not standard pressure, and many thermometers are simply inaccurate. Students should note a difference however when the solute is added.

Questions: The salt will elevate the boiling point and depress the freezing point. Answers will vary as to the exact amount of change recorded.

Page 229. Making Sure

11. Salt reduces the freezing point of water causing the ice to melt.

12. The salt lowers the temperature of the mixture; the ice cream freezes faster.

13. Spaghetti, macaroni, vegetables are some examples.

14. The specific gravity of the coolant solution can tell you the concentration of antifreeze present.

Focus on Skills

Organizing New Terms Using a Chapter Outline

In making students outline text material they become proficient in picking out the important points of a chapter and organizing them in a logical sequence. Looking over a student's outline of a chapter can tell you a great deal about that student's overall comprehension of the material. As stated in the front of this guide, ***Focus on Physical Science*** contains many student aids which help to highlight important ideas and concepts. This skills page enables students to apply the techniques of using these aids.

Answers

B. solid types
  1. ionic compounds—dissolve forming ions
  2. molecular compounds—remain molecules as they dissolve

C. Uses
  1. by lowering the freezing point of a solvent, they can be used as coolants or to melt snow
  2. by raising the boiling point of a solvent, they can be used in cooking to cook foods faster at a higher temperature

Questions for Review

A. True or False

1. False (To form a solution, a solute must be dissolved by a solvent.) **2.** True **3.** False (A gaseous solution can be formed by dissolving a gas in another gas.) **4.** False (Water is a solvent that will dissolve almost everything.) **5.** True **6.** False (Organic solvents usually dissolve organic solutes.) **7.** True **8.** True **9.** True **10.** False (A substance which will not dissolve is insoluble.)

B. Multiple Choice

1. lighter fluid **2.** silver **3.** organic **4.** ions **5.** supersaturated **6.** $NaNO_3$ **7.** decrease **8.** naphtha **9.** dilute **10.** unsaturated

C. Completion

1. Water **2.** dissociate (separate) **3.** Sugar **4.** organic **5.** organic **6.** water **7.** lowers **8.** specific gravity **9.** lower **10.** Energy

D. How and Why

1. a. soluble **d.** soluble
b. insoluble **e.** insoluble
c. soluble **f.** insoluble

12 Chemical Reactions

Overview

Students are introduced to equation writing using a step-by-step process. The types of reactions are introduced and students see the mass relationships shown by a balanced equation when studying the Law of Conservation of Mass. The student moves on to look at the energy exchanges which take place during reactions and their effects on reaction rate in a study of catalysis.

Performance Objectives

Goal: Students will gain an understanding of conservation of matter and energy in chemical reactions and the means by which these are communicated to others.

Objectives: Upon completion of the reading and activities and when asked to diagram, demonstrate, or respond either orally or on a written test, students will:

12:1-4	K/P	define, describe, and give examples of decomposition, synthesis, and displacement reactions.
	K/S	write and balance equations representing each type of reaction.
12:5	K/S	use the Law of Conservation of Mass to solve problems involving unknown amounts of reactants or products.
12:6	K	distinguish between exothermic and endothermic reactions.
12:7	K/P	explain the role of catalysts in chemical reactions.
	S/A	demonstrate the proper use of equipment and materials.
	A	attempt at least one *More Ideas to Explore.*

Equipment for Activities

The amounts listed are for a class of 30 students broken into groups of 2.

balance—5
beaker, 100 mL—15
flashbulbs—30
flash unit—5
graduated cylinder, 25 mL—15
matches
test tubes—15
wooden splints

Chemicals

copper(II) sulfate, powdered—50 g
hydrogen peroxide, 4% fresh—100 mL
manganese dioxide—50 g
zinc strips—15

12:1 Equations for Reactions

Proceed slowly through this section as the material is important and may require some time for students to grasp. Throughout this chapter students should be encouraged to use a handbook to determine the physical state of reactants and products when writing equations.

Page 238. Making Sure

1. $4Fe(c) + 3O_2(g) \rightarrow 2Fe_2O_3(c)$
2. a. $2Ca(c) + O_2(g) \rightarrow 2CaO(c)$
   b. $S(c) + O_2(g) \rightarrow SO_2(g)$

12:2 Synthesis Reactions

Remind students that the material produced in Activity 9-3, page 173 was rust. The reaction that occurred was a synthesis reaction. Point out that a synthesis reaction can generally be recognized by the fact that only one product is formed.

Page 238. Making Sure

3. $2H_2(g) + O_2(g) \rightarrow 2H_2O(l)$
4. $2Mg(c) + O_2(g) \rightarrow 2MgO(c)$

12:3 Decomposition Reactions

Point out that a decomposition reaction can be recognized by the fact that there is one reactant and two or more products.

Activity 12-1

The Activity demonstrates a test for the presence of oxygen.

Materials needed: hydrogen peroxide (4%), MnO_2, test tube, splint, matches

You may want to point out here that the MnO_2 acts as a catalyst in the decomposition. There are enzymes in the blood which perform this same function. When hydrogen peroxide is put on a cut, oxygen is released rapidly due to the presence of these enzymes in the blood. The released oxygen destroys anaerobic bacteria thus preventing an infection.

Questions: The glowing splint bursts into flame as bubbles of O_2 leave the tube.

Page 240. Making Sure

5. $MgCl_2(c) \rightarrow Mg(c) + Cl_2(g)$
6. $2NaCl(c) \rightarrow 2Na(c) + Cl_2(g)$

12:4 Displacement Reactions

You could perform the silver and iron reactions listed in this section to emphasize the definition of a precipitate.

You might demonstrate the removal of tarnish (Ag_2S) from silver. Make a saturated warm water solution of sodium hyposulfite. Dip the tarnished silver into the solution.

Activity 12-2

The Activity demonstrates a single replacement reaction.

Materials needed: beaker, strip of zinc metal, copper(II) sulfate, balance, graduated cylinder

You can have students do the same reaction using magnesium and/or an iron nail in place of the zinc.

Questions: Copper forms on the zinc strip.

$Zn(c) + CuSO_4(aq) \rightarrow Cu(c) + ZnSO_4(aq)$

Page 242. Making Sure

7. a. $NaBr(aq) + AgNO_3(aq) \rightarrow AgBr(c) + NaNO_3(aq)$
   b. $Ca(NO_3)_2(aq) + K_2SO_4(aq) \rightarrow CaSO_4(c) + 2KNO_3$
   c. $2KCl(aq) + Pb(NO_3)_2(aq) \rightarrow 2KNO_3(aq) + PbCl_2(c)$
   d. $3Ca(OH)_2(aq) + 2Fe(NO_3)_3(aq) \rightarrow 2Fe(OH)_3(c) + 3Ca(NO_3)_2(aq)$
   e. $3MgSO_4(aq) + 2Na_3PO_4(aq) \rightarrow 3Na_2SO_4 + Mg_3(PO_4)_2$
   f. hydrogen sulfide plus mercury(II) chloride yields $HgS(c) + 2HCl(aq)$
8. a. displacement (double)
   b. decomposition
   c. synthesis
   d. displacement (single)
9. a. potassium hydroxide plus aluminum chloride yields aluminum hydroxide plus potassium chloride
   b. mercury(II) oxide yields mercury plus oxygen
   c. sulfur trioxide plus water yields sulfuric acid
   d. calcium bromide plus chlorine yields calcium chloride plus bromine

12:5 Conservation of Mass

Use several examples to make sure students know how to determine the formula mass of a compound or atom using the periodic table. Provide extra drill and be sure to go over the *Making Sure* questions with students.

You might have students bring in some recipes from home and discuss the ratios of ingredients required to obtain a good product. Though the parallel is not exact, relating conservation of mass to cooking and baking may make this concept easier to understand.

Activity 12-3

The Activity demonstrates the Law of Conservation of Mass. You may want to do this Activity as a demonstration.

Materials needed: double pan balance, 2 flashbulbs, camera flash holder

Questions: The mass of the bulb does not change.

The flashbulb undergoes a chemical change evidenced by the fact that heat and light are given off.

Page 245. Making Sure

10. a. 2 Na @ 23 = 46
    1 S @ 32 = 32
    4 O @ 16 = 64
    142

    b. Ca @ 40 = 40
    C @ 12 = 12
    3 O @ 16 = 48
    100

    c. 2 N @ 14 = 28
    4 H @ 1 = 4
    3 O @ 16 = 48
    80

    d. 1 Cu @ 64 = 64
    1 S @ 32 = 32
    4 O @ 16 = 64
    160

    e. 1 Ag @ 108 = 108
    1 Br @ 80 = 80
    188

    f. 3 K @ 39 = 117
    1 P @ 31 = 31
    4 O @ 16 = 64
    212

11. 32 grams of oxygen will produce 2 × 28 or 56 grams of carbon monoxide.
12. From the equation 116 grams of NaCl forms 46 grams of Na, therefore half the amount of NaCl (58 grams) will produce half the amount of Na 46/2 or 23 grams.

12:6 Energy and Reactions

Have students recall the demonstrations you did in Chapter 11 to illustrate endothermic (ammonium nitrate and water) and exothermic reactions (sulfuric acid and water).

12:7 Catalysts

You can demonstrate a catalytic converter. Place a small amount of alcohol (methanol) in a beaker. Heat a platinum wire in a beaker until it glows. When the wire is removed from the flame students should observe that it stops glowing. Heat the wire again and immediately place it in the vapor in the beaker. Note that the wire will continue to glow. Heat is generated by the hydrocarbon molecules which are adsorbed on the wire. The catalyst (platinum) promotes a more complete oxidation of the hydrocarbon at a much lower temperature than would be possible without the catalyst.

An automobile equipped with a catalytic converter requires unleaded fuel. Using regular gasoline causes lead to deposit on the catalyst, thus reducing its effectiveness.

You can have students check food labels at home and bring in lists of preservatives. You can use this as a starting point to do a bulletin board on food additives. Preservatives are of two types: Antimicrobials which prevent spoilage from bacteria, molds, fungi, and yeast; Antioxidants which prevent or delay changes in color, flavor, or texture due to oxidation.

Antimicrobials

ascorbic acid (vitamin C)	calcium propionate
benzoic acid	potassium propionate
sodium benzoate	sodium propionate
citric acid	sodium diacetate
lactic acid	sodium erythorbate
calcium lactate	sodium nitrate
butylparaben	sodium nitrite
heptylparaben	sorbic acid
methylparaben	calcium sorbate
propylparaben	potassium sorbate
propionic acid	sodium sorbate

Antioxidants

ascorbic acid
BHA (butylated hydroxyanisole)
BHT (butylated hydroxytoluene)
citric acid
EDTA (ethylenediaminetetraacetic acid)
propyl gallate
TBHQ (tertiery butylhydroquinone)
tocopherols (vitamin E)

In Focus

Chemical Technology

Ask students to prepare montages depicting the benefits and hazards of chemical technology. Use the photo essay and the montages to start a discussion about the wise use of chemical technology. Ask students to write a brief description of the world without chemical technology, as they imagine it. A good source of information on chemical technology is *The Chemical Facts of Life* program by Monsanto Company. For more information contact the Public Relations Department at 800 N. Lindbergh Blvd. St. Louis, Missouri 63166. Information is also available from other chemical companies. Other information on the chemical industry is available from various conservation and environmental organizations.

Focus on Frontiers

Mobile Lab Cleans Spills

Discuss the relationship between chemistry and water treatment. In the discussion consider the importance of the mobile lab and treatment system. Many of the spills handled by the lab are large concentrations of chemicals which in small amounts are useful and safe. Consider this idea in a discussion of pesticide use. Ask the question, "Should pesticides be used?"

As an added project, some students may want to build a model of a water treatment system.

Questions for Review

A. True or False

1. False (Silver chloride is insoluble in water.) **2.** True **3.** True **4.** True **5.** True **6.** False (An equation is balanced by changing coefficients.) **7.** False (The molecular mass of H_2 is 2.) **8.** True **9.** False (An enzyme is a catalyst.) **10.** True

B. Multiple Choice

1. exothermic **2.** iodine **3.** catalyst **4.** remains the same **5.** 85 **6.** 44 **7.** coefficients **8.** exothermic **9.** decomposition **10.** displacement

C. Completion

1. synthesis **2.** mass **3.** endothermic **4.** 136 **5.** AgCl **6.** mass **7.** displacement **8.** decomposition **9.** CO **10.** H_2O

D. How and Why

1. A balanced equation agrees with conservation of mass because the number and kinds of atoms are the same on both sides of the equation.
2. Endothermic reactions require continuous application of energy in order to proceed. Exothermic reactions may require some energy to begin, but give off more energy as they proceed spontaneously.
3. Changing a chemical formula indicates a new chemical compound. As a result the reaction that takes place is not accurately described.
4. **a.** $Na_2S(aq) + 2AgNO_3 \rightarrow 2NaNO_3(aq) + Ag_2S(c)$
   b. $3H_2(g) + N_2(g) \rightarrow 2NH_3(g)$
   c. $2KClO_3(c) \rightarrow 2KCl(c) + 3O_2(g)$
   d. $3CuSO_4(aq) + 2Al(c) \rightarrow Al_2(SO_4)_3(aq) + 3Cu(c)$
   e. $2Na(c) + 2H_2O(l) \rightarrow 2NaOH(aq) + H_2(g)$
5. **a.** displacement **d.** displacement
   b. synthesis **e.** displacement
   c. decomposition

13 Acids, Bases, and Salts

Overview

The study of solutions and chemical reactions is now applied in looking at the properties of acids, bases, and salts. The study of neutralization reactions and pH shows the relationship among these three classes of compounds.

Performance Objectives

Goal: Students will gain an understanding of the properties of common acids, bases, and salts and the use of indicators to distinguish among them.

Objectives: Upon completion of the reading and activities and when asked to diagram, demonstrate, or respond either orally or on a written test, students will:

13:1	K	list and distinguish properties of the common acids.
13:2	K	list and distinguish properties of the common bases.
	P	compare and contrast properties of acids and bases.
13:3	K/P	use ionization to describe the strength of acids and bases.
13:4	K/P	describe the relationship among ion concentration, pH, and acid-base strength.
13:5	K	list some common indicators and describe how they change color.
13:6	K/P	explain and give examples of neutralization reactions.
	K/P	relate neutralization reactions to salts.
13:7	K/P	apply knowledge of acids and bases to their respective anhydrides.
	S/A	demonstrate the proper use of equipment and materials in performing activities.
	A	attempt at least one *More Ideas to Explore.*

Equipment for Activities

The amounts listed are for a class of 30 students broken into groups of 2.

balance—5
Bunsen burner—15
evaporating dish—15
goggles—30
graduated cylinder
 10 mL—15
 25 mL—15
glass, plastic drinking—60
litmus paper
laboratory apron—30
matches
medicine dropper—30
ring stand and ring—15

soda straw—15
stirring rod—15
test tube—75
test tube rack—15
Universal indicator paper
wire screen—15

Chemicals
ascorbic acid—100 mL
fruit and vegetable juices, assorted
household liquids, assorted
hydrochloric acid, dilute—300 mL
indophenol solution, 0.1%—1000 mL
lemon juice—100 mL
milk—100 mL
milk of magnesia—250 mL
petroleum jelly—1 jar
phenolphthalein solution—50 mL
soda pop—100 mL
sodium bicarbonate—30 g
sodium hydroxide
  dilute—200 mL
  0.1*M*—250 mL
vinegar—200 mL
water
zinc, mossy—60 pieces

13:1 Common Acids

You can begin the chapter by demonstrating the corrosive nature of acids by showing the activities in Figure 13-1.

You might spend time here reviewing the safety precautions students should observe when handling acids. Refer to Appendix B for proper procedures and safety rules.

Activity 13-1

The Activity demonstrates the reaction of various acids with zinc.

Materials needed: 4 test tubes, zinc, dilute HCl, vinegar, lemon juice, graduated cylinder

You can substitute other metals and study the results as an extension to this Activity.

Questions: The HCl gives the most observable reaction.

Water is used as a control in the Activity.

Page 260. Making Sure

1. HF, HBr, HI
2. All are organic acids; all contain carbon, hydrogen, and oxygen.

13:2 Common Bases

As shown in Figure 13-4, many cleaning substances found in the home contain bases. Have students check labels at home and bring in a listing of products and the bases they contain.

Activity 13-2

The Activity compares the strengths of various bases.

Materials needed: 4 plastic cups, aqueous ammonia solution—diluted 1:10, sodium hydroxide solution—0.1*M* 4 g per liter, milk of magnesia, petroleum jelly

Questions: The petroleum jelly is in various stages of dissolving. It is most soluble in the sodium hydroxide.

Water is used as a control in this Activity.

Page 261. Making Sure

3. All are found in the home; all contain hydrogen.
4. Bases dissolve fats and oils.

13:3 Ions in Acids and Bases

Use a conductivity apparatus to show that acids and bases do conduct electricity. Use this apparatus also to compare the conductivity of strong acid and weak acid solutions of equal concentration. This demonstration should establish the definition of the words *strong* and *weak* when used in describing acid-base properties. It is important to emphasize that strong and weak are not synonymous with dilute and concentrated.

Emphasize the difference in reaction path between the acids shown in Figure 13-7.

13:4 pH of a Solution

Point out that the consecutive numbers of the pH scale do not differ by a factor of 1 but by a factor of 10. The pH scale is an exponential scale. A pH of 3 denotes a solution that has 10 times more available hydronium ions than a solution with a pH of 4. You may want to use the following table to illustrate this point.

pH	H_3O^+ conc.	Exponent
0	1	10^0
1	0.1	10^1
2	0.01	10^2
3	0.001	10^3
4	0.0001	10^4
5	0.00001	10^5
6	0.000001	10^6
7	0.0000001	10^7
	and so on	

Page 264. Making Sure

5. Acids—stomach contents, vinegar, apples, orange juice, carrots, urine, and milk
   Bases—blood, seawater, milk of magnesia, and ammonia
   Water is neutral.

13:5 Indicators

Emphasize the difference between indicators such as litmus, which merely detect the presence of an acid or base, and highly specific indicators such as methyl violet (Figure 13-13) which can show a specific pH.

Red cabbage juice is an excellent indicator and easy to prepare. Boil red cabbage leaves in 250 mL of water. Boil until the water is deep red-violet in color. You can use this indicator in testing various products students bring in from home.

Activity 13-3

The Activity demonstrates the use of indicators. If you do not have indophenol, you can prepare it by boiling 5 mL of starch in 250 mL of water. Remove 10 drops of this starch solution and add it to 1 drop of tincture of iodine and 100 mL of water. When testing the food juices, add them drop by drop. Count the number of drops required to make the blue color disappear.

Summing Up

1. All in Part A are acids.
2. carbonic acid
3. Universal Indicator paper changes colors over the entire pH range. It not only determines whether a substance is acidic or basic, but it also determines the approximate pH.
4. Testing the ascorbic acid is a control.

13:6 Salts

Using the conductivity apparatus, show that 0.1*M* $Ba(OH)_2$ and 0.1*M* H_2SO_4 conduct an electric current. With the apparatus still in the beaker of $Ba(OH)_2$ slowly add the sulfuric acid. The lamp will cease to glow as the precipitate, $BaSO_4$, forms and removes the ions from solution. A test with litmus paper or Universal Indicator paper should show a pH of 7.

Activity 13-4

The Activity demonstrates the preparation of a salt by neutralization.

Materials needed: 0.1*M* NaOH solution—4 g per liter, 0.1*M* HCl solution—8.55 mL concentrated reagent per liter, phenolphthalein, dropping pipet, graduated cylinder, evaporating dish, burner, stirring rod, ring stand, metal ring, wire gauze, goggles and aprons

Questions: The remaining residue is NaCl. Phenolphthalein is used to show that the base has been neutralized.

Page 268. Making Sure

6. The hydronium ion concentration is reduced because the hydronium ions from the acid combine with the hydroxide ions of the base to form water.
7. **a.** $2KOH(aq) + H_2SO_4(aq) \rightarrow K_2SO_4(aq) + 2H_2O(l)$
   b. $HNO_3(aq) + NaOH(aq) \rightarrow NaNO_3(aq) + H_2O(l)$
   c. $Ca(OH)_2(aq) + 2HNO_3(aq) \rightarrow Ca(NO_3)_2(aq) + 2H_2O(l)$
   d. $Mg(OH)_2(aq) + 2HCl(aq) \rightarrow MgCl_2(aq) + 2H_2O(l)$
   e. $Zn(c) + 2HCl(aq) \rightarrow ZnCl_2(aq) + H_2(g)$
8. **a.** potassium sulfate
   b. sodium nitrate
   c. calcium nitrate
   d. magnesium chloride
   e. zinc chloride

13:7 Anhydrides

Demonstrate acid-forming elements. Ignite a piece of sulfur about half as large as a pea in a deflagrating spoon. Lower the spoon into a wide-mouth bottle containing 25 mL of water. Do not let the sulfur touch the water. Cover the bottle for about 1 minute. Remove the spoon and allow the gas formed to mix with the water. Test the resulting solution with litmus or hydrion paper. You can use this demonstration when presenting the acid rain diagram on page 269.

Demonstrate base-forming elements. Burn a piece of magnesium ribbon. Add the MgO (white powder) that is formed to a few mL of water in a test tube. Heat to boiling. Test the resulting solution with litmus. The product is the same as that in the commercial product milk of magnesia.

You might have students bring in newspaper and magazine articles concerning acid rain. It is now a controversial issue as to how to eliminate it.

Page 269. Making Sure

9. **a.** basic **c.** acidic
   b. acidic **d.** basic
10. $2Mg(c) + O_2(g) \rightarrow 2MgO(c)$

Focus on People

Paula Moyer, Chemist

Ask a technologist from a medical lab or a pathologist to give a presentation on the use of analytical chemistry in their work. Have the students research and discuss other jobs that use or produce chemical analyses. Some examples are farming, plastic production, electronic part production, and the fabric industry. Through the discussion, show that most areas of modern life use the information found by analytical chemists in some way.

Questions for Review

A. True or False

1. True **2.** True **3.** False (Ammonia is a weak base.) **4.** True **5.** False (A solution which has a pH of 4 is an acid.) **6.** True **7.** True **8.** True **9.** True **10.** True

B. Multiple Choice

1. sour **2.** 2 **3.** Benzene **4.** basic anhydride **5.** more than 7 **6.** calcium oxide **7.** HCl **8.** water **9.** more **10.** high hydronium

C. Completion

1. Taste **2.** hydronium ion **3.** an indicator **4.** acid **5.** H_2 **6.** decreases **7.** salt and/or hydrogen **8.** increases **9.** decreases **10.** neutralizes

D. How and Why

1. The reaction is a neutralization reaction.
2. **a.** sodium hydroxide and sulfuric acid
   b. sodium hydroxide and hydrochloric acid
   c. sodium hydroxide and nitric acid
3. Acids and bases may be detected through the use of indicators which exhibit different colors at different pHs.
4. Sulfuric acid—used to make other acids, paints, batteries, fertilizers
   Hydrochloric acid—cleans metals for plating, algaecide
   Nitric acid—preparation of explosives, fertilizers
5. **a.** acid **d.** salt
   b. acid **e.** base
   c. base **f.** salt
6. Lye—used to break up grease and dirt in sink drains
   Ammonia–used as a cleaning agent

Unit 5 Light and Sound

Overview

The unit begins with a study of the general characteristics of waves by utilizing various models. The student then moves on to look at visible and invisible radiation in studying the parts of the electromagnetic spectrum. Practical uses of radiant energy are emphasized in discussing X rays, microwaves, infrared, ultraviolet, radio and TV.

In the next two chapters, the student focuses on the visible light part of the spectrum. The behavior of light in relation to mirrors and prisms is studied in the chapter on light and color. The next chapter covers the behavior of light through lenses and applies this knowledge in a study of eyeglasses, telescopes, microscopes, cameras, and lasers.

The final chapter covers a comparison of the characteristics of compressional and transverse waves and the applications of this knowledge in making devices used to produce and detect compressional waves. The final section of the chapter covers ways of controlling sound waves.

Teaching Tips

- ▶ You can do a bulletin board display using colored yarns on construction paper. Use this model to identify crest, trough, wavelength, and amplitude of transverse waves as you discuss these basic characteristics.
- ▶ You can do a unit bulletin board display of photos, magazine pictures, and posters. Show a surfer, a sunbather, kids playing *Frisbee* on a beach, a rainbow, a cassette tape advertisement showing sound breaking a glass, a person having X rays taken by a doctor and/or a dentist, infrared lamps heating foods in restaurants, microwave oven advertisements, a radio, TV, telescope, microscope, parabolic mirror, camera, laser.
- ▶ Obtain and display large diagrams and/or models of the eye and ear. Sometimes the health office (school nurse) has models and diagrams to lend.
- ▶ Library research project: How is sound put on a record?

14 Waves

Overview

The basic characteristic and properties of waves are introduced to establish the foundation for the study of electromagnetic waves and sound. The relationship among wavelength, frequency, and speed is presented. Water waves are used as a model to explain reflection and refraction. A ball is used as a model to study the angles of incidence and reflection. The content moves from waves you can see to those that cannot be seen. The chapter progresses through X rays, ultraviolet, infrared, microwaves, radio and television waves.

Performance Objectives

Goal: The student will gain an understanding of waves, their motion and properties, and the electromagnetic spectrum.

Objectives: Upon completion of the reading and activities and when asked to diagram, demonstrate, or respond either orally or on a written test, students will:

14:1-3	K	define the characteristics of a wave: length, amplitude, frequency, and speed.
14:3	K/P/S	using the relationship among wavelength, frequency, and speed, find one when the other two are given.
14:4	K/P	relate the water wave model to waves in general.
	K	differentiate between reflection and refraction of waves.
14:5	K	define the electromagnetic spectrum and list examples from various points in the spectrum. Define photon.
14:6-11	K	distinguish properties among familiar waves in the electromagnetic spectrum.
	A/S	demonstrate the proper use of materials.
	A	attempt at least one *More Ideas to Explore.*

Equipment for Activities

The amounts listed are for a class of 30 students broken into groups of 2.

ball, rubber—15
clock with second hand or stopwatch—15
metal, strips—15
pan, shallow—15
rope, 4.5 m—15
tuning fork—15

14:1 Characteristics of Waves

You may want to begin the chapter using the Chapter Preview Skills, page 298.

The most difficult concept for students to grasp involves the motion of the wave. Many think that water travels along with the wave front. Each molecule in the wave path moves vertically but maintains about the same horizontal position.

Ask the students how a surfer "rides" the waves if the water does not move along with the wave front. (Surfers slide down the front of the crest of the waves.)

Emphasize the energy a moving wave possesses. You might have students research articles on obtaining energy from ocean tides and currents.

Page 278. Making Sure

1. The waves may or may not have different wavelengths.
2. Answers will vary. They may be either. If the situation does not arise, you should bring up the fact that waves of the same wavelength do not necessarily have the same amplitude and vice versa.

14:2 Frequency of a Wave

Have students define the word *frequent* (occurring or appearing often at close intervals). Stress that the definition refers to how often something occurs, e.g. the student goes to movies frequently. The frequency of a wave refers to how many waves pass a given point in one second. If a wave is longer, it takes longer to pass. Therefore, fewer waves pass in a given time. Show the inverse relationship between frequency and wavelength.

Activity 14-1

The Activity demonstrates the shape of transverse waves.

Materials needed: Rubber tubing can be used as well as rope. Rubber tubing can be filled with water and clamped off to increase its weight per unit length causing the wave to travel more slowly which is good for demonstration purposes. The tubing should be as long as possible and loosely stretched horizontally.

The wave can be produced by striking the medium with a sharp blow near one end. A light metal object fastened at the other end and dangling against the support will make a clatter at the instant the wave arrives. The transfer of energy and the definite time interval required for the wave to travel the length of the tube are emphasized by the dangling object. The reflection of the wave should also be observed.

Activity 14-2

The Activity demonstrates that any object producing a sound is vibrating.

Materials needed: metal strip, tuning fork, timing device, and a shallow pan of water

If you have a transparency of a graph grid, you can place it underneath the glass dish set on the overhead projector, and you can follow the movement of the waves as they pass the lines on the grid.

Questions: Answers will vary as to the frequencies that students obtain. The vibrating prongs form water waves. The energy of vibration for the tuning fork is transferred to the water.

Page 281. Making Sure

3. The frequency is the number of waves per second. The amplitude is the displacement.
4. 512 Hz is 512 vibrations/second.

14:3 Speed of a Wave

Use the device constructed for Activity 14-1 to show changes in the speed of different waves.

You may want to review the velocity equation given in Chapter 3. You can show students that the speed of a wave is calculated like that of any other moving object.

Page 282. Making Sure

5. Yes, their frequencies may be different. The "rope" wave could have eight times the frequency of the water wave.
6. A radio station of 1000 kilohertz has a frequency of 1 000 000 cycles/second.
7. A "short wave" radio picks up short wavelength, high frequency radio stations.

14:4 Water Wave Model

It would be helpful if you could obtain a ripple tank. Make sure the tank is level. Check the water of each corner. Use a depth of 5-7 mm. Make sure the tank is well supported. Ordinary caulking compound can be used to reseal tanks.

There are also 8 mm filmloops that show the behavior of waves in a ripple tank.

You may want to demonstrate the refraction model shown in Figure 14-11. If you have the equipment spend as much time as possible using models. Students will have a better understanding of the material in the next three chapters if they have a good fundamental background of waves.

Activity 14-3

The Activity demonstrates the reflection of a rubber ball against a wall as a model for reflection of waves.

Materials needed: rubber ball, chalk

If you have a handball court on school property, you can have students perform this Activity there.

A student that has a miniature pool table could bring it in to demonstrate how knowledge of angle of incidence and reflection are important.

Questions: The ball is reflected back on its original path.

The ball leaves the wall at an angle. Students should note that the angles of incidence and refraction look about equal.

Page 286. Making Sure

8.

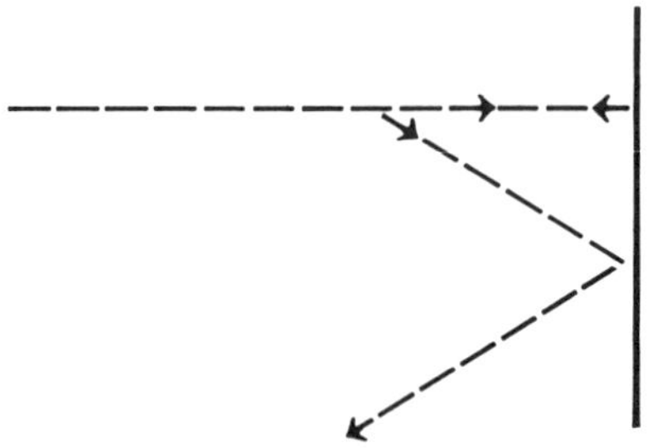

9. These games rely on the "bounce" of the ball from a fixed barrier. "Knowing the angles" improves one's skill at these games.

14:5 Electromagnetic Spectrum

You might also point out that we know light is definitely a form of energy because it causes a response in the light meter. Light causes the pointer to move over a scale. (Light energy is transformed to electrical energy.)

You may wish to review scientific notation 10^{10} is 10 000 000 000, 10^{-16} is 0.000 000 000 000 000 1.

A wall chart of the electromagnetic spectrum can be ordered free of charge from General Electric Lamp Division, Nela Park, Cleveland, Ohio.

Page 287. Making Sure

10. The speed of light in a vacuum is approximately 300 000 000 m/s.

11. The speed of light in air will be slightly less than in a vacuum because air is more dense.

14:6 X rays

Most hospitals have X rays that they discard regularly. Ask for these to use in the classroom. They can be held up against windows and/or used on an overhead projector. You can point out different densities and absorption qualities of some bone structures.

Page 290. Making Sure

12. Flesh does not stop X rays but bone does.

13. They are able to see "inside" using X rays.

14:7 Ultraviolet Radiation

Obtain a "black light" and some mineral samples from the earth science class. Demonstrate the fluorescent properties of some minerals.

You might want to point out to students the importance of protecting their skin from ultraviolet rays while sunbathing. Evidence shows that overexposure to these rays can cause skin cancer. Students should always use some sort of sunscreen protection preferably a product containing PABA. A number of articles on this topic appear every year in consumer magazines. You might have students bring these in.

14:8 Infrared Radiation

If possible, show students how infrared film is used to detect the heat loss from homes and buildings during energy studies. Your community may be involved in a study to determine energy inefficient areas. Aerial photographs using infrared film are taken to determine areas of inefficiency.

If any of your students have a photography hobby, you could ask them to tell the class what sort of special effects can be obtained using infrared film.

You could have students take pictures of each other before and after exercise, or automobiles before and after they've been running using infrared film.

14:9 Microwaves

All microwave ovens come equipped with a basic instruction manual which presents the fundamentals to the consumer. If any of your students have microwave ovens at home, ask them to bring in the instruction manual. You can compare design functions and cooking methods of different ovens. Some manufacturers forbid the use of any metal in the oven while others say aluminum foil or trays may be used as long as the food to metal ratio is quite high.

You might even call a local appliance dealer or the local electric utility and ask if it would be possible to have an educational demonstration.

14:10 Radio

AM = amplitude modulation; FM = frequence modulation. If possible, visit the local broadcasting (radio) station or have a radio engineer come to give a talk to your classes.

14:11 Television

Have students look at the word television to arrive at its meaning (seeing at a distance).

Emphasize that pictures are not sent through the air. Electric impulses are transmitted. Have students locate the element selenium on the periodic table. In 1817, Jons Berzelius discovered this element. It was later found that it would carry electric current depending on the amount of light which struck it (photoelectric properties).

For career emphasis, perhaps the school district Media Specialist (or one from a nearby college) will come to your class to answer questions concerning the job and training. A television service technician can explain the internal workings of a television set and also provide safety information regarding voltage dangers. Television circuitry is covered in Chapter 21.

Page 297. Making Sure

14. Closed circuit TV is not broadcast. The signal travels over wires rather than in the air.

15. The mountain will shield the receiver from the signal.

Focus on Skills

Chapter Preview

The purpose of this section is to show students how all of the aids and graphics integrate with the text to provide a logical presentation of concepts. A chapter preview establishes the scope of the material in students' minds. Generally they can move through the chapter in a more organized manner.

Answers

1. Waves **2.** bird making water waves **3.** shows the chapter title **4.** the properties of waves and the important uses of electromagnetic waves **5.** 14:1 Characteristics of Waves, 14:2 Frequency of a Wave, 14:3 Speed of a Wave, 14:4 The Water Wave Model, 14:5 Electromagnetic Spectrum, 14:6 X rays, 14:7 Ultraviolet Radiation, 14:8 Infrared Radiation, 14:9 Microwaves, 14:10 Radio, 14:11 Television **6.** (In the order in which they appear) wave, crest, trough, wavelength, amplitude, transverse wave, frequency, vibration, hertz, reflection, incident waves, reflected waves, refraction electromagnetic spectrum, photon, X rays, ultraviolet radiation, infrared radiation, microwaves **7.** The photo shows one use of infrared radiation. **8.** Can you measure the frequency of a wave? **9.** strip of metal, pan of water, tuning fork, and timing device **10.** 13

Questions for Review

A. True or False

1. True **2.** True **3.** False (The amplitude of a wave is the same as its displacement.) **4.** True **5.** False (When the speed of a wave changes it is refracted.) **6.** False (You cannot detect X rays with your eyes.) **7.** True **8.** True **9.** True **10.** False (Ultraviolet and infrared rays have the same speed.)

B. Multiple Choice

1. Wavelength **2.** frequency **3.** Light **4.** X ray **5.** bone **6.** shorter **7.** infrared radiation **8.** radar **9.** frequency **10.** electrons

C. Completion

1. Frequency **2.** frequency **3.** speed **4.** reflection **5.** photons **6.** X rays **7.** Ultraviolet **8.** infrared **9.** microwaves **10.** AM, FM

D. How and Why

1. A wave can be made with a rope which has one end secured. The other end is moved up and down rapidly and the wave travels along the length of the rope.

2. Water waves are different from waves in the electromagnetic spectrum in that water cannot travel through a vacuum and water waves are much slower than light.

3. Reflection can be demonstrated in a ripple tank by allowing generated waves to meet a barrier either straight on or at an angle. The waves actually reflect from the barrier. Refraction can be demonstrated by varying the depth of the water. Waves slow down in shallow water and bend if they approach at an angle or get closer together if straight on.

4. Waves in the electromagnetic spectrum in order of increasing wavelength and decreasing frequency: cosmic, gamma, X rays, ultraviolet, visible light, infrared, and radio waves. Facts learned about each will vary with the student.

5. ultraviolet—disinfectant, light shows, tanning
infrared—heat, therapy, night "seeing," chemical analysis
microwave—cooking, communications

15 Light and Color

Overview

Chapter 15 focuses on the visible light part of the electromagnetic spectrum. The beginning of the chapter stresses the importance of light to all living things. Mirrors are used to emphasize reflection. The study of refraction covers prisms and the spectrum of visible light. Color is then further developed in the discussions covering primary colors and pigments. Polarized light and interference are introduced to reinforce the wave properties of light.

Performance Objectives

Goal: Students will gain an understanding of the properties of visible light.

Objectives: Upon completion of the reading and activities and when asked to diagram, demonstrate, or respond either orally or on a written test, students will:

15:1	K/A	explain the importance of light to living things.
15:2	K/S	conduct activities regarding reflective properties of mirrors.
		compare the properties of real and virtual images.
15:3	K/P/S	use index of refraction to determine the direction light is bent in passing through different media.
15:4	K/P	describe the action of a prism in producing the visible light spectrum.
15:5	K	list the spectrum colors by order of wavelength.
		distinguish between primary light colors and primary pigment colors.
		describe how a person sees color.
15:6	K	explain how polarizing filters work.
15:7	K	define interference.
	K/S	construct a spectroscope.
	A/S	demonstrate the proper use of equipment and materials.
	A	attempt at least one *More Ideas to Explore.*

Equipment for Activities

The amounts listed are for a class of 30 broken down into groups of 2.

aluminum foil
candle—30
card, index or sheet of paper—15
cardboard
  tube—15 white sheet—15
coins, assorted—15
glass, plastic drinking—15
knife—5
light ray box—15
matches
meter sticks—15
mirror
  magnifying—15 parabolic—15
  plane, small—15
plastic diffraction grating, 1 cm^2—15
polarizing filter—30
prism, triangular—15
ruler, metric—15
tape, masking
teacup—15

15:1 Light

You might begin the chapter with a discussion of mirages. Students should realize that they see objects because rays of light are reflected from objects to our eyes. These rays reach our eyes in straight lines so we should see only things that are straight ahead above the horizon. Sometimes air above the ground reflects light to our eyes from objects below the horizon. If the sky is reflected by this air, the mirage looks like a lake.

Emphasize that in this chapter students should be trying to form a model (mental image) to explain the behavior of light. You may need to review some of the topics presented back in Chapter 14. You may want to pose the following questions to students as they progress through the chapter.

1. Is sunlight the same as light from a bulb?
2. How does light travel?
3. What is the relationship between light and color?
4. What causes a rainbow?

You may also want to use the theme of the chapter opening photograph to start a discussion on color preference. You could take a survey of what colors students prefer and why. Ask students to share which colors express their different moods. Determine if there are any patterns associated with students' color choices.

Page 304. Making Sure

1. You could not see, take pictures, and enjoy the flavors of green plants (vegetables) and fruits among other things.
2. Plants need light to manufacture food.

15:2 Mirrors and Reflection

Pass around pieces of metal such as bronze, brass, tin, aluminum, and so on. For thousands of years, these metals were used as mirrors. Glass mirrors were introduced about 1300. Craft people in Venice found a way to coat glass with a mercury-tin mixture. Silver is now used. A mixture of ammonia, tartaric acid, and silver nitrate is passed over smooth warm glass. A coating of shellac and paint protects the silver from chipping.

Ask students some of the important uses of mirrors (rearview mirrors in cars, dental mirrors, periscopes in submarines and so on).

Be sure students have a working knowledge of the terminology presented in this section. You may want to spend extra time here on vocabulary.

Activity 15-1

The Activity demonstrates the relationship between a reflected object and its virtual image.

Materials needed: plane mirror, 2 candles (larger than the mirror), matches, meter stick

Be sure students understand the differences between real and virtual images.

Questions: The distance from the first candle to the front of the mirror should equal the distance from the second candle to the mirror.

Activity 15-2

The Activity demonstrates the properties of parabolic mirrors.

Materials needed: magnifying mirror, candle, meter stick, matches

If you prefer, you may use a small electric lamp instead of a candle.

Questions: The image is upright and appears to be behind the mirror.

The second image is a real image. It is inverted and appears in front of the mirror. The real image is smaller than the actual flame.

Activity 15-3

The Activity demonstrates a method for finding the focal length of a parabolic mirror.

Materials needed: candle, index card or sheet of paper, matches, meter stick

A simple parabolic mirror can be made from a coffee can. Cut out the top and bottom then cut the cylinder lengthwise. **CAUTION:** The metal will have sharp edges. You can also use a sheet of aluminum foil taped to a piece of cardboard.

Questions: The first image is inverted, smaller, and real.

The size increases.

The third image is same size, but inverted. Answers will vary as to the focal length of the mirror.

Page 308. Making Sure

3. A real image can be projected on a screen. A virtual image does not actually exist. The image formed from a parabolic mirror may be real; from a plane mirror, virtual.
4. Mirror, spoon, window, coffee pot, toaster, dish, and hubcaps are some examples.
5. In the bowl of the spoon, the image is real and inverted; on the back of the spoon, the image is virtual and upright.

15:3 Refraction

Use Table 15-1 and Figure 15-11 to establish the relationship between a numerical value for the index of refraction and angles at which light is refracted.

Activity 15-4

The Activity demonstrates the bending of light rays as they pass through water.

Materials needed: pencil, clear drinking glass, teacup, coin

Questions: The pencil appears bent at the liquid level.

You should see the coin since the light from the coin is refracted to your field of view.

Page 311. Making Sure

6. Diamond refracts light the most. The brilliance of a cut diamond is due to its high index of refraction.
7. As the light hits the water it is slowed. The light ray is bent as a result of this change in speed.

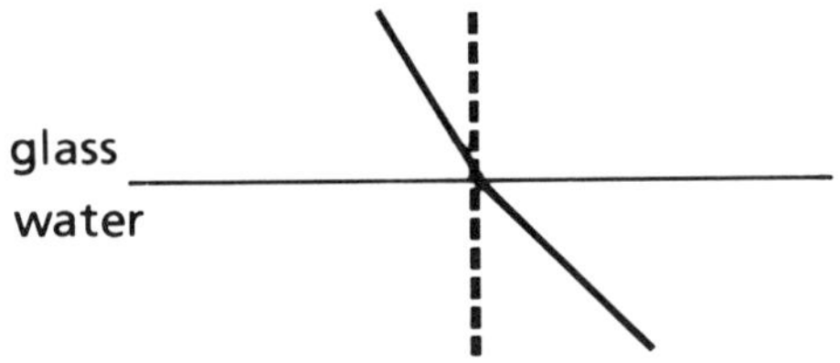

15:4 Prisms

Be sure to establish the relationship among index of refraction, wavelength of each light color, and what the students observe as light passes through the prism.

Activity 15-5

The Activity demonstrates the behavior of light through a prism.

Materials needed: prism, flashlight, white cardboard (for screen)

Question: Students should see the colors listed in Table 15-2.

Page 313. Making Sure

8. violet
9. red
10. violet
11. red

15:5 Color

Demonstrate retinal fatigue. Paint a brilliant red circle on a piece of white paper. Stare at it for 30 seconds. What color do you see around the circle? Shift your eyes quickly to another piece of white paper. Do you see a circle of a different color? Cones in the retina become fatigued to red. White paper around the circle is also reflecting colors to your eyes. The white paper reflects all colors, but the fatigued red cones do not sense red. Therefore, you see white light minus red, which leaves blue-green. Try other colors: yellow circle—blue is seen, orange circle—greenish-blue, violet circle—greenish-yellow, green circle—crimson.

Demonstrate the blending of color using a toy top, or paint a cardboard disc half green and half red. Rotate the disc as rapidly as possible. It should appear yellow.

Expand on the information in Figure 15-21. Do a bulletin board or have students do library research concerning the four-color printing industry. An inexpensive source of information that can be found in most bookstores is

Pocket Pal, A Graphic Art Production Handbook, International Paper Company

You might want to have students report on the different careers associated with the printing industry. Speakers may also be helpful. Some careers and sources of information are listed on page 28T.

Page 317. Making Sure

12. In red light, a grapefruit would appear red because it reflects red light. In blue light, it would appear black since blue is absorbed.
13. Pigments add to form other pigments, colors subtract to form other colors.

15:6 Polarized Light

Polaroid is made of a plastic material containing needlelike crystals of a compound called iodosulfate of quinine. These crystals are parallel to each other. Only those light vibrations which are in the same plane as the parallel slits can get through the material to your eyes.

Sunglasses made with polarized lenses reduce glare when the arrangement of the parallel crystals is vertical, or at right angles to the glare.

If any of your students are interested in photography, you could have them speak on the uses of polarizers in photography.

Activity 15-6

The Activity demonstrates the behavior of light through polarizing filters.

Materials needed: two polarizing filters (you can use the lenses from an old pair of polarized sunglasses)

Question: Eventually, rotation of the second lens will block out all light because the crystals in one lens are lined up at right angles to the crystals of the other.

15:7 Interference

Colors are often seen in thin films (soap bubbles, oil on water, mother of pearl). If you dip a loop of wire into a soap solution, gravity pulls the film down making it thinner at the top than at the bottom. A cross section of the film would show it as a thin wedge.

You can make a permanent film by letting a drop of colorless nail polish fall into a layer of water. The film will dry quickly. Remove it from the water and place it on a piece of white cardboard which has two holes in it about 1 cm in diameter. Look at this film under natural and artificial light. Two surfaces reflect light to your eyes (the upper and lower surfaces of the film). The light rays from the lower surface travel at a longer distance than those from the upper surface. This film works like a diffraction grating. When white light passes through, interference occurs. Interference causes different wavelengths of light to reinforce or cancel out each other. If the two rays reach your retina out of step (phase) the color is destroyed. If the waves of a particular color arrive in step or in phase, the color appears brighter.

Tell students to half close their eyes and look through their lashes at a distant streetlight at night. Can they explain the color fringes? Have them look through the end of a feather, too.

Activity 15-7

The Activity demonstrates the use of a spectroscope to show the wave nature of light.

Materials needed: cardboard tube, diffraction grating, aluminum foil, knife, masking tape, white light source, fluorescent light source

A crude diffraction grating can be made by scratching through the paint or silver on the back of a pocket mirror. Use a ruler and a razor. Make 10-15 lines per inch. Professional gratings have 5000 to 30 000 lines per inch.

Page 321. Making Sure

14. Refraction results from the bending of light because of different speeds in different media. Diffraction results from light interference.

15.

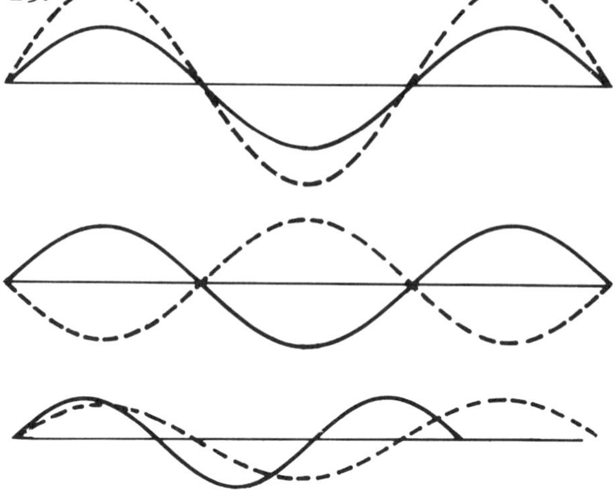

Focus on Careers

Research in Light

Ask students to design and build a simple periscope. Obtain ideas from students for other things they could design. Discuss items in the room that make use of optics, such as lighting, mirrors, windows, and eyeglasses. Extend the discussion to the use of optics to make life easier and more pleasant. Some examples are movies, cameras, laser light shows, laser scanners, car lighting, and telescopes. Talk about the careers associated with each.

Questions for Review

A. True or False

1. True **2.** False (A virtual image is formed in a plane mirror.) **3.** True **4.** True **5.** True **6.** False (All colors of light have different wavelengths and frequencies but the same speed.) **7.** True **8.** True **9.** False (A prism produces a color spectrum through the refraction of light.) **10.** False (Red, blue, and green are the primary colors of light.)

B. Multiple Choice

1. energy **2.** behind **3.** reflects **4.** bent **5.** greater than **6.** triangle **7.** Violet **8.** reflects **9.** all colors other than blue **10.** interference

C. Completion

1. reflects 2. refracts 3. concave 4. transparent 5. element 6. frequency 7. Magenta 8. White 9. Black 10. slits

D. How and Why

1. The parabolic mirror focuses the light and sends it out in a narrow beam which is more intense than without the mirror.
2. The sunlight is refracted by the atmosphere and bent around the horizon.
3. No, the reflected light rays would not necessarily meet at single points.
4. The rods and cones in the eye are stimulated by different wavelengths. The brain mixes the stimulations to produce color.

16 Light and Its Uses

Overview

This chapter expands on the knowledge acquired in Chapter 15 by now exposing students to the properties of lenses and their applications to correct vision problems and other uses in telescopes, microscopes, photography and lasers.

Performance Objectives

Goal: Students will gain an understanding of lenses and their uses.

Objectives: Upon completion of the reading and activities and when asked to diagram, demonstrate, or respond either orally or on a written test, students will:

16:1	K	distinguish between the properties of convex and concave lenses.
	K/P/S	conduct activities demonstrating properties of lenses.
16:2	K	describe how lenses correct vision defects.
16:3	K/P	diagram the workings of a telescope.
16:4	K/P	contrast refracting and reflecting telescopes.
		detail the differences and similarities between a microscope and a telescope.
16:5	K/P	describe the function of a lens or system of lenses in photography.
16:6	K	define laser and describe how it functions.
		list a number of uses for lasers.
	S/A	demonstrate the proper use of equipment and materials.
	A	attempt at least one *More Ideas to Explore.*

Equipment for Activities

The amounts listed are for a class of 30 students broken into groups of 2.

lens, concave—15
prism, triangular—30
ruler, metric—30

16:1 Lenses

Show that a magnifying glass or convex lens converges light rays. Use a pocket comb, a book with a dark color in the path of the sunlight. Place a magnifying glass in the path of the sun (light).

Use the theme of the chapter opening photo to begin a discussion or do a bulletin board on different objects which use lenses.

Activity 16-1

The Activity demonstrates the similarities in the way light behaves when passing through prisms and a concave lens.

Materials needed: two prisms, a concave lens, light source (flashlight—covered with piece of cardboard containing a 1 cm hole)

The prisms and lens should lay on a white piece of paper or cardboard.

Questions: The light is refracted away from the normal to the outside edges of the prisms (see Figure 16-5).

The lens refracts light in the same manner as the prisms.

Activity 16-2

The Activity demonstrates locating a real image using a lens diagram.

Materials needed: metric ruler, pencil, paper

You might do the Activity on the overhead projector as the students do it on their paper.

Page 331. Making Sure

1. Convex lens. It magnifies.
2. Concave lens.
3. Microscope, telescope, magnifying glass are examples.
4. The image gets larger. Image size is proportional to distance from lens, farther from lens the greater the size of the image.

16:2 Lenses and Vision

You might assign an extra credit project doing library research on the chemistry of vision. Students can find out what is known about the interaction between light and the human eye. The following are good sources of information.

Case, J., *Sensory Mechanism,* MacMillan Company, NY, 1966.

Hubbard, R., and Kropf, A., *Bio Organic Chemistry,* W. H. Freeman and Company, San Francisco, 1968.

You may want to invite an optometrist or ophthalmologist to speak to the class.

A pin and a card with a pinhole in it can be used to show that the real image on the retina is inverted. The pin is held erect with its head about 2.5 cm from the eye. The card is held about 2.5 cm beyond the pin, with the pinhole in line with the eye and the head of the pin. The pin seen against the light coming from the pinhole appears to be inverted. The pin is actually so close to the eye that the lens cannot invert its image and its shadow falls erect on the retina. The mental mechanism which reinverts the usual image to make it erect inverts this erect shadow to make it seem inverted.

Page 333. Making Sure

5. A farsighted person holds the object far away from the eyes.
6. A cat cannot see in total darkness because reflected light is necessary to see anything.

16:3 Telescopes

Try to have at least one telescope available in the classroom. Use it to view things in the nearby area.

16:4 Microscopes

Allow students to examine a compound microscope. Show them where the lenses are positioned and how the magnification is calculated. Use a prepared slide to show magnification. If available, allow students to look at insects or crystals under a stereo microscope.

Page 336. Making Sure

7. The refraction of light rays causes the magnification.
8. The light must be able to pass through the specimen.

16:5 Photography

Be sure students understand the point of Figure 16-15. Many more light rays are reflected from the chipmunk in (a). They are not shown to keep the diagram simple. After discussing these illustrations it should be obvious to students why the image on film is inverted.

A simple camera should be available for students to examine. You might want to invite a professional photographer to speak to your class.

You might also want to do a bulletin board illustrating different photographic techniques. Have students collect the pictures for you (from magazines and so on).

Be sure students understand the relationship between the focal length of the lens and the size of the image captured. Use Figures 16-17 and 16-18.

Page 340. Making Sure

9. A short focal length lens could be used to photograph astronauts.
10. A long focal length lens could be used to photograph a kite.
11. A "telephoto" lens takes pictures of objects far away.

16:6 Lasers

Point out that *LASER* is an acronym which stands for Light Amplification by Simulated Emission of Radiation. Try to borrow a laser from a physics lab. Ask the physics teacher to show you how to view holograms, if they have any.

You might have students report on the varied uses of lasers in research, medicine, and industry.

Questions for Review

A. True or False

1. False (A convex lens and a concave lens have different shapes.) **2.** True **3.** True **4.** True **5.** False (A telescope contains two convex lenses.) **6.** True **7.** True **8.** True **9.** False (Laser beams are sent through glass or plastic fibers.) **10.** True

B. Multiple Choice

1. convex **2.** real **3.** concave **4.** convex **5.** convex lenses **6.** mirror **7.** shorter time **8.** refracted **9.** Laser **10.** more

C. Completion

1. concave **2.** concave lens **3.** concave **4.** parabolic **5.** stereo **6.** film **7.** pinhole **8.** greater **9.** Laser **10.** image

D. How and Why

1. A real image can be projected, a virtual does not exist.
2. The muscles of the eye squeeze and stretch the lens changing its shape.
3. A compound microscope has two convex lenses. The first lens magnifies the object. The second lens magnifies the image from the first lens. The actual magnification is a product of the two magnifications.
4. Light is needed to take a picture with a camera because the film is light sensitive. Also there would be nothing on the film if light rays were not reflected from the object. Thus, light is needed in two respects.
5. Lasers have many practical uses. Among these are surgery, photography, welding, communication, and lighting effects. They have also been used to create three dimensional images.

17 Sound

Overview

Chapter 17 focuses on the characteristics of compressional waves. These characteristics are then applied as students study the properties of sound. The topics covered include: volume, pitch, musical instruments, acoustics, and noise pollution.

Performance Objectives

Goal: Students will gain an understanding of sound and its properties through a study of compressional waves.

Objectives: Upon completion of the reading and activities and when asked to diagram, demonstrate, or respond either orally or on a written test, students will:

17:1	K/P	define compressional waves and compare them to transverse waves.
	K	explain how sound waves are formed.
17:2	K/S	solve simple problems relating to speed of sound.
17:3-4	K	explain the relationship of sound, volume, and amplitude; pitch and frequency.
17:5	K/P	list and explain properties of musical sound.
17:6	K/P	compare interference of sound waves with interference of light waves.

17:7	K	define the Doppler effect.
17:8	K/P	explain the relationship of sound to acoustics.
17:9	K/A	list examples of noise pollution and indicate some methods for controlling this kind of pollution.
	S/A	demonstrate the proper use of equipment and materials.
	A	attempt at least one *More Ideas to Explore.*

Equipment for Activities

coil spring (toy)—15

17:1 Compressional Waves

Establish the difference between compressional and transverse waves. Emphasize the long wavelengths of sound waves as compared to the short wavelengths of light waves. Also stress that a medium is necessary for the transmission of sound. If possible, have students in your class who play musical instruments bring them in. Have them give short presentations on the structure and properties of each.

Ask students if they have ever sensed sound without using their ears (loud sounds can cause objects to vibrate to the touch). How then is this energy transferred from the source to the vibrating object? Sound moves through air, yet, it is not a flow of air. The air itself does not move from place to place.

Blow up a paper bag and/or balloon and cause it to burst. Ask students to explain why it makes such a loud noise. Why isn't the sound softer? Why is there any sound at all? Have students give their answers without indicating right or wrong. Can they think of ways to make the sound louder? softer?

Some people have voices which sound similar—mother and daughter, brothers, sisters. The sinus cavities in the head act as a resonating column. People who have similar shaped heads have similar sinus cavities. Thus, their voices sound similar.

Activity 17-1

The Activity demonstrates the characteristics of compressional waves.

Materials needed: toy coil spring

Questions: The resulting wave is a compressional wave. The coils are displaced in the direction of the wave motion. The coil spring wave consists of alternate compressions and rarefactions. The movement is quite unlike that of a transverse wave which consists of alternating crests and troughs. The amplitude of a transverse wave made with a rope is its vertical displacement. The amplitude of a compressional wave is horizontal—in the direction of the wave motion.

Page 350. Making Sure

1. Sound waves are compressional (longitudinal). Electromagnetic waves are transverse. Refer to Figure 17-1.

17:2 Speed of Sound

Emphasize the changes in the speed as sound waves travel through various substances. Particles are needed for sound to travel. Therefore, the closer that particles are, as in solids, the faster the sound travels.

Place a clock at one end of a wooden table. Have students press their ears against the wood at the other end. Cover the table with a cloth and repeat. The cloth should absorb the sound.

Page 351. Making Sure

2. $$wavelength = \frac{speed}{frequency} = \frac{344 \text{ m/s}}{256 \text{ Hz}} = 1.34 \text{ m}$$

3. Other forms of the equation are

$$frequency = \frac{speed}{wavelength} \text{ and}$$

$$speed = frequency \times wavelength$$

4. $$frequency = \frac{speed}{wavelength} = \frac{344 \text{ m/s}}{6 \text{ m}} = 57.3 \text{ Hz}$$

17:3 Volume

Emphasize that it is the amplitude of the wave which controls the volume of sound. This point is especially important in establishing the difference between volume and pitch.

Make a megaphone by rolling a sheet of notebook paper on the diagonal. From a distance, have someone talk in an ordinary voice both with and without the megaphone. The megaphone directs the sound waves directly to your ear. The sound is reinforced by reflection. A megaphone is a resonator.

Blow up a balloon. Place a watch against one side of the balloon and place your ear against the other side. Why do you hear the watch better through the balloon? (Denser air conducts the sound better.)

You might have students do library research to find out how a hearing aid works.

17:4 Pitch

Contrast pitch with volume. Emphasize that pitch is a function of sound wave frequency.

Page 352. Making Sure

5. The amplitude must be greater. It takes more energy to make a wave with a greater displacement.

6. The guitarist can tighten or loosen a string or shorten it by pressing the string against a fret on the neck of the guitar.

17:5 Musical Sounds

See the suggestion concerning musical instruments under Section 17:1. You might also ask the music teacher to visit the class and give a talk and demonstration on different musical instruments.

Note: The frequencies listed for the piano in Figure 17-7 are rounded off to the nearest whole number.

Page 355. Making Sure

7. a. blow across a pop bottle
  b. hum on a comb and wax paper
  c. stretch and pluck a rubber band

8. a. a column of air vibrates
  b. the paper vibrates like a reed
  c. the rubber band vibrates like a guitar or violin string

9. The box increases the amplitude of the waves produced by the strings.

17:6 Interference

You can show interference by rotating a tuning fork over an air column tuned to resonate at the frequency of the fork. If you are moving the fork so that the prongs are in positions A, B, and C when viewed end-on, you will note no response in position C.

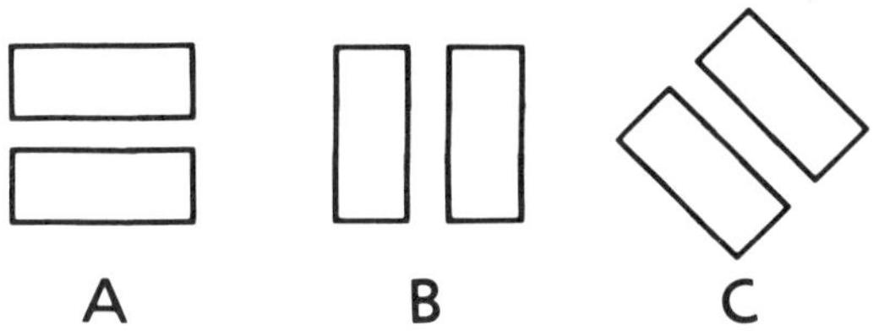

You may want to review light interference at this point to emphasize the addition and cancellation of wave motions.

Page 356. Making Sure

10. Constructive interference increases the amplitude and thus the loudness of sound.

17:7 Doppler Effect

A whistle at the end of a 130 cm piece of rubber tubing can be sounded while swinging it in a horizontal circle. This demonstration illustrates the Doppler effect.

A mechanical analogy can be used to clarify the phenomenon. On a heavily traveled highway, the frequency of passing cars is at maximum when the observer travels against the traffic. (The observer is moving toward the source.) The frequency is reduced when the observer is standing still and at a minimum when the observer moves in the same direction as the traffic.

17:8 Acoustics

Obtain a portable radio. Have students listen to it as it rests on the ground in a small room and outside the school. What differences in sound do they notice?

A distant echo may be heard when a reflecting wall is about 17 meters away. It should take the sound about 0.1 second to travel the 17 meters and back again.

You may want students to do library research into the workings and uses of sonar.

Have students do an acoustics inventory of the school and their homes. What objects are used to control the movement of sound?

The Acoustical Society of America puts out a pamphlet concerning careers in acoustics titled, *Acoustics and You.* Write to:

Acoustical Society of America
335 East 45th Street
New York, NY 10017

You might also have a theater manager come in to speak on the acoustical features of the theater.

Page 361. Making Sure

11. It could be completely carpeted or lined with acoustical tile.
12. People and their clothing break up echoes and absorb the sound.

17:9 Noise Pollution

Stress how serious the problem of noise pollution is. Emphasize the dangers of hearing loss associated with overexposure to loud sounds. Talk about the kinds of jobs that force people to work with loud noise. How can these people be protected?

Page 363. Making Sure

13. Answers will vary. Ask for reasons.
14. The interpretation of many sounds as noise is a matter of personal taste.
15. Answers will vary. Stronger legislation against noise is one example.

Focus on Frontiers

Visible Speech

Ask someone to give a demonstration of American sign language and talk about its history. Discuss the relationship between the ability to hear and learning to speak. How can speech spectrograms help people with hearing disabilities? Have students research various methods of communication. Talk about problems that would appear in trying to communicate with alien beings. Through library research, have students report on the records attached to the Voyager probes for the purpose of communicating with other beings.

Questions for Review

A. True or False

1. True **2.** False (You cannot hear ultrasonic sound.) **3.** False (Sound travels through matter. It cannot travel through a vacuum.) **4.** True **5.** True **6.** True **7.** False (Every note on the musical scale has a different pitch.) **8.** False (The higher the frequency, the higher the pitch.) **9.** False (The Doppler effect changes the frequency, pitch, of a sound.) **10.** True

B. Multiple Choice

1. compressional **2.** decreases **3.** different from **4.** meters **5.** second **6.** 20 000 **7.** frequency **8.** volume **9.** increases **10.** Doppler effect

C. Completion

1. vibrates **2.** glass (solids) **3.** 120 **4.** air **5.** Overtones **6.** beats **7.** Acoustics **8.** reflected **9.** hearing **10.** noise

D. How and Why

1. A compressional wave vibrates in the direction the wave is moving. A transverse wave moves at right angles to the direction of wave motion.
2. There are no particles through which sound can travel in a vacuum.
3. Pitch and volume can help one recognize another's voice.
4. Two tuning forks can produce beats when they vibrate out of phase with each other. The waves alternately cancel and reinforce each other. This interference causes beats, periods of relative loud sounds followed by periods of silence.
5. The speed of sound can be used to find the distance to a nearby mountain. The interval between a shout and the echo can be timed. This time is double the time to the mountain. Applying 340 m/s as the speed of sound, multiply by one half the time to get the distance. The same method can be used to time the distance from a lightning flash.

Unit 6 Energy

Overview

The first chapter of the unit focuses attention on fundamental principles regarding energy. Effects of heat energy on matter are explored using kinetic theory to explain many observations. Melting ice, boiling liquids, and freezing water are familiar to the student. Chapter 18 explains the basic scientific principles behind these processes. Chapter 19 illustrates how the knowledge of heat movement has been applied to provide the way of life to which students have grown accustomed. Cooling systems, heating systems, and heat engines are considered. Chapter 20 illustrates the electrical nature of matter. Static and current electricity are investigated. The student is led to an understanding of potential difference, resistance, Ohm's law, and the characteristics and uses of circuits. Chapter 21 establishes the relationship between magnetism and electricity. The student becomes familiar with the properties of magnets and the nature of magnetic fields. The presentation of material in this chapter leads the student to an understanding of television, integrated circuits, and computer structure.

Teaching Tips

- Construct a bulletin board that shows the effects of heat energy on the world. Include topics such as heating buildings, cars, clothes for hot and cold climates, the water cycle, geysers, and volcanoes. Using this type of display students can see both the positive and negative effects of heat energy.
- Do a bulletin board display entitled "If It Were Not For Electricity. . . ." Use pictures of electric lights, TV, movies, and all kinds of electrical appliances (stoves, toasters, refrigerators, freezers, dishwashers, coffee makers, washing machines, irons, sewing machines, radios, hairdryers, and so on).
- An interesting project for students is mapping their home wiring. This mapping can be accomplished (with parents' permission) by breaking one circuit at a time and checking to see which devices will not operate when turned on. Wall outlets can be checked by plugging a lamp into each. This information can be especially helpful when repair work is necessary.

18 Heat

Overview

This chapter is important because it extends the principle of the conservation of energy introduced in Chapter 3 and provides further evidence that energy can be transformed from one form to another. Groundwork is laid for the development of the idea that heat is a form of energy. The difference between temperature and heat is firmly established. The ability of different substances to absorb heat is explored experimentally as is the heat energy released or absorbed during a change of state. Kinetic theory is used to explain the expansion and contraction of substances. The relationship of temperature, pressure, and volume of a gas is developed.

Performance Objectives

Goal: Students will gain an understanding of heat energy and its effects.

Objectives: Upon completion of the reading and activities and when asked to diagram, demonstrate, or respond either orally or on a written test, students will:

18:1	K	distinguish between potential and kinetic energy.
18:2	K/P	describe the relationship between temperature and heat.
18:3	K	define specific heat.
18:4	K/S	measure changes in heat energy of a material.
18:5	K/P	describe and explain the processes of melting and vaporization.
18:6-7	K/P	explain expansion using kinetic energy. explain Boyle's and Charles' laws.
	S/A	demonstrate the proper use of equipment and materials.
	A	attempt at least one *More Ideas to Explore.*

Equipment for Activities

The amounts listed are for a class of 30 students broken down into groups of 2.

aluminum foil squares, 12 cm x 12 cm—15
ball, iron and ring—15
balloon, round—15
Bunsen burner or candle—15
cans
#2½—15
#1—15
cardboard, heavy squares, 10 cm x 10 cm—15
cloth—15
dowel rod, 0.5 cm x 20 cm—15
flask, 250 mL—15
glass tube—15
glass wool—15
hot plate—10
matches
pan, sauce—15
paper cup—30
stopper, 1-hole for flask—15
tape, masking
tape measure—15
thermometer—15
tongs—15
Chemicals
copper pieces, 50 g—15
ice
sand—1 kg
strips of Al, Cu, Fe of the same mass—15 sets
wax (paraffin), small blocks—45

18:1 Energy

The familiar yo-yo or a simple pendulum can be used to show energy transformations. The students should be able to mention many examples of potential and kinetic energy transformation.

Heat resulting from work can be readily demonstrated. Have a student bend a paper clip back and forth rapidly. A temperature rise should be evident. Another student can quickly stretch a rubber band (temperature rise). Hold it stretched for a couple of minutes. Allow it to return to normal quickly. It will feel cooler as a result of doing work. Rubber molecules are long chains in a state of disorder. Stretching introduces order. Rubber contracts when heated as does cartilage, skin, leather, and many plastics.

Ask, "Why does a piece of metal get hot when you hammer it for a long time?" The faster particles move, the greater their kinetic energy and the more heat they have.

Activity 18-1

The Activity demonstrates that mechanical energy can be converted to heat energy.

Materials needed: 2 paper cups, sand, tape, thermometer

If you prefer, water may be substituted for the sand. Polystyrene cups can be used instead of paper ones.

Questions: The kinetic energy of the moving cups is changed to heat in the sand.

Page 372. Making Sure

1. The kinetic energy is transferred to kinetic energy in the nail and heat. It does work.
2. **a.** The wound spring unwinds.
   b. The stretched rubber band is released, returning to normal.

c. The diver springs from the board and moves toward the water.
d. The drawn string is released, pushing the arrow away.

18:2 Temperature and Heat

Discuss the nature of heat as explained in the second paragraph of the section. Be sure that the students understand the difference between heat and temperature. To illustrate the relationship between mass and heat content, pour equal amounts of water at the same temperature into two beakers. Place thermometers in each beaker. Record the temperatures. Next, pour unequal amounts of boiling water into each. Compare the readings on the thermometers. Although the added water was at the same temperature, the larger amount contained more heat, as evidenced by the greater change in temperature.

Page 373. Making Sure

3. Temperature measures the average kinetic energy of a substance.
4. The pot will have more heat energy since they are both at the same temperature (boiling water).
5. The joule is the modern unit for heat energy.

18:3 Specific Heat

Be sure that the students understand that an increase in the kinetic energy (rise in temperature) of a substance means the total internal energy is increased.

The specific heat, C_p, is measured at constant pressure.

Activity 18-2

This Activity gives students a qualitative understanding of the ability of substances to absorb or release heat energy.

Materials needed: 50-gram pieces of aluminum, copper, and iron, 3 blocks of paraffin, tongs, hot plate, sauce pan

It might be difficult to obtain exactly the same mass of each metal. Before class, you should select pieces that are close in mass. Be sure as little water as possible is carried over to the paraffin after heating. You can use screws made of different materials such as aluminum, steel, brass, or washers made of steel, lead, copper.

Questions: Since the aluminum has the largest specific heat, it will have the most heat energy and melt the most paraffin. The iron is next and the copper, having the smallest specific heat, will melt the paraffin least.

Page 375. Making Sure

6. A gain in heat causes the particles to increase their kinetic energy.
7. Specific heat is the ability of a material to absorb heat.

18:4 Measuring Heat

Work through the example problem with the students. Have them try the *Making Sure* problems for homework.

Activity 18-3

This Activity provides a quantitative view of specific heat, extending the knowledge gained in the previous section.

Materials needed: aluminum foil squares 12 cm by 12 cm, dowel rod 20 cm by 0.5 cm, 50 grams of copper, glass wool, heavy cardboard squares 10 cm by 10 cm, sauce pan, thermometer, tongs, two cans—#2½ and #1

You may not want students to use glass wool. Instead, they may use two polystyrene drinking cups, one inside the other. If a constant temperature oven is available, use it to heat the copper. It will prevent the addition of hot water when the metal is placed in the calorimeter.

Summing Up

3. As long as the temperature rises, the water is still gaining heat.

Page 377. Making Sure

8. $\Delta H = \Delta t \times m \times C_p$
   $\Delta H = 65\ C° \times 40\ g \times 0.7\ J/g \cdot C° = 1800\ J$
9. $\Delta H = \Delta t \times m \times C_p$
   $\Delta H = 60\ C° \times 500\ g \times 0.92\ J/g \cdot C° = 28\,000\ J$

18:5 Melting and Vaporization

Demonstrate that a body of water at 100° C or ice and water at 0° C may be heated without changing its temperature. Discuss what is happening to the heat that is being added.

Ask students if they know why areas around bodies of water tend to have delayed changes in temperature. As each kilogram of water gets colder, it releases 4.18 kilojoules of heat for every Celsius degree drop in temperature. Thus, the water supplies heat to the region and keeps it from getting colder. Water also absorbs heat from the surroundings as the region warms. Thus, it delays the warming of the surrounding region.

Page 379. Making Sure

10. No.

11. Heat added breaks the bonds holding the substance in that state during the change.

18:6 Expansion

The fact that substances expand when heated and contract when cooled helps us to understand the internal structure of matter. Matter must be made up of particles and there must be empty spaces between these particles.

Activity 18-4

The outcome of this Activity, as well as the one following, helps students understand the internal structure of matter. An increase in heat increases the kinetic energy of the particles in a material. As they move faster, they move farther apart. Thus, the material expands.

Materials needed: Bunsen burner or candle, iron ball and ring, matches

Questions: The ball expands and does not fit through the ring. When the ball cools, it contracts and again fits through the ring.

Activity 18-5

Materials needed: cloth, 250-milliliter flask, glass tube, sauce pan, 1-hole stopper for flask

Questions: The water level rises due to the expansion of the water.

18:7 Gases

The concept of pressure as force per unit area can be demonstrated using an air mattress in a swimming pool. When a person lies on the mattress, the weight (force) is distributed over the whole mattress. The person floats. When the person sits on the air mattress, the force is only on part of the mattress. The pressure increases and pushes the air out of that part of the mattress. With no air, that part of the mattress sinks.

Activity 18-6

The Activity demonstrates Charles' law.

Materials needed: round balloon, ice, sauce pan, tape measure, hot water

A piece of string may be used instead of a tape measure. By marking the string for each circumference, the changes can be shown. Alternate methods of heating and cooling are a strong lamp and a refrigerator, if available.

Questions: The balloon expands when heated and contracts when cooled.

The reason for waiting ten minutes in each case is to allow all of the air in the balloon to be heated or cooled.

Page 383. Making Sure

12. Pressure is force per unit area.

13. If the temperature increases, the pressure increases.

14. If the pressure is decreased, the volume is increased.

Focus on Skills

Taking Notes in Outline Form

Have students complete the outline before their final test on the chapter. A chapter outline is an excellent way to review the chapter material.

Answers

1. kinetic **2.** potential **B.** the total internal energy of a substance **2.** joules **A.** the ability of a substance to retain heat **B.** $H = \Delta t \times m \times C_p$ **B.** energy needed to change a substance from the liquid to vapor (gaseous) state **B.** mercury columns used to measure pressure **C.** The volume of a gas decreases as its pressure increases, if the temperature is to remain the same. **E.** The volume of a gas increases as its temperature increases, if the pressure is to remain the same.

Questions for Review

A. True or False

1. True **2.** True **3.** False (As temperature increases, gas particles move faster.) **4.** False (Water has a greater specific heat than iron.) **5.** False (A thermometer measures the average kinetic energy.) **6.** True **7.** True **8.** False (The heat of fusion is the energy needed to change from solid to liquid.) **9.** True **10.** False (Temperature and heat are not the same.)

B. Multiple Choice

1. Motion **2.** joules **3.** kinetic energy **4.** calorimeter **5.** expands **6.** kinetic **7.** absorb **8.** heat **9.** heat of fusion **10.** vaporization

C. Completion

1. increases **2.** work **3.** potential energy **4.** joules **5.** absorb **6.** calorimeter **7.** increases **8.** force **9.** pressure **10.** gained

D. How and Why

1. Heat is the internal energy of a substance. Temperature is the measure of its average kinetic energy.
2. The engine would expand and the parts would not be able to move past each other.
3. Less energy is needed to raise the temperature of iron than is needed to raise the temperature of an equal mass of water. Iron has a lower specific heat than water.
4. $\Delta H = \Delta t \times m \times C_p$
   $\Delta H = 40\ \text{C}° \times 100\ \text{g} \times 0.45\ \text{J/g} \cdot \text{C}°$
   $\Delta H = 1800\ \text{J}$

More Ideas to Explore

3. Many electric irons use bimetallic strips to control temperature. The strip is used as a switch in the heating circuit. As it becomes hot, it bends breaking the circuit. As it cools, it straightens and connects the circuit. This process continues as long as the iron is on.

19 Heat and Its Uses

Overview

The student extends the kinetic theory model to include an explanation of heat movement. With the knowledge of the three methods of heat movement established, the control of heat movement using insulation becomes clear. The student then becomes aware of the application of these principles to cooling and heating systems and engines.

Performance Objectives

Goal: Students will gain an understanding of the transfer of heat and the uses of each transfer.

Objectives: Upon completion of the reading and activities and when asked to diagram, demonstrate, or respond either orally or on a written test, students will:

19:1	K	differentiate among conduction, convection, and radiation as methods of heat movement.
19:2	K/P	explain how insulation controls heat transfer.
19:3	K/P	describe various cooling systems and explain the role of evaporation.
19:4	K/P	contrast various heating systems.
19:5	K	describe how internal combustion engines work.
19:6	K/A	explain the problems of waste heat and the resulting thermal pollution.
	S/A	demonstrate the proper use of equipment and materials.
	A	attempt at least one *More Ideas to Explore.*

Equipment for Activities

The amounts listed are for a class of 30 students broken down into groups of 2.

aluminum foil
beaker, 250 mL—15
bottle (same size)
  glass—25
  vacuum—8

Bunsen burner—15
candle—15
cotton, absorbent—1 pkg
hot plate—10
knitting needle and glass rod of the same size—15 sets
matches
medicine dropper—15
pan, sauce—10
ring stand and ring—15
stopper, 1-hole—15
test tube—15
thermometer—32
wire screen—15
Chemicals
ethanol—100 mL
food coloring—several vials

19:1 Movement of Heat

Stress that transfer of heat by conduction and convection requires the movement of particles. The fact that molecules in liquids and gases are farther apart and are therefore poorer conductors than solids is important to establish so that the student can understand insulators in the following section.

After they have read the section, ask students why there are no convection currents in a lake in summer, but only in late fall. (In fall, cool air near the surface cools the water at the surface of the lake. Heavier, more dense cold water sinks to the bottom. Warmer less dense water rises establishing a convection current. In summer, sun shining on surface water warms the water. The warmed less dense water is already on top.)

Give students a piece of metal and a piece of wood. Or have them touch the faucet of your lab sink and the wooden desk top. Ask them if they observe any difference. (They will probably say the metal feels colder than the wood.) Explain that they must both be at the same temperature because they are at room temperature. Get them to arrive at the fact that metal feels colder because it conducts heat away from their bodies better than wood does.

Activity 19-1

The Activity shows that different materials conduct heat at different rates.

Materials needed: metal knitting needle and glass rod of the same size, candle, matches, 1-hole stopper

Knitting needles can be made of different kinds of metals. You might find several types which would extend this Activity to show that different metals conduct heat at different rates.

Questions: While the rate of conduction for both rods will depend on their length and diameter, the glass rod will not conduct as well as the metal.

Activity 19-2

The Activity demonstrates the effect of heat on a liquid—the creation of a convection current.

Materials needed: 250-milliliter beaker, Bunsen burner, food coloring, matches, medicine dropper, ring stand and ring, wire screen

Questions: As the water near the flame warms, it rises carrying the food coloring along. The resulting pattern is circular until all of the water has been heated.

Page 391. Making Sure

1. Answers will vary; radiator, light bulb, and people are examples.
2. In conduction, kinetic energy is transferred from particle to particle.
3. Convection takes place in liquids and gases and relies on density changes.

19:2 Insulation

Emphasize that insulators retard the transfer of heat. Air is an excellent insulator because it conducts poorly. The absence of air, as in a vacuum bottle, prevents heat transfer by convection. Breaking up the air into many small spaces also reduces convection. A good example is foam. Have students examine a polystyrene cup using a hand lens or a stereo microscope.

Ask students why sweaters keep them warm and why birds ruffle their feathers in cold weather. (Air is trapped in each case, providing insulation.)

Another question is why do several layers of clothing keep you warmer than a single layer? (Using several layers helps to prevent convection, keeping the warm air close to the body.)

Have the students consider the structure of a sponge. Would it make a good insulator? (It would, because it has many spaces for "dead" air.)

Summarize the section with the idea that insulators are simply poor conductors of heat.

Activity 19-3

The Activity demonstrates the advantages in combining different types of insulation.

Materials needed: aluminum foil, 3 clear glass bottles, hot plate, sauce pan, 4 thermometers, vacuum bottle

Use identical bottles with wide mouths (as wide as possible). It might be easier to fill each bottle fully instead of trying to estimate $^2/_3$. Be sure students prepare a data chart before they begin the experiment.

Summing Up

1. The bottle without the foil cools the fastest.
2. Heat travels from the inside of the bottles to the outside.
3. The vacuum bottle is insulated the most.
4. The aluminum foil slows the movement of heat by reflecting heat back into the bottle.
5. The bottles could be put inside similarly covered bottles or covered with foam.

Page 394. Making Sure

4. Clothing can prevent all three methods of heat movement.
5. Double windows prevent convection and conduction; fiber glass insulation prevents conduction and convection; weather stripping prevents convection; siding prevents convection and radiation.

19:3 Cooling Systems

Students should be able to understand how the kinetic theory explains the cooling effect of evaporation. According to the kinetic theory, particles are in constant random motion. As a result of colliding, some particles acquire high velocities, which means high kinetic energies. If the kinetic energy is high enough, particles near the surface may escape into the air. The loss of these rapidly moving particles takes away some of the energy. The loss of energy lowers the average kinetic energy of the remaining particles. Thus, the temperature of the liquid is lowered.

You might invite a refrigeration service person to be a guest speaker for your class.

Evaporation and boiling are both processes by which a liquid changes into a gas. Be sure students realize the difference between the two processes. The temperature and rate at which each occurs is different.

Activity 19-4

The Activity demonstrates the ability of evaporation to lower temperature.

Materials needed: beaker, absorbent cotton, ethanol, medicine dropper, thermometer, water

You might want a second thermometer wrapped in cotton without water or alcohol to use as a control. Ordinary rubbing alcohol can be used.

Questions: In each case the thermometer will show a decrease in temperature. The amount of decrease will be greater with the alcohol.

Page 396. Making Sure

6. The particles absorb heat as they evaporate. This absorption cools the part that is left.
7. The energy comes from inside the refrigerator —from the food and walls.

19:4 Heating Systems

Stress that efficient heating systems rely on the application of convection currents. Be sure students realize why a steam heating system provides more heat than a hot water system.

Page 399. Making Sure

8. The heat pump transfers heat out or into a building rather than changing other forms of energy into heat.
9. One system uses moving water, while the other uses stationary water.
10. All of the heating systems make use of convection.

19:5 Heat Engines

If possible, all students should have the opportunity to see a dismantled engine and various parts. A trip to the school district's automobile shop (if you have one) or a local garage is suggested. You could even ask the students to visit the garage on their own as a homework assignment. Many lawnmowers are driven by a one cylinder, 4-stroke engine. Try to obtain a discarded engine of this type. Even model airplane gasoline engines make good teaching tools.

Page 402. Making Sure

11. The fuel burns inside the engine.

12. In the gasoline engine, the spark plug ignites the fuel. In the diesel, the heat of compression does.

13. The pistons turn the crankshaft, then the driveshaft, then the axle.

19:6 Waste Heat

A visit to a local electric power plant would be beneficial. If field trips are not possible, most companies have educational consultants who will bring a program to your class.

Page 403. Making Sure

14. Thermal pollution damages the environment by waste heat.

15. Examples are: gasoline engines, furnaces, stoves, electric lamps, people, televisions and stereos. The heat produced goes into the atmosphere and eventually into space.

In Focus

Science and Technology

Pick two objects, such as a radio and a microwave oven. Ask the students if science can be used to explain their operation with the same principles. The answer is yes. Both devices use electronics and electromagnetic waves. Technology uses a few basic scientific principles in many ways. Often, the products of technology can be used in many ways. Computers are an example. Have some students research the history of computers. Discuss their use today and how it has changed in the last few decades. Computers were originally calculating devices. Now they are used as control systems, interpreters, data storage systems, and even to supplement teachers in some areas of education. Ask students to speculate on the future uses of computers.

Focus on People

Solar Flight

Have your students research the uses of balloons in the past and in the present. Considering their history and new developments, like Sunstat, ask for speculation on the future uses of balloons. Since their direction and speed are not controllable, balloons are still not feasible as transportation for people, goods, or services. Talk about the relationship among airships, like Germany's zeplins of World War I, the Goodyear blimp, and balloons. An airship is actually a balloon with its own power for propulsion. Balloons have fascinated many people, among them writers of fiction. In fact, some of the ideas for using balloons came from fiction. Two influential stories were written by Jules Verne. They are *Around the World in Eighty Days* and *Five Weeks in a Balloon.* Ask some students to report Verne's ideas and discuss the role of fiction in the development of balloons.

Questions for Review

A. True or False

1. False (Heat is transferred by convection in water.) **2.** True **3.** True **4.** False (Air is a poor conductor.) **5.** False (Conduction is a transfer of heat from particle to particle.) **6.** False (Radiation is movement of heat without moving particles.) **7.** False (Insulation retards heat movement.) **8.** True **9.** True **10.** False (Diesel engines do not use spark plugs.)

B. Multiple Choice

1. cools **2.** conduction **3.** convection **4.** control **5.** changes **6.** Convection **7.** hot air **8.** transfers **9.** gasoline and air **10.** power

C. Completion

1. Conduction **2.** gases **3.** thermal **4.** salt **5.** insulation **6.** freon **7.** solar radiation **8.** water **9.** heat **10.** diesel

D. How and Why

1. As freon evaporates, it gains heat from the surrounding area. Since the area suffers a loss of heat, it becomes cooler. Freon is then pumped on, condensed, and the process is repeated.
2. As a liquid or gas is heated, it expands and becomes less dense. It rises to the top of its container. This movement creates currents which carry heat. For example, air at the bottom of a room is heated and rises. It causes currents which aid in carrying heat upward by other heated air.
3. The explosions in the cylinder of a gasoline engine force the pistons down. The pistons turn the crankshaft which turns the drive shaft. The drive shaft transmits the power to the wheels of a car.
4. In a hot water system, water is heated and moves by convection to the radiators. As it cools, it warms the air surrounding the radiator. The water then returns to the boiler. Steam heat works on essentially the same principle except that water is heated to boiling under pressure. The steam condenses in the radiator and runs back to the boiler as water. Steam heat is far more efficient producing more joules of heat per gram.

20 Electricity

Overview

This chapter provides evidence that matter is indeed electrical in nature. The student begins to develop a feeling for the first law of electrostatics by using rubber, glass rods, and an electroscope. Laws of attraction and repulsion are demonstrated. The phenomenon of current electricity is explored through the investigation of wet and dry cell construction and operation. The battery, explained in simple terms, yields a basic understanding of the device as a source of continuous current. The study of series and parallel circuits completes the chapter.

Performance Objectives

Goal: The student will gain an understanding of the basic concepts of electricity and electron transfer.

Objectives: Upon completion of the reading and activities and when asked to diagram, demonstrate, or respond either orally or on a written test, students will:

20:1	K/P	describe various methods for obtaining and identifying static charges.
20:2	K	explain how an electroscope works.
20:3	K	contrast wet and dry cells.
	K/P	compare conduction (static) and current as sources of electric charge.
20:4	K	define volt.
20:5	K/S/P	use Ohm's law to solve simple problems in current—resistance relationships.
20:6	K/P	compare parallel and series circuits.
	K/S	build several circuits and diagram others using both parallel and series.
20:7	K/S	determine power for lighting various bulbs.
20:8	K	describe some complex circuits.
	S/A	demonstrate the proper use of equipment and materials.
	A	attempt at least one *More Ideas to Explore.*

Equipment for Activities

The amounts listed are for a class of 30 students broken down into groups of 2.

aluminum foil, 0.5 cm x 2 cm—30
ammeter, 0-5 amp DC—15
battery, 6 volt—15
bottle or flask—15
cloth
  silk—15
  wool—15
comb, plastic—15
curtain rod, 20 cm—15
glass friction rod—30
light bulbs and sockets, 6 volt—45
plastic friction rod—30
resistor, 25 Ω slide variable—15
rubber bands
switch—15
voltmeter, 0-10 volt DC—15
wire, 30 cm—120

20:1 Electric Charge

Experimenting with static electricity is most successful in cool, dry weather. Since these conditions cannot always be met, follow these simple directions. Some pieces of equipment, particularly the glass rod, will work best if heated just before use. Place items in a box on a warm radiator before class or in a box containing an operating incandescent lamp for a short while before use.

Several activities involving static charges should be made by pupils at home. (1) Comb hair in front of a mirror in a darkened room to observe sparks. (2) Scuff across the room and touch a doorknob or another person.

Make a list of situations where static charges may be dangerous. (Dry cleaning with a highly volatile combustible substance.) Ask why gasoline trucks dangle a chain at the rear.

Activity 20-1

The Activity demonstrates the attraction of opposite charges and the repulsion of like charges.

Materials needed: plastic comb, 2 glass friction rods, 2 plastic friction rods, silk, wool

Questions: The two charged glass rods repel as do the charged plastic rods. The glass rod attracts the plastic rod and the silk. Paper is attracted to the comb because the negative charge on the comb repels the electrons in the paper. Since the paper is neutral, the electrons move to the part of the paper farthest from the comb. Thus, the part closest to the comb is positive and attracted to the comb. The plastic rods have the same charge and repel while the glass rod and silk have opposite charges and attract.

The distinction between neutral and charged objects should be pointed out. Explain how objects become charged in terms of gain or loss of electrons.

Page 415. Making Sure

1. The balloon gains electrons from the cloth.
2. The rod loses electrons and has a positive charge. It attracts the balloon.

20:2 Conduction

Explain the difference between conductors and insulators. Try to borrow a Van de Graaff generator from the physics lab to use in class. Be sure to keep the belts clean.

Activity 20-2

The Activity demonstrates the working of an electroscope.

Materials needed: bottle, curtain rod 20 cm, two pieces of metal foil 0.5 cm by 2 cm, plastic rod, rubber band, wool, graphite, glass rod, silk

Questions: When the electroscope is touched with a charged rod, it becomes charged and the leaves spread. Touching the scope with a hand allows electrons to enter or leave, discharging it. Nothing happens when the electroscope is touched with the graphite, since carbon is an insulator.

20:3 Current

Make a cell by wetting thoroughly with saliva a piece of paper towel the size of a postage stamp. Place the moistened paper towel between two coins, a penny and a dime. Connect to a galvanometer and observe the deflection. Reverse the connections and note the opposite deflection. Wet another piece of toweling with dilute sulfuric acid. A greater deflection should be observed.

Demonstrate the deposition of copper in an electroplating cell and explain it in terms of ionization.

Showing an actual cutaway section of a lead acid battery would aid students' comprehension of the operation of a battery.

20:4 Potential Difference

Bring in a variety of different batteries. Have students examine them and identify the voltage of each. Keep in mind that a 12-volt battery can do 12 joules of work for each coulomb of charge that it produces. Ask the students which battery can do more work.

Page 421. Making Sure

3. volt
4. Electrons must have a path to flow along.

20:5 Resistance and Ohm's Law

Stress that electrons must move through the conductor in a closed circuit. The conductor is made of atoms. These atoms get in the way of traveling electrons. Different things affect the resistance of a wire. Temperature affects resistance because the higher the temperature, the faster the atoms of the conductor are moving. The electrons collide more often with the atoms. The length of a wire is also a factor because it presents more atoms in the path of the moving electrons.

A good conductor has a low resistance.

Georg Simon Ohm in 1827 found that there was a relationship among current, voltage, and resistance in a circuit. Most appliances have a fixed resistance and current so that they will operate properly. Since resistance and current are fixed, a definite voltage must be used with them. If too much voltage is used, there will be too much current. The voltage can be determined using Ohm's law:

$$\textit{current} = \frac{\textit{potential difference}}{\textit{resistance}}$$

If the voltage is too large, with fixed resistance, the current will be too large. For example, a motor that draws too much current will burn out. It can also start a fire.

Activity 20-3

The Activity demonstrates the relationship of current, resistance, and potential difference.

Materials needed: 0-5 amp DC ammeter, 6-volt battery, switch, 25Ω slide variable resistor, 0-10 volt DC voltmeter, wire

Check the polarity of each item in the circuit. The ammeter must be connected in series with the negative terminal connected to the negative terminal of the battery. The voltmeter is connected in parallel.

Summing Up

1. As the length of the resistor increases, the resistance increases.
2. As the resistance increases, the current decreases.

Page 424. Making Sure

5. $I = \frac{V}{R}$

$I = \frac{12\text{ V}}{50\,\Omega}$

$I = 0.24\text{ A}$

6. $I = \frac{V}{R}$

$I = \frac{6\text{ V}}{50\,\Omega}$

$I = 0.12\text{ A}$

7. $I = \frac{V}{R}$

$I = \frac{120\text{ V}}{200\,\Omega}$

$I = 0.60\text{ A}$

8. $I = \frac{V}{R}$

$R = \frac{V}{I}$

$R = \frac{120\text{ V}}{10\text{ A}}$

$R = 12\,\Omega$

20:6 Circuits

Stress that a series circuit has only one path for current whereas a parallel circuit has two or more paths.

Walk over to the wall light switches and turn one set off, leaving part of the lights burning. Ask students which kind of circuit is wired here and why.

Activity 20-4

The Activity demonstrates the difference between series and parallel circuits.

Materials needed: 6-volt battery, three light bulbs with sockets, switch, wire

You can also have students work with sets of Christmas tree lights. Have them determine if they are wired in series or parallel.

Questions: When one bulb is unscrewed in a series circuit, all of the bulbs go out. When one bulb in a parallel circuit is unscrewed, the rest stay on.

Since a series circuit has only one current path, a switch anywhere can be used to open and close the circuit.

A switch in a parallel circuit will turn off one bulb at a time with two exceptions. If the switch is between the battery and all of the bulbs or is parallel with all of the bulbs, all the bulbs can be turned off by the switch.

Each student's pictures will be different, but the difference between series and parallel should be clearly shown.

Activity 20-5

The Activity introduces circuit diagrams and symbols and gives practice in drawing circuits. *Questions:* The parts of the circuit in Figure 20-17 are a battery, resistor, and switch.

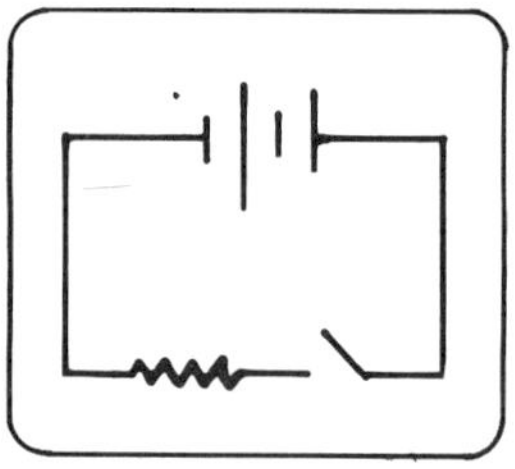

The diagrams for the previous activities will vary, but they should represent the pictures drawn by the students.

The circuit diagram for two light bulbs in parallel with a resistor in series, a switch, and a battery is

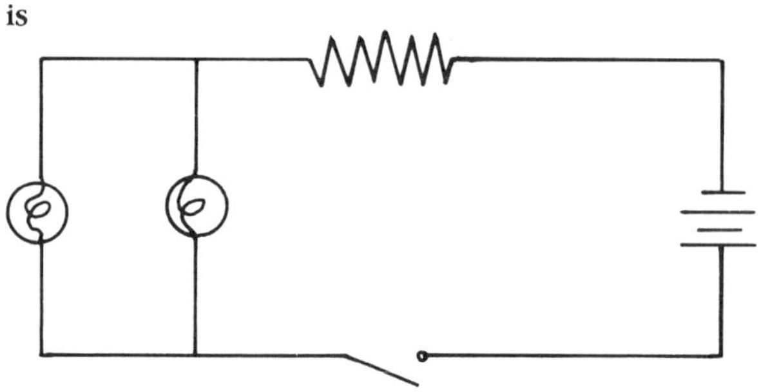

20:7 Power

Allow students to examine various appliances to identify the power rating. Knowing the wattage and the voltage, they can calculate the current going through the appliances.

Page 427. Making Sure

9. $P = VI$	**10.** $P = VI$
$P = 120\text{ V} \times 1.25\text{ A}$	$P = 120\text{ V} \times 0.5\text{ A}$
$P = 150\text{ W}$	$P = 60\text{ W}$

20:8 Complex Circuit

This section demonstrates that complex circuits are nothing more than networks of simple circuits. Every use of electronics from house wiring to computers is a collection of simple circuits. Many of those circuits can be related back to the basic series and parallel networks.

Questions for Review

A. True or False

1. True **2.** True **3.** False (Like charges repel.) **4.** False (The loss or gain of electrons causes a static charge.) **5.** False (Current is charge in motion.) **6.** True **7.** False (Ohm's law relates voltage, current, and resistance.) **8.** True **9.** False (The plates of a wet cell must be connected to have a current.) **10.** False (No current flows in an open circuit.)

B. Multiple Choice

1. negative **2.** positively **3.** lose **4.** volts **5.** resistance and current **6.** too much **7.** insulators **8.** conductors **9.** both wire and solution **10.** charges

C. Completion

1. loses **2.** Like **3.** electroscope **4.** insulator **5.** electric **6.** watts **7.** high **8.** parallel **9.** current **10.** current

D. How and Why

1. $I = \frac{V}{R}; I = \frac{12\text{ V}}{2\,\Omega}; I = 6\text{ A}$

2. $P = VI; P = 12\text{ V} \times 6\text{ A}; I = 72\text{ W}$

3. $I = \frac{V}{R}; I = \frac{60\text{ V}}{140\,\Omega}; I = 0.43\text{ A}$

$P = VI; P = 60\text{ V} \times 0.43\text{ A}; P = 26\text{ W}$

4. Static electricity is produced by an excess or deficit of electrons caused by rubbing one substance with another to cause a transfer.

More Ideas to Explore

4. This poster might include such things as turning lights off, adjusting the thermostat, weather stripping, and using a computer to control power consumption in a house or building.

21 Electricity and Its Uses

Overview

The properties of magnets and magnetic fields are explored in this chapter. The construction and use of the ammeter and voltmeter is explained. The student is shown how current in a wire creates a magnetic field, and how a magnetic field moving across a wire, creates a current. The student is introduced to alternating current, generators, rectifiers, amplifiers, cathode-ray tube, and is led to an understanding of how the parts of a television work together. The chapter concludes with a presentation of integrated circuits and computers.

Performance Objectives

Goal: The student will gain an understanding of the relationship between electricity and magnetism and their use in technology.

Objectives: Upon completion of the reading and activities and when asked to diagram, demonstrate, or respond either orally or on a written test, students will:

21:1	K	describe the behavior of magnets.
21:2	K/P	explain how an electric current and a magnet set up similar magnetic fields.
21:3	K	compare and contrast ammeter and voltmeter.
21:4	K/P	explain how a magnet and coil produce alternating current.
21:5	K	describe a rectifier.
21:6	K	explain the operation of amplifiers.
21:7-10	K	describe various electronic devices.
	A/S	demonstrate the proper use of equipment and materials.
	A	attempt at least one *More Ideas to Explore.*

Equipment for Activities

The amounts listed are for a class of 30 students broken down into groups of 2.

battery, 6-volt —15
compass, small—15
galvanometer—15
iron filings—15
magnet, bar—15
switch (optional)—15
wire, 3.5 m—15

21:1 Magnets

Point out the position of iron, cobalt, and nickel on the periodic table as you discuss their properties. Using a bar magnet, test various materials for magnetic attraction. With a freely suspended magnet, demonstrate how a compass works. Point out that only certain substances can be magnetized and a magnetized object always contains two poles.

Activity 21-1

The Activity shows the lines of force of a magnetic field.

Materials needed: 2 bar magnets, compass, iron filings, paper

You may wish to use a horseshoe magnet, as well.

Questions: The iron filings arrange themselves along lines of force going from end to end.

The compass needle will always point to the north pole along the lines of force.

21:2 Current and Magnetic Fields

Show that a straight wire carrying current has a magnetic field around it. Use iron filings to show lines of force around a straight wire, a circular wire, and a coil in which direct current is flowing. Discuss and demonstrate the electromagnet as a means of producing strong, controllable magnetic fields.

Page 435. Making Sure

1. The two fields oppose each other and force the shaft to turn.
2. Current in the coil sets up a magnetic field in opposition to the magnet. This field causes the coil to rotate.

21:3 Ammeter and Voltmeter

Stress that magnetic fields exert forces. These forces are responsible for the operation of meters and motors in which electric energy is converted into mechanical energy.

Activity 21-2

The Activity demonstrates the effect and use of magnets in electronics by having students construct a current meter.

Materials needed: 6-volt battery, compass, wire

Questions: The needle deflects when placed in the field around the coil. The needle is a magnet and reacts to the magnetic field.

The purpose for trying the Activity in two different positions is to be certain that the students observe the deflection. If the coil were oriented with its field pointing north, there would be no deflection.

21:4 Generators and Alternating Current

If possible, demonstrate a working model of an AC generator connected to a galvanometer. You may also want to discuss the use of commutators to produce direct current from generators.

Activity 21-3

The Activity demonstrates the operation of a generator.

Materials needed: bar magnet, galvanometer, wire

Questions: Putting the bar magnet through the coil in one direction deflects the needle in one direction. Reversing the direction reverses the needle. The faster the magnet moves, the more the needle deflects. Moving the magnet through a larger coil also produces a larger deflection.

21:5 Rectifiers

Stress that rectifiers are used to change alternating current to direct current. Show the students the rectifier circuit from an old radio.

Page 439. Making Sure

3. A rectifier conducts current in only one direction.
4. Stereos operate only on direct current.

21:6 Amplifiers

Relate the word amplify to amplitude of waves. An amplifier makes a signal larger, increasing the amplitude.

Ask the students to name some devices that use amplifiers. Some examples are computers, radios, televisions, and microwave ovens.

Page 440. Making Sure

5. The input signal controls the flow of current.
6. The microphone changes sound to electrical signals.
7. Amplifiers are used to increase signal levels.

21:7 Cathode-ray Tube

Point out that radar and computers also use cathode-ray tubes. In a radar receiver, a bright spot appears on the screen showing the location of a moving object. In a computer, a number or word may appear on the screen.

Page 441. Making Sure

8. The direction of the electron beam is controlled by electric fields.
9. The input signal determines the number of electrons hitting the screen.

21:8 Television Receivers

Stress how the television employs many of the devices now familiar to students. As an aid, explain that a television can be thought of as a radio combined with a cathode-ray tube.

Page 442. Making Sure

10. The sound and picture are the basic parts of a television signal.
11. After the first amplifier, the television signal is separated.
12. The picture signal is the input for the cathode-ray tube.

21:9 Integrated Circuits

If you have a small calculator, carefully open the front and examine the integrated circuit.

Explain that, although an integrated circuit is smaller than a single transistor, it contains many transistors.

Page 443. Making Sure

13. A circuit board is a card mounted with many parts like transistors and resistors.
14. Integrated circuits have one part instead of many and they are small.

21:10 Computers

Many school districts have computer terminals or micro-computers. If your class does not, make arrangements for the students to observe one. Sales representatives from computer companies will probably come to your class to give a demonstration with portable microcomputers. You can also have students go to stores selling home computers and ask to have them explained.

Page 445. Making Sure

15. Five parts of a computer are: input unit, control unit, arithmetic unit, memory unit, and output unit.
16. A program is a set of instructions for a computer.
17. The control unit runs the program through the other three units.

Focus on People

CHAOS

Computers can be used as an aid in instruction. One way is teaching students to program. Another way is testing students. The tests are programmed into the computer. Each student's grades are kept by the computer. Only the teacher can see the grades. Computer games are also useful in helping students become comfortable with computers. What Mary provided was a versatile system that allowed more students to take advantage of these learning opportunities. With the article as a starting place, talk about the potential of computers in educational processes. If you would like information about Mary's company, write: Computer Systems Design Group, 3632 Governor Drive, San Diego, California 92122.

Questions for Review

A. True or False

1. False (North poles attract south poles.) **2.** True **3.** False (Ammeters and voltmeters use the same basic design.) **4.** False (Rectifiers change AC to DC.) **5.** True **6.** True **7.** False (The colors are red, green, and blue.) **8.** False (There are five basic parts to a computer.) **9.** True **10.** False (The control unit moves information from memory.)

B. Multiple Choice

1. Ammeters **2.** iron **3.** electrical **4.** direction **5.** rectifiers **6.** after **7.** control **8.** output **9.** amplifiers **10.** show pictures of

C. Completion

1. charged plates **2.** arithmetic **3.** arithmetic **4.** south **5.** coil **6.** north, south **7.** alternates **8.** cathode-ray **9.** direct current **10.** voltmeter

D. How and Why

1. An electric generator and a meter operate on the same general principle, the relationship between electricity and magnetism. In a meter an electric current sets up a magnetic field which causes a needle to deflect. In a generator, passing a wire through a magnetic field causes a current in the wire. (For more detail see sections 21:2 and 21:4, pages 434 and 437.)
2. A Canadian nickel contains nickel, which is magnetic. The United States nickel is mostly copper and zinc, and thus, is not magnetic.
3. The development of the integrated circuit allows great miniaturization and mass production, and thus, lower prices for electronic appliances.
4. A cathode-ray tube could be set up. As a magnet is brought near the electrons are deflected. This is the general principle behind the television tube.

Unit 7 Energy Resources for the Future

Overview

This final unit focuses on the most complex problem of our times—developing alternate sources of energy and the allocation of existing resources. It is extremely important that your students as future citizens are fully aware of the problems we face in developing and utilizing energy.

Teaching Tips

- Do a bulletin board display of current newspaper articles relating to the energy situation during the last few months.
- Have representatives from public interest groups as well as the local utility companies speak to your class. Students should research information regarding nuclear energy. A debate could be planned between several members of the class. You could ask your media specialist to videotape the debate. Consider having students write a position paper regarding nuclear energy. They should support their opinion with information gathered by literature research and the guest speakers.
- If you live near a nuclear reactor, plan to visit their educational center.
- *The Energy–Environment Sourcebook* is an excellent source of information covering the total energy picture. It can be obtained from the National Science Teachers Association. Write to:

  National Science Teachers Association
  1742 Connecticut Avenue, N.W.
  Washington, D.C. 20009

22 Radioactivity and Nuclear Energy

Overview

The phenomenon of radioactivity is covered in this chapter. Students will study the types of radiation, the behavior of radioactive atoms (half-life), radiation detection methods, and nuclear reactions. The material in the chapter provides the base for the study of nuclear reactors in Chapter 23.

Performance Objectives

Goal: Students will gain an understanding of the properties and uses of nuclear radiation.

Objectives: Upon completion of the reading and activities and when asked to diagram, demonstrate, or respond either orally or on a written test, students will:

22:1	K	list some radioactive elements.
22:2	K/P	identify the characteristics of unstable nuclei.
22:3	K	compare the three kinds of nuclear radiation.
22:4	K/P	define half-life of a radioactive nuclide.
22:5-6	K	describe various methods for detecting radiation.
22:7	K/S	write equations for nuclear reactions involving fission.

22:8 K/P compare fusion and fission.
S/A demonstrate the proper use of equipment and materials.
A attempt at least one *More Ideas to Explore.*

Equipment for Activities

The amounts listed are for a class of 30 students broken into groups of 2.
cardboard box with lid—15
corn kernels—1500

22:1 Radioactive Elements

You may want to have students do some library research into the preparation of one or more of the synthetic elements.

Page 455. Making Sure

1. A synthetic element is one produced in the laboratory.
2. Elements 93 through 105 are synthetic. Element 43, technetium, exists on the stars. It has been produced synthetically here on the earth.

22:2 Radioactive Nuclides

Be sure to point out that the 1:1 ratio holds true for light elements only. As noted in Figure 22-3, the ratio changes slightly for the heavy elements.

You may wish to invite a radiologist in to speak on the varied uses of radiation in medicine, or have students report on the duties of a radiologist.

Page 457. Making Sure

3. 27:33 or 9:11

22:3 Nuclear Radiation

You may wish to write the symbols for radioactive particles on the board.

α alpha β beta γ gamma

It is important that students understand how radiation can harm body cells. Alpha, beta, and gamma particles have a great deal of energy. The radiation can change some of the atoms into ions. These ions can break chemical bonds and can affect the reactions that occur in the cell. Radiation can cause mutations which are changes in cell genes as well and cancer and leukemia. You should also make the point that radiation is useful.

Page 459. Making Sure

4. In order from least to most penetrating power—alpha, beta, and gamma.
5. Gamma rays are shorter in wavelength than X rays and have greater energy.

22:4 Decay and Half-Life

Emphasize that nuclear changes occur within the nucleus of an atom whereas chemical changes are the result of interactions between electron clouds.

Concerning the discussion of radioactive dating: Though useful, radioactive dating using carbon-14 has some limitations. One assumes that the carbon-14 level in the atmosphere has remained constant over time. However, it is now known that changes in the sun's activity can affect the carbon-14 level. This material is presented because of its usefulness in illustrating a method of analysis and as an application of the concept of half-life.

Activity 22-1

The Activity demonstrates a model for the decay of radioactive atoms.

Materials needed: square box with lid, 100 corn kernels

Students could also use pennies, selecting those that land heads up. Have them try to graph the data. To show a substance with a longer half life, you could roll a large number of dice and select those with a specific number appearing.

Questions: Answers will vary, but approximately 1/4 of the kernels will have been removed.

Page 462. Making Sure

6. With a half-life of 86 minutes, 4 hours and 18 minutes is the equivalent of three half-lives. Thus, a ten-gram sample would decay to 5 to 2.5 to 1.25 grams.
7. 140 days

22:5 Radiation Detection

This section describes various methods of detecting radiation. If possible, demonstrate a cloud chamber. Inexpensive cloud chambers are available from a chemical supply house. You may be able to borrow one from the physics department of your school district. Ask the physics teacher to explain how to set it up, or come to your class and give the demonstration.

Page 465. Making Sure

8. The alpha particle is heavier and has less energy than a beta particle.

9. Radiation can be detected using an electroscope, cloud chamber, and nuclear emulsion.

22:6 Radiation Counters

Most school districts have a Geiger counter and a few radioactive samples. Contact the physics teacher to arrange to borrow this equipment.

Page 466. Making Sure

10. A Geiger counter can tell you the intensity of the radiation released by a radioactive substance. An electroscope will only tell you if a substance is radioactive.

22:7 Fission

Demonstrate a chain reaction using a series of wooden matches placed 1 cm apart in clay. Arrange the matches in a bowling pin formation (see Figure 22-18a).

You may need to spend time reviewing the notation used on page 466. Writing symbols for nuclides was covered briefly in Chapter 6. Emphasize once again that these reactions occur in the nucleus of an atom. Therefore, they will be written in a different manner than chemical reactions. Remind students that the law of conservation of mass still holds.

22:8 Fusion

Stress the difference between fission and fusion. Scientists have been experimenting with two methods for containing the hydrogen fuel for fusion. See Teacher Information for Section 23:7.

You may want to write a fusion reaction on the board so students can compare it to a fission reaction. A simple example is the production of tritium from lithium-6.

$$^{6}_{3}\text{Li} + ^{1}_{0}n \rightarrow ^{3}_{1}\text{H} + ^{4}_{2}\text{He}$$

Emphasize that the fusion reaction shown in Figure 22-20 consists of a series of steps.

$$^{1}_{1}\text{H} + ^{1}_{1}\text{H} \rightarrow ^{2}_{1}\text{H} + ^{0}_{+1}e\text{(positron)}$$
$$^{2}_{1}\text{H} + ^{1}_{1}\text{H} \rightarrow ^{3}_{2}\text{He}$$
$$^{3}_{2}\text{He} + ^{3}_{2}\text{He} \rightarrow ^{4}_{2}\text{He} + 2^{1}_{1}\text{H}$$

Remember, Sections 22:7-8 form the base for the discussions of nuclear reactors in Chapter 23.

Focus on Skills

Using Graphic Aids

In covering the material in every chapter, it is important that students utilize the visual aids. These aids are especially important for students who have reading difficulties and when covering topics where students must formulate mental models to comprehend abstract information.

This Skills page focuses on having students look critically at the illustrations for this chapter. Students are asked to determine the purpose and relationship of an illustration to the text material.

Answers

1. radioactive **2.** 88 **3.** lawrencium, rutherfordium

1. no **2.** protons and neutrons **3.** hydrogen

1. when the ratio of protons to neutrons is 1:1 **2.** colored squares—green and orange **3.** neutrons

1. 3 **2.** 3 × 86 minutes **3.** cut in half

1. uranium decay **2.** 24.1 days **3.** three times **4.** alpha and beta particles

1. radon and radium **2.** days **3.** radon—shorter half-life

1. uranium fission **2.** neutron **3.** uranium-236 **4.** barium-144 and krypton-90

1. 3 **2.** 6 **3.** 2 **4.** 4

Questions for Review

A. True or False

1. False (A uranium atom has a different number of protons and neutrons in its nucleus.) **2.** False (The changing of uranium to lead is an example of decay.) **3.** False (A beta particle is actually a positive or negative electron.) **4.** False (A beta ray has a positive or negative charge.) **5.** True **6.** False (Carbon-14 is an unstable nuclide.) **7.** True **8.** True **9.** True **10.** False (The longer the half-life, the more stable the isotope.)

B. Multiple Choice

1. increases **2.** Lead **3.** radiation **4.** alpha **5.** alpha particle **6.** decreases **7.** lead **8.** unite **9.** nuclear forces **10.** stable

C. Completion

1. neutron **2.** plasma **3.** chain reaction **4.** lead **5.** neutrons **6.** positive or negative **7.** time, one half **8.** saturated **9.** emulsion **10.** Geiger counter

D. How and Why

1. Radiation ionizes the gas in the Geiger counter cylinder. This process produces a "flash" of current. The current causes a click which is amplified.
2. Alpha particles are helium nuclei. They have a positive charge and are least energetic of the three particles.
   Beta particles are positively or negatively charged electrons. They have a penetrating ability about 100 times greater than alpha particles.
   Gamma rays are energy waves with shorter wavelengths than X rays. They have the greatest penetrating power.
3. Radioactive nuclides are used as tracers for internal organs, to detect wear of machine parts, to trace the path of chemical reactions, to treat cancer and other diseases. There are other uses.
4. Experimentally, stability can be determined by use of a Geiger counter or other detection device. Theoretically, if the neutron:proton ratio is near 1:1, the nuclide is not radioactive.
5. Nuclear fission breaks nuclei into lighter elements. Nuclear fusion combines nuclei to produce heavier elements.

23 Alternative Energy Resources

Overview

This chapter presents a brief overview of the major energy alternatives presently under development. The chapter begins with a discussion of the limitations of relying solely on fossil fuels for our energy. Students then move on to alternatives which may reduce the demand for fossil fuels. The chapter closes with a section on conservation methods.

Performance Objectives

Goal: Students will gain an understanding of alternate energy sources.

Objectives: Upon completion of the reading and activities and when asked to diagram, demonstrate, or respond either orally or on a written test, students will:

23:1	K	list the major fossil fuels.
23:2	K	explain the use of the sun for energy.
23:3	K/P	diagram the water cycle that leads to the production of hydroelectric power.
23:4	K	describe geothermal power.
23:5	K/P	diagram and explain the six parts of a nuclear reactor.

23:6	K	explain the functioning of a breeder reactor.
23:7	K	contrast thermonuclear power with that from a fission reactor.
23:8	K/A	list the advantages and disadvantages of nuclear energy.
23:9	K/A	list at least three ways to conserve energy.
	A	attempt at least one *More Ideas to Explore.*

23:1 Fossil Fuels

Be sure to emphasize that fossil fuels are an excellent source of energy but there are economic problems associated with its use. Beside the problems of supply vs. demand there is the cost of cleaning up the environment especially when burning coal.

The second paragraph introduces the fact that sulfur is present in coal. When coal burns (oxidation), sulfur is also oxidized forming sulfur dioxide. Sulfur dioxide is soluble in water (vapor present in the air) and forms sulfurous acid which is then further oxidized to form sulfuric acid. The sulfuric acid precipitates as acid rain (Section 13:7). Students have probably read about the increase in the acidity of rain, and the environmental problems it has caused. Have students bring in newspaper and magazine articles dealing with this problem.

Activity 23-1

The Activity emphasizes how one's lifestyle depends on energy.

The actual listings will vary, some examples are waking up to a clock radio, turning on the lights, taking a shower (hot water), using an electric hair dryer, cooking food, riding to school, washing and drying clothes, using appliances, vacuuming carpets, heating and cooling the home and school.

Ask students if they know what the term "energy servant" means. The average person has about 70 energy servants (bus, car, electric appliances and so on). As an extension, you can ask students to list the energy servants they use each day.

Page 476. Making Sure

1. The chemical change is burning.
2. There are great coal reserves, but coal pollutes. Oil is more efficient and easier to store than coal but is in limited supply, expensive, and it also pollutes when burned. Natural gas is convenient and clean but its supply is also limited and expensive.

23:2 Solar Energy

An inexpensive radiometer is a valuable piece of equipment for demonstrating the conversion of solar energy to mechanical energy. It also presents an opportunity to show the effect of light and dark surfaces on reflection and absorption of radiant energy.

It is important to emphasize here that not all solar energy is collected via solar panels. The material on page 478 shows passive solar homes. As stated in the caption, these homes make use of radiation from the sun by their architectural design. Many articles have been published recently in consumer magazines which deal with passive solar housing. Have students look for these and bring them in. If there are any solar homes in your area, you may be able to arrange a field trip or have the builder in to speak to the class.

23:3 Hydroelectricity

Remind students that early settlements and villages were built near water sources because the water could be put to work to turn the paddle wheels of mills.

Page 480. Making Sure

3. The generator uses kinetic energy.
4. Solar energy evaporates water and changes it to vapor which eventually returns as rain or snow. The path of this water through the cycle creates the kinetic energy.

23:4 Geothermal Energy

Be sure students realize that geothermal resources are limited in capacity and are not available everywhere in the world. The fields presently in use in California are "dry steam" fields. Dry steam is so hot that it does not contain water. Technology is being developed for recharging hot dry wells with new water to extend the supply of this resource. You might want to point out that geothermal is not a new resource. The power plant in Italy has been in operation since 1904.

23:5 Nuclear Reactors

A great deal of publicity was given to the Three Mile Island incident. You might have students research the periodicals to gather information about this accident. It is important, however, that students view both sides of the issue concerning nuclear power. This topic would be excellent for a debate. If possible, arrange for speakers to cover both sides of the issue.

You may want to point out to students that there are two types of reactors in operation: pressurized water reactors (PWR) and boiling water reactors (BWR). A PWR is shown in Figure 23-8a. In looking for articles on Three Mile Island, you might have students research the differences between these two types of reactors.

Page 484. Making Sure

5. The control rods stop the chain reaction. In case of emergency, the reaction must be stopped immediately, quick response is necessary.

23:6 Breeder Reactors

There are a number of drawbacks associated with breeder reactors even though they provide a powerful energy source, plutonium. The liquid metal fast breeder reactor (LMFBR) shown in Figure 23-10 uses sodium as a coolant. Review with students the highly reactive properties of sodium. It is important that the coolant never come in contact with water or air as an explosion will result.

There are also security problems associated with breeder reactors. Plutonium fuel can be made easily into nuclear bombs. It is therefore necessary to protect these supplies during shipment and handling from terrorists and hijackers.

Page 486. Making Sure

6. The nucleus of uranium-238 changes to become plutonium-239.
7. A breeder reactor is fast and it produces both energy and fuel.

23:7 Thermonuclear Power

There are a number of advantages to obtaining power from nuclear fusion.

1. Though the process produces radioactive tritium, this material is a fuel for fusion rather than a waste product. Therefore, it is economically feasible to utilize it rather than discard it as waste. Other radioactive products are formed in significantly smaller quantities than those formed during the fission process.
2. The threat of explosion is considerably less than that of a fission reactor.
3. There are no security problems associated with the transportation of fuel.
4. The fuels for the reaction are in great supply.

The major problem is that the technology associated with fusion is still in the experimental stage. As stated in the text, the problem centers around containing the deuterium in a high density, high temperature situation. A number of methods are being investigated. Among those are containing the deuterium in a magnetic bottle and freezing the deuterium sample then bombarding it with a laser beam. Using laser bombardment, the sample temperature increases so quickly that the density remains high due to inertia.

23:8 Nuclear Energy and the Environment

You might have students research the safety precautions necessary in transporting nuclear fuel. As stated previously, the threat of hijacking is an important consideration in transporting plutonium.

As the amount of nuclear waste increases, suitable areas for waste storage must be found. Most people would not want a disposal site located in their area. The reasons should be obvious.

Point out to students that reactors do not release particulates (NO_x and SO_x) into the atmosphere—an advantage over coal. The plant site itself requires less land than a coal plant but must be located next to a water source for cooling.

Page 489. Making Sure

8. Nuclear energy is called "clean" because it doesn't pollute the atmosphere with particulates.
9. Nuclear "accidents," waste disposal, and thermal pollution are some reasons for opposition.
10. Answers will vary. Some may say fusion, solar, wind, tidal, and so on.

23:9 Conserving Energy

Make students conscious of ways they waste energy. Have them list ways they could change their habits in an effort to conserve.

Focus on Frontiers

Wind Power

Have some students research the use of windmills in the Netherlands. Compare this with the common practice of pumping water on ranches in the United States with windmills. To gain some insight into the workings of a windmill, have some students build a model of a mill for grinding grain. Have other students build a model of a mill for grinding grain that uses a water wheel. Compare the two types of mills. Are there any advantages of one over the other? Talk about other uses for wind power, such as sailboats, hang gliders, and balloons.

Questions for Review

A. True or False

1. False (Sulfur oxides in coal cause air pollution.) **2.** True **3.** True **4.** False (Most of the hydroelectric power produced in the United States comes from the west coast.) **5.** True **6.** False (A moderator slows a chain reaction.) **7.** True **8.** True **9.** True **10.** False (Nuclear reactors do not pollute the air with particulates like fossil fuels.)

B. Multiple Choice

1. control rod **2.** nuclear fusion **3.** breeder **4.** fusion **5.** Coal **6.** increase **7.** neutrons **8.** neutrons **9.** thermal **10.** Natural gas

C. Completion

1. Methane (CH_4) **2.** fusion **3.** moderator **4.** turbine **5.** plutonium **6.** neutrons **7.** temperatures **8.** nonrenewable **9.** carbon **10.** crude oil (petroleum)

D. How and Why

1. If the fuel-can absorbs neutrons, it slows the reaction.
2. The heat generated by fission creates steam which turns turbines. In this way, nuclear energy is changed to kinetic energy.
3. Nuclear power plants produce energy cheaply with a renewable source of fuel. However, there are safety factors which mitigate the advantages. These include release of radioactive materials and the threat of a possible uncontrolled reaction.
4. A nuclear plant could harm the environment through release of radioactive material, thermal pollution, and inadequate storage for radioactive waste.

Teacher Questionnaire

Perhaps one of the best ways to ensure that effective educational materials are produced is to let authors and publishers know how you feel concerning the texts you are using. Please help us plan revisions and new programs to meet your needs. Complete and return the form found on the next page. Please attach any additional comments to the questionnaire form. After removing the questionnaire from the book, fold and staple it so that the address label shows. We would certainly appreciate hearing from you.

Focus on Physical Science

Circle the number which corresponds to your opinion of each of the following items for the Merrill Physical Science Program. Please also star (*) those three factors which most influence your evaluation or choice of a text.

Student Text	Excel-lent	Very Good	Satis-factory	Fair	Poor	Comments
1. Readability	5	4	3	2	1	
2. Approach	5	4	3	2	1	
3. Organization	5	4	3	2	1	
4. Factual accuracy	5	4	3	2	1	
5. Coverage of Physical Science	5	4	3	2	1	
6. Concept development	5	4	3	2	1	
7. Visual impact	5	4	3	2	1	
8. Chapter end materials	5	4	3	2	1	
9. Tables	5	4	3	2	1	
10. Illustrations	5	4	3	2	1	
11. Focus pages	5	4	3	2	1	
12. Skills pages	5	4	3	2	1	
13. Student notes	5	4	3	2	1	
14. Activities	5	4	3	2	1	
15. Example problems	5	4	3	2	1	
16. Appendices	5	4	3	2	1	
17. Glossary	5	4	3	2	1	
Teacher's Annotated Edition						
1. Teachability	5	4	3	2	1	
2. Objectives	5	4	3	2	1	
3. Demonstrations and Activities	5	4	3	2	1	
4. Unit and Chapter suggestions	5	4	3	2	1	
5. Planning Guide	5	4	3	2	1	
6. Answers to Questions	5	4	3	2	1	
7. Audiovisual aids	5	4	3	2	1	
8. Annotations	5	4	3	2	1	
9. Suggested readings	5	4	3	2	1	
Supplements						
1. *Evaluation Program*	5	4	3	2	1	
2. *Activity-Centered Program, Teacher's Guide*	5	4	3	2	1	
3. *A Learning Strategy for the Laboratory*	5	4	3	2	1	
4. *A Learning Strategy for the Laboratory, TAE*	5	4	3	2	1	
5. *Review and Reinforcement Guide*	5	4	3	2	1	
6. *Review and Reinforcement Guide, TAE*	5	4	3	2	1	
7. *Physical Science Skillcards*	5	4	3	2	1	

Circle the appropriate information:

1. Grade level of your students	6	7	8	9	10
2. Average number of students in your physical science classes	5-10	11-20	21-30	31-40	40+
3. Total number of students enrolled in physical science	under 100	101-200	201-300	300+	
4. Total school enrollment	under 200	201-500	501-1000	1000+	
5. Locale of the school	rural	small town	suburban	city	
6. Ability level of students	below avg	average	above avg		
7. Appropriateness of the text for your class	easy	about right	difficult		
8. Number of years the text will be used	1	2	3	4	5
9. May we quote you?	yes	no			

Please feel free to attach an additional sheet to make further comments.

Name ____________________ Date ____________

School ____________ City ____________ State ______ Zip ______

Fold

NO POSTAGE NECESSARY IF MAILED IN THE UNITED STATES

BUSINESS REPLY MAIL

FIRST CLASS PERMIT NO. 284 COLUMBUS, OHIO

POSTAGE WILL BE PAID BY ADDRESSEE

CHARLES E. MERRILL PUBLISHING CO.
Managing Editor, Elhi Science
A BELL & HOWELL COMPANY
1300 ALUM CREEK DRIVE
COLUMBUS, OHIO 43216

Focus on Physical Science

Charles H. Heimler
California State University
Northridge, California

Jack Price
Superintendent, Vista Unified School District
Vista, California

Charles E. Merrill Publishing Co.
A Bell & Howell Company
Columbus, Ohio
Toronto • London • Sidney

A Merrill Science Program
Focus on Physical Science
Focus on Physical Science: *Teacher's Annotated Edition*
Focus on Physical Science: *Evaluation Program (Spirit Duplicating Masters)*
Focus on Physical Science: *Activity-Centered Program, Teacher's Guide*
Focus on Physical Science: *A Learning Strategy for the Laboratory*
Focus on Physical Science: *A Learning Strategy for the Laboratory, Teacher's Annotated Edition*
Focus on Physical Science: *Review and Reinforcement Guide*
Focus on Physical Science: *Review and Reinforcement Guide, Teacher's Annotated Edition*
Physical Science Skillcards
Focus on Earth Science Program
Focus on Life Science Program

Project Editor: Ellen M. Lappa
Editor: Eric Smith

Project Designer: Larry P. Koons
Project Artist: Katie White
Artist: Barbara A. Kauffman

Photo Editor: M. Lisy Boren
Russell T. Lappa

Illustrators: Bert Dodson
Kathie Kelleher
Heidi Palmer
Jim Shough

Teaching Specialists:

Annette M. Saturnelli
Marlboro Schools
Marlboro, New York

Robert C. Smoot
McDonogh School
McDonogh, Maryland

Reviewers:
Harold H. Hankins, *Fulton Junior High School, Indianapolis, Indiana*
Joseph G. Krajkovich, *Science Supervisor—Edison Schools, Edison, New Jersey*
Bud H. Larsen, *Rocky River Junior High, Rocky River, Ohio*
Karen E. Reynolds, *Havenscourt Junior High School, Oakland, California*
Garline D. Shaw, *Pearl C. Anderson Middle School, Dallas, Texas*
Nuclear Consultant: John Lamarsh, *American Nuclear Society*

Reading Consultants:
Sally Kovacik, Reading Coordinator, Mequon-Thiensville School District, Mequon, Wisconsin
Pat Chase, Reading Consultant, Mequon-Thiensville School District, Mequon, Wisconsin

Cover Photo Credits and Description:
The cover photographs show the theme of *Focus on Physical Science*: Physical Science can be applied to everyday happenings in your environment. The rainbow shows a realistic example of one way light behaves. You will study this behavior in Chapter 15. The water droplet on the leaf shows how a miniature rainbow can be formed when sunlight passes through it. The leaf can be used as a model to explain how the large rainbow is formed from water droplets in the sky. The sun is the light source as well as a symbol for energy. You should notice the four states of matter are also represented on the cover. Physical science is the study of matter, energy, and their relationship. *Rainbow:* **G. Harrison/Tom Stack and Assoc.**
Water droplet: **Roger K. Burnard** *Sun:* **Tom Stack/Tom Stack and Assoc.**

ISBN 0-675-02817-5
Published by
Charles E. Merrill Publishing Co.
A Bell & Howell Company
Columbus, Ohio 43216

Printed in the United States of America

Preface

Focus on Physical Science is a practical study of the relationship between matter and energy. Applications of physical laws and chemical processes are current and meaningful. Fundamental physical science principles are introduced through student involvement rather than by rote memorization.

This program offers a well-balanced introduction to the chemical and physical properties of matter, forms of energy, and the laws of motion. The content has been updated to focus on the interests and needs of today's students. Information concerning photography, lasers, radio, television, computers, and musical sound have been added as relevant subjects of high interest. The world energy problem is dealt with at length. Current energy sources as well as resources for the future are presented. Complex ideas are presented simply and then are developed logically. These ideas are reinforced when students use the "hands on" *Activities* placed throughout the text. Students repeatedly use their experience in observation, in data gathering, and in studying cause and effect relationships to interpret happenings in their environment. The *Activities* have been designed to be effective without being time consuming or costly.

Focus on Physical Science consists of seven units. Each of the twenty-three chapters is divided into short numbered sections of related information. These sections form manageable, logical teaching blocks for student assignments. Chapters can be studied in a variety of sequences and can be easily organized into courses to fit any school calendar.

Throughout the program, reading level has been carefully controlled. Photographs, illustrations, charts, graphs, and tables enable students to visualize ideas presented in the text and thus increase their comprehension. New science words are printed in boldface type and are then spelled phonetically.

Focus pages, *People • Careers • Frontiers,* are special pages which feature articles and photographs on current topics. They give additional contemporary emphasis to ***Focus on Physical Science.*** Career opportunities in physical science and related fields are highlighted through job descriptions or brief biographical sketches.

Focus on Skills pages are designed to emphasize reading in the content area. Practical language arts skills that are applicable to the study of physical science are presented. These pages enable the teacher to put added emphasis on important skills such as reading tables, graphs, illustrations, and problems. Vocabulary building and study skills are emphasized as well.

Questions in the margin help students identify important concepts as they read. Margin questions also may be used to preview new topics and to review sections or chapters.

Making Sure questions and problems interspersed throughout the chapters enable students to apply newly-learned concepts immediately. *Making Sure* can be used to identify individual difficulties and to ensure that basic concepts are mastered before more complicated topics are introduced. Mathematics required to do problems is integrated within the text. Thus, students learn basic mathematical skills as they need them. The International System of measurement (SI) is emphasized throughout the text.

Chapter-end features of ***Focus on Physical Science*** encourage student involvement and increase the flexibility of the program. These features are

- *Points to Remember*—a summary list of important concepts
- *Words to Use*—vocabulary list of important science terms
- *Questions for Review*—questions and additional problem-solving applications of scientific knowledge
- *More Ideas to Explore*—selected thought-provoking problems, projects, and investigations
- *Readings to Discover*—literature references to topics discussed in each chapter.

Focus on Physical Science presents material which is basic for understanding physical science concepts and principles. The material is also meaningful to the everyday lives of the students. Thus, the text involves the students in a relevant, purposeful study of physical science.

During the writing of ***Focus on Physical Science,*** the authors have had many helpful suggestions from students, teachers, and colleagues. To them, as well as to the editors and reviewers, the authors offer their thanks and appreciation for the time and effort involved in coordinating the materials within the text.

To the Student

You are embarking on an adventure into the study of physical science that will be both interesting and practical. This subject presents endless opportunities to learn about solar energy, machines, chemical changes, radiation, electricity, and many other aspects of your environment. Physical science will help you understand why many things occur the way they do. Also, you will learn how many things work, such as a television set, electric motor, and a nuclear power plant.

Most people would like to make the world a better place to live. What you learn in physical science is the kind of knowledge used to help conserve natural resources and solve the world's energy problems. Basic physical science principles are used in designing the equipment to clean up our air and water and decrease pollution. They are also used in producing inventions that make work easier, communication faster, and transportation systems more efficient.

Scientists use certain methods in solving problems and developing new ideas. In this course you will learn about these scientific methods and how to use them. You will discover that you can use the methods of science in your own daily life. They will increase your success in solving problems and getting things done.

One of the important decisions you will make in the future is a choice of a career or job. A background in physical science is either required or very useful in many jobs. In your physical science class, you will have a chance to explore your interests and abilities as they relate to different types of jobs. Careers in chemistry, physics, health services, home economics, engineering, mechanics, environmental protection, and many other fields make use of basic physical science principles.

As you already know, learning something worthwhile takes time and effort. This is true for physical science. ***Focus on Physical Science*** contains many features that will help you learn. Each chapter begins with a photograph and brief introduction to the theme of the chapter. A *Goal statement* identifies the major objectives of your study of the chapter. Throughout the chapter, *margin questions* emphasize the main ideas. Use these questions as self-checks to evaluate your progress. Major terms are highlighted in boldface type and are often respelled phonetically. Review questions and/or problems have been placed at the end of many sections throughout the chapters.

These, too, provide a means of self-evaluation. At the end of each chapter, *Points to Remember* provide a list of the major ideas presented. A word list serves as a reminder of the most important terms.

Also at the end of each chapter are sets of questions and problems. *Questions for Review* contains questions and problems that are useful as a review of the chapter's concepts. In addition, a set of project ideas is presented in *More Ideas to Explore.* The *Appendices* contain additional tables and background information to help you in setting up the Activities. A *Glossary* contains definitions of the major terms in the text. The *Index* will help you to locate particular topics quickly. *Focus* pages will introduce you to People, Careers, and Frontiers in physical science. *Focus on Skills* pages offer you tips on how to have a successful learning experience in physical science.

This textbook has been written and organized to help you be successful in your science class. As you do your classwork and complete your assignments you will gain the satisfaction of understanding physical science and its use in everyday life.

See the Teacher's Guide at the front of this book for additional information on teaching reading in the content area using the Focus on Skills pages. To administer the inventory, we recommend the following:

1. *Administer the inventory at the time books are distributed.*
2. *Allow enough time so all students will complete the inventory.*
3. *Emphasize that it is not a graded activity but an aid to better understand their new text.*
4. *Correct the inventory in class. Encourage group discussion.*
5. *Provide additional practice for students who have difficulty with one or more segments of the inventory.*

Textbook Inventory

Your textbook is your primary learning tool. Therefore, an inventory is an excellent way to introduce you to your text. How does answering the questions on the inventory help you?

(a) You will see how your book is structured.

(b) You will see the various features of the text that have been added to help you learn.

1. What is the title of this book? *Focus on Physical Science*
2. Who is the publisher? *Charles E. Merrill Publishing Company*
3. Name the 7 Units that your text contains. *Measurement and Motion; Classification of Matter; Changes in Matter; Patterns in Matter; Light and Sound; Energy; Energy Resources for the Future*
4. What aspect of science does this book focus on? *Physical Science*
5. Who are the authors of this book? *Charles Heimler and Jack Price*
6. What is the most recent copyright date? *1981*
7. How many chapters are in the Unit called *Patterns in Matter*? *3*

8. Where could you find information on *work*?
   a. Chapter 2
   b. Section 2:2
   c. Text page 24-25
9. Turn to page 23, line 3.
   a. What is the boldfaced word on this line? force
   b. What does this word mean? a push or pull
10. Look at the *Examples* on pages 30 and 49. Why have these been included? to show you how to apply your math skills in physical science
11. Turn to page 13. What do the photos on this page show? how to read a graduated cylinder
12. Turn to page 18.
    a. What will you learn from the *Activity* on this page? how to construct a time/temperature graph
    b. What kind of information do you find under *Setting Up*? materials list
    c. What kind of information do you find under *Getting Started*? how to do the activity
    d. What do you do under *Keeping Track*? record your data
    e. Why have the authors included FIGURE 1-15? to show you how to set up your equipment for the Activity
13. On what pages can you find pictures of convex lenses? 328, 329, 331, 332
14. What is the author's purpose for including
    a. the photo on page 8? to show you how to set up the Activity
    b. *Goals* found in the left margins at the beginning of each chapter? know your purpose for reading the chapter
    c. the blue-inked marginal questions? highlight important points, help you review
    d. *Points to Remember* at the end of each chapter? highlight important points
    e. the blue numbers after each of the *Points to Remember*? to show you which numbered section each point comes from
    f. *Readings to Discover* at the end of each chapter? sources for additional information
    g. words in bold type throughout the text? to highlight important science terms
    h. *Activities*? to give you practical experiences
15. What is the title of *Appendix A*? Units of Measurement and the International System
    Appendix B? Laboratory Techniques
16. What word does the abbreviation km stand for? kilometers
17. How many centimeters are there in a kilometer? 10 000
18. K is the abbreviation for which temperature scale? kelvin
19. You must locate a table showing the types of simple machines. How can this be done quickly and efficiently? using the index
20. Why has the author included the diagrams in Appendix B? to show you good technique, which may give you better results in the Activities
21. Turn to Appendix B:6. What do you do if
    a. you spill acid on yourself or your clothing? wash with plenty of water and notify your teacher
    b. you burn yourself? immerse in cold water and notify your teacher
22. Does this book have a glossary? yes
23. What is the purpose of a glossary? provides definitions and pronunciations for new terms you may not know

Table of Contents

Unit 1

This unit begins the study of your physical environment. You may wonder what skateboarding, riding a roller coaster, or running a race have to do with physical science. Each activity makes use of measurement, motion, and shows applications of physical laws.

Measurement and Motion

teacher insert George Anderson/ICOM *skate insert Colour Library International (USA) Ltd.* *Rick Norton/Kings Island*

The person pictured here may be similar to your idea of a scientist, but is it a correct idea? Is a scientist someone who merely works in a laboratory or studies science? Could you be considered a scientist? Chapter 1 will give you some idea of what science is and what a scientist does.

Eric Hoffbines

The Nature of Science

1

Chapter 1 introduces physical science as the study of matter and energy. Measurements and their applications are emphasized as they relate to science and everyday life. See the Teacher's Guide at the front of this book for additional teaching strategies for this chapter.

1:1 Physical Science

GOAL: *You will learn how measurements, experiments, and other scientific methods are used in physical science.*

Physical science is the study of matter and energy. **Matter** is the "stuff" that makes up the universe. Your body, this book, and your desk are matter. Anything that takes up space and has mass is matter. In physical science, you will learn the properties of metals, water, air, and many other kinds of matter. A **property** describes how matter behaves. Hardness is a property of diamonds. They are difficult to scratch. The color black is a property of coal. It appears black because it absorbs light well.

What is physical science?

List three examples of matter.

You will also learn the properties of electricity, sound, heat, and light. These are forms of **energy.** Matter and energy are related to each other. *Anything that has energy can move itself or some other object*. For example, you can measure your body temperature with a thermometer. The heat energy in your body causes the liquid in the thermometer to rise.

Name three kinds of energy.

Making Sure

1. When you pedal a bicycle, what supplies the energy? *the rider* What moves? *the bicycle and the rider*
2. What supplies your body with energy? *food*

George Kufrin/FPG

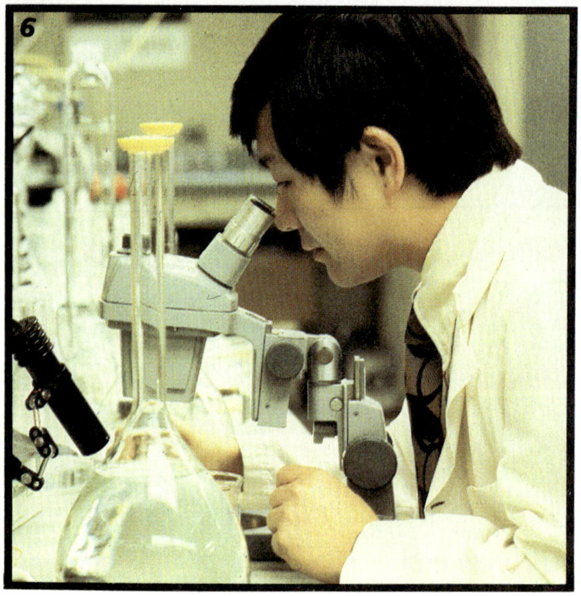

K. Brown

FIGURE 1-1. Not all scientific tools are found only in a laboratory. What measurement tool would you use at a swim meet that could be considered a scientific tool?

A stopwatch or other timing device

1:2 Methods of Science

In science certain methods are used to develop and test ideas. A scientist will make observations, propose and test ideas, and form conclusions.

Name three tools used to make observations.

Observation is basic to science. For example, you look at the sky. You say it is cloudy. This statement is an observation. Special tools are often used to make observations. Some of these tools are a ruler, thermometer, and microscope. What are some tools you have used to make observations? *answers will vary*

What is a hypothesis?

Using observations and facts, a scientist can propose a hypothesis (hi PAHTH uh sus). A **hypothesis** is a scientific "guess." It is a suggested answer to a question or a solution to a problem. Once a hypothesis is proposed it must be tested. For example, a scientist makes this hypothesis: A homing pigeon uses the sun to find its way home. To test the hypothesis, the scientist releases 25 pigeons from some point on a sunny day. The scientist waits to see how many pigeons return. Next, 25 pigeons are released at the same point on a cloudy day. Again, the scientist waits to see how many birds come home. All 25 pigeons came home on the sunny day. On the cloudy day, only 10 pigeons returned.

What is a conclusion? Give two examples.

The scientist concluded that pigeons use the sun in finding their way home. A **conclusion** is a judgment based on observations. However, the conclusion may not be correct. Perhaps a storm prevented the flock from returning on the cloudy day. Can you think of other reasons? *answers will vary*

You see the sun shining when you wake up in the morning. You might conclude that it is going to be a nice day. You have made a judgment based on what you observed. You may be right or wrong.

In actual practice, the methods of science are not exact. The work of successful scientists shows it is not always a step-by-step process. Skill, luck, trial and error, and intelligent guessing all play a part.

1-1

ACTIVITY *How well do you observe?*

Have someone place 15 to 20 small objects on a tray. Cover the tray. When the tray is uncovered each student will get 10 seconds to observe the objects on the tray. Your teacher or someone in the class will keep time. Once you have seen the objects on the tray go back to your seat and list as many as you can. Compare your list with others in the class to see who has named the most objects.

How could a tape recorder or camera help you in this activity?

Any number of objects can be used: pencil, thimble, tape, paper clips. Simple objects will be easier to remember.

A camera would take pictures for further study later. A person could "read" the contents from the tray to the tape recorder. These are becoming important tools to the scientist.

1:3 Using Experiments

How can you keep a record of an experiment?

In your study of physical science you will conduct experiments. You might want to keep a record of your experiments in a notebook. Scientists must always keep accurate records of their work. Your experimental work could be organized as follows:

(1) **Problem.** What question do you hope to answer in doing this experiment?

(2) **Procedure.** What things are you doing?

(3) **Observations.** What do you see, hear, or smell? What changes have occurred?

(4) **Conclusion.** Based on your observations, what is your answer to the question?

Stress the importance that scientists attach to a notebook. Students should try to keep a notebook of classroom Activities and notes. Time spent now in helping students organize information will benefit them throughout the whole year.

Background information concerning the structure and types of activities in this text can be found in the Teacher's Guide at the front of this book.

1-2 **ACTIVITY**

Background information concerning the structure and types of activities in this text can be found in the Teacher's Guide at the front of this book.

Does air expand or contract when heated?

Hickson-Bender Photography

FIGURE 1-2.

Carefully insert glass tubes into two one-hole rubber stoppers. **CAUTION:** *Moisten the tubes with water or mineral oil and hold the glass tubes with a towel. Attach two balloons which are not inflated to the tubes using a piece of string. Obtain two flasks. Label them* **A** *and* **B.** *Insert a stopper into each flask. Use a hot plate to heat flask* **A** *until a change occurs in the balloon. What do you observe about flask* **A?** *Cool flask* **A** *for a short time, then place it in a pan of ice.*

What changes do you observe? Why?

the balloon expands

the balloon contracts, gases contract when cooled

Lab Report

Problem: Does air expand or contract when heated?

Procedure: Use a hot plate to heat the assembly for flask A. Flask B is used as a control. Flask A is cooled and placed in a pan of ice.

Observations: The balloon on Flask A expands when the flask is heated. The balloon contracts when flask A is cooled. Flask B remains unchanged.

Conclusion: Air in a balloon expands when heated.

FIGURE 1-3. Sample lab report

What is a control in an experiment?

Describe an example of a control in an experiment.

Many experiments have a control. A **control** is a standard for comparison. The control can be part of the procedure. In the heated air experiment, you assembled two balloons and flasks. Both flasks are exactly alike. The unheated flask, flask **B,** is your control. *Note that flask B does not change.*

Making Sure

See the Teacher's Guide at the front of this book.

3. List the problem, procedure, observations, and conclusion for the pigeon experiment.
4. A medical scientist tests a new drug. Two groups of people are selected who have the disease the drug is intended to cure. One group is given the drug. The other is not. What is the control? *group not given the drug*

1:4 Theories and Laws

A scientific **theory** (THEE uh ree) is an explanation based on observations and experiments. For example, there are several theories to explain how birds find their way when they travel. One theory is that they use the earth's magnetic field. Another is that they are guided by the sun. Birds that travel long distances may be guided by the stars.

What is a scientific theory?

A scientific **law** is a description of how the universe behaves. It is based on the information collected by many people. For example, matter can be changed to energy. This statement is a scientific law.

Point out that theories are different than laws. A law is a description of an observed phenomenon. A theory is an explanation for what is observed.

Theories and laws can be changed. They are tested often. If a new observation shows a theory or law to be wrong, it is changed or discarded. For example, at one time the following was a law: Matter can neither be created nor destroyed. New observations showed this statement was not always true. Under certain conditions, matter changes to energy.

When are theories and laws changed?

1:5 Measurement

Measurement is a basic part of science. Numbers and units are used to make measurements. You are already aware of some of the numbers and units used in measuring things.

How do you measure something?

The use of English units will be kept to a minimum in this text. Students are encouraged to use SI as the principal system of measurement. Conversions between measurement systems are generally not used in order to get students to think in terms of SI.

Think about how you would measure the length of any object. You might think you need a ruler. However, you could pick any object and use its length as your ruler. You could use the length of your shoe as a ruler to measure long distances. You could measure the distance from your seat to your teacher's desk by walking with one foot directly in front of the other.

This distance may be 25 shoe lengths. If others in your class measured the same distance, would they get the same measurement? The sizes of shoes for all the people in your class could be quite different. You can see that your measurement unit, though usable, is not practical. To make practical measurements, a measurement standard must be used. A **standard** is a fixed quantity used by everyone when measuring.

What is a measurement standard?

Point out that any unit will work as long as everyone agrees on the unit.

You might ask why is it important for the people of the world to have the same measurement systems. Obviously, scientists are not the only people affected by measurement.

FIGURE 1-4.

What system of measurement is used by scientists?

Some of the measurement standards you have used are part of the English system of measurement. The foot, yard, and mile are all English units for measuring length. However, most of the people in the world do not use English units to express their measurements. Most people use another system of units called the **metric system.** Scientists in all countries use these units in their work. Scientists everywhere can understand each other's measurements. The modern form of the metric system is called the **International System of Units** or **SI.** Prefixes are used to change the units by multiples of 10. Changing from one unit to another is easier than with English units.

Table 1-1

Important Measurement Prefixes

Prefix	Symbol	Factor by which unit is multiplied
kilo-	k	1000
centi-	c	0.01
milli-	m	0.001

1:6 Measuring Length

What metric units are used to measure length?

The **meter (m)** is a unit of length. A meter is about the distance from a doorknob to the floor. A golf club is also about a meter in length.

The meter is divided into 100 equal parts called **centimeters (cm).** The prefix *centi-* is similar to cent. There are 100 cents in a dollar. There are 100 centimeters in a meter.

An even smaller unit is a **millimeter (mm).** There are 1000 millimeters in a meter. The prefix *milli-* means 1/1000 (one thousandth). There are 10 millimeters in 1 centimeter.

Explain the meaning of these prefixes: centi-, milli-, kilo-

Long distances are measured in **kilometers (km).** A kilometer is 1000 meters. The prefix *kilo-* means 1000. A kilometer is about 5 city blocks in length.

Changing from one unit to another is easy. You divide or multiply by multiples of 10. For example, 945 millimeters equal 94.5 centimeters or 0.945 meters. *Remind students that division by multiples of ten moves the decimal point to the left; multiplication moves it to the right.*

Thomas Russell

Background information concerning the structure and types of activities in this text can be found in the Teacher's Guide at the front of this book.

FIGURE 1-5.

1-3

ACTIVITY How do you measure distances using a map?

Figure 1-6 is a map of one section of a park. Use a metric ruler to measure the distances between the points listed in the table. Using the scale provided on the map, convert your measurements to kilometers.

HOW FAR IS IT FROM THE	mm	cm	using scale Km
ROCK MASS TO THE LAKE			
MEADOW TO THE PICNIC AREA			
HICKORY GROVE TO THE LAKE			
PINE FOREST TO THE PICNIC AREA			

FIGURE 1-6.

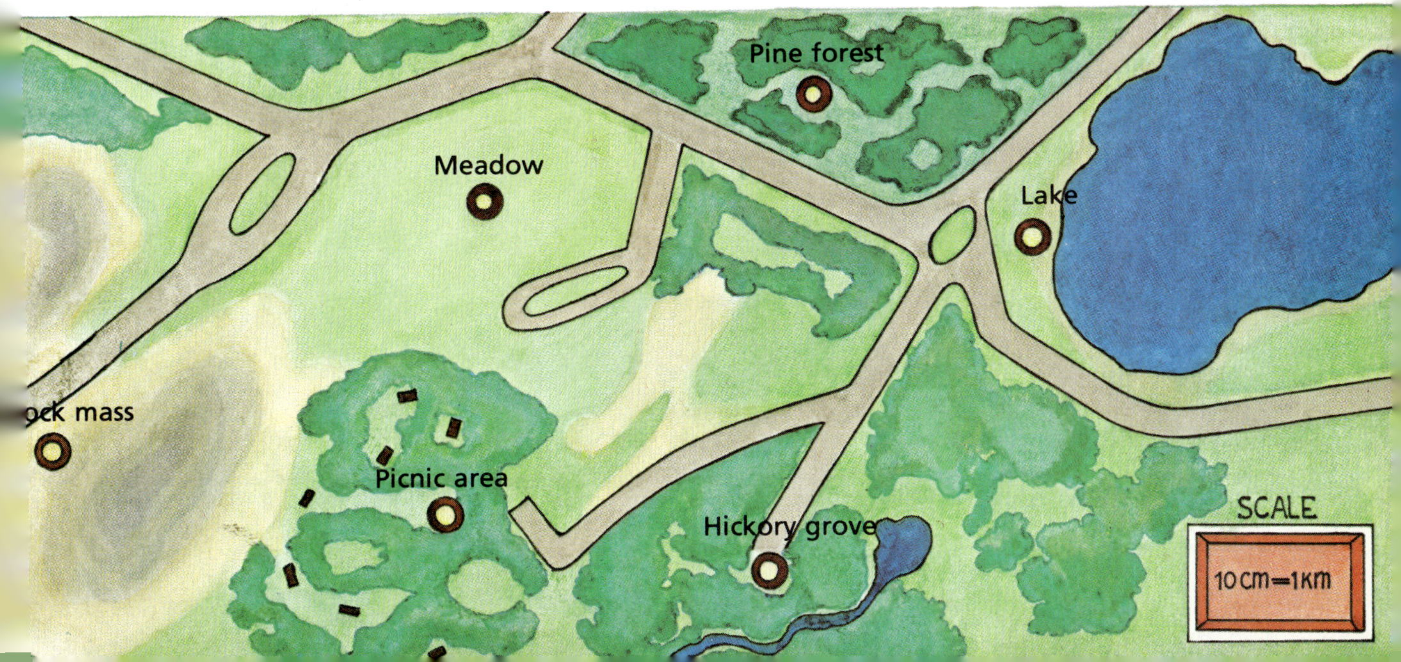

Making Sure

88 km/h

5. What is the speed limit on a state highway in kilometers per hour?
6. Name three things that are about one meter long.
7. Name three things that are measured in centimeters.
8. Name three things that are small enough to be measured in millimeters.

golf club, bath towel are two examples

fingernail, book cover, notebook paper are some examples

wire diameter, film, thickness of a book, tape are some examples

1:7 Measuring Volume

For reference, point out that a quart is slightly less than a liter.

Name three units used to measure volume.

A unit of volume often represents the length, width, and height of an object. The units for volume are derived from units of length. A cubic meter (m^3) is a unit of volume. However, a cubic meter is a very large unit, Figure 1-7. Throughout this book, smaller volume units will be used. The liter (L) is one such unit. Many soft drinks are now available in liter bottles. For even smaller volume measurements, we will use the milliliter (mL) or cubic centimeter (cm^3). One liter contains 1000 milliliters or 1000 cubic centimeters.

FIGURE 1-7. The cubic meter is a large unit of volume. Smaller volume units are more useful for everyday activities.

a

Hickson-Bender Photography

b

Thomas Russell

Graduated cylinders are the tools used for measuring liquid volumes. They are made in many sizes like measuring cups for the kitchen. The level of a liquid in a graduated cylinder shows the volume of the liquid. In Figure 1-8a, you see that the level of the liquid is curved. To read the volume of the liquid, note the level at the bottom of the curve.

How can you measure volume with a graduated cylinder?

The curve is called a meniscus. Only mercury has a convex meniscus. Caution students to read volume at the bottom of the curve from eye level.

Hickson-Bender Photography

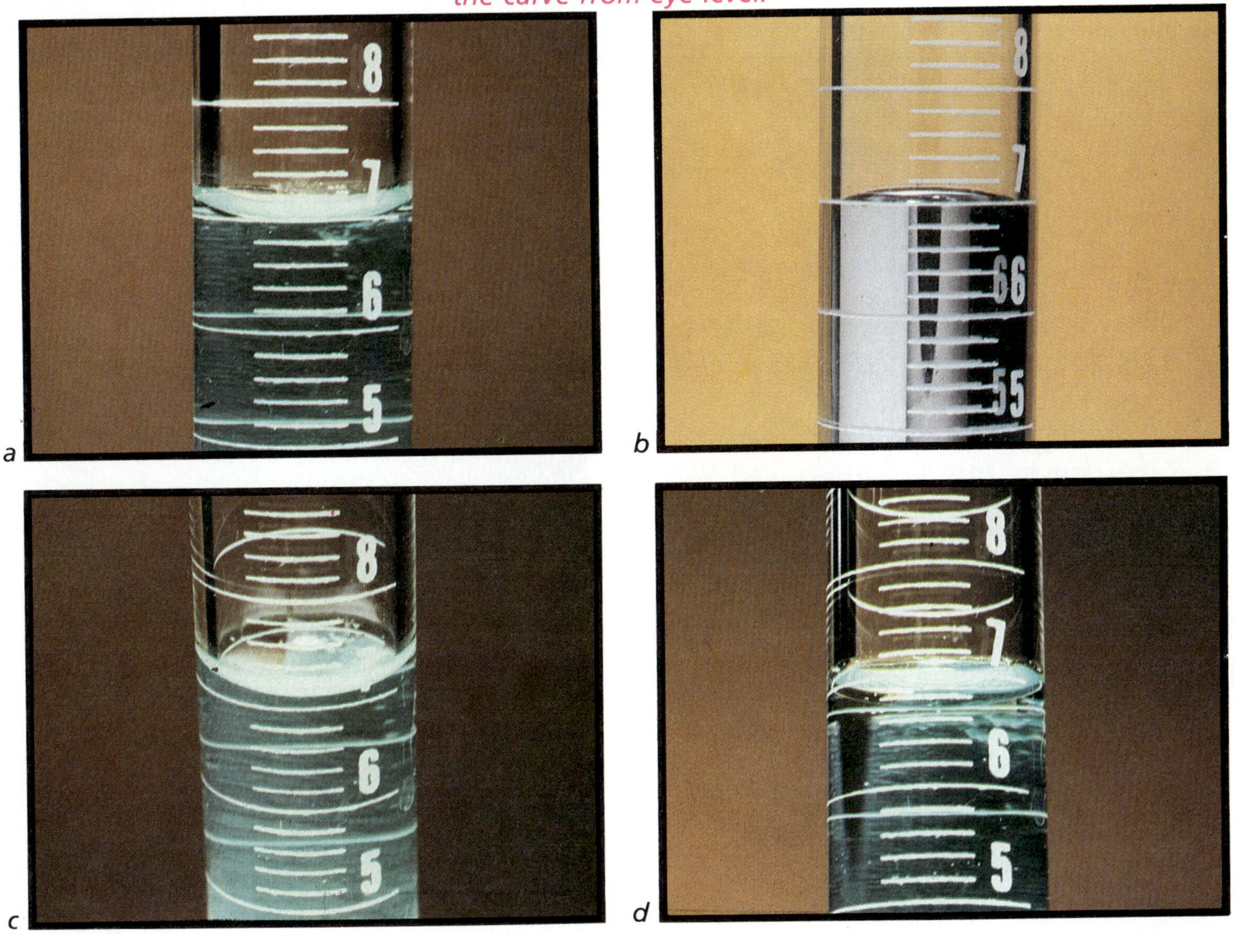

FIGURE 1-8. The volume of liquid in (a) is 7 mL. The volume of mercury in (b) is 7 mL. In reading the liquid level, keep the liquid surface at eye level. Photos (c) and (d) show errors you can make in reading the same liquid level shown in (a).

1-4

Activity

How do you measure volume?

Setting Up

250 mL beaker
400 mL beaker
blocks of wood or metal
lead sinker
string
3 test tubes (different sizes)

You may wish them to work in pairs or trios for this Activity. Students will measure volumes using three different methods.

They should record any data collected under "Keeping Track" in their notebooks.

Getting Started

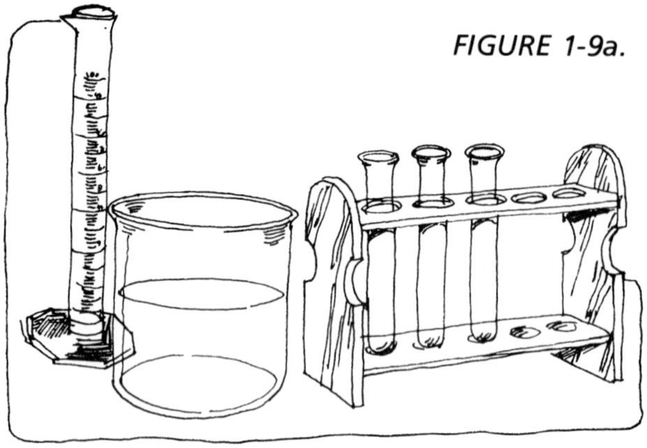

FIGURE 1-9a.

Part A

1. *Obtain three test tubes of different sizes, a 25 mL graduated cylinder, and a beaker.*
2. *Fill the beaker half full with water.*
3. *Take one of the test tubes and fill it with water from the beaker.*
4. *Now pour the water from the filled test tube into the graduated cylinder. Set up a table like the one on page 15. Record the volume of the water.*
5. *Repeat Steps 3 and 4 with the other test tubes.*

FIGURE 1-9b.

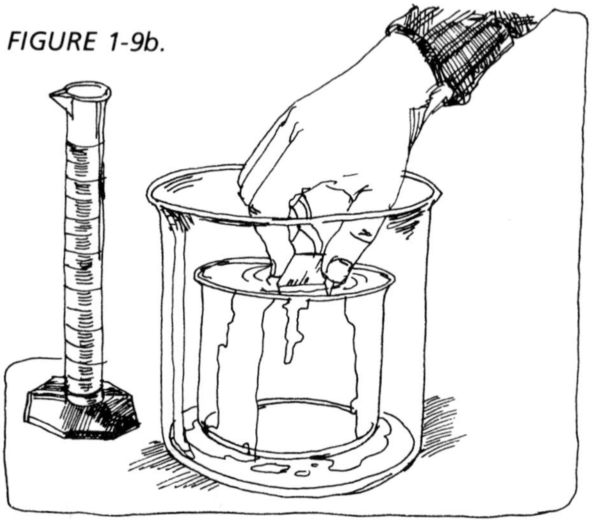

Part B

1. *Place a 250 mL beaker inside a 400 mL beaker. Fill the smaller beaker to the top with water.*
2. *Measure the length, width, and height of a block of wood or metal. Record these measurements in the table.*
3. *Gently place the block in the 250 mL beaker. You may have to push the wood block under the water. Some of the water will overflow into the larger beaker.*
4. *Remove the 250 mL beaker and pour the overflow water from the larger beaker into a graduated cylinder.*
5. *Record the volume of the overflow in the table.*
6. *Repeat Steps 1 through 5 with other blocks. Record all measurements.*

Part C

1. *Fill a 25 mL graduated cylinder to the 10 mL mark with water.*
2. *Obtain a small lead sinker and tie a string to it.*
3. *Lower the sinker into the cylinder until it is submerged, Figure 1-9c.*
4. *Read the level of the water. Record the amount the water level rises.*
5. *Record the volume of the sinker.*

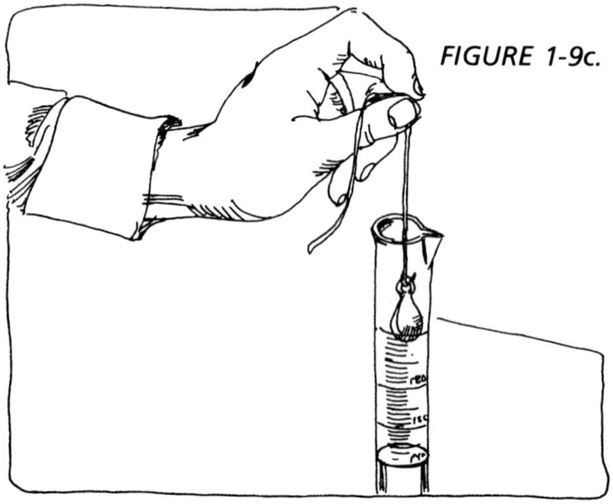

FIGURE 1-9c.

Keeping Track

Part A	1	2	3
volume of test tubes			

Part B

volume of block 1 (length x width x height) ______ cm^3
volume of overflow ______ mL

Part C

volume of water level rise ______ mL
volume of sinker ______ mL

Summing Up

See the Teacher's Guide at the front of this book.

1. *In Part B, how does the volume of the block compare with the volume of the overflow? Should they be the same? Why might they be different?*
2. *In Part C, how does the volume of the sinker compare with the rise in the water level? Should they be the same? Why might they be different?*
3. *Which procedure (Part A, B, or C) would you use to measure the volume of a vase?* *A*
4. *Which procedure would you use to measure the volume of a handful of sand?* *A*
5. *Which procedure would you use to measure the volume of an aquarium?* *B or C*

Making Sure

9. What is the volume of liquid shown in Figure 1-8a? *7 mL*

10. What are some of the units of volume used in cooking? Why is it easier to use metric units?

teaspoon, tablespoon, cup are some examples

11. How much water will fill a dish 25 cm × 25 cm × 5 cm? *3125 cm^3*

Metric units are multiples of ten so conversion from one unit to another is easy. With English units, conversion factors between units must be memorized.

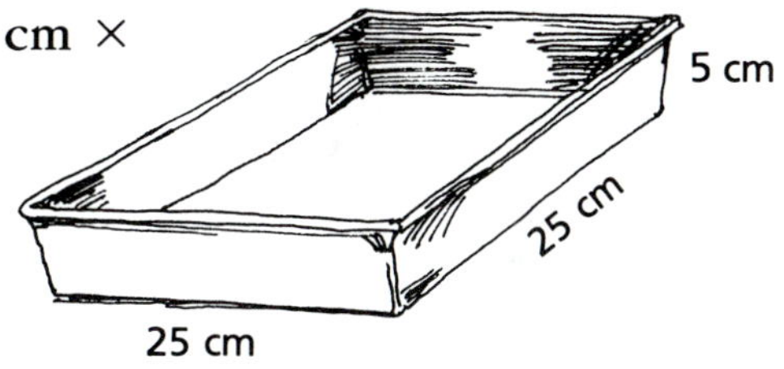

1:8 Measuring Weight and Mass

How is weight different from mass?

Weight is a measure of the force or pull of gravity on an object. Your own weight is the force of gravity that pulls you down to the earth. The unit of force is the **newton (N).** Weight may be measured with a spring scale, Figure 1-10a. Pounds and ounces are English units of weight or force.

Hickson-Bender Photography

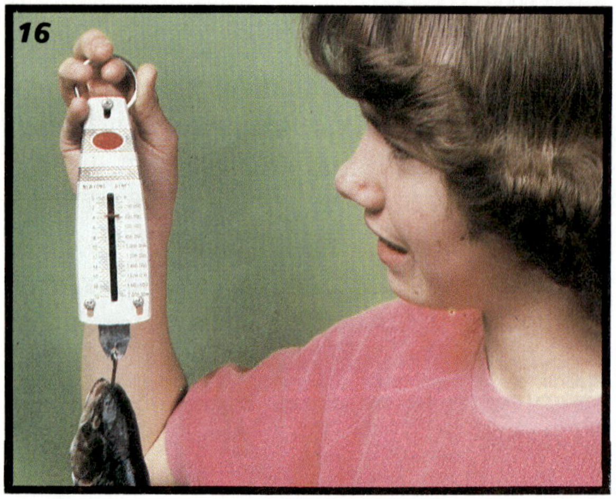

Thomas Russell

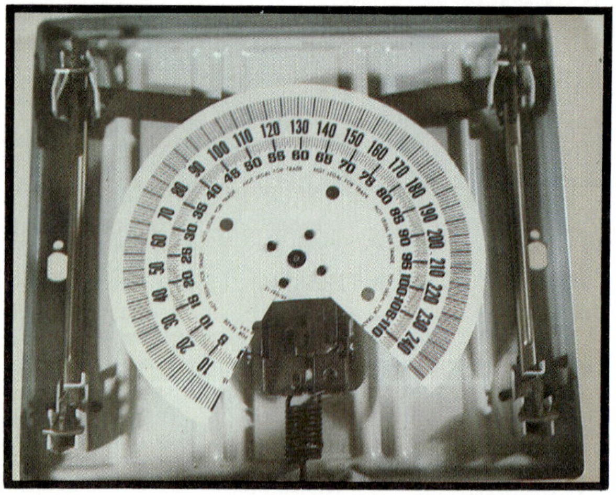

FIGURE 1-10. Weight is measured with a spring scale. Your bathroom scale is also a spring scale.

Mass is the amount of matter in an object. Mass does not depend on gravity. The **kilogram (kg)** is a unit of mass. Your book has a mass of about 1.2 kilograms. The kilogram is divided into 1000 equal parts called **grams (g).** A paper clip has a mass close to 1 gram. One milliliter of water has a mass of a gram at room temperature. What do you think the mass of your book is in grams? *about 1200 grams*

What units are used to measure mass?

Mass may be measured with a **balance,** Figure 1-12. An object of unknown mass is placed on the left pan of the balance. Objects of known mass are placed on the right pan. When the two pans are in balance, the mass of the objects on the right pan equals the mass of the objects on the left pan.

FIGURE 1-11. One liter of water has a mass of one kilogram. One milliliter of water has a mass of one gram. The masses shown by the riders on the balances account for the masses of the containers.

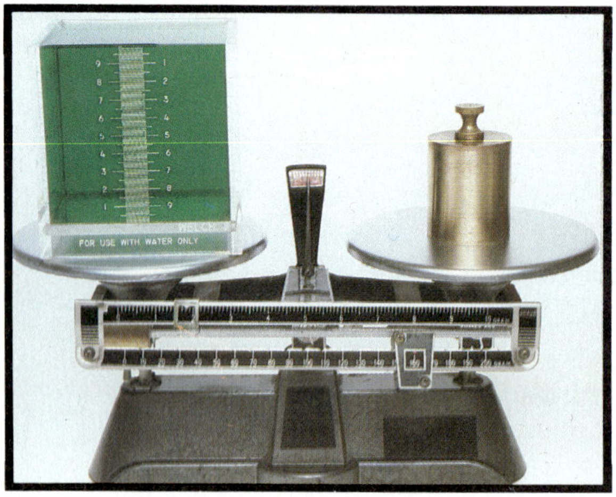

Hickson-Bender Photography

1-5 *Detailed information concerning this Activity can be found in the Teacher's Guide at the front of this book.*

ACTIVITY *How do you measure mass with a balance?*

Craig Kramer

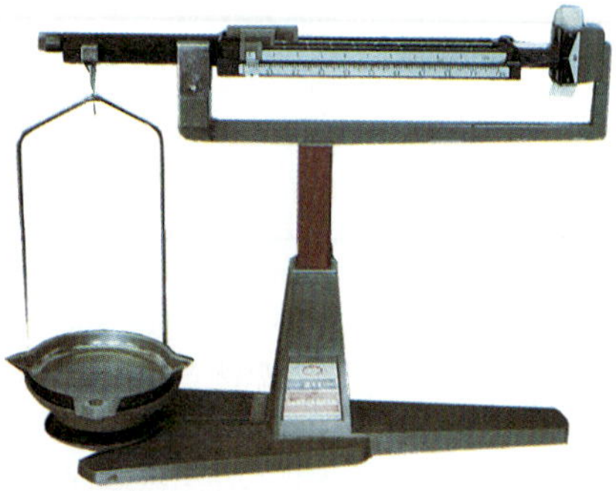

FIGURE 1-12. A balance.

***(1)** Obtain a balance and refer to the Appendix for instructions on how to use it. **(2)** Your teacher will give you three objects. Measure the mass of each. Make a table for recording these masses. **(3)** Obtain a clean, dry beaker. Find the mass of the beaker. **(4)** Fill the beaker half full of water. Find the mass of the water and beaker. Record all measurements.*

What is the mass of the water? How did you get this number? How would you find the mass of air in a balloon?

FIGURE 1-13.

1:9 Measuring Temperature

How is temperature measured?

In science, temperature is measured using the **Celsius temperature scale.** The temperature in the weather report is often listed in degrees Celsius. This temperature scale is based on the freezing and boiling points of water. The freezing point of water is given the value of 0°C. The boiling point of water is labeled as 100°C.

FIGURE 1-14. Measuring temperature

1-6 **Activity** *How do you construct a time/temperature graph?*

Setting Up

400 mL beaker, ice, ring stand, Bunsen burner, wire screen, metal ring, thermometer

Getting Started

1. *Fill the beaker half full of ice and water.*
2. *Set up the apparatus as in Figure 1-15.*
3. *Heat the beaker and record the temperature in a table like the one below at the end of every minute. Do this until the temperature of the water reaches 100°C.*

Keeping Track

Time	Temperature

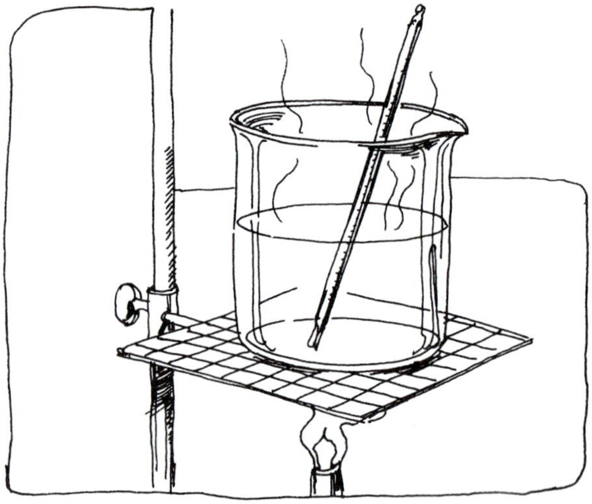

FIGURE 1-15.

Summing Up

1. *Make a graph of the temperature and time data in the table. Label the y-axis for temperature and the x-axis for time.*
2. *When does the temperature begin to rise?* *after all the ice melts*
3. *When does the temperature stop rising?* *after the water begins boiling*

Points to Remember

1. Physical science is the study of matter and energy. *1:1*
2. A hypothesis is formed based on observations and facts. *1:2*
3. Hypotheses, theories, and scientific laws are tested by experiments. *1:3*
4. Scientists use the metric system as standards for measurement. *1:5*
5. Prefixes are used to change metric units by multiples of ten. *1:5*
6. Weight is the measure of force on an object. Mass is the amount of matter in the object. *1:8*
7. The Celsius temperature scale is based on the freezing and boiling points of water. *1:9*

Words to Use

Write a sentence in which you correctly use each of the following words.

conclusion	hypothesis	meter
control	law	observation
experiment	liter	standard
kilogram	mass	theory

Questions for Review

Do not write in this book.

A. True or False *Have students rewrite the false statements to make them true.*

Determine whether each of the following sentences is true or false.

T **1.** A ruler, graduated cylinder, microscope are tools used in science.

F **2.** A hypothesis is always true. *not*

T **3.** Every experiment has a procedure.

F **4.** The control in an experiment is the same as a conclusion. *not*

F **5.** A scientific law can ~~never~~ be changed.

T **6.** Metric units are used by scientists.

F 7. The liter is the unit of ~~mass.~~ volume

F 8. Mass is measured in ~~newtons.~~ kilograms

F 9. Mass and weight are ~~the same.~~ different

T 10. Temperature is measured in degrees Celsius.

B. Multiple Choice

Choose the word or phrase that correctly completes each of the following sentences.

1. A meter equals *(10, 100, 1000, 10 000)* centimeters.
2. The prefix centi- means *(10, 100, 1/100, 1/1000)*.
3. There are *(1, 10, 100, 1000)* millimeters in a centimeter.
4. The prefix milli- means *(10, 100, 1000, 1/1000)*.
5. The prefix kilo- means *(10, 100, 1000, 1/1000)*.
6. There are *(10, 100, 1000, 1/1000)* grams in a kilogram.
7. One cubic centimeter equals one *(milliliter, liter, kilogram, kilometer)*.
8. A milliliter of water has a mass of *(0.1, 1, 10, 100)* grams.
9. There are *(10, 100, 1000)* milliliters in a liter.
10. A meter stick is used to measure *(length, volume, mass)*.

C. Completion

Complete each of the following sentences with a word or phrase that will make the sentence correct.

1. One centimeter equals __1/100__ meter (s).
2. __100__ centimeters equal one meter.
3. A liter is a unit of __volume__.
4. A stone is dropped into a graduated cylinder. The volume of the water rises from 18 to 22 milliliters. The volume of the stone is __4__ milliliters.
5. A graduated cylinder contains 15 milliliters of water. The mass of this water is __15__ grams.
6. Metric units can be changed by multiples of __10__.
7. The __Celsius__ temperature scale is used in science.
8. The cubic centimeter (cm^3) is a unit of __volume__.

9. In the metric system, weight is measured in *newtons*.
10. One liter contains *1000* cubic centimeters.

Detailed answers to these questions are given in the Teacher's Guide at the front of this book.

D. How and Why

1. Name five tools used to make measurements. What units are used with each?
2. What is physical science?
3. What are the advantages to the use of metric units?
4. What tools do you use to measure mass and volume in the laboratory?
5. Change the following to liters: 250 mL, 100 mL, 500 mL.
6. Change the following to milliliters: 1 L, 0.5 L.
7. Change the following to meters: 55 cm, 550 cm, 5500 mm.

Detailed answers to these questions are given in the Teacher's Guide at the front of this book.

More Ideas to Explore

1. Through library research, prepare a report on metrology, the study of measurement.
2. Write to the National Bureau of Standards, Washington, D.C. for information about this agency. Make a report to your class.
3. Snow and water skis are sold in centimeter lengths. Find out how you would go about purchasing the proper length skis.
4. How does the scale used in the doctor's office differ from your bathroom scale?

Readings to Discover

Bendick, Jeanne, *Measuring.* NY: F. Watts, 1971.

Gallant, Roy A., *Man the Measurer: Our Units of Measure and How They Grew.* Garden City, NY: Doubleday and Co., 1972.

Klein, A. Arthur, *The World of Measurements: Masterpieces, Mysteries, and Muddles of Metrology.* NY: Simon and Schuster, Inc., 1974.

Moorman, Thomas, *How to Make Your Science Project Scientific.* NY: Atheneum Publishers, 1974.

Norris, Jane, "Metrics and Me." Indianapolis, IN: *Youth Publications, Saturday Evening Post,* 1976.

A watch is a measurement tool we use to measure time. As you can see, a watch is much more than a measurement tool. A watch is a machine. Chapter 2 will tell you how machines, like the watch, make our work easier.

Larry Hamill

Force and Work 2

Chapter 2 develops the concepts of force, work, and power. Simple and compound machines are presented with an emphasis on how work is made easier and power is increased by using machines. See the Teacher's Guide at the front of this book for additional teaching strategies for this chapter.

2:1 Force

GOAL: *You will learn how machines change forces and do work.*

Kick a soccerball. Throw a baseball. Pound a nail into a board. In each case an object is moved. It takes a force to put an object into motion. A **force** is a push or pull.

List three examples of forces.

Does a force always produce motion? Push down on your desk top as hard as you can or push against the wall in your room. Does the desk or wall move? Press the palms of your hands together and push hard. The force of one hand opposes the force of the other hand. Your hands will not move if the two opposing forces are balanced. **Balanced** means the forces are equal and opposite each other. **Unbalanced** means one force must be greater than the force that opposes motion. *Motion occurs when the opposing forces are unbalanced.* When you push down on your desk, you can think of the desk pushing up with an equal force. The opposing forces are balanced, so the desk does not move.

When does a force produce motion?

The force required to set an object in motion can be calculated. The size of the force depends on the mass of the object being moved and the rate at which the motion of the object changes. It takes less force to move your book than to move your desk. Your book has less mass.

Point out that force is related to both mass and rate.

What unit is used to measure force?

The weight of an object is also a measure of force, Section 1:8. Weight is measured with a spring scale. The unit of force is the newton (N). The exact definition of a newton will be discussed in Chapter 4.

2-1 Detailed information concerning this Activity can be found in the Teacher's Guide at the front of this book.

ACTIVITY *How do you make your own spring scale to measure force?*

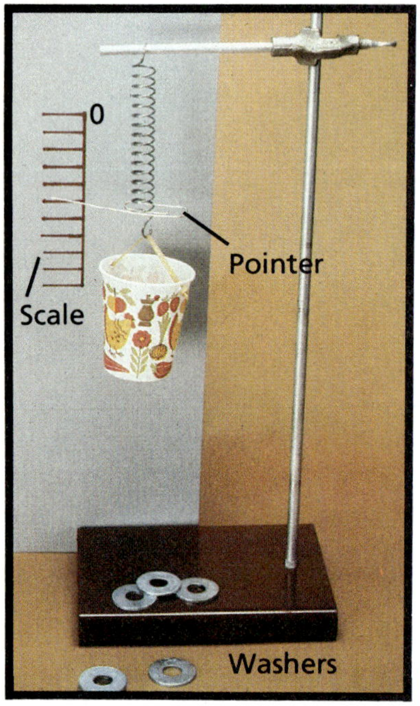

FIGURE 2-1. Hickson-Bender Photography

(1) *Set up the ring stand and extension clamp as shown in Figure 2-1.* **(2)** *Use string to tie the spring to the extension clamp.* **(3)** *Bend a paper clip to form a pointer and attach it to the bottom end of the spring.* **(4)** *Cut off the bottom end of a paper cup. Use string to attach the bottom of the cup to the spring.* **(5)** *Set up a piece of cardboard behind your apparatus as in Figure 2-1. Mark the position of the pointer and label it zero.* **(6)** *Now add a metal washer to the cup. Mark the new position of the pointer on the cardboard.* **(7)** *Repeat Step 6 adding another washer each time until you have ten washers in the cup. DO NOT OVERLOAD THE SPRING.* **(8)** *Use your spring scale to determine the force needed to hold a marble, pencil, and ruler. Record the force (weight) of each object in terms of your washer-weight scale.*

Why aren't washers used as standard units of force instead of newtons? If you overloaded the spring, how would it affect your results?

washers vary in size and shape

The spring would not return to the zero point. Lighter objects would appear to weigh less.

Making Sure

1. What force moves your body parts? muscles on bones
2. How could you exert a force to lift yourself? How large would this force be in comparison to your weight? See the Teacher's Guide.

2:2 Work

What is the definition of work?

Mowing a lawn is work. Washing a car and lifting weights are other examples of work. In science, work has a precise definition. **Work** is the product of the force applied to an object and the distance the object moves.

$$work = force \times distance$$

$$W = F \times d$$

Force is measured in newtons and distance is measured in meters. The unit for work is the **joule** (JEWL) **(J).** One joule is the amount of energy or work required to maintain a force of one newton through a distance of one meter. If you lift a box 1 meter using 10 newtons of force, you do 10 joules of work.

The SI unit, joule, will be used throughout the book as the unit for work and energy.

How much work is in one joule?

stress 1 J = 1 N·m

Example

A force of 100 newtons is applied in lifting a concrete block 1.5 meters. How much work is done in lifting the block?

Solution:

(a) Write the equation for work.

$$W = F \times d$$

(b) Substitute the values for force and distance given in the problem.

$$W = 100 \text{ N} \times 1.5 \text{ m}$$
$$W = 150 \text{ N}\cdot\text{m} = 150 \text{ J}$$

Making Sure

3. A suitcase which weighs 60 newtons is lifted 0.5 meter. How much work is done in lifting the suitcase? *30 J*
4. A force of 14 newtons is used to push the suitcase in problem 3 a distance of 0.5 meter across the floor. How much work is done? *7 J*
5. Which is more work, lifting a suitcase 0.5 meter or pushing it a distance of 0.5 meter? Why? *friction exerts less force than gravity*
6. A force of 40 newtons is used to push a desk 4 meters across a room. Calculate the work done. *160 J*

2:3 Machines

A machine makes work easier by changing the direction or distance through which a force moves. Suppose you want to dig a hole to plant a tree. Can you do it using just your fingers? A shovel would make it much easier. A shovel is an example of a simple machine. There are six types of simple machines. They are listed in Table 2-1. A bicycle is a compound machine. A bicycle is made of more than one simple machine.

Name the six types of simple machines.

Table 2-1
Simple Machines

Don Parsisson Don Parsisson Don Parsisson

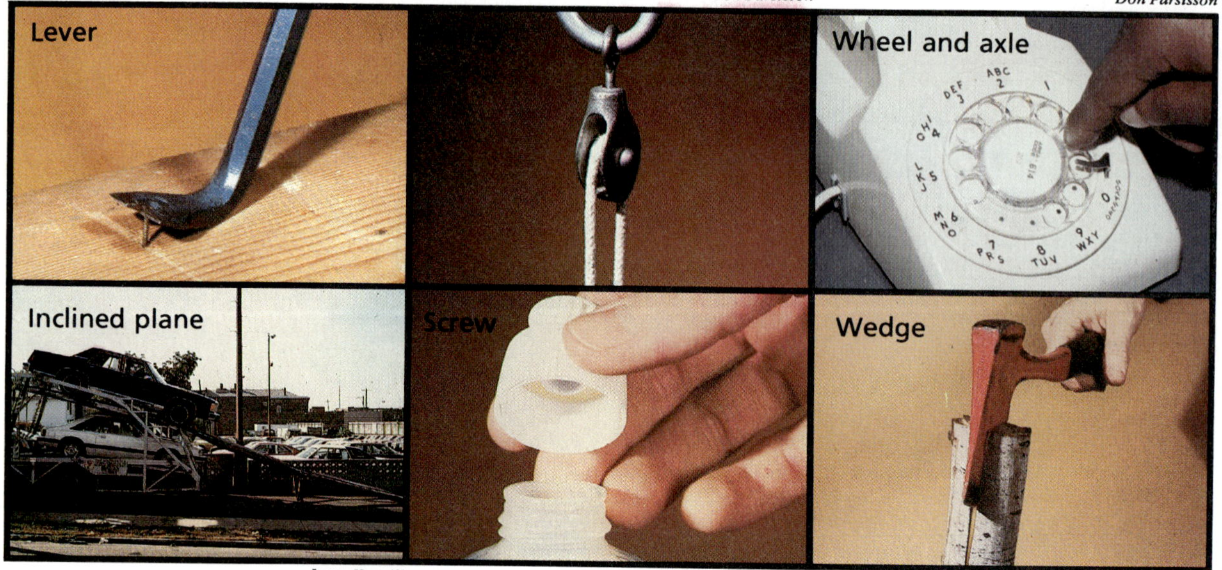

Larry Hamill Don Parsisson Don Parsisson

Table 2-2
Compound Machines

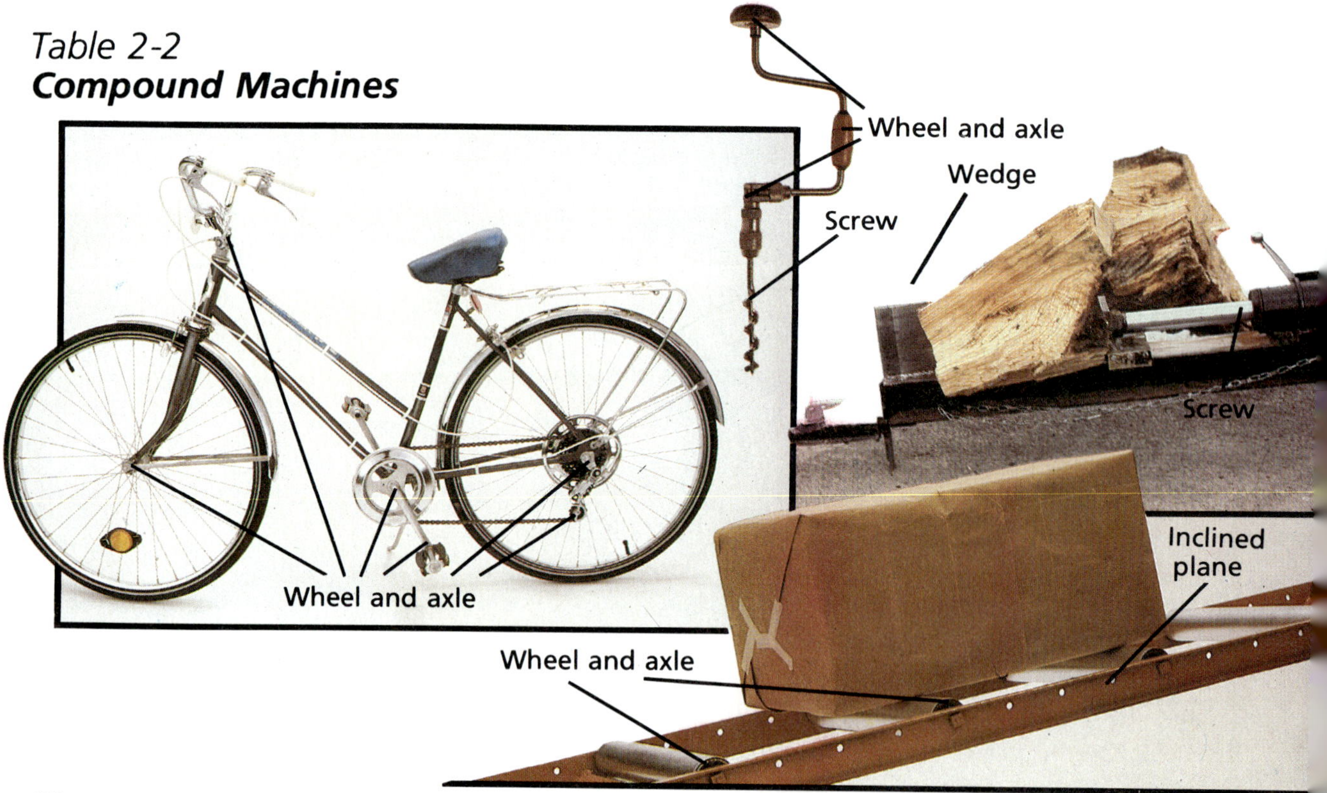

Hickson-Bender Photograp

Some machines make work easier because they increase the amount of force that is applied. For example, a screwdriver increases the force you use to pry the lid from a paint can. The amount by which a machine increases a force is called the **mechanical advantage.** The mechanical advantage of a machine is not always greater than one. Sometimes a gain in force is lost to gain speed or change the direction of the force. For example, the blades of an eggbeater move faster than the handle that turns them.

How does a machine make work easier?

What is the mechanical advantage of a machine?

Friction decreases the mechanical advantage of a machine. **Friction** is a force that opposes motion. It can slow down and wear out the parts of a machine. If you rub your hands together you can feel heat caused by friction. When a machine does work there is friction. Friction always changes work to heat. The energy changed to heat reduces the energy changed to work by the machine. The mechanical advantage of the machine is reduced.

List three examples of friction.

Some machines could not be used to do work without friction. Think of riding a bicycle on an icy surface. There is very little friction between the tires and the ice. The bicycle may not move forward at all. Most tires are designed to increase friction for better traction on the road.

FIGURE 2-2. In basketball, players make use of friction by wearing shoes that grip the floor. In skiing, skis are waxed to reduce friction between them and the snow.

a

Zimmerman/FPG

b

Mr. & Mrs. Pantages

See the Teacher's Guide at the front of this book for detailed answers.

Making Sure

7. How does each of the following machines make work easier?
   (a) bicycle
   (b) oar
   (c) sewing machine
   (d) elevator
8. How does friction interfere in using an oar to move a boat? How does friction help?

Friction opposes the action of lifting the oars out of the water. However, the friction between the oars and water during the stroke moves the boat forward.

Explain how a lever is used to do work.

Bruce D. Sampsel

FIGURE 2-3.

2:4 Levers

A **lever** is a bar that is free to turn about a fixed point. The point at which a lever rotates is called the **fulcrum** (FUL krum). A lever can make work easier. When an effort force is applied to a lever, a resistance force can be overcome. In Figure 2-3, a screwdriver is used as a lever to open a can of paint. The fulcrum of the lever is the inside edge of the can. The effort force is applied to the handle of the screwdriver. The screwdriver pivots about the edge of the can to remove the lid. The resistance force is the friction between the lid and the can.

2-2 Detailed information concerning this Activity can be found in the Teacher's Guide at the front of this book.

ACTIVITY *Can a ruler be a lever?*

(1) Lay a ruler on a pencil so the ruler is balanced. **(2)** *Place a metal washer on the ten centimeter mark of the ruler.* **(3)** *Place another washer on the opposite side of the ruler.* **(4)** *Move the second washer until the ruler is balanced again. Record the position of the second washer.* **(5)** *Lay two washers on top of each other at the ten centimeter mark.* **(6)** *Move the washer on the opposite side until the ruler balances. Record the position of the second washer.*

How do the positions of the washers compare? Why is the ruler in this activity a lever?

The single washers are twice as far from the pencil as the double washers.

The ruler is free to turn on a fulcrum.

There are three types or classes of levers, Table 2-3. These classes are based on the position of the fulcrum, resistance, and effort. In a first class lever, the fulcrum is between the effort and resistance. In a second class lever, the resistance is between the effort and fulcrum. In a third class lever, the effort is between the fulcrum and resistance.

Table 2-3
Levers

Every lever has two parts, an effort arm and resistance arm. The **effort arm** is the distance from the fulcrum to the effort force. The **resistance arm** is the distance from the fulcrum to the resistance force. The **resistance force** is the weight of the object the lever will move. For example, a lever is used to lift a rock weighing 1000 newtons. The resistance force is 1000 newtons, the weight of the rock.

What are the parts of a lever?

2:5 Mechanical Advantage for a Lever

The amount by which a lever increases a force is the mechanical advantage for the lever. Suppose a machine produces 100 newtons of force when the effort force applied is 10 newtons. The machine multiplies the force 10 times.

$$\frac{100\text{ N}}{10\text{ N}} = 10$$

Its mechanical advantage is 10.

The mechanical advantage of a lever depends upon the lengths of the effort arm and resistance arm. A short effort arm together with a long resistance arm gives a high mechanical advantage. To find the mechanical advantage for a lever use the equation

How do you calculate the mechanical advantage for a lever?

$$\textit{mechanical advantage} = \frac{\textit{effort arm}}{\textit{resistance arm}}$$

$$M.A. = \frac{\textit{effort arm}}{\textit{resistance arm}}$$

Example

A screwdriver is used to pry the lid off a paint can. The resistance arm is 0.5 centimeter. The effort arm is 15 centimeters. What is the mechanical advantage of the screwdriver?

Solution:

(a) Write the equation for mechanical advantage.

$$M.A. = \frac{\textit{effort arm}}{\textit{resistance arm}}$$

(b) Substitute the values for the effort arm and resistance arm given in the problem.

$$M.A. = \frac{15\text{ cm}}{0.5\text{ cm}}$$

$$M.A. = 30$$

Making Sure

9. An automobile jack has an effort arm of 45 centimeters. The resistance arm is 6 centimeters. What is the mechanical advantage of the jack? 7.5

10. A crowbar, 1 meter long, is used to pry open a box. The fulcrum of the crowbar is 0.2 meter from the resistance end. What is the mechanical advantage of the crowbar? 4

2:6 Pulleys

A **pulley** is a simple machine. It is used to move objects and do work. A pulley is really a form of a lever. It can be fixed in one spot or movable, Figure 2-4.

a Mr. & Mrs. Pantages b Don Parsisson c Susan Marquart

FIGURE 2-4. Pulleys may be either fixed (a), or movable (b). A pulley may have more than one support rope (c).

How does a pulley make work easier?

A pulley makes work easier by changing the direction of a force. For example you could use a rope wound around a fixed pulley to raise a heavy object. You pull the object up while standing on the ground. With a fixed pulley, the effort force is applied in one direction. The resistance moves in the opposite direction.

Two or more pulleys can be used together to decrease the force needed to move an object. The

How do you find the mechanical advantage for a set of pulleys?

mechanical advantage of a set of pulleys is about equal to the number of supporting ropes or strands, Figure 2-4c. In actual use the mechanical advantage is less than the number of supporting ropes. Friction and stretching of the rope lowers the mechanical advantage.

2-3 Detailed information concerning this Activity can be found in the Teacher's Guide at the front of this book.

Activity *What is the advantage in using a pulley?*

FIGURE 2-5.

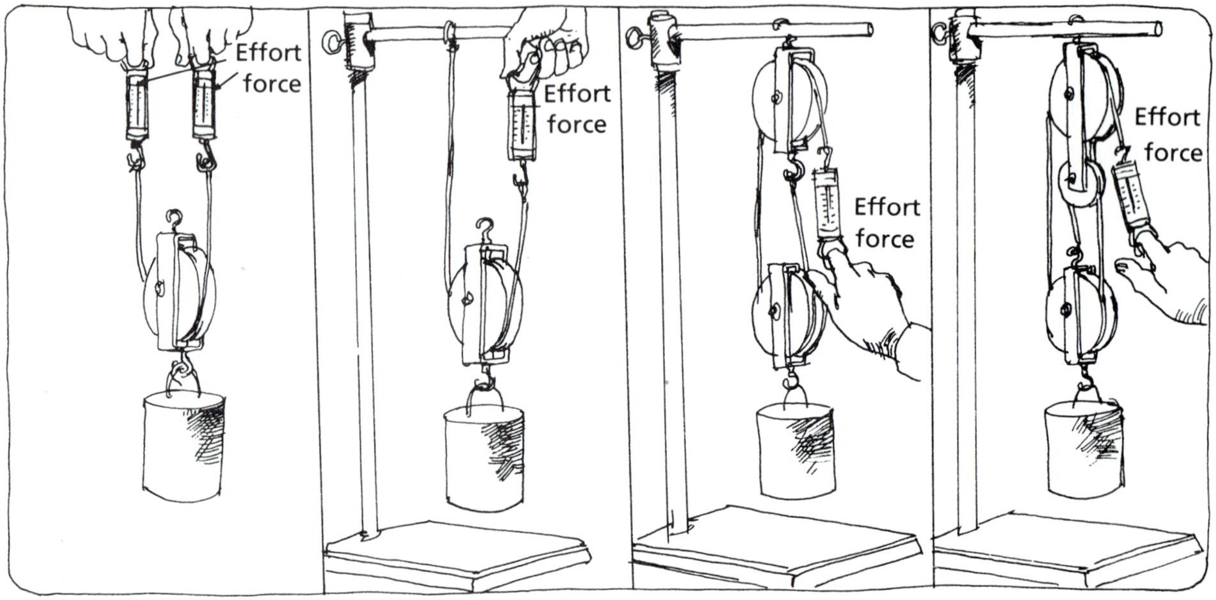

Setting Up

2-newton weight
meter stick
string
2 spring scales
3 pulleys
ring stand
extension clamp
paper clips

Getting Started

1. *Cut a piece of string 1 meter long. Run the string through a single movable pulley.*
2. *Attach each end of the string to a different spring scale as in Figure 2-5a.*
3. *Attach the 2-newton weight to the pulley.*
4. *Lift the weight to a height of 20 centimeters. Record the force readings on the spring scales in a table like the one below.*
5. *Now set up the pulley as in Figure 2-5b. Attach the weight and lift it 20 centimeters also. Use the spring scale to record the force for this pulley system.*
6. *Repeat Step 5 for the pulley system in Figure 2-5c. Record the force in the table.*

Keeping Track

pulley system 2-5a	______
pulley system 2-5b	______
pulley system 2-5c	______

Summing Up

1. *How does the number of supporting strings affect the force needed to lift the weight?*
2. *How much work is done to lift the weight using pulley system 2-5a?*
3. *How much work is done to lift the weight using pulley systems 2-5b and 2-5c?*
4. *How much work is done in lifting the weight using the pulley system in Figure 2-5d?*

See the Teacher's Guide at the front of this book.

2:7 Wheel and Axle

Cars, trains, and bicycles all contain wheels and axles. The crank used to lift a bucket from a well is a **wheel and axle.** The wheel has a larger radius than the axle. The **radius** of a wheel is the distance from the center to the edge, Figure 2-6. The wheel and axle act like a first class lever. The effort arm is the radius of the wheel. The resistance arm is the radius of the axle. The fulcrum is the center of the axle. The radius of the axle is less than the radius of the wheel. As a result, a small effort force can be used to move a larger resistance force. The mechanical advantage of the wheel and axle is equal to the radius of the wheel divided by the radius of the axle.

$$M.A. = \frac{\textit{radius of wheel}}{\textit{radius of axle}}$$

Hickson-Bender Photography

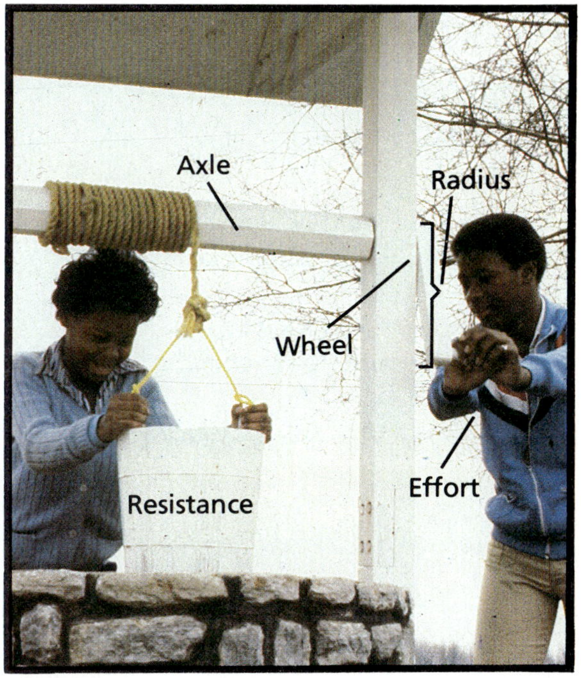

FIGURE 2-6.

How is a wheel and axle like a first class lever?

How can you find the mechanical advantage for a wheel and axle?

Example

What is the mechanical advantage of the wheel and axle in Figure 2-6? The wheel has a radius of 0.4 meter. The axle has a radius of 0.1 meter.

Solution:

(a) Write the equation for the mechanical advantage of a wheel and axle.

$$M.A. = \frac{\textit{radius of the wheel}}{\textit{radius of the axle}}$$

(b) Substitute the values for the radius of the wheel and of the axle.

$$M.A. = \frac{0.4 \text{ m}}{0.1 \text{ m}}$$

$$M.A. = 4$$

Making Sure

11. List three machines having a wheel and axle which you use. Which part of the machine is the wheel? Which part is the axle? *answers will vary: auto, bicycle, steering wheel*

12. A screwdriver is also a wheel and axle system. The handle of the screwdriver is the wheel; the shaft is the axle. The handle of a screwdriver has a radius of 1.5 centimeters. The radius of the shaft is 0.25 centimeter. It takes an effort force of 20 newtons to turn a screw into a piece of wood. What is the mechanical advantage of the screwdriver? *6*

13. A force of 6 newtons is used to turn a doorknob which has a radius of 3.5 centimeters. The shaft of the doorknob has a radius of 1.5 centimeters. What is the mechanical advantage of the doorknob? *2.33*

FIGURE 2-7. A screwdriver and doorknob are used as a wheel and axle.

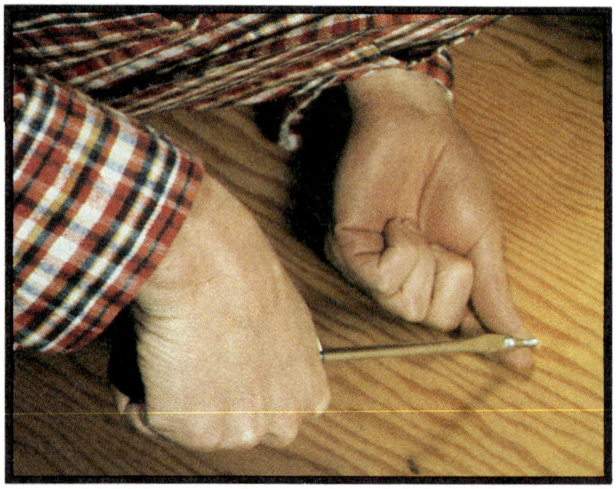

Eric Hoffhines

2:8 Inclined Planes

What is an inclined plane?

A ramp and flight of stairs are both examples of an inclined plane. An **inclined plane** is a slanted surface used to raise objects. Less force is needed to lift an object using an inclined plane. However the object is moved through a longer distance using the inclined plane, than if it were moved straight up. For example, you want to move a box weighing 200 newtons from the floor to the top of a table. The table is 1 meter high. If you use a ramp which is 2 meters long, it will take 100 newtons of force to move the box. Without the ramp, it takes a force of 200 newtons to lift the box. Using the ramp, you push with a force of 100 newtons through a distance of 2 meters. Without the ramp, you lift the box with a force of 200 newtons through a distance of 1 meter.

How does an inclined plane make work easier?

FIGURE 2-8. What force is used to move the 200 newton box to the top of the table, one meter from the floor?

Under actual conditions you must consider friction. It would take more force than 100 newtons to move the box up the ramp. The friction between the surfaces of the box and the ramp will have to be overcome.

The mechanical advantage of an inclined plane is its length divided by its height. The longer the inclined plane, the smaller the force needed to move an object.

What is the mechanical advantage of an inclined plane?

A **wedge** is made of two inclined planes, Figure 2-9. How is an inclined plane different from a wedge? In doing work the wedge always moves. A knife blade and an ax blade are wedges. A **screw** is also a form of inclined plane. It is like a spiral staircase where the steps are wound around the center, Figure 2-10.

Hickson-Bender Photography

FIGURE 2-9. A wedge is two inclined planes.

Hickson-Bender Photography

FIGURE 2-10. A screw is an inclined plane.

2-4 **Activity** *Does the inclined plane make work easier?*

Setting Up

wooden block or brick
spring scale
smooth board at least 0.5 meter long
string
books

Getting Started

1. *Set up a stack of books as in Figure 2-11.*
2. *Measure the height of the stack in centimeters. Record this number in a table like the one below.*
3. *Set up the inclined plane on the books. Measure the distance from the base of the plane to the stack of books as in Figure 2-11.*
4. *Tie a string to the block. Use the spring scale to lift the block the same height as the stack of books. Record in the table the force needed to lift the block.*
5. *Use the scale to drag the brick slowly up the inclined plane. Read the scale while the brick is moving and record.*

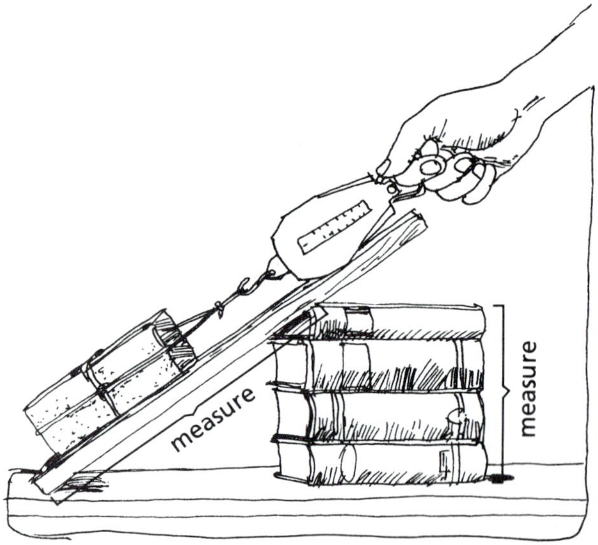

FIGURE 2-11.

Keeping Track

height of books	______
length of plane	______
force needed to lift the block	______
force needed to drag the block	______

Summing Up

See the Teacher's Guide at the front of this book.

1. *Does it take more or less force to move the block using the inclined plane?*
2. *How much work is done in lifting the block without the inclined plane?*

   work = force to raise the block × distance the block is raised

3. *How much work is done using the inclined plane?*

   work = force to drag the block × length of the plane

4. *Does it take more or less work to move the block using the inclined plane?*

Making Sure

14. Why is a flight of stairs an inclined plane? *changes the direction of force*
15. Why is the road up a side of a mountain an inclined plane? *changes the direction of force*
16. List some tools that have a wedge. What tasks are they used for? *scissors, can opener, knife, etc.*
17. Some people put soap or wax on a screw before putting it into wood. Why? *reduces friction*
18. How is the screw different from an inclined plane? *the plane is wrapped around a shaft*

2:9 Efficiency

When you push on a lever, you are putting work into the machine. When you pull the rope on a pulley, you are putting work into the machine. Work must be put into a machine before it can do any work for you. A machine converts this work into more useful work by changing the size of the force, the distance, or the direction through which the force moves.

Why is work output less than work input?

What is the efficiency of a machine?

The useful work obtained from a machine is always less than the work put into it. Why? Some of the input work is used to overcome friction. The ratio of work output to work input is called the **efficiency** (ih FIHSH un see) of a machine. High efficiency means much of the work input is changed to useful work done by the machine. Low efficiency means much of the work input is lost and not changed to useful work. Efficiency is more commonly expressed as a percent. The equation is

$$\textit{percent efficiency} = \frac{\textit{work output}}{\textit{work input}} \times 100$$

How can you increase the efficiency of a machine? Efficiency is increased by reducing friction. Sanding or waxing smooths a surface and reduces friction. Oil and grease are used in many machines to reduce friction. Ball bearings in bicycle wheels and other machines reduce friction.

Increasing the efficiency of machines is an important step in conserving natural resources. Many machines are run by electricity or fuels such as gasoline. When efficiency is increased, less fuel or electricity is needed to do a given amount of work. Thus, resources are conserved. For example, steps are being taken to improve the gasoline engine. Moving parts are made so there is less friction between them. These parts will last longer.

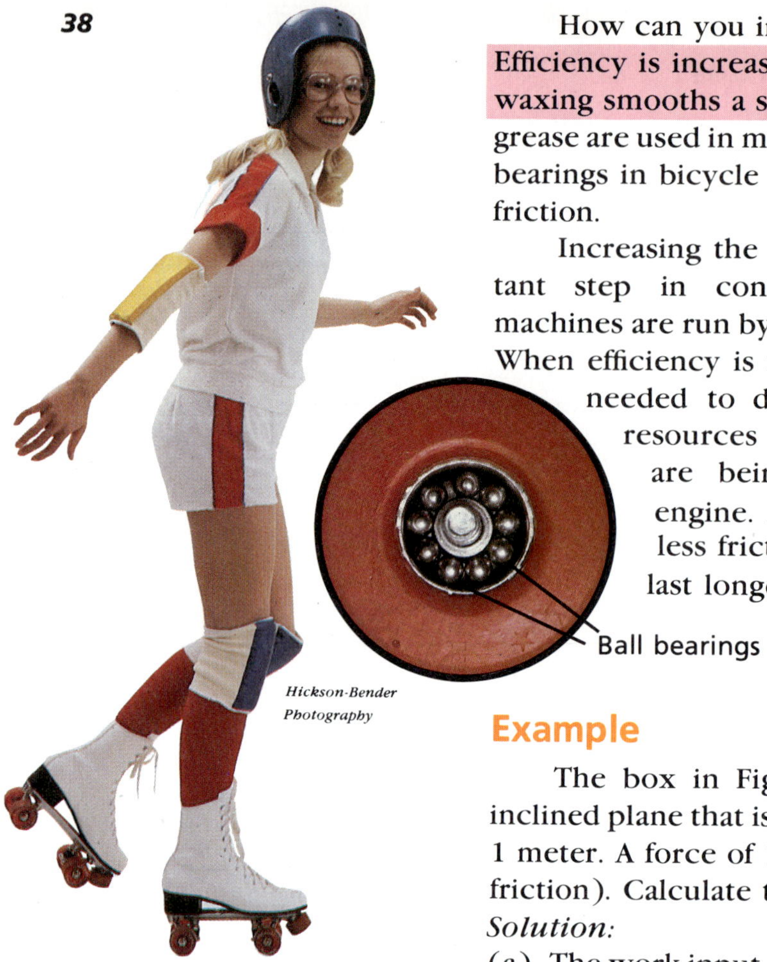

FIGURE 2-12. Ball bearings are used to reduce friction in roller skates.

Example

The box in Figure 2-8 weighs 200 newtons. An inclined plane that is 2 meters long is used to lift the box 1 meter. A force of 140 newtons is required (including friction). Calculate the efficiency of the inclined plane.

Solution:

(a) The work input is the force needed to move the box multiplied by the distance the box is moved.

$$140 \text{ N} \times 2 \text{ m} = 280 \text{ J}$$

(b) The work output is the weight of the box multiplied by the distance it is moved without using the inclined plane.

$$200 \text{ N} \times 1 \text{ m} = 200 \text{ J}$$

(c) Write the equation for the percent efficiency of the machine.

$$\textit{percent efficiency} = \frac{\textit{work output}}{\textit{work input}} \times 100$$

$$= \frac{200 \text{ J}}{280 \text{ J}} \times 100 = 71.4\%$$

Making Sure

19. Is the efficiency of a bicycle increased or decreased when the air in the tires is low? *decreased*

20. How does the shape of a car affect its efficiency?

Cars are designed to minimize air resistance.

21. Which would use more fuel, an engine with a high or low efficiency? *low*

2:10 Power

What is power?

Power has a precise meaning in science. **Power** is the amount of work done per unit of time. For example, a large engine is more powerful than a small engine. The large engine can do more work in less time. The less time it takes to do work, the more power is used. The unit for power is the **watt (W)**. One watt is equal to one joule of work per second (J/s). This unit was named in honor of James Watt, the inventor of the steam engine. To find the power of a machine, use the following equation:

$$\text{power (watts)} = \frac{\text{work (joules)}}{\text{time (seconds)}} \qquad P = \frac{W}{t}$$

Horsepower is a unit of power in the English system. This unit was based on the amount of work the average horse could do. One horsepower is equal to 746 watts.

FIGURE 2-13. The power used by some appliances is listed below.

2-5 Detailed information concerning this Activity can be found in the Teacher's Guide at the front of this book.

Activity

How much power do you use when you go up a flight of stairs?

George C. Anderson

FIGURE 2-14.

(1) *Measure the height of a single step. Multiply this value by the number of stairs. Your answer is the height of a flight of stairs.* **(2)** *Have someone measure the time it takes for you to walk up the stairs.* **(3)** *Your teacher will give you the value of your weight in newtons.* **(4)** *Using your weight and the height of the stairs, calculate the amount of work done in walking up the stairs.* **(5)** *Using your calculated value for work and the time it took to walk up the stairs, calculate the power you used. (One watt is one joule per second.)*

Extension: Have students vary their speeds and compare power.

Example

A set of pulleys is used to lift a boat weighing 900 newtons. The boat is lifted 2 meters in 50 seconds. How much power is used?

Solution:

(a) In order to calculate, we must first calculate the amount of work done in lifting the boat. The equation for work is

$$W = F \times d$$

(b) Substitute the values for force and distance into the work equation.

$$W = 900 \text{ N} \times 2 \text{ m} = 1800 \text{ J}$$

(c) Substitute the value for work and time into the power equation.

$$P = \frac{1800 \text{ J}}{50 \text{ s}} = 36 \text{ W}$$

Note: Students should have a working knowledge of important SI prefixes. The kilowatt question is an application of that knowledge.

Making Sure

22. Convert the following to kilowatts.

(a) 4500 watts *4.5 kW* **(c)** 10 000 watts *10 kW*

(b) 1 watt *0.001 kW* **(d)** 0.25 watts *0.00025 kW*

23. What is the power of a small appliance motor which can do 4000 joules of work in 20 seconds? *200 W*

Points to Remember

1. Work is done when a force is exerted through a distance. *2:2*
2. Machines can change the size, direction, or the distance through which a force moves. *2:3*
3. Machines can decrease the amount of force needed to do work. *2:3*
4. The six simple machines are the lever, pulley, wheel and axle, inclined plane, wedge, and screw. *2:3, 2:4, 2:6, 2:7, 2:8*
5. The work output of a machine is always less than the work input. *2:9*
6. Power is the amount of work done in a unit of time. *2:10*

Words to Use

Write a sentence in which you use correctly each of the following words.

compound machine	friction	radius
efficiency	fulcrum	resistance
effort arm	joule	simple machine
force	mechanical advantage	watt
	power	work

Questions for Review

Do not write in this book.

A. True or False *Have the students rewrite the false statements to make them correct.*

Determine whether each of the following sentences is true or false.

T **1.** A compound machine is more complex than a simple machine.

F **2.** A pulley is an example of a ~~compound~~ machine. *simple*

F **3.** The mechanical advantage of a machine is always greater than one. *not*

T **4.** A force is a push or pull.

F **5.** An eggbeater is an example of a ~~simple~~ machine. *compound*

T **6.** Newton is the unit of force.

T **7.** There are six simple machines.

F **8.** One watt is one joule of work per ~~minute~~. *second*

T 9. To do work an object must be moved.

F 10. Friction ~~increases~~ the mechanical advantage of a machine. decreases

B. Multiple Choice

Choose one word or phrase that completes each of the following sentences.

1. Work is done when a body is moved through a distance by a *(force, mechanical advantage, fulcrum).*
2. $F \times d$ is the equation used to determine *(power, mechanical advantage, work).*
3. A *(sewing machine, gasoline engine, lever)* is a simple machine.
4. A compound machine has *(one, two, two or more)* simple machines.
5. *(Mechanical advantage, Work, Friction)* is a force that opposes motion.
6. *(Resistance, Effort, Fulcrum)* is the point around which a lever rotates.
7. You can measure force with a *(ruler, pulley, spring scale).*
8. If the fulcrum of a lever is between the effort and resistance, the lever is a *(first, second, third)* class lever.
9. A doorknob is an example of a *(pulley, lever, wheel and axle).*
10. A wedge can be considered a(n) *(inclined plane, screw, lever).*

C. Completion

Complete each of the following sentences with a word or phrase that will make the sentence correct.

1. A force that slows down or prevents motion is friction.
2. The effort arm on a lever is 4 meters and the resistance arm is 1 meter long. The mechanical advantage of the lever is 4.
3. The work output of a machine is always less than the work input.
4. Reducing friction increases the efficiency of a machine.
5. The mechanical advantage of a pulley system is equal to the number of ______. supporting strands or ropes
6. Motion occurs if two opposing forces are unbalanced.
7. Friction changes the useful work of a machine to heat.
8. A crowbar is an example of a(n) lever.

9. A wedge is made from <u>two</u> inclined planes.
10. A machine has a(n) <u>low</u> efficiency if much of its input work is lost to friction. *Detailed answers to these questions are given in the Teacher's Guide at the front of this book.*

D. How and Why

1. In what ways are a lever, wheel and axle, and pulley alike? *all are simple machines*
2. How much work is done when a force of 25 newtons is used to slide a 150-newton sofa 10 meters across the floor? *250 J*
3. An electric mixer does 21 600 newton-meters of work in 3 minutes. What is the power of the electric mixer? *120 W*
4. A 500-watt gasoline engine and a 250-watt motor both do 1.5 newton-meters of work. Which machine can do the work faster? Explain your answer. *500-watt engine, power $\propto$ speed*
5. A pole vaulter weighing 780 newtons leaps 5 meters over a bar. How much work is done? *3900 J*

More Ideas to Explore

1. Make a mobile to hang in class. How does a knowledge of levers help you in making a mobile? Hint: Refer to the Activity on page 28.
2. Look up "perpetual motion" in the library. Prepare a report on perpetual motion machines.
3. Which appliances in your home use motors to do work? Prepare a report on the power rating of each.
4. Make a comparison of fuel economy and horsepower in several types of cars. Report your findings to the class.
5. Obtain advertising material for different kinds of motorcycles, dirt bikes, and minibikes. Make a chart comparing horsepower and gear ratios.

Readings to Discover

James, Elizabeth, and Baskin, Carol, *The Simple Facts of Simple Machines.* NY: Lothrop, Lee, and Shepard Co., 1975.

Landels, J.G., *Engineering in the Ancient World.* Berkeley: University of California Press, 1978.

Munch, Theodore W., *Man the Engineer: Nature's Copycat.* Philadelphia: Westminster Press, 1974.

The motorcycle racer depends on much more than speed to win a race. The bike is designed to be lightweight so the racer accelerates faster. The tires are made to grip the course. What kinds of forces must the racer consider in going around curves and up and down hills?

Thomas Zimmerman/FPG

Moving Objects

3

Chapter 3 introduces the concept of motion and the forces that cause or alter it. Speed, velocity, acceleration, and deceleration are defined and related to each other. The energy relationship between objects in motion and at rest is discussed. See the Teacher's Guide at the front of this book for additional teaching strategies for this chapter.

3:1 Weight and Mass

GOAL: *You will learn how weight, mass, and gravity are related to moving objects.*

The earth pulls on all things. A skydiver leaping from an airplane falls swiftly toward the ground. If you jump up in the air you come down again. If you drop your book it falls to the ground. Objects fall because the earth exerts a force on them. This force is gravity. Gravity acts upon all objects. The force of gravity is measured by weight. The weight of an object can be measured using a spring scale. The standard unit of weight is the newton.

What unit is used to measure the force of gravity?

Mass is different from weight. Mass is the quantity or amount of matter in an object. All matter has mass. The mass of an object does not change. However, the weight of an object can change. A change in the force of gravity causes a change in weight. For example, on the moon you would weigh $^1/_6$ of your weight on the earth. Why the difference? The pull of gravity on the moon is only $^1/_6$ as great as the pull of gravity on the earth. Yet your mass would be exactly the same on the moon as it is on the earth. Two masses that balance on the earth would balance on the moon.

How can the weight of an object change when it is moved?

Your weight can also change on the earth. The earth is not a perfect sphere. The earth is slightly flattened at the poles and fatter at the equator. At the equator, the distance from the surface to the center of the earth is about 20 kilometers greater than at the north pole. As an object moves away from the center of the earth, the force of gravity decreases. A person who weighs 600 newtons at the north pole would weigh 597 newtons at the equator. Weight decreases by 0.5 percent when an object is moved from the north pole to the equator.

The reading would not be your normal weight since water has buoyancy. However, your mass remains the same. Reinforce the idea that the mass does not change because it is not affected by these forces.

If you stood on a scale in a swimming pool, would the reading be your normal weight? Does your mass change in the pool? How does the water change the force of gravity which pulls you toward the earth?

3-1 Detailed information concerning this Activity can be found in the Teacher's Guide at the front of this book.

Activity *Does an object lose mass or weight when submerged in water?*

Setting Up

25-mL graduate
double pan balance
lead sinker
rubber band
spring scale
string

Getting Started

1. *Fill a 25-mL graduate to the 15-mL mark with water. Record the water level.*
2. *Determine the mass of the graduate. Record.*
3. *Attach a string to a lead sinker or some other object your teacher provides. Record the weight of the object using a spring scale.*
4. *Lower the sinker into the graduate until it is submerged.*
5. *Again record the weight of the sinker using the spring scale as in Figure 3-1.*
6. *While the sinker is still submerged record the new water level.*
7. *Remove the sinker. Add water to the graduate to raise the water level to the level in Step 6.*
8. *Record the new mass of the graduate and water.*

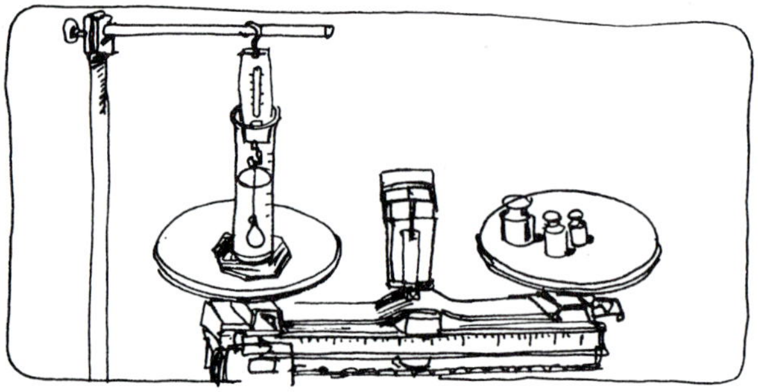

FIGURE 3-1.

Keeping Track

mass of graduate and water ______
weight of sinker ______
weight of sinker submerged ______
mass of graduate + additional water ______

Summing Up

See the Teacher's Guide at the front of this book.

1. *Does the graduate gain mass, weight, or both when the water is added?*
2. *Does the sinker lose mass when it is submerged? Does it lose weight?*
3. *What is the change in mass for the graduate and water?*
4. *What is the change in weight of the sinker when it is submerged?*

3:2 Gravity

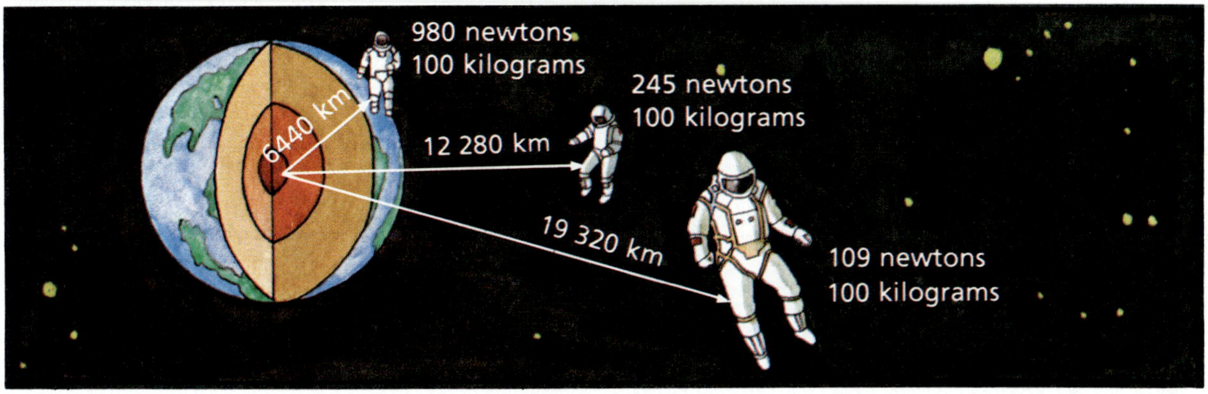

FIGURE 3-2. The weight of the astronaut changes as gravity decreases, but the mass remains the same.

Most objects fall down if you drop them. Gravity pulls objects to the earth. However, gravity is a property not only of the earth but of all matter. Every object in the universe pulls on every other object. Every object exerts its own force on other objects. The pull between most objects is very small. For example, a lead ball with a mass of 5000 kg attracts a baseball at its surface with a force less than the weight of a mosquito.

How does mass affect gravitational force?

How does the distance between two objects affect the force of attraction between them?

The more mass an object has the greater its gravitational force. For example, the earth exerts a greater force on objects near its surface than does the moon. The earth has a greater mass than the moon. As the distance between two objects increases, the attraction between them decreases. As the distance between a rocket and the earth increases, the pull of gravity decreases. If the distance between two objects is doubled, the force of attraction between them becomes $^1/_4$ of what it was originally. Triple the distance and the attraction becomes $^1/_9$ the original force.

Making Sure

1. Suppose you were 6400 kilometers above the surface of the earth. You would be twice as far from the center of the earth as you are now. The force of gravity on your body would decrease to $^1/_4(^1/_2)^2$. How would the decrease in gravity affect your weight? *$^1/_4$ the weight on earth*
2. What would you weigh if you were 12 800 kilometers above the earth's surface? *$^1/_9$ the weight on earth*

3:3 Speed

What is the definition of speed?

When you throw a ball, you put it in motion. How fast the ball moves is its speed. **Speed** is defined as the distance an object travels per unit of time. The equation for speed is

How is speed calculated?

$$speed = \frac{distance}{time}$$

$$s = \frac{d}{t}$$

The units given to speed, kilometers per hour or meters per second, are called rates. **Rates** are ratios between two different measurements. Your pulse rate is the number of times your heart beats in one minute. A car speedometer indicates a rate of speed in miles per hour or kilometers per hour. On a highway cars may move at a constant speed. **Constant speed** means that the speed does not change. For example, a car travels at a constant speed of 50 kilometers per hour. The car travels 50 kilometers in the first hour and 50 kilometers in the second hour. Thus, it travels a total of 100 kilometers in two hours. When it goes 50 kilometers every hour, the car maintains a constant speed.

In physical science, speed refers to how fast an object is moving. **Velocity** (vuh LAHS ut ee) refers to both the speed and direction of the object. For example, a plane is traveling to the north pole. The speed of the plane is 220 kilometers per hour. The velocity of the plane is 220 kilometers per hour due north.

Example

What is the speed of a truck which travels 10 kilometers in 10 minutes at constant speed?

Solution:

We can find the speed for one minute by using the rate.

$$\frac{10 \text{ km}}{10 \text{ min}}$$

If we reduce, the rate of speed is

$$1 \text{ km/min}$$

Example

The sound from thunder travels at the rate of 330 meters per second. How long does it take for the sound to travel 1320 meters?

Solution:

There is a constant rate of 330 meters each second. To travel 1320 meters will take

$$s = \frac{d}{t} \quad \text{or} \quad t = \frac{d}{s} \qquad\qquad \frac{1320\ \text{m}}{330\ \text{m/s}} = 4\ \text{s}$$

Making Sure

3. What is the speed of a bicycle that travels 100 meters in 50 seconds at constant speed? *2 m/s*
4. What distance would be covered in 10 minutes by a train that travels at a constant speed of 500 meters per minute? *5000 meters*

3:4 Average Speed

How is average speed calculated?

Cars, trucks, trains, and bicycles seldom travel at a constant speed for very long. The speed of any moving object usually increases or decreases as it moves. It is better to speak of this type of motion in terms of average speed.

$$\textit{average speed} = \frac{\textit{total distance}}{\textit{total time}}$$

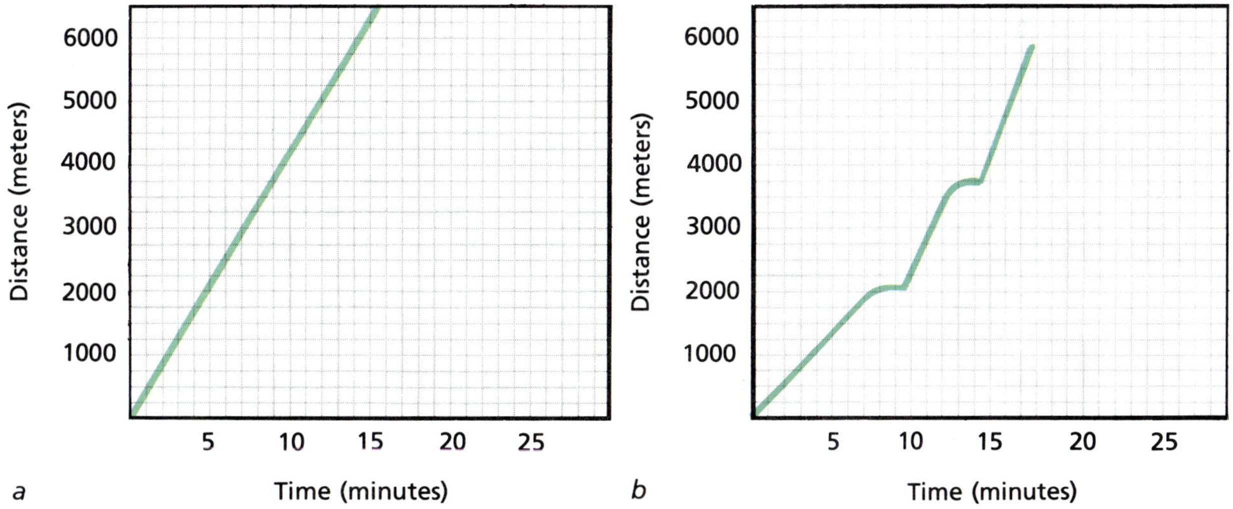

FIGURE 3-3. Graphs (a) and (b) show the same trip. The car in (a) travels at a constant speed. The car in (b) makes the trip through traffic with many stops along the way.

Figure 3-3a after 5 minutes-450 m/min, after 10 minutes-about 450 m/min

Figure 3-3b after 5 minutes-250 m/min, after 10 minutes-225 m/min

Making Sure

5. What is the average speed of the cars in Figures 3-3a and 3-3b at the end of 5 minutes? 10 minutes?
6. What is the average speed of a runner who completes a 10 kilometer race in 45 minutes?

3:5 Acceleration

Define acceleration.

Acceleration (ak sel uh RAY shun) is the rate at which speed increases. Acceleration is caused by a force. For example, the force of your bicycle tires on the road makes the bicycle accelerate. When something accelerates, its speed increases.

How does speed change during acceleration?

You may want to introduce the equation for acceleration. It may help to develop the relationship between velocity and acceleration.

$$a = \frac{v_2 - v_1}{t}$$

A car stopped for a red light is at rest. The speed of the car is zero. When the light turns green, the driver steps on the gas pedal (accelerator) and the car moves forward. In less than a minute, it may reach a speed of 50 kilometers per hour. The driver may increase the speed so the car accelerates to the speed limit of 88 kilometers per hour. The graph in Figure 3-4a represents the motion of the car. From the time the light turns green until it reaches the speed limit, we will assume constant acceleration. Figure 3-4b shows the motion of the car once it has reached the speed limit and as it continues at constant speed. The horizontal line on the graph shows the acceleration of the car is zero.

FIGURE 3-4. The car in (a) shows constant acceleration. The car in (b) shows no acceleration. It maintains a constant speed.

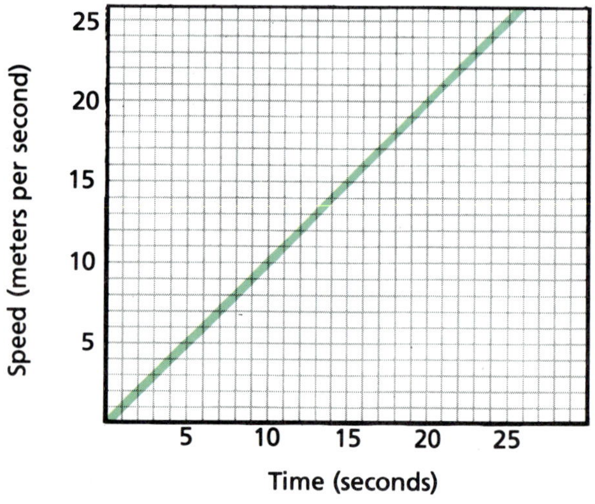

a

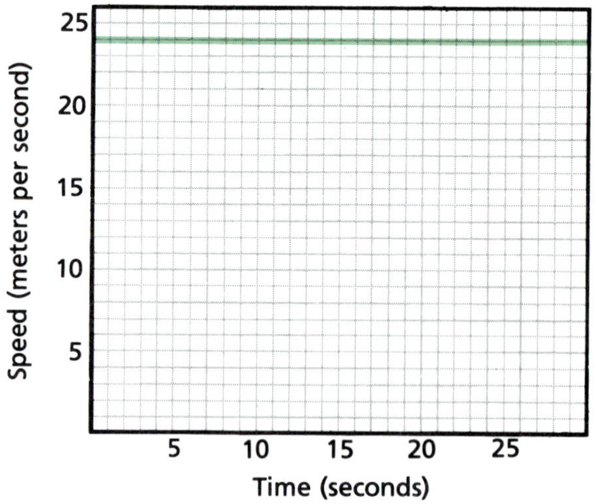

b

How does a pilot stop a jet airliner after it lands? Reversing the engines of a jet plane causes it to slow down. Brakes are used to bring it to a stop. The driver of a car applies the brakes to slow down and stop. Both the airplane and car are stopped by forces. Decreasing speed is the opposite of increasing speed. The rate at which the speed of an object decreases is called **deceleration** (dee sel uh RAY shun). The graph in Figure 3-5 shows the deceleration of a car as it slows to stop for a red light.

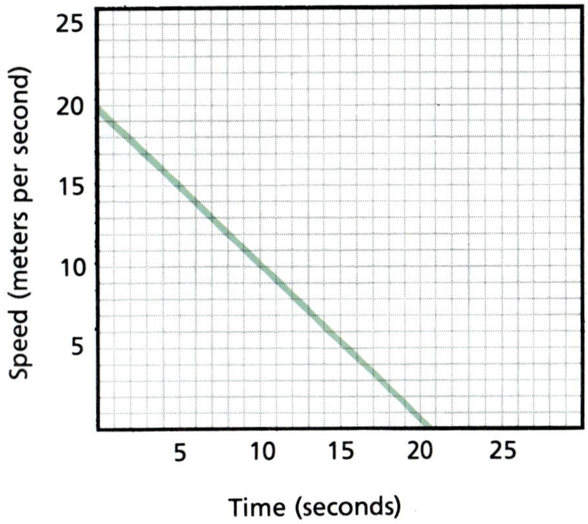

FIGURE 3-5. Deceleration is the opposite of acceleration. How does this graph compare with Figure 3-4a?

Acceleration and deceleration are opposites. Yet both are produced by forces. Any change in the speed of an object requires the application of a force.

The acceleration of the car described in Figure 3-4a is 1 meter per second squared (1 m/s^2). This unit shows the change in the speed of the car each second. At the end of one second, the speed of the car is 1 meter per second. At the end of two seconds, the speed of the car is 2 meters per second. What is the speed of the car after five seconds? *13.3 km/hr*

How does speed change during deceleration?

Making Sure

7. What forces accelerate and decelerate a car, bicycle, and a jet plane? *See the Teacher's Guide at the front of this book.*

8. What is the speed of the car in Figure 3-4a after eight seconds? *8 m/s*

3:6 Energy

Energy is the ability to do work. If an object has energy, it has the ability to exert a force through a distance. For example, a bowling ball rolling down the alley has energy. You can see the result of this energy when the ball strikes the pins. When a flashlight is turned on, you can see the result of the energy stored in the batteries. Energy can be divided into two types—energy of motion and energy of position.

FIGURE 3-6. A more massive ball (a) generally gives the bowler more power because it has more kinetic energy. If the car and train in (b) are traveling at the same speed, which has more kinetic energy? A diver ready to jump (c) and an amusement park ride at the top of a hill (d) have potential energy.

Describe two examples of kinetic energy.

Any object in motion has **kinetic** (kuh NET ihk) **energy.** The amount of kinetic energy an object has depends on the speed and mass of the object. For example, a train moving at 90 kilometers per hour has more kinetic energy than a car moving at the same speed. The train has a greater mass. A car traveling at 90 kilometers per hour has more energy than a car traveling at 40 kilometers per hour. Why?

What is potential energy?

Describe two examples of potential energy.

An object at rest has energy too. This energy depends upon the position of the object. For example, an 8-centimeter rubber band is stretched to a length of 30 centimeters. Once the rubber band is at the 30-centimeter mark, it is no longer in motion. Yet, the rubber band has the ability to do work when you let it go. The rubber band has energy at 30 centimeters with respect to its position at 8 centimeters. Energy of position is called **potential** (puh TEN chul) **energy.** An object with potential energy is capable of doing work because of its position.

Focus On

Skills

Using and Interpreting Graphs

The information graphs contain can be very useful if you know how to interpret them.

Bar graphs

Figure A shows the average MPG's (miles per gallon) that automobiles have reached over the years.

1. Which years are compared? *1930-1970*
2. What do the numbers on the vertical scale represent? *MPG's (miles per gallon)*
3. In which year were cars most efficient? *1940*
4. Estimate the MPG's for the following years.
   a. 1930 *13.2* **b.** 1940 *15.2* **c.** 1950 *14.5* **d.** 1960 *13.8*
5. Between which 10 year period was there the largest increase in MPG? *1930-1940* *2 MPG*

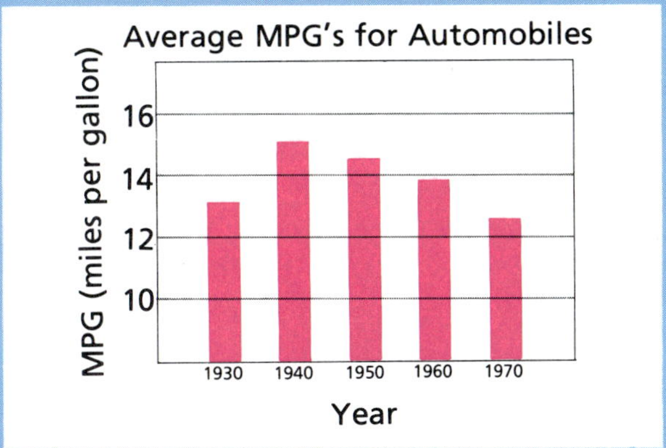

Refer students to Figures 3-3, 3-4, and 3-5.

Line graphs

Line graphs are also used to show change. The graphs you use throughout this chapter are line graphs. The graph in Figure B shows changes in the price of gasoline.

1. During which 5 year period did gasoline prices increase the most? *1975-1980*
2. During which 5 year period did gasoline prices stay about the same? *1960-1965*
3. Estimate the price of gasoline for the following years. **a.** 1965 *14* **b.** 1970 *36* **c.** 1980 *$1.15*
4. What is the increase in price for the 5 year period between 1975 and 1980? *60*

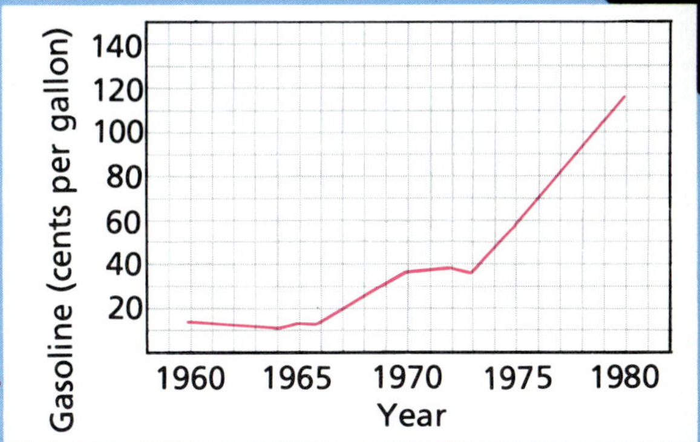

Circle graphs

Circle graphs allow you to compare parts of a whole. The data on most circle graphs is usually expressed as percentages. Figure C is a circle graph showing how transportation energy is used.

1. What is the sum of the percents shown on the graph? *100%*
2. Which type of transportation uses the most energy? the least? *automobiles* *boats*
3. If the total amount of energy available for transportation is 10 000 barrels of fuel, how much would be used for **a.** boats? *481* **b.** trains? *620* **c.** jets? *1412*

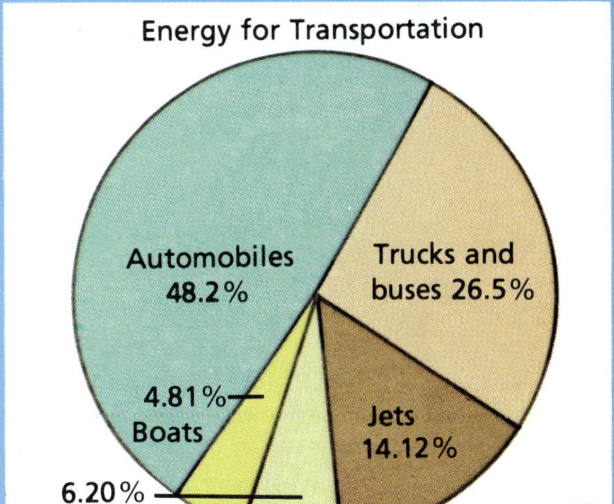

You may also wish to refer students to Figure 23-1 on page 476 for other circle graphs.

Teen Energy Saver

Nick Naumovich Jr.

At age 17, Nickey Naumovich became the president of his own company, Parsec Inc. Parsec makes a product called Thermo-Brite. Thermo-Brite was invented by Nickey to cut down on heat lost by houses. Builders say Thermo-Brite could save a homeowner thousands of dollars in energy bills over many years.

Many houses lose heat through cracks or gaps in walls. For example, air could flow through a gap between the boards in wood siding. In winter warm air moves through the gaps. Because heat is escaping, more energy is needed to heat the house. One way to prevent this heat loss is to seal the cracks. Sheets of Thermo-Brite are used to seal the cracks. One side has a shiny aluminum surface. The other side is covered with a sticky substance. Sheets of Thermo-Brite are stuck onto the frame before the brick or wood walls are put on.

When Thermo-Brite is placed between the outer wall and the frame, it cuts down the amount of air that leaks through cracks. In winter the aluminum helps keep the heat inside. During summer, heat from the sun penetrating the walls is reflected to keep the house cool.

Nickey developed Thermo-Brite because of his interest in conservation. With the help of his own computer, Nickey tackled the problem of energy conservation in homes. He began by studying typical houses. He recorded the type and thickness of the walls for each house. He determined the amount of dead-air space between the inside and outside walls. The size and numbers of windows and the size and location of the houses were also recorded. All this information was fed into his computer.

Nickey found that about forty percent of all energy used to heat or cool a house is lost through air leaks. Something was needed to seal up a house and stop the leaks. What Nickey came up with was Thermo-Brite.

How does he feel about his success?

"I've been lucky," he says. "I've had the right tools to put together the information I needed. These tools, such as the small computer, just weren't available to an earlier generation."

Points to Remember

1. Weight is the amount of force exerted on an object due to gravity. *3:1*
2. Mass is the amount of matter in an object. Mass is unaffected by gravity. *3:1*
3. Speed is the distance covered per unit time. Velocity is speed in a given direction. *3:3*
4. Acceleration and deceleration are rates at which speed changes. *3:5*
5. Motion starts and stops through the action of forces. *3:5*
6. The energy an object has while in motion is kinetic energy. *3:6*
7. The energy an object has because of its position is potential energy. *3:6*

Words to Use

Write a sentence in which you correctly use each of the following words or terms.

acceleration	kinetic energy	speed
deceleration	mass	velocity
gravity	potential energy	weight
	rate	

Questions for Review

Do not write in this book.

A. True or False *Have the students rewrite the false statements to make them correct.*

Determine whether each of the following sentences is true or false.

T **1.** It takes a force to produce motion.

T **2.** An object would have the same mass on the moon as it has on the earth.

T **3.** It takes a force to change the speed of an object.

T **4.** Force is measured in newtons.

T **5.** Gravity is an attraction.

T **6.** Weight is measured in newtons.

T **7.** The mass of an object may be measured in kilograms.

T **8.** Speed is a rate.

F 9. The kilometer is a unit of ~~speed~~. length or distance

F 10. A moving object has ~~potential~~ energy. kinetic energy

B. Multiple Choice

Choose one word or phrase that correctly completes each of the following sentences.

1. The *(newton, centimeter, kilogram)* is a unit of force.
2. A car traveling 60 kilometers in 2 hours has an average speed of *(30 km/2 h, 30 km/h, 30 km/min, 30 km/s)*.
3. The equation for speed is $\left(s = \frac{d}{t}, s = \frac{t}{d}, s = \frac{v}{d}\right)$.
4. When the driver of a car steps on the brake pedal, the car *(accelerates, loses speed, changes direction)*.
5. Mass is measured in *(meters, kilograms, newtons)*.
6. *(Speed, Acceleration, Gravity)* produces a force.
7. Ratios between two different measurements are *(forces, rates, laws)*.
8. The force of gravity *(increases, decreases, stays the same)* as the distance between two objects increases.
9. Deceleration is a decrease in *(force, time, speed)*.
10. The unit for energy and work is the *(joule, newton, kilogram)*.

C. Completion

Complete each of the following sentences with a word or phrase that will make the sentence correct.

1. The weight of an object changes at different places on the earth.
2. The force of mass is greater on the earth than on the moon.
3. Velocity has both speed and direction.
4. Speed is distance covered per unit time.
5. When a runner leaves the starting line and increases speed, the runner accelerates.
6. A(n) newton is the unit of force.
7. Acceleration is produced by a(n) force.
8. Deceleration occurs when the brakes of a bicycle cause it to slow down or stop.

9. Deceleration is negative acceleration.
10. The energy an object at rest has due to its position is potential.

Detailed answers to these questions are given in the Teacher's Guide at the front of this book.

D. How and Why

1. A car travels 120 kilometers in 2 hours. What is its average speed in kilometers per minute? 1 km/min
2. A bobsled has a rate of acceleration of 1 meter per second squared ($1 m/s^2$) starting from rest. How fast is it going after 6 seconds? 6 m/s
3. In 6 seconds a bobsled travels 18 meters. What is the average speed of the bobsled? 3 m/s
4. A sledgehammer can exert more force than a tack hammer. Why? the sledgehammer has more mass
5. How long will it take a bobsled with a speed of 6 meters per second (6 m/s) to stop if it decelerates at a rate of 3 meters per second squared ($3 m/s^2$)? 2 seconds

More Ideas to Explore

See the Teacher's Guide at the front of this book.

1. Obtain a library book on rockets. Find out how forces can make a rocket accelerate, decelerate, and change direction in flight.
2. Obtain a book on sailboats and learn how a sailboat can sail against the wind.
3. Obtain information on research into automobile accidents. Find out how the study of forces and motion in accidents helps improve auto safety.
4. All sports involve forces and motion. Do research on your own to learn about the kinds of forces and motion in different sports. Prepare a report for your class. What kinds of safety equipment are used to absorb forces?

Readings to Discover

Drake, S., "Galileo and the Rolling Ball; excerpt from Galileo at Work." *Science Digest,* October 1978, pp. 74-76.

Lefkowitz, R.J., *Forces in the Earth: A Book About Gravity and Magnetism.* NY: Parents', 1976.

A gymnast practices long and hard in order to give a good performance. The approach to the horse is as important as the vault from the horse. What laws of motion must the gymnast consider in trying to make a perfect vault?

Zimmerman/Alpha

Laws of Motion 4

Chapter 4 presents Newton's laws of motion and relates them to common examples. Projectile motion, centripetal force, and momentum are also introduced. See the Teacher's Guide at the front of this book for additional teaching strategies for this chapter.

4:1 First Law of Motion

GOAL: *You will learn how motion is changed by forces.*

You are riding in a car. The driver suddenly steps on the brakes. Your body tends to keep moving. The tendency of a moving object to keep moving is called **inertia** (ihn UR shuh). Inertia keeps your body moving in a straight line, even though the car begins to stop. The pull of the seat belt keeps your body from flying forward. If you do not wear a seat belt, you can get hurt. Your body may continue to move forward and hit the windshield. Inertia is also the tendency of an object at rest to remain at rest. An object that is not moving will stay at rest unless a force acts on it.

What is inertia?

Sir Isaac Newton (1642-1727) stated three laws which explain the way objects move. Newton's first law of motion states: *An object which is moving or at a state of rest does not change its state of motion unless a force acts on it.* Objects at rest tend to remain at rest. It takes a force to start and stop motion. Objects in motion tend to remain in motion. It takes a force to change the speed or direction of an object in motion. The following cases illustrate Newton's first law of motion.

FIGURE 4-1. Inertia causes you to be lifted off your seat in going down a hill on a roller coaster.

Case I

The electric motor in a slot car makes the wheels turn. The force of the wheels against the track makes the car move forward. As the car rounds a curve, the force of the track against the car makes it change direction. When the power is shut off, friction slows the car and makes it stop.

Greg Miller

a b

FIGURE 4-2. The force of friction between the tires and the track makes the slot car move forward.

Case II

A sailboat floats on a lake. A breeze exerts a force on the sails. The boat moves. The skipper moves the rudder right or left to change direction. The force of water on the rudder makes the boat turn.

Paul Brown Steve Lissau

a b

FIGURE 4-3. The force of the water against the rudder of the sailboat makes the boat turn.

Case III

A person is standing in a bus. The bus moves forward suddenly and the person falls backward. The person tends to remain at rest (motionless) while the bus moves. When the bus stops suddenly, the person tends to fall forward because of inertia.

4-1 Detailed information concerning this Activity can be found in the Teacher's Guide at the front of this book.

ACTIVITY *Do coins have inertia?*

(1) *Set a plastic drinking glass on a desk or table. Lay a card flat on top of the drinking glass. Place a coin on the center of the card. Hold the base of the glass with your hand. Flick the card with your finger so it moves out from under the coin. If you do this quickly, the coin will fall into the drinking glass when the card flies away.* **(2)** *Stand a nickel or quarter on edge on a piece of paper. Try to jerk the paper from under the coin without upsetting the coin.*

Does the coin have inertia in Step 1? How do you know? Does the coin have inertia in Step 2? How do you know? yes, the coin remains at rest

FIGURE 4-4.

Making Sure

Detailed answers to these questions are given in the Teacher's Guide at the front of this book.

1. Identify the forces in Cases I, II, and III. What effect does each force have on speed and direction of the moving object?
2. What forces put the following objects in motion: basketball, arrow?
3. What forces stop or change the motion of the following objects: bicycle, surfboard, ball?
4. Why are seat belts used in cars and airplanes?

4:2 Second Law of Motion

Hit a ball with a bat and the ball flies away. The ball is accelerated. Acceleration of the ball depends on the mass of the ball and the force with which the ball is hit. The harder you hit the ball, the faster it moves. How far can you hit a baseball? A professional baseball player may hit a homerun ball over 130 meters.

What is Newton's second law of motion?

Newton's second law of motion states: ***Acceleration of an object increases as the amount of force causing the acceleration increases.*** The larger the mass of the object, the larger the force needed to produce acceleration. In equation form, Newton's second law is

$$\textit{force} = \textit{mass} \times \textit{acceleration}$$

$$F = ma$$

A large force is required to move a bookcase filled with books. What happens if you empty the bookcase? If you are able to push the empty bookcase with the same amount of force, you can move it across the room faster. Decreasing the mass of the bookcase makes it easier for you to increase its acceleration.

How are force, mass, and acceleration related?

The unit of force, the newton, is defined by Newton's second law of motion. One **newton** is the force needed to cause a one kilogram mass to be accelerated at the rate of one meter per second each second.

Stress this relationship. It explains weight and force.

$$F = ma$$

$$F = 1\ \text{kg} \times 1\ \text{m/s}^2$$

$$F = 1\ \text{N}$$

Describe two examples of the second law of motion.

A ball has a mass of 0.5 kilograms. It is hit with a force of 50 newtons. It accelerates at the rate of 100 m/s^2. If the mass of the ball had been 1 kilogram, it would have accelerated at the rate of 50 m/s^2. If the force on the 0.5-kilogram ball had been 100 newtons, it would have accelerated twice as fast or 200 m/s^2. As the force increases, the acceleration increases. As the mass increases, the acceleration decreases. The following cases illustrate this point.

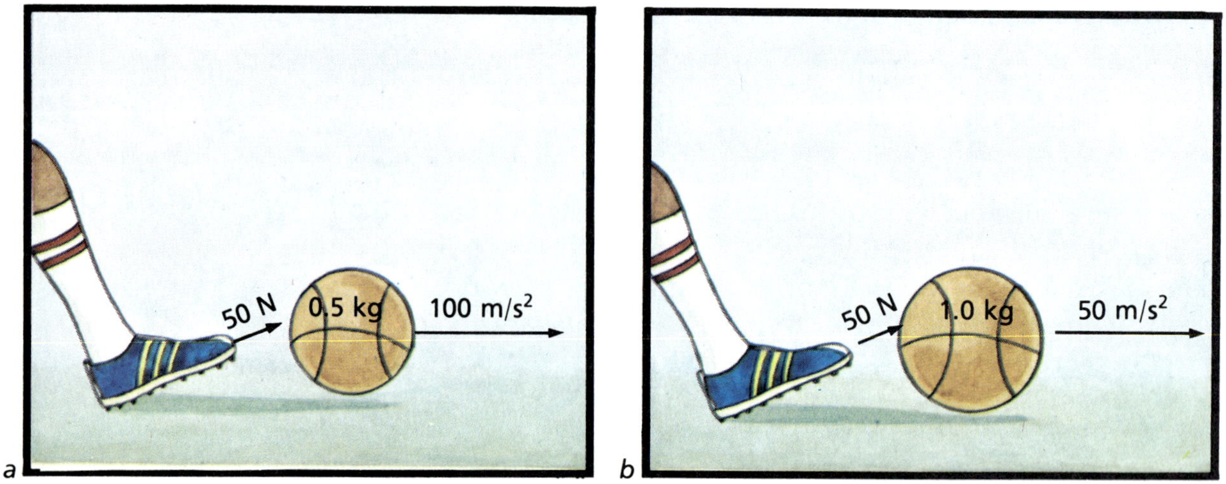

FIGURE 4-5. The 0.5 kilogram ball accelerates at a faster rate than the 1.0 kilogram ball when kicked with the same force.

Case I

A driver controls the speed of a car with the gas pedal, or accelerator. By feeding more gas into the engine, more force is created. The car speeds up.

Case II

Heavy football players often play on the line. The line players must apply force to stop players on the other team. Less massive players are often used in the backfield. They carry the ball and catch passes. Backfield players must be able to accelerate quickly. Less mass makes for faster acceleration since there is less mass to put in motion.

Case III

The fastest racing cars have light bodies with powerful engines for rapid acceleration.

Greg Miller

FIGURE 4-6. Racing cars have light bodies and a sleek design for rapid acceleration.

Making Sure

5. A sports car and a moving van are traveling at a speed of 30 kilometers per hour. Which vehicle requires more force to stop? Why? *The van has greater mass.*
6. List three examples of the second law of motion. *bunting or hitting a ball, pedaling a bike harder, increasing pressure on an accelerator*

4:3 Third Law of Motion

Imagine that you are skating at a rink. Hold on to the railing with both hands and push off. What happens? In Figure 4-7, the sprinkler arm turns when the water is turned on. Water is pushed out of the sprinkler by a force. The water exerts a force that makes the sprinkler arm turn. Push down on your desk top as hard as you can. The desk exerts an upward force on your hand at the same time.

Paul Brown

FIGURE 4-7.

What are action and reaction forces?

Newton's third law of motion states: *For every force, there is an equal and opposite force.* When a force is exerted on an object, the object exerts an equal force in the opposite direction. The two forces are called action and reaction forces. The **reaction force** is equal to the **action force** and acts in the opposite direction.

4-2 Detailed information concerning this Activity can be found in the Teacher's Guide at the front of this book.

ACTIVITY *How can action and reaction forces be measured?*

(1) *Take two spring scales. Fasten them together. One person holds one scale while another person pulls on the other scale. Look at the readings on the scales and see who is pulling harder.* **(2)** *Fasten three scales together in a line, as in Figure 4-8. Again, one person holds the scale on one end while another person pulls on the scale on the other end.*

What are the readings on all three scales? How are the readings different from those in Step 1?

The reading of the middle scale should equal the sum of the other two.

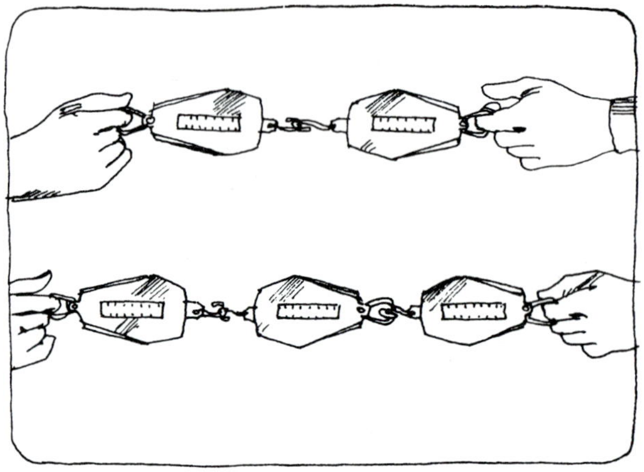

FIGURE 4-8.

Making Sure

7. As you stand, you exert a force on the floor. What is the reaction force? *the floor on your feet*
8. How is the bounce of a basketball an example of Newton's third law? *the force of the floor against the ball, ball against the floor; compression of the ball, release of the compression*
9. How are action and reaction forces produced as you press a pencil against paper while writing? *the paper forces up with the same force that the pencil pushes down*
10. How would the motions of a toy balloon and a rocket engine be different if there were no gravity? *they would have the same straight line motion into space*
11. Which law of motion is illustrated by each of the following?
    - **a.** A person jumps to a dock from a boat. The boat moves away from the dock. *third*
    - **b.** A galloping horse comes to a sudden stop. Its rider is thrown over the head of the horse and lands on the ground. *first*
    - **c.** A ping-pong ball can be accelerated faster than a golf ball when hit with the same force. *second*

4:4 Falling Objects

From a tenth-story window, a bowling ball and golf ball are dropped. Which ball strikes the ground first? Many people think because the bowling ball is heavier it will fall faster.

Galileo (gal uh LAY oh, 1564-1642), an Italian scientist, had a different idea. He thought all objects fall at the same rate. Galileo performed an experiment to test his hypothesis. He timed the motion of a ball rolling down an inclined plane. The movement of the ball is caused by gravity. The speed of the ball can be measured in the same way as an object falling freely through the air. At equal time intervals, Galileo marked the distance the ball traveled.

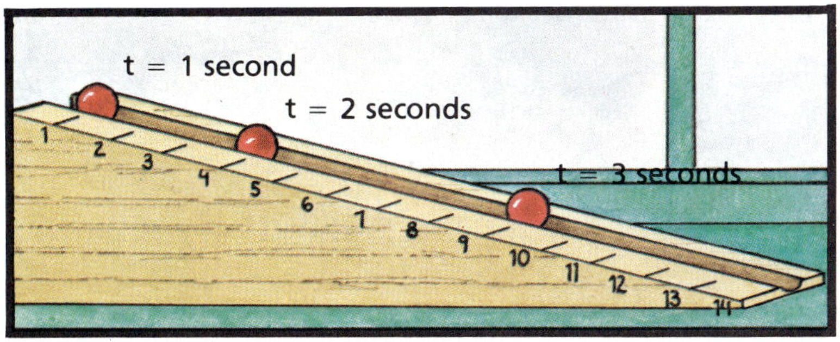

FIGURE 4-9. Galileo's experiment

Galileo found that the speed of the ball increased as it rolled down the ramp. The distance the ball traveled increased with each unit of time. If the same experiment is done with a bowling ball or a golf ball, the time intervals are the same. The distance traveled in each second is the same for the bowling ball and the golf ball. When dropped, both balls accelerate at the same rate.

Near the surface of the earth, falling objects accelerate at a rate of 9.8 meters per second squared (9.8 m/s^2). This value means the speed of the falling object increases 9.8 meters per second for each second it falls. If the object starts at rest, it is traveling 9.8 meters per second at the end of one second. At the end of the next second, its speed is 19.6 meters per second (2×9.8 m/s). How fast will the object be falling after three seconds?

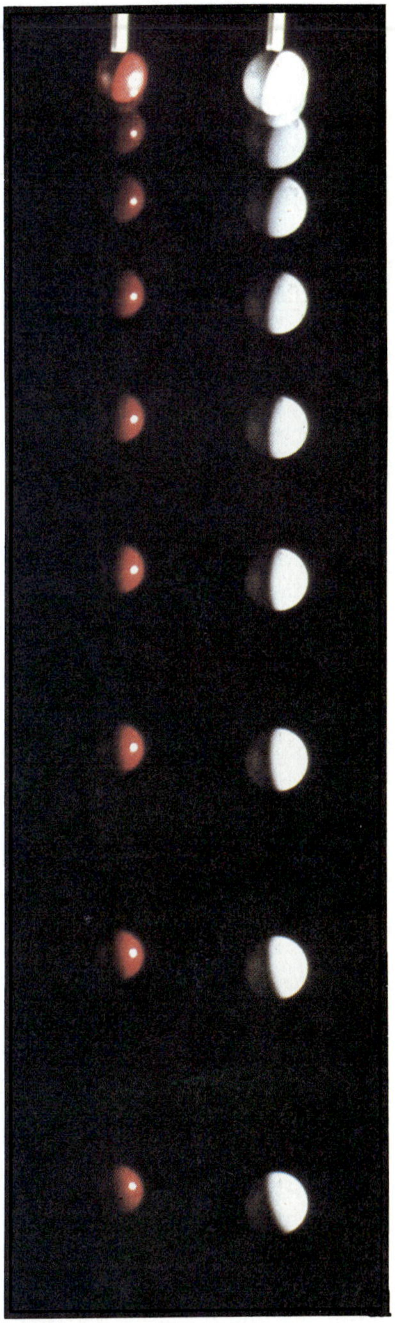

Kodansha

FIGURE 4-10. Though the white object is larger than the red, both fall at the same rate.

Stress the idea that all falling objects fall at the same rate of acceleration in a vacuum.

How does air affect the rate at which an object falls?

The upward force of air against the object is equal to the downward force of gravity at **terminal speed**. It is the highest speed reached by a falling object. The net force on the object is zero. The object will keep falling at a constant speed and no longer accelerates.

Objects such as feathers, Ping-Pong balls, and open handkerchiefs fall more slowly. These objects meet more air resistance when they fall. **Air resistance** is the upward force of air against an object. In a vacuum, there is no air. Therefore, all objects accelerate continuously.

FIGURE 4-11. A rocket is designed to reduce air resistance. A parachute is designed to make use of air resistance.

FPG

a

Greg Miller

b

Making Sure

12. A billiard ball is dropped from the roof of a building. It takes three seconds to strike the ground. What is the speed of the billiard ball at the instant before it strikes the ground? *3 x 9.8 m/s = 29.4 m/s*

4:5 Motion in Two Directions

Suppose you are standing in a moving jet airplane. You jump up two feet off the floor. Will you land in the same spot on the floor when you come down from your jump? Remember, you are moving forward when you go up and come down. On a sheet of paper, draw the path of your jump.

Give two examples of an object moving forward and downward at the same time.

A large stone is dropped from the top of the mast of a moving ship. Does the stone fall to the deck directly below the point from which it was dropped? Or does the stone land in front or behind the mast? Assume that the mast is straight. Also, remember the ship is moving forward as the stone falls.

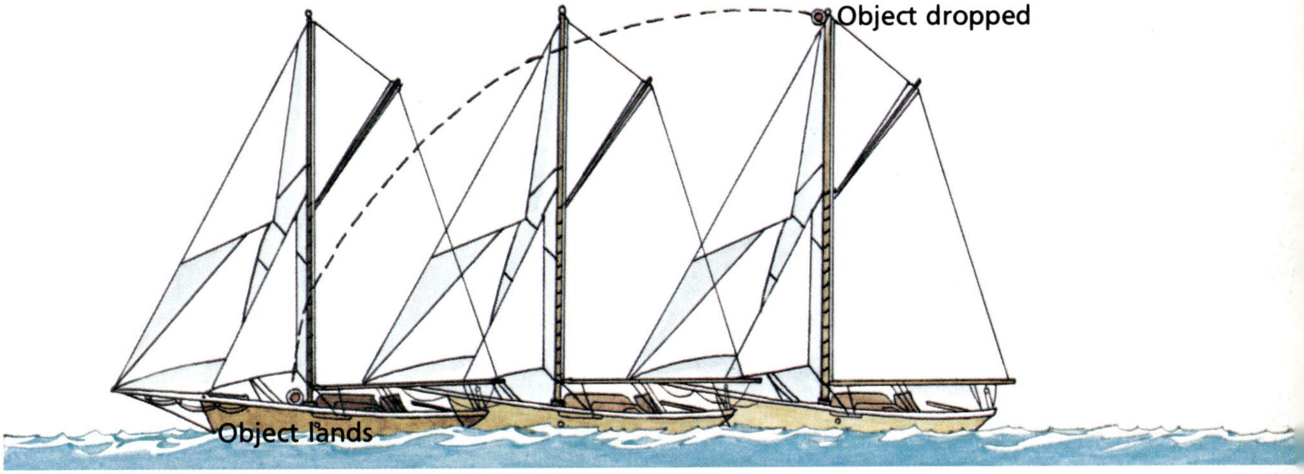

FIGURE 4-12. The path of the falling stone is curved because the ship is in motion.

The falling stone lands on the deck directly below the point from which it was dropped. Before it was released, the stone was moving forward at the same velocity as the ship. The stone kept its forward velocity during its fall. While falling, the stone had two velocities: forward and downward. The forward motion caused it to continue in the same path as the boat during its fall.

An arrow is shot parallel with the ground, Figure 4-13. How long does it take for the arrow to fall to the earth? The time depends on the acceleration of gravity. The forward motion of the arrow has no effect on the time it takes to fall. In an experiment, the time it takes for an arrow to strike the ground is measured. Then the time

Kodansha

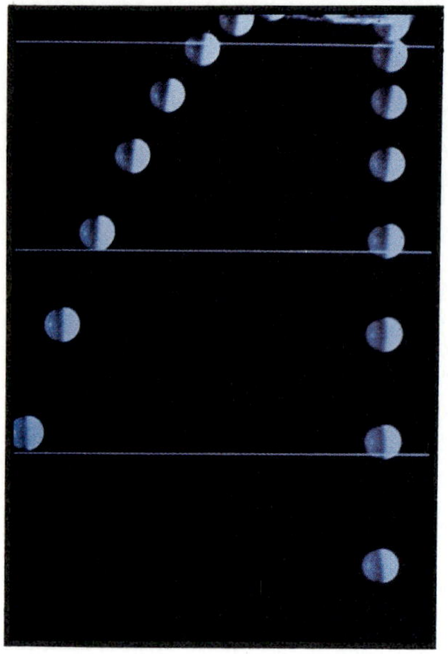

a

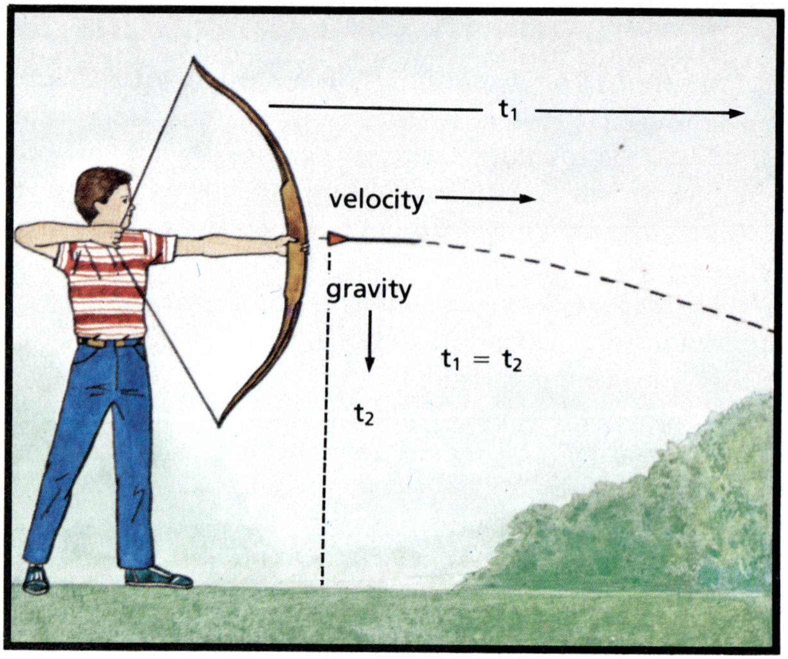

b

FIGURE 4-13. In (a), the free falling object and the projectile (the object on the right) are falling at the same rate. In (b), if the archer drops an arrow at the same time another is shot, both will reach the ground at the same time.

What is the difference between horizontal and vertical?

is measured for an arrow to strike the ground when it is dropped from the same height as the bow. Both times are the same.

Objects such as stones, balls, and arrows when thrown or shot have two kinds of motion—horizontal and vertical. To hit a target, you cannot throw or shoot straight at it. You must allow for the object's fall.

4-3 Detailed information concerning this Activity can be found in the Teacher's Guide at the front of this book.

ACTIVITY *How does the velocity of a ball change during its flight?*

Figure 4-14 shows a ball in motion. The time interval between each position of the ball is 1/30 second. **(1)** *Place a piece of thin, centimeter-graph paper on top of the drawing. Mark each position of the ball with a dot.* **(2)** *Remove the graph paper. Draw straight lines connecting every third position of the ball. The time between three positions of the ball is 0.1 second. Why? The length of each straight line shows the average velocity during each 0.1 second of flight. At what point is the velocity the greatest? At what point is the change in velocity the greatest? What two forces act on the ball?*

3 x 1/30 = 1/10 = 0.1 s

at the beginning and end of the motion

the highest point in the curve

gravity, the forward thrust of the ball

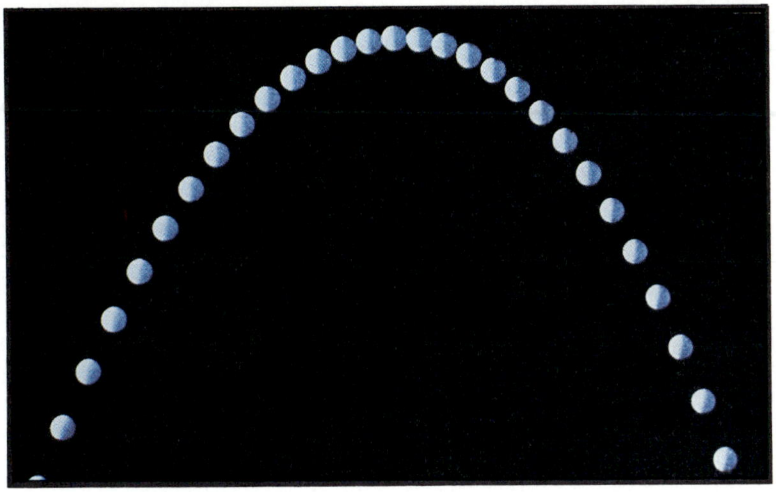

FIGURE 4-14. The motion of a projectile

4:6 Motion in Curves

Centrifugal force is a fictitious force and is not referred to in this text.

What kind of push or pull do you feel in a car when it rounds a sharp curve? Your body may slide sideways. You feel as though you are being pushed outward.

What is a centripetal force?

It takes a force to keep an object moving in a circle. This force is called **centripetal** (sen TRIHP ut ul) **force.** Centripetal force acts toward the center of a circle, Figure 4-15. The centripetal force of the road on a car's tires pushes inward on a car rounding a curve. If the car goes around the curve too fast, inertia may cause it to go off the road. Highways are banked on curves to improve contact between the tire and the road. Banked means the outside edge is higher than the inside edge. Banked roads increase highway safety because the amount of friction between the tire and the road is increased.

Describe two examples of an object moving in a curved path.

FIGURE 4-15.

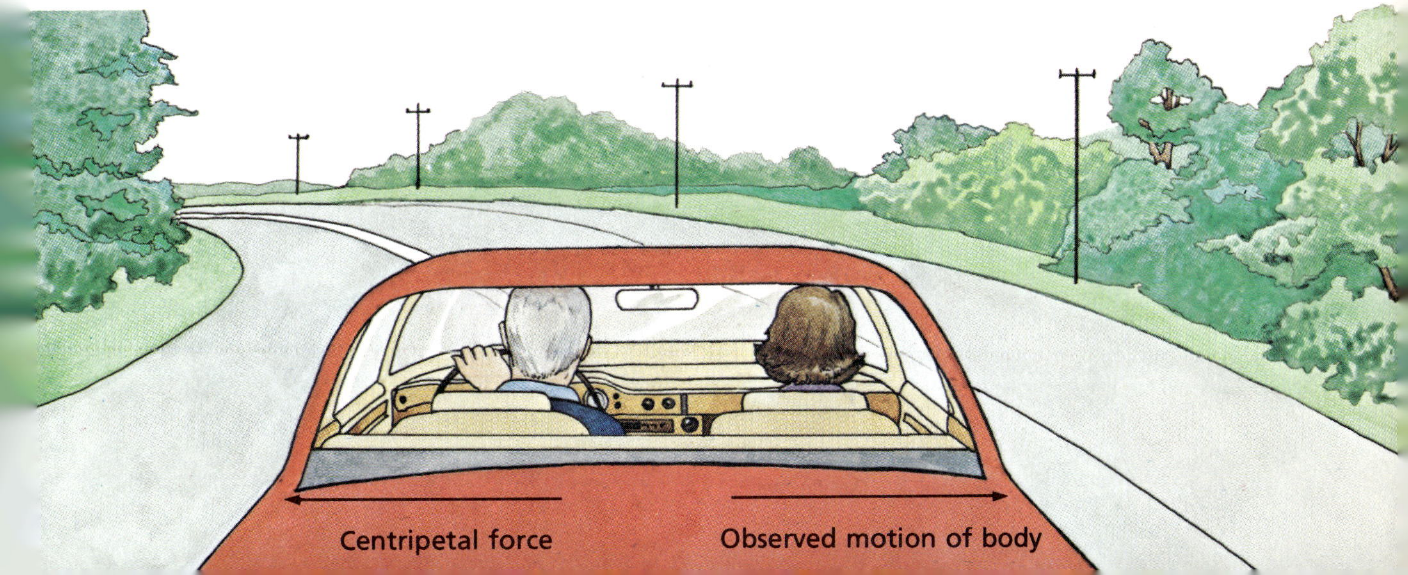

4-4 Detailed information concerning this Activity can be found in the Teacher's Guide at the front of this book.

Activity How does centripetal force affect the velocity of an object?

Setting Up

1.5 meters of fishing line
washers
15-centimeter piece of glass
glass tubing wrapped with tape (fire polished)
paper clip
two-hole rubber stopper

Getting Started

1. *Arrange the equipment in Figure 4-16a.*
2. *Hold the tube with one hand and the string with the other hand. Whirl the stopper over your head.*
3. *Now add six washers to the paper clip as in Figure 4-16b. Whirl the stopper at a rate which keeps the clip in the same position. Have a classmate count the number of revolutions in 30 seconds. Record this value in a table.*
4. *Repeat Step 3 using three and nine washers. Record the number of revolutions in 30 seconds.*

FIGURE 4-16.

Keeping Track

1. *Calculate the period of revolution for three, six, and nine washers.*

$$\text{period} = \frac{\text{number of revolutions}}{\text{30 seconds}}$$

Record these values in the table.

2. *Draw a graph plotting the period and number of washers.*

Number of Washers	Number of Revolutions	Period

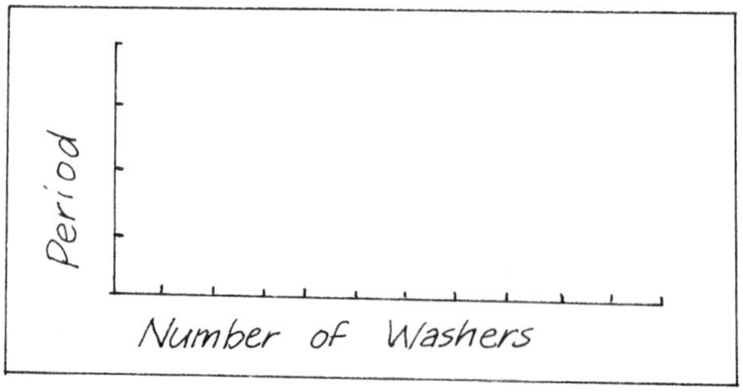

Summing Up

1. *How is the period related to the mass of washers on the end of the string?*
2. *The number of washers on the string is a measure of centripetal force. How is the centripetal force affected by changes in stopper velocity?*

Making Sure

13. Why might a car slide off an icy road when the car rounds a curve? *Ice reduces centripetal force. Inertia keeps the car moving in a straight line.*

14. Hold on to a rubber band tied to a small lead sinker. Whirl the sinker in a circle. Why does the rubber band stretch? *The inertia of the sinker pulls the rubber band. The centripetal force that keeps the sinker moving in a circle also causes it to stretch.*

15. How does the banking of a road on a curve affect the centripetal force which acts on a car? *Driving on a banked curve puts more of the weight of the car over the wheels. Thus, the centripetal force is increased.*

4:7 Momentum

How do mass and speed affect the momentum of an object?

To simplify the introduction of forces and motion it is assumed in the problems and examples that the objects mentioned are inelastic.

Every object in motion has a property called **momentum** (moh MENT um). The amount of momentum depends on the mass and velocity of the object. As the mass or velocity of an object increases, so does the momentum. A baseball has more momentum than a tennis ball when they travel at the same velocity. Why? The baseball has more mass. Suppose a truck and a sports car go down a freeway together at a speed of 88 kilometers per hour. Which vehicle has more momentum? *The truck has a greater mass.* The truck has more momentum because it has more mass.

Which has more momentum, a fast-pitched softball or a slow-pitched softball? The fast-pitched softball has more momentum because its velocity is greater. A rock falls off a cliff. Does the rock gain or lose momentum as it falls? Momentum increases because the velocity of the rock increases during the fall.

Air friction is not considered in explaining the rate of fall.

FIGURE 4-17. If the two skaters push against each other, they will roll away in opposite directions. Which skater will be moving faster?

Hickson-Bender Photography

a

b

Zimmerman/FPG

FIGURE 4-18. (a) When the swinging object on the left loses momentum what happens to the object on the right? (b) If the child and adult ski down the hill together, which will have more momentum?

The greater the momentum of an object, the more force it takes to stop it. An object at rest has zero momentum. Doubling the speed of an object doubles its momentum. A 3600-kilogram truck moving at 8 kilometers per hour has the same momentum as a 1800-kilogram car moving at 16 kilometers per hour. When they are both moving with the same speed, the truck has the greater momentum. Why?

A moving object gains or loses momentum when its speed changes. The law of conservation of momentum states that *momentum is never created or destroyed.* When an object loses momentum, something else gains it. If an object gains momentum, something else loses it.

Suppose a baseball player swings a bat to hit a ball. The momentum gained by the ball as it flies off is equal to the momentum lost by the bat. If two billiard balls collide on a pool table, there is no net gain or loss of momentum. The speed of one ball increases and the speed of the other decreases. The change in speeds causes one ball to gain momentum and the other to lose it.

Hickson-Bender Photography

FIGURE 4-19. Momentum is transferred when the billiard balls collide. However, some momentum is lost because of friction between the balls and the table.

Making Sure

16. Which ball has more momentum at a forward speed of 5 meters per second, a billiard ball or a tennis ball? Why? *billiard ball has more mass*

17. A golf ball and a tennis ball of the same mass are both traveling at 10 meters per second. Compare the momentum. *the momentum of both is equal*

18. How is momentum related to the mass and velocity of an object? *directly proportional*

19. A bowling ball and a golf ball are dropped from a tenth-story window. Which has more momentum when it reaches the ground? *bowling ball*

20. How do the velocities of the bowling ball and golf ball compare in problem 19? *they are the same*

Frontiers
Imitating a Hip

Researchers at the Massachusetts Institute of Technology are using a special machine to study a crippling disease. It is a form of arthritis called osteoarthritis (ahs tee oh ar THRITE us) of the hip. In this form the hip joint simply wears out. Often there seems to be no reason for the hip to fail. To study the disease, enginers at MIT developed a machine that imitates hip movement. A machine that imitates something is called a simulator.

The hip simulator has a small metal ball that is placed in a hip socket. On one side, the ball has a rod which is connected to the equipment that moves the ball. The ball is a Moore prosthesis. A prosthesis is a device used to replace damaged or missing parts of a body. A Moore prosthesis replaces the top of the thigh bone in correcting some kinds of hip problems. Since pressure produces stress on a joint, engineers placed 14 sensitive pressure gauges on the ball. The gauges are connected to a computer. Using the gauges, researchers can find the pattern of stress in a hip socket.

The simulator moves the ball within a hip socket, imitating a normal walk. A normal walking cycle exerts pressures three to five times the weight of a body on the joint. Using the readings of the pressure gauges, the computer produces a map of the stress on the joint. To study the stress on real hip sockets, scientists use sockets removed from dead bodies.

Researchers thought that the pressure on a hip socket would be even throughout the joint. However, results from the simulator showed that the pressure is not even. In fact the researchers found that the pattern is quite irregular. By studying the stress on the hip joint, researchers hope to find the cause of osteoarthritis. Finding the cause is the first step in finding a cure.

Points to Remember

1. Inertia is the tendency of an object at rest to remain at rest. It is also the tendency of an object in motion to remain in motion. *4:1*
2. It takes a force to start an object moving and a force to stop motion. It also takes a force to change the speed or direction of an object. *4:1*
3. Rate of increase or decrease in speed depends on the amount of force and amount of mass. *4:2*
4. For every action force, there is an equal and opposite reaction force. *4:3*
5. Objects which are thrown or shot (baseballs, arrows) have horizontal and vertical motion. *4:5*
6. Centripetal force on an object moving in a curve acts inward towards the center of the curve. *4:6*
7. Every moving object has momentum which depends on its mass and speed. *4:7*

Words to Use

Write a sentence in which you use correctly each of the following words or terms.

acceleration	deceleration	momentum
action force	gravity	reaction force
air resistance	horizontal	terminal speed
centripetal force	inertia	vertical

Questions for Review

Do not write in this book.

A. True or False *Have the students rewrite the false statements to make them correct.*

Determine whether each of the following sentences is true or false.

T **1.** A force is needed to stop a moving object.

T **2.** Acceleration is always caused by a force.

T **3.** It takes a force to accelerate a golf ball.

T **4.** Reaction force is equal and opposite to the action force.

F **5.** ~~Inertia~~ makes a lawn sprinkler turn. *The force of the water*

F **6.** As the speed of a moving objcct increases, momentum ~~decreases~~. *increases*

F 7. Speed and acceleration are the same. not

F 8. To hit a distant target, an arrow is aimed directly ~~at~~ the target. above

T 9. Centripetal force increases as a merry-go-round increases speed.

T 10. A baseball gains momentum when hit with a bat.

B. Multiple Choice

Choose the word or phrase that correctly completes each of the following sentences.

1. Force is measured with a *(scale, meter stick, graduated cylinder).*
2. It takes *(more, less, the same)* force to accelerate a car as/than it does to keep it at constant speed.
3. A rocket accelerates because of *(action-reaction, inertia, centripetal)* force.
4. Traveling at 5 km/h, a *(tennis ball, golf ball, bowling ball)* would have the most momentum.
5. The size of action-reaction forces is *(equal, different).*
6. When an object falls, its rate of acceleration *(increases, decreases, does not change).*
7. When you throw a ball to a friend, the ball shows *(2, 3, 4)* kinds of motion.
8. According to Newton's first law, every moving object has *(motion, acceleration, inertia).*
9. According to Newton's second law, acceleration of an object *(increases, decreases, stays the same)* as the amount of force causing the acceleration increases.
10. According to Newton's third law, when a force is exerted on an object, the object exerts an equal force in the *(same, opposite)* direction.

C. Completion

Complete each of the following sentences with a word or phrase that will make the sentence correct.

1. Centripetal force keeps a car moving in a curved path on a highway.
2. A(n) newton is a unit of force.

3. The attractive force between two objects is called gravity.
4. For every action force, there is an equal and opposite reaction force.
5. An arrow in flight has two motions: horizontal and vertical.
6. The point in which a falling object stops accelerating is known as terminal velocity.
7. As an object falls, its downward velocity increases.
8. As an object falls, its rate of acceleration does not change.
9. An object at rest has zero momentum.
10. Deceleration is caused by forces opposing motion.

Detailed answers to these questions are given in the Teacher's Guide at the front of this book.

D. How and Why

1. Give an example of Newton's second law.
2. How can you use a falling stone to judge the height of a bridge?
3. How does an automatic washing machine remove water from wet clothes?
4. Compare the falling speed of two sheets of paper, one crumpled, one not. Is there a difference? Explain.

More Ideas to Explore

1. Make a model of an airplane. Make a drawing of your model. Label the parts of the airplane that control the speed and direction of the airplane's flight. Explain the forces involved in changing speed and direction.
2. Using the library, prepare a short biography of Isaac Newton. Report your findings to the class.

Readings to Discover

Chase, Sara B., *Moving to Win: The Physics of Sports.* NY: Messner, 1977.

Gardner, Robert, and Wegster, David, *Moving Right Along: A Book of Science Experiments and Puzzles About Motion.* Garden City, NY: Doubleday and Co., 1978.

Helman, Hal, *Energy and Inertia.* NY: Lippincott and Co., 1970.

Legunn, Joel, *Motion.* Makato, MN: Creative Education Press, 1971.

Unit 2

You go to the grocery store and find the shelves disorganized. What are some of the problems you encounter? Matter can be thought of as a grocery store containing billions of items. Unit 2 will show you the ways matter can be classified to make it easier to study.

combustion Hickson-Bender Photography

Classification of Matter

glassware Francek/FPG

George Anderson/Media Group

This mass of dust clouds and gases can be found thousands of light years from the earth. As this matter changes over millions of years, new stars will be born. What is matter? How many kinds of matter are there? What kinds of changes can matter undergo? How do these changes affect the way matter behaves?

Tersch

Properties of Matter

5

Chapter 5 is an introduction to matter. The states of matter are discussed. Physical and chemical properties are defined and contrasted. The differences between chemical and physical changes are also discussed. See the Teacher's Guide at the front of this book for additional teaching strategies for this chapter.

5:1 Matter

GOAL: *You will learn the basic properties of all matter and the changes that occur in matter.*

Look around you. Everything around you is matter. You are matter. Matter is anything that has mass and takes up space. Mass is the amount of material an object contains. It can be measured. Can you think of anything that is not matter? Are thoughts and ideas matter? Is heat matter? Is air matter?

What is matter?

Two pieces of matter cannot occupy the same space at the same time. This characteristic is one property of all matter. When you get into the bathtub, your body pushes water away. The water level in the tub rises. When a nail is pounded into a board, the nail makes a hole in the wood.

5-1 Detailed information concerning this Activity can be found in the Teacher's Guide at the front of this book.

ACTIVITY *Does the water level change?*

(1) *Obtain a 25-mL graduated cylinder and 5 marbles.* **(2)** *Fill the graduate to the 10-mL mark with water.* **(3)** *Gently drop a marble into the water. Note the change in the water level.* **(4)** *Add 4 more marbles to the water, one at a time. Now read the water level.*

Why does the water level rise when you add the marbles? How much space is taken by the marbles? How much space does one marble occupy? As you added the marbles, did the amount of air in the cylinder increase or decrease? Why?

FIGURE 5-1.

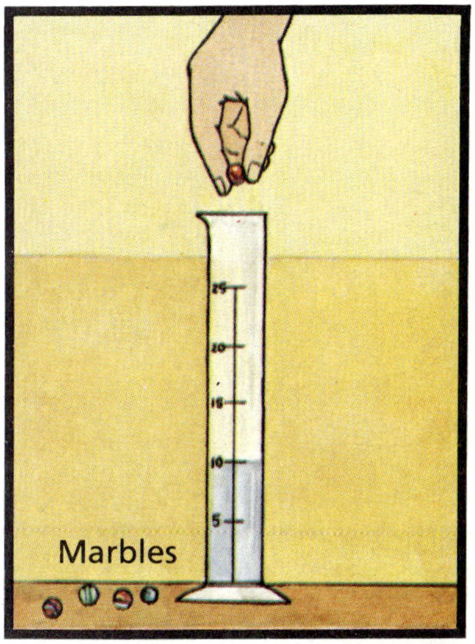

5:2 States of Matter

Name the four states of matter.

All matter exists in one of four states. These are solid, liquid, gas, and plasma. Each state of matter has a specific set of properties. A **solid** has a definite shape and volume. Ice is a solid. Salt, aluminum, and carbon are other examples of solids.

A **liquid** does not have a definite shape. Think of the times you've filled a glass with water. The water takes the shape of its container. Water, mercury, and gasoline are examples of liquids. Liquids have a definite volume.

How is gas different from a liquid?

A **gas** does not have a definite shape or volume. Fill a balloon with air. You can change the shape of the balloon by squeezing it. By increasing the force (squeezing), the balloon pops out in different directions. The air fills the new shape. When you allow air to escape from a balloon, the volume of the air increases. A gas can be compressed to a smaller volume by increasing the force on it. A gas such as air always takes the shape of its container. What shape does air take in a basketball?

What is plasma?

Plasma, the fourth state of matter, exists only at very high temperatures. The surface of our sun is in the plasma state. Plasma has some of the properties of a gas. However, unlike a gas, plasma consists of electrically charged particles. Scientists are trying to learn more about this state. There are some nuclear reactions which occur only in the plasma state. These reactions can be an important source of energy. This energy can be converted to electricity.

FIGURE 5-2. All matter can be classified as a solid, liquid, gas, or plasma.

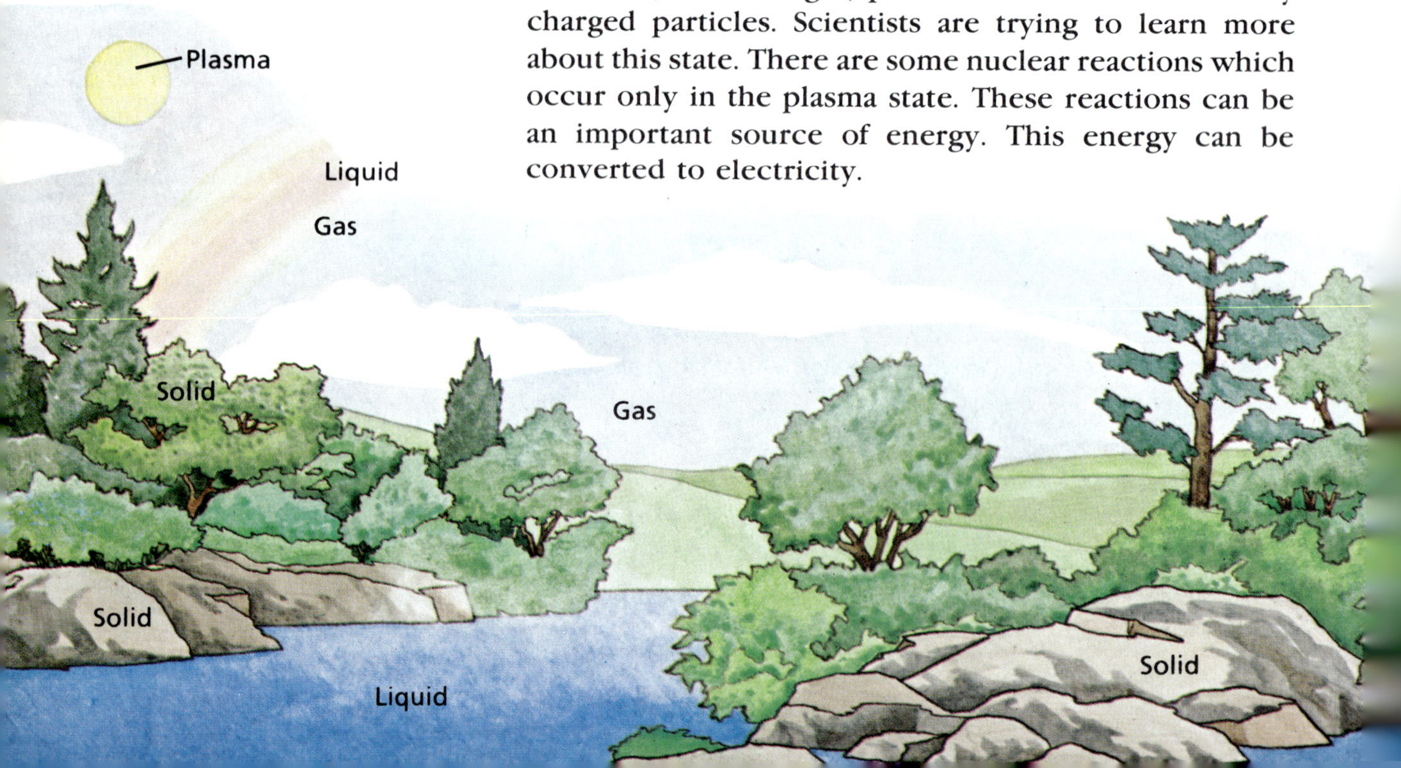

Liquids
take the shape of their container.

Young/Hoffbines

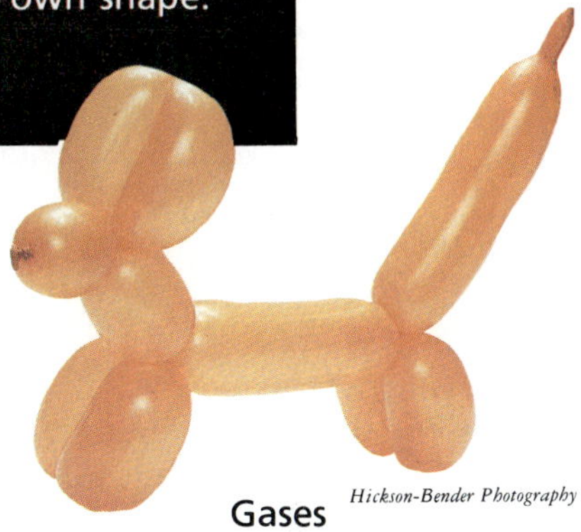

Hickson-Bender Photography

Gases
expand to fill any shape.

FIGURE 5-3. Solids have their own shape. Liquids take the shape of their container. Gases expand to fill any shape.

5:3 Physical Properties

Suppose you have four test tubes in a rack. Each test tube is filled with a liquid. The liquid in the first test tube is blue. In the second test tube, the liquid has a bad odor. A small steel ball floats on the liquid in the third test tube. When you hold the fourth test tube in your hands, the liquid evaporates rapidly. How can you determine whether any of the liquids is water?

One way to decide if a liquid is water is to compare the properties of the liquid with water. Is water normally blue? Does it have a bad odor? Will a steel ball float in it? Does it evaporate rapidly? These properties are called physical properties. A **physical property** of matter depends only upon matter itself.

What is a physical property?

Physical properties include state, color, taste, odor, freezing point, and boiling point. These properties may be observed without changing the chemical composition of the substance.

List four kinds of physical properties.

You observe the physical properties of matter everyday without ever realizing it. What kind of shoe is worn for playing basketball? What kind of shoe is worn for ballet dancing? The physical properties of each type of shoe make it suitable for a particular activity.

Table 5-1
Some Physical Properties of Matter

Frank Psaute

Density:
A hot air balloon rises as the density of air changes.

Thomas Russell

Melting Point:
Low melting metals are useful as solder to hold matter together.

Eric Hoffhines

Physical State:
Mercury remains a liquid over a broad range of temperatures making it useful in thermometers.

Greg Miller

Luster:
The reflective quality of silver makes it useful as a backing for mirrors.

Linda Young

Malleability:
Tin can be pounded and shaped into art objects like this lantern.

Young/Hoffhines

Electrical Conductivity:
The ability of copper to carry current and be drawn into thin wire makes it useful in electrical wiring.

Eric Hoffhines

Thermal Conductivity:
Aluminum is an excellent conductor of heat making it useful for pots and pans.

Thomas Russell

Odor: The pleasant odor of a rose makes it useful as a base for perfumes.

Frank V. Lisy

Taste:
The taste of berries provides us with a natural energy source.

Color:
Tree bark and roots are useful in making natural dyes.

Making Sure

1. What physical properties could you use to tell the difference between the following pairs of matter?
   a. coal—snow
   b. strawberry ice cream—vanilla ice cream
   c. vinegar—water
   d. lead—aluminum
   e. salt—sugar
   f. a baseball—a football

a. color, melting point
b. color, taste
c. taste, density
d. taste
e. taste
f. shape

2. What physical property do all of the following have in common: glass, water, carbon dioxide, plastic wrap, air? *all are transparent*
3. Classify the substances in problem 2 as solids, liquids, or gases. *solids-glass, plastic wrap; liquids-water; gases-air, carbon dioxide*

5:4 Density

What is density?

Density is also a physical property. **Density** is the mass of a substance per unit of volume. It may be expressed in grams per cubic centimeter (g/cm^3). Water has a density of 1 g/cm^3. Density is an important physical property of a substance. A substance may be identified by its density. Steel and polished aluminum may look alike, but they have different densities. The density of a pure substance remains constant for a specific temperature. The density does not depend on how much of the substance you have. Why? *Every bit of it has the same density.* The density of a pure substance can change with changes in temperature. A mineral, such as quartz, also has a certain density by which it can be identified. Densities of different minerals may be used to identify unknown mineral samples.

Hickson-Bender Photography

FIGURE 5-5. Though the volumes of both substances are equal, the balance shows the masses are not. Which substance is more dense?

List three examples of the densities of substances.

Table 5-1

Densities of Some Common Substances

Substance	Density	Substance	Density
hydrogen	0.00009	aluminum	2.7
oxygen	0.0013	iron	7.9
water	1.0	copper	8.9
sugar	1.6	lead	11.3
table salt	2.2	mercury	13.6
quartz	2.6	gold	19.3

How is density calculated?

To find the density of a substance, you must know its mass and volume. Since density is mass per unit volume, the equation is

$$density = \frac{mass}{volume} \qquad D = \frac{m}{V}$$

Example

A rectangular object measures 3 cm × 2 cm × 1 cm, Figure 5-6. The volume of this object ($l \times w \times h$) is 6 cm^3. The object has a mass of 4 grams. What is its density?

Solution:

(a) Write the equation for density.

$$D = \frac{m}{V}$$

(b) Substitute the values for mass and volume given in the problem.

$$D = \frac{4\ g}{6\ cm^3} \qquad D = 0.67\ g/cm^3$$

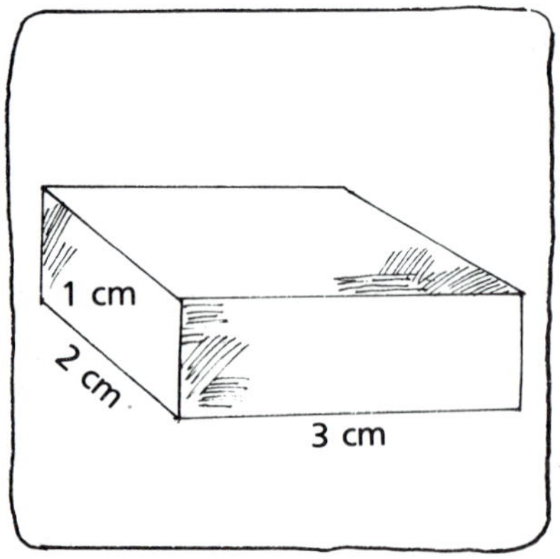

FIGURE 5-6.

5-2 Detailed information concerning this Activity can be found in the Teacher's Guide at the front of this book.

Activity

What does it mean for a substance to be more dense than another?

Setting Up

balance
100-mL beaker or other clear container
graduated cylinder
3 small paper or plastic drinking cups
cooking oil, molasses, water

Getting Started

1. *Label the cups A, B, and C. Use the balance to find the mass of each cup. Record these values in a table.*
2. *Use a clean graduated cylinder to measure 25 mL of water. Pour the water into cup A.*
3. *Find the mass of the cup and water.*
4. *Use the graduated cylinder to measure 25 mL of cooking oil. Pour the oil into cup B.*
5. *Find the mass of the cup and oil.*
6. *Repeat Steps 2 and 3 using cup C and molasses.*

Keeping Track

	A	B	C
mass of cup & liquid			
mass of cup			
mass of liquid			
volume of liquid			
density of liquid			

FIGURE 5-7.

Summing Up

1. *Which liquid has the greatest density?* molasses
2. *If you carefully poured each liquid into a 100-mL beaker, which liquid would be on top? Which liquid would be on the bottom? Try it and see.* cooking oil on top, molasses on the bottom
3. *How do the densities of the liquids compare with their positions in the beaker?* low to high, top to bottom

Making Sure

4. What is the density of 10 cm^3 of corn syrup that has a mass of 10.8 grams? *1.08 g/cm^3*
5. What is the density of 25 cm^3 of salad oil that has a mass of 23 grams? *0.92 g/cm^3*
6. What is the density of 30 cm^3 of vinegar that has a mass of 30.3 grams? *1.01 g/cm^3*
7. Vinegar and salad oil are two liquids which do not mix. Which liquid floats on top of the other? Why? *Salad oil floats because it is less dense than the vinegar.*

5:5 Physical Changes

When a pane of glass breaks, the size of the glass changes. However, the pieces still contain the same substances as the original pane of glass. When wood is used for a shelf or chair, it is still wood. Only its size and shape have changed. When matter changes in size, shape, or state, it undergoes a **physical change.**

What is a physical change?

FIGURE 5-8. Some types of physical changes.

Define: boiling, melting, evaporation, and freezing.

Boiling, melting, evaporation, and freezing are changes in the state of matter. When a substance such as water boils, it changes from the liquid to the gaseous state. The **boiling point** is the temperature at which this change occurs. Melting is a change from the solid to liquid state. **Melting point** is the temperature at which this change occurs. When a liquid freezes, it changes to the solid state. This temperature is the **freezing point.** Water changes to ice at its freezing point.

Boiling point and freezing point are specific physical properties of a substance. Unknown substances can often be identified by these temperatures. The boiling and freezing points of the unknown substance can be compared to those of known substances.

What is condensation?

Water vapor is water in the gaseous state. When a gas is cooled to a low temperature it changes into a liquid. The change in state is called **condensation.** You can see the condensation of water vapor if you blow on a mirror.

A change of state can occur if the pressure is changed. Have you ever packed a snowball? The pressure and warmth of your hands caused the snow to melt. The water then refroze to ice when you released the pressure.

Thomas Zimmerman/FPG

Thomas Russell

FIGURE 5-9. A skater is able to glide over the ice because the pressure exerted by the skate blades melts the ice. The water acts as a lubricant between the ice and the blade.

Table 5-2

Freezing and Boiling Points of Some Substances (in °C)

Substance	Freezing point	Boiling point
carbon dioxide	−56.57	−78.47
lead	327.4	1751.0
mercury	−38.8	356.5
oxygen	−218.8	−182.9
table salt	808.0	1473.0
water	0.0	100.0

5-3 Detailed information concerning this Activity can be found in the Teacher's Guide at the front of this book.

ACTIVITY *What changes in state do you see?*

Fill a beaker ⅓ full of hot water. Place an ice cube in the water. Cover the beaker with a watch glass. Place an ice cube on the watch glass.

What change of state occurs at the surface of the water in the beaker? What change of state is occurring on the underside of the watch glass? What change of state is occurring in the ice cubes? melting

FIGURE 5-10.

liquid to gas at the surface, gas to liquid on the underside of the watch glass

5-4 Detailed information concerning this Activity can be found in the Teacher's Guide at the front of this book.

Activity *How cold is water when it freezes?*

Setting Up

clock
600-mL beaker
ice
salt
stirring rod
test tube
2 thermometers

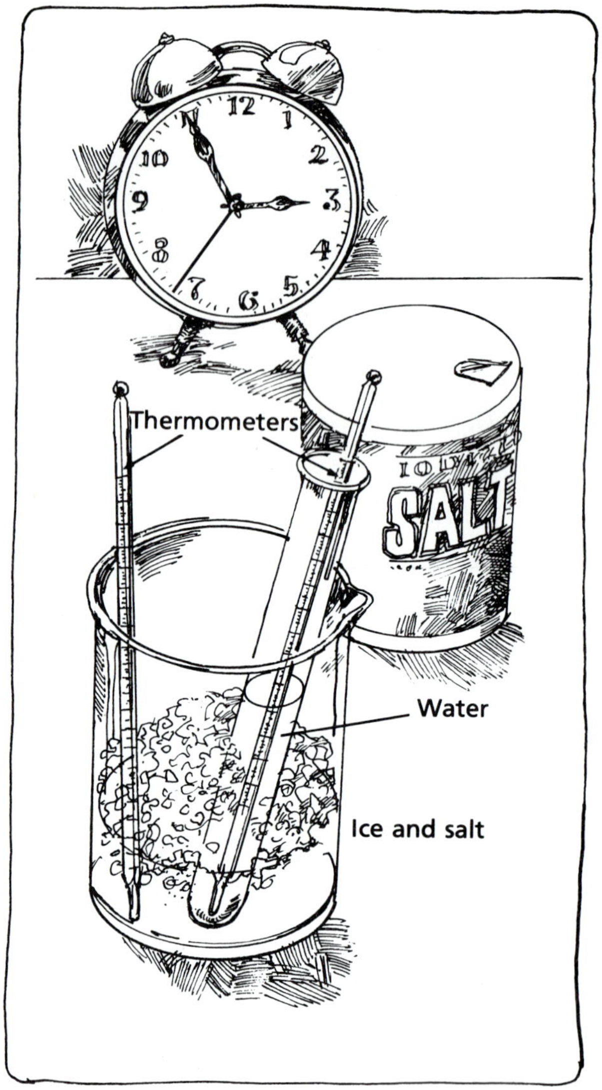

FIGURE 5-11.

Getting Started

1. *Fill the beaker with ice.*
2. *Sprinkle about 250 grams of salt over the ice.*
3. *Add 5 mL of water to a test tube. Place the test tube in the beaker.*
4. *Place one thermometer in the test tube and the other in the ice-salt mixture. Stir the ice-salt mixture gently with a glass stirring rod as it cools the test tube.*
5. *At the end of every minute, record the temperatures of the water and the ice-salt mixture in a table like the one below. Do this until the temperature readings on both thermometers are equal.*

Keeping Track

Time	Temperature of water	Temperature of ice-salt

1. *Draw a graph plotting the time and temperature of the water in the test tube.* The graph should go down in a nearly straight line.

Summing Up

1. *Does the water in the test tube undergo a physical change?* yes, change of state
2. *Why do you think salt was mixed with the ice?* lowers the freezing point of the ice
3. *What is the freezing point of the water in the test tube? How does your graph look at this temperature?*
about 0°C; the graph flattens

5:6 Chemical Properties

Hickson-Bender Photography

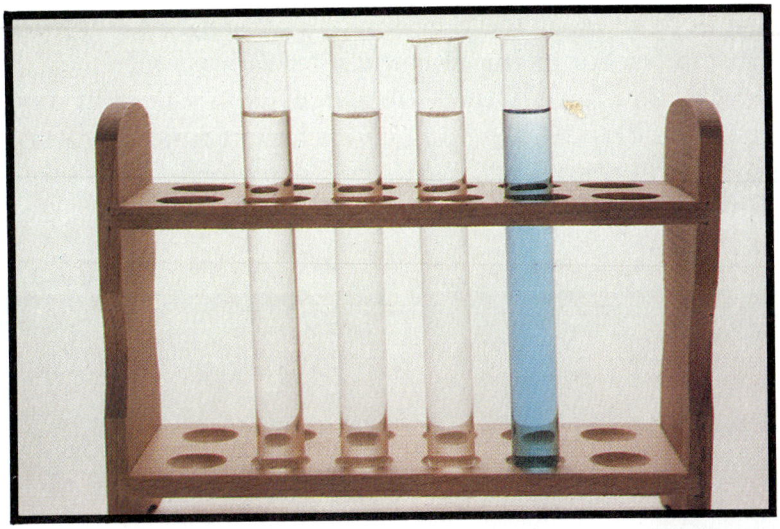

FIGURE 5-12. Are any of the liquids water?

Suppose you have four test tubes, Figure 5-12. Each contains a liquid. How could you find out if any one of the four liquids is water? One way is to see how each reacts with other substances. Then, compare your observations with the way water reacts. When iron filings are sprinkled into the first test tube, the liquid bubbles and a gas escapes, Figure 5-13a. This gas burns with a blue flame when tested with a flaming splint. When small pieces of iron are sprinkled into the second test tube, another gas is given off, Figure 5-13b. This gas has an unpleasant odor. What does water do when iron is added to it? Try it. Observe any change that takes place. Does either of these two test tubes contain pure water?

The liquid in the third test tube turns black when iron is added, Figure 5-13c. If a small nail is placed in the fourth test tube, it takes on a coating, Figure 5-13d. This coating appears to be some other metal. Is either of these two liquids pure water? How do you know?

No, water does not react in that way. Test water to see.

FIGURE 5-13.

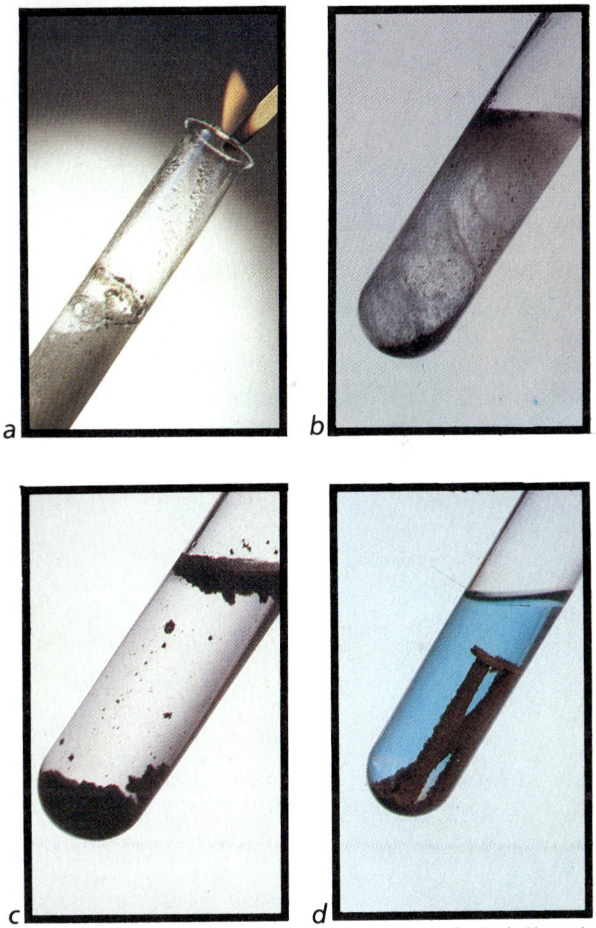

Hickson-Bender Photography

What is a chemical property? List two examples of a chemical property.

The properties described for these liquids are chemical properties. **Chemical properties** are those that depend upon the reaction of a substance with other substances. For example, some substances combine with oxygen and burn. Other substances combine with oxygen and corrode. A rusting nail is an example of **corrosion.** Iron combines with oxygen to form rust. Some substances react with other substances to produce gases or metals.

Don Parsisson Hickson-Bender Photography Hickson-Bender Photography

a b c

FIGURE 5-14. Silver reacts with air to form a silver compound, tarnish (a). Sugar reacts with acid (b). Sodium reacts with water (c). All three pictures show chemical properties.

Making Sure

wood, coal, paper, cloth, magnesium, hydrogen are examples

8. Name five substances that burn.

9. Why is burning a chemical property?

Burning, in most cases, requires oxygen to occur.

10. The following paragraph is a description of the properties of silver. Determine whether each of the underlined properties is chemical or physical. Use a dictionary to find the definitions of words you do not know.

***Silver**

White metal, more malleable and ductile than any other metal except gold. Silver is an excellent conductor of heat and electricity. Melting point 960.5°C; boiling point about 2000°C. Silver is not attacked by water or atmospheric oxygen . . . Inert to most acids; reacts readily with dilute nitric acid. . . .

Physical	**Chemical**
white	*not attacked by water*
malleable	*not attacked by O_2*
ductile	*inert to most acids*
conductor	*reacts with dilute HNO_3*
melting point	
boiling point	

*Merck Index (Merck & Co., Inc., 1976) p. 8239.

5:7 Chemical Changes

What is a chemical change?

What happens when a piece of wood is burned? Heat, light, and smoke are given off. A small pile of ashes is left. Has the substance been changed? It is more than just a change in the appearance of the wood. The composition of the wood has changed. In a **chemical change** new substances with different properties are formed. Chemical changes usually cause the release of heat, light, or electricity.

yes

FIGURE 5-15. A chemical change can produce light (a). Water can be separated into hydrogen and oxygen by electrolysis (b). A permanent wave chemically changes the protein structure of hair (c).

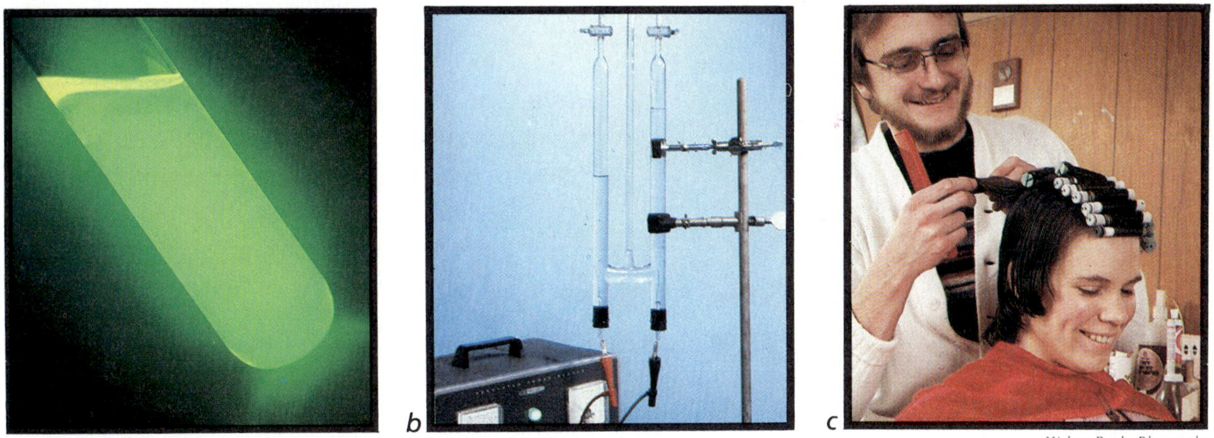

a b c

Hickson-Bender Photography

Describe two examples of a chemical change.

Substances can be broken down, or decomposed, by chemical change. For example, an electric current can be passed through water. The water will decompose into hydrogen and oxygen. The properties of hydrogen and oxygen are different from the properties of water. Pour a few drops of vinegar on some baking soda. What happens? Is the result a physical or chemical change?

bubbling occurs, chemical change

Table 5-3

Physical and Chemical Changes

Physical Change	Chemical Change
Little energy lost or gained when compared to chemical change	*Heat, light, or some other form of energy lost or gained*
Original substances remain; size, shape, or state may change	*Substances are changed to other substances with new properties*
Can be used to separate mixtures	*Can be used to break up or form compounds*

5-5 See the Teacher's Guide at the front of this book for a detailed equipment list.

ACTIVITY How does zinc react with dilute hydrochloric acid?

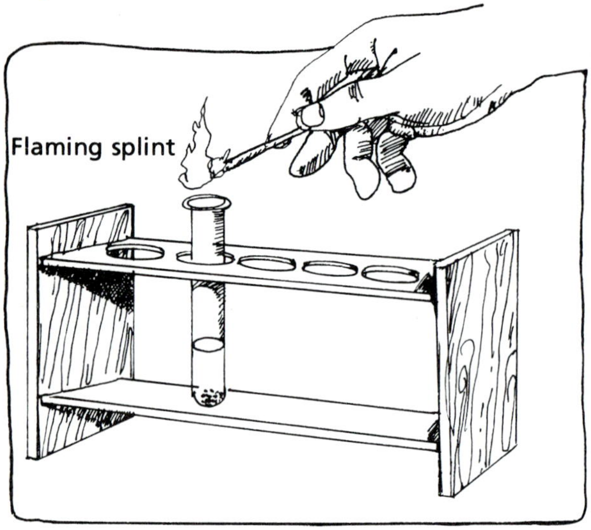

FIGURE 5-16.

CAUTION: *Wear protective glasses. Handle hydrochloric acid with care.*

Place 3 mL of dilute hydrochloric acid in a test tube. Stand the test tube in a test tube rack or beaker. Add a piece of mossy zinc to the acid. Light a wooden splint and bring the flame to the mouth of the test tube. small explosion

What happens to the splint? A positive splint test shows the presence of hydrogen gas. Did a chemical change take place? How do you know? Yes, heat and light are given off. A positive splint test indicates that hydrogen is produced.

Making Sure

11. Label each of the following as a physical or chemical change.

a. building a bookcase
b. burning sulfur
c. breaking a window
d. baking a cake
e. opening an envelope
f. burning paper
g. paneling a room

See the Teacher's Guide.

FIGURE 5-17. Many of the foods you eat everyday are mixtures. How can this mixture be separated?

Greg Miller

5:8 Mixtures

Two or more substances can be mixed together without combining chemically. Such a combination is called a **mixture.** Soil, air, milk, a salad, and iced tea are mixtures. Each component in a mixture keeps its identity. Mixtures can be separated by physical change or mechanical means. For example, salt water is a mixture of salt and water. If the mixture is heated, the water can be boiled off. The salt remains. Thus, salt water is separated by a physical change, the evaporation of water. A wire screen can be used to separate a mixture of pebbles and sand. This mixture is separated by mechanical means.

Describe two examples of a mixture.
Name two gases present in air.

Hickson-Bender Photography

FIGURE 5-18. Whole grain breads are mixtures.

A mixture may or may not have the same composition throughout. Air is a mixture of nitrogen, oxygen, and several other gases. The exact amounts of nitrogen and oxygen in air can vary from place to place. Also, air in a large industrial city may contain smoke and dust particles.

FIGURE 5-19. A centrifuge can be used to separate a mixture of substances of different densities (a). Chromatography is useful as a method of separating colored mixtures (b). Distillation is used in separating mixtures of substances with different boiling points (c).

Hickson-Bender Photography — U.S. Food and Drug Administration — Hickson-Bender Photography

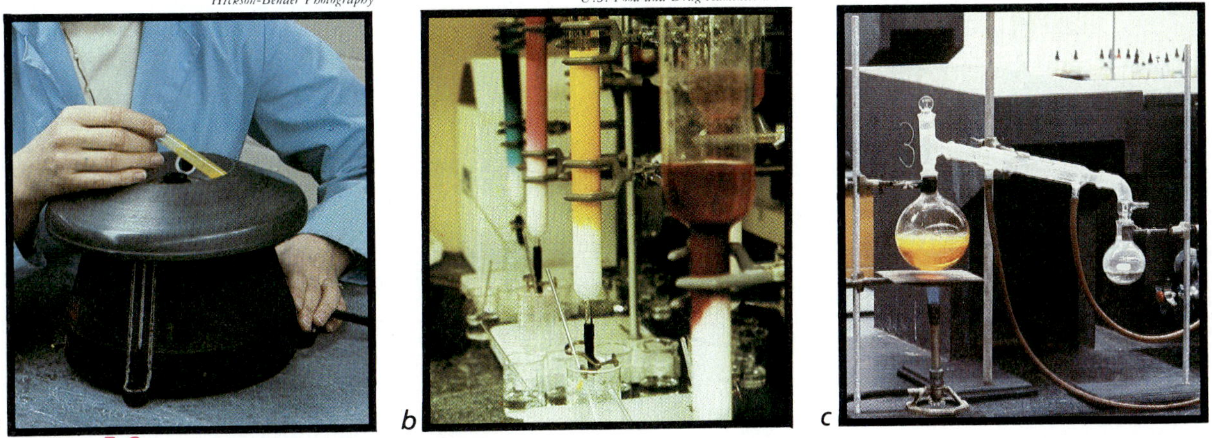

a b c

5-6
ACTIVITY *How can you separate a mixture?*

Mix 25 grams of sand and 25 grams of table salt on a piece of paper. Add the mixture to 250 mL of hot water in a beaker. Refer to the Appendix on how to set-up a filtration system. Pour off the water into a funnel fitted with filter paper. Catch the filtrate in a clean, 400-mL beaker. Evaporate the filtrate on a warm hot plate. What substance is in the funnel? sand *What substance is in the beaker?* salt *Name another mixture that you could separate in this way.* sand and sugar

FIGURE 5-20.

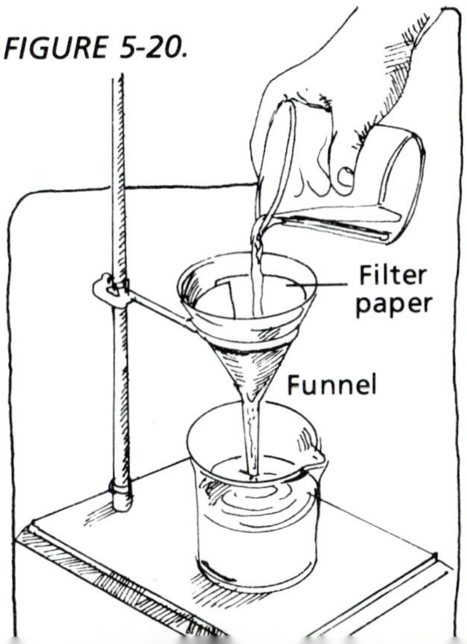

Careers
The Scrap Industry

Institute of Scrap Iron and Steel

Carolyn Fowler was the first woman to work in her company's nonferrous warehouse. Nonferrous means the metal does not contain iron. Her job encompasses a wide variety of duties which include sorting metals, operating a shear, and operating a briquetter. A shear is a device for cutting sheets of metal. A briquetter makes brick-like objects from powdered metal. Metal is easier to handle as briquettes.

Ann Robinson does a different job for her company. She is responsible for industrial safety. In this position she teaches employees to operate machines, like cranes and shears, safely. Safety inspections are another of Ann's duties. She locates hazards and determines how to avoid them. Even with these precautions, accidents do happen. Ann investigates the accidents to learn how they happened. She uses what she learns to prevent further accidents.

As our natural resources dwindle, the need to recycle increases. Recycling our resources means reusing our paper, cans and other wastes. We can reuse paper by making more paper from it. We can also use it as fuel for heating a building or making electricity. A can might be made into a new can or perhaps made into a bar of metal for use in a car.

The idea of recycling is not new. One industry that has been using recycled material for years is the metal industry. The recycled metal comes from scrap companies. Scrap companies take all kinds of metal wastes from cans to cars. They separate the different kinds of metal and tear or cut or shred it down to a useable size. Heavy machinery is needed to do these operations. Because of the heavy machinery, the scrap industry was long thought to be just for men. However, there are women in all parts of the scrap industry.

Adapted from *Phoenix Quarterly, Volume 11, Number 1,* Spring 1979, the Institute of Scrap Iron and Steel, Inc.

Points to Remember

1. Matter is anything that has mass and takes up space. *5:1*
2. Matter exists as solid, liquid, gas, or plasma. *5:2*
3. A physical property depends on the substance itself. *5:3*
4. A physical change alters the size, shape, or state of matter. *5:5*
5. A chemical property tells how a substance reacts with another substance. *5:6*
6. A chemical change alters the composition of matter. *5:7*
7. Mixtures are made of substances which are not chemically combined. *5:8*

Words to Use

Write a sentence in which you correctly use each of the following words or terms.

boiling point
chemical change
chemical property
condensation
corrosion
density
evaporation
freezing point
gas
liquid
melting point
mixture
physical change
physical property
plasma
solid

Questions for Review

Do not write in this book.

A. True or False *Have the students rewrite the false statements to make them correct.*

Determine whether each of the following sentences is true or false.

T **1.** Water is matter because it has mass and takes up space.
F **2.** Ideas are matter ~~because they have mass~~. *not*
F **3.** Making ice cubes is a ~~chemical~~ change. *physical*
T **4.** Boiling point and freezing point are physical properties of matter.
F **5.** The composition of a mixture is always the same. *not*
F **6.** Mixtures are separated by chemical means. *and mechanical*
T **7.** Chemical changes produce new substances with new chemical and physical properties.

T **8.** A substance in the solid state can be changed to the liquid state.

F **9.** Density is a ~~chemical~~ property. physical

T **10.** The melting point and freezing point of a substance are the same.

B. Multiple Choice

Choose the word or phrase that correctly completes each of the following sentences.

1. *(Breaking, Melting, Burning)* is an example of a chemical change.
2. *(Density, Burning, Color)* is not a physical property.
3. Iron usually exists as a *(solid, liquid, gas).*
4. At room temperature, air is usually a *(liquid, gas, solid).*
5. *(Rusting, Freezing point, Boiling point)* is a chemical property.
6. A *(solid, liquid, gas)* has a definite shape.
7. When a substance changes from the solid to liquid state *(boiling, freezing, melting)* occurs.
8. When a gas is cooled to form a liquid *(condensation, evaporation, boiling)* occurs.
9. The decomposition of water is a *(physical change, chemical change, physical property).*
10. The density of a pure substance can change if the *(mass, volume, temperature)* of the substance is changed.

C. Completion

Complete each of the following sentences with a word or phrase that will make the sentences correct.

1. Matter which varies in composition is called a(n) mixture.
2. Freezing point and boiling point are physical properties.
3. Matter can be broken down by a(n) chemical change.
4. Shape is a(n) physical property.
5. Density may be measured in grams per cubic centimeter.
6. Heat and light are often released in a(n) chemical change.
7. Anything that has mass and takes up space is matter.

8. Corrosion is a(n) *chemical* change.
9. The state of matter on the surface of the sun is *plasma*.
10. A substance which has a definite volume but takes the shape of its container is in the *liquid* state.

D. How and Why *Detailed answers to these questions are given in the Teacher's Guide at the front of this book.*

1. What are some chemical and physical properties of water?
2. What properties would help you describe an apple?
3. Name three common mixtures.
4. What properties would a manufacturer look for in a material for auto seat covers?
5. How could you find out if a liquid is pure water or salt water without tasting it?
6. Why does oil float on water?
7. Why does ice float on water?

More Ideas to Explore

1. Obtain information on the use of ethylene glycol and alcohol as antifreeze. Make graphs showing the amount needed to prevent freezing at different temperatures.
2. Visit a materials testing laboratory. Learn what a Brinell test is. Find out how it is used in the laboratory.
3. Obtain a chemistry handbook. What kinds of properties are listed as physical properties for each substance? How could this information be used?
4. Prepare a report on the plasma state. Why is plasma important in the search for alternative sources of energy?

Readings to Discover

Asimov, Isaac, *How Do We Find Out About Atoms?* NY: Walker and Company, 1976.

"Fingerprinting Marble." *Science Digest,* December 1972.

Pringle, Laurence, *Recycling Resources.* NY: Macmillan Publishing Co., Inc., 1974.

The gourds in the picture are all in the same family. Yet they can be broken down into smaller groups by size, shape, or color. At this time there are over 104 elements. This large number can also be broken down or classified into smaller groups or families. How are the elements classified?

Frank Psaute

Elements and the Periodic Table

6

Chapter 6 begins with a discussion of the elements and the arrangement of the periodic table. Atomic models are introduced to further reinforce the logic behind the periodic table. See the Teacher's Guide at the front of this book for additional teaching strategies for this chapter.

6:1 Elements

GOAL: *You will learn how the elements are classified using a model for the atom.*

All matter is made up of basic substances called elements. Carbon, iron, and aluminum are common elements. An **element** cannot be broken down into simpler substances by a chemical change. Eighty-eight elements have been found on the earth. At least fifteen more have been produced in the laboratory. The air we breathe is mostly the elements, oxygen and nitrogen.

What is an element?

There is a shorthand way to write the names of elements. Table 6-1 gives the names of some of the common elements and the symbols used to represent them. Note that some elements have one letter for their symbol. This letter is always uppercase. *If the symbol for an element is two letters, the second letter is always lowercase.* Some of the symbols of the elements are quite different from their English names. The symbol for iron, Fe, is taken from the Latin word for iron, *ferrum.*

Name five elements.

Write the symbols for five elements.

Table 6-1

Names and Symbols for Some Common Elements

Element	Symbol	Element	Symbol	Element	Symbol
aluminum	Al	hydrogen	H	nitrogen	N
carbon	C	iron	Fe	oxygen	O
chlorine	Cl	magnesium	Mg	silver	Ag
copper	Cu	mercury	Hg	sodium	Na
				sulfur	S

Oak Ridge National Laboratory

FIGURE 6-1. Curium is a synthetic element.

The element hydrogen is a gas. It is the lightest and most abundant element in the universe. The element mercury is a liquid. What is mercury used for? The element copper is a shiny solid. It is used as wire to carry electricity. Some of the elements produced in the laboratory exist in amounts too small to be seen. These elements are unstable and may break down into other elements very quickly.

Don McCoy from Rainbow

FIGURE 6-2. Particle accelerators, like the four-mile ring shown, are used to produce new elements and discover other particles in the atom.

6:2 The Periodic Table

How are the elements classified on the periodic table?

Dmitri Mendeleev (men duh LAY uf) (1834-1907), a Russian chemist, attempted to classify the elements known at his time. He organized these elements into an eight-column table. In this order, certain chemical properties of the elements were repeated. There were some blank spots in this table. However, Mendeleev believed these blank spots would be filled with elements yet to be discovered. He was able to predict the properties of these undiscovered elements. His chart, showing the classification of elements according to properties, is known as the **periodic table.**

What is the periodic table?

FIGURE 6-3. How have the stamps been classified? Are there other ways to classify the stamps?

As new elements were discovered, Mendeleev's classification system was later revised. The periodic table on pages 104-105 shows how the elements are classified today. Each box represents one element. The name and symbol for the element are in the center of the box. As you read through this chapter, you will learn more information about the elements from the periodic table.

FIGURE 6-4. An early version of Mendeleev's table.

Sovfoto USSR

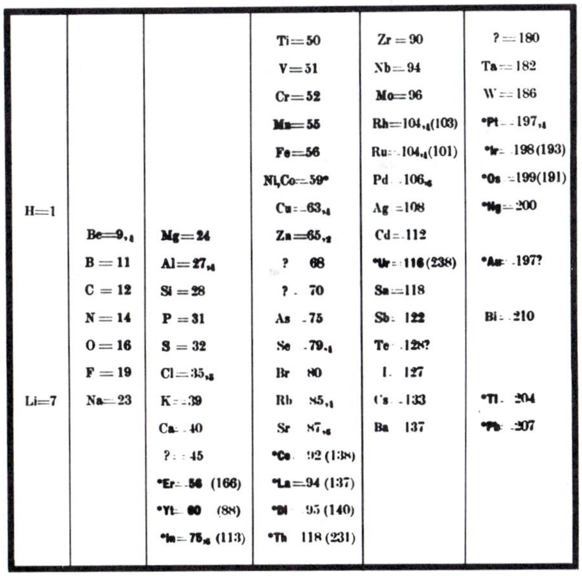

			Ti=50	Zr=90	?=180
			V=51	Nb=94	Ta=182
			Cr=52	Mo=96	W=186
			Mn=55	Rh=104,4(103)	*Pt=197,4
			Fe=56	Ru=104,4(101)	*Ir=198(193)
			Ni,Co=59*	Pd=106,6	*Os=199(191)
H=1			Cu=63,4	Ag=108	*Hg=200
	Be=9,4	Mg=24	Zn=65,2	Cd=112	
	B=11	Al=27,4	?=68	*Ur=116(238)	*Au=197?
	C=12	Si=28	?=70	Sn=118	
	N=14	P=31	As=75	Sb=122	Bi=210
	O=16	S=32	Se=79,4	Te=128?	
	F=19	Cl=35,5	Br=80	I=127	
Li=7	Na=23	K=39	Rb=85,4	Cs=133	*Tl=204
		Ca=40	Sr=87,6	Ba=137	*Pb=207
		?=45	*Ce=92(138)		
		*Er=56 (166)	*La=94 (137)		
		*Yt=60 (88)	*Di=95 (140)		
		*In=75,6 (113)	*Th=118 (231)		

Making Sure

Use the periodic table on pages 104-105.

1. Write symbols for the following.
   - a. gold *Au*
   - b. tin *Sn*
   - c. sodium *Na*
   - d. iron *Fe*
   - e. aluminum *Al*
   - f. fluorine *F*
   - g. uranium *U*
   - h. lanthanum *La*
2. Write the names of the following elements.
   - a. K *potassium*
   - b. Zn *zinc*
   - c. O *oxygen*
   - d. As *arsenic*
   - e. S *sulfur*
   - f. Cu *copper*
   - g. Fe *iron*
   - h. N *nitrogen*
3. Which of the following is the symbol for cobalt? iron? silver? *a, d, e*
   - a. Co
   - b. CO
   - c. Ir
   - d. Fe
   - e. Ag
   - f. Si

Table 6-2
The Periodic Table

(Based on Carbon 12 = 12.0000)

Metals

Transition Elements

	IA	IIA	IIIB	IVB	VB	VIB	VIIB	VIIIB	
1	1 **H** Hydrogen 1.0079								
2	3 **Li** Lithium 6.941	4 **Be** Beryllium 9.01218							
3	11 **Na** Sodium 22.98977	12 **Mg** Magnesium 24.305							
4	19 **K** Potassium 39.0983	20 **Ca** Calcium 40.08	21 **Sc** Scandium 44.9559	22 **Ti** Titanium 47.90	23 **V** Vanadium 50.9414	24 **Cr** Chromium 51.996	25 **Mn** Manganese 54.9380	26 **Fe** Iron 55.847	27 **Co** Cobalt 58.9332
5	37 **Rb** Rubidium 85.4678	38 **Sr** Strontium 87.62	39 **Y** Yttrium 88.9059	40 **Zr** Zirconium 91.22	41 **Nb** Niobium 92.9064	42 **Mo** Molybdenum 95.94	43 **Tc** Technetium 96.90639	44 **Ru** Ruthenium 101.07	45 **Rh** Rhodium 102.9055
6	55 **Cs** Cesium 132.9054	56 **Ba** Barium 137.34	71 **Lu** Lutetium 174.97	72 **Hf** Hafnium 178.49	73 **Ta** Tantalum 180.9479	74 **W** Tungsten 183.85	75 **Re** Rhenium 186.207	76 **Os** Osmium 190.2	77 **Ir** Iridium 192.22
7	87 **Fr** Francium 223.09176	88 **Ra** Radium 226	103 **Lr** Lawrencium 256.099	104 ____ 257	105 ____ 260				

Atomic number — 12
Element symbol — **Mg**
Magnesium
Average atomic mass — 24.305

LANTHANIDE SERIES	57 **La** Lanthanum 138.9055	58 **Ce** Cerium 140.12	59 **Pr** Praseodymium 140.9077	60 **Nd** Neodymium 144.24	61 **Pm** Promethium 144.91279	62 **Sm** Samarium 150.4
ACTINIDE SERIES	89 **Ac** Actinium 227.0274	90 **Th** Thorium 232.0381	91 **Pa** Protactinium 231.03590	92 **U** Uranium 238.029	93 **Np** Neptunium 237.04819	94 **Pu** Plutonium 244.06424

SYNTHETICS—green SOLIDS—blue GASES—orange LIQUIDS—white

	IB	IIB	IIIA	IVA	VA	VIA	VIIA	Noble Gases VIIIA
								2 **He** Helium 4.00260
			5 **B** Boron 10.82	6 **C** Carbon 12.011	7 **N** Nitrogen 14.0067	8 **O** Oxygen 15.9994	9 **F** Fluorine 18.998403	10 **Ne** Neon 20.179
			13 **Al** Aluminum 26.98154	14 **Si** Silicon 28.0855	15 **P** Phosphorus 30.97376	16 **S** Sulfur 32.06	17 **Cl** Chlorine 35.453	18 **Ar** Argon 39.948
28 **Ni** Nickel 58.70	29 **Cu** Copper 63.546	30 **Zn** Zinc 65.38	31 **Ga** Gallium 69.72	32 **Ge** Germanium 72.59	33 **As** Arsenic 74.9216	34 **Se** Selenium 78.96	35 **Br** Bromine 79.904	36 **Kr** Krypton 83.80
46 **Pd** Palladium 106.4	47 **Ag** Silver 107.868	48 **Cd** Cadmium 112.41	49 **In** Indium 114.82	50 **Sn** Tin 118.69	51 **Sb** Antimony 121.75	52 **Te** Tellurium 127.60	53 **I** Iodine 126.9045	54 **Xe** Xenon 131.30
78 **Pt** Platinum 195.09	79 **Au** Gold 196.9665	80 **Hg** Mercury 200.59	81 **Tl** Thallium 204.37	82 **Pb** Lead 207.2	83 **Bi** Bismuth 208.9804	84 **Po** Polonium 208.98244	85 **At** Astatine 209.98704	86 **Rn** Radon 222

Nonmetals: IIIA–VIIA

Rare Earth Elements

63 **Eu** Europium 151.96	64 **Gd** Gadolinium 157.25	65 **Tb** Terbium 158.9254	66 **Dy** Dysprosium 162.50	67 **Ho** Holmium 164.9304	68 **Er** Erbium 167.26	69 **Tm** Thulium 168.9342	70 **Yb** Ytterbium 173.04
95 **Am** Americium 243.06139	96 **Cm** Curium 247.07038	97 **Bk** Berkelium 247.07032	98 **Cf** Californium 251.07961	99 **Es** Einsteinium 254.08805	100 **Fm** Fermium 257.09515	101 **Md** Mendelevium 258	102 **No** Nobelium 255.093

6:3 Atoms

What is an atom?

Suppose you could divide a copper wire into two pieces. Then you continued to divide each piece into smaller and smaller pieces. Finally, you would not be able to divide a piece and still have the element copper. The smallest piece of an element which still has the properties of that element is called an **atom.** *All elements are composed of atoms.*

Scientists often use models to explain a scientific idea. A scientific **model** is simply a way of looking at an idea. Models are usually based on the observations of many people. The model is used to help explain these observations. The pictures of atoms in this book are models. When you read about the parts of the atom, the mental picture you have of an atom is also a model. The model for the atom has changed many times. As experiments continue, our present model of the atom may be changed again.

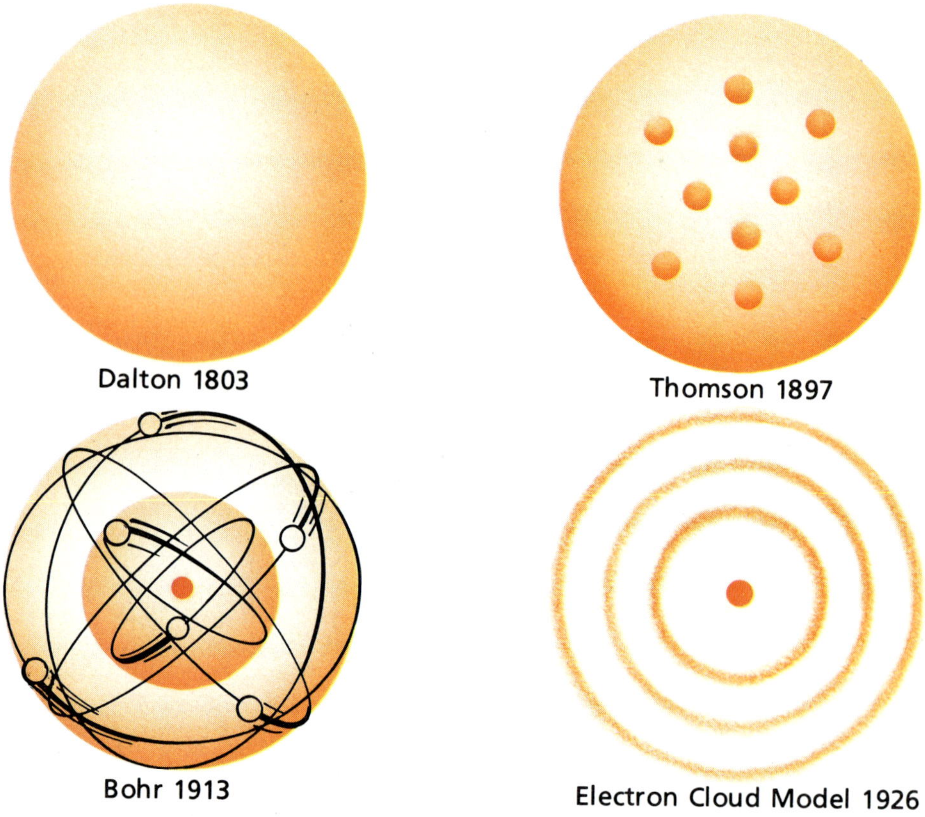

FIGURE 6-5. The model of the atom has changed over time. Dalton thought the atom was simply like a billiard ball.

An atom consists of a central positive core surrounded by a cloud of negative electric charge. The central core is called the **nucleus** of the atom. The nucleus is a center of positive electric charge. Almost all of the mass of an atom is in the nucleus. The cloud of negative charge surrounding the nucleus is like the blades of an electric fan. When you turn on an electric fan, the rapid motion of the blades looks like a cloud.

How is the nucleus different from the electron cloud?

Larry Hamill

FIGURE 6-6. Moving electrons are like the blades of an automobile engine. The blades are moving fast enough to give a blurred appearance.

6:4 Parts of the Atom

Atoms are electrically neutral. That is, atoms have no overall electric charge. The cloud of negative charge exactly balances the positive nucleus.

Why is an atom electrically neutral?

Experiments with electricity in the late 1800's led to the discovery of electrons. The movement of **electrons** forms the cloud of negative charge that surrounds the nucleus. Having discovered electrons, scientists then began looking for a positive particle. About ten years later this particle was discovered. It was named the **proton.** The positive charge of the proton is equal but opposite the negative charge of the electron.

Name the particles found in an atom.

The third basic particle of the atom, the **neutron,** was not discovered until 1932. A neutron has no charge, which is why it was difficult to find. Both protons and neutrons are in the nucleus of the atom. A proton and a neutron are about equal in mass. However, a proton has a mass more than 1800 times that of an electron.

All atoms of an element have the same number of protons. For example, every hydrogen atom has one proton in its nucleus. Every carbon atom has six protons in its nucleus. The number of protons in the nucleus of an atom determines what the element will be. The number of protons of an atom is called the **atomic number.** For every element the atomic number is listed on the periodic table (pages 104-105). You should notice that *the elements on the periodic table are arranged according to increasing atomic number.*

An atom is electrically neutral. Therefore, the number of protons must equal the number of electrons. For each proton in the nucleus, there is one electron moving about the nucleus. Thus, the atomic number of an element is also the number of electrons.

Scientists have found that protons and neutrons seem to be made of other particles. The electron is thought of as a basic particle. Research is being done to discover the properties of these particles. Scientists are continually trying to perfect our model of the atom.

6-1 Detailed information concerning this Activity can be found in the Teacher's Guide at the front of this book.

ACTIVITY *How do you draw a model for an atom?*

(1) *Use the periodic table to find the number of protons, neutrons, and electrons in a lithium atom.* ***(2)*** *On a piece of paper draw a circle about 1 cm in diameter.* ***(3)*** *Write the number of protons in the circle next to a positive (+) sign.* ***(4)*** *Write the number of neutrons in the circle next to a letter n.* ***(5)*** *Now draw another circle around the circle you have already drawn. On this circle write the number of electrons next to a negative (–) sign.* ***(6)*** *Using the steps given above, draw a diagram of a boron atom, oxygen atom, and neon atom.*

What part of your diagram is the nucleus? *[the inner circle]* *How is the model you have drawn different from a real atom?*

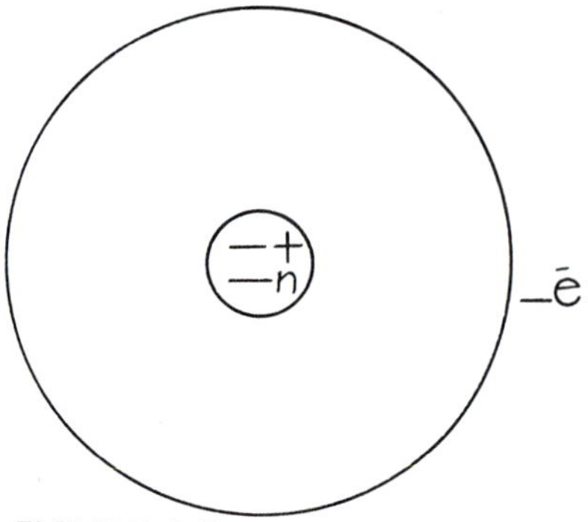

FIGURE 6-7.

Answers will vary, but impress upon the student that the atom is 3-dimensional and that electrons do not orbit the nucleus like planets around the sun.

Making Sure

Use the periodic table on pages 104-105 to answer the following questions.

4. List the name and symbol of the elements that have the following atomic numbers.

a. 8 *oxygen, O* **b.** 12 *magnesium, Mg* **c.** 20 *calcium, Ca* **d.** 27 *cobalt, Co* **e.** 50 *tin, Sn* **f.** 79 *gold, Au*

5. How many protons do atoms of each of the following elements have?
   a. copper 29 c. neon 10 e. mercury 80
   b. iron 26 d. sodium 11 f. uranium 92
6. How many electrons do atoms of each of the following have?
   a. He 2 b. C 6 c. Ag 47 d. I 53 e. K 19 f. Zn 30

6:5 Electron Clouds

Electrons move very quickly about the nucleus. This region around the nucleus is an **electron cloud.** Look at Figure 6-8. Our model of an electron cloud looks much like a galaxy in space. Notice the galaxy is brighter and more dense at the center. The outer edges of the galaxy are not clearly defined. They fade out into space. The region occupied by electrons is much the same as our picture of a galaxy. Some areas of the electron cloud are more dense than others. The density of the cloud decreases as we move away from the nucleus. An electron is more likely to be found in the areas of high density. This is not to say that the electron cannot also be found at the outer edges of the cloud. The electrons making up the cloud should be thought of as being everywhere in the cloud at once.

FIGURE 6-8. A galaxy can be used as a model for an electron cloud.

Tersch

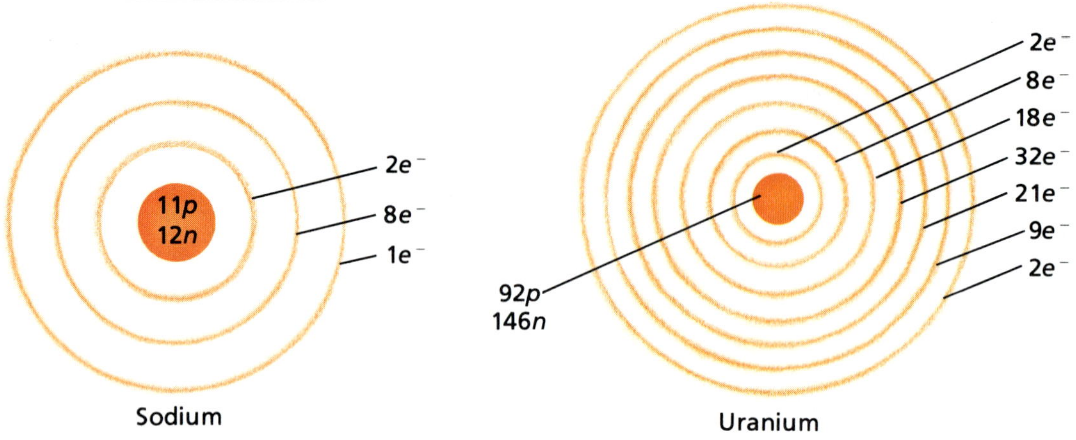

FIGURE 6-9. Energy level models for sodium and uranium showing the electron arrangements.

What are energy levels in an atom?

Every electron cloud has one or more **energy levels.** The first energy level is closest to the nucleus. Only 2 electrons can be in the first energy level. The second energy level of an atom can hold up to 8 electrons. The third energy level can hold up to 18 electrons. Energy levels farther from the nucleus can hold 32 or more electrons.

A magnesium atom contains 12 electrons. The 12 electrons are arranged in pairs within the energy levels. The first energy level has one pair (2) of electrons. The second energy level has four pairs (8) of electrons. The two remaining electrons are in the third energy level. Note that magnesium does not have enough electrons to fill the third energy level.

Most atoms have more than three occupied energy levels. Lawrencium (law REN see um) has 103 electrons in seven energy levels. Many of the properties of the elements are based on the number and arrangement of electrons in atoms.

Making Sure

7. How many electrons are in an atom of each of the following elements?

   a. oxygen *8* **c.** hydrogen *1*

   b. carbon *6* **d.** chlorine *17*

8. How many electrons are in each energy level for an atom of each element listed in problem 7?
a. 2, 6 b. 2, 4 c. 1 d. 2, 8, 7

6:6 Atomic Mass and Isotopes

The mass of an atom depends upon the number of protons and neutrons. The masses of a proton and neutron are nearly the same. They are each assigned a mass of one **atomic mass unit** (a.m.u). Electrons have almost no mass in comparison.

If you know the number of protons and neutrons in an atom, you can find the atomic mass number. The **atomic mass number** is the sum of the protons and neutrons for an atom. For example, beryllium has 4 protons and 5 neutrons. Its atomic mass number is 9.

Be
Beryllium
4 protons
+5 neutrons
9 mass number

I
Iodine
53 protons
+74 neutrons
127 mass number

FIGURE 6-10. Atomic mass numbers for beryllium and iodine are shown.

Table 6-3

Atomic Mass Units of Some Elements

Element	Protons	Neutrons	a.m.u
carbon (C)	6	6	12
oxygen (O)	8	8	16
sodium (Na)	11	11	22
potassium (K)	19	20	39
iron (Fe)	26	29	55

All atoms of an element have the same number of protons. However, some of these atoms may have more neutrons than others. Atoms of the same element with different numbers of neutrons are called **isotopes** (ɪ suh tohps). For example, hydrogen has three isotopes. A hydrogen atom may contain none, one, or two neutrons. Every atom of carbon has six protons. Some carbon atoms have six neutrons and some have eight neutrons. These carbon atoms are isotopes. Every atom of oxygen has eight protons. Some isotopes of oxygen have seven, eight, or nine neutrons.

What is an isotope?

Isotopes of some elements can be produced in the laboratory. Every element has at least two isotopes. Some, like tin, have as many as ten natural isotopes.

Table 6-4

Naturally Occurring Isotopes of Tin (Sn)			
Electrons	**Protons**	**Neutrons**	**Mass number**
50	50	62	112
50	50	64	114
50	50	65	115
50	50	66	116
50	50	67	117
50	50	68	118
50	50	69	119
50	50	70	120
50	50	72	122
50	50	74	124

There are two ways to write the symbol for an element to show the difference between isotopes. In one way, the name of the element is followed by the atomic mass. For example, oxygen-16 means the isotope of oxygen which has an atomic mass of 16. Carbon-12 is the isotope of carbon which has an atomic mass of 12. The numeral indicates the mass number of the isotope being discussed. The symbol of the element can be used with the atomic mass number and atomic number to show an isotope. For example, $^{12}_{6}C$ is the carbon-12 isotope. $^{39}_{18}Ar$ is argon-39.

Atomic mass ——— $^{12}_{6}C$ ——— Element symbol
Atomic number ———

FIGURE 6-11.

Every element is usually found in nature as a mixture of isotopes. For example, a sample of chlorine gas is likely to be a mixture of two isotopes. These are chlorine-35 and chlorine-37. The average mass of the atoms in this sample would be greater than 35 but less than 37. Thus, the atomic masses given for elements in the periodic table (page 104) are average atomic masses. They are based upon the atomic masses of the element's isotopes.

Making Sure

9. Use the periodic table to find the atomic number of
   a. fluorine 9 c. bromine 35 e. oxygen 8
   b. chlorine 17 d. iodine 53 f. sulfur 16
10. How many protons, neutrons and electrons does $^{23}_{11}Na$ contain? 11 protons, 11 electrons, 12 neutrons
11. Use the periodic table to find the atomic number and atomic mass of
    a. Li b. N c. K d. Al e. Ar f. Fe

a. 3, 6.941
b. 7, 14.0067
c. 19, 39.0983
d. 13, 26.98154
e. 18, 39.948
f. 26, 55.847

6:7 Groups of Elements

What is a group of elements in the periodic table?

In the periodic table, elements are arranged in vertical columns. These columns are called **groups** or **families.** Each group contains elements with similar chemical properties. For example, Group VIIA contains fluorine, chlorine, bromine, iodine, and astatine. This group of elements is known as the **halogen family.** In Group VIIA, the elements have electrons in different energy levels. However, each element in this group has seven electrons in its outer energy level. The outer energy level is that which is farthest from the nucleus. Because these elements have the same number of electrons in the outer energy level, they react the same.

The elements of Group VIIIA are called the **noble gas family.** Until 1962, it was believed that noble gases did not react with other elements to form compounds. However, compounds of krypton and xenon have now been formed. All but one of the elements in Group VIIIA have eight electrons in their outer energy level. Helium, the first element in Group VIIIA, has two electrons in its outer energy level.

From the CHEM Study film, A Research Problem: Inert Gas (?) Compounds

FIGURE 6-12. Xenon tetrafluoride is the easiest noble gas compound to prepare. However, it decomposes rapidly in water.

Locate the A and B columns on the periodic table (pages 104-105). The Roman numerals of the A columns show the number of electrons in the outer energy level of each element. The elements in the B groups are called the **transition elements.** Nearly all of them have two electrons in their outer energy level.

Making Sure

they increase

12. What change occurs in atomic number and mass number as you read down a group of elements?
13. Which element in each of the following is not a member of the group in the periodic table?
    - **a.** hydrogen, calcium, sodium, cesium
    - **b.** calcium, barium, magnesium, vanadium
    - **c.** uranium, neon, xenon, helium
    - **d.** sulfur, phosphorus, nitrogen, arsenic

6:8 Periods of Elements

What is a period in the periodic table?

The horizontal rows of the periodic table are called **periods.** Period two begins with lithium and ends with neon. Each element in a period has different properties. The elements on the left side of the table are metals. An atom of a **metal** has three or less electrons in the outer energy level. Elements such as copper, iron, tin, and zinc are metals. What properties do these metals have in common?

Table 6-5

Reading the Periodic Table—Left to Right

	lithium Li	beryllium Be	boron B	carbon C	nitrogen N	oxygen O	fluorine F	neon Ne
Atomic number (Z)	3	4	5	6	7	8	9	10
Atomic mass number (A)	7	9	11	12	14	16	19	20
Group	IA	IIA	IIIA	IVA	VA	VIA	VIIA	VIIIA
Number of outer electrons	1	2	3	4	5	6	7	8
How compounds are formed	gives up electrons	gives up electrons	shares electrons	shares electrons	shares electrons	usually shares electrons	gains an electron	shares electrons
Type of element	metal	metal	metalloid	nonmetal solid	gas	gas	gas	gas

Table 6-6

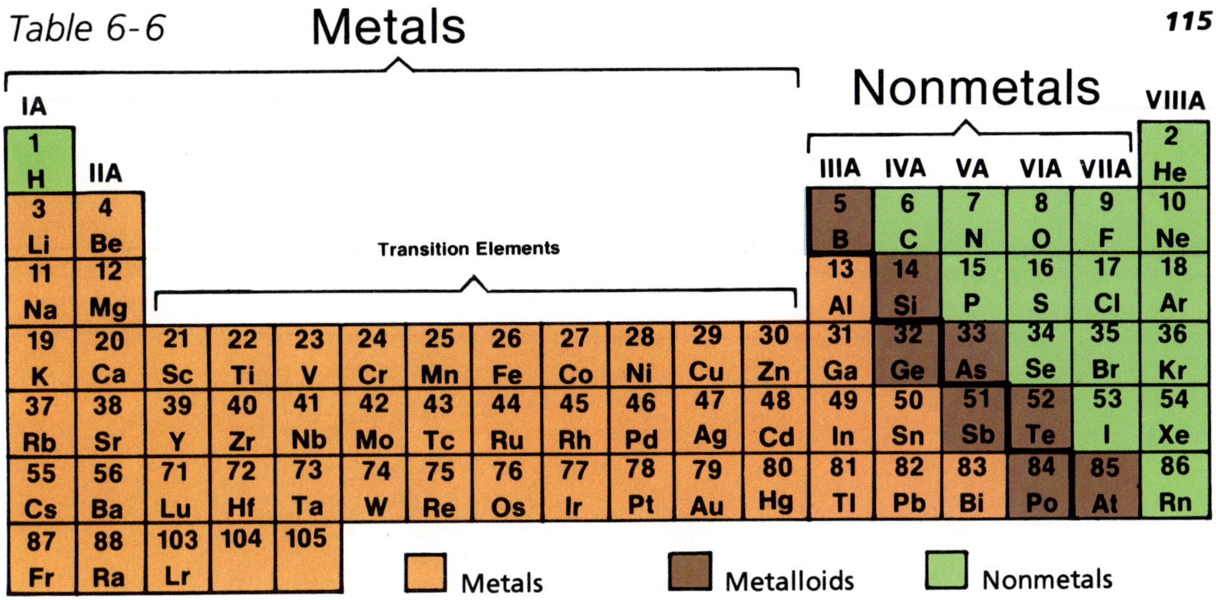

The last five elements of period two are nonmetals. **Nonmetals** usually have five or more electrons in their outer energy levels. Nonmetals also have characteristic properties, Table 6-7. Note the stair step line which divides the periodic table on page 115. The elements to the left of the line are metals. Those to the right of the line are nonmetals. Metalloids are usually found directly on either side of the line. The element boron is considered a metalloid (MET ul oyd). **Metalloids** have properties of both metals and nonmetals. Other metalloids are silicon, germanium, arsenic, antimony, tellurium, polonium, and astatine.

FIGURE 6-13. Mendeleev predicted the existence of the element germanium before it was discovered. He called this element "Ekasilicon." He believed its properties were similar to silicon.

Linda Young

Predicted		Actual
72	Atomic mass	72.6
5.5 g/mL	Density	5.35 g/mL
dark grey	Color	grey-white
	Effect of water	
none		none
	Effect of acids	
slight		no effect by HCl
	Effect of bases	
slight		no effect by KOH

Table 6-7

Some Characteristic Properties of Metals and Nonmetals

Linda Young

Young/Hoffhines

Linda Young

Metals

Physical properties

good conductors of heat and electricity
solids are malleable and ductile
high density
metallic luster

Chemical properties

one to three electrons in the outermost energy level
form positive ions by losing electrons

Nonmetals

Physical properties

poor conductors of heat and electricity
solids are brittle and nonductile
low density

Chemical properties

five to eight electrons in the outermost energy level
form negative ions by gaining electrons except Group VIIIA

Eric Hoffhines

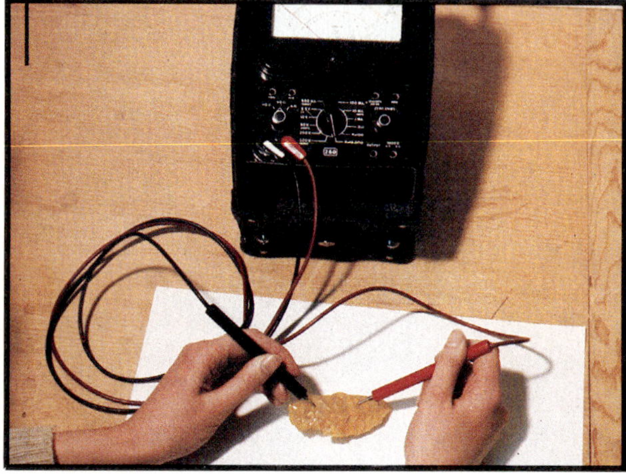

Hickson-Bender Photography

Gold Information Center

a

Hager/Alpha

b

FIGURE 6-14. Gold is used in making this fireproof suit (a). Tungsten is used as the filament for light bulbs (b).

The electron arrangement of the elements at the end of each period is very stable. Noble gases are found at the end of periods on the right side of the table. All but helium have eight electrons in their outer energy levels. Eight electrons in the outer energy level is the most stable arrangement of electrons.

Period four contains the first row of transition metals. The common elements you know as metals are found in this section.

6-2 Detailed information concerning this Activity can be found in the Teacher's Guide at the front of this book.

ACTIVITY *What are some properties of metals and nonmetals?*

Obtain a sample of each of the following elements: aluminum, copper, carbon, iodine, iron, lead, sulfur, and zinc. On a piece of paper, write down the name and symbol for each element. Use the periodic table to find out if each element is a metal or nonmetal. Study each sample carefully and make a list of its physical properties, Section 5:3. Find one use for each element.

Making Sure

14. What change in atomic number occurs from left to right in the periodic table? *it increases*

15. Which element in each set is not in the period in which the other elements are found?

a. aluminum, carbon, boron, neon

b. vanadium, copper, iron, oxygen

c. cobalt, zinc, calcium, uranium

d. argon, cadmium, silver, tin

Focus On

Skills

Using Activities

Activities play an important part in science classes. They provide you with experience in following directions, using scientific methods, and developing concepts. Activities help you to visualize some of the ideas that the authors are presenting in the reading. In order to get the most from an *Activity,* it is important for you to understand the authors' purpose for including it.

ACTIVITY *What are some properties of metals and nonmetals?*

Obtain a sample of each of the following elements: aluminum, copper, carbon, iodine, iron, lead, sulfur, and zinc. On a piece of paper, write down the name and symbol for each element. Use the periodic table to find out if each element is a metal or nonmetal. Study each sample carefully and make a list of its physical properties, Section 5:3 Find one use for each element.

1. What materials will you need to perform this *Activity*? *samples of aluminum, copper, carbon, iodine, lead, sulfur, zinc; paper and pencil*
2. What is the purpose of the *Activity*? *to see the differences between metals and nonmetals*
3. Rewrite the *Activity* as a series of numbered steps.
4. What references in your text do the authors tell you to use in performing the *Activity*? *periodic table and Section 5:3*
5. Why do the authors tell you to refer back to Section 5:3? *to refresh your memory concerning physical properties*
6. How can you use Table 6-7 in this *Activity*? *Table 6-7 tells you some general physical and chemical properties for metals and nonmetals*
7. Why do you think this *Activity* was included in Chapter 6? *to allow you to look at some elements to actually see the difference between metals and nonmetals*
8. What other books would help you find a use for each of the elements in the *Activity*? *encyclopedias, science handbooks*

Points to Remember

1. Elements cannot be broken down by ordinary means. All elements are made of atoms. *6:1*
2. The elements are arranged in order of increasing atomic number on the periodic table. *6:4*
3. Three particles of an atom are the proton, neutron, and electron. *6:4*
4. Electrons occupy energy levels outside the nucleus of the atom. *6:5*
5. The atomic number of an element is the number of protons in the nucleus. *6:4*
6. Isotopes are atoms with the same number of protons but different numbers of neutrons. *6:6*
7. Groups of elements have similar properties. *6:7*
8. Elements can be classified as metals, nonmetals, or metalloids. *6:8*

Words to Use

Write a sentence in which you correctly use each of the following words or terms.

atom	halogen	nonmetal
atomic mass	isotope	nucleus
atomic number	metal	periodic table
electron	metalloid	proton
electron cloud	model	transition metal
element	neutron	
energy level	noble gas	

Have the students rewrite the false statements to make them correct.

Questions for Review

Do not write in this book.

A. True or False

Determine whether each of the following sentences is true or false.

T **1.** Electrons have a negative electric charge.

F **2.** The mass of an electron is ~~greater~~ than the mass of a proton. *less*

T **3.** All atoms of the same element contain the same number of protons.

T **4.** Atoms of the same element may contain different numbers of neutrons.

F **5.** All atoms of the same element have the same mass. do not

T **6.** The positive charge of the protons in an atom is equal to the negative charge of the electrons.

F **7.** The ~~electron~~ is found in the nucleus of the atom. proton/neutron

F **8.** Most of the mass of the atom is contained in the ~~electron cloud surrounding the~~ nucleus.

T **9.** A mental picture of an atom is a model.

T **10.** The electron cloud contains energy levels for an electron.

B. Multiple Choice

Choose the word or phrase that correctly completes each of the following sentences.

1. A(n) *(neutron, proton, electron)* has a positive charge.
2. The first energy level can contain up to *(2, 6, 8)* electrons.
3. The *(electron, proton, neutron)* is the lightest particle in an atom.
4. The elements in the periodic table are arranged according to *(symbol, atomic number, atomic mass).*
5. An atom is *(positive, negative, neutral).*
6. Electrons are arranged in energy levels in groups of *(2, 4, 8)* electrons.
7. Carbon has 6 protons and 6 neutrons. Its atomic mass number is *(6, 12, 36)*
8. On the periodic table, the Roman numerals show the number of *(protons, electrons, neutrons)* in the outer energy level of an element.
9. A vertical column on the periodic table is call a(n) *(group, period, energy level).*
10. Most transition metals have *(2, 6, 8)* electrons in their outer energy level.

C. Completion

Complete each of the following sentences with a word or phrase that will make the sentence correct.

1. Elements which have the same number of protons but different numbers of neutrons are called isotopes.
2. The charge on the nucleus of an atom is positive.

3. Mendeleev developed a periodic table based on atomic mass.
4. Lithium is found in Group IA.
5. Group IIIA elements have 3 electrons in the outer energy level.
6. Two members of the transition elements are iron and cobalt.
7. Iron-56 has 26 protons, 26 electrons, and 30 neutrons.
8. Metals in the B columns of the periodic table are called transition elements.
9. Nonmetals have 5 or more electrons in their outer energy level.
10. Hydrogen has 3 natural isotopes.

D. How and Why *Detailed answers to these questions are given in the Teacher's Guide at the front of this book.*

1. Why is the periodic table of value to scientists?
2. What are the differences among a proton, electron, and neutron?
3. What are some differences between metals and nonmetals?
4. Using the periodic table, tell how magnesium differs from chlorine.
5. Why are the noble gases not very active chemically? Name two noble gases.

More Ideas to Explore

1. John Newlands and Johann Dobereiner made early attempts at classifying the elements. Find out about their work.
2. The search for helium is an interesting story. Find out how helium got its name. Why was its discovery so unusual?

Readings to Discover

Asimov, Isaac, *Building Blocks of the Universe.* rev. ed., NY: Abelard, 1974.

Frazier, K., "Superheavy Elements." *Science News,* April 15, 1978, pp. 236-238.

MacFall, Russell P., *Gem Hunter's Guide: How to Find and Identify Gem Minerals.* 5th ed., NY: Thomas Y. Crowell Co., 1975.

Have you ever thought much about the foods you eat everyday? What are they composed of? Are they elements, compounds, or mixtures? After reading this chapter, look at some food labels. What compounds do you recognize? How do atoms change when compounds are formed?

INGREDIENTS: ROLLED OATS, SOY PROTEIN, WHOLE WHEAT FLOUR, MALT SYRUP, NONFAT MILK, WHEAT GERM, SALT, SODIUM CASEINATE, BREWER'S YEAST, CINNAMON, BAKING SODA, AMMONIUM BICARBONATE, EGGS, TRICALCIUM PHOSPHATE, IRON PHOSPHATE, CALCIUM PANTOTHENATE, PYRIDOXINE HYDROCHLORIDE

Hickson-Bender Photography

Compounds and Bonding

7

Chapter 7 builds on the ideas of models and atomic structure presented in Chapter 6. Bonding models are introduced along with a discussion on how to name compounds and write formulas.

7:1 Compounds

GOAL: *You will learn how elements combine to form compounds.*

What is a compound?

A **compound** is formed when two or more elements combine chemically. "Combine chemically" means the elements join together in a way that makes it impossible to separate them by physical changes. A compound has an identity all its own. It may be much different from the elements that form it.

Elements in a compound combine in the same ratio. The ratio between sodium and chlorine in sodium chloride is always one atom of sodium to one atom of chlorine (1:1 ratio). The ratio between carbon and oxygen in carbon dioxide is always one atom of carbon to two atoms of oxygen (1:2 ratio). Water is another example of a compound. Every sample of water contains two atoms of hydrogen to one atom of oxygen (2:1 ratio).

What does a formula show?

Chemical formulas are used to represent compounds. A formula shows the kinds of atoms in a compound. It also shows the ratio between atoms. In chemical formulas, symbols are used to show the elements present. The formula for sodium chloride is NaCl. NaCl shows a ratio of one atom of sodium to one atom of chlorine.

The formula for carbon dioxide is CO_2. The small number 2 in the formula for carbon dioxide is called a **subscript.** A subscript gives the ratio in which the atoms are combined in a compound. The subscript 2 in CO_2 means two atoms of oxygen. Absence of a subscript next to C means one atom of carbon. *The numeral 1 is never used as a subscript.* The symbol for the element stands for one atom of that element.

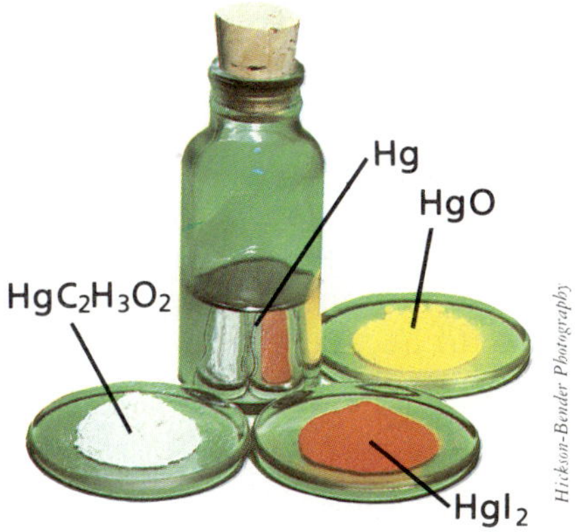

FIGURE 7-1. The element mercury forms many different compounds. Each appears unlike mercury itself.

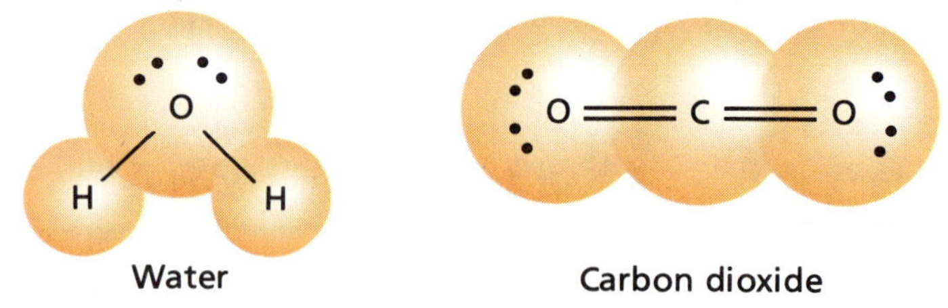

FIGURE 7-2. Models for water and carbon dioxide show the ratio of atoms.

Young/Hoffhines

FIGURE 7-3. Most toothpastes contain the compound stannous fluoride to help prevent tooth decay.

Table 7-1

Some Compounds and Their Formulas

Compound	Chemical name	Chemical formula
cane sugar	*sucrose*	$C_{12}H_{22}O_{11}$
baking soda	*sodium hydrogen carbonate*	$NaHCO_3$
hydrogen peroxide	*same*	H_2O_2
sand	*silicon dioxide*	SiO_2
rubbing alcohol	*2-propanol*	C_3H_7OH
chalk	*calcium carbonate*	$CaCO_3$
"stannous" fluoride	*tin(II) fluoride*	SnF_2

Making Sure

1. NH_3 is the formula for ammonia. What elements does ammonia contain? What is the ratio between the atoms of these elements? *nitrogen and hydrogen, 1 to 3*
2. Laughing gas is a compound containing a ratio of two atoms of nitrogen to one atom of oxygen. What is the formula? *N_2O*
3. Name the elements in each of the compounds in Table 7-1.

See the Teacher's Guide

4. What are the ratios of elements present in each of the following compounds?
   a. H_2O_2 **c.** $NaC_2H_3O_2$ **e.** H_2SO_4
   b. KCl **d.** NaOH **f.** HF
5. What is the number of atoms for each compound in problem 4?

7:2 How Atoms Combine

An atom with a complete outer energy level of electrons is chemically stable. The noble gases, Group VIIIA, on the periodic table have complete outer energy levels. Group VIIIA elements are considered chemically stable. They are generally not reactive and rarely form compounds. The compounds that are formed decompose easily. The elements of Group VIIIA (except helium) have eight electrons in their outer energy levels.

The elements of Group IA are reactive. They do not have eight electrons in their outer energy level. These elements are found in nature in compounds. They are combined chemically with other elements. All of the Group IA metals have one electron in their outer energy level.

The halogens, Group VIIA, are also highly reactive. These elements are also found in nature in a combined state. For example, the main source of the element chlorine is the salt, sodium chloride. All of the Group VIIA elements have seven electrons in their outer energy level.

Most atoms combine to complete an outer energy level of electrons. Atoms may share, gain, or lose electrons in order to become chemically stable. When atoms combine chemically, a **bond** is formed that holds the atoms together.

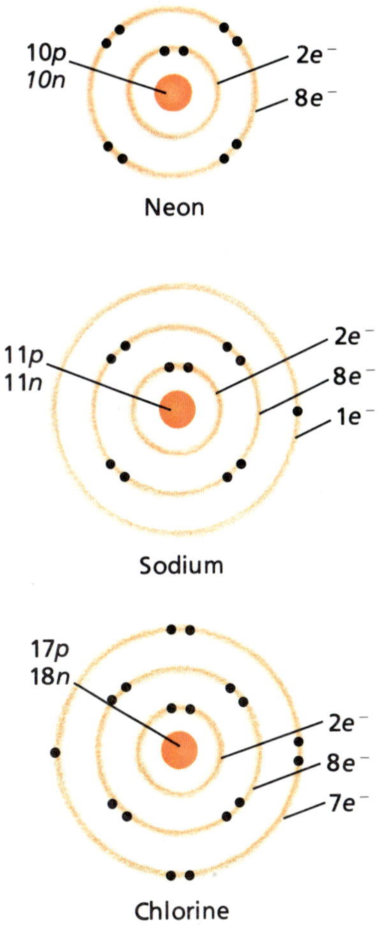

FIGURE 7-4. Electron diagram models for neon, sodium, and chlorine.

courtesy of Morton Salt Div. of Morton-Norwich

FIGURE 7-5. The elements sodium and chlorine are found as salt deep in mines below the surface.

Making Sure

6. How many electrons are in the outer energy levels of the elements in the following groups?
   a. Group IVA *4*
   b. Group IA *1*
   c. Group IIA *2*
   d. Group VIA *6*

7:3 Electron Transfer

How can the energy levels of atoms be completed?

Some compounds are formed by a transfer of electrons between atoms. Sodium chloride is formed by a transfer of electrons between sodium and chlorine atoms. A sodium atom has one electron in its outer energy level. A chlorine atom has seven electrons in its outer energy level. Sodium would need seven electrons to complete its outer energy level. If sodium were to lose its outermost electron, it could become chemically stable. The preceding energy level is already filled. If that electron were transferred to chlorine, both atoms would have filled outer energy levels. Figure 7-6 is a model for the transfer of electrons between sodium and chlorine.

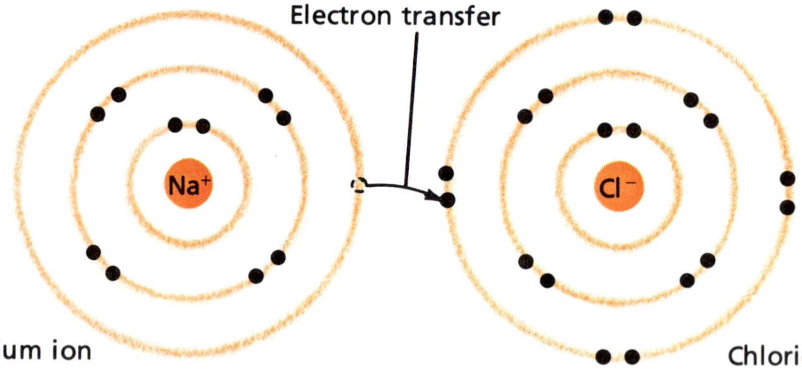

FIGURE 7-6. Bonding model for NaCl showing electron transfer.

After the transfer, the sodium atom no longer has an equal number of protons and electrons. The sodium atom is now positively charged. Why? The chlorine atom is now negatively charged. Why? Sodium and chlorine now have opposite charges. Opposite charges attract each other. The charged atoms bond together to form a new compound. When an atom gains or loses an electron, the resulting charged particle is called an **ion.** Bonding which occurs between ions is called **ionic bonding.**

more protons than electrons

more electrons than protons

How is an ion different from an element?

Sodium chloride is composed of ions. The positive sodium ion is shown as Na^+. The negative chloride ion is shown as Cl^-. Sodium chloride has properties which are quite different from sodium and chlorine. Sodium is a soft metal. It can be cut with a knife. It is highly reactive and must be stored in oil. The oil covers the metal to keep it from reacting with the air. Chlorine is a greenish gas. Both elements are poisonous. Yet, sodium chloride is used to season food.

Why is sodium metal stored under oil?

Hickson-Bender Photography

Linda Young

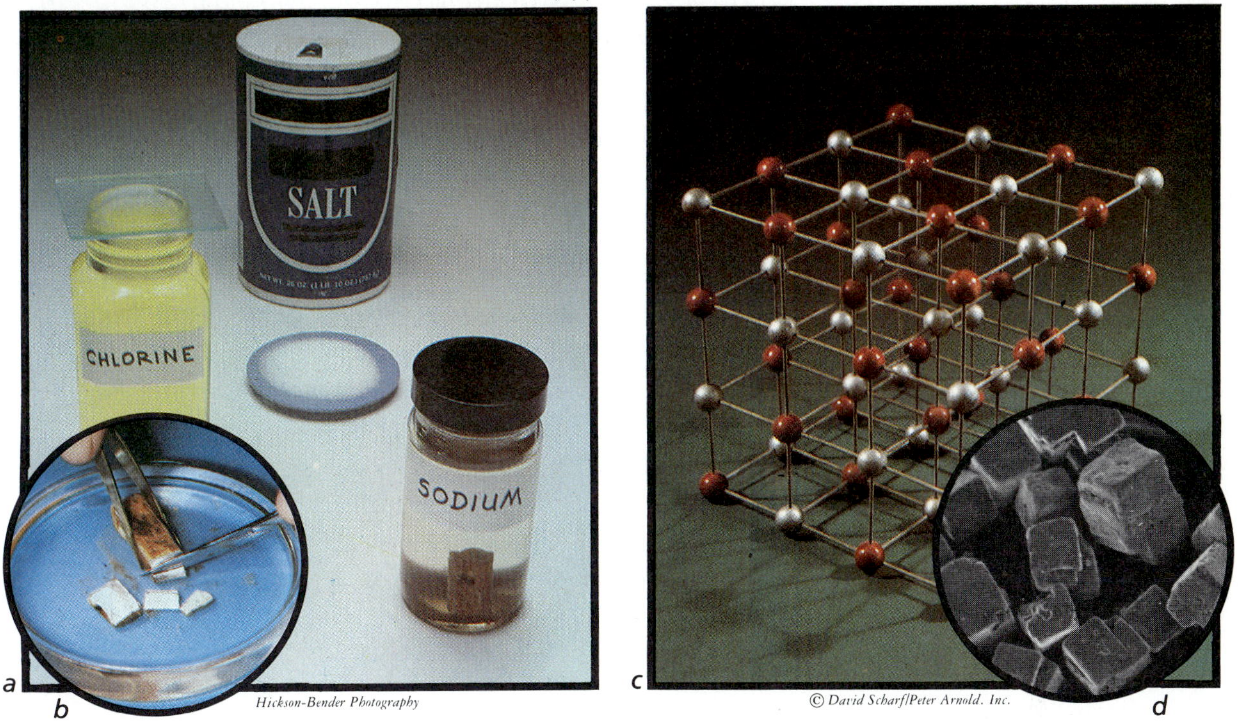

Hickson-Bender Photography

© David Scharf/Peter Arnold, Inc.

FIGURE 7-7. The compound NaCl appears quite different from the elements that form it (a). Sodium is so soft that it can be cut with a knife (b). The arrangement of ions in a salt crystal shows each ion to be surrounded by 6 ions of the opposite charge (c). The crystals have a cubic shape (d).

7-1 **ACTIVITY** *How do you draw a model to show ionic bonding?*

Draw a diagram of a lithium atom. Next to it draw a diagram of a chlorine atom. Now draw an arrow to show that the outer electron in lithium moves to the outer energy level in chlorine. Draw a diagram of a calcium atom. Next to it draw diagrams of two bromine atoms. Draw arrows to show how the outer two electrons in the calcium are lost to the bromine atoms. What kind of bond is formed between lithium and chlorine? ionic *What is the formula for the compound formed from calcium and bromine?* $CaBr_2$

Detailed information concerning this Activity can be found in the Teacher's Guide at the front of this book.

7-2 Detailed information concerning this Activity can be found in the Teacher's Guide at the front of this book.

ACTIVITY *Can you identify the shapes of some crystals?*

***(1)** Pour a few crystals of table salt on a piece of colored paper. Examine the crystals with a magnifying glass. Draw the shape of a salt crystal on a piece of paper. **(2)** Place several Rochelle salt crystals on a glass slide. Observe with a microscope. Make a drawing of their shape. **(3)** Observe alum, nickel sulfate, and sodium nitrate crystals with a microscope. Make a drawing showing the shape of each.*

Are the crystals alike or different in shape? different *All of the crystals you observed are compounds containing ions. State a reason why the crystals might be different in shape.*

The formulas for the compounds used are different. The ions are arranged in various patterns.

7:4 Electron Sharing

Hydrogen chloride, HCl, is a compound in which electrons are shared. The hydrogen atom has one electron. The outer energy level of hydrogen could be filled if it could get another electron.

How is a covalent bond formed?

The chlorine atom has seven electrons in its outer energy level. If chlorine could get one more electron (for a total of 8), its outer energy level would be filled. Figure 7-8 is a model of how hydrogen and chlorine combine to share electrons. Hydrogen has two electrons in its outer energy level. This level is now complete. Chlorine has eight electrons in its outer energy level. Atoms which combine by sharing electrons form a **covalent bond.**

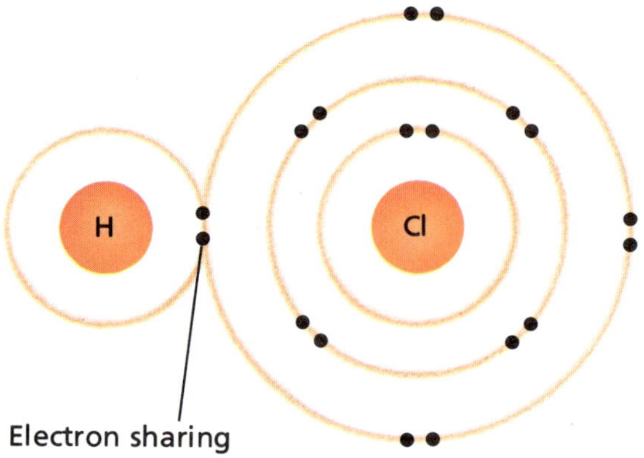

FIGURE 7-8. Bonding model for HCl showing electron sharing.

When atoms bond covalently, the resulting particle is called a **molecule.** Some elements exist in nature as covalent molecules. Oxygen in the air we breathe is a molecule. It is formed from two oxygen atoms. The formula for oxygen gas is O_2.

The properties of molecules are usually quite different from the elements that make them up. The water molecule has the formula H_2O. The properties of water are different from the properties of hydrogen and oxygen. Hydrogen is flammable when mixed with air. Many substances burn in oxygen. However, water is used to put out fires.

FIGURE 7-9. The element hydrogen is flammable (a) while the compound water, H_2O, is used to put out fires (b).

a 

The Bettman Archive Inc.

b 

Abraxas

7-3

ACTIVITY *How do you draw a model to show covalent bonding?*

On a piece of paper write the symbol for hydrogen. Place a dot next to the symbol to show the outer electron in a hydrogen atom. Write the symbol for fluorine. Place dots around the symbol to show the number of outer electrons in fluorine. Now combine the hydrogen and fluorine into one diagram that shows one pair of shared electrons.

Draw a diagram to show how carbon can form four covalent bonds with four hydrogen atoms. What is the formula for the compound formed from hydrogen and carbon? What is the formula for the compound formed from hydrogen and fluorine?

Detailed information concerning this Activity can be found in the Teacher's Guide at the front of this book.

7:5 Oxidation Numbers

What is the oxidation number of an element?

Oxidation number is the name given to the combining ability of an atom. This number tells how many electrons an atom gains, loses, or shares in forming a compound. In sodium chloride, NaCl, sodium has lost one electron so it has an oxidation number of 1+. Chlorine has gained one electron so it has an oxidation number of 1−. In water, H_2O, each hydrogen atom shares one electron with the oxygen atom. The oxidation number for each hydrogen is 1+. The oxidation number for oxygen is 2− because the oxygen atom shares two of its outer electrons with hydrogen.

How are oxidation numbers used to write formulas?

The sum of the oxidation numbers for the atoms in a compound is zero. Therefore, when Na^+ and Cl^- combine, one sodium bonds with one chlorine. Thus, the formula is NaCl.

Hydrogen has an oxidation number of 1+. One atom of hydrogen (1+) will bond with one atom of chlorine (1−) to form HCl. Magnesium has an oxidation number of 2+. One atom of magnesium combines with two atoms of chlorine. Each chlorine atom has an oxidation number of 1−. Thus, the formula is $MgCl_2$.

Some elements have more than one oxidation number. Iron can have oxidation numbers of 2+ or 3+. It forms two different compounds with bromine: $FeBr_2$ and $FeBr_3$. If an element has more than one oxidation number, the number intended is written in parentheses after the element's name. For example, iron(II) means 2+; iron (III) means 3+. Note Roman numerals are used to indicate the number. If bromine has an oxidation number of 1−, which compound above contains iron(II)? iron(III)? *$FeBr_2$ $FeBr_3$*

In writing formulas for compounds, *the symbol of the metal or element with the positive oxidation number is written first.* For example, aluminum chloride, $AlCl_3$, is a compound formed between aluminum and chlorine. Aluminum is written first because it is a metal. Chlorine is a nonmetal. When writing formulas you can check the periodic table on page 115 to determine which elements are metals. The oxidation numbers of some common elements are listed in Table 7-2.

Example

What is the formula for a compound composed of silver and sulfur?

Solution:

(a) Use Table 7-2 to find the oxidation numbers of silver and sulfur.

silver 1+ sulfur 2−

(b) Two atoms of silver are needed to combine with one atom of sulfur. Silver is a metal and is written first.

$$Ag_2S$$

Table 7-2

Oxidation Numbers of Some Elements

1+	2+	3+
copper(I), Cu^+ hydrogen, H^+ lithium, Li^+ potassium, K^+ silver, Ag^+ sodium, Na^+	barium, Ba^{2+} calcium, Ca^{2+} copper(II), Cu^{2+} iron(II), Fe^{2+} magnesium, Mg^{2+} zinc, Zn^{2+}	aluminum, Al^{3+} chromium, Cr^{3+} iron(III), Fe^{3+}
1−	**2−**	**3−**
bromine, Br^- chlorine, Cl^- fluorine, F^- iodine, I^-	oxygen, O^{2-} sulfur, S^{2-}	nitrogen, N^{3-} phosphorus, P^{3-}

a

Hickson-Bender Photography

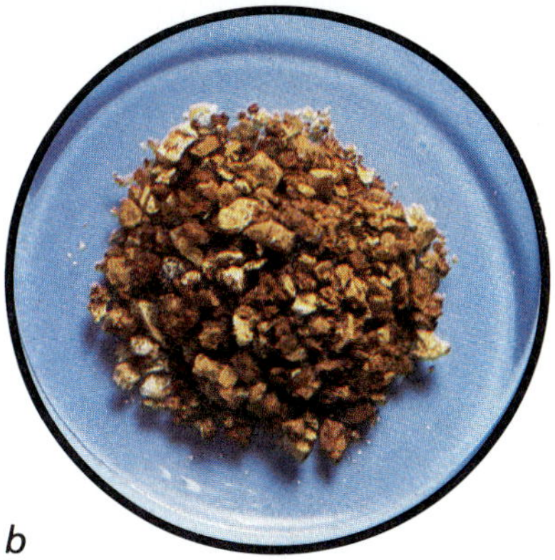

b

FIGURE 7-10. The compound $FeBr_2$ (a) is different in appearance and properties from $FeBr_3$ (b).

Making Sure

7. Using Table 7-2, write formulas for compounds formed from the following:

   a. sodium and bromine *NaBr*

   b. potassium and iodine *KI*

   c. hydrogen and bromine *HBr*

   d. hydrogen and sulfur *H_2S*

   e. magnesium and fluorine *MgF_2*

   f. calcium and chlorine *$CaCl_2$*

   g. lithium and sulfur *Li_2S*

   h. copper(II) and sulfur *CuS*

7:6 Binary Compounds

What is a binary compound?

Binary (BI nuh ree) **compounds** are composed of two elements. Binary compounds are named beginning with the element with the positive oxidation number. The name of the second element will end in *-ide.* For example, $MgCl_2$ is magnesium chlor*ide.* HCl is hydrogen chlor*ide.* $FeCl_2$ is iron(II) chlor*ide.* CuF is copper(I) fluor*ide.*

Example

What is the name for FeS?

Solution:

Using Table 7-2, we see that Fe exists as iron(II) or iron(III). The oxidation state of sulfur is 2−. The formula indicates only one atom of each element. Therefore, the oxidation state of iron must be 2+. The name of the compound is iron(II) sulfide.

Making Sure

8. Using Table 7-2, name each of the following:

a. NaCl *sodium chloride*
b. CuBr *copper(I) bromide*
c. BaS *barium sulfide*
d. MgO *magnesium oxide*
e. KI *potassium iodide*
f. $MgBr_2$ *magnesium bromide*
g. CaS *calcium sulfide*
h. CuO *copper(II) oxide*
i. $FeCl_3$ *iron(III) chloride*
j. FeO *iron(II) oxide*

9. Using Table 7-2, write formulas for each of the following:

a. calcium bromide $CaBr_2$
b. potassium oxide K_2O
c. aluminum chloride $AlCl_3$
d. iron(III) iodide FeI_3
e. copper(I) sulfide Cu_2S
f. lithium fluoride LiF
g. sodium bromide NaBr
h. copper(II) chloride $CuCl_2$

7:7 Polyatomic Ions

A **polyatomic ion** is a group of atoms which act together as one ion or charged atom. Compounds containing polyatomic ions are named in much the same way as binary compounds. The positive part of the compound is given first. For example, the compound formed by sodium and the sulfate ion has the formula Na_2SO_4. It is called sodium sulfate. The compound formed from the ammonium ion and sulfur is $(NH_4)_2S$. Its name is ammonium sulfide. Parentheses and the subscript 2 show two ammonium ions. Table 7-3 lists some polyatomic ions and their oxidation numbers.

Table 7-3

Some Polyatomic Ions and Their Oxidation Numbers		
1+ *ammonium, NH_4^+*		
1− *acetate, $C_2H_3O_2^-$* *chlorate, ClO_3^-* *hydroxide, OH^-* *nitrate, NO_3^-*	**2−** *carbonate, CO_3^{2-}* *sulfate, SO_4^{2-}*	**3−** *phosphate, PO_4^{3-}*

Making Sure

10. Using Tables 7-2 and 7-3, write formulas for each of the following compounds:

a. sodium nitrate $NaNO_3$
b. silver sulfate Ag_2SO_4
c. iron(II) chloride $FeCl_2$
d. potassium phosphate K_3PO_4
e. sodium hydrogen carbonate $NaHCO_3$
f. sodium acetate $NaC_2H_3O_2$

11. Name the following compounds:

a. Na_2SO_4 sodium sulfate
b. $(NH_4)_3PO_4$ ammonium phosphate
c. FeO iron(II) oxide
d. $AgNO_3$ silver nitrate
e. KBr potassium bromide
f. NaOH sodium hydroxide

12. What elements and how many atoms of each are present in the formulas of the compounds listed in problems 10 and 11? See the Teacher's Guide.

Focus On

Frontiers

The Search for a Nondigestible Sweet

Thomas Russell

People crave a sweet taste. But, many people want the taste without the calories that go with it. One solution to this problem is artificial sweeteners. Saccharine is one example of an artificial sweetener. However, saccharine is suspected of causing cancer. Thus, it is not a good solution. Scientists at Dynapol are approaching this problem in a new way. They want to make a sweetener that is not digested.

In order to develop a sweetener, the scientists must understand the taste process. They found that taste occurs when a stimulus molecule in the food bonds with a receptor molecule in the tongue. The reaction takes place in the membranes of the taste cells. Each cell has many finger-like projections, called microvilli. The receptor molecules are in these projections. When the stimulus and receptor molecules bond, the electrical potential of the cell membrane changes. The change leads to the generation of a sweet taste sensation. Each stimulus molecule must have precise features in order to react with a receptor molecule. This process is the same for each kind of taste.

Scientists know that large molecular mass polymers are not digested. A polymer is a carbon compound that has a repeating structure. Dynapol's first approach was to combine a low molecular mass sweetener with a polymer. The result was a tasteless substance. They had to change the structure of the sweetener too much when they bound it to a polymer.

The solution to this problem was to find a new sweetener. One new sweetener can be made from a molecule found in citrus fruits. In early experiments with this new sweetener, a strong aftertaste was found. Further experiments yielded an acceptable sweetener. The final challenge to the scientists at Dynapol is to make a sweetener that tastes like sugar and is not digested.

Points to Remember

1. Two or more elements can combine to form a compound. 7:1
2. Atoms combine to complete their outer levels. 7:2
3. Molecules are formed by atoms that share electrons. 7:4
4. Atoms that form ions bond by a transfer of electrons. 7:3
5. The oxidation number of a bonded atom is the number of electrons lost, gained, or shared. 7:5
6. Binary compounds are named by adding -ide to the name of the element with the negative oxidation number. 7:6
7. A polyatomic ion acts as a single unit. 7:7

Words to Use

Write a sentence in which you correctly use each of the following words or terms.

binary compound	ion	oxidation number
chemical formula	ionic bond	polyatomic ion
compound	molecule	subscript
covalent bond		

Questions for Review

Do not write in this book.

A. True or False *Have students rewrite each false statement to make it correct.*
Determine whether each of the following sentences is true or false.

T **1.** Molecules are formed when atoms bond covalently.
T **2.** Electrons have a negative electric charge.
T **3.** The oxidation number of an element represents the number of electrons which may be lost, gained, or shared by its atoms.
T **4.** A subscript is the ratio of electrons in a compound.
T **5.** The elements of Group IA are reactive.
F **6.** When atoms share electrons ~~ions~~ are formed. *molecules*
F **7.** The elements of Group VIIA have ~~eight~~ electrons in their outer energy level. *seven*
T **8.** A charged atom is called an ion.
T **9.** A binary compound contains two elements.
F **10.** Every element has only one oxidation number. *Some elements have more than one oxidation number.*

B. Multiple Choice

Choose the word or phrase that correctly completes each of the following sentences.

1. The compound $Mg(NO_3)_2$ contains *(mercury, neon, <u>oxygen</u>)*.
2. A molecule is *(positive, negative, <u>neutral</u>)*.
3. The compound iron(II) sulfide has the formula *(<u>FeS</u>, Fe_2S, FeS_2)*.
4. A polyatomic ion is a group of atoms which act together as *(<u>one</u>, two, three)* unit(s).
5. A magnesium atom can form a compound by giving up *(one, <u>two</u>, three)* electrons.
6. The compound $Al_2(SO_4)_3$ contains *(3, 4, <u>12</u>)* atoms of oxygen.
7. In the compound $CuCl_2$, the oxidation number of chlorine is *(1+, <u>1−</u>, 3−)*.
8. Nitrate, NO_3^-, is a *(compound, molecule, <u>polyatomic ion</u>)*.
9. A small number in a formula is called a(n) *(ion, <u>subscript</u>, symbol)*.
10. Sodium chloride is a(n) *(element, mixture, <u>compound</u>)*.

C. Completion

Complete each of the following sentences with a word or phrase that will make the sentence correct.

1. Potassium has an oxidation number of __1+__.
2. In forming compounds, potassium __loses__ electrons.
3. The formula X_3Y shows that for each atom of Y, there are __3__ atoms of X.
4. When electrons are shared by atoms in a molecule, __covalent__ bonding occurs.
5. When an atom gains or loses an electron, a(n) __ion__ is formed.
6. A binary compound contains atoms of __2__ elements.
7. __Ionic__ bonding occurs when electrons are transferred.
8. Like sodium, lithium will form compounds by __transferring__ electrons.
9. An example of a compound formed between elements of Group IA and Group VIA is __Na_2O__.
10. The elements in a certain compound always combine in the same __ratio__.

Detailed answers to these questions are given in the Teacher's Guide at the front of this book.

D. How and Why

1. How does covalent bonding differ from ionic bonding?
2. Name the compounds represented by the following formulas:
   a. $NaCl$ **b.** NH_4NO_3 **c.** $Ca_3(PO_4)_2$
3. Write formulas for the following compounds:
   a. potassium sulfate **b.** sulfur dioxide **c.** mercury(I) sulfide
4. An atom of an element has electrons distributed in energy levels in this manner: 2, 8, 2. What would you expect the oxidation number of this element to be? Why?
5. What kind of atoms and how many of each are represented by the formula $Mg(NO_2)_2$?
6. What are the differences among an element, compound, and mixture?
7. How can iron form the two compounds $FeCl_2$ and $FeCl_3$?

More Ideas to Explore

1. Construct models of atoms. Use clay or styrofoam balls to represent electrons, protons, and neutrons. Thin copper wire will hold the balls in place.
2. Do a library report on how the atomic theory has changed from the time of John Dalton until today.

Readings to Discover

Taylor, L.B. Jr., *Chemistry Careers.* NY: F. Watts, 1978.

Hausen, James, "Forensic Science: The Labs Are No Place Like Holmes." *Science Digest,* October 1979, pp. 33-36.

"Nitrogen Oxides in Polluted Air." *Science News,* Vol. 113, May 19, 1978, p. 199.

Unit 3

In this unit we will look at one of the subgroups of matter, the elements. You have learned that the elements are further classified into families. These families each show a pattern of similar properties. The pattern is as regular as that in the pictures shown here.

pattern *Bruce D. Sampsel*

Patterns in Matter

spectrum Mr. & Mrs. Pantages   Larry Hamill

How many of the objects around you are made of metal? What properties do metals have that make them so important? What are some of the properties of the metal used to form the dome in the picture?

Mr. & Mrs. Pantages

Families of Elements—Metals

8

Chapter 8 contains descriptive material concerning the important elements of the metals section of the periodic table. Uses, chemical and physical properties, and similarities among elements in a family are discussed. See the Teacher's Guide at the front of this book for additional teaching strategies for this chapter.

8:1 Properties of Metals

GOAL: *You will learn the characteristics of metals and the uses of some important metals.*

Most people have some idea of what metals are. They are generally hard and shiny and can be rolled into sheets or pulled into wires. They conduct an electric current and heat. An electric current is a flow of charged particles.

List three properties of metals.

Most metals are elements which have three or fewer electrons in the outer energy level of their atoms. Metals tend to give up electrons readily. This property makes metals good conductors. Electrons can move through the metal. Usually metals combine with other elements by giving up electrons and forming ionic bonds.

8:2 Alkali Metals

Name the alkali metals.

The **alkali** (AL kuh li) **metals** are the family of elements in Group IA of the periodic table. They have all the properties of metals except they are soft. They are usually shiny, reflect light and can be pounded into sheets and pulled into wires. Alkali metals are good conductors of electricity and heat. Group IA elements are the most reactive of all the metals. They are never found in the free state in nature. In pure form, the alkali metals are kept under oil so they will not react directly with oxygen or water vapor in the air.

Table 8-1

Alkali Metals

Eric Hoffhines

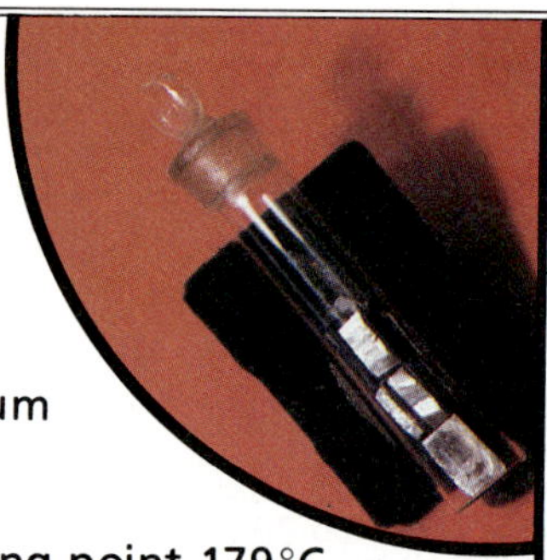 $^{7}_{3}$**Li** Lithium Melting point 179°C Boiling point 1336°C	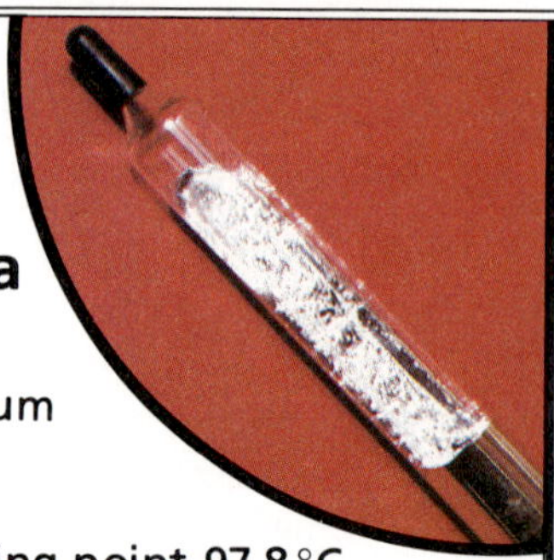 $^{23}_{11}$**Na** Sodium Melting point 97.8°C Boiling point 883°C	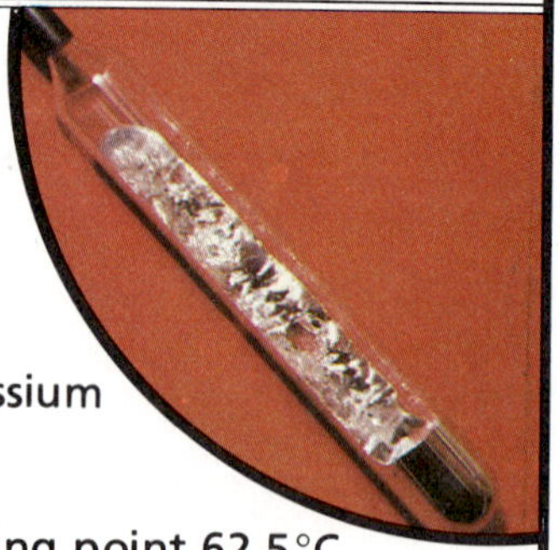 $^{39}_{19}$**K** Potassium Melting point 62.5°C Boiling point 758°C
 $^{85}_{37}$**Rb** Rubidium Melting point 39.0°C Boiling point 700°C	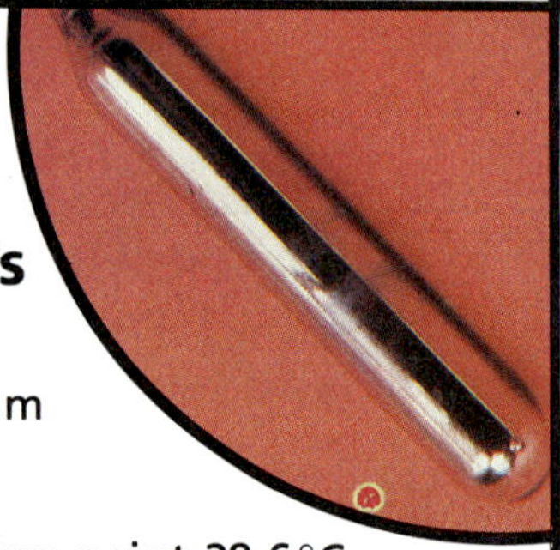 $^{133}_{55}$**Cs** Cesium Melting point 28.6°C Boiling point 670°C	$^{(223)}_{87}$**Fr** Francium Radioactive element, 223 is the mass number of the most stable isotope.

FIGURE 8-1. The metals of Group IA react violently with water. Cesium is shown here.

Hickson-Bender Photography

All the alkali metals form compounds by ionic bonding. They readily give up their one outer electron to form ions. In fact, they give up their outer electron when hit with a beam of light. This type of reaction is used in a cesium photocell to convert light energy into electric energy. Reactions of this type are called **photoelectric** reactions.

One way to identify the alkali metals is by flame tests. When ions or vapors of these elements are heated in a flame, some of their electrons gain energy. These electrons move to higher energy levels. As they return to their previous state, these electrons then lose this energy in the form of light. Figure 8-2 shows flame tests for some of the elements. The names for rubidium and cesium are derived from Latin words describing the color they give off in a flame test.

Lester V. Bergman & Assoc. Inc.

Copper

Calcium

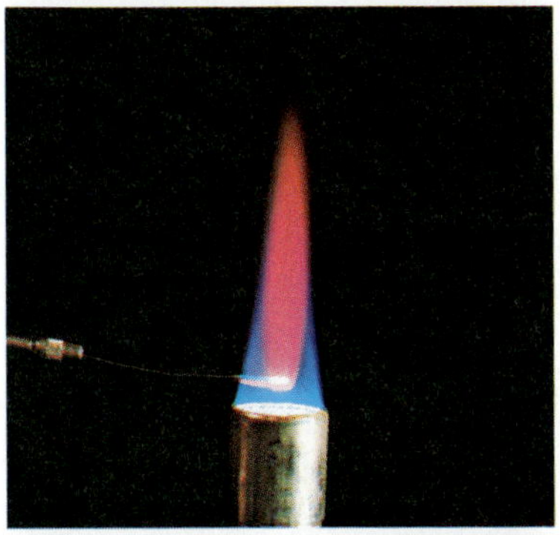

Strontium

Barium

Sodium

Potassium

Rubidium

Cesium

FIGURE 8-2. Flame tests for various elements.

8-1 Detailed information concerning this Activity can be found in the Teacher's Guide at the front of this book.

Activity *How do you identify a metal using a flame test?*

Setting Up

Bunsen burner
platinum or nichrome wire
test solutions
test tubes
test tube rack

Getting Started

CAUTION: *Handle acids with care. Wear eye and clothing protection.*

1. *Label each of the seven test tubes with one of the following chlorides: lithium, potassium, sodium, barium, calcium, strontium, and copper.*
2. *Place 5 mL of the first test solution in a test tube.*
3. *Clean the platinum or nichrome wire by dipping it in hydrochloric acid, then distilled water and drying it in the burner flame.*
4. *Repeat Step 3 until the wire no longer colors the burner flame.*
5. *Dip the clean wire into the test solution. Hold the wire at the tip of the inner cone of a burner flame, Figure 8-3.*
6. *Record the color of the flame test. Clean the wire in acid and then distilled water as in Step 3.*
7. *Repeat Steps 5 and 6 for the other test solutions.*
8. *Obtain an unknown solution from your teacher. Identify the metal in the unknown using the flame test.*

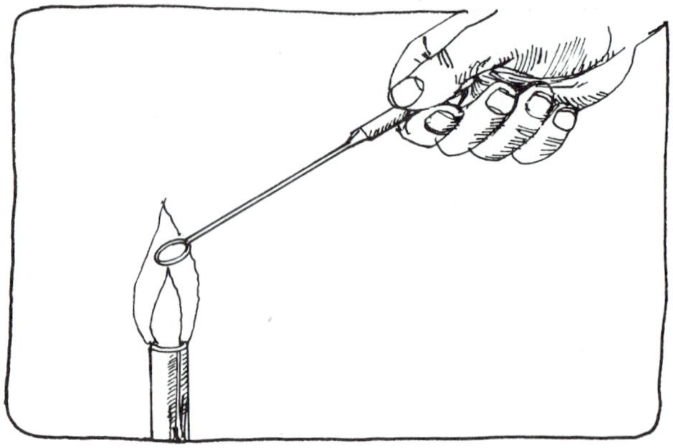

FIGURE 8-3.

Keeping Track

Solution	Color

Summing Up

1. *How can you be sure the chloride ion is not causing the color in the flame?*
2. *Suppose your test solution was a mixture of two metal ions. Could you identify both in the flame? Try the flame test with a mixture and see.*
3. *Why is it necessary to clean the wire between tests?*

Making Sure

1. How many electrons are in the outer energy level of an atom of each of the alkali metals? *one*
2. Why are these elements stored under oil? *They react with water and air.*

8:3 Alkaline Earth Metals

Name the alkaline earth metals.

The elements in Group IIA of the periodic table are called the **alkaline** (AL kuh lun) **earth** metals. The alkaline earth metals are very reactive and are not found in the free state in nature. Most of these elements give up their two outer electrons and form ions. For this reason, they tend to form compounds by ionic bonding. Some of these metals react with water.

Beryllium is found chemically combined in the form of a green mineral. The element itself is usually obtained by passing an electric current through molten beryllium chloride. Beryllium forms compounds with all of the elements of Group VIIA.

In nature, magnesium is found chemically combined in mineral deposits and as an ion dissolved in seawater. Pure magnesium burns with a very bright flame. For this reason, it is used in some photographic flashbulbs.

Magnesium is one of the elements found in the green plant pigment, chlorophyll (KLOR uh fihl). Some compounds of magnesium are used as medicines. An example is magnesium sulfate which is marketed as *Epsom salt.* Many stomach antacids (ant AS ud) contain magnesium hydroxide.

Linda Young

FIGURE 8-4. The mineral beryl is a source of beryllium.

FIGURE 8-5. Magnesium burns brightly (a) making it useful for photographic flashbulbs. Used in baseball bats (b), magnesium is lightweight and strong. The chlorophyll in green plant leaves (c) is a magnesium compound (d).

a
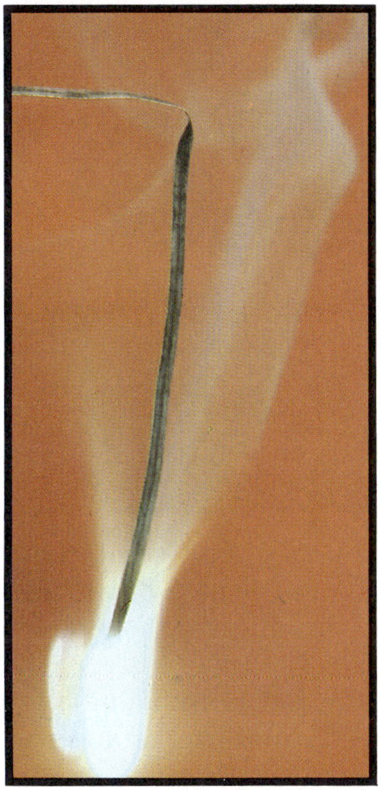

Hickson-Bender Photography

b

Eric Hoffhines

c
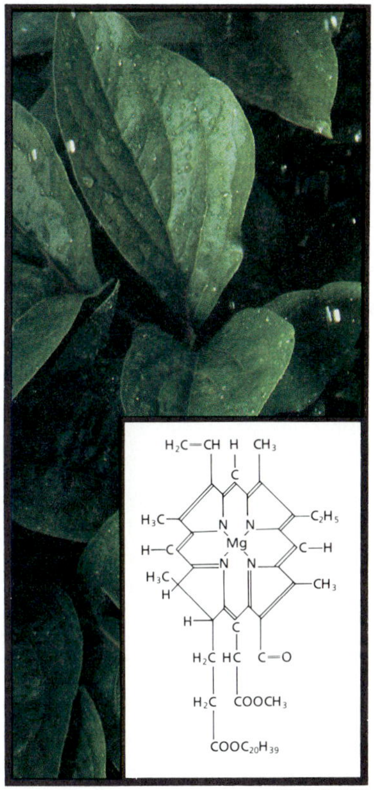

Larry Hamill

What are three compounds formed by the alkaline earth metals?

Calcium is one of the most abundant elements in the earth's crust. Slightly less than four percent of the mass of the earth's crust is calcium compounds. Calcium is never found in the free state in nature. It is usually prepared by passing an electric current through molten calcium chloride.

Lime is calcium oxide. Lime is mixed with sand, water, and other materials for making plaster and mortars for buildings. Lime is also used in making glass, dehairing hides, and softening hard water. Calcium sulfate is used in making paints and plasterboard. Calcium compounds are also used in treating soils that are too acid for crops to grow.

Young/Hoffhines

FIGURE 8-6. These foods are good sources of calcium, an essential nutrient.

Hal Yaeger/Alpha

FIGURE 8-7. The colors in a fireworks display are made from salts of barium, calcium, copper, sodium, and strontium.

Calcium is an important part of bones and teeth. Calcium is essential to the diet of humans and other animals. Milk and other dairy products are excellent sources of calcium.

The flame test for strontium and its compounds is a beautiful shade of red, Figure 8-2. For this reason, strontium compounds are often used in fireworks.

Table 8-2

The Alkaline Earth Metals

Eric Hoffbines

 $^{9}_{4}$**Be** Beryllium. Melting point 1285°C. Boiling point 2970°C	 $^{24}_{12}$**Mg** Magnesium. Melting point 650°C. Boiling point 1117°C	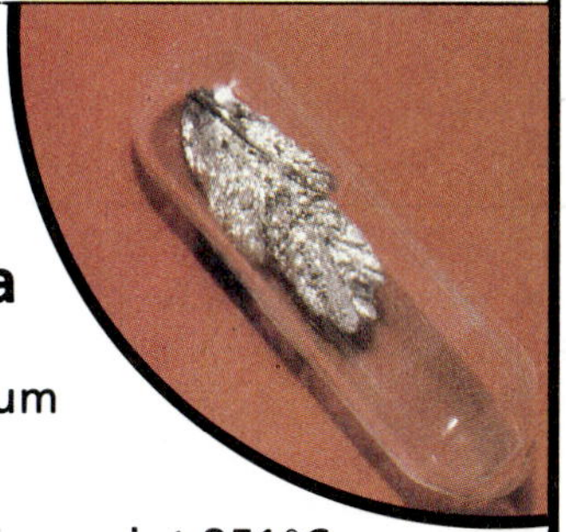 $^{40}_{20}$**Ca** Calcium. Melting point 851°C. Boiling point 1487°C
 $^{88}_{38}$**Sr** Strontium. Melting point 774°C. Boiling point 1366°C	 $^{137}_{56}$**Ba** Barium. Melting point 850°C. Boiling point 1537°C	Silvery-white radioactive element. The physical properties listed are those of the most stable isotope. $^{226}_{88}$**Ra** Radium. Melting point (700°C). Boiling point (1525°C)

Like the other alkaline earth metals, barium is always found in the combined state in nature. Barium has chemical properties similar to calcium and strontium. However, it tends to react more rapidly than calcium and strontium. Barium reacts readily with water, oxygen, and the Group VIIA elements. It is often stored under oil or kerosene to keep it from reacting with air. The flame test for barium and its compounds is green, Figure 8-2.

Barium sulfate is used to study the digestive tract. Patients swallow a liquid mixture containing barium sulfate. Because barium sulfate absorbs X rays, a doctor can study the digestive tract as the chemical moves through it.

FIGURE 8-8. X ray of the digestive tract of someone having ingested barium sulfate.

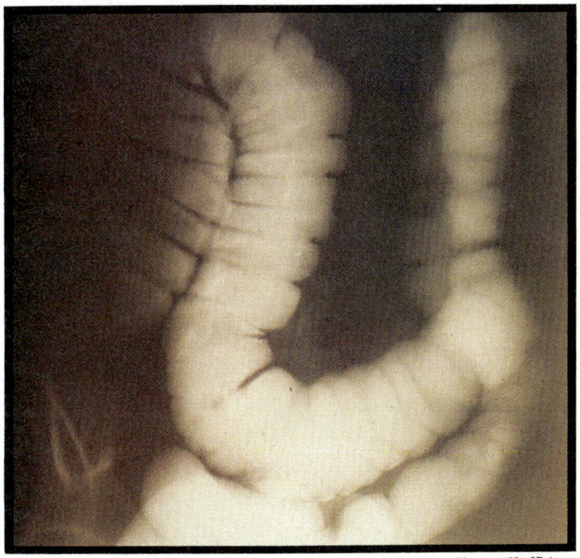

Young/Hoffbines

Radium is more chemically reactive than barium. In nature, it is found in uranium ores. It is also radioactive. It can be obtained in the free state by passing an electric current through radium salts. The metal is silvery white but turns black when exposed to air.

Radium is used in medicine to treat cancer. At one time, it was used to make luminous (LEW muh nus) watch dials. Luminous means to glow in the dark. It was later found that using radium for this purpose presented a health hazard to workers making the dials.

Making Sure

3. What are some of the common uses for calcium, barium, and strontium? *See the Teacher's Guide*
4. How many electrons are in the outer energy level of each of the alkaline earth metals? *two*
5. Chlorine combines with all of the alkaline earth metals. Write a chemical formula for the chloride of each of the alkaline earth metals. $BeCl_2$, $MgCl_2$, $CaCl_2$, $SrCl_2$, $BaCl_2$, $RaCl_2$

8:4 Transition Elements

The **transition elements** are in Group IIIB through IB of the periodic table. These elements are metals. They all have one or two electrons in their outer energy level. Unlike the alkali and alkaline earth families, the transition metals are "heavy" metals.

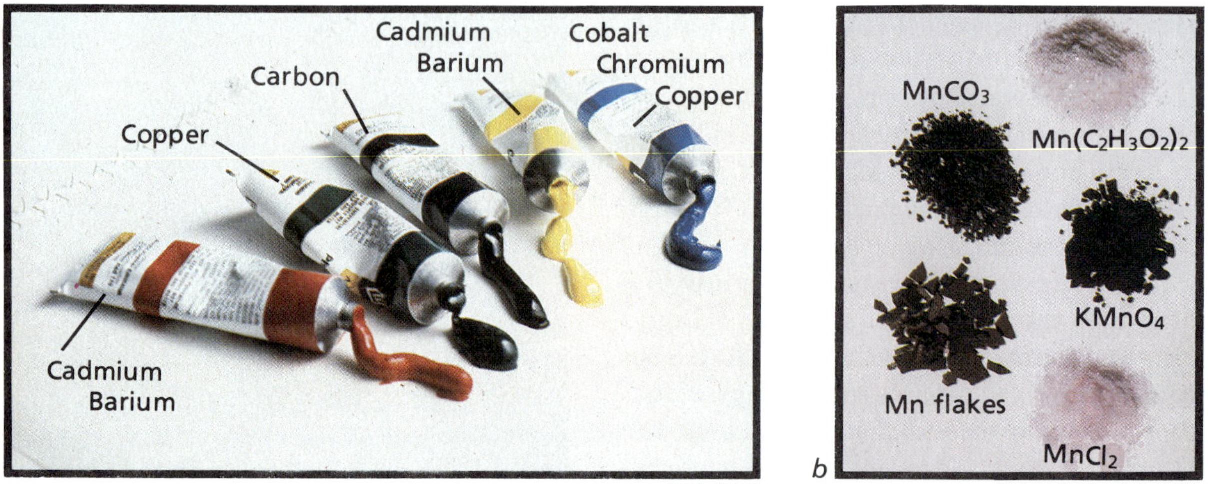

Linda Young

Hickson-Bender Photography

FIGURE 8-9. The colors of many paint pigments are due to transition metals (a). The transition metal, manganese, forms a variety of compounds of different colors (b).

Most of the transition metals have high melting points and are hard. In compounds, the ions of these metals are usually colored. There is often little difference in properties between a transition metal and its nearest neighbors on the periodic table.

List three properties of the transition metals.

Many transition metals also have more than one oxidation state. Iron, for example, forms both iron(II) and iron(III) compounds. Copper can be found in copper(I) and copper(II) oxidation states. Generally, the compounds formed by the different oxidation states have characteristic colors. It is easy to tell which form is in the compound.

8-2 Detailed information concerning this Activity can be found in the Teacher's Guide at the front of this book.

ACTIVITY *Are all transition metal ions the same color?*

With samples that your teacher provides, complete the following chart.

Compound	Oxidation State of the Metal	Color
$FeSO_4$	2	green
$FeCl_3$	3	orange
$FeCl_2$	2	green
$Fe_2(SO_4)_3$	3	orange
$CuCl_2$	2	blue green
$CuSO_4$	2	blue

What would you guess for the color of $Fe(NO_3)_2$? $Cu(NO_3)_2$? blue green

8:5 Metal Alloys

One of the most interesting properties of metals is their ability to form alloys. An **alloy** is a combination of two or more metals or a metal and one or more nonmetals. Alloys may be formed in a number of ways. The most common is to melt the metals, mix, and let the mixture cool. Actual metallic compounds can be formed. Alloys can be mixtures or compounds.

FIGURE 8-10. The photo shows a microscopic view of a gold-copper alloy.

Manfred Kage/© Peter Arnold Inc.

Table 8-3

Some Alloys and Their Uses		
Alloy	**Metals**	**Typical Uses**
Wood's metal	*Bi, Pb, Sn, Cd*	*automatic sprinklers*
Commercial bronze	*Cu, Sn*	*jewelry, screens, nuts, and bolts*
German silver	*Cu, Zn, Ni*	*silver platings, jewelry*
Gold, 14 carat	*Au, Cu, Ag*	*jewelry*
Solder	*Sn, Pb*	*electrical wire solderings*
Dentist's amalgam	*Hg, Ag*	*dental fillings*
Nichrome	*Ni, Cr*	*electrical heating elements*
Monel metal	*Ni, Cu, Fe*	*household appliances*
Dow metal	*Mg, Al, Mn*	*aircraft parts*

National Bureau of Standards

FIGURE 8-11. The International Standard kilogram is made from a platinum alloy.

Alloys may have properties that pure metals do not. For example, platinum is a soft transition metal. It expands the least of any metal when heated. Iridium is one of the hardest metals and one of the least reactive. The alloy of platinum and iridium is used for the International Standard kilogram. Why do you suppose the properties of both metals are needed? *A substance which does not expand or react is needed.*

8:6 Iron, Cobalt, and Nickel

Iron, cobalt, and nickel make up one of the most important metallic families. Iron is the most widely used metal. More iron is used than all of the other metals combined. It is the second most abundant metal in the earth's crust and the fourth most abundant of all the elements. Nearly every animal, vegetable, or mineral in the

Table 8-4

Iron, Cobalt, and Nickel		
$^{56}_{26}$**Fe** Iron  Melting point 1530°C Boiling point 3000°C	$^{59}_{27}$**Co** Cobalt  Melting point 1495°C Boiling point 3550°C	$^{59}_{28}$**Ni** Nickel  Melting point 1455°C Boiling point 2840°C

Hoffbines/Young

a

FPG

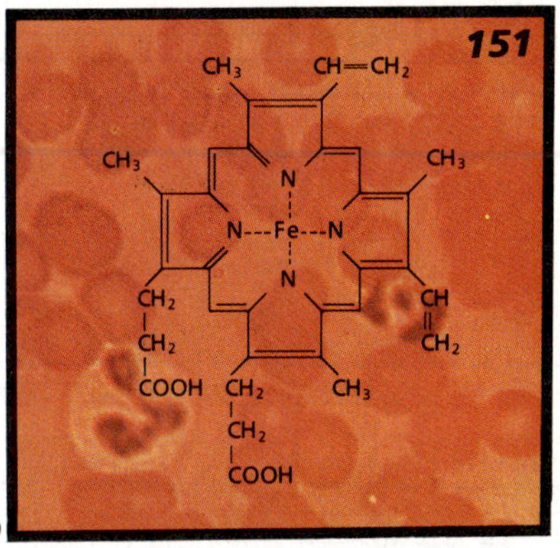

b

FIGURE 8-12. These foods are good sources of iron (a), an essential nutrient and part of blood cells (b).

world contains some iron. Hemoglobin in red blood cells is a compound containing iron.

Cobalt and nickel are far less abundant than iron. Both are difficult to mine and refine. Cobalt is used to produce special heat-resistant steel for use in cutting tools. Nickel can be polished to a high gloss and is often used to coat other metals to make them shiny. It is also alloyed with other metals to make them strong.

Transition elements can form compounds using electrons in the next to the outer energy level. As a result, a number of different compounds can be formed. Most of them form brightly colored solutions.

8-3 Detailed information concerning this Activity can be found in the Teacher's Guide at the front of this book.

Activity

What colors do you observe for some transition metal compounds?

Setting Up

Bunsen burner
2 test tubes
test tube holder

Getting Started

1. *Place a few crystals of cobalt(II) chloride in a test tube. Heat the tube gently at first, then strongly. What appears to be driven off? Record any color change you observe.*
2. *Cool the test tube. Add a few drops of water to the cooled test tube. Record any changes you observe.*
3. *Heat the solution in the test tube. Allow the solution to cool. Record any change.*
4. *Add a few drops of hydrochloric acid to the solution in the test tube.* **CAUTION:** *Handle acids with care; they can cause burns. Record any changes.*
5. *Place about 3 mL of nickel(II) sulfate solution in a test tube. Add about 1 mL of dilute sodium hydroxide to the solution in the test tube.* **CAUTION:** *Handle with care; hydroxides can cause burns. Record any changes you observe.*
6. *Add a few mL of ammonia solution. Record any changes in the solution.*

Keeping Track

Substance	Color

Summing Up *See the Teacher's Guide.*

1. *What do you think caused the color to change in Step 2?*
2. *Why do you think the color of the solution changed when you added hydrochloric acid?*
3. *Why do you think the color of the nickel(II) sulfate solution changed in Step 6?*

How is steel made?

8:7 Steel

Most alloys of iron are called **steels.** Steel contains carbon in varying amounts. Carbon steels become less flexible as more carbon is added. Other metals may be added to make steels with certain properties. The uses can range from wire and pipe to railroad rails, razor blades, springs, and knives. Table 8-5 shows uses of some steel alloys which contain other elements.

Table 8-5

Some Steel Alloys

Name	Composition	Properties	Uses
Manganese	*10-18% Mn*	*very hard*	*railroads, armor plate, conveyors*
Silicon	*1-5% Si*	*magnetic*	*magnets*
Duriron	*12-15% Si*	*acid resistant*	*pipes, condensors, containers*
Nickel	*2-4% Ni*	*elastic, corrosion resistant*	*gears, drive shafts, cables*
Invar	*36% Ni*	*does not expand or contract*	*measuring tapes, pendulums*
Permalloy	*78% Ni*	*magnetic*	*cables*
Stainless	*14-19% Cr 7-9% Ni*	*strong, corrosion resistant*	*surgical instruments, knives, flatware*
Chrome-vanadium	*1-10% Cr 0.15-0.18% V*	*strong, stain-resistant*	*ball-bearings, tools, axles*
High Speed	*14-20% W, 4% Cr or 6-12% Mo, 4% Cr*	*keeps hardness at high temperatures*	*cutting tools, drill bits, saw blades*

Making Sure

6. Would steel used in auto bodies be high- or low-carbon steel? *low*
7. What advantage does a coating of nickel provide? *protects and shines*
8. What is one use for a low-carbon flexible steel? *razor blades, watch springs, auto bodies are some examples*

8:8 The Copper Family

The copper family is made up of three well known metals: copper, silver, and gold. None of the three is very reactive and they are all found free in nature. Copper and silver can be mined as free elements or in ores combined with other compounds. Gold is almost always found in the free state.

List the properties of copper, gold, and silver.

Table 8-6

The Copper Family		
$^{64}_{29}$Cu	$^{108}_{47}$Ag	$^{197}_{79}$Au
Copper	Silver	Gold
		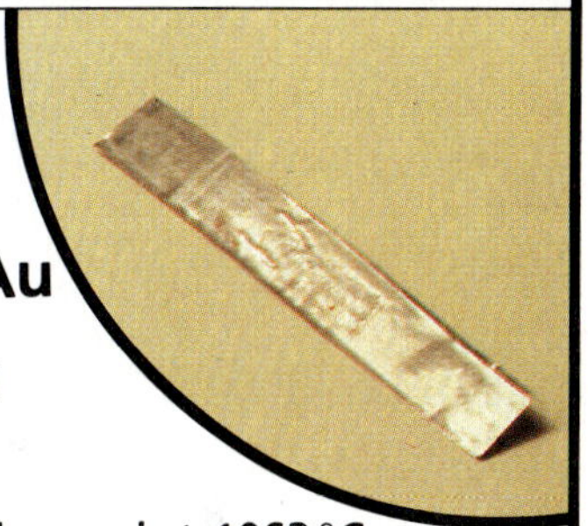
Melting point 1083°C	Melting point 960°C	Melting point 1063°C
Boiling point 2582°C	Boiling point 2177°C	Boiling point 2707°C

Linda Young

Copper is an orange metal and is a good conductor of heat and electricity. It is easily drawn into wires and pounded or rolled into sheets. Copper is most widely used in electrical wiring and plumbing. It is often used to protect other materials since it forms a protective coating when exposed to air.

Gold is a yellow, soft metal. It is often used with other metals in jewelry because it can be shaped easily. "White gold" is an alloy with copper, nickel, and zinc. "Yellow gold" contains silver and copper. Gold has always been valuable since it is rare. It is used as a base

What are some uses for copper, gold, and silver?

for money systems all over the world. Gold is not reactive chemically. It only dissolves in aqua regia. Aqua regia is a mixture of concentrated nitric and hydrochloric acids.

Of all metals, silver is the best conductor of heat and electricity. Silver can also be shaped easily and is used for jewelry and other ornaments. It is a white, soft metal that reflects light well. Silver is sometimes used as a backing for mirrors.

Silver does not react with oxygen but does tarnish when exposed to hydrogen sulfide. Tarnish is a form of corrosion. The tarnish is a coating of silver sulfide. Silver compounds are used in photography because they turn black when exposed to light. This property of silver makes it useful in making photosensitive (foht oh SEN sut ihv) glass. This type of glass is made into eyeglasses which darken in bright sunlight.

Linda Young

FIGURE 8-13. Silver compounds are used in making photosensitive eyeglasses. These glasses darken as the result of a chemical change when they are exposed to light.

8-4

ACTIVITY *What are some properties of copper(II) sulfate?*

***(1)** Place some copper(II) sulfate crystals in a test tube. Heat the tube gently, then strongly. What do you observe? **(2)** Cool the test tube; then add a few milliliters of water. What happens? Why do you think it happened? **(3)** Partially fill two test tubes with copper(II) sulfate solution. Add a few drops of sodium hydroxide solution to one test tube. What happens? Add a few drops of ammonia water to the other test tube. What happens?*

How are the reactions of copper compounds similar to those of cobalt and nickel in the Activity on page 151?

Color changes occurred when compounds from NH_3 and NaOH were formed.

Detailed information concerning this Activity can be found in the Teacher's Guide at the front of this book.

8:9 The Zinc Family

Table 8-7

The Zinc Family		
 $^{65}_{30}$**Zn** Zinc Melting point 419°C Boiling point 907°C	 $^{112}_{48}$**Cd** Cadmium Melting point 320.9°C Boiling point 767°C	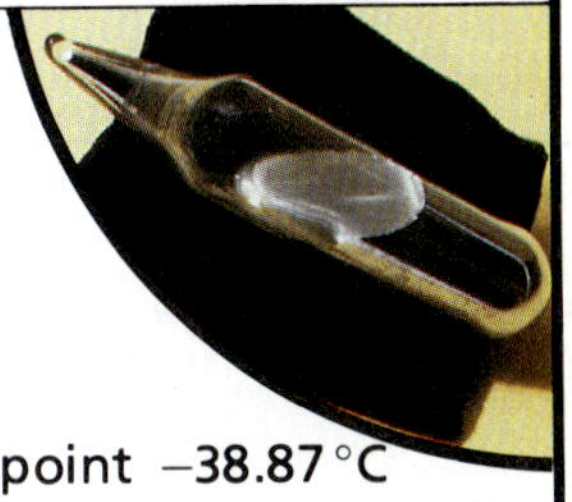 $^{201}_{80}$**Hg** Mercury Melting point −38.87°C Boiling point 357°C

Linda Young

The zinc family is found in Group IIB and immediately follows the transition metals. This family has many properties similar to those of the transition metals.

Zinc is a silvery metal which tarnishes in the air. The tarnish forms a protective coating and prevents further corrosion. For this reason, zinc is often used to coat other metals, such as iron, to protect them from corrosion. Zinc compounds are used in paint, medicines, fiberboard, and automobile tires.

Cadmium is generally obtained during the refining process for zinc. It has many of the same uses including plating on other metals for protection. Cadmium sulfide is a pigment in paint. Cadmium rods are used in nuclear reactors. They can absorb neutrons. Thus, they "control" the reactions. The more neutrons absorbed, the slower the reaction.

Mercury is the only metal that is a liquid at room temperature. It is a dense silvery metal that has a low freezing point and a high boiling point. These properties make mercury useful in thermometers, barometers, and electrical switches. Mercury forms alloys with most metals. Mercury alloys of tin, silver, and gold are used in dentistry for filling teeth. Mercury is a poison and should not be handled. Mercury compounds dumped as waste can be absorbed by plants and animals. These compounds can accumulate in the body. People have died as a result of mercury poisoning.

FIGURE 8-14. Deodorants contain zinc and aluminum compounds.

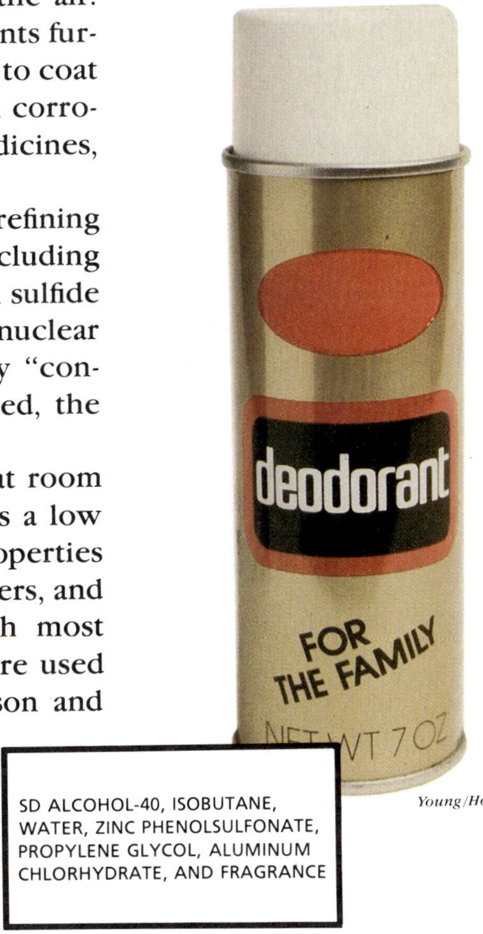

Young/Hoffbines

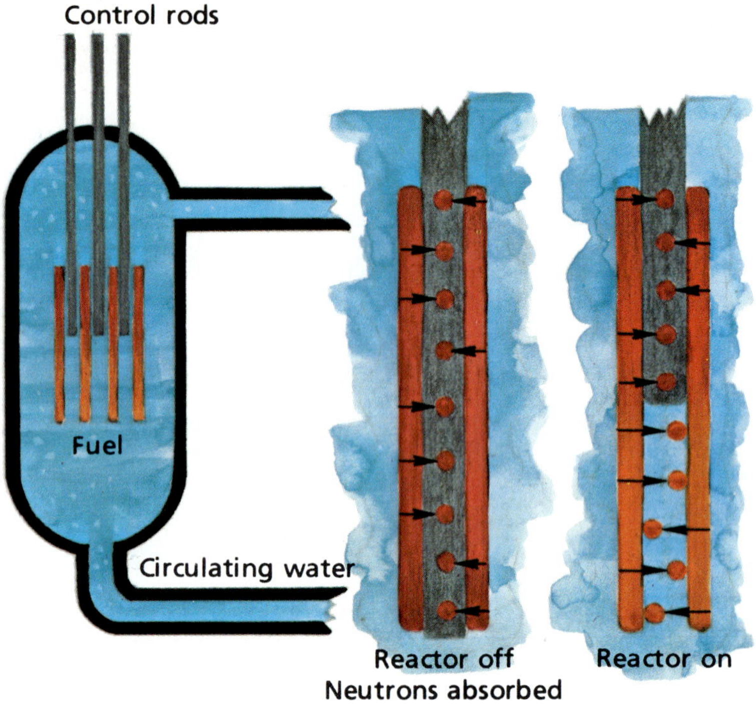

FIGURE 8-15. Boron compounds are used in control rods for nuclear reactors. Boron is a good neutron absorber. Thus, it helps control nuclear reactions.

8:10 Aluminum and Boron

Aluminum is the most abundant metallic element in the earth's crust. It is usually found as aluminum oxide and for years presented chemists with a problem in refining it. The aluminum is removed using an electric current. This process, called **electrolysis** (ih lek TRAHL uh sus), produces aluminum which is ninety-nine percent pure. Aluminum has a silvery appearance but forms a protective coating on its surface in combining with oxygen. It is very light but strong and is a good conductor of heat and electricity. It is used in kitchen pots and pans, in making airplanes, in electrical wire, and as a foil for wrapping.

How is aluminum obtained from its ore?

Much of the aluminum produced is used in alloys. *Duralumin* is made of aluminum, copper, manganese, and magnesium. It is light, but strong as steel. *Alnico* is an alloy of iron, aluminum, nickel, and cobalt. It makes extremely strong magnets. Aluminum compounds are used in medicines, deodorant, and in the manufacture of pigments and dyes.

What are some uses of aluminum?

Table 8-8

Boron and Aluminum

Eric Hoffhines

$^{11}_{5}B$	$^{27}_{13}Al$
Boron	Aluminum
Melting point 2074°C	Melting point 660.2°C
Boiling point 3675°C	Boiling point 2447°C

Even though boron has three electrons in its outer energy level, it is primarily nonmetallic in its chemical properties. Boron is included in the elements usually referred to as metalloids. Metalloids are between metals and nonmetals on the periodic table. They have some properties characteristic of metals and nonmetals. Boron is never found free in nature although its compounds are mined extensively in the West. Common compounds of boron are boric acid, a mild antiseptic, and borax, a water softener.

FIGURE 8-16. Aluminum is used in a variety of ways in the home.

Focus On

Skills

Taking Notes in Chart Form

Information from this chapter can be organized in a chart form to help you see patterns of thought. This form of note taking is easy to do once you have identified your topics. As you read *Families of Elements—Metals* complete the chart below.

Metals (add a general description - see page 141)					
	Examples	Uses	Description	Combining Qualities	Electrons
Alkali Metals	cesium rubidium lithium sodium potassium francium	photo electric reactions	Refer students to Table 8-1.	not found in free state stored in oil	form compounds by ionic bonding give up 2 outer electrons
Alkaline Earth Metals	beryllium magnesium calcium barium radium strontium	flashbulbs, Epson salt lime used in glass+mortar study digestion treat cancer fireworks	Refer students to Table 8-2.	not found in free state, usually chemically combined with other minerals	form compounds by ionic bonding give up 2 outer electrons
Transition Metals	copper	good conductor of heat and electricity drawn into wires + made into sheets		found free	has 2 oxidation states · Copper(1) and Copper(2)
conductor of heat and electricity, jewelry, backing for mirrors, photography, and eyeglasses sensitive to light	gold silver	jewelry, money	Refer students to Table 8-6.	not reactive tarnishes when exposed to hydrogen sulfide	—— gives up 1 electron; + 1+ oxidation state
	iron Cobalt nickel	hemoglobin, making steel protective coating on other metals, paint ·heat-resistant steel for cutting ·coat other metals to make them shiny polished to high gloss	Refer students to Table 8-4.	all form highly colored compounds both are alloyed with other metals	has 2 oxidation states Iron (II) and Iron (III) Refer students back to Chapter 7 where the oxidation states of these metals are discussed
Zinc Family	zinc cadmium mercury	plating; rods in nuclear reactors thermometers, barometers	Refer students to Table 8-7.	forms alloys with most metals	has 2 oxidation states · mercury(I) and mercury(II)
Aluminum and Boron	aluminum boron	pots, airplanes, foil, and wire antiseptics and water softeners	Refer students to Table 8-8.	both form metal alloys	

Points to Remember

1. Metals generally have three or fewer electrons in the outer energy level of their atoms. 8:1
2. Group IA, the alkali metals, are the most reactive metals. 8:2
3. Most transition metals have more than one oxidation state. 8:4
4. Alloys may have properties that pure metals do not. 8:5
5. Transition elements form compounds by sharing electrons. 8:6
6. Steels are alloys of iron. 8:7
7. The copper family—gold, silver, copper—are not very reactive. 8:8
8. Mercury is the only liquid metal. 8:9
9. Metalloids have properties of metals and nonmetals. 8:10

Words to Use

Write a sentence in which you correctly use each of the following words or terms.

alloy	metal	steel
electrolysis	metalloid	transition metal
flame test	photoelectric	

Questions for Review

Do not write in this book.

A. True or False *Have the students rewrite the false statements to make them correct.*

Determine whether each of the following sentences is true or false.

T **1.** Alkali metals are the most reactive metals.
F **2.** Calcium is an ~~alkali~~ metal. *alkaline earth*
T **3.** Silver and copper are in the same metal family.
F **4.** Solutions of transition metal compounds are usually ~~colorless~~. *colored*
F **5.** Nickel ~~is often coated with~~ other metals to make ~~it~~ stronger. *coats them*
F **6.** Boron is a true ~~metal~~. *metalloid*
T **7.** Alkali metals form compounds through ionic bonding.
T **8.** Copper's greatest use is in electric wiring and plumbing.
T **9.** Steels are alloys of iron.
F **10.** The ~~transition~~ metals are stored under oil. *alkali*

B. Multiple Choice

Choose the word or phrase that correctly completes each of the following sentences.

1. *(Iron, Boron, Oxygen, Cadmium)* is in the zinc family.
2. "Yellow gold" contains gold, copper, and *(zinc, mercury, silver)*.
3. The International Standard kilogram is an alloy of platinum and *(iron, iridium, gold)*.
4. To create a shiny steel, iron should be alloyed with *(cobalt, chromium, nickel)*.
5. Duralumin is an alloy of aluminum and many other metals including *(copper, iron, sodium, lead)*.
6. Control rods in nuclear reactors are made of *(cobalt, carbon, calcium, cadmium)*.
7. *(Sodium, Lithium, Potassium, Selenium)* is not a member of the alkali family.
8. Transition metals generally have *(0, 1, 2, 3, 4)* electrons in the outer energy level.
9. Chlorophyll contains *(calcium, magnesium, iron)*.
10. Boron is a *(metal, metalloid, nonmetal)*.

C. Completion

Complete each of the following sentences with a word or phrase that will make the sentence correct.

1. Alkali metals can be identified by a(n) flame test.
2. Alkaline earth metals have 2 electron(s) in their outer energy level.
3. Transition metals form compounds by sharing electrons.
4. The greater the amount of carbon in a steel, the less flexible it becomes.
5. One use of barium sulfate is in medicine.
6. Some compounds of magnesium are used as medicines.
7. Mercury is the only liquid metal.
8. Silver sulfide is the tarnish on silver utensils.
9. An alloy of iron and chromium creates a very hard steel.
10. A boron compound called borax is used as a water softener.

D. How and Why

Detailed answers to these questions are given in the Teacher's Guide at the front of this book.

1. What are some uses for the alkaline earth family members?
2. How are the alkali family and the copper family different?
3. What happens to the melting points of the alkali metals as the mass number increases? Why do you think this occurs?
4. What metals named in this chapter are used to coat other metals? Why is this done?
5. What kind of bonding do you think each of the following compounds would have? **a.** sodium—chlorine **b.** iron—oxygen **c.** magnesium—chlorine **d.** copper—sulfur
6. What are the properties that distinguish metals from nonmetals?

More Ideas to Explore

1. Prepare a report on some uses of the alkali metals.
2. Use your library to find out more information about "mercury pollution."
3. The activities in this chapter resulted in the formation of coordination compounds. Use the library to find out more about these compounds.

Readings to Discover

Luedtke, Peggy, "Hydrogen." *Science Digest,* October 1977, pp. 68-72.

Pearl, R.M., "Platinum." *Earth Science,* Vol, 31, Autumn 1978, p. 228.

Smith, Norman F., *The Inside Story of Metal.* NY: Messner, 1977.

"Xenon Now a Rare Metal." *Science News,* Vol. 114, November 25, 1978, p. 358.

In studying the last chapter, you saw the metallic elements look physically similar. Most nonmetals are quite different from each other. Some are gases, like the helium used in this balloon. One is a liquid and the others are solids. How are nonmetals different from metals? What are some of the properties and uses of helium?

Colour Library International (USA) Ltd.

Families of Elements —Nonmetals

9

Chapter 9 contains descriptive material concerning the elements of the nonmetals section of the periodic table. Uses, chemical and physical properties, and similarities among elements in a family are discussed. See the Teacher's Guide at the front of this book for additional teaching strategies for this chapter.

9:1 Properties of Nonmetals

GOAL: *You will learn the characteristics of nonmetals and the properties and uses of some important nonmetals.*

Nonmetals are at the right on the periodic table. At room temperature, they are solids or gases. One nonmetal, bromine, is a liquid. Oxygen, nitrogen, sulfur, and chlorine are examples of nonmetals. Nonmetals tend to hold electrons tightly. As a result, nonmetals are good insulators and do not conduct heat or an electric current well. Most elements whose atoms have five or more electrons in the outer energy level are considered to be nonmetals.

FIGURE 9-1. Members of the noble gas family give off light when connected to a source of electricity.

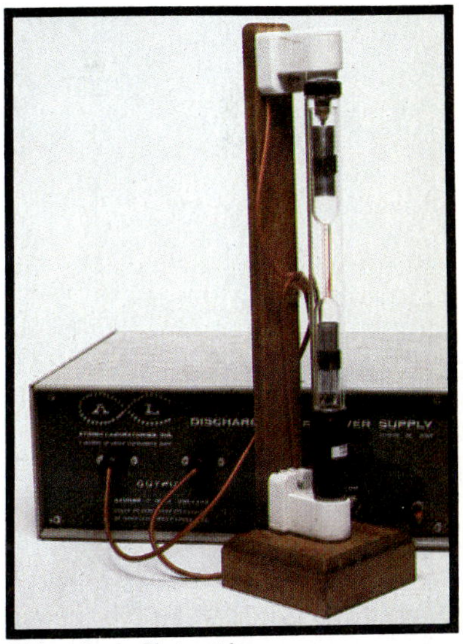

Hickson-Bender Photography

9:2 Noble Gases

The elements of Group VIIIA are known as the noble gases. Most of the members of this family were found by chance. For example, helium was found in a study of sunlight before it was discovered on the earth. Argon was found when not all of a sample of a distillation of liquid air could be accounted for. Xenon, neon, and krypton were found using the techniques that led to the discovery of argon. The last member of the family, radon, is the heaviest gas known. It is formed when the nuclei of radium atoms break down.

Table 9-1

Element	Atomic Number	Mass Number	Melting Point (°C)	Boiling Point (°C)	Description
			Noble Gases		
helium (He)	2	4	−272	−269	All are colorless gases
neon (Ne)	10	20	−249	−246	
argon (Ar)	18	40	−189	−186	
krypton (Kr)	36	84	−157	−153	
xenon (Xe)	54	131	−112	−108	
radon (Rn)	86	(222)	−71	−62	

What are the properties of helium?

What is cryogenics?

The density of helium is less than that of air. This low density makes it useful as a lifting gas in airships and balloons. Helium is also used in **cryogenics** (kri uh JEN ihks). Cryogenics is the study of physical and chemical properties of materials at very low temperatures. Cryogenic temperatures are usually indicated on the **kelvin temperature scale.** On the kelvin temperature scale, 0 is called **absolute zero.** Absolute zero is the lowest temperature to which a substance can be cooled. Zero kelvin is equivalent to −273°C. Cryogenic temperatures are about 90 K (−183°C) or colder.

Helium can be compressed and cooled to form a liquid at 4 K (−269°C). The liquid helium is kept in insulated containers.

Professor Ollie V. Lounasmaa courtesy of "Physics Today"

FIGURE 9-2. The nuclear refrigerator at the Low Temperature Laboratory in Helsinki, Finland, has reached a world record low temperature of 0.000 000 05 kelvins.

Liquid helium is used in refrigeration. For example, it is used to cool metals to extremely low temperatures. When supercooled, some metals offer no resistance to the flow of an electric current.

Cryogenics is also used in the medical field. Preservation of cells, tissues, and whole organs is a current area of research. Tissues can be preserved by freezing, storing, and later thawing for use in research. Whole blood, cooled to the temperature of liquid nitrogen, can be preserved for more than two years. Donated human eye corneas (KOR nee uz) can be kept by freezing. They are later thawed and made available for cornea transplants.

Helium, neon, and argon are used in making lighted signs. Krypton is added to light bulbs to extend the life of the filament. Xenon is used in lamps where short flashes of light are needed for high-speed photography.

FIGURE 9-3. Noble gases are used in making lighted signs for advertising (a) and in runway lighting because of their brightness (b).

a

Jack Zehrt/FPG

b

Eric Hoffhines

Making Sure

1. What is cryogenics? Why is it useful? — *study of materials at low temperature; useful in medicine for storing and preserving body parts*
2. What element is used to form radon? *radium*

Table 9-2

The Halogen Family

Eric Hoffbines

Melting point −220°C Boiling point −188°C Fluorine $^{19}_{9}\mathrm{F}$ Colorless gas	Melting point −101°C Boiling point −34.1°C Chlorine $^{35}_{17}\mathrm{Cl}$ 	Melting point −7.08°C Boiling point 58.8°C Bromine $^{80}_{35}\mathrm{Br}$ 
	Melting point 114°C Boiling point 184°C Iodine $^{127}_{53}\mathrm{I}$ 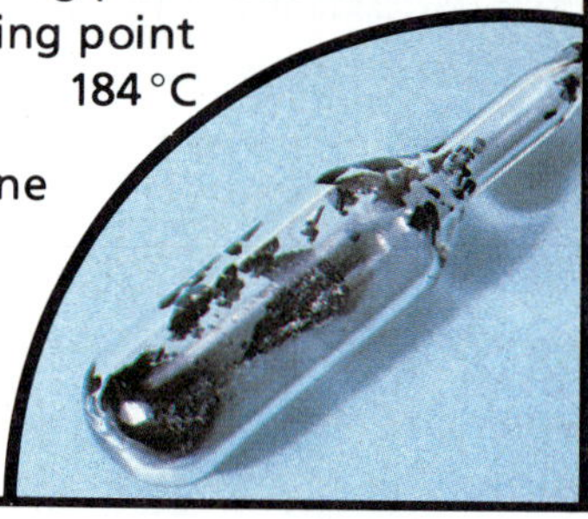	Radioactive solid, produced only in minute quantities. Astatine $^{(210)}_{85}\mathrm{At}$

9:3 Halogen Family

Why are halogens called "salt producers"?

Group VIIA of the periodic table is called the halogen family. Halogen means *"salt-producer."* Halogen elements combine with metals to form compounds called salts. Sodium chloride, NaCl, is the salt with which you are most familiar. In the element form, all of the halogens are poisonous and burn the skin.

How does a halogen combine with a metal?

A halogen combines chemically with a metal by ionic bonding. Each halogen has seven electrons in its outer energy level. One more electron is needed to complete the outer energy level. When a halogen atom combines with a metal, the halogen atom gains that one electron and an ionic bond is formed.

Halogens can also form covalent bonds. In the gaseous state, the halogens exist as **diatomic** molecules. Two atoms of a halogen can share one pair of electrons. The halogens can also bond covalently with each other. In addition to the properties common to this family, each halogen has special properties of its own.

9:4 Fluorine

Fluorine is the most reactive element. It is an extremely corrosive, pale yellow gas. It is never found free in nature. Compounds containing fluorine are called fluorides. Some fluoride salts are added to drinking water in an attempt to prevent tooth decay. Free fluorine is obtained by passing an electric current through molten fluorides.

Why is fluorine never found free in nature?

Fluorine reacts explosively with hydrogen to form hydrogen fluoride, HF. A water solution of hydrogen fluoride can be used to etch glass. The "nonstick" material on cooking utensils is a compound made from fluorine and carbon.

FIGURE 9-4. Hydrogen fluoride is used to etch glass (a) The "nonstick" coating on this wok is made from a carbon-fluorine polymer (b).

a

Larry Hamill

b

Linda Young

9:5 Chlorine

Chlorine is the most abundant halogen. It does not occur free in nature. Chlorine is usually found chemically combined with sodium, potassium, magnesium, or calcium. It is usually obtained by the electrolysis of molten sodium chloride or saltwater brine*. It is only slightly less active than fluorine. Unlike fluorine, chlorine can be liquefied easily under pressure.

Name four properties of chlorine.

**Brine is a concentrated saltwater or ocean water solution. Chlorides and other compounds such as bromides may also be present in brine.*

Mead Paper, Dayton, Ohio

FIGURE 9-5. Chlorine is used as a bleaching agent in the paper industry. Brown paper pulp is bleached white in bleaching vats like those shown.

Chlorine forms compounds with hydrogen and oxygen. Many cleaning products and bleaches contain chlorine compounds. Chlorine bleach is used to whiten clothes. Another type of chlorine product is used to bleach flour and paper. Chlorine compounds are also used to disinfect drinking water.

9:6 Bromine, Iodine, and Astatine

How is bromine separated from seawater?

In nature, bromine is never found as a free element. It is found in compounds called bromides. Bromides are generally found in seawater and brine wells. Bromine is prepared by treating seawater or brine with chlorine. Chlorine is more reactive than bromine. Thus, chlorine replaces bromine in compounds and free bromine is released. At room temperature, bromine is a dark red liquid.

Bromine in the form of silver bromide, AgBr, is used in making photographic film. Ethylene dibromide is added to gasoline to carry off lead compounds formed during engine combustion.

Iodine, like the other halogens, is found only in the combined state in nature. Iodine can be obtained from seawater. Free iodine can change directly to a gas without passing through a liquid state. This type of change is

Hickson-Bender Photography

a

b

FIGURE 9-6. Iodine sublimes when it changes directly from a solid to a gas (a). Iodine is an essential nutrient which is often added to table salt (b).

called **sublimation** (sub luh MAY shun). Iodine is purified by sublimation. The pure vapor is allowed to crystallize on a cool surface.

At room temperature, iodine is a gray, shiny solid. It has many of the physical properties of a metal. Iodine compounds are essential to the human diet and are also used in medicines. Tincture of iodine is a solution of iodine and alcohol. The element iodine is poisonous as are all other halogens.

The last member of the halogen family, astatine, is not found in nature. However, it has been made in the laboratory. It has properties similar to iodine but is a radioactive element. The nucleus of a radioactive element breaks down. Particles and energy are given off and new elements formed. Most astatine isotopes have short half-lives. This statement means the nuclei of these atoms break up rapidly to form other elements. Astatine can form compounds with other halogens.

How is astatine different from the other halogens?

9-1 ACTIVITY *How is iodine used in testing foods for starch?*

Obtain a potato, a piece of bread, a banana, a carrot, and some tincture of iodine. Place a small piece of each food in a dish. Put a drop of iodine on each. Record your observations. Iodine is used to test for the presence of starch. Which of these foods contains starch? Try this test on other foods.

drop turns dark blue on potato and bread

Detailed information concerning this Activity can be found in the Teacher's Guide at the front of this book.

9-2 Detailed information concerning this Activity can be found in the Teacher's Guide at the front of this book.

ACTIVITY Does iodine dissolve in liquids?

Set up a series of labeled test tubes. Each should contain a single liquid: water, alcohol, and mineral oil. Add a crystal of iodine to each liquid. Mix. Does the iodine dissolve in any of the liquids?

Add a drop of liquid starch solution to each and observe any change. Devise an activity to determine whether it is the iodine or the liquid which reacts with starch.

FIGURE 9-7.

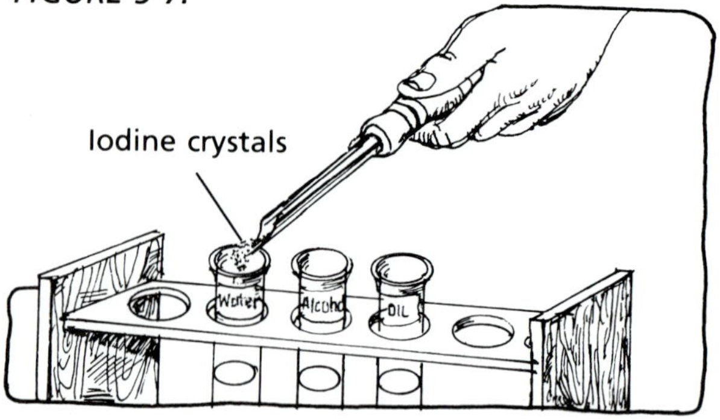

Making Sure

3. Write the chemical formula for a molecule of fluorine, chlorine, bromine, and iodine. F_2, Cl_2, Br_2, I_2
4. Draw a diagram of an atom of fluorine and an atom of bromine. How are they alike?
5. Name one use for the first four elements in the halogen family.

Each have 7 electrons in the outer energy level.

fluorine–etching glass
chlorine–bleach
bromine–photography
iodine–dietary need

9:7 Oxygen Family

Group VIA on the periodic table is called the oxygen family. These elements are all found in nature both in the free state and chemically combined. Most members form covalent compounds. Each atom has six electrons in its outer energy level. Thus, it must share two electrons with other elements to form compounds.

What is an allotrope?

How is O_3 different from O_2?

The elements of the oxygen family can exist as molecules with different numbers of the same atoms. These forms are called **allotropes** (AL uh trohps). Oxygen, for example, exists as a diatomic molecule, O_2. Diatomic means two atoms are bonded together in one molecule. However, under certain conditions, some molecules of O_2 can be changed to ozone, O_3. During thunderstorms some oxygen in the air is changed to ozone. Both diatomic oxygen molecules and **triatomic** (composed of three atoms) ozone molecules are allotropes of oxygen. Oxygen is the only member of Group VIA which exists as a diatomic gas at room temperature. All other members are solids.

Table 9-3

The Oxygen Family

Linda Young

$^{16}_{8}$**O** Colorless gas Oxygen Melting point −219°C Boiling point −183°C	$^{32}_{16}$**S** 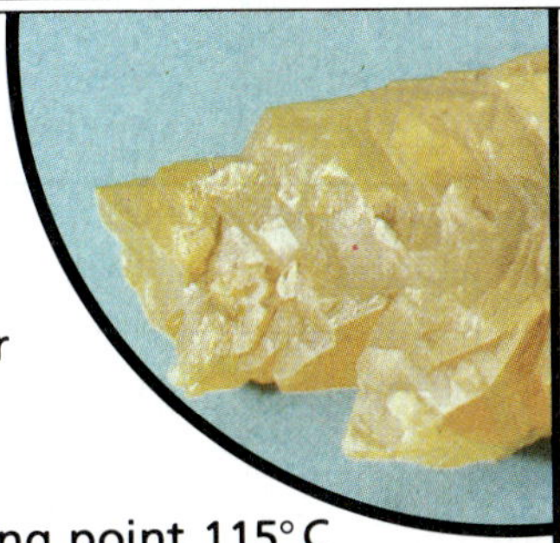 Sulfur Melting point 115°C Boiling point 445°C	$^{79}_{34}$**Se**  Selenium Melting point 217°C Boiling point 685°C
$^{128}_{52}$**Te**  Tellurium Melting point 450°C Boiling point 994°C	Radioactive solid, 210 is the mass number of the most stable isotope. $^{(210)}_{94}$**Po** Polonium Melting point 254°C Boiling point 962°C	

9:8 Oxygen

Oxygen is one of the most reactive nonmetallic elements. Oxygen forms compounds with nearly every other element. Oxygen compounds compose nearly fifty percent (by mass) of the earth's crust. About twenty percent of the total volume of air is O_2.

Why is oxygen an important element?

Without free oxygen, most life on the earth could not exist. Animals breathe O_2. The ozone layer around the earth shields us from radiation from the sun. Compounds of oxygen are also extremely important to people. Water, H_2O, is perhaps the most important oxide. Another compound of hydrogen and oxygen is hydrogen peroxide, H_2O_2. It is used to kill germs and as a bleach. Common sand is an oxygen compound called silicon dioxide, or silica, SiO_2. Rust is iron(III) oxide, Fe_2O_3.

Kodansha

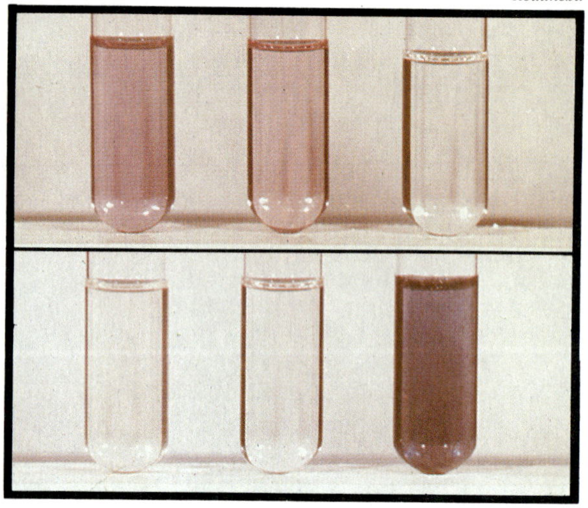

FIGURE 9-8. Ozone has strong bleaching power. The blue and red solutions in the top test tubes are bleached clear when ozone is added. The third solution, starch, turns blue.

Oxygen is most often prepared in large amounts by the **distillation** (dihs tuh LAY shun) of liquid air. In distillation, gases or liquids are separated by differences in their boiling points. Air is a mixture of gases including oxygen and nitrogen. Each gas has a different boiling point. Air is liquefied by pressure and cooling. Then it is allowed to warm. Each gas boils off at a different temperature. Liquid oxygen begins to boil at −183°C. It is drawn off into another container. Repeating this process produces an oxygen sample which is almost pure. Oxygen also can be produced by electrolysis of water. Here, an electric current is passed through water. However, this method is expensive when used to produce large amounts of oxygen.

FIGURE 9-9. The distribution of elements by percent in the in body (a) and on the earth and the atmosphere (b).

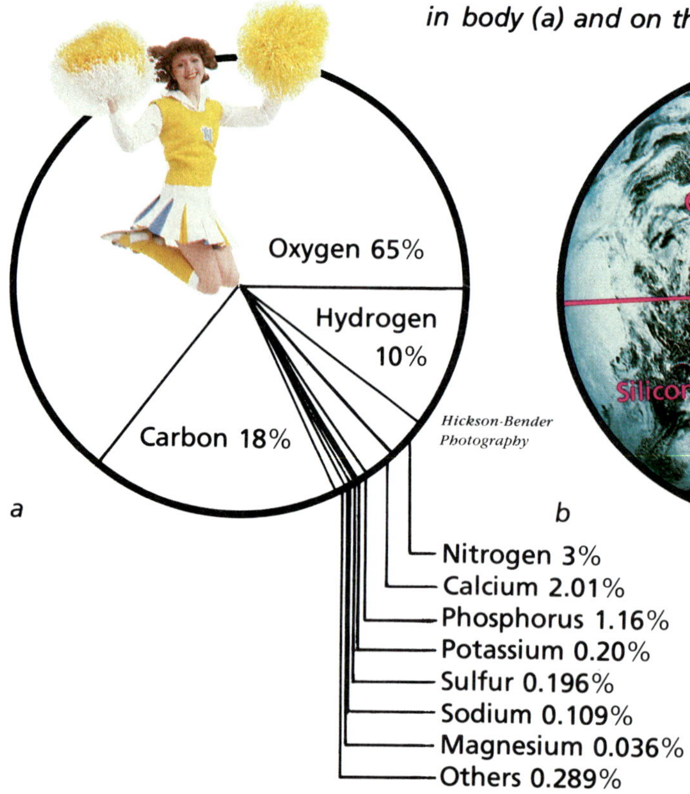

Hickson-Bender Photography

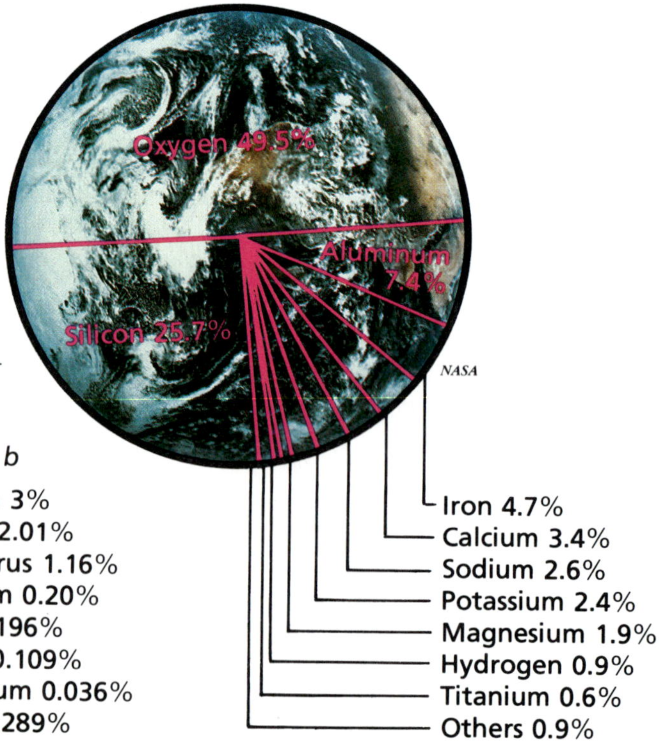

NASA

Table 9-4

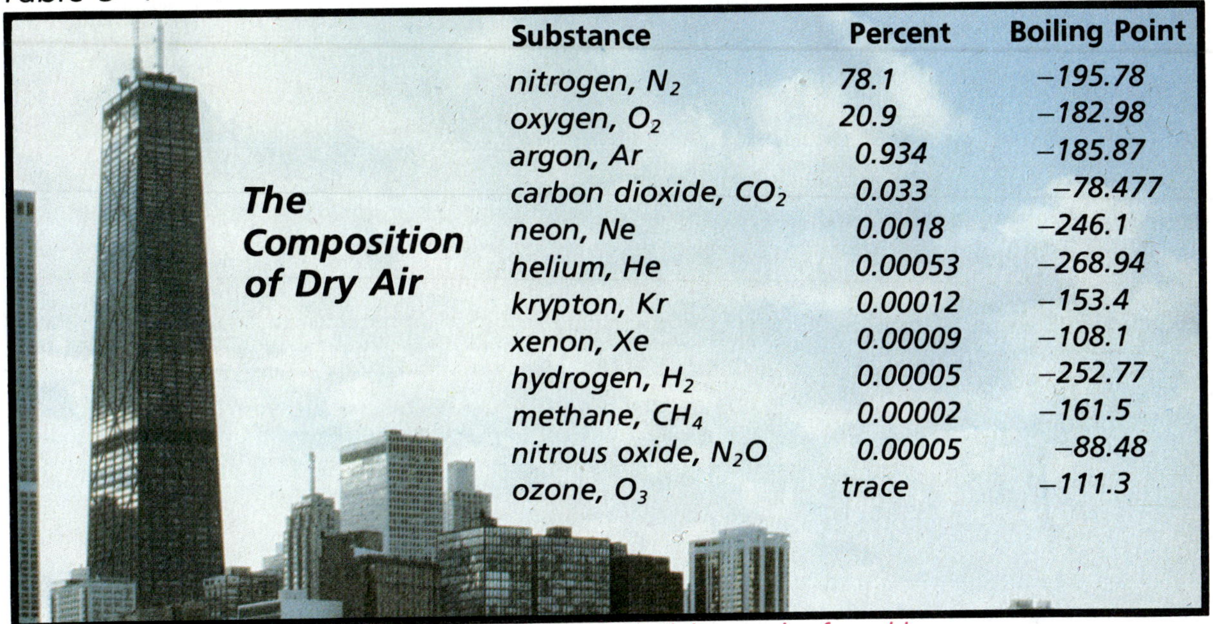

The Composition of Dry Air

Substance	Percent	Boiling Point
nitrogen, N_2	78.1	−195.78
oxygen, O_2	20.9	−182.98
argon, Ar	0.934	−185.87
carbon dioxide, CO_2	0.033	−78.477
neon, Ne	0.0018	−246.1
helium, He	0.00053	−268.94
krypton, Kr	0.00012	−153.4
xenon, Xe	0.00009	−108.1
hydrogen, H_2	0.00005	−252.77
methane, CH_4	0.00002	−161.5
nitrous oxide, N_2O	0.00005	−88.48
ozone, O_3	trace	−111.3

R. Brommer

FIGURE 9-10.

9-3 Detailed information concerning this Activity can be found in the Teacher's Guide at the front of this book.

ACTIVITY *Can you determine the percent of oxygen in air?*

(1) *Place a piece of steel wool on a cork floating in a deep pan of water.* ***(2)*** *Cover it with an inverted 25-mL graduated cylinder, Figure 9-11.* ***(3)*** *Suspend the graduate so the water level is at the 25-mL mark.* ***(4)*** *Allow to stand for one week.*

What do you observe at the end of a week? How many milliliters does the water level rise in the cylinder? What percent is this number of 25 mL?

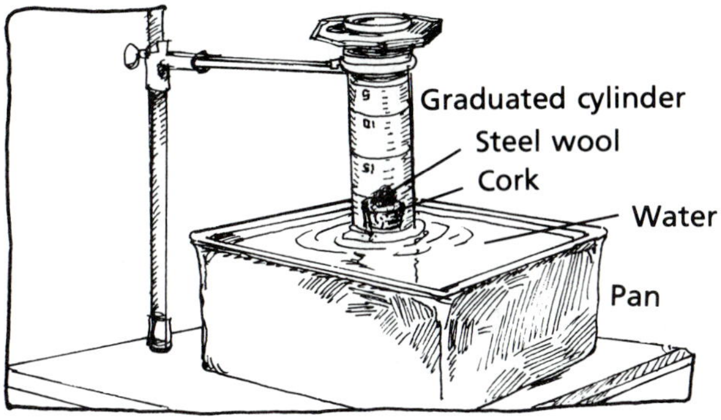

FIGURE 9-11.

9:9 Sulfur

Sulfur, like oxygen, is found free and combined in nature. Sulfur is generally found chemically combined with metals in the form of mineral ores. Most sulfur is obtained from deposits of the free element in southern and southwestern United States. Sulfur is mined by the Frasch process, Figure 9-12a. This process produces sulfur which is more than ninety percent pure.

How is sulfur mined?

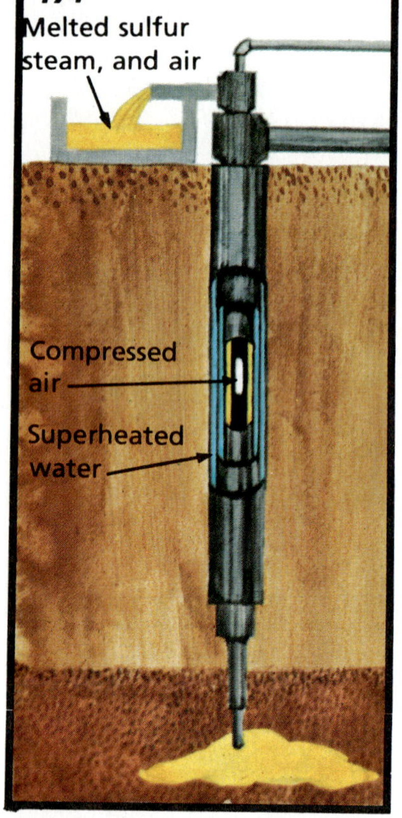

Farrell Grehan/Photo Researchers

FIGURE 9-12. Superheated water and compressed air are used in the Frasch process for mining sulfur.

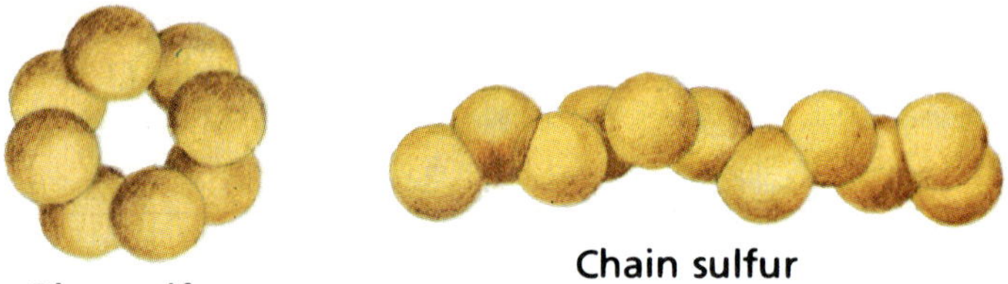

FIGURE 9-13.

Sulfur also exists in several allotropic forms. Some allotropes of sulfur consist of eight sulfur atoms joined in a ring, Figure 9-13. The most common form is rhombic (RAHM bihk) sulfur. Another allotrope of sulfur exists as a long chain of sulfur atoms.

Sulfur unites with some metals to form compounds called sulfides. It also unites directly with oxygen. Sulfur compounds in the air, such as hydrogen sulfide, H_2S, cause the tarnish on silver. Products which contain sulfur include insecticides, fertilizers, drugs, and rubber.

FIGURE 9-14. Matches contain sodium sesquisulfide. Acid rain made from water and sulfur pollutants is a hazard to aquatic life. Healthy hatched salmon (b) are compared to those which have been exposed to acid rain (c).

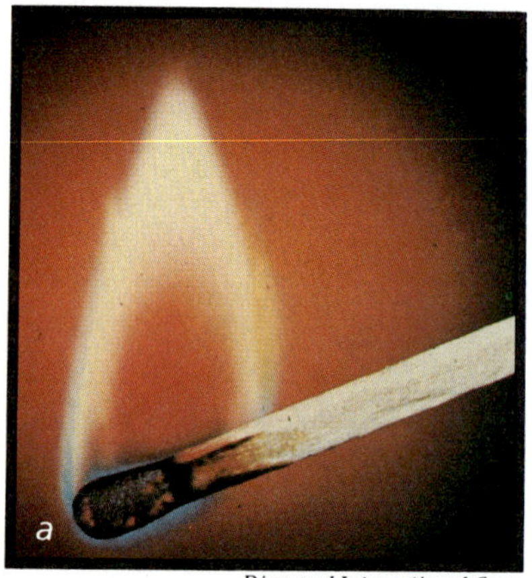

Diamond International Corp.

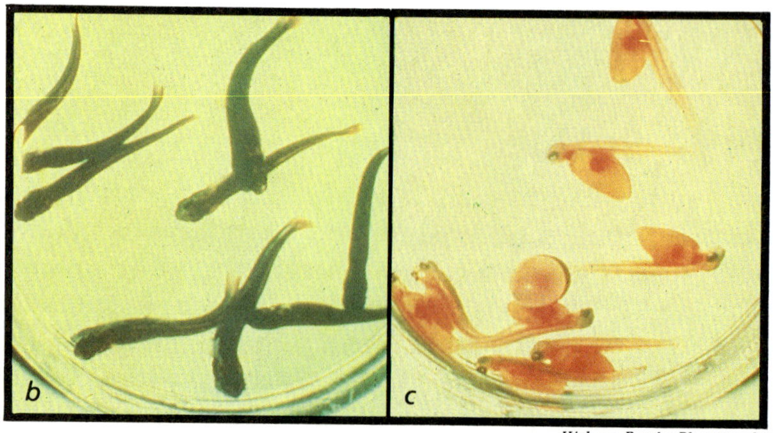

Hickson-Bender Photography

Table 9-5

Sulfides		
Element	**Sulfide Compound**	**Color**
antimony	Sb_2S_3	*orange*
arsenic	As_2S_3	*yellow*
bismuth	Bi_2S_3	*brown*
cadmium	*CdS*	*yellow*
copper	*CuS*	*black*
lead	*PbS*	*black*
silver	Ag_2S	*black*
zinc	*ZnS*	*white*

9-4 Detailed information concerning this Activity can be found in the Teacher's Guide at the front of this book.

ACTIVITY *Can you identify the metal in a sulfide?*

(1) *Place 5 mL of cadmium nitrate, zinc sulfate, antimony chloride, and copper(II) sulfate solutions separately in four test tubes, Figure 9-15.* **(2)** *Label each tube.* **(3)** *Cover the label with a blank piece of paper.* **(4)** *Have a classmate arrange the test tubes in a rack so you do not know the contents of each.* **(5)** *Add a few drops of hydrogen sulfide solution to each.*

What metal is present in each test tube? Table 9-5 lists the colors of various metal sulfides. Check your results against the labels.

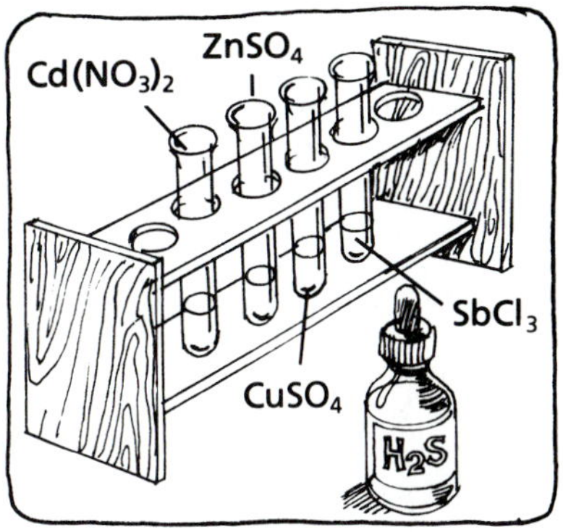

FIGURE 9-15.

9:10 Selenium

Selenium can be found in deposits of free sulfur. It is also an impurity in sulfides and in copper. Most selenium is obtained as a by-product in the electrolysis of copper ore to produce copper.

Selenium is a poison. Plants absorb selenium from the soil and pass it to animals that eat the plant. Insects which feed on plants are often killed in this way. Small amounts of selenium insecticide are put in the soil or sprayed on plant leaves. Selenium then passes through the entire plant without harming it. However, insects eating the plant are poisoned.

Name three properties of selenium.

Selenium has some metallic properties such as conducting an electric current. In the dark, selenium is a poor conductor. However, when exposed to light, selenium gives up electrons and becomes a good conductor. For this reason, selenium is called a **photoconductor.** A photoconductor's ability to pass along electrons is controlled by light.

Photoconductors are used in photographic light meters. One kind of light meter uses a selenium photocell. This photocell is made with a small copper plate, a selenium layer, and a gold film that transmits light. Electric wires go to both the copper film and the gold film. Electricity does not flow through the wires until light hits the meter. Then the electrons in the selenium move and an electric current is produced. An arm on a dial moves to indicate the light intensity. As the light intensity increases, the current increases, and the arm moves a greater distance. Selenium photocells are also used in counting people as they enter buildings and for setting off burglar alarms.

When added to glass, selenium counteracts the green color due to iron impurities in glass. If a large amount of selenium is used, the glass becomes red. This red glass is used in traffic lights.

FIGURE 9-16. Selenium is used in making red glass (a) and as the photosensitive material in light meters (b) and photocopy machines (c).

from Xerox Corporation

a *Thomas Russell*

b *Mr. & Mrs. Pantages*

c

Making Sure

6. What are some of the common uses of the elements in the oxygen family? *See the Teacher's Guide.*
7. How many electrons are in the outermost energy level of each element of the oxygen family? *6*
8. Why is there a similarity in the chemical properties of the elements of the oxygen family? *similar outer energy level electron structure*
9. What properties does selenium have that make it similar to a metal? *solid, conducts electricity*

9:11 Nitrogen Family

How are the elements in the nitrogen family similar?

Group VA on the periodic table is called the nitrogen family. Each member of the nitrogen family has five electrons in its outer energy level. Thus, these elements usually form covalent compounds. Elements in the nitrogen family are not very reactive. The five electrons in the outer energy level are responsible for this property. It is unlikely that these elements will gain three electrons or lose five electrons. However, they do share electrons with atoms of other elements. In some instances, they share three or even all five electrons.

Table 9-6

The Nitrogen Family		
$^{14}_{7}N$ Colorless gas Nitrogen Melting point −210°C Boiling point −196°C	 $^{31}_{15}P$ Phosphorus Melting point 44.2°C Boiling point 280°C	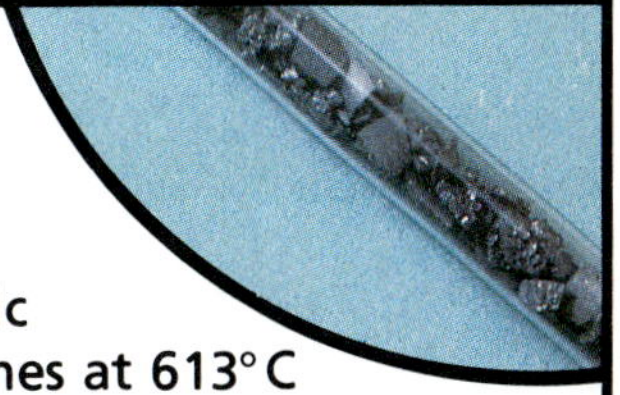 $^{73}_{33}As$ Arsenic Sublimes at 613°C
 $^{122}_{51}Sb$ Antimony Melting point 631°C Boiling point 1640°C	 $^{209}_{83}Bi$ Bismuth Melting point 271°C Boiling point 1560°C	

Linda Young
Eric Hoffhines

This family contains a wide range of physical properties. For example, nitrogen is a gas. Both nitrogen and phosphorus are nonmetals, but bismuth is a metal. Arsenic and antimony have some properties of both metals and nonmetals. These two elements are metalloids, Section 6:8.

Larry Hamill

FIGURE 9-17. Liquid nitrogen is used when low temperatures are required.

9:12 Nitrogen

Nitrogen is required by every living thing. Air is nearly seventy-nine percent free nitrogen. However, most living things cannot get nitrogen directly from the air. Nitrogen for life comes from compounds found as minerals in the ground, formed during electrical storms, or produced by bacteria.

Nitrogen is usually prepared by the distillation of liquid air. Liquid nitrogen boils at −196° C. Liquid nitrogen is used in the treatment of skin disorders. It reduces the size of scars, removes warts, and helps clear severe acne. Pure nitrogen can be produced by heating some nitrogen compounds.

Free nitrogen is found as a diatomic molecule. The two nitrogen atoms are held together with a triple covalent bond. Two nitrogen atoms each share three electrons. Nitrogen forms many compounds which are important to people. One of these compounds is ammonia, NH_3, found in many cleaning products. Industry uses nitrogen compounds in making fertilizers and explosives. "Laughing gas," a common anesthetic (an us THET ihk), is also a nitrogen compound. Many different nitrogen-oxygen compounds exist.

Table 9-7

Nitrogen Oxides

Formula	Chemical Name	Common Name
N_2O	nitrogen(I) oxide	nitrous oxide
NO	nitrogen(II) oxide	nitric oxide
N_2O_3	nitrogen(III) oxide	dinitrogen trioxide
NO_2	nitrogen(IV) oxide	nitrogen dioxide
N_2O_5	nitrogen(V) oxide	dinitrogen pentoxide

9-5 Detailed information concerning this Activity can be found in the Teacher's Guide at the front of this book.

ACTIVITY *How can you identify compounds containing the nitrate ion?*

CAUTION: *This activity should be done only under the supervision of your teacher. Concentrated sulfuric acid must be handled with care.*

(1) *Add 5 mL of a solution of sodium nitrate or potassium nitrate to a large Pyrex test tube.* **(2)** *Add 5 mL of a freshly prepared saturated iron(II) sulfate solution. Mix.* **(3)** *Slant the tube, Figure 9-18. Carefully add 1-2 mL of concentrated sulfuric acid by allowing it to run down the inside of the test tube.* **(4)** *Look for a brown ring at the line between the acid and mixed solutions.* **(5)** *Repeat Steps 2 through 4 using distilled water in place of the nitrate solution.*

Does a brown ring form in Step 5? Explain. distilled water is a control, no ring forms

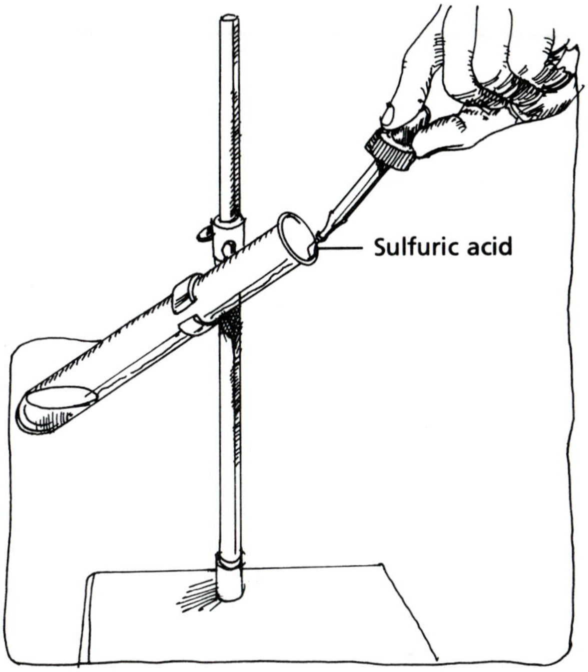

FIGURE 9-18.

9:13 Phosphorus

Like oxygen and sulfur, phosphorus has allotropes. The two most common are white phosphorus and red phosphorus. White phosphorus is produced from calcium phosphate, $Ca_3(PO_4)_2$. It is formed as a gas. The gas is then condensed under water in the form of P_4 molecules. The water prevents the phosphorus from reacting immediately with the oxygen in the air.

Red phosphorus is formed slowly from chains of white phosphorus molecules. Red phosphorus is more stable than white phosphorus. At room temperature, red phosphorus has little chemical activity. However, at higher temperatures it forms many compounds. The ease with which phosphorus burns makes it useful in matches.

Like nitrogen, phosphorus forms a number of oxides. Phosphates are an important class of phosphorus compounds. For example, calcium phosphate is present in bones. Some phosphates serve as water softeners.

FIGURE 9-19. Allotropes of phosphorus.

Eric Hoffhines

Linda Young

Eric Hoffhines

FIGURE 9-20. Phosphate compounds are used in fertilizer to provide essential nutrients for plants.

Name some important phosphates.

Some are used as fertilizers. Ammonium phosphate, $(NH_4)_3PO_4$ is an important fertilizer. It is used because it contains nitrogen and phosphorus; both are needed for plant growth. In small amounts, phosphorus compounds provide a means for transferring energy in both plants and animals. It is also found in deoxyribonucleic acid (DNA), a compound found in genes.

Excessive use of phosphates in detergents may contribute to water pollution. Waste water from the laundry is joined by the runoff from fields fertilized with phosphates and nitrates. These wastes often end up in lakes and rivers. As a result, water plants are fed a diet rich in nutrients. These plants multiply rapidly. When they die, their decomposition uses up the supply of oxygen dissolved in the water. Thus, they deprive fish and other aquatic life of oxygen. Many soap industries are reducing the amount of phosphate in detergents. This step is important in solving the problem.

FIGURE 9-21. The growth of aquatic plants increases rapidly (a) as a result of phosphate pollution (b).

b

a

Nancy Hamilton/FPG

Hickson-Bender Photography

9:14 Arsenic, Antimony, and Bismuth

Arsenic compounds are widespread in nature. The most common consist of arsenic and sulfur. Two allotropic forms of arsenic exist. Yellow arsenic, a nonmetal, exists as As_4 molecules. Yellow arsenic will change slowly to gray arsenic, a metal. Perhaps you know that arsenic is a poison. However, it is also used in medicine. *Salvarsan* (SAL vur san), an arsenic compound, was the forerunner of many modern drugs.

Both antimony and bismuth have metallic properties. Bismuth is a true metal. These two elements have properties and compounds similar to phosphorus and arsenic. Bismuth is found in antacids. Both antimony and bismuth can be used in alloys with other metals. Bismuth is often included in alloys because it has a low melting point. It is used in automatic sprinkler systems. Heat from a fire melts the alloy plugs in water pipes.

Linda Young

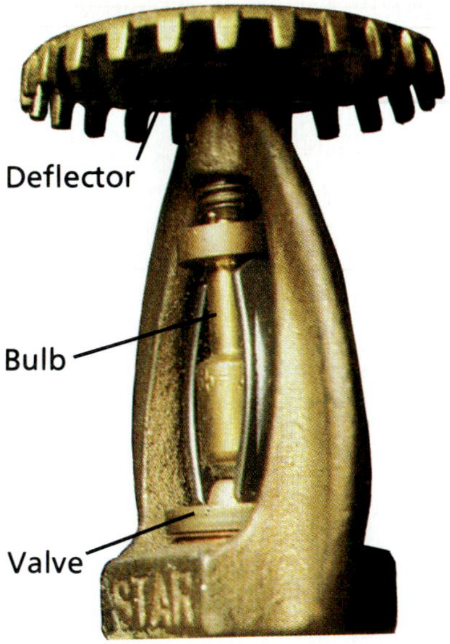

FIGURE 9-22. Wood's metal, a bismuth alloy, melts at low temperatures making it useful in fire sprinkler systems.

9-6 Detailed information concerning this Activity can be found in the Teacher's Guide at the front of this book.

ACTIVITY *What is the melting point of Wood's metal?*

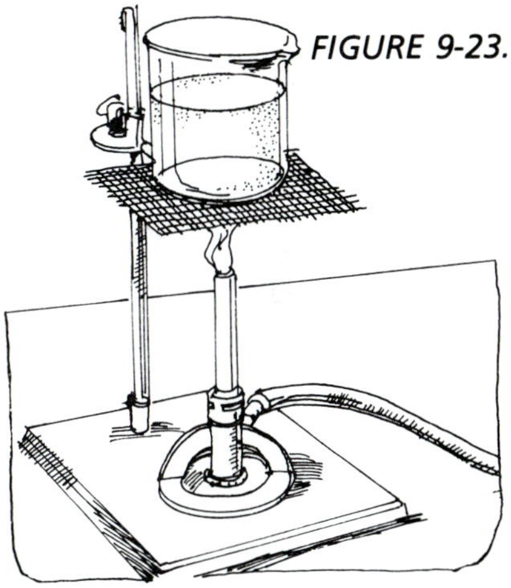

FIGURE 9-23.

(1) *Obtain a piece of Wood's metal, an alloy of bismuth, lead, tin, and cadmium.* **(2)** *Using the set-up in Figure 9-23, heat the water to 40°C.* **(3)** *Place the Wood's metal in the water and continue heating.*

At what temperature does the Wood's metal melt? Why would Wood's metal be used in automatic sprinkler systems? *low melting solid, the metal would melt when exposed to fire*

Making Sure

10. What can you do to help reduce phosphate pollutants in the environment? *use phosphate-free detergents*

11. Give five examples of how the nitrogen family is useful to people. *fertilizers, medicines, water softeners, detergents, matches are examples*

12. In the distillation of air, does N_2 or O_2 boil first? *N_2*

Focus On

Frontiers

Alcohol for Cars

Bruce D. Sampsel

People use oil products everyday. Often they do not realize the products are made with oil. Take, for example, your pen. If it has a plastic case it is probably an oil product. Another example is the sole of your shoe. If it is plastic, it, too, is probably an oil product. Many of today's plastics use oil. Another major use of oil is fuel. We use it to make electricity and to heat homes. As fuel, a major use of oil is gasoline. But, the supplies of oil are decreasing. Because of the shortage of oil, the search is on for new fuels. One of the new fuels is alcohol.

Alcohol, as a fuel, is not really new. After World War I, France used a mixture of gasoline and alcohol for government cars. In the United States, alcohol was used in farm machinery and cars during the depression. And in World War II, the Allies cut off Germany's oil supplies. Germany was forced to operate its military vehicles on alcohol. However, in each case, alcohol was used for only a few years. Oil was plentiful and cheap, so gasoline became the major fuel for vehicles. Alcohol was too expensive to compete.

With the rise in oil prices, research on alcohol fuels has increased. Mixing alcohol with gasoline is one way it can be used. This is called gasohol. In Brazil a mixture of gasoline and alcohol has been used since 1931. The Brazilians began using the mixture to create a market for excess sugar cane. The excess cane is used to make alcohol. In the United States, gasohol began to appear late in the 1970's. But, gasohol is not a solution to decreasing oil supplies. For this reason, much of the research is on the use of alcohol alone.

Research has found that alcohol does not release as much heat energy as gasoline. This means that a car uses more alcohol per mile than gasoline. However, engines burning alcohol are as much as twenty percent more powerful. To use alcohol, some modifications should be made to a car. For example, a noncorrosive gas tank and fuel line are needed. Lower temperature spark plugs are also needed. With these and other minor changes, alcohol can be used as a fuel. The greatest problem with alcohol is learning to produce large quantities at low cost.

Points to Remember

1. Noble gases are the least reactive elements. *9:2*
2. The halogens are the most reactive of the nonmetal families of elements. *9:3*
3. Cryogenic temperatures are indicated on the kelvin temperature scale. *9:2*
4. Members of the oxygen family can exist as allotropes, different molecular forms of the same element. *9:7*
5. The air we breathe contains many gases including oxygen, nitrogen, and most of the noble gases. *9:8 9:2*
6. A photoconductor can pass along electrons when struck by a beam of light. *9:10*
7. Elements in the nitrogen family are not very reactive. Some of these elements also exist as allotropes. *9:11 9:13*
8. Some phosphorus and sulfur compounds have been found to pollute the environment. *9:13*

Words to Use

Write a sentence in which you correctly use each of the following words or terms.

absolute zero
allotrope
cryogenics
diatomic
distillation
electrolysis
kelvin temperature
photoconductor
sublimation
triatomic

Questions for Review

Do not write in this book.

A. True or False *Have the students rewrite the false statements to make them correct.*
Determine whether each of the following sentences is true or false.

T **1.** The elements in the halogen family are all poisonous or harmful in the uncombined state.

F **2.** Under normal room temperature and pressure, all of the halogen elements form ~~triatomic~~ molecules. *diatomic*

F 3. Uncombined fluorine is found free in nature. not

T 4. At room temperature, bromine is a red liquid.

F 5. At room temperature, ~~iodine~~ is a red liquid. bromine

F 6. All elements in the oxygen family have ~~two~~ electrons to share in chemical bonds. 6

T 7. Arsenic is used in some medicines.

T 8. Selenium is a good electrical conductor when exposed to light.

T 9. Heavy growth of water plants in lakes and streams may result from excess phosphate in the water.

F 10. The ~~high~~ melting point of bismuth makes it suitable for use in automatic sprinkler systems used for fire prevention. low

B. Multiple Choice

Choose the word or phrase that correctly completes each of the following sentences.

1. *(Nitrogen, Arsenic, Oxygen)* is a solid at room temperature.
2. An element which is a photoconductor is *(bismuth, selenium, phosphorus).*
3. All of the halogens have *(0, 1, 2, 3, 4, 5, 6, 7, 8)* electrons in their outer energy levels.
4. Halogen atoms form compounds with other elements by *(covalent, ionic, covalent and ionic)* bonding.
5. Phosphorus is not used in the manufacture of *(matches, fertilizers, ice cream).*
6. Ammonia contains *(oxygen, nitrogen, helium).*
7. *(Bismuth, Sulfur, Antimony)* is a true metal.
8. Sulfur is a member of the *(halogen, oxygen, nitrogen)* family.
9. Phosphorus is a member of the *(halogen, oxygen, nitrogen)* family.
10. *(Nitrogen, Antimony, Helium)* is a noble gas.

C. Completion

Complete each of the following sentences with a word or phrase that will make the sentence correct.

1. Nitrogen is found free as diatomic molecules.
2. Oxygen can be found as both the O_2 molecule and the O_3 molecule.

3. Selenium can conduct electrons in the presence of light.
4. Twenty percent of air is oxygen.
5. Pure nitrogen is produced by the distillation of air.
6. Argon is a by-product of the distillation of air.
7. The O_3 molecule of oxygen is called ozone.
8. The most metallic member of the nitrogen family is bismuth.
9. Selenium is the element most like sulfur in physical and chemical properties.
10. Phosphorus is an essential part of bones and genes.

D. How and Why *Detailed answers to these questions are given in the Teacher's Guide at the front of this book.*

1. What are the names and formulas of three nitrogen compounds?
2. What kind of bonding is present in compounds containing nitrogen? How does this compare with compounds between the alkali metal and halogen families?
3. How can you distinguish between metallic and nonmetallic members of a family of elements?
4. How do allotropes differ from isotopes?
5. Why do you think the noble gases were difficult to discover?
6. What is a diatomic gas? Name three and give their formulas.

More Ideas to Explore

1. Visit a nursery or garden shop. (a) From the labels on the pesticides, determine which elements are most used. (b) From the labels on the fertilizers, determine which elements are most often used.
2. Conduct a survey in your local grocery store to determine which detergents are low in phosphates.
3. Obtain information from a library on the nitrogen cycle in nature. Draw a poster that shows the stages in the nitrogen cycle.

Readings to Discover

Fisher, A., "From Krypton: A New Blue Laser Detective." *Popular Science,* Vol. 213, September 1978, p. 93.

Pearl, R.M., "Helium." *Earth Science,* Vol. 31, January 1978, p. 33.

"Putting a Check on Ozone Predictions." *Science News,* Vol. 115, May 19, 1979, p. 325.

Carbon is a unique element. Its compounds serve as fuels for transportation and heating as well as fuels for our bodies. Scientists have been able to use the unique properties of carbon to synthesize substitutes for these fuels. Silicon has now become important because it is a major component of solar cells. How are carbon and silicon alike? How are they different?

Michael Collier

Families of Elements—Carbon and Silicon

10

Chapter 10 introduces some of the chemistry of carbon and silicon. The importance of carbon compounds to living systems is discussed in sections on carbohydrates, proteins, and vitamins. The importance of carbon compounds as fuels is also considered. See the Teacher's Guide at the front of this book for additional teaching strategies for this chapter.

10:1 Carbon

GOAL: *You will learn the properties of carbon and silicon, and some important uses of their compounds.*

How are a diamond and a pencil alike? A diamond and the "lead" in a pencil are made of carbon. The wood that holds the "lead" is a mixture of carbon compounds. Plastics, foods, fibers, and most fuels contain carbon. Coal and charcoal are mostly carbon. Carbon is also present in all living things. The paper and ink on this page contain carbon.

Why is carbon an important element?

Carbon is a nonmetal. In graphite (GRAF ite), carbon is black in color. In a diamond, carbon is colorless. Carbon combines mostly with hydrogen, oxygen, and elements in the halogen family. Over eighty percent of all known compounds contain carbon. Over three million different carbon compounds have been discovered.

Name two forms of carbon.

Graphite and diamonds are allotropes of carbon. Graphite is the form of carbon in a "lead" pencil. Graphite crystals are thin and flat. The structure of graphite crystals makes it easy for the atoms to slip and slide over each other. Therefore, graphite is used as a lubricant. Carbon atoms in a graphite crystal are bonded in a triangular pattern. The resulting crystal has a hexagonal structure, Figure 10-1b. The bonds between these atoms are covalent.

Remind students what allotropes are.

Hickson-Bender Photography Tom Stack/Tom Stack & Assoc.

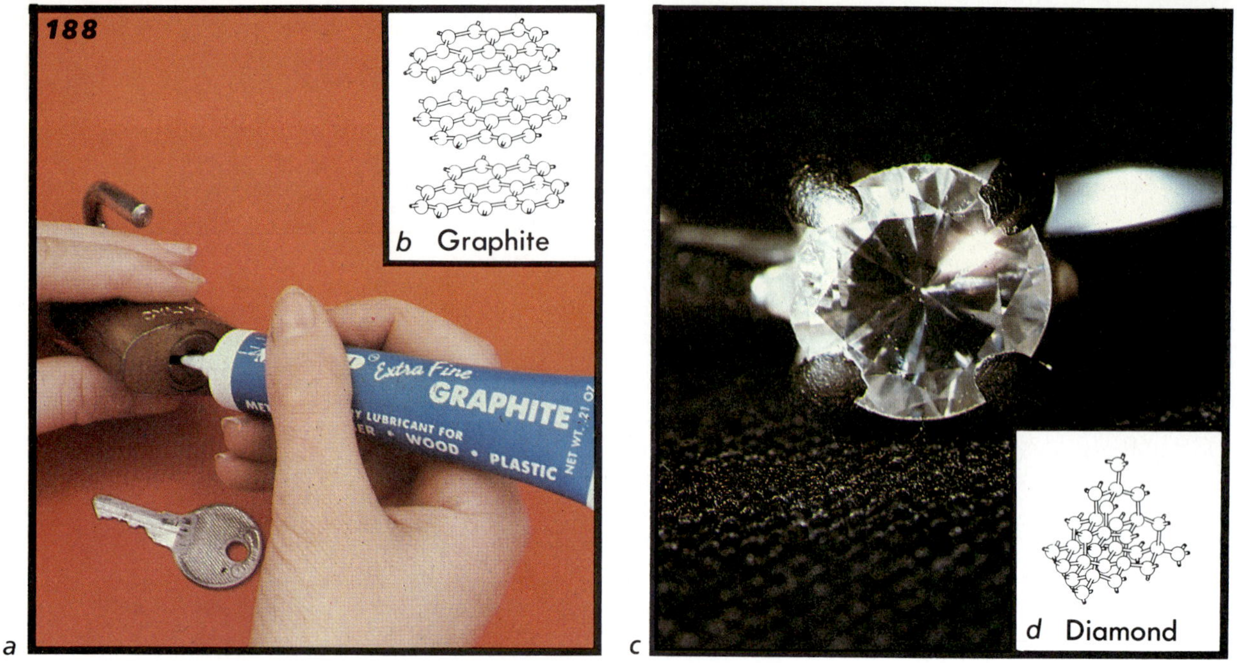

FIGURE 10-1. Graphite (a) is used as a lubricant. Notice the graphite structure (b) consists of parallel planes of carbon atoms which can slide over one another. Diamond (c) is one of the hardest substances known. Its structure (d) consists of a network of carbon atoms.

extremely hard, brilliant, reflects light.

Diamond is the hardest substance known. Each carbon atom in a diamond is bonded covalently to four other carbon atoms. The atoms are arranged in a tetrahedral pattern, Figure 10-1d. Diamonds are used in cutting tools and as gems in jewelry. What properties of a diamond make it suitable for these two uses?

Making Sure

1. Locate carbon in the periodic table. What is its atomic number? Mass number? *6, 12*
2. What other elements are in the carbon family? *silicon, germanium, tin, lead*

10:2 Organic Compounds

What is an organic compound?

Organic compounds are compounds that contain carbon. At one time people thought organic compounds came only from living things. But this idea has been changed. For many years, chemists have known how to make organic compounds without using plants or animals. For example, plastics are organic compounds that can be made from coal, air, and water.

How can carbon form so many compounds?

Carbon has four electrons in its outer energy level. Carbon atoms form covalent bonds with other carbon

Greg Miller

a 

b 

FIGURE 10-2. Plastics can be shaped into siding (a), or molded into toys (b)

atoms. Atoms of carbon join together in long chains or rings. The chains may be continuous or branching, and short or long in length. Atoms of other elements can be bonded to carbon atoms in the chain at many different points.

The properties of an organic compound depend upon the number and types of atoms in the compound. The structure or pattern in which the atoms are bonded is also important. Two organic compounds can have the same chemical formula. Yet, the compounds have different properties because of a difference in the structure of their molecules.

Stress this point as it is the foundation for the section on isomers, 10:4.

10:3 Formulas for Organic Compounds

A formula for an organic compound can be written in the same way you write the formula for any other compound. For example, the formula for methane is CH_4. The methane molecule contains one carbon atom and four hydrogen atoms. Methane is also known as natural gas. It is used as fuel in stoves and furnaces.

How is ethane different from methane?

Ethane, C_2H_6, is another example of an organic compound. How many atoms of carbon and hydrogen are in an ethane molecule?

The formula for an organic compound can be written in such a way as to show its structure. The structural formula shows the pattern or form in which the atoms are bonded. For example, the structural formula for methane is

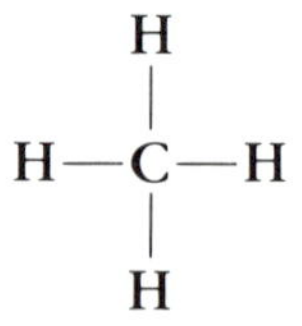

How many covalent bonds are in the molecule? Remember each covalent bond is a shared pair of electrons.

The structural formula for ethane is

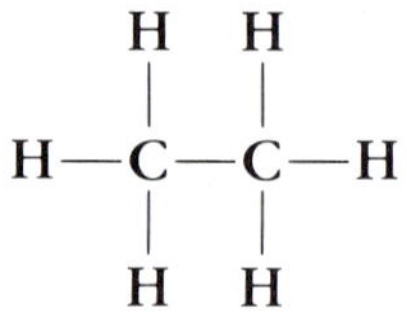

One covalent bond links the two carbon atoms together. How many hydrogen atoms are bonded to each carbon atom?

How is ethyne different from ethane?

Carbon atoms also bond with a double covalent bond. In a double covalent bond, four electrons (two pairs) are shared. Ethene is an example of an organic compound with a double covalent bond. Its formula is C_2H_4. Its structural formula has two lines showing the two covalent bonds between the carbon atoms.

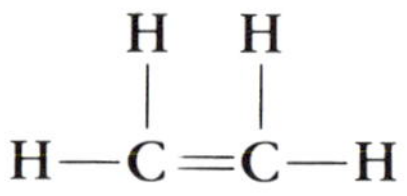

Carbon atoms can also bond by sharing three pairs or six electrons. This bond is a triple covalent bond. One example of a compound with a triple bond is ethyne, C_2H_2. The common name for ethyne is acetylene (uh SET uleen). Its structural formula is

$$H—C \equiv C—H$$

Notice the difference in the endings of the names ethane, ethene, and ethyne. The ending, or suffix, gives a clue to the structure of the compound. The suffix *-ane* refers to a hydrocarbon in which the carbon atoms all have single covalent bonds. Hydrocarbons with the ending *-ene* have a double covalent bond between carbon atoms. The suffix *-yne* means a triple covalent bond is present.

Making Sure

3. How is ethene different from ethane?
4. How many covalent bonds can a carbon atom form? *4* Double covalent bonds? *2* Triple covalent bonds? *1*

ethene–double bond, 4 hydrogen atoms

ethane–single bond, 6 hydrogen atoms

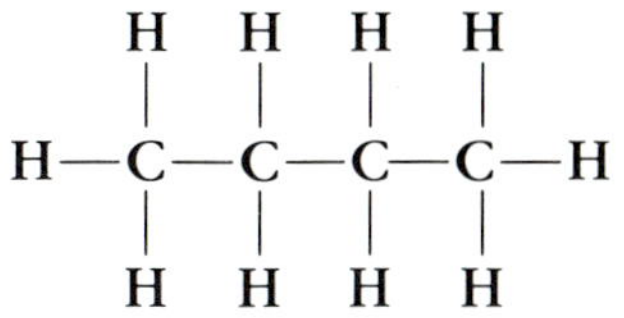

butane

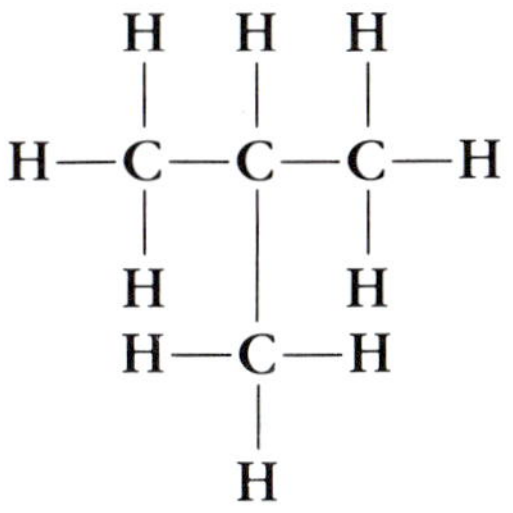

isobutane

10:4 Isomers

The formulas of two different carbon compounds can be the same. For example, C_4H_{10} is the formula for both butane and isobutane. Both compounds have four atoms of carbon and ten atoms of hydrogen. However, the two compounds have different properties because the structure of their molecules is different.

Butane and isobutane are isomers. **Isomers** are compounds with the same formula but different structures. The carbon atoms in butane are in a continuous chain. Isobutane has a different structure. Its carbon atoms are in a branched chain. The branch in isobutane is bonded to the carbon atom at the center of the chain.

Stress this definition of isomers.

What are isomers?

FIGURE 10-3. Butane (a) and isobutane (b) have the same chemical formula. The models show they are structurally different.

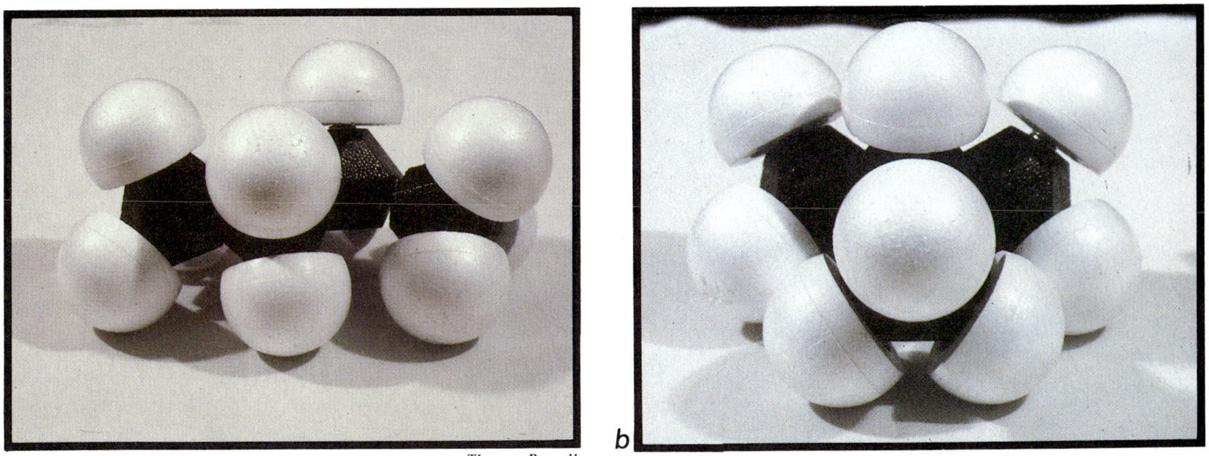

a b

Thomas Russell

Table 10-1

Properties of Butane and Isobutane

	Butane	**Isobutane**
Description	*colorless gas*	*colorless gas*
Density	*0.6 g/cm³*	*0.6 g/cm³*
Melting point	*−135°C*	*−145°C*
Boiling point	*−0.8°C*	*−10.2°C*

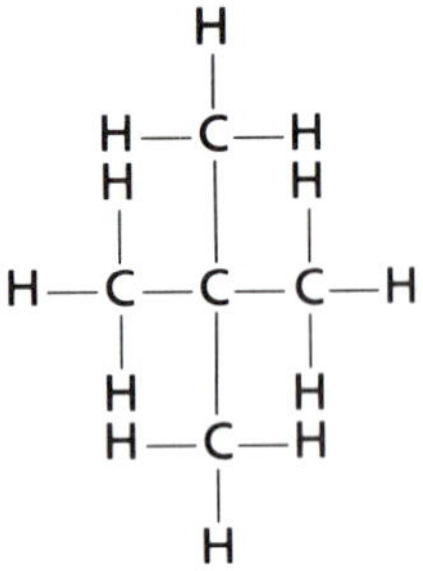

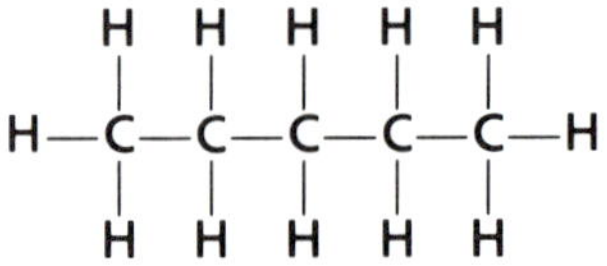

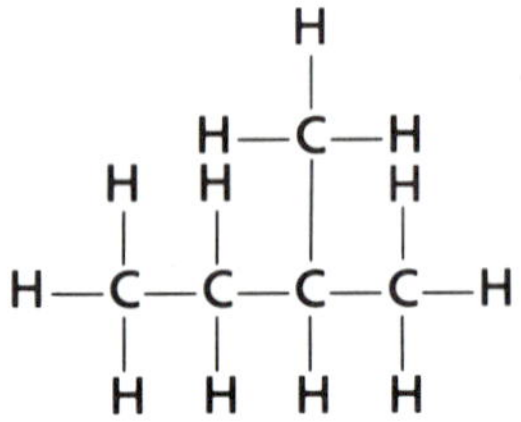

FIGURE 10-4. The formula for these three isomers is C_5H_{12}. They are called 2,2-dimethyl propane, pentane, and 2-methyl butane.

As the number of carbon atoms increases, the number of possible isomers also increases. There are eighteen isomers for octane, C_8H_{18}. The ability of carbon to form isomers is one reason why there are so many carbon compounds.

FIGURE 10-5. Butane is used as a fuel for lighters.

D.A. Davidson/Tom Stack & Assoc.

Making Sure

isobutane–branched chain
butane–continuous chain

5. How is the structure of isobutane different from butane?
6. What is the chemical formula for the three compounds in Figure 10-4? neopentane or 2, 2-dimethyl-propane, pentane, isopentane or 2-methylbutane

10:5 Hydrocarbons

A **hydrocarbon** is a compound containing only hydrogen and carbon. Methane and butane are both hydrocarbons. Crude oil is a mixture of hydrocarbons.

Hydrocarbons are **saturated** if all the carbon atoms are joined by single covalent bonds. One group of saturated hydrocarbons is the alkane series. The eight simplest compounds in the alkane series are listed in Table 10-2. All of the short chain compounds in the alkane series will burn and can be used as fuel. Octane, C_8H_{18}, is one kind of gasoline. Notice that the names of all compounds in the alkane series end in *-ane.*

An **unsaturated hydrocarbon** has one or more double or triple covalent bonds. For example, ethene has a double covalent bond between its two carbon atoms. Acetylene has a triple covalent bond between its two carbon atoms.

How is an unsaturated different from a saturated hydrocarbon?

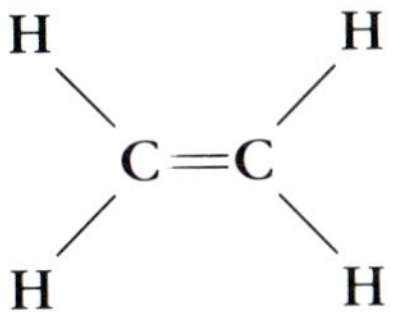

ethene

acetylene

Some vegetable oils are described as being unsaturated. This word means the compounds in the oils have double covalent bonds. Unsaturated oils are present in corn oil and safflower oil. Animal fat, such as lard, contains saturated hydrocarbons. There is some medical evidence that a diet high in saturated fats may be harmful. In some people, it may cause hardening of the arteries, high blood pressure, and heart disease.

a b

Thomas Russell

FIGURE 10-6. Foods high in saturated fat (a) contain fats from animal sources. Foods containing unsaturated fats (b) are usually made from vegetable oils.

Table 10-2

Alkane Series of Hydrocarbons

methane	CH_4	pentane	C_5H_{12}
ethane	C_2H_6	hexane	C_6H_{14}
propane	C_3H_8	heptane	C_7H_{16}
butane	C_4H_{10}	octane	C_8H_{18}

Craig Kramer

FIGURE 10-7. Many of the products we use everyday are made from polymers.

10:6 Polymers

What is a polymer?

Small organic molecules can combine to form very large molecules. These compounds are called **polymers** (PAHL uh mur). An example of a polymer is rubber. Rubber contains long chains of carbon atoms formed by joining small chains together.

Many plastics, such as polyethylene (pahl ee ETH uh leen), are polymers. Also, synthetic fibers such as nylon, orlon, and polyester are polymers. The properties of latex paint that make it resist wear are due in part to polymer compounds.

FIGURE 10-8. Paint manufacturers test samples of paint to determine its resistance to weathering. Polymer products are added to improve the properties of paint.

Pittsburg Paint, Delaware, Ohio

10:7 Soap and Detergent

Soap is an organic compound that dissolves in water. The cleaning ability of water is increased if soap is added. A soap molecule is a long hydrocarbon chain. At one end of the chain is a sodium or potassium atom.

Why is soap a good cleaning agent?

Soap is a good cleaning agent because the carbon end of the soap molecule dissolves grease and oil. When you wash grease or oil off your hands with soapy water, the soap "cuts" the grease. The water then washes the grease away.

How is soap made?

Soap is made in a chemical reaction. Lye (sodium hydroxide) and fat are mixed and heated. Soap and an organic compound called glycerol (GLIHS uh rawl) are formed. The soap is then separated from the glycerol and pressed into bars.

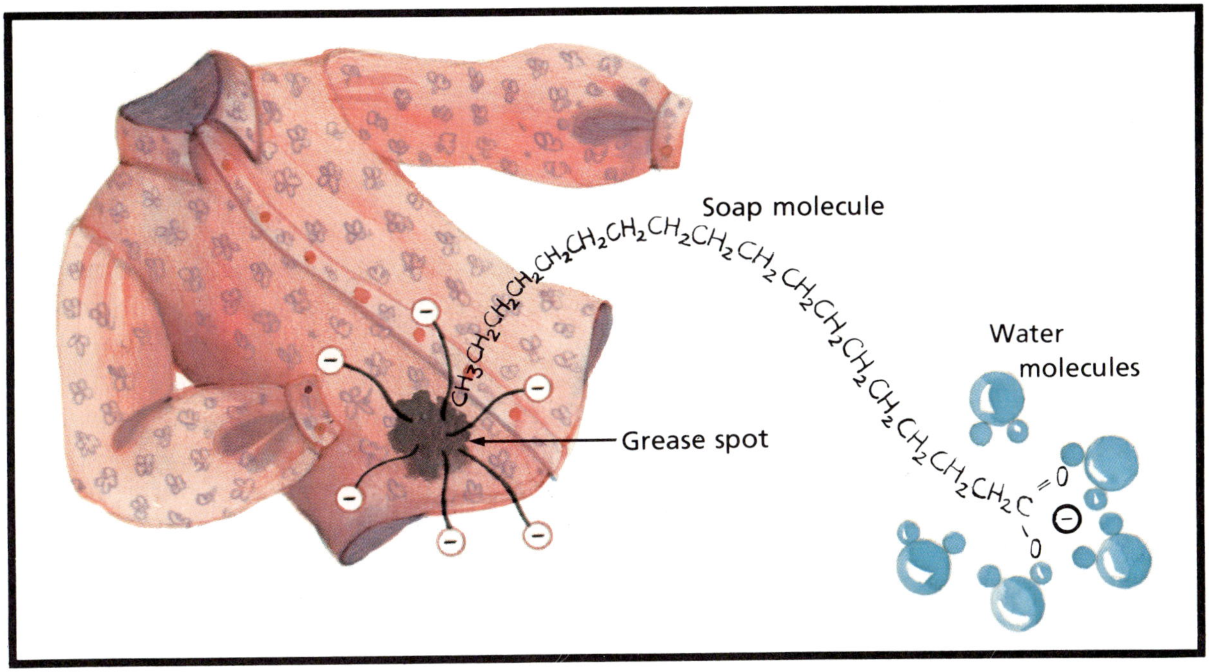

FIGURE 10-9. One end of a soap molecule dissolves grease. The other end dissolves in water. The addition of soap allows grease or oil to dissolve in water.

Synthetic detergents are organic compounds that make water "wetter." Detergents make water do a better job of washing oil, grease, and dirt. Like soap, they are long carbon chains with a metal at one end of the chain. Unlike soap, synthetic detergents work well in hard water. Hard water contains minerals that reduce the cleaning action of soap.

10-1 Detailed information concerning this Activity can be found in the Teacher's Guide at the front of this book.

ACTIVITY How do you make soap?

CAUTION: *Wear protective goggles and clothing.* **(1)** *Place 50 mL of lard in a beaker and add 150 mL of a 20% sodium hydroxide solution.* **(2)** *Heat the mixture with a laboratory burner and boil gently for about 20 minutes.* **(3)** *After heating, let the solution stand for a few minutes.* **(4)** *Then add 10 grams of salt. Stir.* **(5)** *Skim off the soap and let it dry on a paper towel.* **(6)** *Place a small amount of the soap in a test tube and fill it ¼ full of water. Stopper the test tube and shake it hard for 30 seconds. Does your soap make suds?*

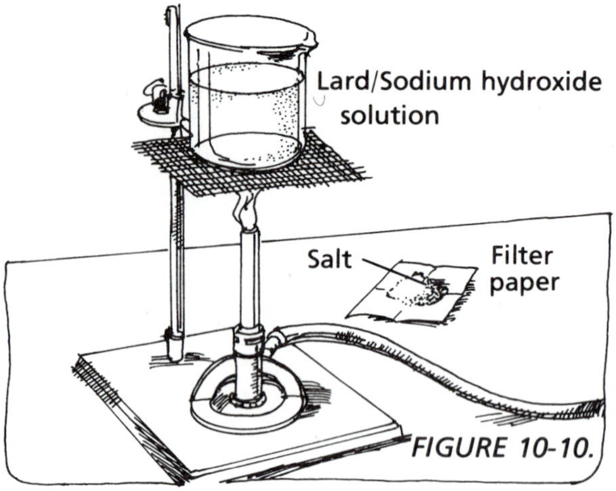

FIGURE 10-10.

10-2 Detailed information concerning this Activity can be found in the Teacher's Guide at the front of this book.

ACTIVITY How well do soap and detergent work in hard water?

(1) *Obtain two test tubes.* **(2)** *Label one test tube with an "H" and add 5 mL of hard water to the test tube.* **(3)** *Mark the second test tube with a "D" and add 5 mL of distilled water to it.* **(4)** *Add 5 drops of liquid soap to each test tube. Stopper each tube and shake it. Do suds appear in either test tube?* **(5)** *Repeat the procedure using liquid detergent instead of soap.*

How does the action of detergent differ from the soap? Which would be better to use in areas where the water is hard?

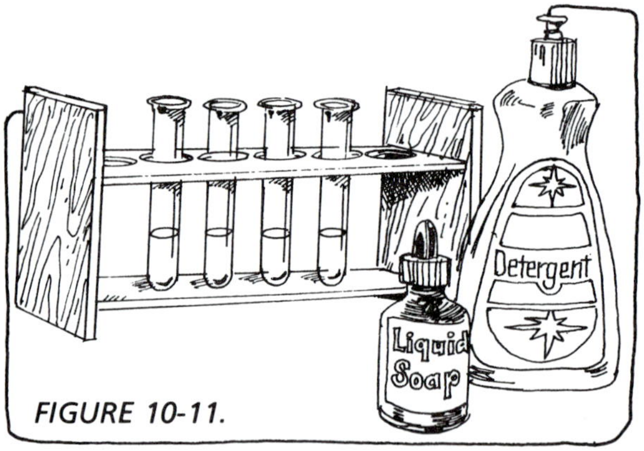

FIGURE 10-11.

Shostal Associates Inc.

FIGURE 10-12. Detergents are often used in the clean-up of accidental oil spills.

10:8 Other Organic Compounds

Many hydrocarbon compounds are composed of molecules in the form of rings. The carbon atoms are bonded in a ring instead of a chain. For example, benzene has six carbon atoms in a ring.

benzene 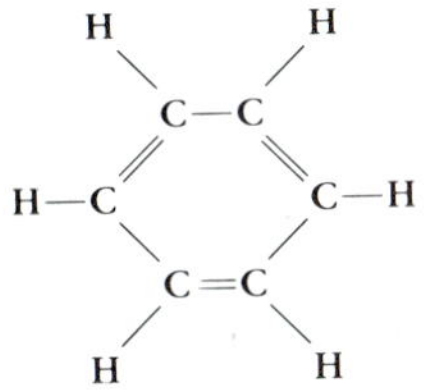

FIGURE 10-13. Ethanol, an alcohol, is used as a fuel for some airplanes.

Alcohols are organic compounds that contain an —OH group. Methanol, CH_3OH, is called wood alcohol because it can be made by heating wood in a sealed container. Methanol is a poison and causes blindness. Ethanol, C_2H_5OH, is the alcohol obtained from grains such as wheat and corn. The alcohol in beverages such as beer and wine is ethanol.

Many carbon compounds contain one or more elements in the halogen family. Carbon tetrachloride, CCl_4, is composed of one carbon atom and four chlorine atoms. It was once used to dry-clean clothing. However, the vapors from carbon tetrachloride are poisonous. Tetrachloroethene, C_2Cl_4, is now used. Chloroform, $CHCl_3$, is used to dissolve organic substances such as fat, oil, and rubber. Iodoform (i OHD uh form) is a yellow solid used to kill germs.

FIGURE 10-14. Fermentation involves the conversion of sugar to alcohol. Fermentation vats similar to the one shown will be used to produce ethanol for fuel.

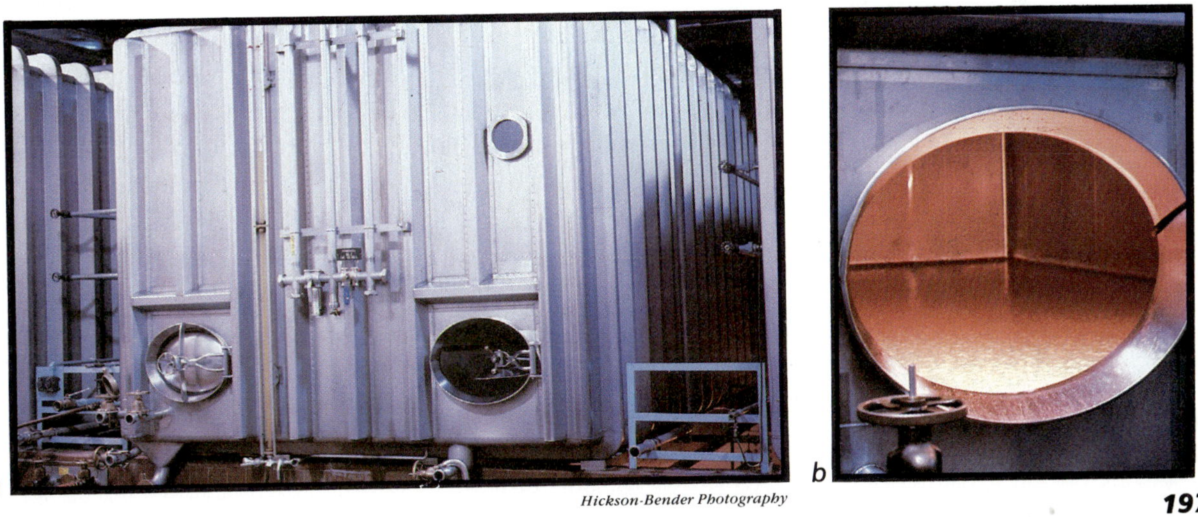

a b

Hickson-Bender Photography

a

H. Carroll/FPG

b

FIGURE 10-15. Antifreeze (a) is made from ethylene glycol, an alcohol. Organic acids are used in home canning (b) to keep foods from spoiling or turning brown.

Most foods and substances used in cooking contain organic compounds. Food colors, flavors, and preservatives are usually organic compounds. One substance used to preserve food is vinegar. Vinegar contains acetic acid. Acetic acid slows the growth of organisms that spoil food.

10:9 Organic Compounds in Living Things

The matter that makes the bodies of living things is mostly water and organic compounds. In fact, the term organic means living. Fat is one kind of organic compound in living things. **Fat** contains the elements carbon, hydrogen, and oxygen. Some fat is needed in the diet for good health. In your body, fat is used to store energy.

Carbohydrates, like fats, contain carbon, hydrogen, and oxygen. However, in carbohydrates the hydrogen and oxygen are present in a ratio of two hydrogen atoms to one oxygen atom. This ratio is the same as in water. Two kinds of carbohydrates are sugar and starch. The sugar in blood, called glucose, has the formula $C_6H_{12}O_6$. Starch is a large molecule made of smaller sugar molecules. Both fat and carbohydrates in food are important sources of energy for the body. Fats contain more energy per gram than carbohydrates.

Name five organic compounds present in living things.

Thomas Russell

a

b

FIGURE 10-16. Foods high in carbohydrates (a) usually have a high sugar content. Good sources of protein are shown in (b).

You could not walk, run, play, read, think, or do anything else without energy. Sugar and fats are broken down in chemical changes that release energy.

What is the source of energy in food?

Protein is an organic compound that contains hydrogen, oxygen, and nitrogen. Some proteins also contain sulfur. Body tissues are built and repaired with protein. A protein is a polymer made from smaller molecules called amino acids. The hemoglobin (HEE muh gloh bun) that gives blood its red color contains a protein and iron. Meat, fish, and beans are good sources of protein in the diet. Protein can also be used to supply energy for the body.

Vitamins are complex organic compounds. Many vitamin molecules contain carbon rings. Vitamins are needed for chemical changes in the body that are necessary for good health. All the vitamins you need can be gained from a good diet.

All the energy in the food you eat came originally from the sun. Sunlight is needed for plants to make food through a chemical change called photosynthesis. Animals obtain energy by eating plants and their products such as fruits and seeds. The plants and animals we use for food contain fats, carbohydrates, proteins, and vitamins.

FIGURE 10-17. The sun is the primary energy source of the foods we eat.

Food chain: energy from the sun is transferred to plants, to animals, to people.

The oxygen/hydrogen ratio is 1:2 in carbohydrates but not in fats. Fats contain more energy per kilogram. Both contain C, H, and O and are found in the body.

Making Sure

7. Why is it correct to say that the energy in meat comes from the sun?
8. How are fats different from carbohydrates? How are they alike?

10:10 Petroleum

What is petroleum?

Petroleum is a mixture of hydrocarbons. It is obtained from wells driven deep into rock formations. Another name for petroleum is crude oil. Petroleum is the major source of fuels such as gasoline and kerosene. Also, the hydrocarbons in petroleum are used to make fertilizer, plastics, paint, and synthetic fibers.

How is gasoline obtained from petroleum?

The mixture of hydrocarbons in petroleum is separated by a method called **fractional distillation.** In fractional distillation, the petroleum is heated. The hydrocarbons in the mixture boil at different temperatures. As the temperature increases, each fraction changes to a vapor and is collected separately. Cooling changes the vapors back to liquid hydrocarbons, Figure 10-18.

Table 10-3

Hydrocarbons from Petroleum

Fraction	Boiling range
liquefied petroleum gas	*below 40°C*
gasoline	*40°C to 180°C*
kerosene and jet fuels	*180°C to 230°C*
home heating oils	*230°C to 305°C*
diesel oil	*305°C to 405°C*
asphalt, wax	*405°C to 515°C*

Making Sure

9. Are the compounds in petroleum separated by chemical or physical changes? *physical changes*
10. What are some products, other than gasoline, that are made from petroleum? *plastics, asphalt, synthetic fibers are examples*

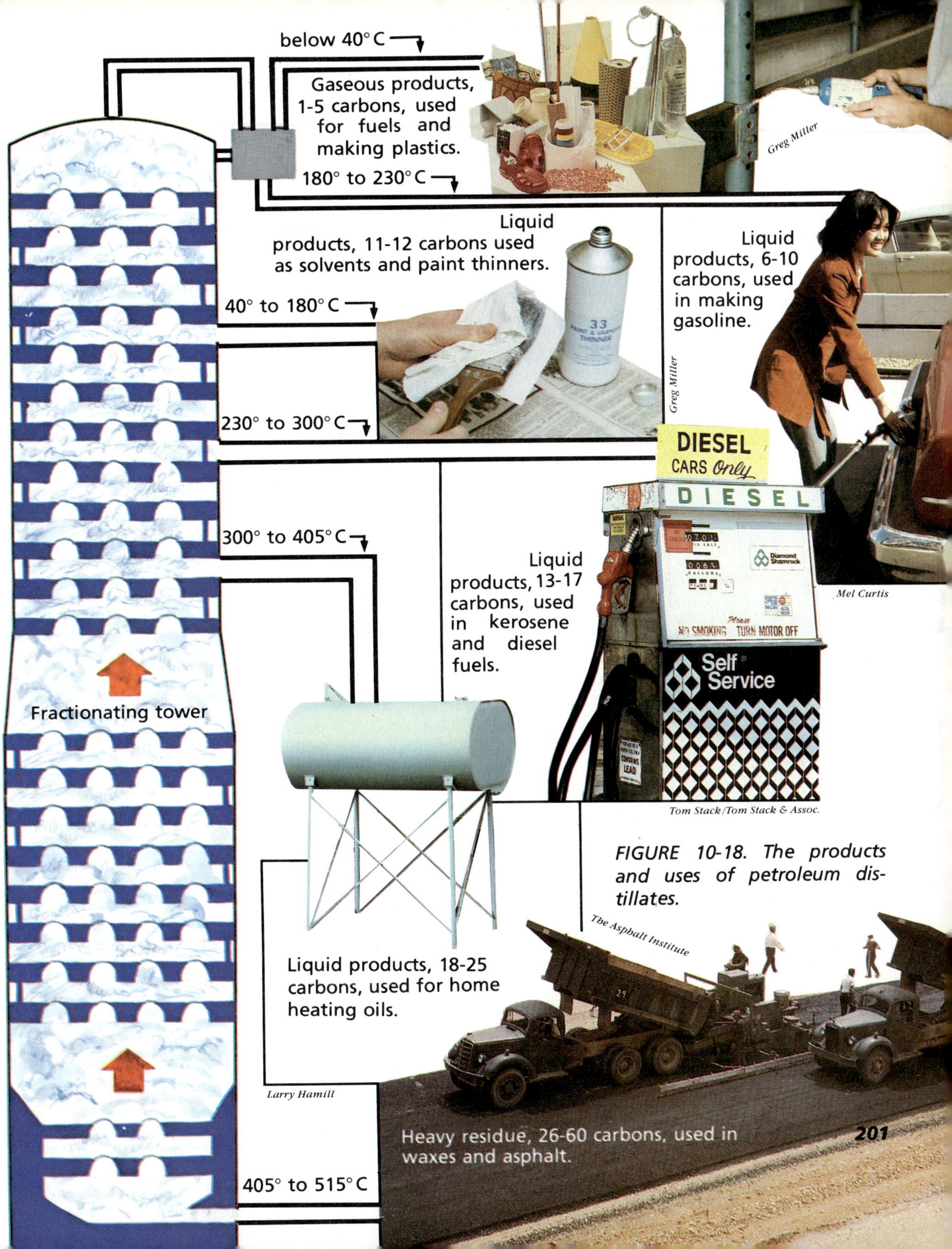

FIGURE 10-18. The products and uses of petroleum distillates.

10:11 Energy from Organic Compounds

Organic compounds in food provide the energy living things need to stay alive. Energy is also obtained from fuels. Coal, natural gas, crude oil, and gasoline are fossil fuels that contain carbon. Fossil fuels are the remains of animals and plants that lived long ago. When a fossil fuel is burned, carbon and hydrogen in the fuel combine with oxygen. Carbon dioxide and water are formed and energy is released as light and heat. The energy in fossil fuels came originally from the sun.

How is energy obtained from fossil fuels?

Most of the matter in coal is carbon. When a fuel such as coal, oil, or gasoline is burned in insufficient oxygen, carbon monoxide is formed. Carbon monoxide is a deadly poisonous gas. When taken into the lungs, it enters the blood by replacing oxygen. As a result, a person's oxygen supply is reduced. Carbon monoxide poisoning causes a person to die from a lack of oxygen in the body.

How is gasoline different from fuel oil?

Fuel oil used for heating is a mixture of long chain hydrocarbons. Gasoline is a mixture of short chain hydrocarbons. The density of gasoline is less than that of fuel oil. Gasoline evaporates faster than fuel oil. Diesel engines use fuel that is similar to the fuel oil used in oil furnaces. Diesel engines are now used in many cars because they are more efficient than gasoline engines. One drawback to a diesel engine is the high level of nitrogen oxides in the exhaust. These nitrogen oxides form acids when dissolved in water in the atmosphere. These acids are harmful.

PROTEIN	7 grams	8 grams	15 grams
CARBOHYDRATE	23 grams	11 grams	34 grams
FAT	1 gram	8 grams	9 grams
PERCENTAGES OF RECOMMENDED DAILY ALLOWANCES			
VITAMIN A	20%	4%	25%
VITAMIN C	40%	4%	25%
CALCIUM	10%	30%	40%
IRON	25%	0%	25%
VITAMIN D	0%	25%	25%
PHOSPHORUS	15%	20%	35%
IODINE	2%	30%	30%

FIGURE 10-19. Food labels provide nutritional information. You need more nutrients than the energy from fats, carbohydrates, and proteins.

Approximate Energy Equivalents of Fuels (in kJ/kg)					
Body fuels		**Heat and transportation fuels**			
carbohydrates	17 000	methane	55 000	fuel oil	44 000
fats	38 000	propane	50 000	methanol	24 000
protein	17 000	butane	49 000	ethanol	31 000
		gasoline	48 000	coal	28 000
				wood	15 000

10-3 Detailed information concerning this Activity can be found in the Teacher's Guide at the front of this book.

ACTIVITY *How does a burner use gas as fuel?*

(1) *Obtain a gas burner and connect it to a gas outlet. Turn on the gas and light the burner.* **(2)** *Find the valve that controls the height of the flame.* **(3)** *Adjust the burner so the air intake decreases and the flame becomes yellow. Use metal forceps to hold a glass plate in the yellow flame. What forms on the plate?* **(4)** *Increase the air intake so the flame is blue in color.*

Is the blue flame hotter than the yellow flame? Explain. Draw a diagram of the burner system and label its parts.

Making Sure

11. Why does a gas burner mix air with the fuel? — *to have the oxygen necessary for combustion*
12. How is your home heated? What type of fuel is used? *answers will vary*
13. List five things people can do to cut down the use of energy. *Answers will vary, see the Teacher's Guide for examples.*

10:12 Synthetic Fuels

What is a synthetic fuel?

Fuels made from coal, plants, and other sources of hydrocarbons are called synthetic fuels. To make a fuel from coal, the coal is heated to a high temperature under high pressure. Steam is then passed over the hot coal. Carbon in the coal combines with hydrogen in the steam to form hydrocarbons. About fifty percent of the synthetic gas produced is methane, CH_4.

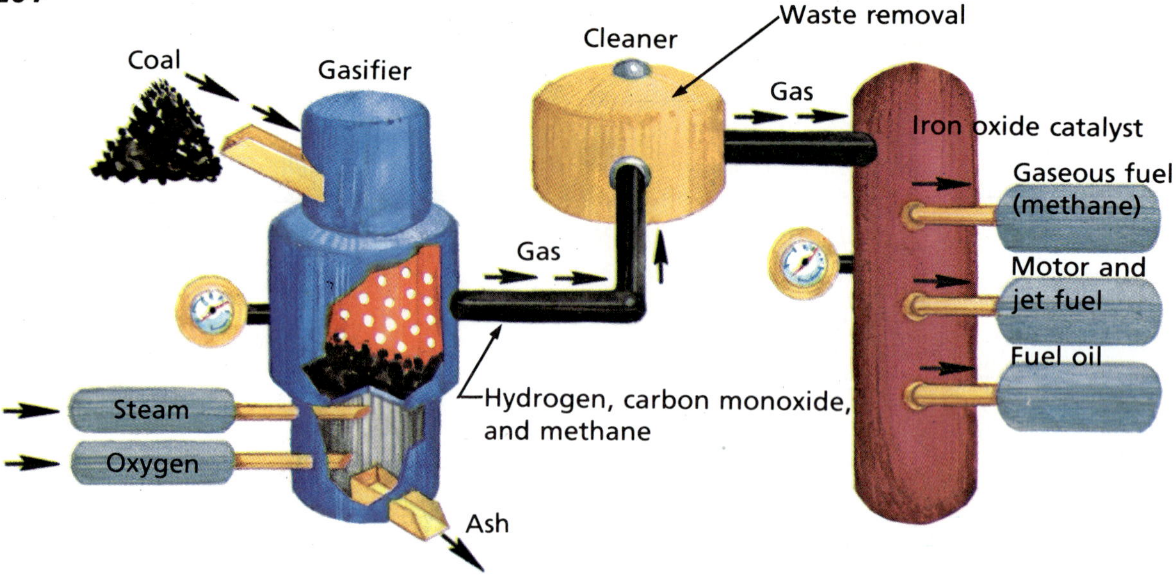

FIGURE 10-20. One alternate source of energy is converting coal to natural gas and oil. Natural gas burns cleaner and produces little air pollution compared to coal.

FIGURE 10-21. The use of gasohol as fuel for automobiles will decrease our demand for fossil fuels.

Bruce D. Sampsel

Oil can be removed from a rock called oil shale. Oil shale is a reddish-brown rock containing hydrocarbons. Huge amounts of oil shale are found in Colorado, Utah, and Wyoming. These hydrocarbons are the remains of prehistoric animals and plants. About one-half barrel of oil can be removed from one metric ton of oil shale.

One method of removing oil from shale is to heat it to about 500°C. The heating is done in a steel container with no oxygen present. Heating causes the hydrocarbons to change to a vapor. The vapor is then cooled and condensed to form oil. This oil is like the crude oil pumped from oil wells. Gasoline, heating oil, and other useful products can be separated from synthetic oil.

Alcohol is a fuel that can be made from the sugar in corn. Corn is ground and mixed with water and yeast. Yeast changes the sugar to ethanol, C_2H_5OH. The pure alcohol is removed. Gasohol, a mixture of gasoline and about ten percent alcohol, can be used as a fuel in gasoline engines.

There is one disadvantage to the use of alcohol from corn and other grains as a fuel in automobiles. Heat is needed to distill the liquid to purify the alcohol. At present, it takes more heat energy to make the alcohol than is obtained when the alcohol is burned as a fuel.

FIGURE 10-22. Fuels which can be used as alternatives to oil are shown.

Making Sure

14. How may synthetic fuels help to solve the world's energy problems? *cuts the demand for fossil fuels*

15. What are some of the disadvantages in using synthetic fuels? *Often more energy is used to make the fuel than would be obtained from using it.*

Linda Young

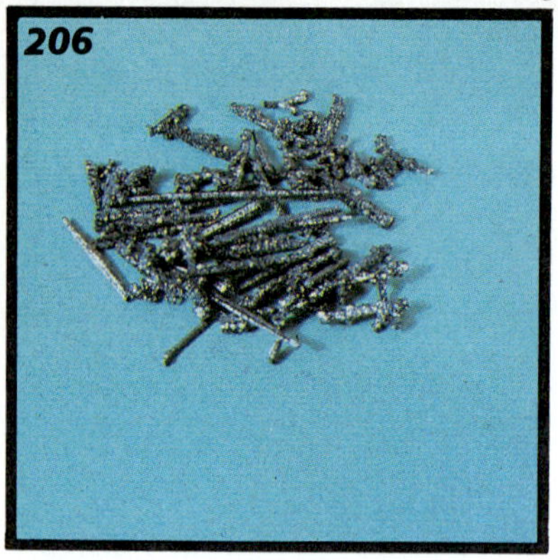

FIGURE 10-23. Silicon

10:13 Silicon

Silicon is the second most abundant element in the earth's crust. It is a nonmetal and takes the form of a brown powder or a hard grey solid. Silicon is present in many rocks and minerals. For example, quartz and sand are composed of silicon dioxide, SiO_2. Gems such as opal, amethyst, and onyx contain silicon.

Steve Lissau

a

b

Craig Kramer

c

Stewart/FPG

FIGURE 10-24. Sand (a), amethyst (b), and opal (c) are natural sources of silicon.

Silicon has many practical uses. For example, *Carborundum* (kar buh RUHN duhm), a very hard compound of silicon and oxygen, is used in grindstones. Silicon is used to make the transistors found in radios, television sets, and computers. Window glass is made by heating a mixture of sand and limestone to a high temperature.

© Dan McCoy from Rainbow

D. Briskin/Tom Stack & Assoc.

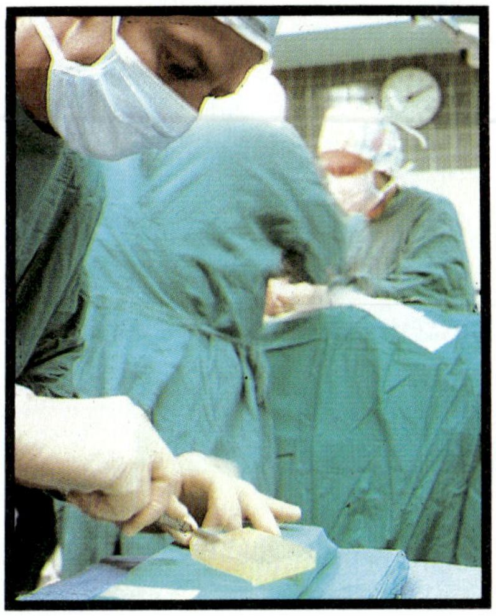

a

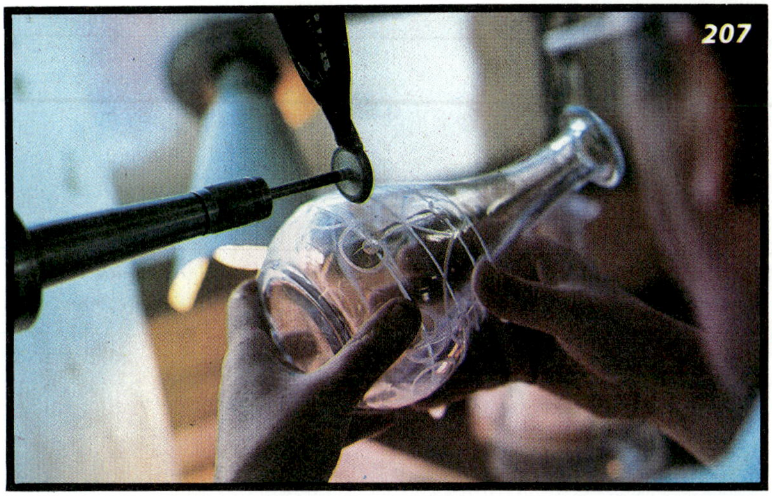

b

A silicon crystal which has been manufactured with certain impurities has the ability to absorb energy from light. This property makes these types of silicon crystals useful in solar cells which convert sunlight to electricity.

Like carbon, silicon has four electrons in its outer energy level. It forms compounds with oxygen and other elements by covalent bonding. Silicones (SIHL uh kohnz) are compounds containing long chains of silicon and oxygen bonded to side chains of hydrocarbons. Silicones are used as lubricants, electric insulators, water repellents, and synthetic motor oil.

FIGURE 10-25. Silicone materials are used in bone restructuring (a) and in grinding wheels (b) because they are durable, hard, and strong.

FIGURE 10-26. Silicones are used as caulking for windows (a) and bathroom tile because they are water resistant. Silicon is a major component of glass (c).

a

Greg Miller

b

c

Wendler/FPG

Focus On

Frontiers

Composites, Lighter Than Steel

Graftek/Division of Exxon Enterprises Inc.

Car makers are under pressure to make lighter cars in order to increase mileage. One way this can be done is to use composites. A composite is a substance made of two different materials. Each material contributes certain advantages and the combination is better than either alone. A common example of a composite is reinforced concrete. Steel rods within the concrete supply strength. The concrete supplies resistance to compression. The result is a better building material.

The composites under study for use in cars are usually made of fine, high strength strands of carbon embedded in a plastic bonding material. A composite bar might have one-fifth the weight and the same strength as a steel bar. Composites similar to those being studied were originally developed for aircraft. They are used to save weight in airplanes. Graphite fibers were used in the early 1960's. Today most of the carbon fibers come from an acrylic material, much like that used in fabrics.

You would think that composites can save an enormous amount of weight in a car. However, there are some problems to overcome. Carbon materials are "anisotropic." Anisotropic means that, unlike steel, the fibers are not equally strong in all directions. Designers must always keep in mind the direction of the stress on a part. The direction of stress determines the direction of the fibers. One example is a push rod in a car. A push rod moves the valves in the engine. The stress on a push rod is in one direction. This means that the fibers can be in one direction. The stress on a crankshaft is in many directions. Here fibers must be in many directions to handle the stress. This is a much more complex problem. Even with the complex problems, composites will be used increasingly in the next few years.

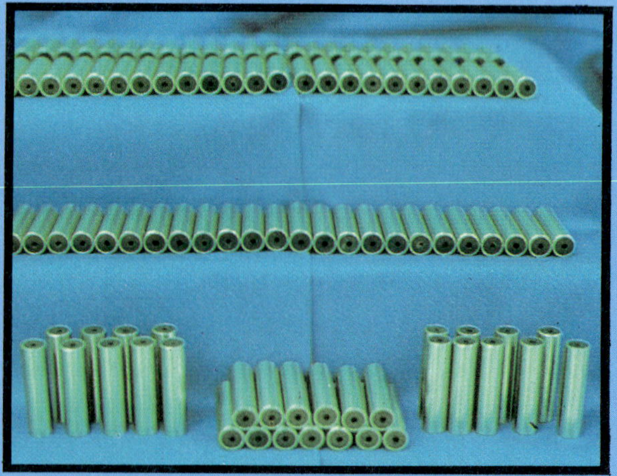

Points to Remember

1. An organic compound is a compound containing carbon. *10:2*
2. Carbon atoms bond covalently. *10:2*
3. Organic molecules can be chains or rings of carbon atoms. *10:2, 10:8*
4. Hydrocarbons contain only hydrogen and carbon. *10:5*
5. Rubber, synthetic fibers, and many other organic compounds are polymers. *10:6*
6. In addition to carbon and hydrogen, many organic compounds contain oxygen and one or more halogens. *10:8*
7. Fossil fuels contain hydrocarbons. *10:10*
8. Synthetic fuels can be made from coal or grains. *10:12*
9. Oil can be produced from oil shale. *10:12*
10. Organic compounds in food and fuel are a source of energy. *10:9, 10:11*

Words to Use

Write a sentence in which you correctly use each of the following words or terms.

alcohol
amino acid
carbohydrate
fat
fossil fuel
fractional distillation
hydrocarbon
isomer
organic compound
petroleum
polymer
protein
saturated hydrocarbon
structural formula
synthetic fuel
unsaturated hydrocarbon
vitamin

Questions for Review

Do not write in this book.

A. True or False *Have the students rewrite the false statements to make them correct.*
Determine whether each of the following sentences is true or false.

T **1.** Graphite is a form of carbon.
F **2.** Carbon ~~never~~ combines with hydrogen.
T **3.** All organic compounds contain carbon.
T **4.** The formula for methane is CH_4.

T 5. Two pairs of electrons are present in a double covalent bond.

F 6. Butane and isobutane have ~~the exact same~~ properties. different

F 7. Methane is an example of ~~a polymer~~. an alkane

T 8. A soap molecule contains carbon and hydrogen atoms.

T 9. Foods contain organic compounds.

F 10. The boiling point of gasoline is ~~higher~~ than the boiling point of kerosene. lower

B. Multiple Choice

Choose the word or phrase that correctly completes each of the following sentences.

1. *(Carbon, Graphite, Diamond)* has atoms bonded together in a tetrahedral pattern.
2. *(CCl_4, CH_3OH, C_2H_6)* is a hydrocarbon.
3. *(C_2H_6, C_3H_8, C_2H_2, CH_4)* is unsaturated.
4. Butane and isobutane are *(unsaturated, isomers, carbohydrates)*.
5. *(Methane, Butane, Octane, Benzene)* is one kind of gasoline.
6. Plastics, soap, and detergents are *(polymers, organic compounds, isomers)*.
7. An example of a ring compound is *(benzene, methane, ethyl alcohol, acetylene)*.
8. Alcohol is a(n) *(isomer, hydrocarbon, organic compound)*.
9. A source of energy in the human body is *(carbohydrates, hydrocarbons, fossil fuels)*.
10. Quartz and sand contain *(carbon, hydrogen, silicon)*.

C. Completion

Complete each of the following sentences with one word or phrase that will make the sentence correct.

1. Diamond is the hardest substance known.
2. Natural gas is another name for methane.
3. Ethanol is an alcohol made from corn.
4. The formula for carbon tetrachloride is CCl_4.
5. Petroleum is a mixture of hydrocarbons.
6. CO is a poisonous gas made of carbon and oxygen.

7. Coal, oil, and gas are examples of fossil fuels.
8. A synthetic fuel can be made from corn.
9. Silicones are long chains of silicon and oxygen atoms.
10. SiO_2 is the formula for sand.

D. How and Why

Detailed answers to these questions are given in the Teacher's Guide at the front of this book.

1. How is graphite different from diamond?
2. How is it possible for carbon to form so many organic compounds?
3. Write two structural formulas for saturated organic compounds.
4. Write the structural formula for an unsaturated hydrocarbon.
5. Name five polymers that have practical uses.
6. Why is carbon important to living things?
7. Describe two examples of the use of organic compounds to obtain energy.
8. How might synthetic fuels increase the world's energy supply?
9. How is gasoline obtained from petroleum?
10. How is silicon like carbon? How is it different?

Readings to Discover

Burt, Olive W., *Black Sunshine: The Story of Coal.* NY: Messner, 1977.
Chase, Sara H., *First Book of Diamonds.* NY: F. Watts, 1971.
Hahn, Lynn and James, *Plastics.* NY: F. Watts, 1974.

Unit 4

Iron has many undesirable properties. However, steel, which is made from iron, is very versatile and has many desirable properties. The pictures show the changes iron must undergo in the process of making steel. How is matter changed to give us useful products?

Changes in Matter

molten steel J. P. Conrardy/Tom Stack & Assoc. girders Larry Hamill J. P. Conrardy/Tom Stack & Assoc.

You can go without food for a much longer period of time than without water. Treatment plants, like the one in the picture, supply us with the water we need. Water contains many substances in solution. What is a solution? Why is water important in a study of solutions? How can undesirable substances be removed from drinking water?

James N. Westwater

Solutions

11

Chapter 11 discusses the formation of solutions and physical interaction of solute and solvent. Factors relating to rate of solution are presented. The concepts of solubility, concentration, and saturation are discussed. See the Teacher's Guide at the front of this book for additional teaching strategies for this chapter.

11:1 Types of Solutions

GOAL: *You will learn how solutions are formed and some important uses for solutions.*

A **solution** is a mixture in which one substance is dissolved in another substance. The **solute** (SAHL yewt) is the substance being dissolved. The **solvent** (SAHL vuhnt) is the substance in which a solute is dissolved. In a sugar-water solution, sugar is the solute and water is the solvent. In a solution, two or more substances are uniformly mixed. The solution formed is the same in all parts. In the sugar-water solution, molecules of sugar are spread evenly throughout the molecules of water.

What is a solution?

The most common solutions are liquid solutions. The solvent is a liquid. The solute can be a solid, liquid, or gas. Water is the most common solvent. Unless some other solvent is named, assume the solvent is water. For example, a salt solution is considered to be salt and water.

Solutions can also be formed by dissolving solids, liquids, or gases in gases. In this case, a gaseous solution is formed. Air is a gaseous solution (see Table 9-4, page 173).

Name three kinds of solutions.

A third type of solution is a solid solution. Solid solutions are formed by dissolving solids, liquids, or gases in solids. Sterling silver is a solution of copper in silver. A solid solution like sterling silver is an alloy, Section 8:5.

Some solids contain water molecules as part of their crystalline structure. For example, when copper(II) sulfate, $CuSO_4$ crystallizes out of solution, four water molecules attach to each Cu^{2+} ion. One water molecule is attached to each sulfate ion. The crystal is called a **hydrate.** Many ionic substances form hydrated crystals.

Keith Turpie

FIGURE 11-1. White gold is a solution of gold, copper, nickel, and zinc. Yellow gold is a solution of gold, silver, and copper.

11-1

ACTIVITY *What happens to hydrated crystals when heated?*

Place a few crystals of copper(II) sulfate in a test tube. Heat strongly over a burner flame until a change occurs. What happens to the crystals? What happens at the mouth of the test tube?

Now add a few drops of water to the powder in the test tube. What happens? What do you think causes the color of the copper(II) sulfate crystals? *water causes the color*

crystals become a white powder; water forms at the mouth of the test tube

Tom Stack/Tom Stack & Assoc.

FIGURE 11-2. The anhydrous form of cobalt chloride is blue. The hydrated form is deep pink. Objects treated with this chemical are used to indicate changes in humidity.

11:2 The Solution Process

What happens when a solute dissolves? A sugar crystal is placed in a glass of water. The dissolving action begins on the outside surface of the crystal. The outer layer of sugar molecules of the crystal is pulled away by the water, Figure 11-3. As these outer molecules leave, the next layer of sugar molecules come in contact with the water. These molecules also come off and mix with the water. This process goes on until all the sugar molecules are mixed with the water. The crystal has dissolved completely. A clear solution has been formed.

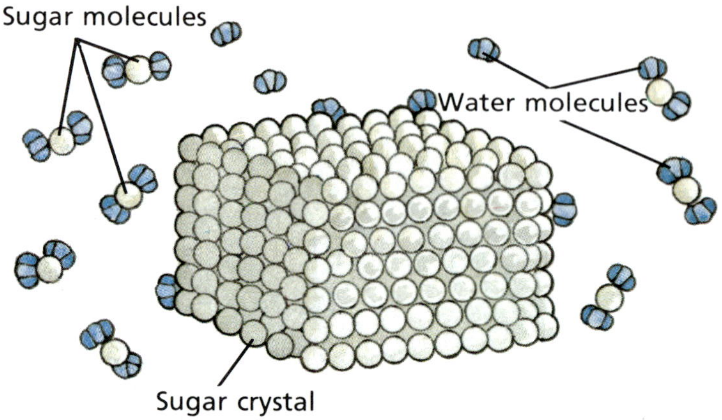

FIGURE 11-3. As sugar dissolves, sugar molecules are pulled away from the crystal.

Greg Miller

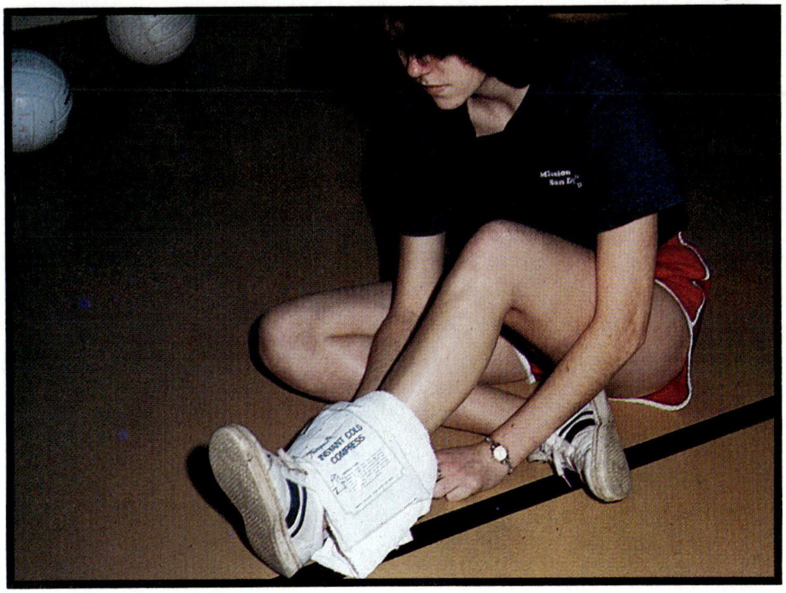

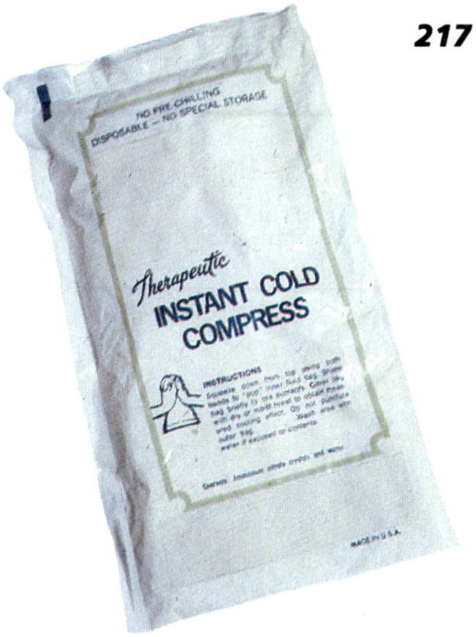

FIGURE 11-4. Instant ice packs used by athletes absorb energy as a solute dissolves.

When a solute is dissolved in a solvent, a change in the temperature of the solvent may occur. For example, when ammonium chloride is dissolved in water, the temperature decreases. Just the opposite occurs when sodium hydroxide is dissolved in water. The temperature of the solution increases. The temperature change is caused by mixing solute and solvent particles. Particles of the solute pull apart from each other and attach to particles of solvent. During this change energy may be absorbed or released.

11-2 Detailed information concerning this Activity can be found in the Teacher's Guide at the front of this book.

ACTIVITY *Do all substances dissolve?*

__(1)__ Add 5 mL of water to each of four test tubes. __(2)__ In the first test tube, place a small amount of table salt. To the second, add 4 drops of mineral oil. To the third, add 4 drops of ethanol. To the fourth, add a small amount of sugar. __(3)__ Stopper each tube and shake. Record what you observe in each tube. __(4)__ Clean the test tubes and repeat Steps 2 and 3 using 5 mL of ethanol in each test tube. Add water to the third test tube instead of ethanol. salt, sugar, ethanol dissolve in water

What solutes dissolved in water? What solutes dissolved in ethanol? mineral oil, water dissolve in ethanol

FIGURE 11-5. A food blender can be used as a time-saving device for making solutions at home.

Hickson-Bender Photography

11:3 Rate of Solution

Suppose you stir some lemonade after adding sugar to it. Does the stirring help the sugar dissolve? Will granulated sugar dissolve faster than sugar cubes? The answers to these questions tell you something about the rate at which a substance dissolves.

When a solution is stirred, surface particles of the solute are pulled away faster. Thus, the solute dissolves faster. The rate of solution is increased.

If a large crystal is crushed, the small pieces have more surface area than the large crystal. Surface area is the total outer part or exterior of something. For example, a cube of sugar is crushed. The crushed sugar will dissolve faster than the sugar cube. Why? The increased surface area brings more of the sugar particles in contact with the water. Thus, the particles pull apart and mix with the water faster than if they were all in one sugar cube.

Energy is needed for the particles of a solid to separate. Adding energy in the form of heat should cause the particles to separate faster. Therefore, solids dissolve faster in hot water.

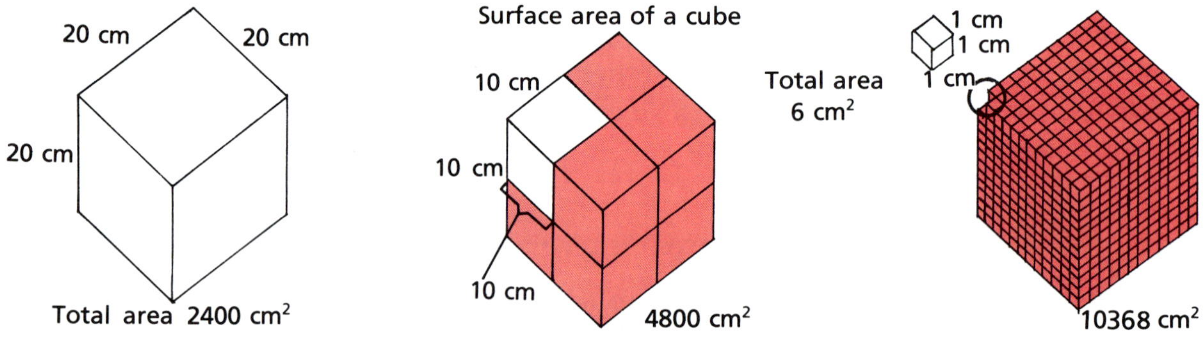

FIGURE 11-6. As a crystal is cut into smaller pieces, the total surface area of the crystal increases. Thus, smaller crystals dissolve faster because more surface area is exposed to the solvent.

To summarize, three ways to increase the rate at which a solid dissolves are (1) heat the solution, (2) stir or shake the solution, and (3) crush the solid solute.

How does heat and pressure affect the solution of gases in liquids?

Although heat usually increases the amount of solid that can dissolve in a liquid, the opposite is true for gaseous solutions. More gas can be dissolved in a cold liquid than in a hot one. The amount of gas that dissolves can also be increased by increasing the pressure on the solution.

Does stirring speed or slow the rate at which a gas dissolves in a liquid? Carbon dioxide gas is dissolved in many kinds of beverages. Have you ever stirred a glass of soda pop? Does the gas stay in solution? Before the bottle of soda pop is opened, the gas inside is under pressure. What happens when the cap is removed from a warm bottle of soda pop that has been shaken? Gas rushes out of the bottle and usually takes some of the liquid along with it. *Detailed information concerning this Activity can be found in the Teacher's Guide at the front of this book.*

11-3

ACTIVITY *How does size affect the rate of solution?*

(1) *Find the mass of a large crystal of copper(II) sulfate using a balance.* **(2)** *Use a balance to measure an equal mass of small copper(II) sulfate crystals.* **(3)** *Place each sample into separate 250-mL flasks filled with water.* **(4)** *Stopper both flasks and allow to stand for one week. Check the flasks several times during the week and record your results.*

Hickson-Bender Photography

FIGURE 11-7. As a bottle of soda is opened, the pressure is reduced and the gas comes out of solution.

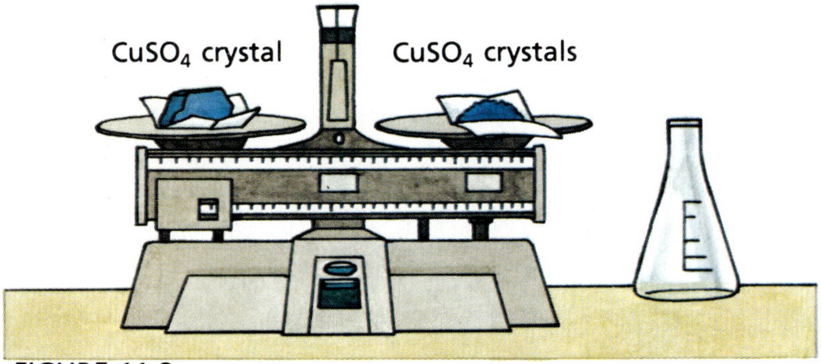

FIGURE 11-8.

Making Sure

1. You are given two 1-gram samples of copper(II) sulfate. One sample contains tiny crystals. The other contains large crystals. Which will dissolve faster? Explain. *tiny crystals; more solute surface area*
2. What causes soda pop to get "flat" after standing at room temperature? *CO_2 gas comes out of solution at a higher temperature*
3. Why is hot water sometimes used to wash soiled clothing? *grease dissolves better in hot water*

11:4 Solvents

Why is water called a "universal solvent?"

There is no known solvent that will dissolve everything. Water is closest to being a "universal solvent." A universal solvent is something that will dissolve everything. Water can dissolve many gases, liquids, and solids. However, water will not dissolve a number of substances. Oil, varnish, and iodine are three materials that do not dissolve in water.

Water dissolves both organic and inorganic substances. An inorganic substance usually does not contain carbon. For example, salt is an inorganic compound that dissolves in water. Water will dissolve soap, an organic compound. However, most organic substances such as fat and oil will dissolve in organic solvents. Acetone (AS uh tohn) used as a nail polish remover is an organic solvent. Other organic solvents are used in dry cleaning of garments that could be damaged by water.

How are solvents used to remove stains?

A knowledge of solvents can be useful when removing stains from clothing. Some stains will dissolve in water while others will not. Use of hot water may cause the stain to "set" and make it more difficult to remove. Heat can cause some stains to enter the threads of fabric. A solvent that will remove chewing gum may also dissolve a fabric. Therefore, it is important to read the label on a cleaner to make sure it is right for both the stain and the fabric. Generally, a solvent will dissolve a solute which is chemically like the solvent.

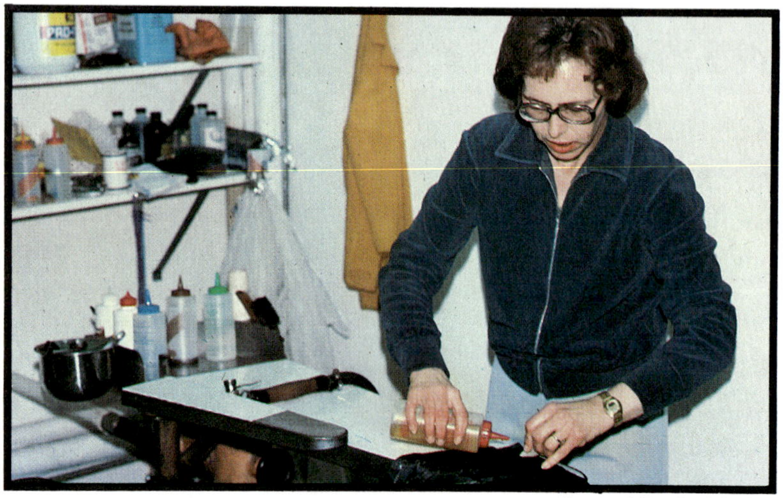

FIGURE 11-9. A dry cleaner knows the types of solvents that will dissolve and remove various stains.

Tom Stack/Tom Stack & Assoc.

11-4 *Detailed information concerning this Activity can be found in the Teacher's Guide at the front of this book.*

ACTIVITY Does vegetable oil dissolve?

Obtain four test tubes. Place 10 mL of water in 3 test tubes and 10 mL of naphtha (lighter fluid) in the fourth test tube. To one of the test tubes containing the water, add a piece of soap and 5 drops of vegetable oil. Shake. Now add 5 drops of liquid detergent to the second test tube containing the water. Add 5 drops of oil and shake again. Now add 5 drops of oil to the last test tube containing the water and the test tube containing the naphtha. Shake and record your results.

Does the oil dissolve in any of the solvents? Explain your observations for each test tube.

The oil partially dissolves in soap and detergent. It dissolves completely in naphtha, but does not dissolve at all in water.

Making Sure

4. Is water an organic or inorganic compound? *inorganic*
5. You can clean spilled latex paint with water. Does latex paint dissolve in water? *yes*
6. Do you think latex paint would dissolve better in soapy water? *yes*
7. What kinds of paints do not dissolve in water? What kinds of solvents are used to clean these spills?

Oil base paints require turpentine or some other organic solvent to dissolve them.

11:5 Particles in a Solution

What kinds of particles are in solution when a ionic solid dissolves?

Depending on the solute, a solution can contain molecules or ions. For example, sugar is made of sugar molecules. When sugar dissolves in water, the molecules separate and form a solution.

A water solution of table salt contains sodium and chloride ions. Recall that an ion is a charged atom or group of atoms. A sodium ion has a 1+ charge. A chloride ion has a 1− charge. The solution contains the same number of sodium and chloride ions. Therefore, it is neutral. It does not have a charge.

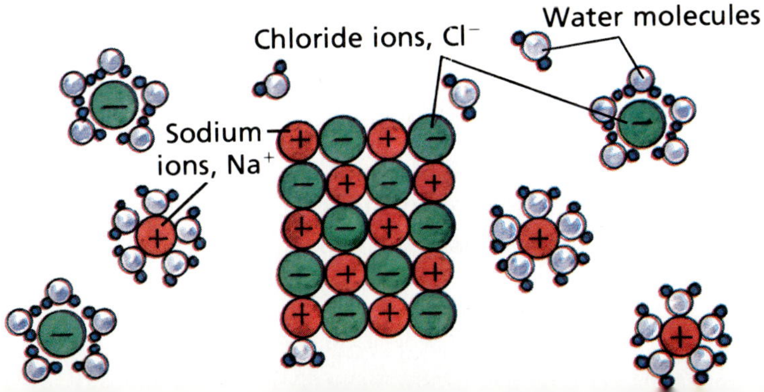

FIGURE 11-10. As sodium chloride dissolves, the positive end of the water molecule attaches to the negative chloride ions. The negative oxygen end pulls the positive sodium ions from the crystal.

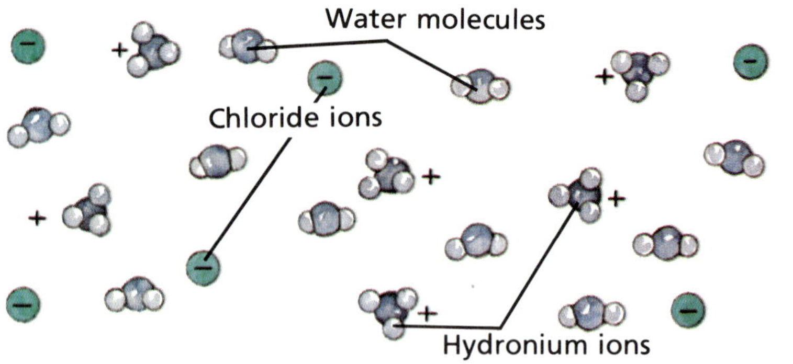

FIGURE 11-11. When an acid solution is formed, the positive hydrogen ion from the acid attaches to a water molecule.

a

b

Tom Stack/Tom Stack & Assoc.

FIGURE 11-12. A sodium chloride solution (a) contains ions. These ions complete the circuit and the bulb lights. A molecular substance like sugar (b) does not contain ions.

When hydrogen chloride gas, HCl, dissolves in water it forms ions. The hydrogen chloride molecule separates. Both hydrogen and chloride ions are formed. The hydrogen ions combine with water molecules to form hydronium ions, Figure 11-11. You will study more about hydronium ions in Chapter 13.

11:6 Solutions as Conductors

Electric current in a wire is a flow of electrons. In a solution, an electric current is a movement of ions. For an electric current to pass through a solution, ions must be present in the solution. A conductor allows electricity to pass through. The wire and solution of ions are conductors of electricity.

Putting wet hands on anything that uses electricity is dangerous. A person can receive a severe shock or even be killed. Tap water can be a good conductor of electricity. It contains many ions in the form of minerals and salts that make it a good conductor. Any solution which contains ions will conduct an electric current.

Sugar in distilled water does not release ions. A sugar solution contains molecules. The solution does not conduct electricity. An alcohol-distilled water solution does not conduct a current. Alcohol, like sugar, does not form ions when mixed with distilled water.

Making Sure

8. Will distilled water conduct a current? Why or why not? *No, it does not contain ions.*
9. What precautions should you take before using a hair dryer after a bath? *Make certain you are dry and not standing in any water that could conduct electric current.*

11:7 Solubility

Solubility (sahl yuh BIHL uht ee) is the amount of solute that can be dissolved in a specific amount of solvent. When table salt is added to water, the salt dissolves to form a saltwater solution. In contrast, iodine crystals do not dissolve readily in water. When iodine crystals are added to ethanol, they dissolve. However, only a tiny amount of table salt dissolves in ethanol.

It is said that iodine is insoluble in water. **Insoluble** means a substance does not appear to dissolve. Table salt is soluble in water and insoluble in ethanol. In what substance is iodine soluble?

A few solubility rules have been determined which can be used to predict whether an inorganic compound will dissolve. These rules are based upon observations that have been made during laboratory experiments.

Tom Stack/Tom Stack & Assoc.

FIGURE 11-13. Iodine is insoluble in water (a) but dissolves in alcohol (b).

Table 11-1

Solubility of Common Compounds in Water
Common compounds which contain the following ions are soluble:
(a) sodium (Na^+), potassium (K^+), ammonium (NH_4^+)
(b) nitrates (NO_3^-)
(c) acetates ($C_2H_3O_2^-$), except silver acetate, which is only moderately soluble
(d) chlorides (Cl^-), except silver, mercury(I), and lead chlorides. $PbCl_2$ is soluble in hot water
(e) sulfates (SO_4^{2-}), except barium and lead sulfates. Calcium, mercury(I), and silver sulfates are slightly soluble
Common compounds which contain the following ions are insoluble:
(a) silver, (Ag^+), except silver nitrate and silver perchlorate
(b) sulfides (S^{2-}), except those of sodium, potassium, ammonium, magnesium, barium, and calcium
(c) carbonates (CO_3^{2-}), except those of sodium, potassium, and ammonium
(d) phosphates (PO_4^{3-}), except those of sodium, potassium, and ammonium
(e) hydroxides (OH^-), except those of sodium, potassium, ammonium, and barium

The solubility of most solids can be increased by raising the temperature of the solution. Sugar is more soluble in hot water. The reverse is true for gases. The solubility of a gas decreases as the temperature rises.

How can the solubility of a solid be increased?

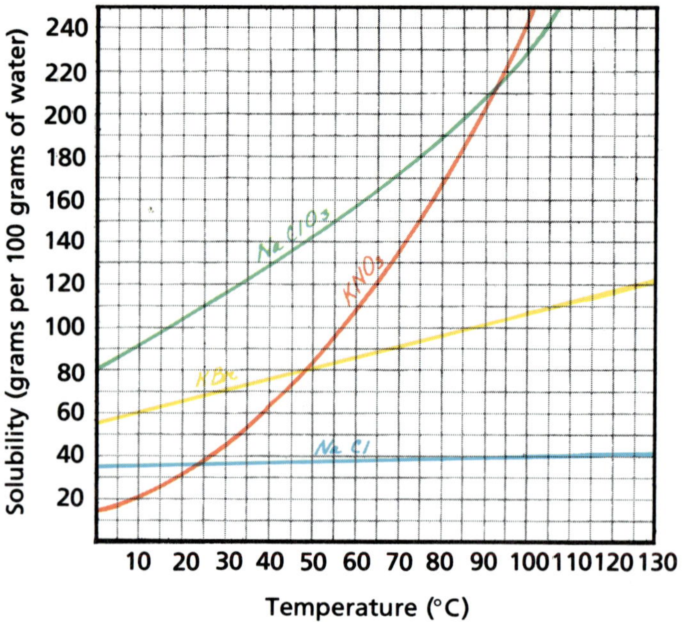

FIGURE 11-14. Solubility graph

Temperature does not affect the solubility of all compounds by the same amount. For example, at 60° C about 110 grams of potassium nitrate, KNO_3, dissolve in 100 milliliters of water. Less than 40 grams of sodium chloride, NaCl, dissolve in the same amount of water at the same temperature.

At room temperature, 100 milliliters of water will hold about 40 grams of KNO_3. If any more KNO_3 is added to the solution, it falls to the bottom of the container undissolved. The solution is said to be saturated. **Saturated** means all the solute the solution can hold is dissolved. However, if the solution is heated to 60° C, the same amount of water can hold nearly three times as much KNO_3, Figure 11-14. At 60° C the solution is unsaturated. **Unsaturated** means that more solute can be dissolved in the solution at that temperature.

If the same solution is cooled slowly to 10° C so that no crystals form, this solution is **supersaturated.** It contains more solute than is expected at that temperature. According to Figure 11-14, at 10° C, only 25 grams of KNO_3 will dissolve in 100 milliliters of water. The supersaturated solution contains 40 grams of KNO_3.

11-5 Detailed information concerning this Activity can be found in the Teacher's Guide at the front of this book.

Activity *How do you find the solubility of a salt?*

Setting Up

balance, *250-mL beaker*, *metal ring, ring stand*, *Bunsen burner*, *evaporating dish*, *filter paper, funnel*, *stirring rod*, *table salt*

Getting Started

1. *Place 20 mL of water in the beaker.*
2. *Add table salt slowly with constant stirring until only a very small amount lies on the bottom of the beaker.*
3. *Set up a filtration system, Figure 11-15a. (Refer to the appendix for additional instruction on how to set up this system.) Filter the salt solution.*
4. *Using the balance, determine the mass of an evaporating dish. Record.*
5. *Place the filtrate in the evaporating dish.*
6. *Use the balance to determine the mass of the dish and salt solution. Record.*
7. *Heat the dish and solution until all the liquid has evaporated, Figure 11-15b.*
8. *After the dish and contents have cooled, find the mass again. Record.*

FIGURE 11-15.

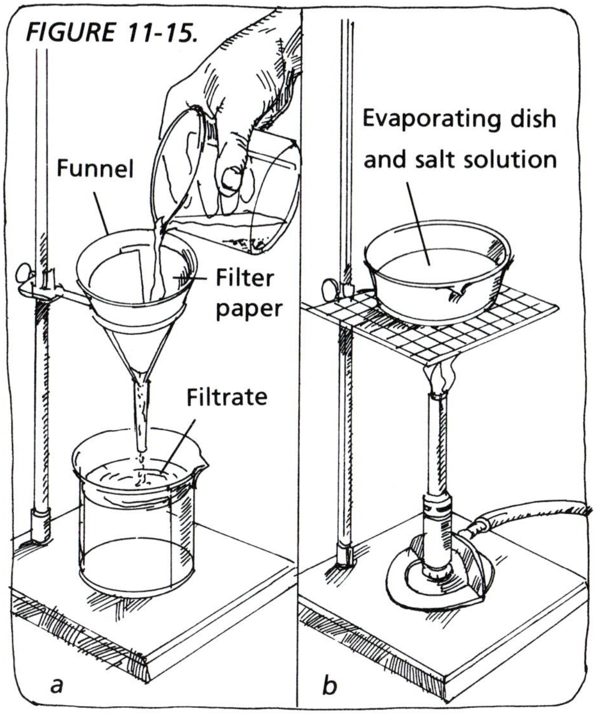

Keeping Track

mass of dish and solution	
mass of dish	
mass of dish and residue	

Summing Up

1. *What is the mass of the salt solution?*
2. *What is the mass of the salt that dissolved in 20 mL of water? How did you get this value?* Subtract the mass of dish from the mass of the dish plus the residue.
3. *How could you increase the solubility of salt in 20 mL of water?* heat the water

Making Sure

10. Using Figure 11-14, what is the solubility of each of the following compounds at the specified temperature? See the Teacher's Guide.

a. KBr at 50°C
b. $NaClO_3$ at 70°C
c. KBr at 100°C
d. NaCl at 100°C

11:8 Concentration

How is a concentrated solution different from a dilute solution?

To some people, a glass of lemonade may be too sour. To others, the same lemonade may not be sour enough. To describe a solution such as lemonade, people often use the terms "dilute" or "concentrated." Concentrated generally means there is a lot of solute dissolved. Dilute is just the opposite. It means there is little solute dissolved.

The concentration of a solution can be determined and expressed in many ways. For example, the concentration of a solution is often expressed as a percent. A glass of orange drink which is ten percent fruit juice, contains 10 milliliters of fruit juice for every 100 milliliters of orange drink.

One liter of a five percent sugar solution contains 50 grams of sugar per liter of water. Since the sugar is spread evenly in the solution, there are 25 grams of sugar in 500 milliliters of the solution. If you need 5 grams of sugar, you pour out 100 milliliters of the solution and evaporate the water.

What is the specific gravity of a solution?

The concentration of some solutions can be determined by testing the specific gravity of the solution. The specific gravity of a solution is the ratio of its density to the density of water. Since the density of water is 1 g/cm^3, the specific gravity of a substance is numerically the same as its density. If the density of a liquid is 2.5 g/cm^3, its specific gravity is 2.5.

Hickson-Bender Photography

FIGURE 11-16. A hydrometer is used to test the specific gravity of battery acid.

11-6 Detailed information concerning this Activity can be found in the Teacher's Guide at the front of this book.

Activity

How does the specific gravity of a solution affect the soda straw hydrometer?

Setting Up

beaker | *lead shot* | *tape*
graduated cylinder | *soda straw*

Getting Started

1. *Obtain a soda straw. Squeeze one end shut and tape it closed.*
2. *Hold the straw, taped-end down, in a graduated cylinder which is ¾ full of water. Add a few pellets of lead shot until the straw sinks down about 4 centimeters in the water. Mark the water level with a pen, Figure 11-17.*
3. *Now place the straw in a graduate that is ¾ full of alcohol. How does the level of the alcohol compare with that which you marked for the water?* It floats lower.
4. *Dissolve as much salt as possible in 35 mL of water.*
5. *Pour the salt solution into a graduated cylinder. Float the soda straw hydrometer in the salt solution.*

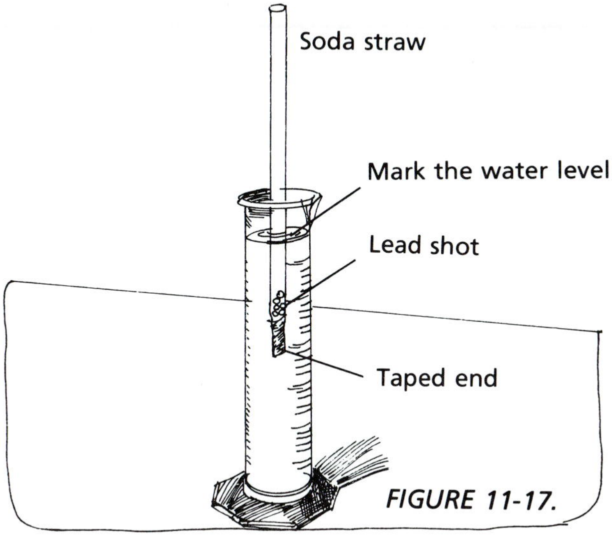

FIGURE 11-17.

Summing Up

1. *Does the soda straw float lower or higher in salt water?* higher
2. *Is salt water more or less dense than fresh water?* more dense
3. *Would your body float lower or higher in salt water compared to fresh water?* higher

11:9 Using Solutions

How can you change the freezing and boiling points of water?

A radiator in a car usually contains antifreeze mixed with water. Antifreeze prevents water in the cooling system from freezing. Many cooking recipes tell you to add salt to water. The salt makes the boiling water hotter.

When you dissolve a solute in a liquid, the liquid's boiling point is raised. The amount the boiling point is increased depends on how much solute is added. The more solute added, the higher the boiling point. The type of particle in the solution is unimportant, the number of solute particles in the solution is very important. As the number of dissolved particles in the solution increases, more heat is needed to cause the solvent to evaporate. Thus, the boiling point is raised.

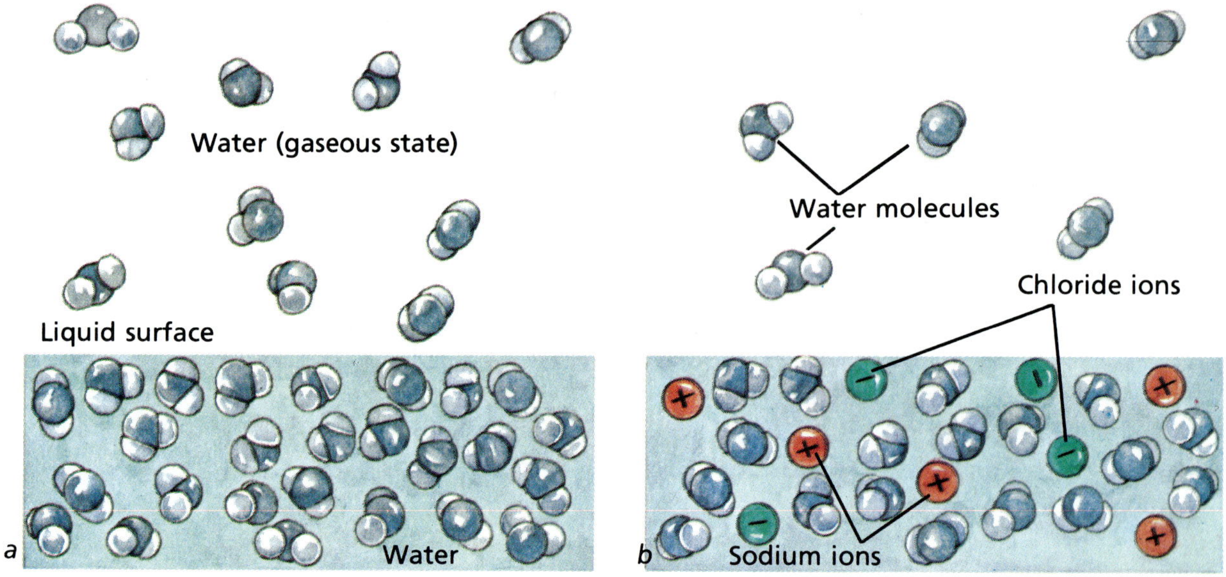

FIGURE 11-18. A molecular view of the boiling process is shown by a model (a). The addition of salt (b) can be thought of as adding small magnets which prevent the water molecules from leaving the liquid surface. Thus, a higher temperature is required to boil the water.

An increase in the number of particles in solution also affects crystal formation. The solute particles interfere with crystal formation. More heat energy must be removed in order to get the solution to crystallize. Thus, the freezing point of the solution is lowered.

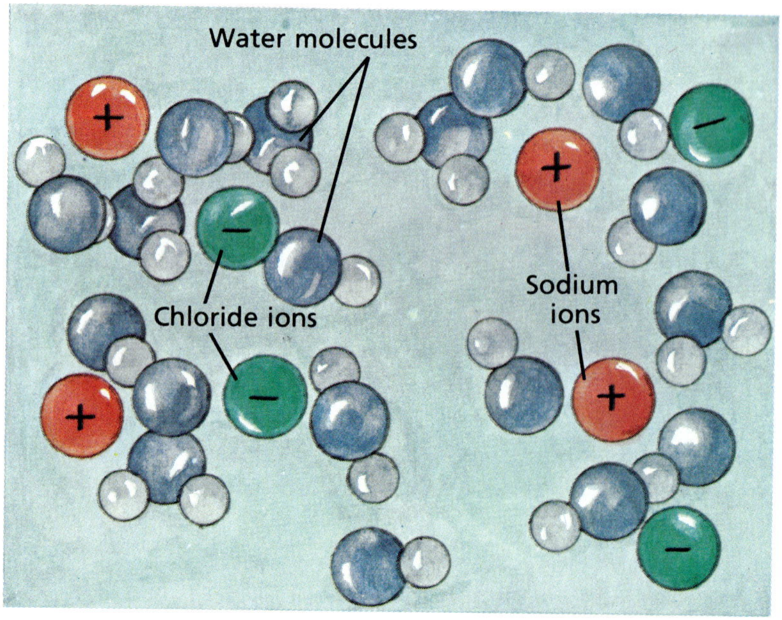

FIGURE 11-19. The addition of salt keeps water from freezing at the freezing point. The salt interferes with the formation of ice crystals. A lower temperature is required to get the ice to freeze completely.

11-7 Detailed information concerning this Activity can be found in the Teacher's Guide at the front of this book.

ACTIVITY *Can you measure the change in freezing point and boiling point for a solution?*

(1) *Fill a beaker half-full with water. Heat the water to boiling using a burner or hot plate.* **(2)** *Using a thermometer, record the boiling point of the water.* **(3)** *Cool the water slightly, then add 10 grams of salt and stir.* **(4)** *Reheat the solution until it boils, then record the temperature.*

(5) *Now fill a beaker half-full of ice and add a small amount of water.* **(6)** *Use the thermometer to record the temperature of the mixture after stirring for one minute.* **(7)** *Add 25 grams of salt to the ice water. Stir. Once again record the temperature of the mixture.*

How much did the salt change the boiling point of the water? How much did it change the freezing point?

Making Sure

11. Why is salt spread on ice-covered sidewalks? — *It lowers the freezing point of water so the snow melts.*

12. Why is salt mixed with ice in making homemade ice cream? *It lowers the temperature of the ice-water mixture.*

13. Make a list of some of the foods you have at home that use salt in the cooking process. *Macaroni, frozen vegetables, boiling potatoes, and spaghetti are some examples.*

14. Why does one check the specific gravity of the radiator fluid during cold weather? — *To make certain the concentration of antifreeze is high enough to protect against freezing.*

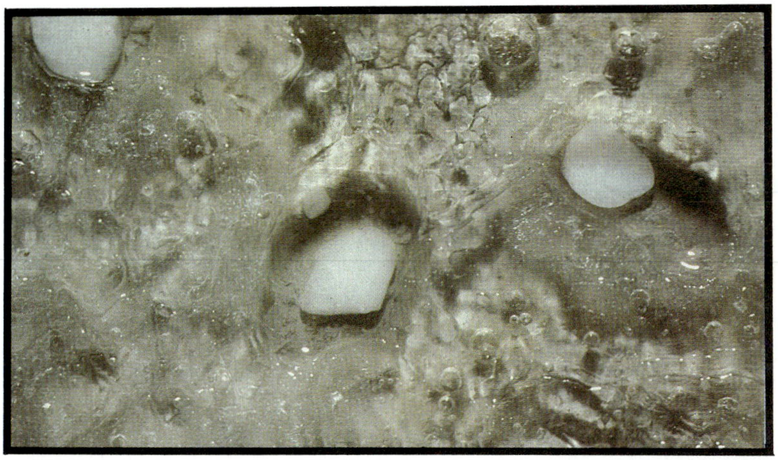

Hickson-Bender Photography

FIGURE 11-20. Salts are used to melt snow and ice. They lower the freezing point of water.

Focus on

Skills

Organizing New Terms Using a Chapter Outline

The vocabulary in this chapter centers around the definitions of three basic terms: **solution, solute,** and **solvent.** These terms are defined in the first paragraph of the chapter. These definitions are expanded as the chapter progresses. The following outline shows how you can organize the vocabulary in this chapter. Try to follow the process used in Parts I and II. See if you can complete Part III yourself.

I Solution
- A. Definition: a mixture in which one substance is dissolved in another substance
- B. Types:
  1. liquid: formed by dissolving solids, liquids, or gases in a liquid
  2. gaseous: formed by mixing gases
  3. solid: formed by dissolving solids, liquids, or gases in a solid
- C. Process by which they are made: solvent particles pulling away each layer of molecules or particles until all are dissolved
- D. Properties:
  1. solutions of ionic substances conduct an electric current
  2. raise the boiling point and lower the freezing point of the solvent
  3. affects crystal formation

II Solvent
- A. Definition: substance in which the solute is dissolved
- B. Properties of water as a solvent:
  1. can dissolve many gases, liquids, and solids
  2. will not dissolve most organic solvents such as oil, varnish, and molecules such as iodine
- C. Uses:
  1. removing stains
  2. dissolving a solute which is chemically like the solvent, such as in cleaning paintbrushes with turpentine

III Solute
- A. Definition: substance being dissolved

See the Teacher's Guide.

Points to Remember

1. Solutions are mixtures consisting of a solute dissolved in a solvent. 11:1
2. Energy may be absorbed or released in making a solution. 11:2
3. Heating, crushing the solute, or stirring increases the rate of solution for a solid solute. 11:3
4. The solubility of a gas in a liquid can be increased by decreasing the temperature or increasing the pressure. 11:3
5. Organic solvents usually dissolve organic solutes. Inorganic solvents usually will dissolve inorganic solutes. 11:4
6. Solutions containing ions will conduct an electric current. 11:6
7. The concentration of a solution can be expressed by percent, specific gravity, or saturation level. 11:7 11:8
8. Dissolving a solid in a liquid increases the liquid's boiling point and lowers its freezing point. 11:9

Words to Use

Write a sentence in which you correctly use each of the following words or terms.

concentration	solubility	solvent
hydrated crystal	solute	supersaturated
insoluble	solution	unsaturated
saturated		

Questions for Review

Do not write in this book.

A. True or False *Have the students rewrite the false statements to make them correct.*

Determine whether each of the following sentences is true or false.

F **1.** To form a solution, a ~~solvent~~ must be dissolved by a ~~solute~~. *solute* *solvent*

T **2.** Oil will not dissolve in water.

F **3.** A ~~solid~~ solution can be formed by dissolving a gas in another gas. *gaseous*

F **4.** Water is a solvent that will dissolve everything. *almost*

T **5.** Ethanol and water can form a solution.

F **6.** Organic solvents usually dissolve ~~inorganic~~ solutes. organic

T **7.** Stirring increases the rate of solution.

T **8.** Ions conduct electricity in a solution.

T **9.** The addition of solute raises the boiling point of a pure liquid.

F **10.** A substance which will not dissolve is ~~soluble~~. insoluble

B. Multiple Choice

Choose the word or phrase that correctly completes each of the following sentences.

1. Water will not dissolve *(copper sulfate, lighter fluid, alcohol).*
2. Most *(nitrate, silver, sulfate)* compounds are insoluble in water.
3. Dry cleaning solvents are usually *(inorganic, organic).*
4. A solution conducts electricity through its *(electrons, ions, atoms).*
5. If you could dissolve 5 kilograms of salt in a liter of water, the solution would probably be *(saturated, unsaturated, supersaturated).*
6. *(Ag_2S, Sugar, $NaNO_3$)* would produce the most ions when added to water.
7. Adding solute to a solution causes the freezing point to *(decrease, remain the same, increase).*
8. Organic solids will generally dissolve in *(water, ammonia, naphtha).*
9. One gram of salt in ten liters of water would make a *(dilute, concentrated, supersaturated)* solution.
10. A solution which will accept more solute is *(saturated, unsaturated, supersaturated).*

C. Completion

Complete each of the following sentences with a word or phrase that will make the sentence correct.

1. Water is the most common solvent.
2. When ionic compounds dissolve in water, the particles separate into ions.

3. <u>Sugar</u> does not form ions when it dissolves.
4. Organic solvents generally dissolve <u>organic</u> solutes.
5. Acetone is a liquid <u>organic</u> solvent.
6. Adding <u>water</u> to orange juice makes the solution more dilute.
7. Adding alcohol to water <u>lowers</u> the freezing point.
8. A straw hydrometer can be used to determine <u>specific gravity</u>.
9. Adding a solute to a liquid will <u>lower</u> the freezing point of the liquid.
10. <u>Energy</u> is needed to break bonds to dissolve an ionic substance.

D. How and Why

1. Using Table 11-1, which of the following compounds is soluble in water?

   a. sodium nitrate
   b. silver phosphate
   c. barium chloride
   d. ammonium chloride
   e. aluminum hydroxide
   f. magnesium carbonate

Readings to Discover

Asimov, Isaac, "Are Oceans Getting Too Salty?" *Science Digest,* Vol. 72, April 1972, pp. 73-74.

Berger, Melvin, *Consumer Protection Labs.* NY: John Day Co., Inc., 1975.

Kleintob, J., "Water Recycler Purifies Entire Household Supply." *Popular Science,* Vol. 212, June 1978, p. 162.

To stay healthy, you should take in food everyday. Food provides the fuel to keep your body going. You can think of yourself as a large scale chemical factory. Thousands of reactions are occurring each second. What is a chemical reaction? How do you get energy from chemical reactions?

Hickson-Bender Photography

Chemical Reactions

12

Chapter 12 presents the guidelines for writing chemical equations. The four common types of chemical reactions are introduced followed by a discussion of conservation of mass. The role of energy in chemical reactions is presented in the closing discussion of the effects of catalysts. See the Teacher's Guide at the front of this book for additional teaching strategies for this chapter.

12:1 Equations for Reactions

GOAL: *You will learn the types of chemical reactions, how to write a chemical equation, and how reactions take place.*

A **chemical equation** is used to show the changes that take place during a chemical change. A chemical equation is made of symbols and formulas. Recall that a symbol stands for an element and formula shows the elements in a compound. Here is the chemical equation for the reaction between carbon and oxygen to form carbon dioxide.

What is a chemical equation?

$$C + O_2 \longrightarrow CO_2$$

Using word equations, you can describe the chemical change between silver nitrate and table salt.

silver nitrate plus sodium chloride yields
silver chloride plus sodium nitrate

However, it is faster to write

$$AgNO_3 + NaCl \longrightarrow AgCl + NaNO_3$$

Symbols in a formula equation describe how atoms are rearranged in a chemical reaction. The arrow which points to the right ($\rightarrow$) means "yield" or "produces."

How is an equation balanced?

Substances to the left of the → are called **reactants.** Substances to the right of the → are called **products.**

$$AgNO_3 + NaCl \longrightarrow AgCl + NaNO_3$$

reactants products

Equations are balanced to show that atoms are not lost or created during a reaction. A chemical equation shows the same number of each kind of atom to the left and right of the arrow (yields sign). Numbers are used in front of the symbols and formulas. These numbers, called **coefficients,** keep the numbers of atoms in balance. To balance a chemical equation, you change coefficients. *Never change a formula.* When you change a formula, you change the substance and the equation for the reaction is no longer correct.

Example

Chlorine gas contains molecules of chlorine, formula Cl_2. When chlorine combines with sodium, the compound formed is sodium chloride. Write the balanced equation for this reaction.

Solution:

Word equation

sodium plus chlorine yields sodium chloride

Formula equation

$$Na + Cl_2 \longrightarrow NaCl$$

Balanced formula equation

$$2Na + Cl_2 \longrightarrow 2NaCl$$

The 2 in front of Na in the balanced equation shows 2 atoms of sodium. The 2 in front of NaCl shows two formula units of NaCl. Note there is the same number of sodium and chlorine atoms on both sides of the arrow.

To write a chemical equation follow these steps:

1. *Write a word equation.*

Example: carbon plus oxygen yields carbon dioxide

Example: magnesium plus oxygen yields magnesium oxide

2. *Write symbols and formulas for the substances in the reaction.* Put the reactants on the left. Put the

products of the reaction on the right. (Use plus signs and an arrow to complete the outline.)

Example: $C + O_2 \longrightarrow CO_2$

Example: $Mg + O_2 \longrightarrow MgO$

3. ***Check the number and kinds of atoms on each side to see whether the equation is balanced.***

Example: $C + O_2 \longrightarrow CO_2$
one C atom and two O atoms on each side OK

Example: $Mg + O_2 \longrightarrow MgO$
two O atoms on the left, one on the right NO

4. ***If the atoms are not in balance, use coefficients to balance the equation.***

Example: $Mg + O_2 \longrightarrow 2MgO$
There are now two O atoms on each side. Mg is not balanced, two Mg atoms are needed on the right.

$$2Mg + O_2 \longrightarrow 2MgO \qquad \text{OK}$$

One other piece of information that a chemical equation should give is the state of the substances in the reaction. For example, in the carbon dioxide reaction,

$$C + O_2 \longrightarrow CO_2$$

carbon is a solid, oxygen is a gas, and carbon dioxide is a gas. This reaction could be written

$$C(c) + O_2(g) \longrightarrow CO_2(g)$$

The symbol (g) means gas and (c) means solid or crystal.

Many substances do not react unless they are dissolved in water. For example, in the silver nitrate and sodium chloride reaction

$$AgNO_3 + NaCl \longrightarrow AgCl + NaNO_3$$

the products would not form unless the reactants are present in a solution. This reaction should be written

$$AgNO_3(aq) + NaCl(aq) \longrightarrow AgCl(c) + NaNO_3(aq)$$

The symbol (aq), aqueous, means a compound dissolved in water. The symbol (l) would be used to show a liquid substance such as bromine, mercury, or water.

$4Fe(c) + 3O_2(g) \rightarrow 2Fe_2O_3(c)$

Making Sure

1. Iron rusts in oxygen to form iron(III) oxide. The formula for this compound is Fe_2O_3. Write a balanced chemical equation for the reaction.

$2Ca(c) + O_2(g) \rightarrow 2CaO(c)$

$S(c) + O_2(g) \rightarrow SO_2(g)$

2. Complete and balance the following.
   a. $Ca(c) + ? \longrightarrow CaO(c)$
   b. $? + O_2(g) \longrightarrow SO_2(g)$

12:2 Synthesis Reactions

Many chemical reactions can be classified as one of four types. When you think of chemical reactions, you might first think of a synthesis process. A **synthesis reaction** occurs when two or more elements or compounds unite to form one compound. The formation of carbon dioxide from the elements carbon and oxygen is a synthesis reaction.

$$C(c) + O_2(g) \longrightarrow CO_2(g)$$

What are two examples of synthesis reactions?

The formation of table salt and the rusting of iron are both synthesis reactions.

$$2Na(c) + Cl_2(g) \longrightarrow 2NaCl(c)$$
$$4Fe(c) + 3O_2(g) \longrightarrow 2Fe_2O_3(c)$$

J. R. Schnelzer

FIGURE 12-1. Rust occurs as the result of a chemical reaction between iron and oxygen.

Making Sure

$2H_2(g) + O_2(g) \rightarrow 2H_2O(l)$

3. Water can be formed in a synthesis reaction between hydrogen and oxygen gases. Write a balanced equation for the synthesis of water.

4. Magnesium oxide, MgO, is formed when a flashbulb flashes. Write a balanced equation for the synthesis of MgO from magnesium and oxygen gas.

$2Mg(c) + O_2(g) \rightarrow 2MgO(c)$

12:3 Decomposition Reactions

Hydrogen peroxide is an unstable compound. Upon standing for a period of time, it decomposes to form water and oxygen. A **decomposition reaction** is the breakdown of one substance into two or more other substances. The oxygen released is a diatomic molecule, O_2. The equation for the decomposition of hydrogen peroxide is

What happens in a decomposition reaction?

$$H_2O_2(l) \longrightarrow H_2O(l) + O_2(g)$$

Oxygen can also be prepared by heating a compound called potassium chlorate. This compound decomposes to form two compounds, potassium chloride and oxygen.

$$KClO_3(c) \longrightarrow KCl(c) + O_2(g)$$

Recall from Chapter 8 that some metallic elements are obtained in pure form from electrolysis reactions. Electrolysis is used to decompose salts to obtain pure elements. Barium is obtained by the decomposition of barium chloride.

$$BaCl_2(c) \longrightarrow Ba(c) + Cl_2(g)$$

Hydrogen and oxygen can be obtained by the decomposition of water.

$$2H_2O(l) \longrightarrow 2H_2(g) + O_2(g)$$

Camilla Smith from Rainbow

FIGURE 12-2. Baked goods rise as the result of a chemical reaction producing carbon dioxide gas.

12-1 *Detailed information concerning this Activity can be found in the Teacher's Guide at the front of this book.*

ACTIVITY *How do you test to see if oxygen is formed in a decomposition reaction?*

Place 5 mL of hydrogen peroxide in a test tube (use a fresh bottle). Drop a pinch of manganese dioxide, MnO_2, into the mouth of the test tube. Insert a glowing wooden splint into the mouth of the test tube.

What happens to the splint? What else do you observe that indicates a gas is produced?

Note: The MnO_2 increases the rate at which hydrogen peroxide decomposes. It is not changed by the reaction, Section 12:7.

FIGURE 12-3.

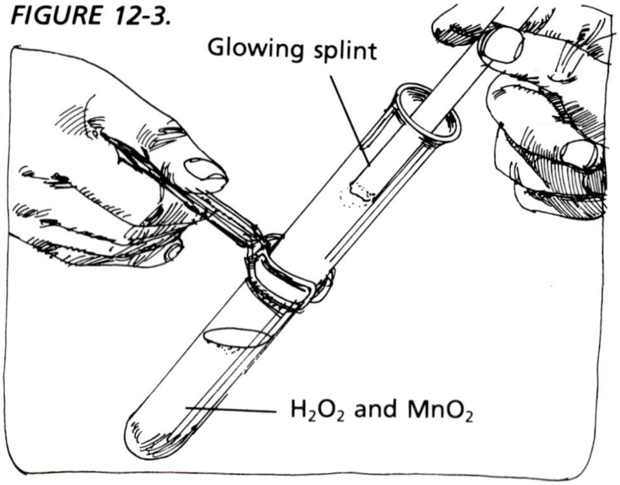

Making Sure

5. Write and balance the equation for the formation of magnesium from the electrolysis of magnesium chloride. *See the Teacher's Guide.*
6. Write and balance the equation for the formation of chlorine from the electrolysis of sodium chloride. *See the Teacher's Guide.*

12:4 Displacement Reactions

What happens when a copper wire is placed in silver nitrate?

There are two types of displacement reactions. In one type, one element may replace another element in a compound. For example, if a copper wire is placed in a solution of silver nitrate, silver metal forms on the wire. The copper displaces the silver in silver nitrate and sets the silver free. Copper(II) nitrate is also formed in the reaction.

$$Cu(c) + 2AgNO_3(aq) \longrightarrow 2Ag(c) + Cu(NO_3)_2(aq)$$

This reaction is called a **single displacement reaction.**

The element beryllium can be obtained in pure form through a single displacement reaction involving beryllium fluoride and magnesium.

$$BeF_2(c) + Mg(c) \longrightarrow MgF_2(c) + Be(c)$$

Sometimes it is difficult to determine whether one substance can displace another. Fortunately, experiments show which substances will actually displace others.

The reaction between silver nitrate and sodium chloride is called a **double displacement reaction.**

$$AgNO_3(aq) + NaCl(aq) \longrightarrow AgCl(c) + NaNO_3(aq)$$

When water solutions of these two substances are mixed a white precipitate is formed. A **precipitate** is an insoluble substance. In this case the precipitate is silver chloride. In the reaction silver and sodium atoms replace each other. The sodium nitrate formed in the reaction is soluble in water. If the silver chloride were removed by filtration and the filtrate evaporated, the residue would be sodium nitrate.

Hickson-Bender Photography

FIGURE 12-4. Silver chloride is a precipitate formed in a double displacement reaction.

Example

Sodium hydroxide, NaOH, and iron(III) chloride, $FeCl_3$, react to form sodium chloride, NaCl, and iron(III) hydroxide, $Fe(OH)_3$. The NaOH, $FeCl_3$, and NaCl are present as aqueous solutions. $Fe(OH)_3$ is a precipitate. Write a balanced equation for this reaction.

Solution:

(a) Write the formulas for the reactants and products.

$$NaOH(aq) + FeCl_3(aq) \longrightarrow NaCl(aq) + Fe(OH)_3(c)$$

(b) Check to see if the atoms on both sides of the arrow are in balance. Chloride ions and hydroxide ions do not balance. Three chlorine atoms are needed on the right, place a 3 in front of NaCl.

$$NaOH(aq) + FeCl_3(aq) \longrightarrow 3NaCl(aq) + Fe(OH)_3(c)$$

Now three sodium atoms are on the right. To have three sodium atoms on the left, place a 3 in front of NaOH.

$$3NaOH(aq) + FeCl_3(aq) \longrightarrow 3NaCl(aq) + Fe(OH)_3(c)$$

Tom Stack/Tom Stack & Assoc.

FIGURE 12-5. Iron(III) hydroxide is formed in a double displacement reaction.

Three hydroxide ions are needed on the right. The formula already has three. The iron atoms are equal. The equation is balanced.

12-2 Detailed information concerning this Activity can be found in the Teacher's Guide at the front of this book.

ACTIVITY *Does zinc displace copper?*

Dissolve three grams of powdered copper(II) sulfate in 20 mL of water in a beaker. Place a strip of zinc metal in the water. Wait at least ten minutes for a reaction to occur.

What substance forms on the zinc? Write the equation for the reaction.

Making Sure

7. Complete and balance the following equations. Use the tables on pages 131 and 133 to find the oxidation numbers of elements and polyatomic ions.

a. NaBr(aq) + $AgNO_3$(aq) → *Ag* Br(c) + *Na* NO_3(aq)

b. $Ca(NO_3)_2$(aq) + K_2SO_4(aq) → Ca *SO_4* (c) + *2* K *NO_3* (aq)

c. *2* KCl(aq) + $Pb(NO_3)_2$(aq) → *2* K *NO_3* (aq) + Pb *Cl_2* (c)

d. *3* $Ca(OH)_2$(aq) + *2* $Fe(NO_3)_3$(aq) → *2* Fe *$(OH)_3$* (c) + *3* Ca *$(NO_3)_2$* (aq)

e. *3* $MgSO_4$(aq) + *2* Na_3PO_4(aq) → *$3Na_2SO_4$(aq)* + *$Mg_3(PO_4)_2$(c)*

f. Hydrogen sulfide plus mercury(II) chloride in water yields *HgS(c)* + *2HCl(aq)*

8. Recall that reactions can be classified as one of four types. Which type of reaction is represented by each equation?

double displacement **a.** 3KOH(aq) + $AlCl_3$(aq) → $Al(OH)_3$(c) + 3KCl(aq)

decomposition **b.** HgO(c) → Hg(l) + O_2(g)

synthesis **c.** SO_3(g) + H_2O(l) → H_2SO_4(l)

single displacement **d.** $CaBr_2$(aq) + Cl_2(g) → $CaCl_2$(aq) + Br_2(l)

9. Write word equations for each formula equation in problem 8. *See the Teacher's Guide.*

12:5 Conservation of Mass

In ordinary chemical changes, no matter is lost. *The mass of all the substances before a reaction equals the mass of all the substances after the reaction.* This statement is called the **law of conservation of mass.** As iron rusts, it combines with oxygen to form red iron(III) oxide. The mass of the oxide is equal to the combined mass of the iron and oxygen. No mass is lost or gained in the reaction. In the same way, mass is conserved when hydrogen and oxygen react to form water. The mass of the water is equal to the total mass of hydrogen and oxygen that combine.

Is mass conserved in a chemical reaction?

Ohio Wesleyan University

FIGURE 12-6. The mass of the reactants on the left side of the balance equals the mass of the products on the right side.

When carbon burns in air to form carbon dioxide, the equation is

$$C(c) + O_2(g) \longrightarrow CO_2(g)$$

Suppose 12 grams of carbon combine with oxygen. How much carbon dioxide is formed? You can predict the amount of carbon dioxide formed from its molecular mass. **Molecular mass** is the sum of the atomic mass numbers for the atoms in a molecule. Atomic masses may be obtained from the periodic table on page 104.

What is the molecular mass of a compound?

Carbon dioxide contains one atom of carbon and two atoms of oxygen. Carbon has a mass of 12 and oxygen has a mass of 16. Thus, the molecular mass of CO_2 is

$$12 + 16 + 16 = 44$$

The equation for the formation of CO_2 shows that one atom of C combines with one molecule of O_2 to yield one molecule of CO_2. The ratio between the atomic mass of C and the molecular mass of CO_2 is

$$C:CO_2 \qquad 12:44$$

The ratio 12:44 indicated the number of grams of reactants and products. Thus, 12 grams of carbon react with oxygen to yield 44 grams of carbon dioxide.

Hydrogen gas burns in oxygen to form water. The equation for the reaction is

$$2H_2(g) + O_2(g) \longrightarrow 2H_2O(l)$$

How much water is formed when 32 grams of oxygen react with hydrogen? The molecular mass of H_2O can be used to predict the answer.

The equation shows that two molecules of H_2 combine with one molecule of O_2 to yield two molecules of H_2O. The molecular mass of O_2 is

$$2 \times 16 = 32$$

The molecular mass of H_2O is 18 (16 + 1 + 1). However, the coefficient 2 in front of water shows that two molecules of water are formed when one molecule of oxygen combines with hydrogen. Therefore, the molecular mass of water (18) is multiplied by 2.

$$2 \times 18 = 36$$

The ratio between the mass of O_2 and the mass of H_2O is

$$O_2:H_2O \qquad 32:36$$

Thus, 36 grams of water are formed from 32 grams of oxygen. How many grams of hydrogen react with 32 grams of oxygen? *4 g H_2*

Define the term formula mass.

In reactions involving ionic compounds, recall that they do not exist as molecules. The mass of the smallest unit of an ionic compound is called the formula. **Formula mass** is the sum of the mass numbers of the atoms present in a formula of an ionic compound. Though they are calculated the same way, molecular mass is a term to be used only for molecular compounds. Formula mass may be used for all compounds. Formula mass is a more general term than molecular mass.

OATMEAL RAISIN ROLLS

2⅓ C wheat flour
1 C rolled oats
1 C wheat bran
¾ C raisins
2 PKGS dried Yeast
½ t salt
2 C water
½ C honey
¼ C butter
2 ¼ C unbleached flour

Stir together 1 c of the wheat flour and all of the oats, bran, raisins, yeast, and salt. In a saucepan warm butter, water, and honey; add to the flour mixture. Mix well. Add remaining flour. Knead 6 to 8 minutes. Shape into a ball. Cover. Let rise till double. Punch down. Shape into 24 rolls. Cover. Let rise till nearly double. Bake at 350° for 25 minutes.

FIGURE 12-7. A cooking recipe shows the proper ratios of ingredients. A balanced chemical equation can be used to show the required amounts of reactants needed to obtain specific amounts of product.

12-3 — *Detailed information concerning this Activity can be found in the Teacher's Guide at the front of this book.*

ACTIVITY *Is mass conserved when a flashbulb reacts?*

Obtain two flashbulbs and place each on opposite pans of a double pan balance. The two pans should be in balance showing the masses of the two flashbulbs to be the same. Put one bulb in a camera flash holder and flash it. Allow the bulb to cool then place it on the balance.

Has the mass of the bulb changed? Does the flashbulb undergo a chemical or physical change when it flashes? How do you know? — *No, the bulb undergoes a chemical change, light and heat are given off.*

Making Sure

10. Using the periodic table on page 104, find the formula mass for each of the following compounds.

a. Na_2SO_4 *142*
b. $CaCO_3$ *100*
c. NH_4NO_3 *80*
d. copper(II) sulfate *160*
e. silver bromide *188*
f. potassium phosphate *212*

11. Thirty-two grams of oxygen combine with carbon to form carbon monoxide gas. The equation for the reaction is

$$2C(c) + O_2(g) \longrightarrow 2CO(g)$$

How many grams of carbon monoxide are formed? *56 grams*

12. How many grams of sodium are formed from the electrolysis of 58 grams of sodium chloride? The equation for the reaction is *23 grams*

$$2NaCl(l) \longrightarrow 2Na(c) + Cl_2(g)$$

12:6 Energy and Reactions

How is an exothermic reaction different from an endothermic reaction?

Energy is either gained or lost during a chemical change. In some reactions, such as burning, energy is released. In other reactions, energy must be added for a chemcial change to occur. If energy is released, the reaction is called **exothermic** (ek soh THUR mihk). If energy must be added during a reaction, the reaction is called **endothermic** (en duh THUR mihk).

The burning of magnesium is an exothermic reaction. Though some heat is needed to start the reaction, the heat given off when magnesium bonds with oxygen is more than enough to keep the reaction going.

Dissolving ammonium nitrate, NH_4NO_3, in water is an endothermic reaction. Energy is absorbed as the NH_4NO_3 dissolves. The temperature of the solution decreases. Energy is absorbed to keep the reaction going. A small amount of energy is given up as the products form. Thus, the reaction is endothermic.

12:7 Catalysts

The time it takes for a reaction to occur can vary greatly. The chemical change that occurs when silver tarnishes may take place over a few months. The formation of silver chloride from silver nitrate and sodium chloride solutions takes place in an instant. In some cases, a reaction may be too slow to be of use.

AC Spark Plug Division of GM Corp.

FIGURE 12-8. The catalytic converter on an automobile contains a metallic catalyst. Carbon monoxide and unburned hydrocarbons in the car's exhaust are quickly converted to carbon dioxide and water.

Shell Development Company

FIGURE 12-9. Some catalysts simply provide a site for a reaction to occur. Catalysts are often porous substances having large surface areas.

Recall the Activity on page 240 involving the decomposition of hydrogen peroxide. Since the decomposition of a dilute solution of hydrogen peroxide is a slow process, manganese dioxide is added. The MnO_2 speeds the reaction so the oxygen is formed faster. However, the MnO_2 is unchanged. In this case, MnO_2 acts as a catalyst. A **catalyst** speeds up a reaction without being permanently changed itself.

What is a catalyst?

Some of the reactions inside your body occur because of catalysts. All enzymes serve as catalysts. The way that many catalysts work in speeding a reaction is not known. Scientists also study substances which can prevent a reaction. These substances are used in foods as preservatives. Preservatives help to slow the spoilage process in foods.

Thomas Russell

FIGURE 12-10. Preservatives in foods slow the growth of organisms which spoil food. Such substances are called inhibitors.

IN FOCUS

Chemical Technology

How are the colors for our clothes made? How do we know if our water is safe to drink? A knowledge of chemistry is important in answering these questions. In fact, we use the results of the science of chemistry everyday.

Using or applying the results of a science on a large scale is called technology. The colors for clothes come from dyes. The dyes are developed in chemical laboratories. The production of dyes is a part of chemical technology. Water is tested in laboratories. The process by which water is purified is also a result of chemical technology.

Imagine a town or city in the 1920's. It is full of life. People are wearing new styles of clothing and the car is still new. The cars are made of steel with natural rubber tires. Windows are plate glass. The new styles of clothing are made of wool, cotton, linen, or even silk. These are natural fibers. They come from plants or animals.

Hickson-Bender Photography

Gary Stallings/Tom Stack & Assoc.

Don Parsisson

Steve Lissau

In the 1980's, many of our clothes are made from synthetic fibers, like nylon. These fibers are made from coal or oil. Our cars have changed since the 1920's, too. We have metal alloys that give them strength and light weight. Some of the parts are made with plastic. Even the tires are made with plastics. Plastics give the tires strength and longer life.

Chemical technology is not limited to cars and clothes. For example, small boats are given added strength by using synthetic materials like fiberglass. Airplanes also use synthetic materials. In fact, we use synthetics almost everywhere. Carpets are made of nylon for long life. Nylon is also easy to care for. We protect tables and other furniture with plastic coatings.

Hickson-Bender Photography

International Harvester

Tracy Borland

Another use of chemical technology is energy conservation. One example is office buildings. Often, they have many windows. Sunlight coming through the windows heats the rooms. To keep the buildings cool, air conditioners must be on all the time. A chemical coating on the windows reduces the amount of sunlight entering the rooms. With less sunlight, the building stays cooler.

Perhaps the most important uses of chemical technology are protection and food production. Chemicals are used to make materials fire resistant. For example, lining a chair with special plastic can keep it from burning violently. We also use chemicals to stop fires when they start. A forest fire is a spectacular example. Airplanes spray the fire with chemicals. The chemicals take the oxygen that the fire needs. Without oxygen, the fire dies.

burning chairs courtesy of DuPont

Monsanto

Chemicals are used in several ways to produce food. We enrich the soil with fertilizers. Insects are killed with pesticides. Weeds are prevented with chemicals, called herbicides. After the food is produced, we use chemicals to preserve it. Without chemicals much of our food would rapidly spoil. Spoiled food is the cause of many serious diseases. The use of chemical technology makes our life easier and safer.

Don Parsisson

Tracy Borland

Frontiers

Mobile Lab Cleans Spills

EPA, Edison Facility

A laboratory on wheels is helping the Environmental Protection Agency respond quickly to spills of oil and hazardous chemicals. The mobile spills laboratory is designed to help chemists identify the chemicals where they spilled. This way they don't have to wait several days to get the results from the EPA's laboratory in New Jersey. As a result, the proper treatment for the spill can be started right away.

Housed in a 35-foot long van semi-trailer, the lab contains a variety of equipment to identify chemicals. For example, it has two gas chromatographs. These help identify chemicals by their colors. An atomic absorption spectrophotometer helps to identify chemicals by using light. Every chemical absorbs different colors of light. The laboratory also has glassware and chemicals which are used to identify chemical spills.

Since the lab is working with dangerous chemicals, it carries a full range of safety equipment. One piece is a fume hood which is used to remove poisonous gases. A safety shower is used to wash off dangerous chemicals, if they are spilled on the chemist. The lab also carries fire extinguishers. For further safety the lab has special air conditioning and heating systems. Most air conditioning and heating systems use the same air over and over. In the lab the air is used once and replaced with fresh air. This prevents a build up of poisonous gases.

The mobile laboratory is also equipped with a small water treatment system. With this system it can treat or remove dangerous chemicals from water supplies. It has treated such incidents as a chemical spill that contaminated the Kernersville, North Carolina reservoir. Another incident was a spill of pesticides in Pennsylvania. By treating these spills, the mobile lab is helping to prevent damage to the environment from hazardous chemicals.

Adapted from *Chemecology,* January 1980, the Chemical Manufacturers Association.

Points to Remember

1. In a chemical reaction, matter is not gained or lost. *12:1*
2. Chemical equations are used to describe chemical changes. *12:1*
3. Water, gas, or a precipitate may be formed in a chemical change. *12:1*
4. Reactions that can be represented by chemical equations include:
   (a) double displacement reactions *12:4*
   (b) single displacement reactions *12:4*
   (c) decomposition reactions *12:3*
   (d) synthesis reactions *12:2*
5. Energy is gained or lost in a chemical change. *12:6*
6. The mass of a substance involved in a chemical reaction can be found by using molecular mass or formula mass. *12:5*
7. Catalysts speed a chemical reaction. *12:7*

Words to Use

Write a sentence in which you correctly use each of the following words or terms.

catalyst	equation	product
coefficients	exothermic	reactant
decomposition	formula mass	synthesis
displacement reaction	molecular mass	
endothermic	precipitate	

Questions for Review

Do not write in this book.

A. True or False *Have the students rewrite the false statements to make them correct.*

Determine whether each of the following sentences is true or false.

F **1.** Silver chloride is ~~soluble~~ in water. *insoluble*

T **2.** In ordinary chemical reactions, no mass is lost.

T **3.** A gas can be formed in a chemical reaction.

T **4.** A precipitate is an insoluble solid that forms during a chemical reaction.

T **5.** Electrolysis is decomposition of a compound by electricity.

F **6.** An equation may be balanced by changing ~~formulas~~. *coefficients*

F **7.** The molecular mass of H_2 is ~~1~~. *2*

T **8.** The molecular mass of O_2 is 32.

F **9.** An enzyme is a ~~preservative~~. catalyst

T **10.** The formula mass of potassium bromide, KBr, is 119.

B. Multiple Choice

Choose the word or phrase that correctly completes each of the following sentences.

1. A reaction that gives off heat is *(exothermic, endothermic, stable).*
2. Bromine can displace *(fluorine, iodine, iron)* in a chemical reaction.
3. In the decomposition of hydrogen peroxide, the compound MnO_2 acts as a(n) *(ion, catalyst, coefficient).*
4. In a chemical change, the total mass *(increases, decreases, remains the same).*
5. The formula mass of $NaNO_3$ is *(85, 170, 180).*
6. The molecular mass of CO_2 is *(20, 30, 44).*
7. To balance equations, *(coefficients, subscripts, formulas)* should be changed.
8. Burning of magnesium is an *(endothermic, exothermic)* reaction.
9. $2KClO_3(c) \rightarrow 2KCl(c) + 3O_2(g)$ is a *(replacement, decomposition, synthesis)* reaction.
10. $AB + CD \rightarrow AD + CB$ is a *(displacement, decomposition, synthesis)* reaction.

C. Completion

Complete each of the following sentences with a word or phrase that will make the sentence correct.

1. $C(c) + O_2(g) \rightarrow CO_2(g)$ is an equation which represents a(n) synthesis reaction.
2. A chemical change involves no change in mass.
3. Electrolysis of water is an example of a(n) endothermic reaction.
4. Calcium sulfate has a formula mass of 136.
5. If silver nitrate solution reacts with potassium chloride solution, AgCl is the precipitate that forms.
6. A balanced equation shows that mass is conserved.

7. The reaction in question 5 is a(n) ___double displacement___ reaction.
8. Some elements can be obtained in pure form through ___decomposition___ reactions.
9. ___CO___ is the compound of carbon and oxygen with a molecular mass of 28.
10. The compound of hydrogen and oxygen with a molecular mass of 18 is ___H_2O___.

D. How and Why

Detailed answers to these questions are given in the Teacher's Guide at the front of this book.

1. Why does a balanced equation agree with the law of conservation of mass?
2. How do endothermic reactions differ from exothermic reactions?
3. Why are formulas not changed when balancing equations?
4. Balance the following equations:
   a. $Na_2S(aq) + AgNO_3(aq) \longrightarrow NaNO_3(aq) + Ag_2S(c)$
   b. $H_2(g) + N_2(g) \longrightarrow NH_3(g)$
   c. $KClO_3(c) \longrightarrow KCl(c) + O_2(g)$
   d. $CuSO_4(aq) + Al(c) \longrightarrow Al_2(SO_4)_3(aq) + Cu(c)$
   e. $Na(c) + H_2O(l) \longrightarrow NaOH(aq) + H_2(g)$
5. What type of reaction is represented by each equation in question 4?

More Ideas to Explore

1. Through library research, obtain information about the Solvay process. Prepare a report showing the steps in the process and its commercial importance.
2. Find the Haber process in a reference book. Determine what catalysts and other factors are used to speed the reaction.

Readings to Discover

Coulson, E.H., Trinder, A.E.J., and Kleith, Aaron E., *Test Tubes and Beakers: Chemistry for Young Experimenters.* Garden City: Doubleday and Co., 1971.

Fisher, A., "Splitting Water With Sunlight." *Popular Science,* Vol. 212, June 1978, pp. 66-68.

Grosswirth, Marvin, "The Wonders of $NaHCO_3$ (baking soda)." *Science Digest,* March 1976, pp. 70-75.

You may use salt everyday to season your food. The picture shows one way salt is obtained. How is salt made? Is table salt the only kind of salt? Chapter 13 tells you about salts and the compounds that react to form them.

Shostal Associates

Acids, Bases, and Salts

13

Chapter 13 defines and discusses the properties of acids, bases, and salts. The use of indicators for identifying acids, bases, and neutralization reactions is introduced. See the Teacher's Guide at the front of this book for additional teaching strategies for this chapter.

13:1 Common Acids

GOAL: *You will learn the properties of acids, bases, and salts and how these compounds are produced and tested.*

Acids are substances which produce hydronium ions, H_3O^+, in solution. Acids have certain properties. Acids have a sour taste and react with metals. Every acid contains hydrogen. Almost all acids are formed from nonmetals. Many acids are poisonous and corrosive to the skin. For this reason, extreme care should be used when handling acids.

What are the properties of acids?

Common acids play an important part in daily life. Vinegar contains acetic acid. Buttermilk contains lactic acid. We eat citric acid in lemons, oranges, and grapefruits. Hydrochloric acid in the stomach aids digestion. Some household bleaches are weak solutions of hypochlorous (HI puh klor uhs) acid. Automobile batteries contain sulfuric acid. Three major acids are used in industry and the laboratory. They are sulfuric acid, nitric acid, and hydrochloric acid.

Name three important acids.

Sulfuric acid, H_2SO_4, is an oily, thick liquid. The production of sulfuric acid is greater than any other chemical in the United States. It is used in the manufacture of paints, plastics, and fertilizers. It is also used to make other acids and as a dehydrating agent. Dehydrate means to remove water. A wooden stick placed in sulfuric acid turns black as the acid removes water from it. Sulfuric acid can burn skin and damage clothing fibers. Always handle it with care.

Why is sulfuric acid important?

Hickson-Bender Photography

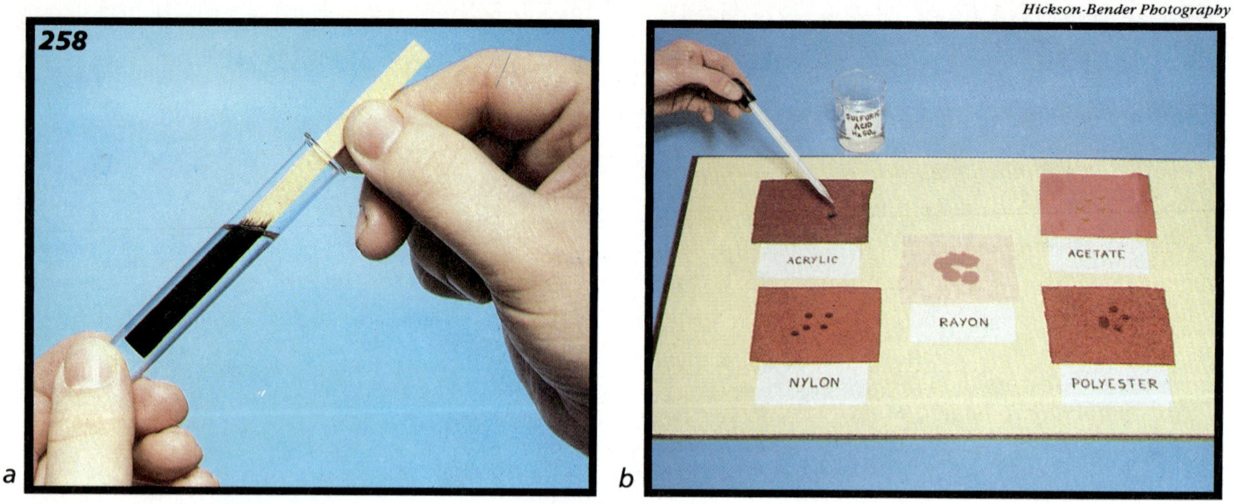

FIGURE 13-1. Wood placed in sulfuric acid turns black (a) as the acid dehydrates the wood. Sulfuric acid affects fabrics in many ways (b).

Sulfuric acid can be produced in the laboratory. First sulfur dioxide is produced by burning sulfur.

$$S(c) + O_2(g) \longrightarrow SO_2(g)$$

The gas is dissolved in water and the solution treated with hydrogen peroxide.

Dilute and concentrated sulfuric acid react in different ways. Dilute sulfuric acid will react with zinc to produce hydrogen.

$$Zn(c) + H_2SO_4(aq) \longrightarrow ZnSO_4(aq) + H_2(g)$$

However, when concentrated sulfuric acid reacts with copper, there is a different reaction. Copper(II) sulfate, water, and sulfur dioxide are produced instead.

$$Cu(c) + 2H_2SO_4(l) \longrightarrow CuSO_4(aq) + 2H_2O(l) + SO_2(g)$$

FIGURE 13-2. Sulfuric acid in a car battery can corrode the terminals.

Tom Stack/Tom Stack & Assoc.

Worthington Industries Corp.

FIGURE 13-3. Hydrochloric acid is used as a pickling agent to remove scale from newly made steel.

Nitric acid, HNO_3, is oily but not as thick as sulfuric acid. Nitric acid should be handled with care. If it touches skin, it combines with protein in the skin. A yellow stain results which will gradually wear away. Nitric acid can be produced in the laboratory. It is produced by heating sodium nitrate with concentrated sulfuric acid. Nitric acid does not always produce hydrogen when it reacts with metals. This property makes it different from most dilute acids.

What are the formulas for three common acids?

Hydrochloric acid, HCl, is made by adding hydrogen chloride gas to water. The hydrogen chloride gas is formed by heating sodium chloride with concentrated sulfuric acid. Hydrochloric acid produces hydrogen when it reacts with metals such as zinc and iron. Care should be taken when using HCl. Hydrochloric acid fumes can harm the lungs and will destroy skin. This acid is used to clean metals.

13-1 Detailed information concerning this Activity can be found in the Teacher's Guide at the front of this book.

ACTIVITY

What happens to zinc metal when it is added to different acids?

Add 5 mL of each of the following liquids to separate test tubes: water, dilute hydrochloric acid, vinegar, and lemon juice. Add a small piece of mossy zinc to each liquid.

What do you observe in each of the test tubes? Compare and explain the reactivity of the acids. What is the control used in this Activity? *water*

Many other acids are also important. Organic acids contain hydrogen, carbon, and oxygen. Formic acid was first found in ants. This acid was first produced by distilling ants. Acetic acid, CH_3COOH, is in vinegar. It is produced by a chemical change in ethanol. Propanoic acid is used to slow spoilage in foods such as bread.

Table 13-1

Acids in Some Common Substances

Substance	Acid present	Acid formula
aspirin	*acetylsalicylic acid*	$CH_3COOC_6H_4COOH$
citrus fruit juice	*ascorbic acid*	$C_6H_8O_7$
milk	*lactic acid*	$C_3H_6O_3$
soda water	*carbonic acid*	H_2CO_3
vinegar	*acetic acid*	CH_3COOH

Making Sure

1. In addition to hydrochloric acid, HCl, other acids are formed from the elements in the halogen family (Group VIIA of the periodic table). What are the formulas for hydrofluoric acid, hydrobromic acid, and hydroiodic acid? *HF, HBr, HI*

all are organic, all contain carbon hydrogen and oxygen

2. How are the acids listed in Table 13-1 alike?

13:2 Common Bases

What are the properties of bases?

All bases have properties that make them alike. **Bases** usually taste bitter and feel slippery. However, taste and touch are not safe methods to identify a base. Strong bases are poisonous and corrosive to skin. Bases also dissolve fats and oils. Except for ammonia, all bases contain hydrogen, oxygen, and at least one metal.

Write the formulas for two bases.

Alkalis or antacids are bases. Lye, ammonia, and milk of magnesia are common household bases. The most widely used base is sodium hydroxide, NaOH. It is also known as lye and is used in making soap. Lye is used to unclog sink drains since it dissolves oil and grease readily. Ammonia solution is used in cleaning compounds. Milk of magnesia is most commonly used as a laxative.

Thomas Russell

FIGURE 13-4. Many of the substances around the home contain bases. Check labels for bases in your home.

Table 13-2

Common Bases and Their Uses

Name	Formula	Use
aluminum hydroxide	$Al(OH)_3$	*deodorants*
ammonia	NH_3	*household cleaner*
calcium hydroxide	$Ca(OH)_2$	*dehairing hides, manufacture of mortar and plaster*
magnesium hydroxide	$Mg(OH)_2$	*laxative, antacid*
sodium hydroxide	$NaOH$	*drain cleaner, soap*

13-2 Detailed information concerning this Activity can be found in the Teacher's Guide at the front of this book.

ACTIVITY *What effect do bases have on oils?*

Fill four plastic cups one-half full of water. Add 15 mL of ammonia to one cup, 15 mL of NaOH to another, and 15 mL of milk of magnesia to another. Put a small lump of petroleum jelly in each cup. Let the cups stand for several hours.

What happens to the petroleum jelly in each cup? Why did you use only water in one cup? *The petroleum jelly dissolves best in the NaOH. Water is the control.*

FIGURE 13-5.

Making Sure

3. How are all of the bases listed in Table 13-2 alike? *all are used in the home, all have the hydroxide ion*
4. What property of a base makes sodium hydroxide useful in making soap? *dissolves fats and oils*

13:3 Ions in Acids and Bases

Name the two ions formed from a water molecule.

Pure water contains both water molecules and ions. About one in every 500 000 000 water molecules breaks up to form ions. The ions formed are the hydronium ion and hydroxide ion.

$$\underset{\text{water}}{2H_2O(l)} \longrightarrow \underset{\text{hydronium ion}}{H_3O^+(aq)} + \underset{\text{hydroxide ion}}{OH^-(aq)}$$

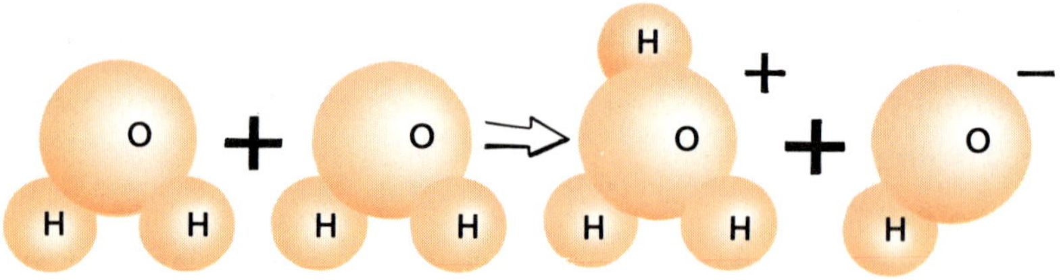

FIGURE 13-6. Two water molecules can split to form a hydronium ion and a hydroxide ion. How is water like an acid? How is water like a base?

What ions do acids add to water?

A hydronium ion has a 1+ charge and a hydroxide ion has a 1− charge. In pure water, there is an equal number of hydronium and hydroxide ions. However, the ratio changes if an acid or base is added to the water. An acid increases the amount of hydronium ions. The hydronium ions come from the hydrogen in the acid which combines with water molecules. For example, here is the equation for the addition of hydrogen chloride to water.

$$HCl(g) + H_2O(l) \longrightarrow H_3O^+(aq) + Cl^-(aq)$$

What ions do bases add to water?

The addition of a base increases the amount of hydroxide ion in water. For example, sodium hydroxide adds hydroxide ions to water when it dissolves. The hydroxide ions come from the OH^- in the base.

$$NaOH(aq) \longrightarrow Na^+(aq) + OH^-(aq)$$

Not all compounds which contain an OH group are bases. Some organic compounds known as alcohols contain an OH group. However, alcohols do not ionize to form hydroxide ions. Therefore, they are not classified as bases. Some metal hydroxides, such as zinc hydroxide or aluminum hydroxide, can act as acids or bases. Reaction conditions determine how each of these compounds will react.

Acids and bases may be classified as strong or weak. In general, a strong acid or base breaks up completely into ions when added to water. A weak acid or base does not break up completely when added to water. Most of the particles of a weak acid or base exist in water in their molecular form rather than as ions. The terms weak and strong acid or base have nothing to do with the concentration of the acid or base in the solution. We can have dilute solutions of strong acids and concentrated solutions of weak acids.

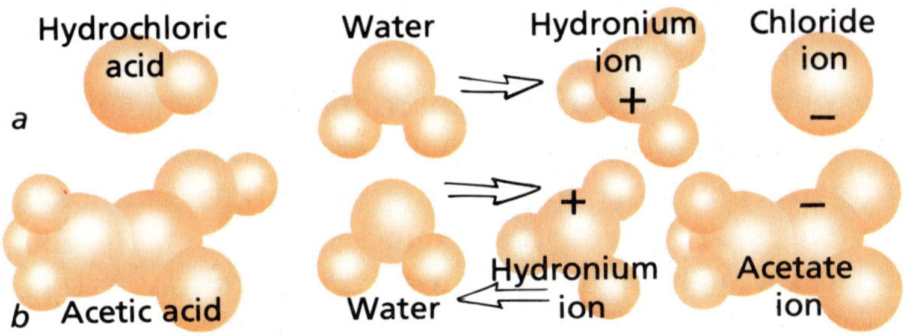

FIGURE 13-7. When added to water, a strong acid breaks up completely into ions (a). Many of the molecules of a weak acid will remain unchanged (b). As a result, fewer hydronium ions are produced.

Table 13-3

Strength of Some Acids and Bases

	Strong	Weak
Acids	*nitric acid, HNO_3* *hydrochloric acid, HCl* *hydrobromic acid, HBr*	*acetic acid, CH_3COOH* *citric acid* *carbonic acid, H_2CO_3* *oxalic acid, $C_2H_2O_4$*
Bases	*sodium hydroxide, $NaOH$* *calcium hydroxide, $Ca(OH)_2$* *potassium hydroxide, KOH*	*ammonia, NH_3* *iron(III) hydroxide, $Fe(OH)_3$* *aluminum hydroxide, $Al(OH)_3$*

13:4 pH of a Solution

How is the pH scale used?

The acidity of a solution can be expressed by using the pH scale. The pH of a solution shows its acidity in terms of its hydronium ion concentration. The pH scale ranges from 0 to 14. Solutions above 7 are basic. Solutions below 7 are acidic. A neutral solution has a pH of 7. A neutral solution is not acidic or basic. Pure water is neutral.

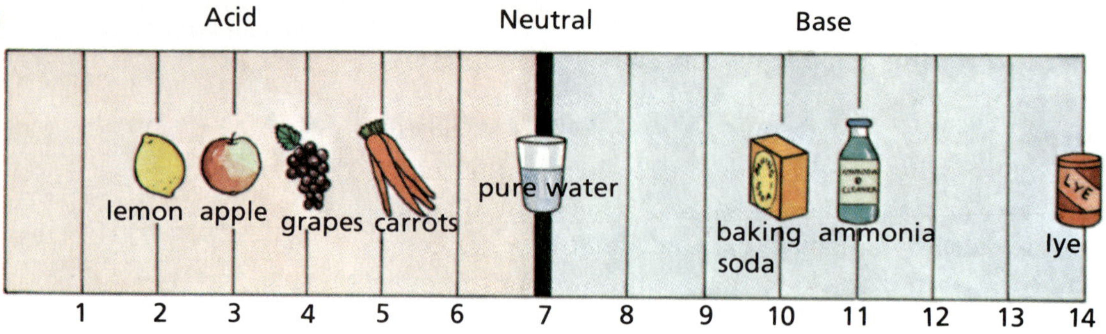

FIGURE 13-8. Approximate pH's of some substances

Concentrated solutions of strong acids have a pH range near 0. Concentrated solutions of weak acids can have a pH range of 2 to 5. A concentrated solution of a strong base has a pH near 14. Concentrated solutions of weak bases can have pH's around 11. A low pH value indicates a high hydronium ion concentration. A high pH value indicates a high hydroxide ion concentration. The pH of a solution can be measured accurately using a pH meter.

Hickson-Bender Photography

FIGURE 13-9. A pH meter is used to give an accurate pH reading.

Table 13-4

Approximate pH Values of Some Common Substances

Substance	pH	Substance	pH
stomach contents	1.6	milk	6.5
vinegar	2.8	pure water	7.0
apples	3.0	blood	7.35
orange juice	3.5	sea water	8.4
carrots	5.0	milk of magnesia	10.5
urine	6.0	household ammonia	11.1

Bill & Joan Popejoy

R. Brommer

FIGURE 13-10. The pigment in both flowers is the same compound. The difference in color is due to a difference in pH.

Making Sure

5. Classify each substance in Table 13-4 as acidic, basic, or neutral. *See the Teacher's Guide.*

13:5 Indicators

How can you test an unknown solution to see whether it is an acid or a base? One easy way is to use an indicator. Acid-base **indicators** are usually organic compounds which turn different colors in acidic or basic solutions. Litmus paper is one indicator you can use to test for an acid or base. Blue litmus paper will turn red in an acid solution. Red litmus paper will turn blue in a base solution. If a solution does not change the color of either paper, the solution is neutral.

Phenolphthalein (feen l THAYL een) is an indicator used to detect an acid or base. Phenolphthalein is colorless in an acid solution and bright pink in a basic solution. Many indicators are more specific than litmus or phenolphthalein. For example, red cabbage juice can tell you the approximate pH of some solutions. Many indicators change colors at narrow pH ranges, Figure 13-13. Some pH test papers are made from mixtures of indicators to cover the whole pH scale.

Tom Stack/Tom Stack & Assoc.

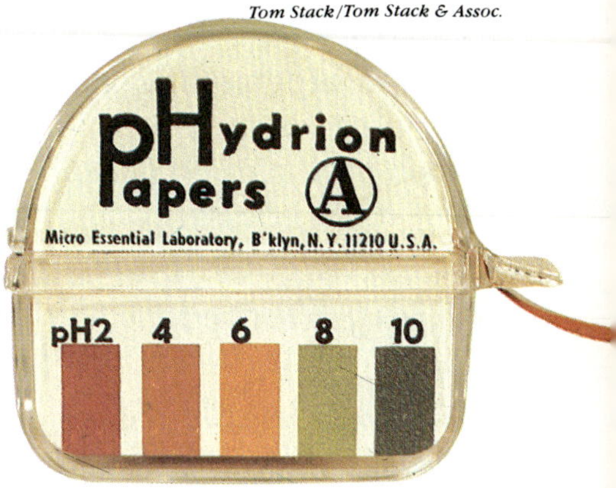

FIGURE 13-11. This indicator can show the approximate pH of a substance. It is more specific than litmus.

George C. Anderson

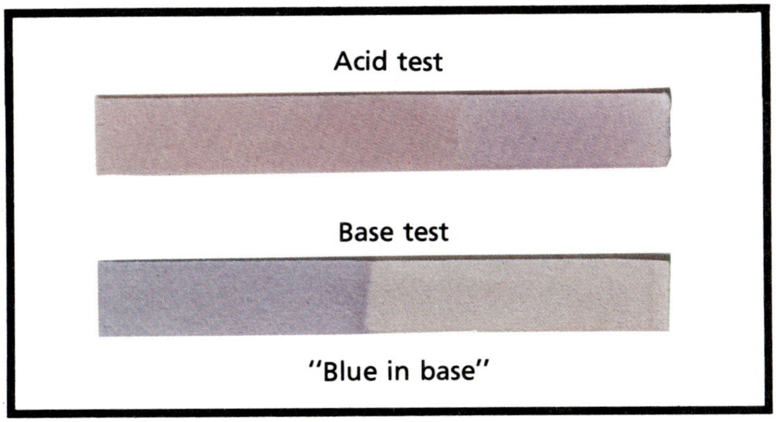

FIGURE 13-12. Litmus is an indicator which turns red in acid and blue in base.

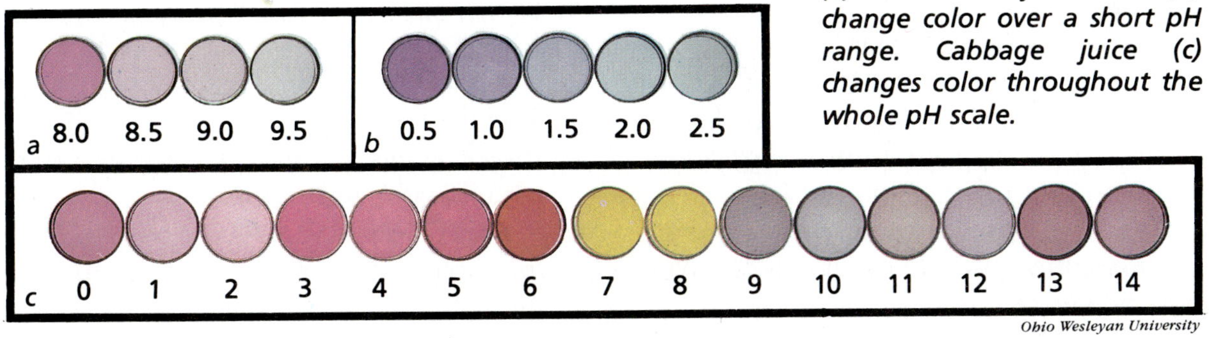

Ohio Wesleyan University

FIGURE 13-13. Phenolphthalein (a) and methyl violet (b) change color over a short pH range. Cabbage juice (c) changes color throughout the whole pH scale.

13-3 Detailed information concerning this Activity can be found in the Teacher's Guide at the front of this book.

Activity How are indicators used in testing acids and bases?

Setting Up

fruit and vegetable juices
household liquids
indophenol solution (0.1%)
5 test tubes and rack
Universal Indicator paper
litmus paper
soda straw

Getting Started

Part A

1. Obtain 5 test tubes. In the first test tube, dissolve 1 gram of sodium bicarbonate in 10 mL of water.
2. Use a soda straw to bubble your breath through 10 mL of water in another test tube.
3. Place 5 mL each of milk, soda pop, and vinegar in the three remaining test tubes.
4. Test the solution in each test tube with red and blue litmus paper. Record your results in a table.

Part B

1. Put samples of various household liquids in test tubes or paper cups.
2. Test each liquid with Universal Indicator paper. Record your results in a table.

Part C

1. Add 10 mL of indophenol to a test tube.
2. Add dilute ascorbic acid (vitamin C) one drop at a time to the test tube. Count the number of drops it takes to change the solution from blue to colorless. Record your results in a table.
3. Repeat Steps 1 and 2 with common fruit and vegetable juices. Record your results.

FIGURE 13-14.

Keeping Track

Part A

Solution	Blue litmus	Red litmus

Part B

Household liquid	indicator paper color	pH

Part C

Solution	Number of drops to change color

Summing Up

1. Which substances in Part A are acids? bases?
2. What acid did you make in Step 3 of Part A?
3. Why is Universal Indicator paper a better indicator than litmus?
4. In Part C, what was the purpose in testing ascorbic acid before testing the juices?

13:6 Salts

If an acid is added to a base, a chemical change called **neutralization** (new truh luh ZAY shuhn) occurs. In neutralization, the properties of both the acid and the base are destroyed. Neutralization explains why bases are used to counteract acids that are spilled on skin or clothing. Baking soda in water is a common base used to neutralize acids. Antacids contain bases to reduce excess stomach acid.

In neutralization, hydronium ions from the acid combine with the hydroxide ions from the base. As a result, water is formed.

$$\underset{\text{hydronium ion}}{H_3O^+(aq)} + \underset{\text{hydroxide ion}}{OH^-(aq)} \longrightarrow \underset{\text{water}}{2H_2O(l)}$$

What is a salt?

Neutralization produces water and a salt. A salt is a substance which is neither acid nor base. For example, when NaOH is neutralized by HCl, a salt is formed. The salt is sodium chloride.

$$HCl(aq) + NaOH(aq) \longrightarrow NaCl(aq) + H_2O(l)$$

Most salts contain a metal and a nonmetal. What metal and nonmetal are in sodium chloride? Some salts, such as ammonium chloride, contain the ammonium ion. Others contain a nonmetal and oxygen. For example, sodium nitrate, $NaNO_3$, contains nitrogen and oxygen in addition to sodium, a metal.

Sulfuric acid reacts with sodium hydroxide to form water and sodium sulfate. Sodium sulfate is a salt.

$$H_2SO_4(aq) + 2NaOH(aq) \longrightarrow Na_2SO_4(aq) + 2H_2O(l)$$

Salts are also formed when metals react with acids. For example, iron filings added to hydrochloric acid produce hydrogen gas. Iron(II) chloride, a salt, is also formed.

$$Fe(c) + 2HCl(aq) \longrightarrow FeCl_2(aq) + H_2(g)$$

FIGURE 13-15. The salt, sodium nitrate, is formed from a reaction between nitric acid and sodium hydroxide. When the water is boiled off, the white crystals of sodium nitrate remain.

Hickson-Bender Photography

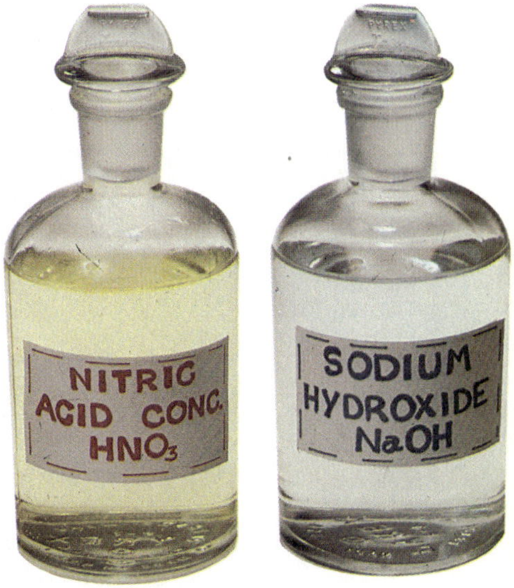

13-4 *Detailed information concerning this Activity can be found in the Teacher's Guide at the front of this book.*

ACTIVITY *Can you prepare sodium chloride by a neutralization reaction?*

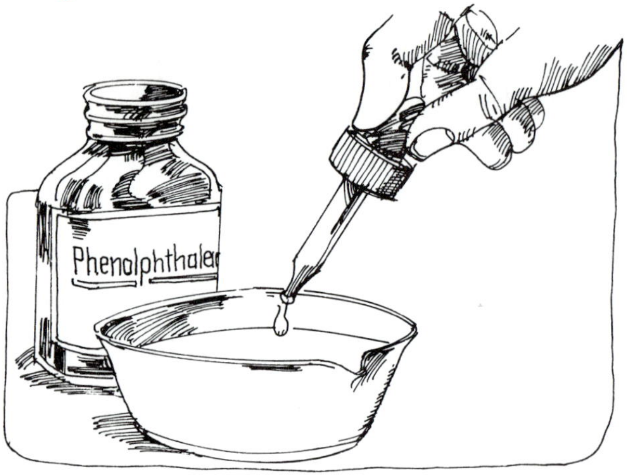

FIGURE 13-16.

Place 10 mL of dilute sodium hydroxide in an evaporating dish. **CAUTION:** *Use care when working with acids and bases. Wear eye and clothing protection. Add 2 drops of phenolphthalein as an indicator. What do you observe? Stir the solution carefully while adding dilute HCl. Add HCl until one drop makes the pink color disappear. Evaporate the solution slowly over a low burner flame. What is the residue that remains? Why did you use phenolphthalein in this Activity?*

NaCl *solution turns pink*

Making Sure

It is used to indicate the neutralization point.

6. How does the addition of a base to an acid affect the hydronium ion concentration? *reduces it*

7. Write a balanced equation for each of the following reactions: *See the Teacher's Guide.*

a. potassium hydroxide + sulfuric acid

b. nitric acid + sodium hydroxide

c. calcium hydroxide + nitric acid

d. magnesium hydroxide + hydrochloric acid

e. zinc + hydrochloric acid

8. Name the salt produced in each of the above reactions. *potassium sulfate sodium nitrate calcium nitrate magnesium chloride zinc chloride*

FIGURE 13-17. The anhydride, MgO, forms a base when added to water.

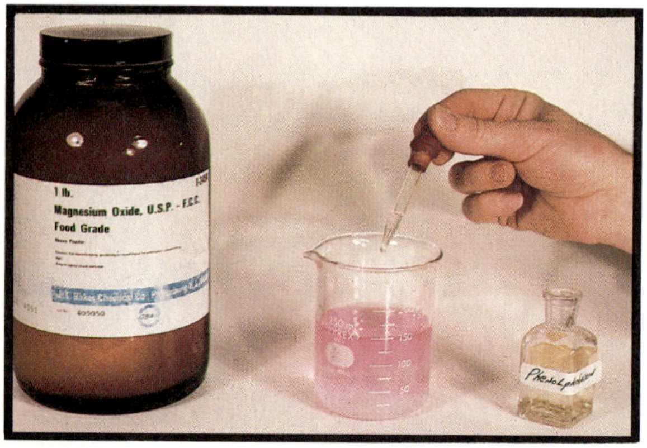

Tom Stack/Tom Stack & Assoc.

13:7 Anhydrides

When magnesium is burned, white magnesium oxide is formed. If the oxide is added to water, it produces a colorless solution. If a drop of colorless phenolphthalein is added to the solution, it turns pink. This color change shows a base has been formed. Magnesium oxide is a basic anhydride. **Anhydride** means without water. A basic anhydride is a substance that forms a base when added to water. Most metallic oxides are basic anhydrides.

George Wuerthner/Tom Stack & Assoc.

FIGURE 13-18. Carbonic acid is formed when carbon dioxide dissolves in water. The action of this acid produces the formations in limestone caves.

Sulfur combines with oxygen when it burns. Sulfur dioxide gas, SO_2, is formed. Sulfur dioxide is soluble in water. A solution of sulfur dioxide is colorless. When a piece of blue litmus paper is added to the solution, the paper will turn red. What does this color change indicate? Most nonmetallic oxides are acidic anhydrides. Sulfur dioxide is an acid anhydride. When added to water, an acid is formed.

Why is sulfur dioxide called an acidic anhydride?

$$SO_2(g) + H_2O(l) \longrightarrow H_2SO_3(aq)$$

Making Sure

9. Identify the following oxides as basic or acidic anhydrides.

a. MgO *base* **b.** SO_3 *acid* **c.** CO_2 *acid* **d.** CaO *base*

10. Write the equation for the formation of magnesium oxide.

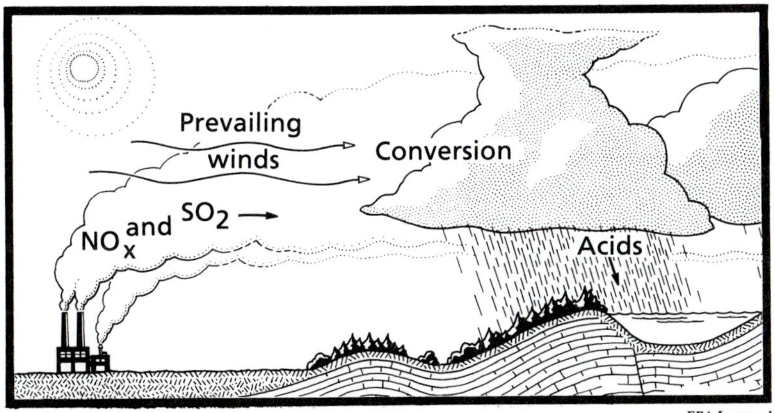

EPA Journal

FIGURE 13-19. Acidic anhydrides of sulfur combine with moisture in the air and later fall as acid rain. This rain damages both plant and animal life.

Focus on

People
Paula Moyer, Chemist

Paula Moyer

Paula Moyer is a research chemist. She works in the Science and Technology Division of Union Oil Company of California. Her job is to identify chemicals in test materials. Two of the methods she uses are gas chromatography and X rays.

Gas chromatography is used to identify organic chemicals. A mixture of chemicals is vaporized and put onto a special column. The column has a material that retains each part of the mixture to different degrees. As the mixture travels through the column, it is separated. Each chromatograph is connected to a computer. Paula writes programs that tell the computer how to identify the parts of the mixture. She also picks the material for the column that will best separate the chemicals in each mixture.

Paula has worked on several projects using gas chromatography. In one project, engineers needed to know how pure a product was. She developed a way to find the amount of raw material left in the final product. Knowing the amount of raw material remaining helps engineers control the quality of the final product. Paula also helped to develop a way to use gas chromatography in oil exploration. Using chromatography, the chemicals in a sample can be identified. This information tells geochemists where to look for oil.

In the X-ray lab, Paula uses X rays to identify chemicals. When an element is hit by X rays, it releases other X rays. Each element releases its own set of X rays. Since each set is known, the elements in a substance can be identified with X rays. Using special counters, the amount of X rays released can be found. From the amount of X rays, chemists can tell how much of an element is present in a substance. Each X-ray unit is controlled by a computer. Paula writes programs telling the computer how to run each test and identify the elements present.

All of the research groups in the Science and Technology Division need to identify chemical compositions. Thus, all of the groups must interact with Paula's department. "This makes my job as a research chemist a fascinating one," she says. "I have the opportunity to work with many different people on all types of projects, both within the research center and throughout the company."

Points to Remember

1. Acids have a sour taste and react with metals. 13:1
2. Bases have a bitter taste and feel slippery. 13:2
3. Acids increase the hydronium ion concentration of a solution. 13:3
4. Bases increase the hydroxide ion concentration of a solution. 13:3
5. The acidity of a solution is rated on the pH scale. 13:4
6. Indicators turn different colors in acidic and basic solutions. 13:5
7. A salt and water are the products of a neutralization reaction. 13:6
8. Anhydrides form acids or bases when added to water. 13:7

Words to Use

Write a sentence in which you correctly use each of the following words or terms.

acid
anhydride
base
hydronium ion
hydroxide ion
indicator
litmus paper
neutralization
pH
phenolphthalein
salt

Questions for Review

Do not write in this book.

A. True or False *Have the students rewrite the false statements to make them correct.*

Determine whether each of the following sentences is true or false.

T 1. The formula for nitric acid is HNO_3.

T 2. Vinegar contains an acid.

F 3. Ammonia is a ~~strong~~ base. *weak*

T 4. The strength of an acid in solution is measured on a pH scale.

F 5. A solution which has a pH of 4 is ~~a base~~. *an acid*

T 6. A neutralization reaction is a reaction between an acid and a base.

T 7. OH is the formula for a hydroxide ion.

T 8. An indicator may be used to determine whether a solution is an acid or a base.

T 9. Strong acids produce more ions than weak acids.

F 10. An acid anhydride contains a ~~metal~~. *nonmetal*

B. Multiple Choice

Choose the word or phrase that correctly completes each of the following sentences.

1. Acids in food taste *(sour, sweet, bitter, salty).*
2. An acid solution would probably have a pH of *(2, 7, 11).*
3. *(Phenolphthalein, Benzene, Litmus)* is not an indicator.
4. An oxide of a metal usually is a(n) *(acid anhydride, basic anhydride).*
5. The pH of a dilute NaOH solution is *(more than 7, less than 7).*
6. An example of a basic anhydride is *(carbon dioxide, sulfur dioxide, calcium oxide).*
7. Which of the following is an acid? *(H_2O, MgO, HCl)*
8. Neutralization reactions produce a salt and *(a gas, light, water).*
9. As the amount of HCl in water increases the solution becomes *(more, less)* acidic.
10. A low pH value indicates a *(low hydronium, high hydronium)* concentration.

C. Completion

Complete each of the following sentences with a word or phrase that will make the sentence correct.

1. Taste should never be a test for an acid or base in a laboratory.
2. A hydrogen ion combines with a water molecule to form hydronium ion.
3. Bases can be tested safely by using an indicator.
4. CO_2 is an example of a(n) acid anhydride.
5. When an active metal reacts with dilute H_2SO_4, H_2 gas is formed.
6. As the acidity of a solution rises, its pH value decreases.
7. When an active metal and an acid react, a(n) salt is formed.
8. When sodium hydroxide is added to water, the pH increases.
9. When carbon dioxide is added to water, the pH decreases.
10. A salt is formed when an acid neutralizes a base.

Detailed answers to these questions are given in the Teacher's Guide at the front of this book.

D. How and Why

1. What kind of reaction is shown by the following equation?

$$HCl(aq) + NaOH(aq) \longrightarrow NaCl(aq) + H_2O(l)$$

2. What are the "parent" acids and bases for these salts?
   a. Na_2SO_4 **b.** NaCl **c.** $NaNO_3$
3. How are acids and bases detected?
4. List three important industrial acids. What are the primary uses of each?
5. Classify each substance as an acid, a base, or a salt:
   a. HNO_2 **c.** KOH **e.** $Ca(OH)_2$
   b. HCOOH **d.** CaI_2 **f.** $Fe(NO_3)_3$
6. Name two common household bases. Give their uses.

More Ideas to Discover

1. Check the labels on many household products such as medicines, kitchen aids, and foods. See how many involve acids or bases.
2. Prepare solutions of different liquid synthetic detergents. Use the same number of drops of each in the same volume of water. Use a Universal Indicator to determine the pH of each.
3. Boil some natural and synthetic fibers for about 5 minutes in a weak solution of sodium hydroxide. Test the same type of fibers in dilute sulfuric acid. What do you conclude?
4. Certain gases in the air form acids when dissolved in water. What gases are they? Where do they come from? How do the acids they form affect the environment?
5. Using information from garden books, farm publications, your local garden store, or florists make a list of plants that require acid soil and those that require basic soil. Find out what methods can be used to make soil basic or acidic.

Readings to Discover

Cecil, George, *Salt.* NY: F. Watts, 1976.

La Bastille, Anne, "The Deadly Toll of Acid Rain: All of Nature Is Suffering." *Science Digest,* October 1979, pp. 61-66.

Salisbury, David F., "Salt: An Untapped Source of Abundant Energy." *Science Digest,* December 1978, pp. 45-47.

Unit 5

A drop of water can be used to capture light waves reflecting off an object. A television satellite can pick up and send TV waves all over the world. The lenses in our eyes and in a camera can produce the star-shaped patterns of light waves. How are light and sound similar?

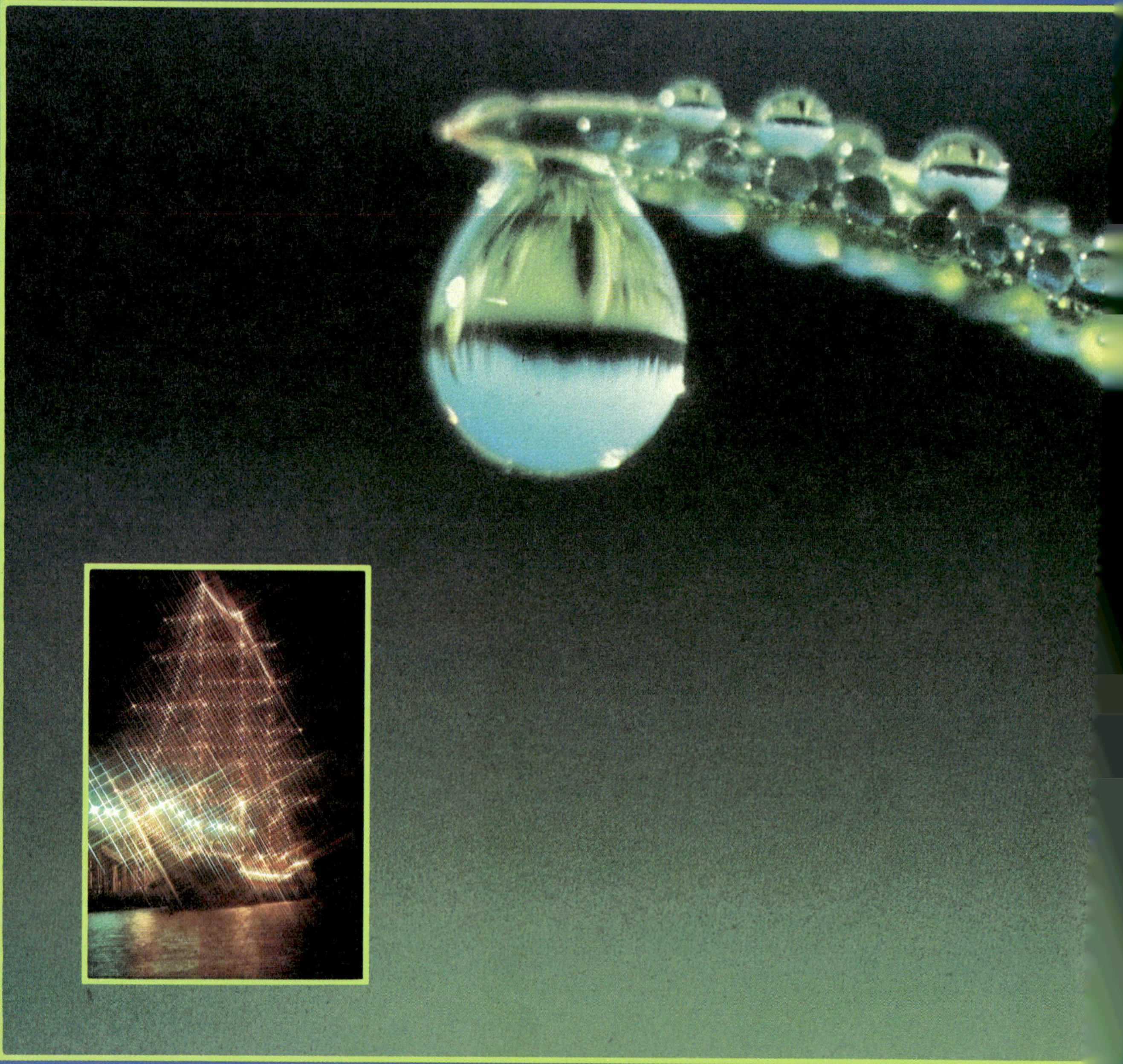

Lighted ship Steve Lissau

Light and Sound

TV satellite relay Tom Stack/Tom Stack & Associates

E. Braun/The Image Bank

***W**hen you think of the word "waves" you probably think of water. Are water waves the only kind of waves? How does the swan in the picture make waves? Chapter 14 tells you some of the properties of water waves and other waves which are invisible. After reading the chapter, make a list of the objects you have that use waves.*

Larry Hamill

Waves

14

Chapter 14 discusses the transfer of radiant energy by transverse waves. Wave properties are introduced along with practical uses for electromagnetic waves. See the Teacher's Guide at the front of this book for additional teaching strategies for this chapter.

14:1 Characteristics of Waves

GOAL: *You will learn the properties of waves and the important uses of electromagnetic waves.*

Have you ever watched waves in an ocean or lake? The waves travel forward as the water moves up and down. As each wave passes a point, the water moves up and down. A **wave** is a rhythmic disturbance which travels through space or matter.

Name three characteristics of waves.

A wave made with a rope has a hill and a valley. The hill is called the **crest.** The valley is called the **trough.** Locate these parts in Figure 14-1. Notice the crests and troughs. Every wave has a certain wavelength. The total distance from one crest through one trough is one **wavelength.**

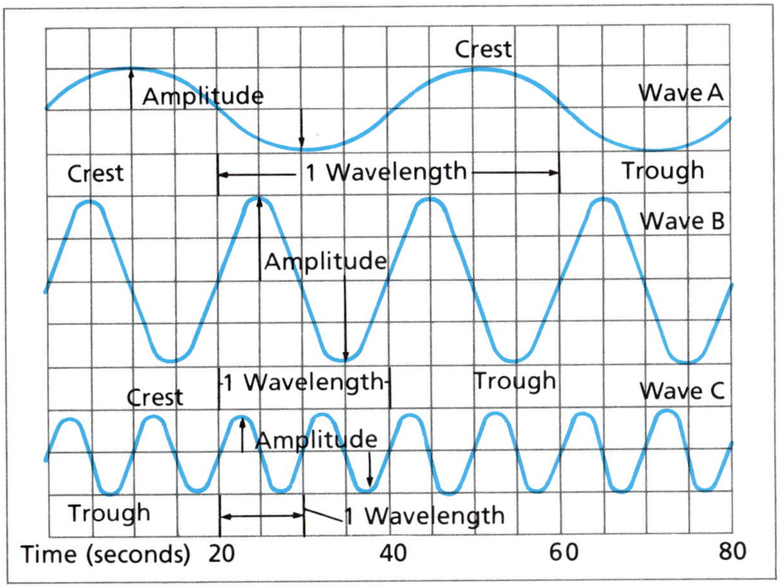

FIGURE 14-1. Parts of a wave

Steve Lissau

Camera Hawaii

FIGURE 14-2. The energy of a wave can cause erosion and destruction.

Amplitude is the distance a wave rises or falls from its usual rest position. Amplitude depends on the amount of energy which creates the wave. As the wave energy increases, the amplitude increases. For example, if you drop a large rock instead of a pebble into a pond, a bigger wave results. The amplitude is greater. How can you produce waves of large amplitude with a rope?

What is a transverse wave?

Waves formed by water or a rope are transverse waves. In a **transverse wave,** matter vibrates at right angles to the direction in which the wave travels. Vibrate means to move back and forth rapidly. In a water wave, the wave travels across the water. The water molecules vibrate up and down.

Making Sure

1. Draw two transverse waves on a piece of paper. Make one with a small amplitude. Make the second with an amplitude three times the first wave.
2. Take a ruler and measure the wavelengths of the two waves you have drawn. Are the wavelengths the same or different?

14:2 Frequency of a Wave

All waves have a certain frequency. **Frequency** is the number of waves that pass a given point in one second. Suppose you throw a pebble into a pond. Three wave crests caused by the splash pass by a rock in 15 seconds. What is the wave frequency? The wave frequency is three waves per 15 seconds, or 0.2 waves per second.

$$\frac{3 \text{ waves}}{15 \text{ seconds}} = \frac{0.2 \text{ waves}}{\text{second}}$$

As the number of waves that pass a given point per second increases, the frequency also increases.

Have you ever stood on a pier and watched water waves pass underneath? The longer the wave, the more time it takes to pass a given point. The shorter the wave, the less time it takes to pass a given point.

The to and fro (back and forth) movement of matter is called a **vibration.** You can feel vibrations if you stretch a rubber band and then pluck the rubber band with your finger, Figure 14-4. It will vibrate back and

FIGURE 14-3. Wave B has a wavelength that is one half the wavelength of A. The frequency of B is twice that of A.

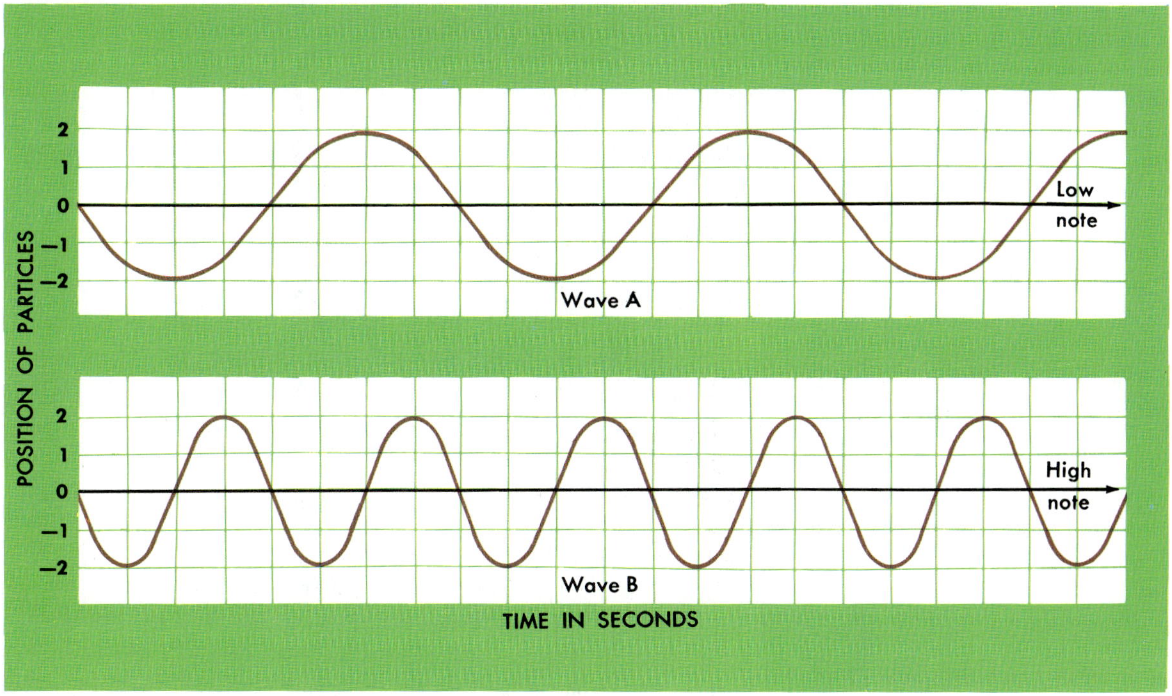

Larry Hamill

FIGURE 14-4. The frequency of vibration for a rubber band can be counted.

forth. The vibration of the rubber band is similar to a wave in water. Vibrations in the rubber band are much faster than water waves. The frequency of a vibration is expressed using a unit called the hertz. One **hertz (Hz)** is one vibration or one cycle per second for a wave. For example, the frequency of the sound made by one kind of tuning fork is 256 hertz. How many times per second does this tuning fork virbrate when someone strikes it?

What unit is used to measure the frequency of a vibration?

There is a relationship between the frequency and wavelength of a wave. As the length of a wave increases, its frequency decreases. Long waves have a low frequency. Short waves have a high frequency.

How does wavelength affect the frequency of a wave?

14-1 Detailed information concerning this Activity can be found in the Teacher's Guide at the front of this book.

ACTIVITY *How can you make a transverse wave?*

Take a rope about 4.5 meters long and tie one end to a doorknob. Hold the other end of the rope with your hand. Shake it up and down so waves begin to form. Make a diagram of the shape of the waves produced.

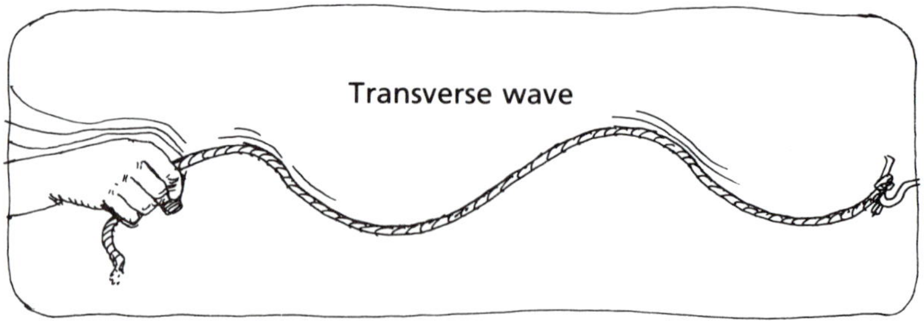

FIGURE 14-5.

14-2 Detailed information concerning this Activity can be found in the Teacher's Guide at the front of this book.

ACTIVITY Can you measure the frequency of a wave?

Hold one end of a thin strip of metal in your hand. Place the other end in a pan of water. Vibrate the metal strip so waves are produced. How do the waves behave? Count the number of waves that strike the side of the pan in 30 seconds. What is the frequency? Obtain a tuning fork and hold it by the stem. Tap it lightly so the prongs vibrate. Dip the vibrating prongs into a pan of water. What happens? Explain your observations.

You can project the waves produced if you use a flat, clear glass dish set on an overhead projector. The waves will project onto a wall or screen.

answers will vary

the water vibrates

FIGURE 14-6.

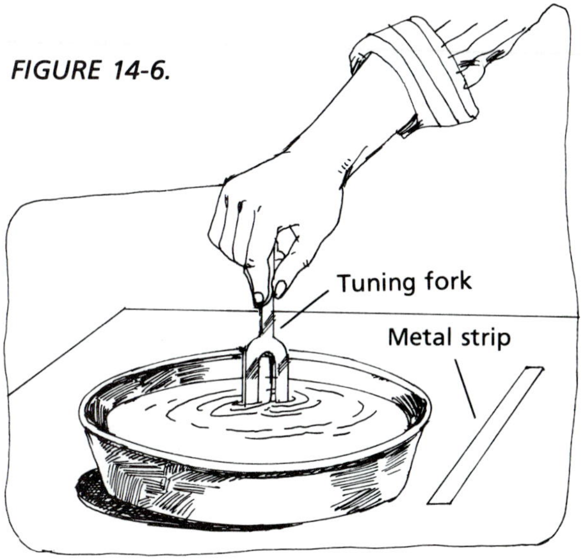

Making Sure

3. How is the frequency of a wave different from its amplitude?

Frequency is the number of waves per second; amplitude is the height or depth of a crest or trough.

4. One kind of tuning fork has a frequency of 512 hertz. How many times per second does it vibrate? 512

14:3 Speed of a Wave

The speed of a wave depends on the wavelength and frequency of the wave. Here is the equation used to calculate the speed of a wave.

How is the speed of a wave calculated?

$$speed = wavelength \times frequency$$

For example, the tuning fork mentioned on page 276 has a frequency of 256 hertz. The wavelength of the sound wave produced by the fork is about 1.3 meters. The speed of the wave is

$$\begin{aligned} speed &= 1.3 \text{ meters} \times 256 \text{ hertz} \\ &= 332.8 \text{ meters per second} \end{aligned}$$

Recall that the hertz is a unit which shows the number of vibrations per second. Therefore, the unit for speed in this case is meters per second.

Example

A wave made with a rope has a wavelength of one meter. The frequency of the wave is measured at 0.5 hertz. What is the speed of this wave?

Solution:

(a) Write the equation for the speed of a wave.

$$speed = wavelength \times frequency$$

(b) Substitute the values for speed and frequency given in the problem.

$$speed = 1 \text{ meter} \times 0.5 \text{ hertz}$$
$$= 0.5 \text{ meter per second}$$

Making Sure

5. A wave made with a rope has a wavelength of 0.25 meters. A water wave has a wavelength of 2 meters. Could these two waves be traveling at the same speed? Explain why.

   Yes, the rope could have a frequency eight times that of the water wave.

6. What does it mean when a radio station has a frequency of 1000 kilohertz? *1 000 000 cycles per second*
7. What do you think a "short wave" radio is?

   It picks up short wavelength, high frequency stations.

14:4 The Water Wave Model

When are waves reflected?

Water waves in a tank can be used as models to explain the behavior of sound, light, and other energy waves. Water waves can be used to show reflection. **Reflection** occurs when a wave strikes an object and bounces off. The waves that strike an object are called **incident waves.** The waves that bounce off are called **reflected waves.** A wave machine, Figure 14-7, also can be used to show reflection of waves. Once the wave hits the edge of the machine, it is reflected back again.

Kodansha

FIGURE 14-7. The wave machine shows that a wave can be reflected back once it hits a barrier.

Think of a wave as a straight line striking a wall at an angle. The angle between the wave and a line drawn normal to the wall is the angle of incidence. It is shown as angle *i* in Figure 14-8. A line drawn normal to the wall means the line is perpendicular to the wall at the point where the wave strikes the wall. The angle between the reflected wave and the normal is the angle of reflection. On Figure 14-8, it is labeled angle *r*.

Kodansha

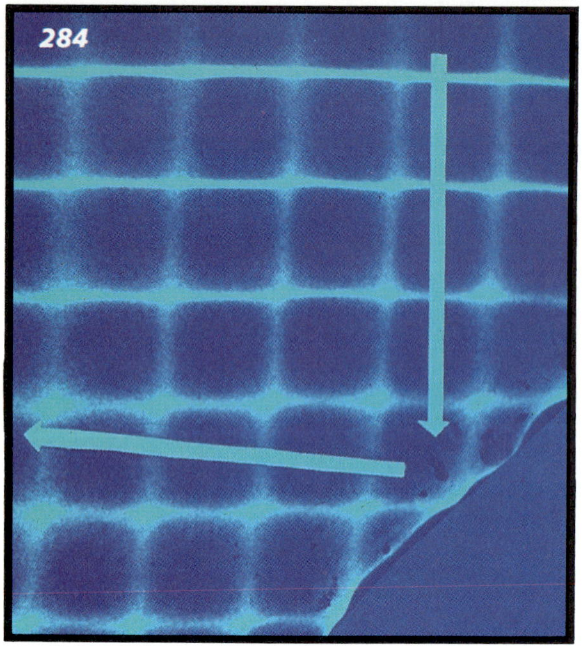

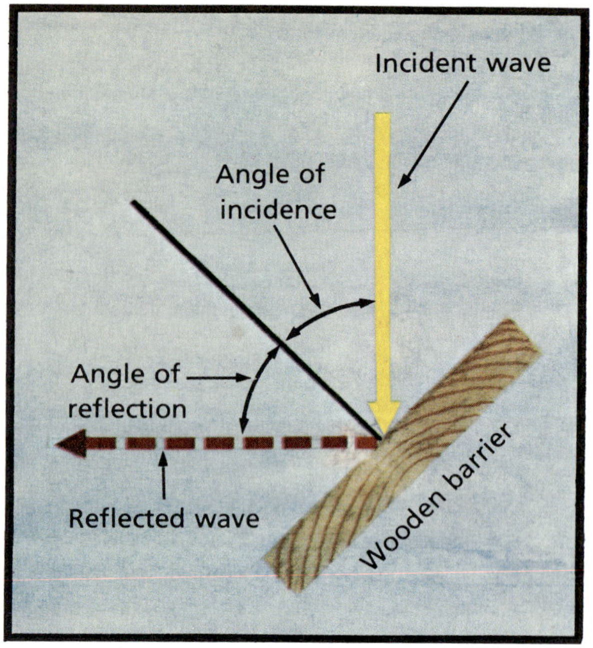

FIGURE 14-8. The angle of incidence equals the angle of reflection.

FIGURE 14-9. The speed of the water waves changes as they pass through the shallow water. The incident wave is bent because the whole wave is not traveling at the same speed.

Refraction is the bending of waves. Water waves can be used to show how refraction occurs. As water waves pass into shallow water, their wavelength becomes shorter. The speed of the waves decreases. Recall that speed equals wavelength multiplied by frequency. If the frequency stays the same and the wavelength becomes smaller, the speed must decrease. The speed of water waves changes as they pass from deep to shallow water.

Craig Kramer

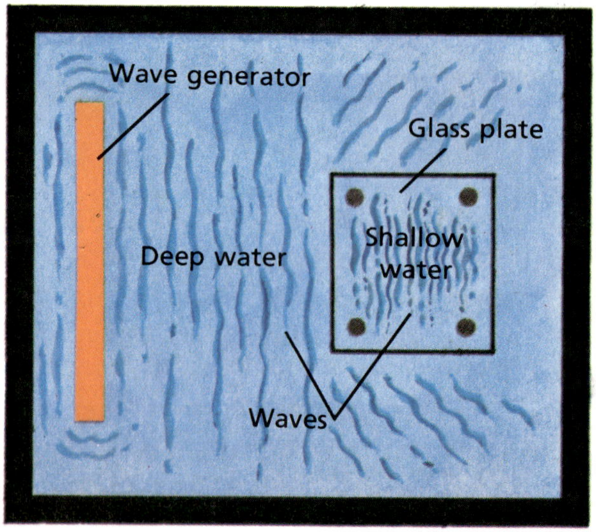

Kodansha

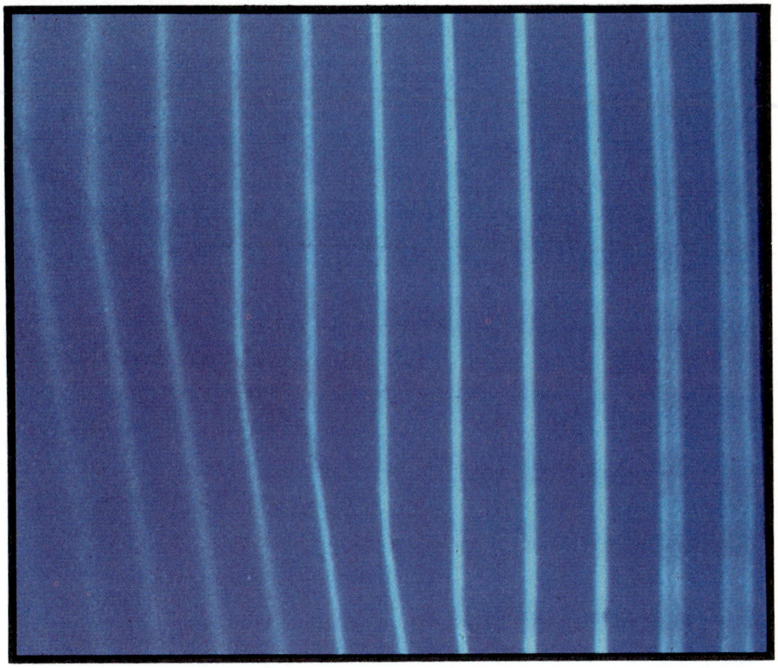

FIGURE 14-10. Water waves are refracted as they pass over a shallow barrier.

When water waves pass into shallow water at an angle, the waves are bent, or refracted, Figure 14-10. Refraction always occurs toward the area in which the speed of a wave slows down. This principle of refraction may be explained by an example. Suppose two small wheels are mounted on an axle. As they roll across a tabletop, one wheel reaches a soft velvet cloth and is slowed down by friction, Figure 14-11. The other wheel continues at its faster speed. It is pulled toward the slower wheel. The change in speed of the wheel on the cloth causes a change in direction of the wheels and axle. The wheels turn toward the soft cloth, the area in which speed is decreased.

Any type of wave can be refracted. Whenever a wave passes from one substance to another substance, its speed changes. If the wave approaches the boundary between two substances at an angle, it is refracted.

FIGURE 14-11. The speed of the wheels changes as they hit the rough surface of the cloth. This model shows how waves are bent as their speed changes.

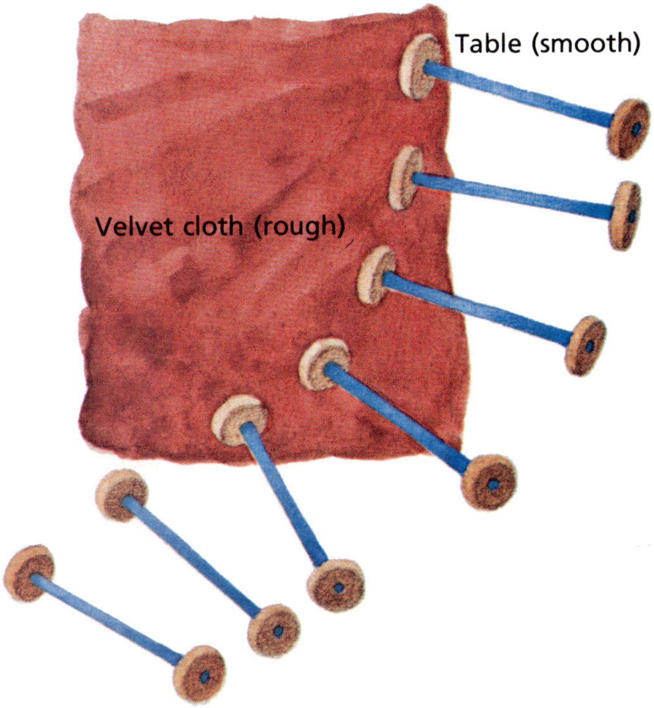

14-3 Detailed information concerning this Activity can be found in the Teacher's Guide at the front of this book.

ACTIVITY *How is a ball reflected?*

Roll a ball so that it strikes a wall head on. How was it reflected? Roll a ball toward the wall at an angle. How is it reflected? Repeat. Chalkmark the path of the ball in both cases. Identify the angles of incidence and reflection.

back along its original path

back at an angle

Making Sure

Remind students that the angles of incidence and reflection are measured from the normal.

8. On a piece of paper make a drawing showing the reflection of a ball off a wall. Draw a straight line for the wall and a dotted line for the path of the ball.
9. Why are the angles of incidence and reflection important in games such as basketball, billiards, and racquetball? *These games rely on the "bounce" of the ball from barriers (floor, walls).*

14:5 Electromagnetic Spectrum

What kinds of waves make up the electromagnetic spectrum?

There are waves all around you. You can detect light waves with your eyes. Water waves are waves you can see. Most waves are invisible. For example, radio, radar, infrared, X ray, and gamma-ray waves are invisible. Infrared waves are radiant energy. Gamma rays are one kind of nuclear radiation.

Each type of wave listed above has a different wavelength and frequency. However, all of these waves travel at the same speed. If the waves are arranged in order of their wavelength and frequency, the waves form what is called the **electromagnetic spectrum.** Why are they called electromagnetic? The waves in the electromagnetic spectrum can be produced by electricity or magnetism.

What is a photon?

All of the waves that make the electromagnetic spectrum, Figure 14-12, are transverse waves. These waves travel as tiny bundles or packets called photons. A **photon** is a particle of radiant wave energy. It is too small to be seen with the most powerful microscope.

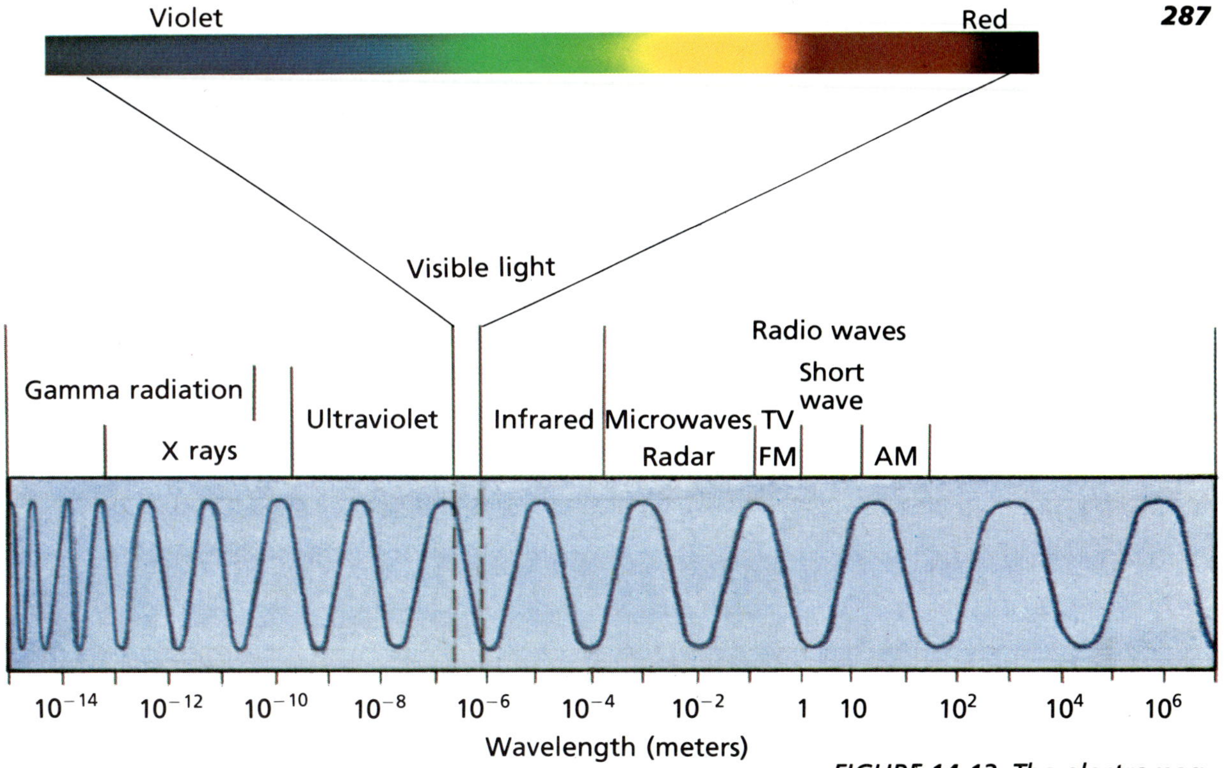

FIGURE 14-12. The electromagnetic spectrum

Photons travel at 300 000 000 meters per second in a vacuum. Photons are so swift they circle the earth more than seven times in one second. Photons of electromagnetic energy can pass through space. Light rays and invisible radiation rays are streams of photons. The ability to travel in a vacuum makes electromagnetic waves different from water or sound waves.

The wavelengths of electromagnetic radiation range from 10^{10} meters (electric waves) to 10^{-16} meters (cosmic rays). Therefore, frequencies range from very low for electric waves, to very high for cosmic rays. Waves with the highest frequencies have the greatest amount of energy.

Remind students that 10^{10} is one followed by ten zeros and 10^{-16} is a decimal point followed by 15 zeros and a one.

Making Sure

10. What is the speed of light? *3×10^{8} m/s*

11. Would the speed of light be greater or less in air? Why? *The speed of light is less in air because air is more dense.*

Who discovered X rays?

14:6 X rays

An important discovery was made in 1895 by the German physicist W. K. Roentgen. Roentgen passed a high voltage electric current through a glass tube in which air was removed. A fluorescent screen near the tube began to glow with a greenish color. Fluorescent material glows when exposed to radiation. Roentgen thought an unknown kind of radiation was given off by the glass tube. He called the radiation X rays. The "X" stood for unknown. Experiments show that a beam of electrons produced X rays when the electrons struck a solid such as glass. **X rays** are a form of electromagnetic radiation.

Ultra-Violet Products, Inc.

a 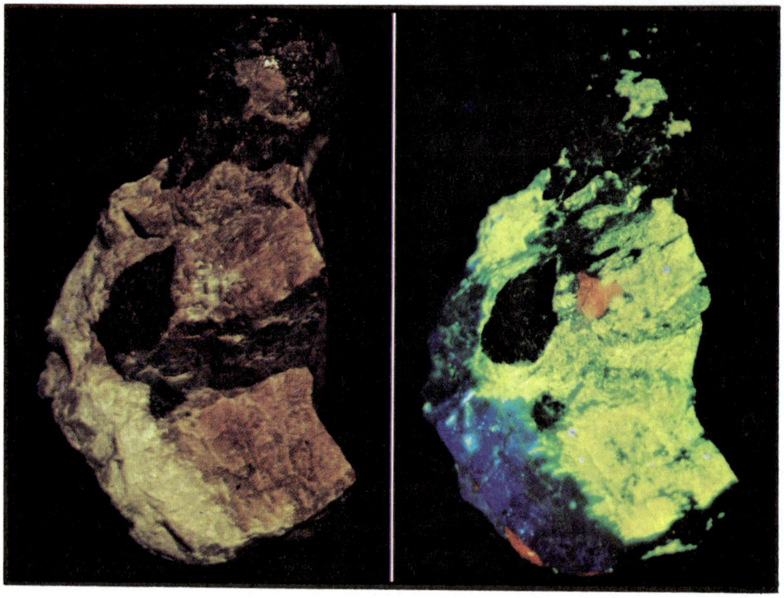 b

FIGURE 14-13. The energy in ultraviolet light causes the rock under normal light (a) to fluoresce when placed under ultraviolet light (b).

X rays can be produced in an X-ray tube. An X-ray tube is a high voltage cathode-ray tube. It contains a metal target and a metal filament, Figure 14-14. When the electrons strike the metal target, X rays are released by the metal.

How are X rays produced? A moving electron has kinetic energy. When a high-speed electron hits the tungsten, it collides with a tungsten atom. Often, the

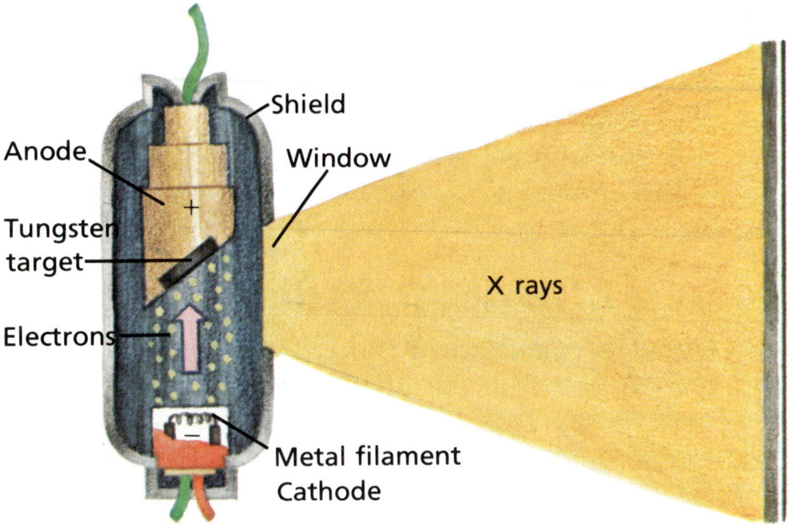

FIGURE 14-14. Moving electrons produce X rays as they strike the tungsten target.

electron must collide with several atoms before it is stopped. Some of the kinetic energy lost by the electron when it is stopped changes into X rays. Actually, one percent or less of the kinetic energy is changed to X-ray radiation. The rest becomes heat energy.

Have you ever had a part of your body X rayed by a doctor or dentist? Like all electromagnetic radiation, X rays travel at the speed of light. X rays can pass through all matter. However, all substances, including gases, absorb X rays to some degree. The amount of absorption depends upon the density of the material. For example, bone absorbs more X rays than flesh. Lead absorbs more than aluminum.

FIGURE 14-15. A tomogram (a) is a type of X ray used to diagnose disease. This tomogram shows a section of the brain. People using X rays (b) must be shielded from the source to avoid overexposure.

a
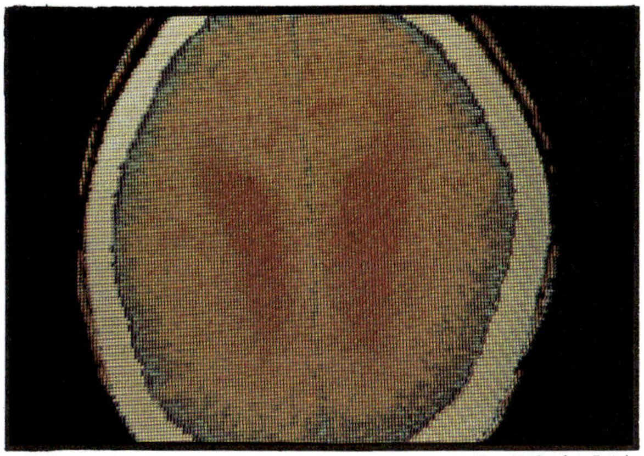

Dan McCoy from Rainbow

b
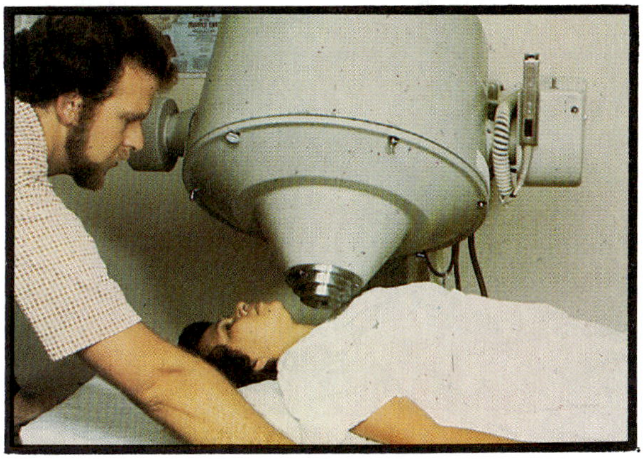

Making Sure

12. How can X rays be used to make pictures of internal body parts? *Flesh does not stop X rays but bone does.*
13. How do X-ray photographs aid doctors and dentists in their work? *They are able to see internal organs and defects.*

14:7 Ultraviolet Radiation

Ultraviolet radiation is present in sunlight. When sunlight strikes your body, the ultraviolet radiation produces vitamin D in your skin. Vitamin D is needed for healthy bones and teeth. The vitamin D content is increased when some foods are exposed to ultraviolet rays. Milk, for example, is exposed to radiation from ultraviolet lamps to increase its vitamin D content.

What are some uses for ultraviolet radiation?

Ultraviolet radiation kills germs. For this reason, hospitals often use ultraviolet lamps to kill germs in operating rooms.

How is ultraviolet radiation different from visible light?

Ultraviolet radiation is invisible and its wavelength is shorter than visible light. In the electromagnetic spectrum, it is next to violet light at the end of the visible light band. Ultraviolet radiation can be detected with a fluorescent material. When struck by radiation, the fluorescent material glows and gives off light. This property of ultraviolet radiation is why it is sometimes called "black light." Overexposure to ultraviolet radiation can be harmful. Frequent overexposure to the sun is known to cause skin cancer.

FIGURE 14-16. A black light generates ultraviolet rays. These rays cause some fabric dyes to fluoresce (a). Overexposure to ultraviolet radiation can cause skin cancer (b).

a
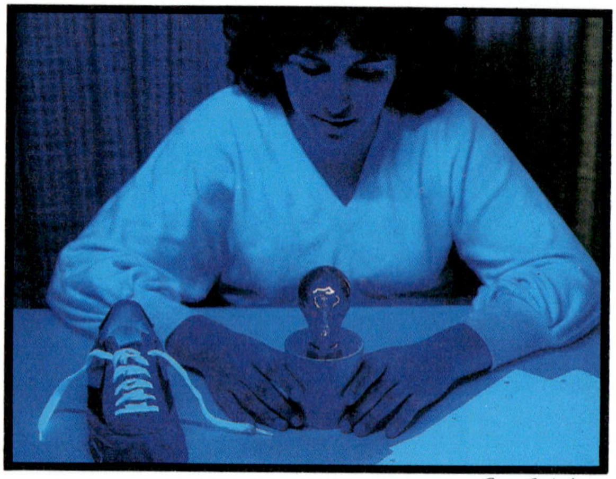
George C. Anderson

b
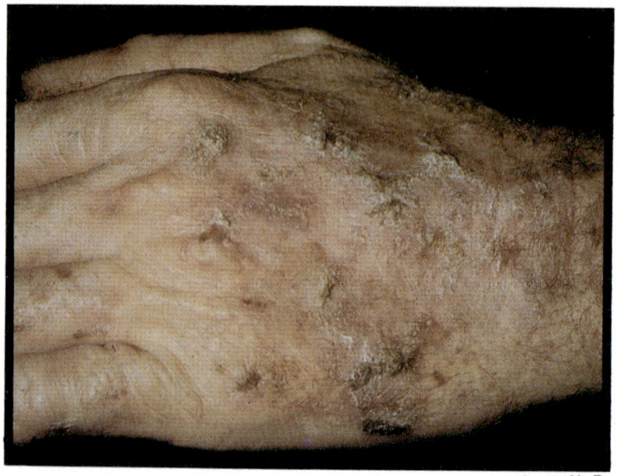
Camera M. D.

Larry Hamill

FIGURE 14-17. Infrared heat lamps are used in restaurants to keep food warm.

14:8 Infrared Radiation

Infrared radiation is used to dry and warm things. For example, infrared lamps are used in industry to dry paint. Cooked food in a restaurant may be kept warm by an infrared lamp. Warm objects emit infrared rays. This fact has military value in the use of heat-seeking missiles. The missiles find their targets by detecting the infrared radiation given off by the target. Infrared radiation is also used in detecting tumors.

FIGURE 14-18. Infrared film is used in photography to produce special effects. This type of film is heat sensitive. The colors produced are related to the amount of heat an object radiates and not the object's natural color.

Larry Hamill

EROS Data Center

FIGURE 14-19. This satellite photo of southern Florida was taken using infrared film. Much of the brown central area represents the Everglades swamp. The tiny red areas within the Everglades represent higher areas of hardwood trees. Heavy population centers are shown along the east coast.

How is infrared radiation different from visible light?

Infrared radiation is invisible and has a longer wavelength than visible light. In the electromagnetic spectrum, it is next to the red light at the end of the visible light band. Infrared radiation produces heat when absorbed. Overexposure can cause the burning of tissue. One way to detect infrared radiation is through the use of special film sensitive to infrared rays.

Infrared radiation is used in industry to identify unknown substances. When a substance is exposed to infrared rays, the atoms in the substance vibrate. The vibrations for each compound in the substance form a spectrum that is recorded by a machine. Every compound has an infrared spectrum that is like a fingerprint. From the infrared "fingerprint," the compound is then identified. Many of the compounds in petroleum were identified in this way.

Beckman Instruments

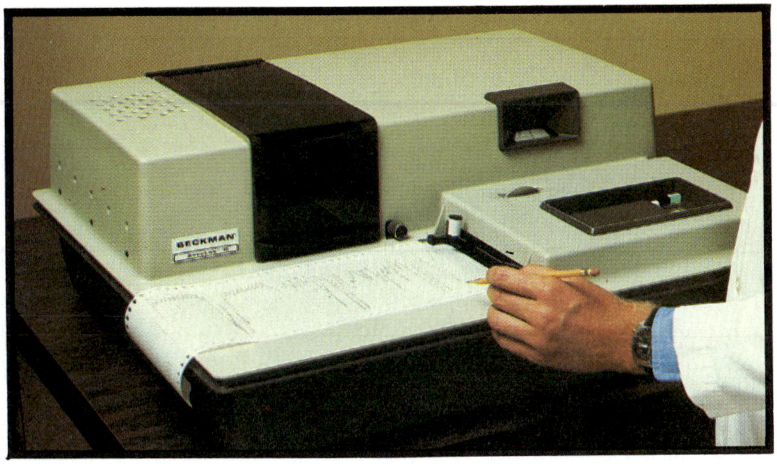

FIGURE 14-20. The infrared spectrum of an unknown compound will give a technician many clues to its identity.

14:9 Microwaves

What are microwaves?

Microwaves are very short radio waves. In the electromagnetic spectrum, microwaves are in between ordinary radio waves and infrared waves. Microwave rays can pass through rain, smoke, and fog. For this reason they are used for communication. For example, beams of microwaves are used to send telephone messages in mountain areas where it is too difficult to put up telephone lines.

Name two uses of microwaves.

A microwave oven contains an electronic tube that produces an intense beam of microwave radiation. When absorbed, the radiation causes the molecules in the food to vibrate. The kinetic energy of the food is increased. The temperature of the food rises and it cooks. The microwaves are absorbed directly by the food, not by the container. Glass or paper cooking dishes are used because they allow microwaves to pass through. Metal containers are not used because they reflect microwaves. Cooking with microwaves is faster than cooking with gas or electricity. A microwave oven has a shield to protect people from exposure to the radiation. Being exposed to too much microwave radiation is harmful and can make people ill.

FIGURE 14-21. High-energy microwaves cook food faster and more efficiently than gas or electricity.

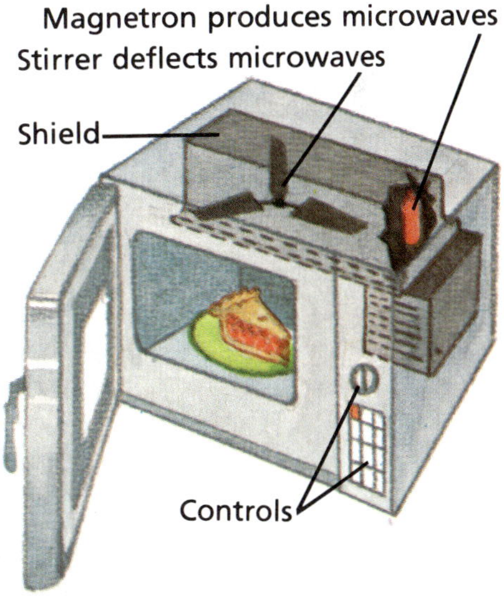

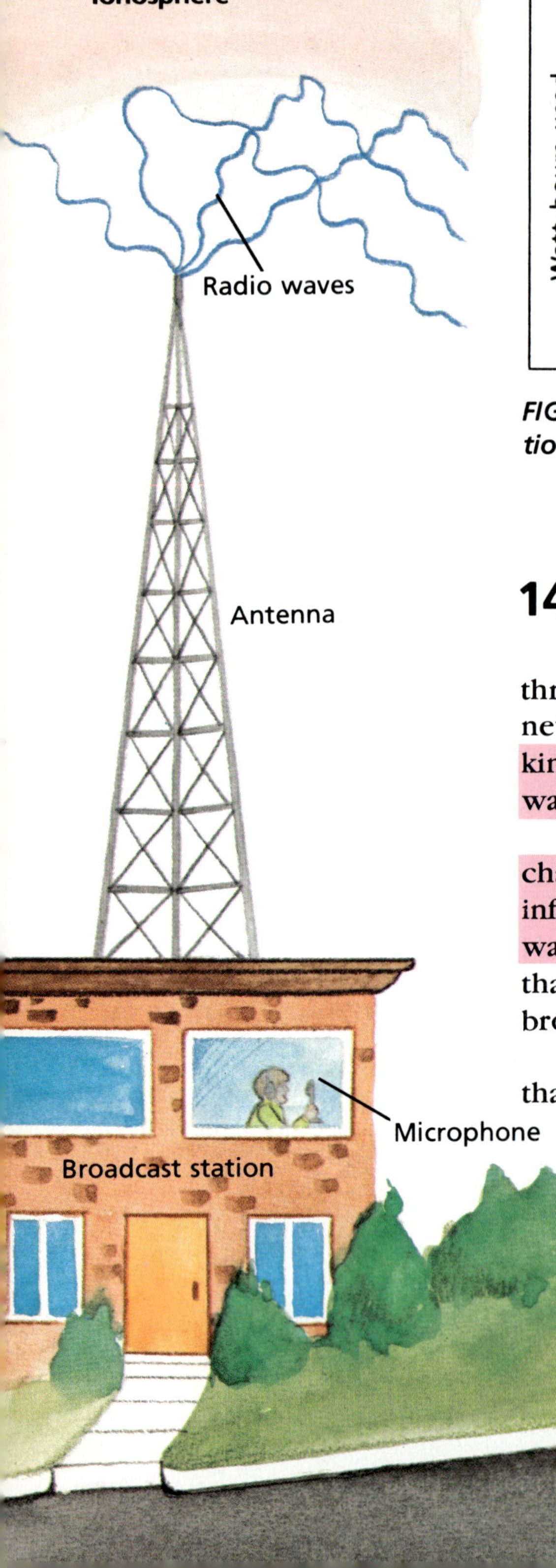

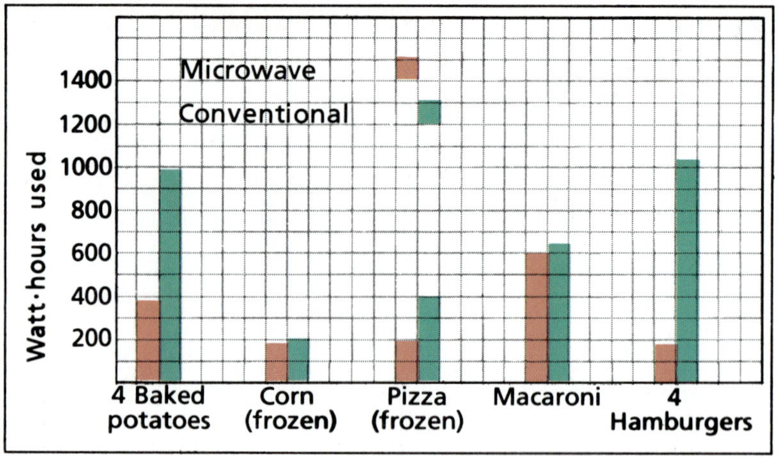

FIGURE 14-22. A comparison of the energy used in conventional cooking versus microwave cooking.

14:10 Radio

Radio programs are broadcast by waves that travel through the air. These waves are part of the electromagnetic spectrum. They travel at the speed of light. Two kinds of radio waves are AM waves and FM waves. AM waves have a shorter wavelength than FM.

Information is sent over AM waves by constantly changing the amplitude of the waves. FM waves carry information through changes in the frequencies of the waves. Also, FM waves carry sounds of higher frequency than AM waves. For this reason, many stations that broadcast music are FM stations.

You can tune in a distant AM station more readily than an FM station. Why? AM radio waves go up into the sky and bounce back down to the earth off the ionosphere. The **ionosphere** is an upper layer of charged particles in the earth's atmosphere. AM waves reflected off the ionosphere are carried great distances around the curve of the earth. Shortwave radio waves bounce back and forth between the ionosphere and the earth many times. They can travel thousands of miles. A shortwave radio receiver can pick up broadcasts from all over the world.

In what ways are AM radio waves different from FM waves?

How is sound changed into radio waves?

The FM stations you tune in on a radio are not too far away. FM waves are not reflected by the ionosphere and do not travel long distances. Most FM stations do not have much power beyond 80 kilometers.

Sound is changed to radio waves at a radio broadcast station. Most people know that radio announcers talk into a microphone. The microphone changes the sound into an electric current. The strength of the current is increased by vacuum tubes or transistors in an amplifier. Next the current goes into the transmitter which is connected to an antenna. The antenna sends out the radio waves. Many small radio stations broadcast with about 5000 watts of power. Others broadcast with as much as 50 000 watts or more.

Further information concerning electric circuitry is found in Chapter 21.

To hear a radio program, you need a radio receiver. As the receiver picks up the radio waves, an electric current is produced in the antenna. This current is amplified and sent to a part called the loudspeaker. Vibrations produced by a thin plate in the loudspeaker, called a diaphragm, produce the sound you hear. Each radio station has a different wave frequency on which it broadcasts. When you tune a radio, you adjust it to pick up the broadcast frequency of a station.

FIGURE 14-23. Radio waves are transmitted at the broadcast station. Your radio is the receiver of these waves.

14:11 Television

TV is used to send pictures as well as sound. The principle of sending pictures is similar to radio transmission. However, with TV, the picture is changed to a signal composed of TV waves. TV waves are like FM waves. Their reception is usually limited to about 80 kilometers from the TV station.

To broadcast pictures, a TV camera is needed. The camera contains a lens and photoelectric cells. The lens focuses an image on the cells, causing them to produce an electric current. This electric current is amplified and carries the image to the broadcast antenna. The antenna sends out the picture through TV waves. In a TV broadcast, the sound part of the program is sent out at the same time with radio waves.

The set you use to watch TV is a receiver. It is attached to an antenna by a wire or cable. The antenna picks up the signal from the TV station. A weak alternating current is produced and carried to the receiver. Here it is amplified and fed to the picture tube.

How does a picture tube form a picture? The inner surface of its screen is coated with fluorescent material. Attached to the tube is a gun that fires a beam of electrons at the screen. When these electrons strike the screen it glows. The electron beam is controlled by electromagnets whose operation is based on the pattern in

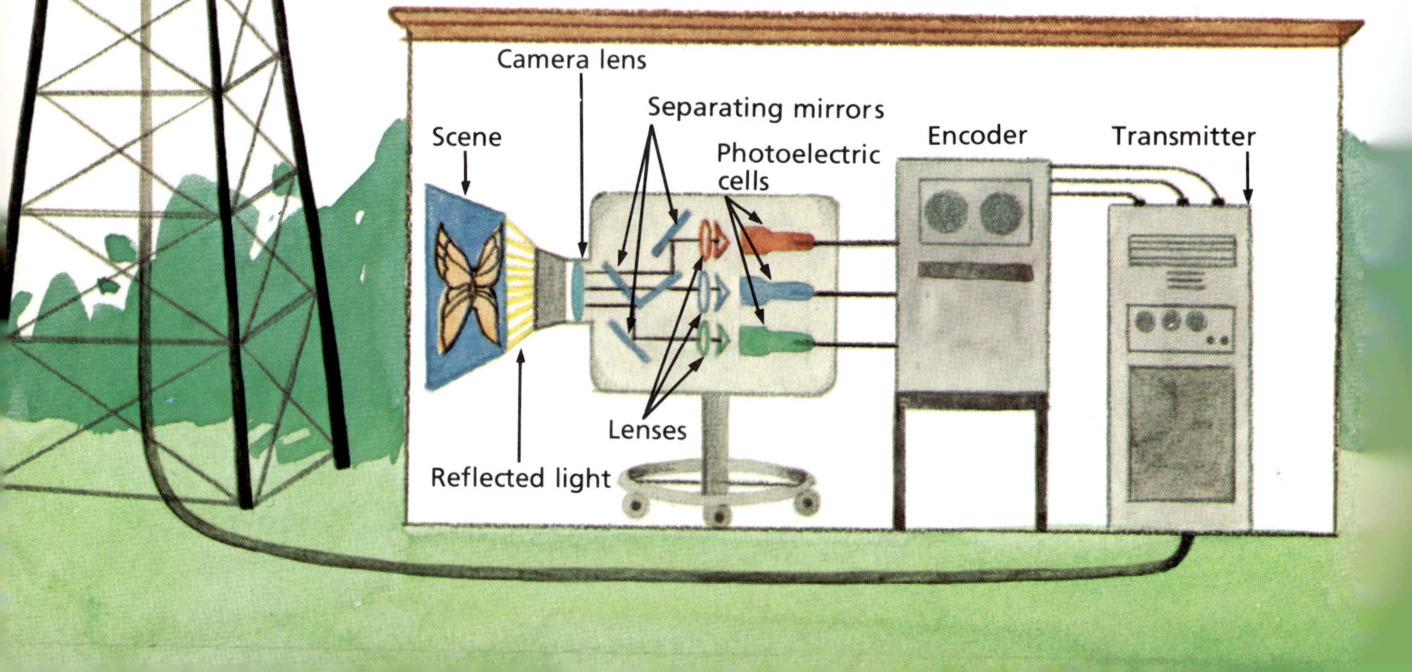

How does a color TV set work?

the TV signal. These electromagnets make the beam of electrons move swiftly back and forth, up and down, across the screen. Different points on the screen light up as they are struck by electrons. Each spot hit by an electron glows for a fraction of a second. The combination of tiny light and dark spots makes the picture. The picture reproduces the scene recorded by the TV camera in the studio.

A color television picture tube has tiny dots all over the inner surface of its screen. There are three kinds of dots and they are arranged in groups. When struck by electrons the dots glow. One glows red. The second glows green and the third glows blue. Three separate guns fire electrons at the dots. One fires electrons at the red dots. The second gun fires at the green dots. The third gun fires electrons at the blue dots. The pattern of lighted dots formed when struck by electrons produces a colored picture.

A color TV camera produces three different color signals. A black and white signal is also produced for black and white TV sets. The four signals are sent out as TV waves by the transmitter at a TV station. The picture on the tube reproduces the scene in the TV studio.

Making Sure

14. What is closed circuit television? *Closed circuit television is not broadcast. The signal travels over wires.*

15. Why might TV reception be poor in a building near a mountain? *The mountain may shield the receiver.*

FIGURE 14-24. The television transmission station sends out four signals—three for color TV and one for black and white TV. Each dot on the TV screen glows as it is hit by electrons from an electron gun of the same color.

Focus On

Skills

Chapter Review

A chapter preview will acquaint you with the material to be presented in this chapter. The preview is to be done quickly to give you a general idea of the information presented in this chapter.

1. The title of Chapter 14 is? *Waves*
2. What is the picture used to start the chapter? *bird making water waves*
3. Why do you think this picture was selected? *shows the chapter title*
4. What are you expected to learn from this chapter? *the properties of waves and the important uses of electromagnetic waves*
5. Use the *Table of Contents* to list the chapter sections in order.
6. List the words in boldface type found in this chapter. Star the ones you know. Keep this list and define the others as you read the chapter.
7. Read the caption under the picture on page 292. Why do you think this picture is included in the chapter? *shows a use of infrared radiation*
8. What is the title of the *Activity* on page 281? *Can you measure the frequency of a wave?*
9. What materials will you need to set up this *Activity*? *strip of metal, pan of water, and a tuning fork*
10. The *Making Sure* sections in each chapter are there to reinforce what you have just read. How many *Making Sure* questions are in this chapter? *13*
11. *Points to Remember*, on page 299, is a summary of the chapter. This section is to be read carefully before you read the chapter. It gives an overview of the chapter and identifies the authors' important points.
12. Read through the *True and False* questions on pages 299-300. What questions do you already know? You will be reading to find the answers to questions you do not know.

After this preview, carefully read the chapter.

Points to Remember

1. Waves travel through space and matter. 14:1
2. Vibrations can produce sound waves. 14:2
3. Every wave has a frequency, amplitude, and wavelength. 14:1-14:2
4. Water waves can be studied in a ripple tank. 14:4
5. Waves in the electromagnetic spectrum can be produced by electricity or magnetism. 14:5
6. Light, radio, television, and X rays are part of the electromagnetic spectrum. 14:5-14:11

Words to Use

Write a sentence in which you correctly use each of the following words or terms.

amplitude	infrared	refraction
electromagnetic spectrum	microwaves	ultraviolet
frequency	photon	wave
hertz	reflection	X rays

Questions for Review

Do not write in this book.

A. True or False Have the students rewrite the false statements to make them correct.

Determine whether each of the following sentences is true or false.

T **1.** Transverse waves can be formed with a rope.
T **2.** The hertz is a unit of frequency.
F **3.** The amplitude of a wave is always the same as its ~~speed.~~ displacement
T **4.** Waves can be reflected and refracted.
F **5.** When the speed of a wave changes it is ~~reflected~~. refracted
F **6.** You ~~can~~ cannot detect X rays with your eyes.
T **7.** All the waves in the electromagnetic spectrum are transverse waves.
T **8.** Light travels at a speed of 300 000 000 meters per second.
T **9.** X rays are produced when a high voltage electron beam strikes a metal target.
F **10.** Ultraviolet and infrared rays have ~~the same~~ a different wavelength.

B. Multiple Choice

Choose the word or phrase that correctly completes each of the following sentences.

1. *(Amplitude, Wavelength, Frequency)* is the linear distance of one wave crest and trough.
2. Vibrations per second refers to a wave's *(amplitude, wavelength, frequency).*
3. *(Light, Water, Sound)* waves can travel through a vacuum.
4. *(X-ray, Radio, TV)* waves can be detected with a fluorescent substance.
5. X rays are absorbed the most by *(flesh, bone, aluminum, lead).*
6. The wavelength of ultraviolet radiation is *(longer, shorter, the same as)* visible light.
7. Warm objects give off *(X rays, ultraviolet radiation, infrared radiation).*
8. Microwaves are a kind of *(X ray, visible light, radar).*
9. When you tune a radio you adjust it to the broadcast *(amplitude, speed, frequency)* of a radio station.
10. A beam of *(ultraviolet radiation, TV waves, infrared radiation, electrons)* produces the picture in a TV receiver.

C. Completion

Complete each of the following sentences with a word or phrase that will make the sentence correct.

1. Frequency is the number of waves that pass a given point in one second.
2. As the wavelength increases, the frequency of the wave decreases if the wave is traveling at the same speed.
3. The speed of a wave equals its wavelength times its frequency.
4. Reflection occurs when a wave strikes an object and bounces off.
5. Electromagnetic radiation consists of tiny bundles or packets called photons.
6. X rays are used to make pictures of the inner parts of the body.

7. Ultraviolet lamps are used to kill germs.
8. Infrared radiation is used to dry and warm things.
9. Microwaves are very short radio waves used to send telephone messages.
10. Two kinds of radio waves are AM and FM.

Detailed answers to these questions are given in the Teacher's Guide at the front of this book.

D. How and Why

1. How can you produce a transverse wave with a rope?
2. In what two ways are water waves different from waves in the electromagnetic spectrum?
3. How can reflection and refraction be demonstrated in a ripple tank?
4. Make a list of the waves in the electromagnetic spectrum. State one fact you have learned about each kind of wave.
5. What are some uses for ultraviolet, infrared, and microwave radiation.

More Ideas to Explore

1. Make a colored chart of the electromagnetic spectrum for a bulletin board. List the different kinds of waves and important facts about each.
2. Obtain a kit for building a radio from a hobby store. Use it to make your own receiver.
3. Do library research on the harmful effects of radiation. Make a report to your class.

Readings to Discover

Field, R., "Microwave Popcorn Debate Warms Up." *Science Digest,* Vol. 85, January 1979, pp. 85-86.

Martens, A.E., "Seeing Machines: Visual Labor Becomes Automated." *Science Digest,* Vol. 83, May 1978, pp. 22-28.

"Microwave Ovens: Advantages Deserve Buyer's Closer Look." *Science Digest,* Vol. 83, February 1978, pp. 80-83.

Color is so much a part of your visual world. We tend to like certain colors and dislike others. Our choice of color can reflect our mood. What is color? The trees in the picture were once green. How did they change color? How do artists change colors in painting beautiful scenes such as this?

James N. Westwater

Light and Color 15

Chapter 15 describes the properties of light. Reflection is presented in the discussions on mirrors. Refraction is used as an introduction to color. See the Teacher's Guide at the front of this book for additional teaching strategies for this chapter.

15:1 Light

GOAL: *You will learn the basic features of light, mirrors, prisms, and color.*

What would life be like without light from the sun? Our world would probably be quite unlike what it is today. Try to imagine a world without green plants. These plants need light to make food through photosynthesis. We could produce light on a small scale, but how could we grow the food we need to live? Oftentimes when we think of light, we think of the things we would not be able to see without it. Life on the earth would be very different without the natural light of the sun. Perhaps it would not exist at all.

What is light?

Visible light is one small part of the electromagnetic spectrum. Like the other waves of the electromagnetic spectrum, light is made of photons. Recall that a photon is a tiny packet of radiant energy. Light travels at the same speed as other radiant energy, 300 000 000 meters per second in a vacuum. Unlike other waves of the electromagnetic spectrum, we can see light.

FIGURE 15-1. The colors of visible light are a very small part of the electromagnetic spectrum.

Making Sure

1. List three things you could not do without light.
2. Why are most houseplants kept near windows?
   Plants need light to manufacture food.

15:2 Mirrors and Reflection

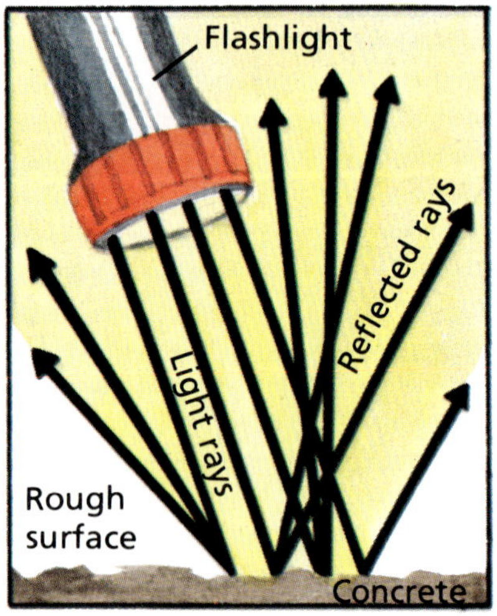

FIGURE 15-2. A piece of concrete reflects light in many directions.

When you look in a mirror, you see an image of yourself. An image forms in the mirror because light travels in a straight line. Light is reflected from your face to the mirror and back to your eyes.

A **plane mirror** is flat and smooth. Usually it is made of a pane of glass with a silver coating on the back. The smooth surface of a mirror causes a beam of light to be reflected. The angle at which light is reflected is the same as the angle it strikes the mirror.

You cannot see an image in a rough surface such as a concrete floor, a grass lawn, or a brick wall. Light is reflected from these surfaces in many directions. The reflected light has no pattern and produces no image.

Dan McCoy from Rainbow

FIGURE 15-3. A plane mirror reflects light in a straight line.

When you look at your reflection in a mirror, your image appears to be behind the mirror. It appears the same distance behind the mirror as you are in front of the mirror. The image produced in a plane mirror is called a **virtual image.** Although you can see it, a virtual image does not really exist. It only appears to exist.

A **parabolic mirror** is a curved mirror. Parabolic mirrors are used as reflectors for searchlights and automobile headlights. A shaving mirror and lighted make-up mirror are parabolic mirrors. If you look in this type of mirror, you see an enlarged image of your face. The image you see of yourself is a virtual image.

George C. Anderson

a

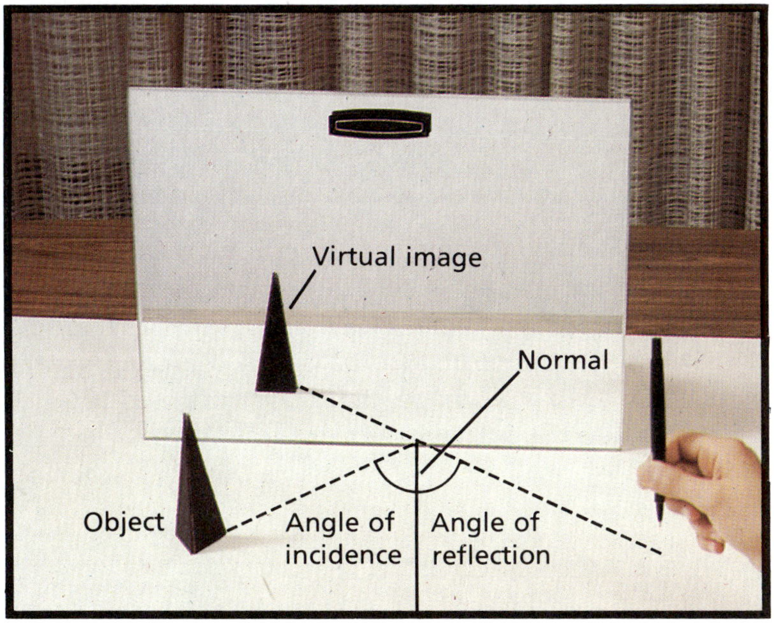

Larry Hamill

b

FIGURE 15-4. The image of the cone (a) is a virtual image. It appears to be behind the mirror. A parabolic mirror (b) magnifies an image.

The surface of a parabolic mirror curves in the shape of a line called a parabola. A line straight out from the center of the mirror is called the **principle axis,** Figure 15-5. Light rays striking a parabolic mirror parallel to its principle axis are reflected toward a common point in front of the mirror. This point is called the **principle focus.** The distance from the center of the mirror to the principle focus is the **focal length** of the mirror.

George C. Anderson

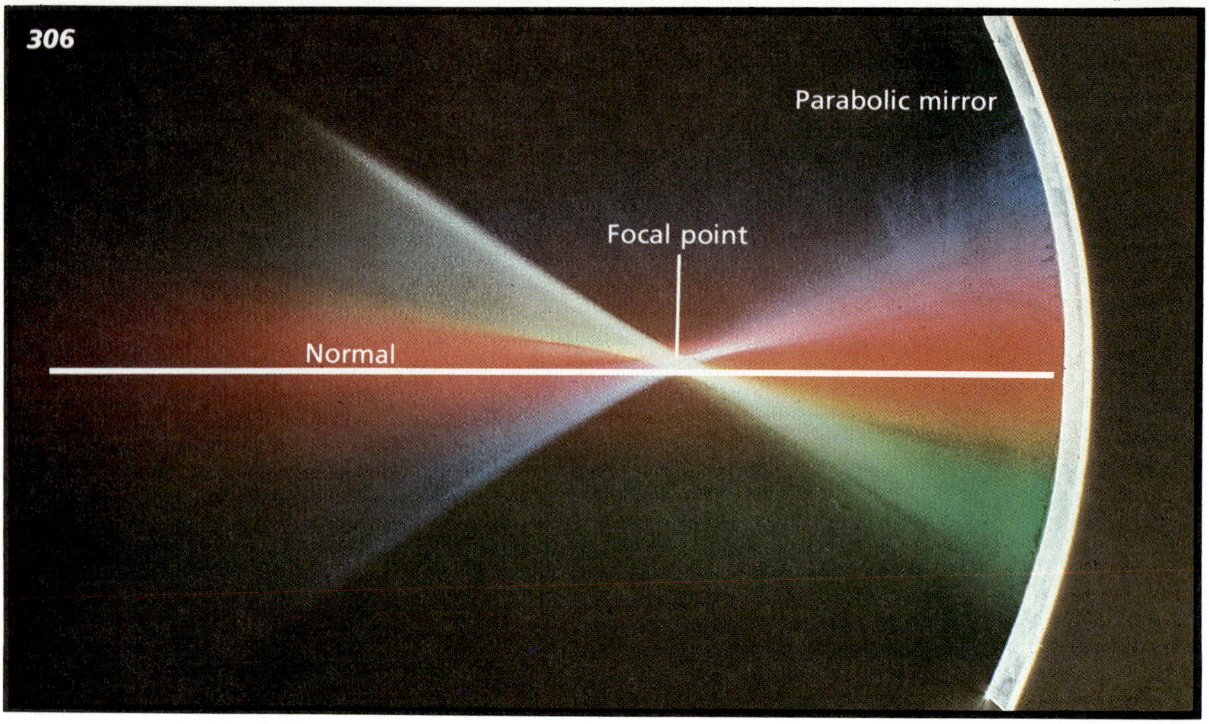

FIGURE 15-5. The focal point of the parabolic mirror is the point where the reflected light rays intersect.

A real image formed by a parabolic mirror appears in front of the mirror. A real image can be formed on a smooth flat surface such as a wall or movie screen. A virtual image cannot be formed on a screen or any other surface. With a real image, light rays reflected from the mirror strike the screen to form the image. A parabolic mirror can produce both virtual images and real images.

What kinds of images can be produced by a parabolic mirror?

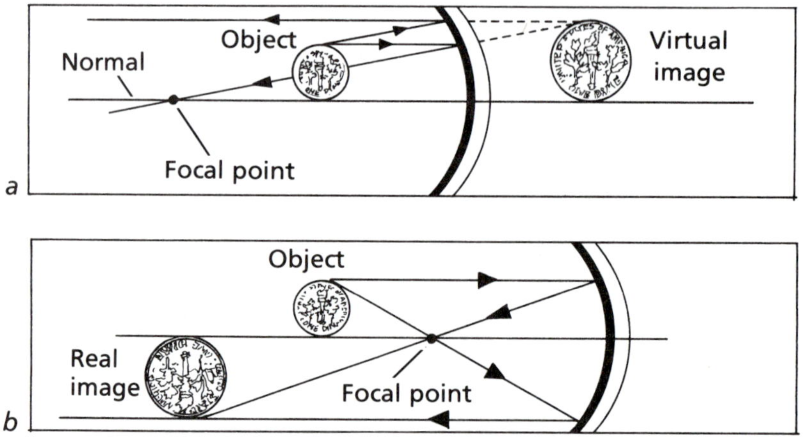

FIGURE 15-6. A virtual image is formed behind the mirror when an object is placed to the right of the focal point (a). An inverted real image is formed in front of the mirror when the object is placed to the left of the focal point (b).

15-1 Detailed information concerning this Activity can be found in the Teacher's Guide at the front of this book.

ACTIVITY Where does an image appear in a plane mirror?

Set up a small plane mirror perpendicular to a tabletop. Place a candle taller than the mirror 20 centimeters in front of the mirror. Place a second candle (the same size as the first candle) behind the mirror. Look at the image of the first candle in the mirror. Move the second candle to the point at which its top part equals (appears at) the top part of the image. How far is the candle beyond the mirror?

It should be 20 centimeters.

George C. Anderson

FIGURE 15-7.

15-2

ACTIVITY What images can be formed using a parabolic mirror?

CAUTION: Use care when working with lighted candles.

(1) Obtain a shaving mirror of the magnifying type to produce a virtual image. **(2)** Place a lighted candle 10 centimeters in front of the mirror. Darken the room. Compare the size of the image to the size of the candle itself. Is the image upright or inverted? Does the image appear to be in back of or in front of the mirror?

upright, in back of the mirror

(3) Set the candle 30 centimeters away from a wall. Hold the mirror 10 centimeters from the candle, facing the wall, Figure 15-8. Slowly move the mirror away from the candle until the image of the candle flame appears on the wall. How is this image different from the image produced in the mirror?

inverted, real image in front of the mirror and smaller than the flame

George C. Anderson

FIGURE 15-8.

15-3 Detailed information concerning this Activity can be found in the Teacher's Guide at the front of this book.

ACTIVITY How do you find the focal length of a mirror?

inverted, smaller, real

larger

same, inverted

answers will vary

(1) *Place a candle about 2 meters in front of a parabolic mirror.* **(2)** *Use a white index card or white sheet of paper to locate the image. Be careful to hold the card slightly off center from the principal axis of the mirror to allow light rays to reach the mirror and be reflected.* **(3)** *Is the image upright or inverted? Is it larger or smaller than the candle? Is it a real or a virtual image?* **(4)** *Now move the candle closer to the mirror. Locate the image. How has the size changed?* **(5)** *Move the candle toward the mirror until the candle and its real image are at the same point.* **(6)** *Compare the size of the candle and its image. Is the image upright or inverted?* **(7)** *Continue to move the candle toward the mirror until the image becomes blurred and begins to turn over. This is the focal point of the mirror. What is the focal length of your mirror?*

FIGURE 15-9. George C. Anderson

Making Sure

Real images can be projected on a screen; virtual images cannot. A real image can be formed from a parabolic mirror and a virtual image can be formed from a plane mirror.

3. How is a real image different from a virtual image? Give one example of each.
4. Name five things in which you can see an image of yourself.

Mirror, spoon, window, chrome coffee pot, and hubcap are examples.

5. Observe your face in both sides of a shiny tablespoon. How are the two images different?

The curved part of the spoon produces a real, inverted image; the back of the spoon produces an upright, virtual image.

15:3 Refraction

Suppose you see a coin on the bottom of a swimming pool and want to dive for it. Where do you aim? Not at the coin! The light rays reflected off the coin are bent as they travel to your eye. Light rays are bent as they pass from water into air. The bending of light rays is called refraction. Refraction changes the direction of the light rays. Refraction explains why it is hard for you to locate the coin. When you dive for the coin, you must aim in front of it.

How does refraction affect a light ray?

George C. Anderson/ICOM

FIGURE 15-10. Light rays are refracted as they pass through water.

Refraction is caused by an increase or decrease in the speed of light. The speed of light changes as it passes from one transparent substance to another. For example, if light passes into glass at an angle, its speed decreases, and it is refracted. Index of refraction tells how much light is refracted by a substance. The greater the change in the speed of light, the larger the index of refraction.

Explain the meaning of the index of refraction.

Table 15-1

Index of Refraction and Speed of Light in Some Substances		
Substance	**Index of Refraction**	**Speed of Light (m/s)**
air	1.00	3.00×10^8
water	1.33	2.23×10^8
ethanol	1.36	2.21×10^8
glycerine	1.47	2.04×10^8
glass	1.50	2.00×10^8
carbon disulfide	1.63	1.71×10^8
diamond	2.42	1.24×10^8

To find the angles formed by a refracted ray, a line is drawn perpendicular to the transparent surface. This line is called a normal. When light enters a transparent surface at an angle and its velocity is decreased, the light is bent toward the normal. For example, when light

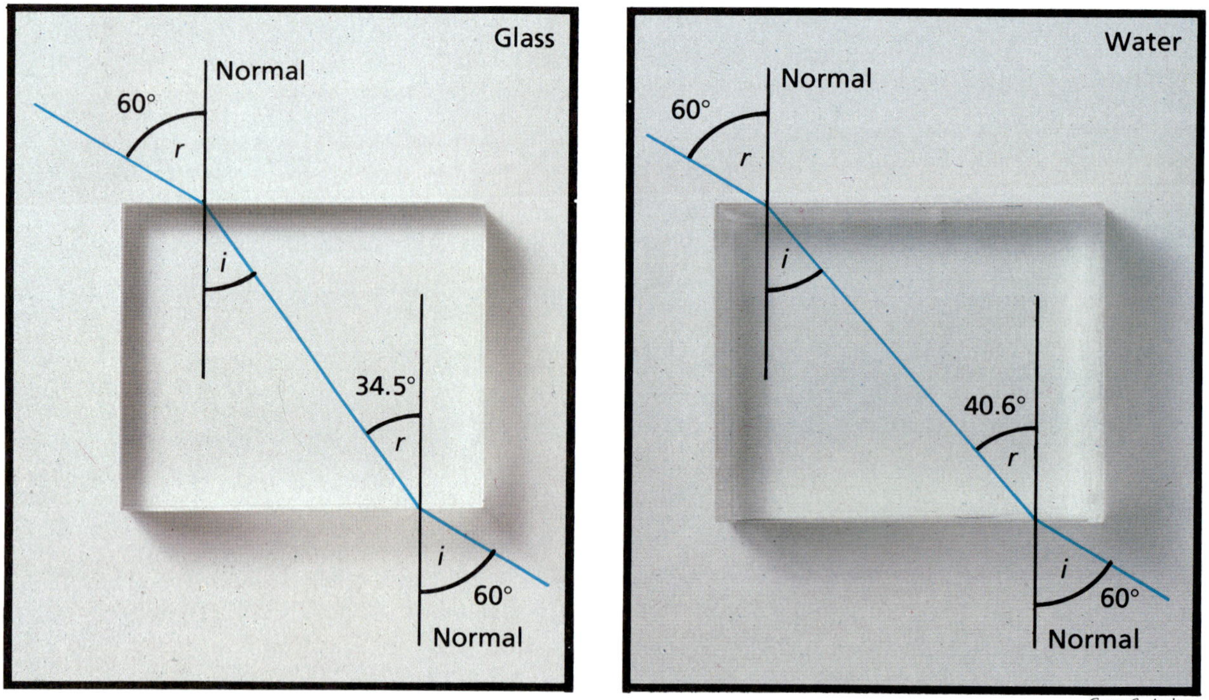

George C. Anderson

FIGURE 15-11. The index of refraction for glass is greater than that of water. Note that the refracted angle for glass (a) is less than that of water (b).

passes from air into glass, the light is bent toward the normal. When light strikes a transparent surface at an angle and its velocity increases, it is bent away from the normal. For example, when light passes out of glass into air, the light is bent away from the normal.

15-4 Detailed information concerning this Activity can be found in the Teacher's Guide at the front of this book.

ACTIVITY *What do you observe when light is refracted?*

Hold a pencil in a glass of water so that the upper half of the pencil is above the water surface. View the pencil with your eye level to the water's surface. What do you observe? Place a coin in a teacup. Place your eye so the coin is just out of sight. Now have someone fill the teacup with water. Can you see the coin? Explain.

It appears disjointed.

The water refracts light allowing you to see the coin.

Making Sure

6. Which material in Table 15-1 will refract light the most? How is refraction related to the use of this material?

Diamond refracts light the most. As a result, diamond has a sparkling brilliance.

7. How is light bent as it passes from glass into water? To find the answer, you must know the speed of light in glass and the speed of light in water, Table 15-1. Make a drawing with a light ray to show the refraction.
See the Teacher's Guide.

15:4 Prisms

A **prism** is made of transparent material with two straight faces at an angle to each other. From a side view, a prism has the shape of a triangle, Figure 15-12. The path of a light beam changes when it goes through a prism. The light is refracted twice; once as it enters and once as it leaves. Both refractions are in the same direction, Figure 15-13.

White light is a mixture of colors. When white light is passed through a prism, the colors are separated. The beam of white light that enters the prism spreads out into a band of colors. The colors are violet, blue, green, yellow, orange, and red. The band of colors produced by a prism is called a visible light spectrum.

FIGURE 15-12. A prism is a triangular piece of glass.

Larry Hamill

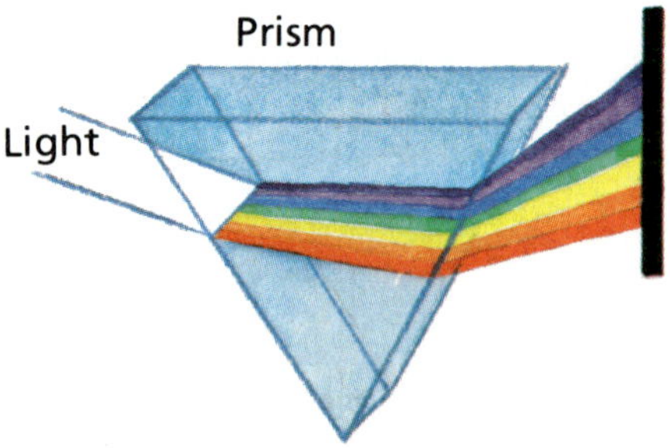

FIGURE 15-13. As light waves pass through the prism, each color that composes white light is bent. Red light, which has the longest wavelength, is refracted least. Violet light, which has the shortest wavelength, is refracted most.

Eastman Kodak Company, 1977

How does a glass prism produce a spectrum? White light is composed of the different colors of the rainbow. Each color of light has an index of refraction in glass that is slightly different from the other colors. When light passes through the angled faces of a glass prism, it is refracted. The light is refracted twice in the same direction; once as it enters and once as it leaves the prism. Each color is refracted differently. For example, red light is refracted least. Violet light is refracted most. As a result of the refraction, all the colors are separated.

Table 15-2

Index of Refraction in Glass for Spectrum Colors

Color	Index of Refraction	Color	Index of Refraction
violet	1.532	yellow	1.517
blue	1.528	orange	1.514
green	1.519	red	1.513

Recall that a chemical element can be identified by a flame test. The flame color can be used to produce a spectrum for that element, Figure 15-14. Elements in the stars have been identified by the spectra of light they give off.

Kodansha

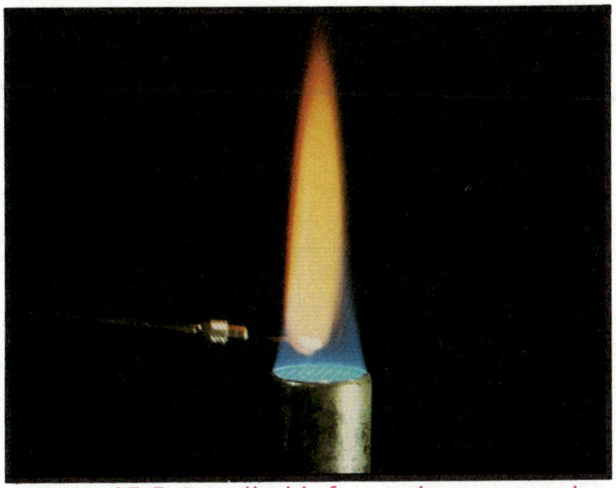

Lester V. Bergman & Associates

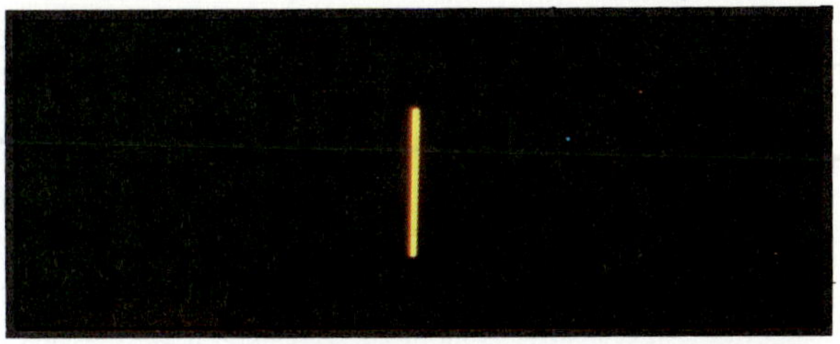

FIGURE 15-14. The sodium spectrum consists of one bright yellow line. This spectrum is produced by looking at a sodium flame test through a spectroscope.

15-5 Detailed information concerning this Activity can be found in the Teacher's Guide at the front of this book.

ACTIVITY *How do you form a spectrum?*

White light may be separated into a color spectrum. Darken the room and pass a narrow beam of light through a prism. Form a spectrum on white cardboard or a screen. What colors do you see?

Making Sure

8. Which color in the visible light spectrum has the largest index of refraction for glass? *violet*

9. Which color has the smallest index of refraction? *red*

10. Which color in the visible light spectrum is refracted most by a glass prism? *violet*

11. Which color is refracted the least? *red*

15:5 Color

What is the connection between the color and frequency of a light wave?

Each color of light has a different wavelength and frequency. The frequency of a light wave determines its color. Frequency is a physical property of a light wave. Color is what you sense with your eyes and your brain when light enters your eyes. Each color of the visible spectrum has its own wavelength.

Light waves have very short wavelengths compared to radio or television waves. The wavelength of violet light waves is 0.00004 centimeters. At the opposite end of the spectrum are the red light waves which are longer. The wavelength of a red light wave is 0.00007 centimeters. Light waves with shorter wavelengths have higher frequencies.

Table 15-3

Color and Wavelength	
violet	*short light waves*
blue	↓
green	*increasing*
yellow	*wavelength*
orange	↓
red	*long light waves*

FIGURE 15-15. A red filter (a) absorbs all other colors but reflects red light. A green filter (c) absorbs all other colors but reflects green light.

A filter is a transparent material which absorbs some colors and allows others to pass through. The color of the filter is shown by the color of light it transmits, Figure 15-15. The other colors that do not pass through a filter are absorbed.

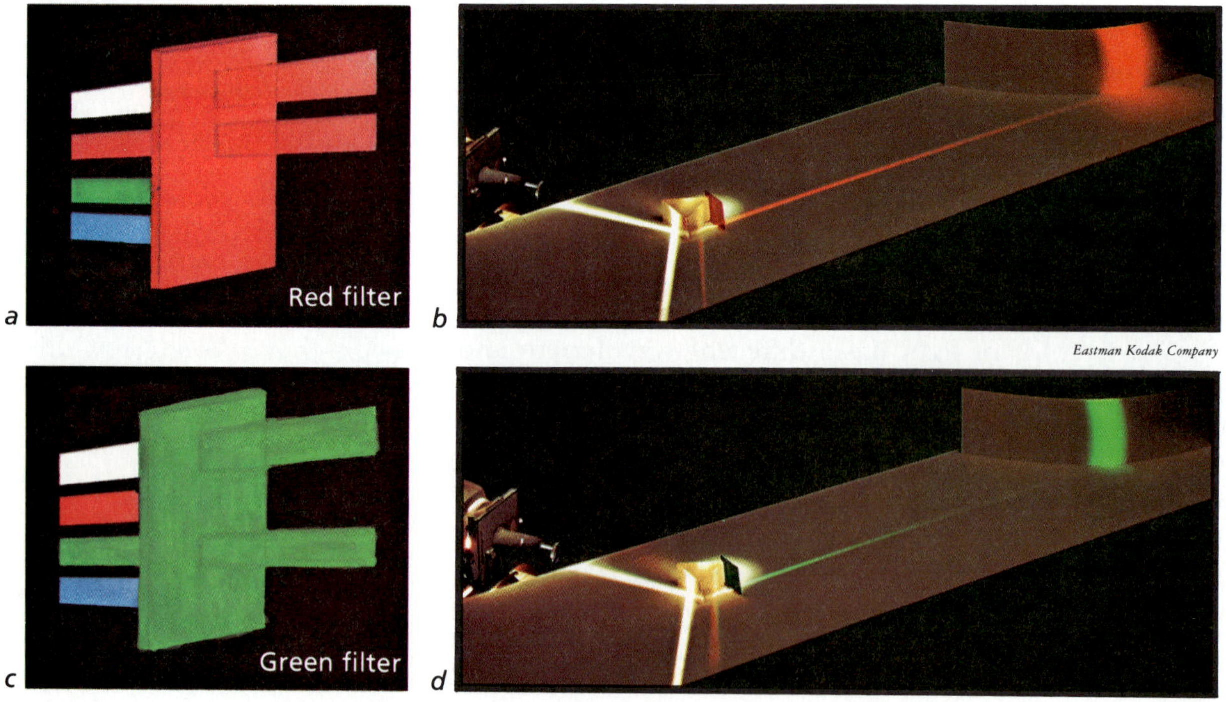

Eastman Kodak Company

Eastman Kodak Company

FIGURE 15-16. A blue filter absorbs all other colors.

How can a person see colors? The nerves in the human eye have three kinds of color receptors. These receptors are stimulated by red, blue, and green light waves. Any color can be produced by mixing together the proper proportions of these colors. Therefore, the colors a person sees depends upon the amount and proportion of red, blue, and green light that enters their eyes.

Red, blue, and green are known as the primary colors of light. When mixed in equal amounts they produce white light.

Fisher Scientific Co.

FIGURE 15-17. The primary colors of light produce white light when mixed.

Why is an apple red? Why is a grapefruit yellow? These objects are not transparent. They reflect light. The color we see depends on the kind of colored light that is reflected. The molecular composition of a grapefruit skin is different from that of an apple. When struck by white light, the particles of a grapefruit will reflect green and red but absorb blue. As a result, the grapefruit is yellow. The particles of an apple will reflect red and some green but absorb blue.

FIGURE 15-18. An apple absorbs the colors of white light and reflects red (a). In red light, the apple still appears red (b). In blue light, the apple appears black (c). The blue light is absorbed.

Larry Hamill

How does a person see colors?

Stress the difference between the primary colors of light and the primary pigment colors. Pigments are additive; light colors are subtractive.

How does your eye sense the color that is reflected by an object? The color receptors in your eyes are called cones. There are three kinds of cones. Each is sensitive to either red, blue, or green light. To see the yellow color of a grapefruit, the red and green cones are stimulated. Your brain reads the message as yellow. This color mixing is the same process that occurs with color television. A color television screen is covered with tiny dots. Each dot is a cluster of smaller dots. In each cluster, there is one red, one blue, and one green dot. The dots light up in various combinations to produce the color picture on the screen.

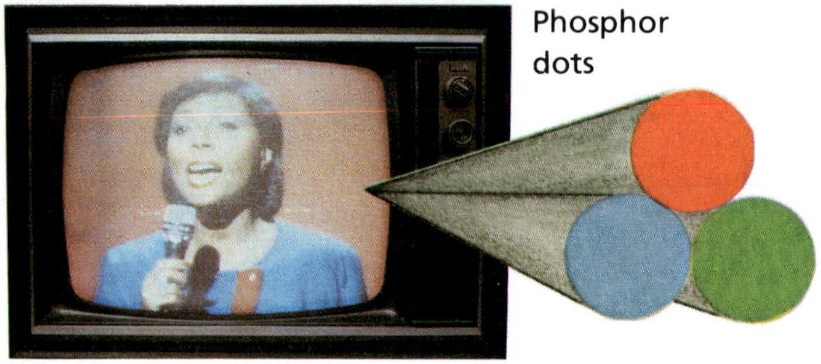

Hickson-Bender Photography

FIGURE 15-19. A color television screen consists of thousands of three-dot clusters. These dots glow in various combinations to produce the picture on the screen.

What does an artist have to know about color in order to mix paint? An artist needs only three pure pigments to mix any color. The three basic or primary pigment colors are magenta, yellow, and cyan. These three colors are mixtures of the primary colors, Figure 15-20. Magenta is formed by mixing red and blue. Cyan is formed by mixing green and blue. Yellow is formed by mixing red and green. When light strikes one of these dyes, it reflects two of the primary colors. The third primary color is absorbed.

Here is an important point for you to remember. When the primary colors of light are mixed, white light is produced. When the primary pigment colors are mixed, black is produced.

FIGURE 15-20. The primary pigment colors are shown. How are they different than the primary colors of light?

Colour Library International (USA) Ltd.

FIGURE 15-21. A color photograph can be separated into four separate pieces of film—yellow (a), magenta (b), cyan (c), and black. These films can be put together to produce the original photograph (d). Thus, a printing press needs only four colors of ink to produce full color photographs.

Making Sure

12. What color would a grapefruit appear in red light? in blue light? *red, black*
13. How are primary pigments different from primary colors of light? *pigments are additive; colors are subtractive*

15:6 Polarized Light

What is polarized light? How can it be produced?

Polarized light can be produced by passing light through a special kind of filter. **Polarized light** is light in which the waves vibrate in a certain uniform pattern. You may have worn sunglasses that contain filters which block out polarized light. The sunglasses cut down the glare on a bright sunny day. The glare from shiny surfaces is usually polarized light.

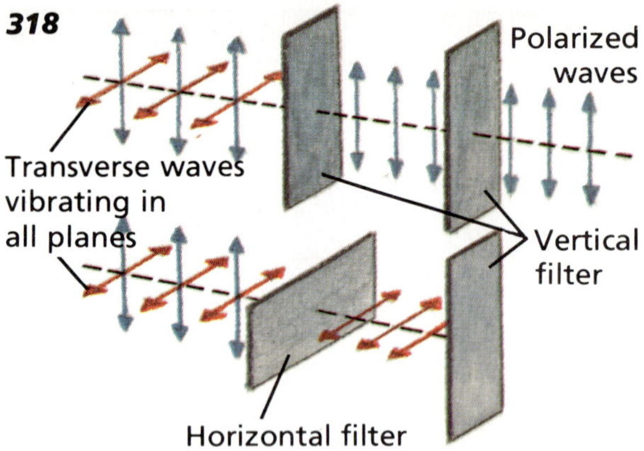

FIGURE 15-22. A polarizing filter allows only parallel light waves to pass through.

Think of light as transverse waves. A polarized light filter permits waves vibrating in the same plane to pass through, Figure 15-22. In effect, the filter has an endless number of parallel slits. Light waves vibrating in the same plane as the slits can pass through. Light not vibrating in the same plane as the slits is reflected or absorbed. Light that passes through the filter is vibrating only in one plane. It is called polarized light.

Why are polarizers used in photography?

Polarizers are used in photography. They control the intensity of light that enters a camera when taking a picture. There is more contrast between colors in photographs taken on a very bright sunny day when polarizing filters are used. Polarized light can be used to show areas of strain on an object. For example, an area of strain in a part for an airplane. Parts are more likely to bend or break where there is strain. This property of polarized light is useful to engineers who design things.

FIGURE 15-23. A comparison of photographs taken without a polarizing filter (a) and with a polarizing filter (b) is shown. What differences do you see?

a b

Larry Hamill

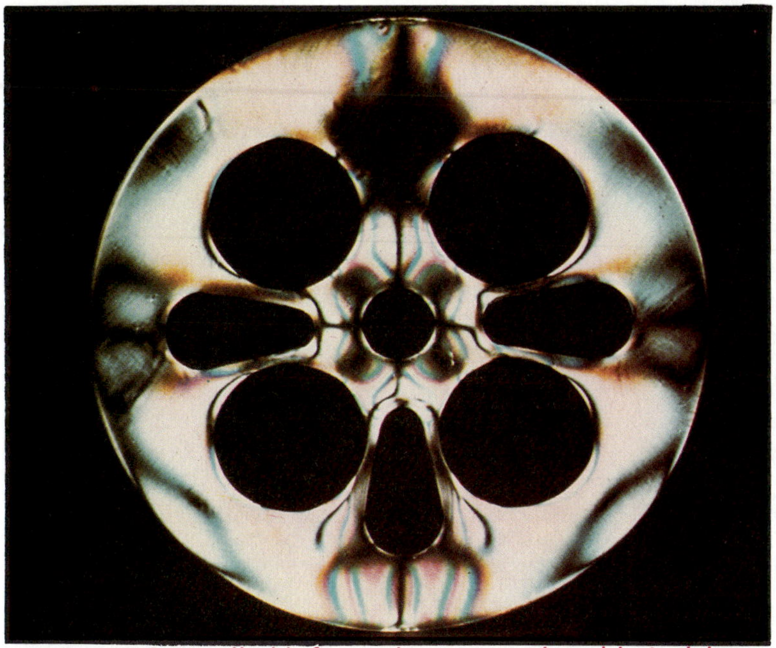

FIGURE 15-24. The disc shown is under pressure. Points of stress are shown using polarized light.

15-6 Detailed information concerning this Activity can be found in the Teacher's Guide at the front of this book.

ACTIVITY *How does a polarizing filter affect light?*

Hold two polarizing filters against each other. Look through them toward a lamp or window. Rotate one filter slowly. How does the brightness change?

The light should dim and brighten as the filters are rotated.

15:7 Interference

In 1801, Thomas Young, an English scientist, performed an experiment with light. In his experiment, Young passed light through a narrow slit, Figure 15-25. The light passing through the slit spread out and passed through two more narrow slits set side by side. These two slits were the same distance from the first slit. The light went through the slits and again spread out. Young observed that this light had a series of light and dark bands, Figure 15-26.

FIGURE 15-25. Young's interference experiment.

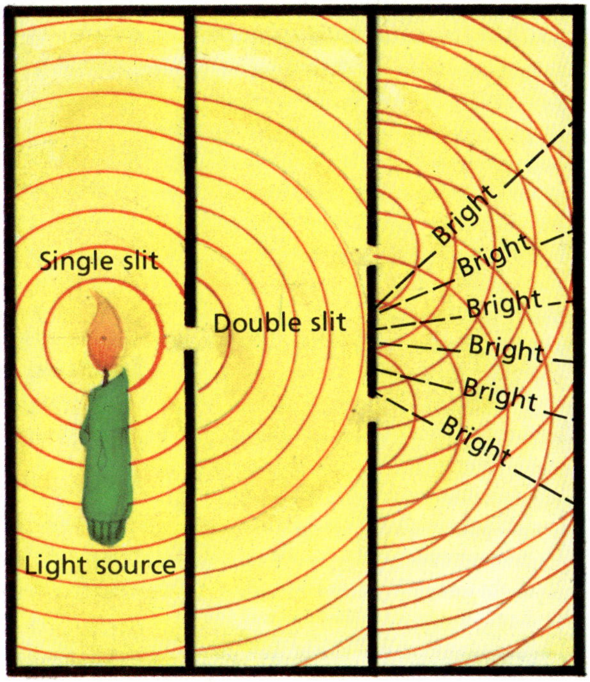

Kodansha

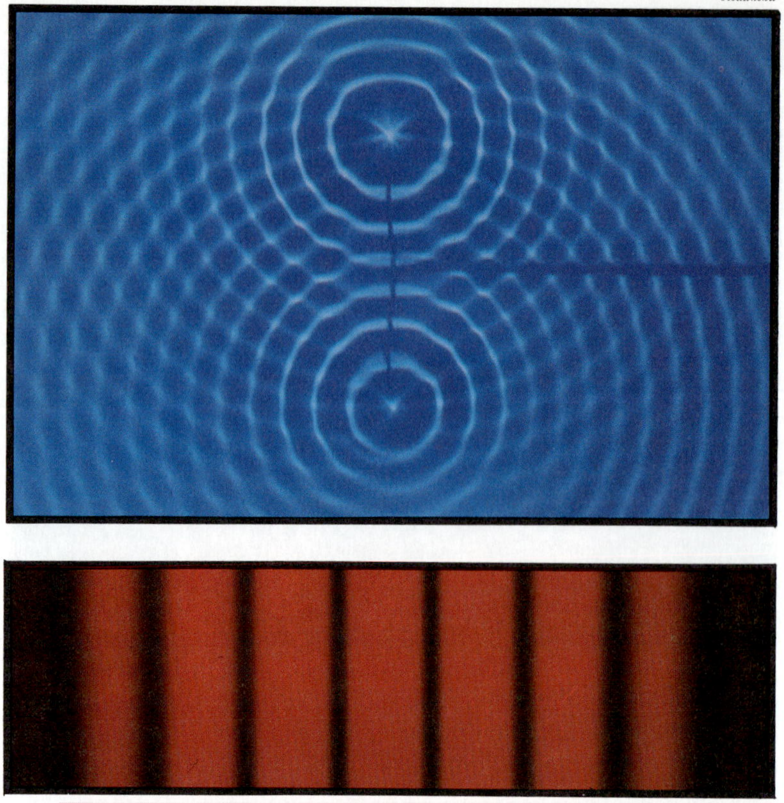

a

b

FIGURE 15-26. The light and dark bands in Young's experiment can also be produced by interfering water waves (a). An actual photograph of a light interference pattern (b).

What is interference of light?

The light and dark bands are caused by **interference.** In the areas of the light bands, the waves were in phase. They combined to make the light brighter. In the areas of the dark bands, the waves were out of phase. Here the waves cancelled or destroyed the effect of each other. Thus, there were dark bands.

How can interference produce a color spectrum?

Like a prism, a diffraction grating can be used to produce a color spectrum. However, the diffraction grating does not produce a color spectrum by refraction of light. The colors are separated by interference. A **diffraction grating** is a piece of glass or plastic containing many parallel slits, Figure 15-27b. There may be as many as 25 000 slits in a piece 2.5 centimeters long. The slits are produced by a machine which makes parallel scratches on the glass with a diamond needle. When white light passes through the slits of the diffraction grating, interference occurs. This interference causes different wavelengths of light to reinforce or cancel each other. The net result is a spectrum of colors.

Kodansha

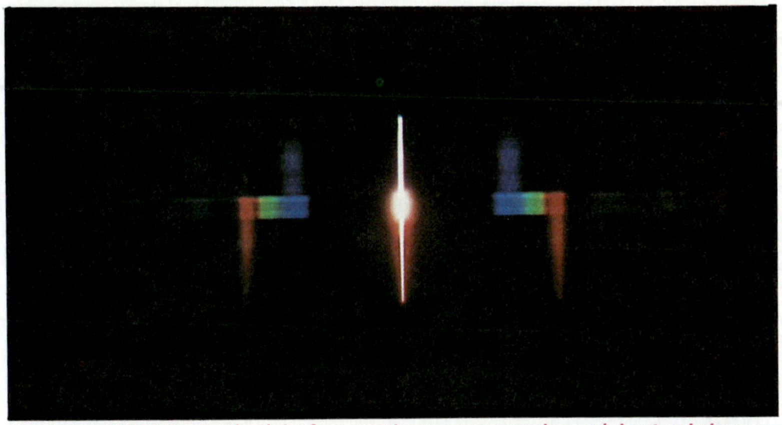

Hickson-Bender Photography/Ohio Wesleyan Univ.

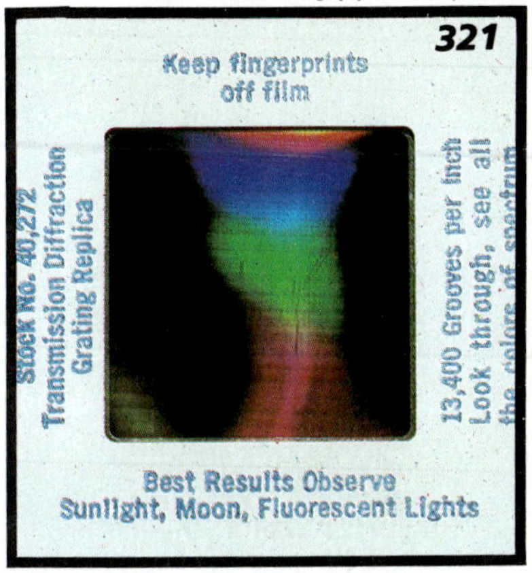

FIGURE 15-27. A diffraction grating produces a spectrum by forming an interference pattern.

15-7 Detailed information concerning this Activity can be found in the Teacher's Guide at the front of this book.

ACTIVITY *How do you make a spectroscope?*

Construct a diffraction grating spectroscope, Figure 15-28. Use a piece of cardboard tubing or a cardboard box. Cover one end of the tube with aluminum foil containing a slit cut with a knife. Mount a square piece of plastic diffraction grating, measuring 1 cm^2, in the opposite end. The lines in the grating must be parallel to the slit. Observe white light from a lamp through the spectroscope. Observe light from a fluorescent lamp. What colors are formed? *answers will vary*

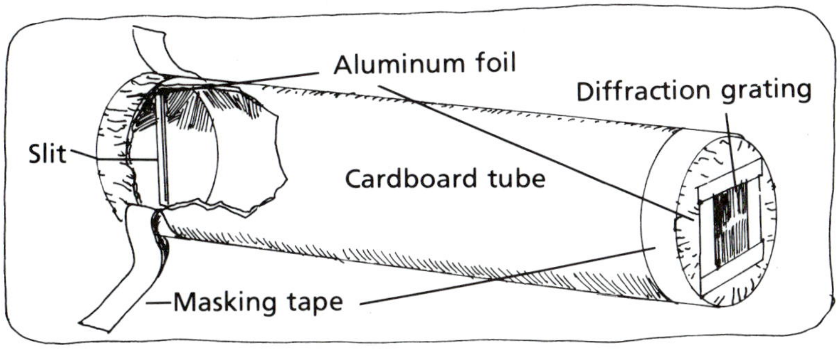

FIGURE 15-28.

Making Sure

14. How is refraction of light different from diffraction of light?

Refraction results from the bending of light; diffraction from interference.

15. On a piece of paper, draw two waves that are in phase. Now draw two waves that are out of phase.

Focus On

Careers
Research in Light

Dan McCoy from Rainbow

In the next few years telephones, televisions, and even some parts of computers will use light. Instead of using wires, light will be used to carry information. The light will flow through special fibers. This field is called fiber optics. It is finding uses in many industries. Where do ideas, like fiber optics, come from? How are they developed? Such ideas are developed in an optics laboratory.

Imagine you are working in an optics lab. Someone asks the question, "Can light be used to carry telephone calls?" After some thought, you decide that, if you can find a way to control the light, it will work. Now you must find a way to control the light. Lasers would be a good light source. So, you design a system you think will work.

All of your work, so far, is on paper. It is ideas. Now you must test them. To test them, you set up a series of experiments. Suppose one experiment is to test different glass and plastic fibers. You want to see which one carries the laser light best. You use lenses to focus the laser on one end of a fiber. At the other end place a detector. The detector is connected to a computer. The results of each trial are recorded by the computer. By studying the results, you can pick the best fiber.

Another experiment would test a method of putting sound on the laser beam. You would use things like amplifiers, lenses, microphones, and speakers. All of your data would be put into the computer. After the experiment the data would be used in making a better experiment. If the experiment failed, the data would help to show why it failed. Knowing why an experiment failed helps in designing a better one.

It is not always possible to make an idea work. When one does, researchers help to make it a part of everyday life. Many of the ideas using fiber optics and lasers have worked. There are several test systems using fiber optics with telephones.

Optics is not limited to lasers and fibers. New lenses for cameras or telescopes are also developed in an optics lab. Developments in optics are used in many kinds of research. But they are not limited to research. They can be found in things like ordinary car mirrors and satellites.

Points to Remember

1. Visible light consists of tiny packets of radiant energy called photons. 15:1
2. Images can be formed with mirrors. 15:2
3. Light is refracted as it passes from one transparent substance into another. 15:3
4. White light contains a mixture of colors that can be separated into a spectrum. 15:4
5. The color of an object depends on the color of light it reflects. 15:5
6. Polarized light consists of waves vibrating in the same plane. 15:6
7. Interference of light waves as they pass through a diffraction grating produces a color spectrum. 15:7

Words to Use

Write a sentence in which you correctly use each of the following words or terms.

diffraction grating	parabolic mirror	reflection
image	photon	refraction
index of refraction	polarized light	spectrum
interference	prism	

Questions for Review

Do not write in this book.

A. True or False Have the students rewrite the false statements to make them correct.

Determine whether each of the following sentences is true or false.

T 1. Visible light is part of the electromagnetic spectrum.

F 2. A ~~real~~ image is formed in a plane mirror. virtual

T 3. A real image can be formed on a screen.

T 4. Refraction occurs when the speed of a light beam changes.

T 5. A glass prism can produce a spectrum of colors.

F 6. All colors of light have ~~the same~~ wavelength and frequency. a different

T 7. Mixing equal amounts of red, blue, and green light produces white light.

T 8. Some sunglasses have filters that block out polarized light.

F 9. A prism produces a color spectrum through the ~~diffraction~~ of light. refraction

F 10. White and black are primary colors. not

B. Multiple Choice

Choose the word or phrase that correctly completes each of the following sentences.

1. A photon is a tiny packet of *(matter, energy)*.
2. Your image in a plane mirror appears to be *(in front of, behind, on the surface of)* the mirror.
3. A mirror *(refracts, reflects)* light.
4. Light is refracted when it is *(bent, reflected, absorbed)*.
5. The index of refraction for glass is *(the same as, greater than, less than)* the index for water.
6. From a side view, a prism has the shape of a *(square, rectangle, triangle)*.
7. *(Violet, Green, Red)* light is refracted the most when it passes from air into glass.
8. An apple appears red because it *(absorbs, reflects, refracts)* red light.
9. When white light passes through a blue filter *(white, blue, all colors other than blue)* are absorbed.
10. A diffraction grating separates light by *(reflection, refraction, interference)*.

C. Completion

Complete each of the following sentences with a word or phrase that will make the sentence correct.

1. A mirror reflects light rays.
2. A glass prism refracts light rays.
3. A parabolic mirror has a shiny, concave surface.
4. A prism is made of glass or some other transparent material.
5. The color in a flame test is used to identify an element.
6. Each color of the light spectrum has a different wavelength and frequency.

7. Magenta is a pigment color formed by mixing red and blue.
8. White is produced when the primary colors of light are mixed.
9. Black is produced when the primary pigment colors are mixed.
10. A diffraction grating has many parallel slits through which light passes.

D. How and Why Detailed answers to these questions are given in the Teacher's Guide at the front of this book.

1. Why does a searchlight or headlamp have a parabolic mirror behind the light bulb?
2. Why can you still see a sunset on the horizon for a short time after the sun is actually below the horizon?
3. Could you see an image in a mirror if light did not travel in straight lines? Explain why.
4. What causes a person to see colors?

More Ideas to Explore

1. Make a periscope out of a shoebox and two pocket mirrors. Tape the mirrors at 45° angles at opposite ends of the box. Cut a window opposite each mirror and then tape the cover on. Use your periscope to see around corners.
2. Obtain a camera and a light meter. Use the camera to take photographs of the same scene at different times during the day. Make a poster with your prints. Label each print with the light meter reading.
3. Colors have different effects on people. Obtain information on the use of colors in designing new products.

Readings to Discover

Gardner, Robert, and Webster, David, *Shadow Science.* Garden City, NY: Doubleday and Co., 1976.

Heyer, Kenneth, *Rainbows, Halos, and Other Wonders: Light and Color in the Atmosphere.* NY: Dodd, Mead, 1978.

Leven, Edith M., *The Penetrating Beam, Reflections on Light.* NY: Richards Rosen, 1978.

Do you wear eyeglasses or contact lenses? If not, you may think lenses are not important to you. Have you ever looked at the stars through a telescope or a cell through a microscope? Do you ever take pictures or watch television? Is the water in the glass a lens?

Steve Lissau

Light and Its Uses

16

Chapter 16 describes the behavior of light passing through lenses. This information is developed further in practical discussions of telescopes, microscopes, photography, and lasers. See the Teacher's Guide at the front of this book for additional teaching strategies for this chapter.

16:1 Lenses

GOAL: *You will learn some of the practical uses of light, lenses, and images.*

A **lens** is a curved transparent object, usually made of glass or clear plastic. There are two kinds of lenses: convex and concave. A **convex lens** is thicker in the middle than at the edges. Magnifying glasses are examples of convex lenses. A **concave lens** is thinner in the middle than at the edges. Each surface of a concave lens is shaped like the inside of an orange peel.

Name two kinds of lenses and tell how they differ from each other.

Light is refracted as it passes through a convex lens. The bending of the light rays brings them together at a point called the principal focus. When a light beam is passed through a convex lens, the principal focus can be found with a piece of paper. It appears as a tiny point of light. Light is refracted as it enters and leaves the lens. Thick convex lenses refract light more than thin lenses. For this reason, a thick convex lens has greater magnifying power.

L.D. Franga

Larry Hamill

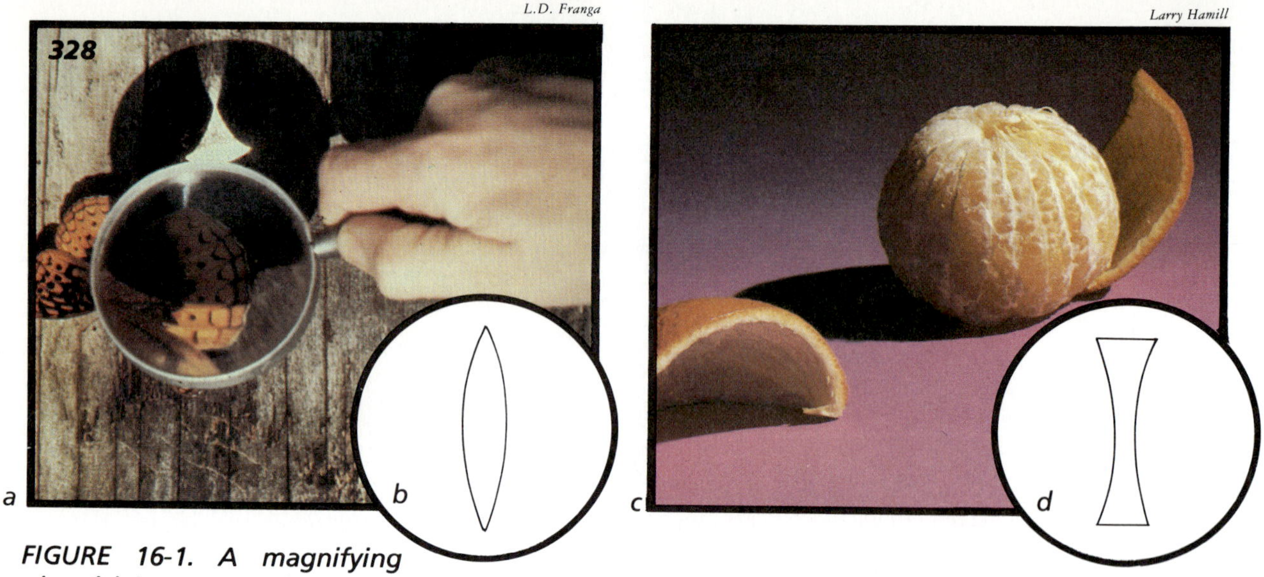

FIGURE 16-1. A magnifying glass (a) is a convex lens. Each surface of a concave lens is shaped like the inside of an orange peel (c).

A convex lens can be used to form a real image. The image on a movie screen is a real image formed with a convex lens. The image formed by an overhead projector is also a real image. Have you ever seen slides shown with a slide projector? A convex lens inside the projector forms the real image you see.

An image produced by a convex lens may be larger than the actual object. It also can be the same size or smaller than the actual object. When the image is larger than the object, the object is said to be magnified. Magnification is the number of times an image is larger than the actual object. Microscopes, telescopes, binoculars, and slide projectors use convex lenses to magnify objects.

Kodansha

FIGURE 16-2. The principal focus is that point where light rays intersect.

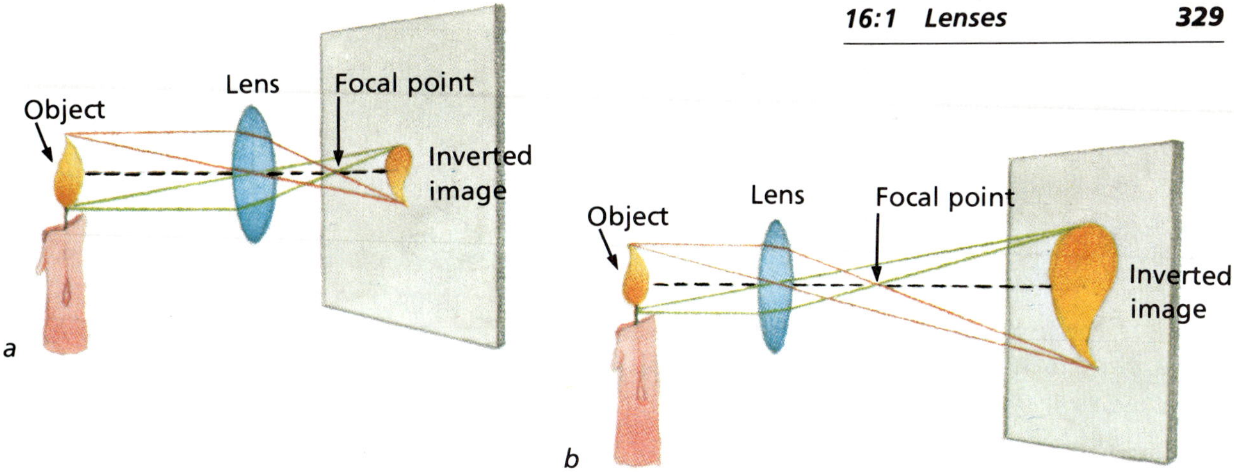

FIGURE 16-3. The principal focus of a thick lens is closer to the lens (a) than that of a thin lens (b).

When the image is twice as large as the object, the magnification is two power (2x). When the image is three times as large, the magnification is three power (3x). The lens in the eyepiece of a microscope usually magnifies about 10x.

If an object is placed between a convex lens and its principal focus, the lens produces a virtual image. When someone uses a magnifying glass to read fine print, they see a virtual image of the print. The virtual image formed by a convex lens is larger than the object and is upright, Figure 16-1. Remember, a virtual image cannot be projected on a screen.

How does a convex lens form a virtual image?

FIGURE 16-4. A magnifying glass produces a virtual image which is larger than the object.

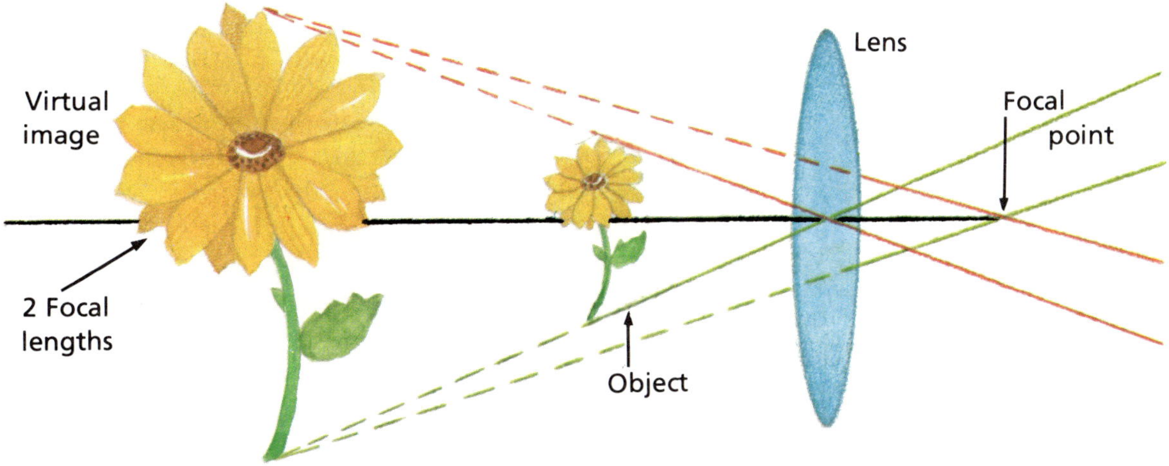

16-1 Detailed information concerning this Activity can be found in the Teacher's Guide at the front of this book.

ACTIVITY How is a lens like a prism?

Hold two triangular prisms point to point, Figure 16-5. Pass a narrow beam of light through the prisms. How is the light bent? Repeat using a concave lens. How is the effect of the lens similar to the two prisms? The effects are similar.

Hold the concave lens over this page. Move it toward and away from the page until you can see an image. Is the image real or virtual? Why is a concave lens sometimes called a reducing lens?

Virtual image which is reduced in size.

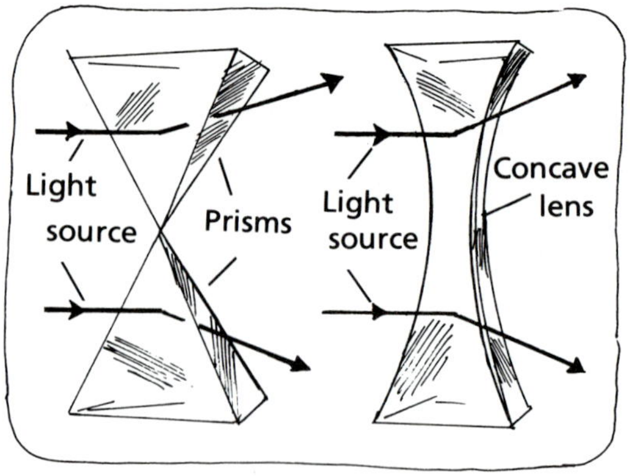

FIGURE 16-5.

16-2 Detailed information concerning this Activity can be found in the Teacher's Guide at the front of this book.

ACTIVITY Can you find a real image on a diagram?

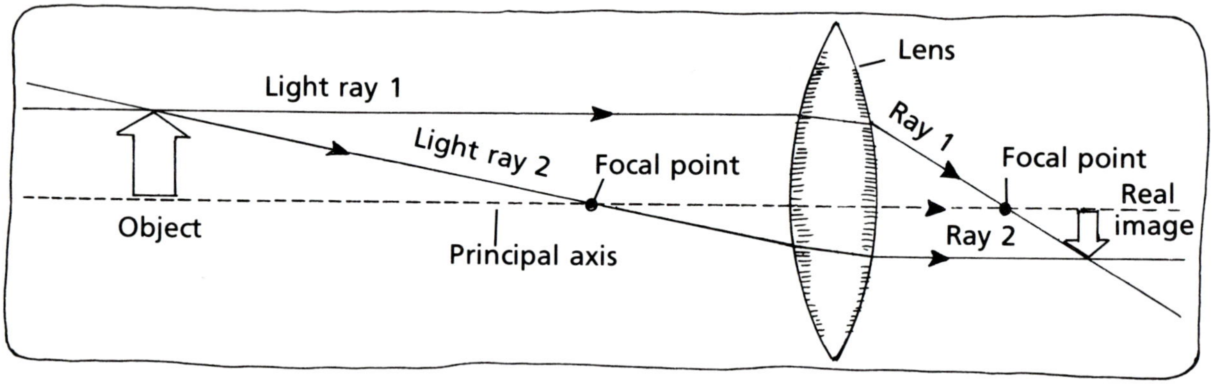

FIGURE 16-6.

(1) On the left side of a piece of paper, draw an upright 2-cm arrow. The arrow represents the object. **(2)** Fifteen centimeters to the right of the arrow, draw a side view of a convex lens 5 cm high. **(3)** With a ruler, draw a dotted line across the paper through the center of the lens to show its axis. **(4)** Then measure two 5-cm focal lengths: one to the right of the lens and one to the left of the lens. **(5)** Mark the principal focus to the left as F_2. Mark the principal focus to the right as F_1. **(6)** Now draw a line parallel to the axis from the top of the arrow to the lens. This line represents a light ray. **(7)** Continue the line *from the lens to the principal focus F_1.* **(8)** *Draw a second line from the top of the arrow through the principal focus F_2. Continue the line until it meets the lens.* **(9)** *As the ray leaves the lens on the opposite side, continue the ray parallel to the principal axis. The point at which the two lines cross is the top of the real image. Compare your drawing to Figure 16-6.*

Making Sure

1. What kind of lens would you use to study a bee's leg? Why? *See the Teacher's Guide.*
2. What kind of lens is shaped like the inside of an orange peel? *See the Teacher's Guide.*
3. What are some objects that use lenses? — *Cameras, microscopes, telescopes, magnifying glasses, and binoculars are some examples.*
4. Close-up pictures may be made by using an extension tube between the lens and a camera. This moves the lens toward the object and away from the film. How does the image size change when the lens is extended? *gets larger*

16:2 Lenses and Vision

Lenses may be used to correct vision problems. For example, farsightedness and nearsightedness can be corrected with glasses. The human eye has a convex lens. The lens is attached to muscles which can either relax or tighten. When the muscles are relaxed, they allow the lens to thicken at the center. However, when the muscles tighten, they pull on the sides of the lens. As a result, the center of the lens becomes thinner. Changing the shape of a lens changes the focus of the lens. If the muscles cannot properly control the shape of the lens in the eye, a person has poor vision. The person may be farsighted or nearsighted.

What causes a person to be farsighted or nearsighted?

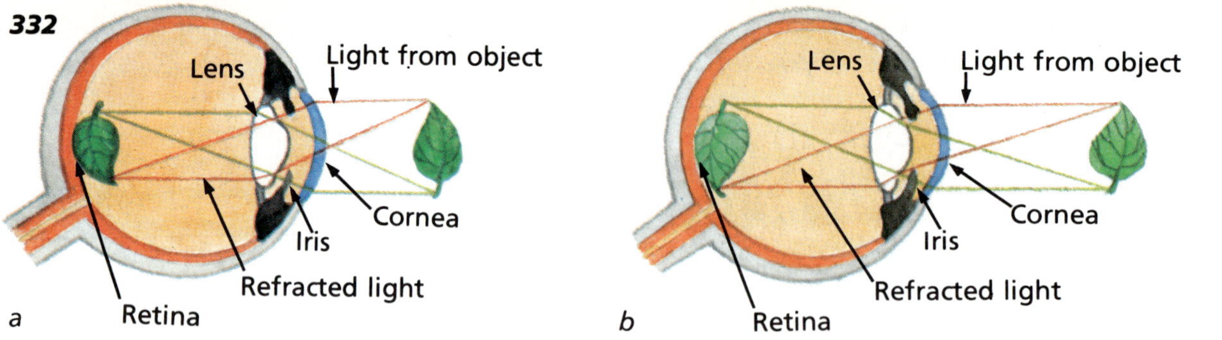

FIGURE 16-7. In order to see close objects, muscles in the eye cause the lens to thicken (a). The inverted image of the object is then focused on the retina in the back of the eye. In order to see distant objects, the muscles relax and the lens becomes thinner (b). The inverted image of the object is still focused on the retina.

A farsighted person can see things far away better than things up close. The view of nearby objects is not clear. Farsighted vision can be corrected with convex lenses, Figure 16-8. The lenses sharpen the image of nearby objects so they can be seen more clearly.

A nearsighted person can see things up close better than things far away. Distant objects are not seen clearly. Nearsighted vision can be corrected with concave

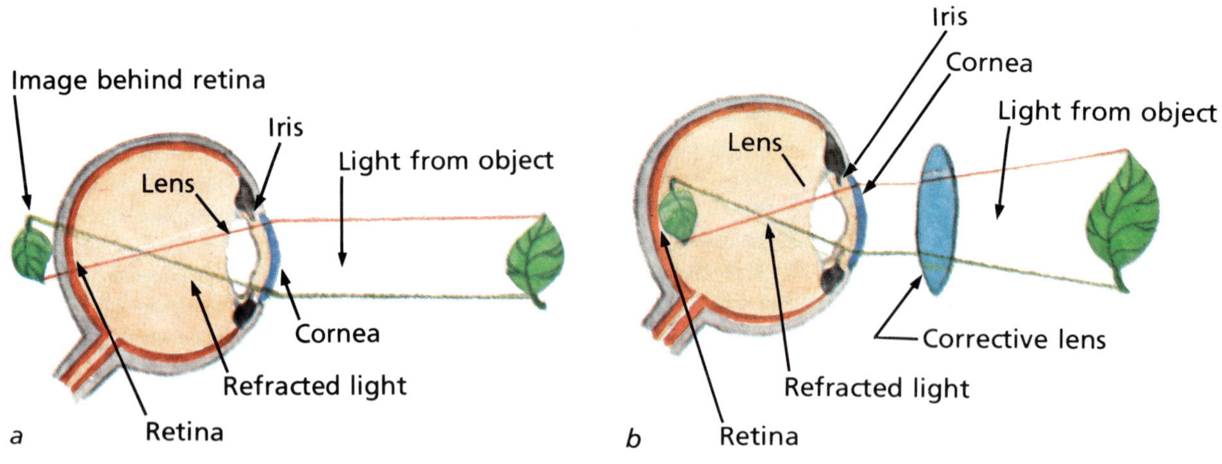

FIGURE 16-8. A farsighted person cannot see close objects well. The lens focuses the image behind the retina (a). A convex lens (b) is used to refract light at the proper angles to focus the image on the retina.

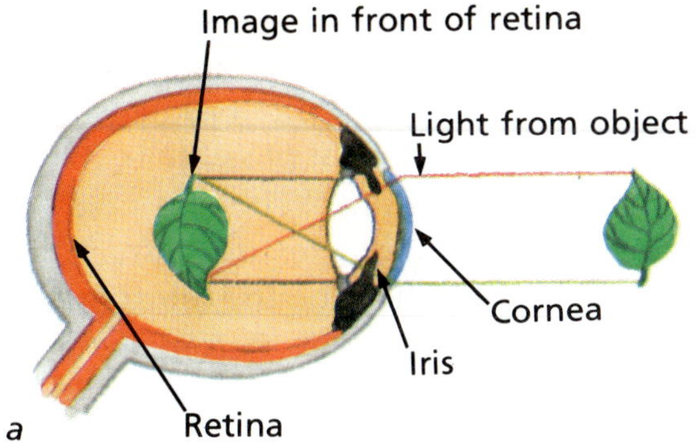

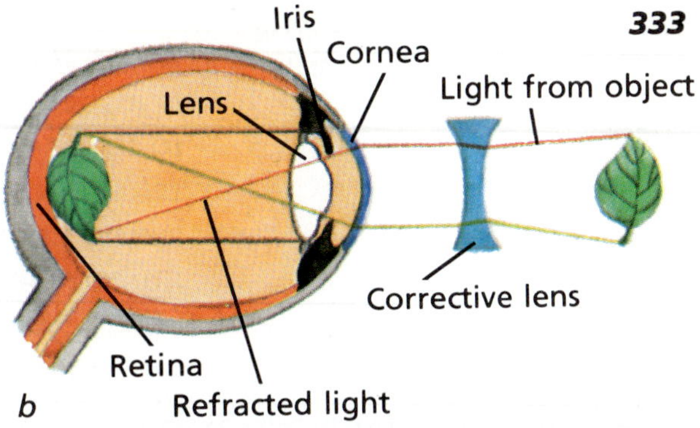

FIGURE 16-9. A nearsighted person cannot see distant objects well. The image of a distant object is focused in front of the retina (a). A concave lens is used to refract light at the proper angles to focus the image on the retina.

lenses, Figure 16-9. The proper concave lens produces a clear, sharp image inside the eye. As a result, the person can see things at a distance better.

Making Sure

5. Suppose you are a farsighted person reading a book without glasses. Are you likely to hold it close or far from your eyes? *far*
6. Can a cat see in total darkness when there is no light? Why? *No, reflected light is required to see.*

16:3 Telescopes

Telescopes are used to view things that are far away. For example, astronomers use telescopes to study the moon, sun, and stars. Lenses are used in telescopes to produce enlarged images of distant objects. A simple telescope has two convex lenses: the eyepiece lens and objective lens. The eyepiece lens has a short focal length. The objective lens has a long focal length. Because its lenses refract light, this type of telescope is called a refracting telescope, Figure 16-10.

FIGURE 16-10. A refracting telescope

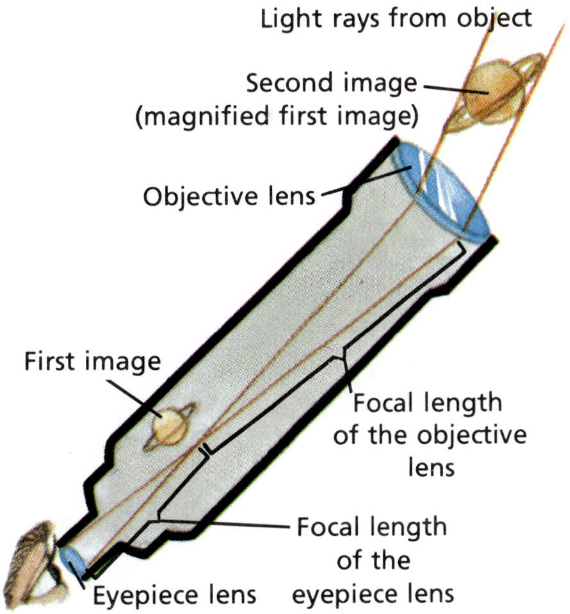

Convex lenses cannot be made much larger than about 100 centimeters in diameter. When a convex lens is made larger than this, the weight of the lens causes it to sag. It slowly loses its shape. How is it possible to have telescopes with high magnifications? The very large astronomical telescopes in observatories use parabolic mirrors. Such telescopes are called reflecting telescopes, Figure 16-11. The Hale telescope at Mt. Polomar, California contains a parabolic mirror.

a

California Institute of Technology, Carnegie Institute of Washington

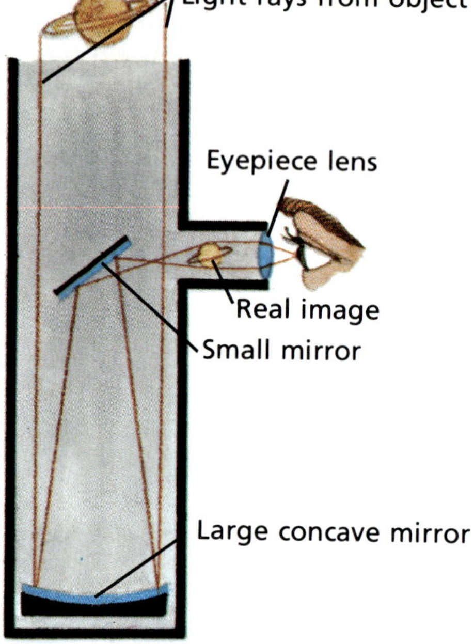

b

FIGURE 16-11. The Hale telescope (a) is a reflecting telescope. It contains a parabolic mirror (b).

16:4 Microscopes

Explain how a microscope produces an enlarged image.

A microscope works in much the same way as a telescope. The microscope magnifies extremely small objects. The image produced is much larger than the object being magnified. In using a microscope, a thin slice of an object is placed on a glass plate called a slide. The slide is then set on a flat part of the microscope called a stage. Light rays are directed up through a hole in the stage and through the specimen. The convex lens bends these rays to form a larger image of the object, Figure 16-12.

E.J. Cable/Tom Stack & Associates

E.J. Cable/Tom Stack & Associates

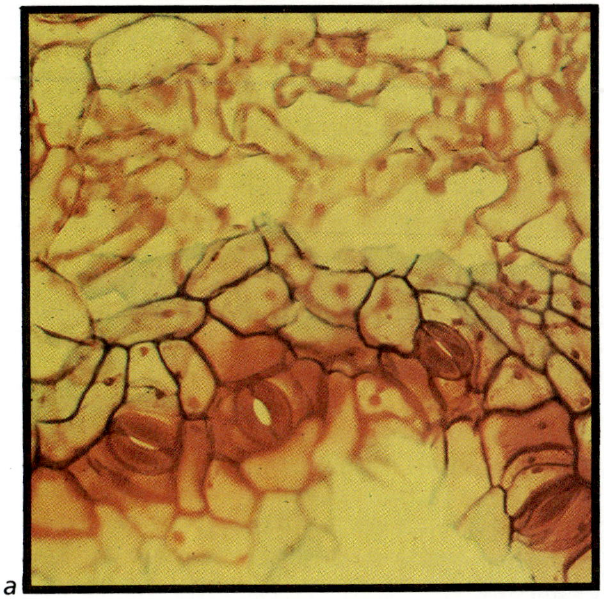

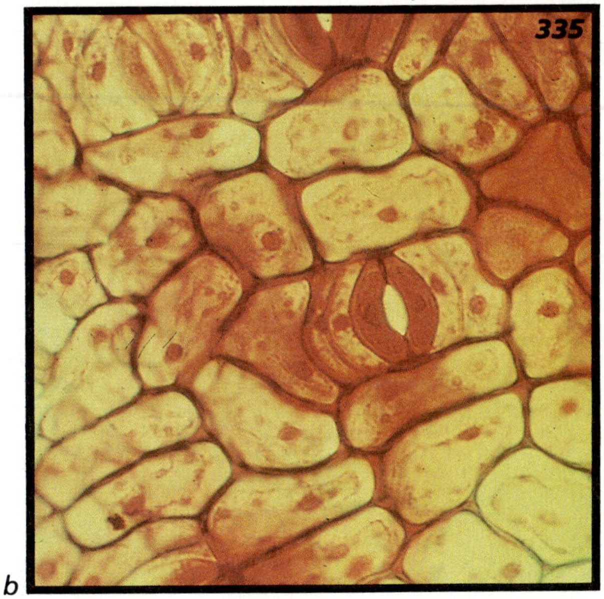

FIGURE 16-12. A section of a leaf is shown as viewed under a microscope at 250x (a) and 450x (b). How does the field of view change as the magnification increases?

A compound microscope has two lenses. The eyepiece lens magnifies the magnified image from the objective lens, Figure 16-13. An objective lens may magnify a blood cell forty-five times (45x). The eyepiece lens may have a 10x magnification. Using a compound microscope, the blood cell would be magnified four hundred fifty times (450x).

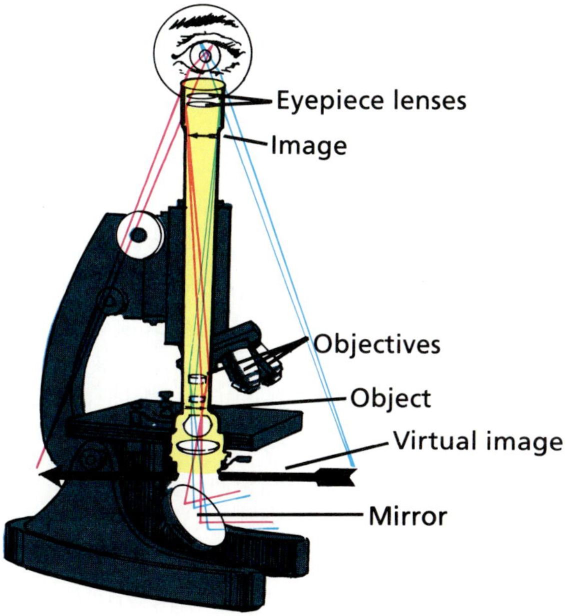

FIGURE 16-13. A compound microscope contains a system of lenses. The eyepiece lens further magnifies the image seen through the objective lens.

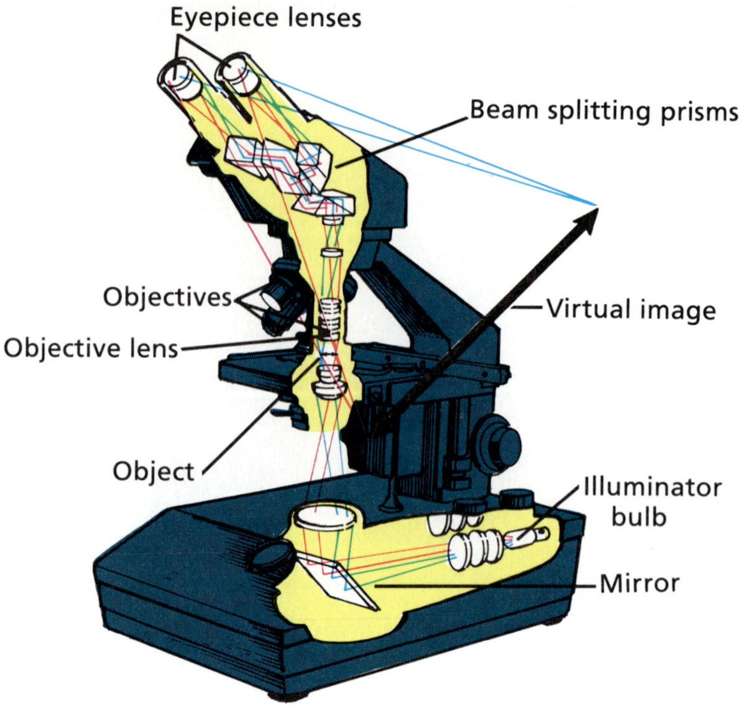

FIGURE 16-14. A stereo microscope contains a complex system of lenses and prisms. The image produced appears 3-dimensional. Why is this type of microscope called a stereo microscope?

A stereo microscope consists of two microscopes, Figure 16-14. There is one microscope for each eye. Each eye views an object from a different angle. The combined image of the object looks 3-dimensional. This type of microscope gives the user a larger field of view. Stereo microscopes are used in performing dissections and in assembling small parts.

Making Sure

Light rays are refracted to produce the magnification.

7. Why is light needed when using a microscope?
8. You can see the parts inside a plant stem if you observe a thin slice with a microscope. Why must the slice you use be thin and not thick?

The light must be able to pass through the slice.

16:5 Photography

How does a camera make a picture?

Taking pictures with a camera is just one use of light and lenses. Every camera works by allowing light to enter through a very small opening. This light passes through a convex lens and strikes the surface of the film

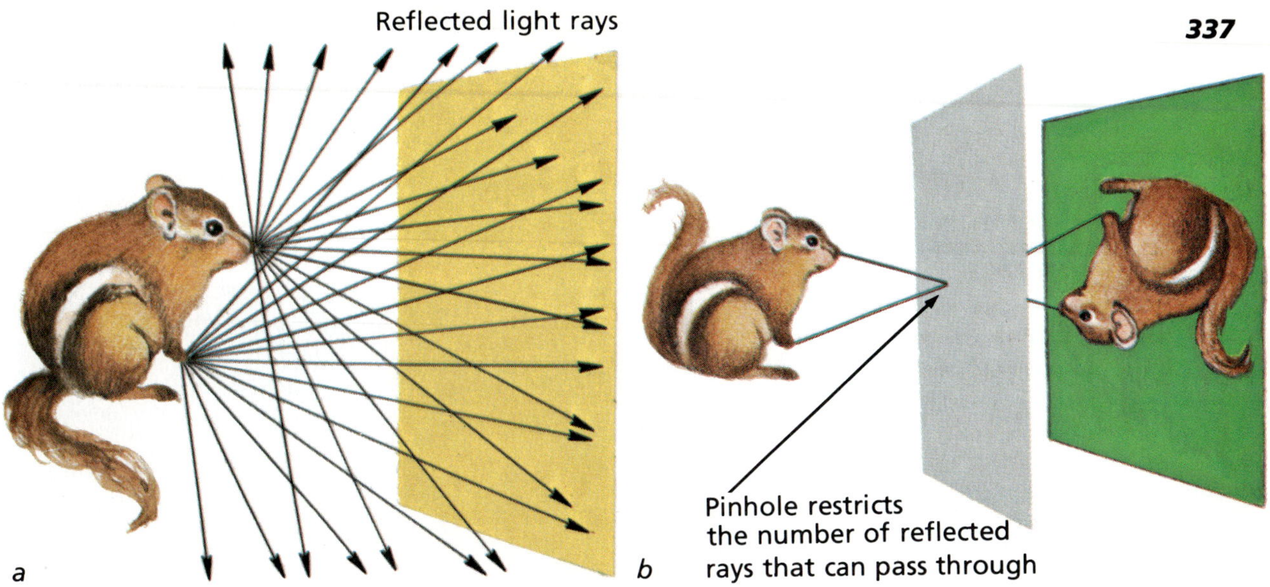

FIGURE 16-15. Light is reflected off an object in many directions (a). A pinhole allows only certain light rays to pass through (b). An inverted image can then be produced on film.

inside. Film contains chemicals which are sensitive to light. Because the lens is convex, the real image formed on the film is upside-down.

Why is the opening in a camera so small? Light is reflected from an object in many different directions, Figure 16-15a. An image could never be produced if the light rays were not controlled. The small hole restricts the amount of light that can pass through the lens. It may surprise you to know that a camera need not have a lens. If the opening is very tiny, tiny as a pinhole, an image can be formed without a lens, Figure 16-15b.

Why is a lens used if pictures can be taken through a pinhole? The lens serves to sharpen the image. It also cuts down the time needed to expose the film. Using a pocket camera, you can take a picture in a fraction of a second. Convex lenses are most often used in cameras. Recall that a convex lens can form a real image of an object when reflected light rays pass through the lens. The refracted rays will converge at the focal point of the lens, Figure 16-2.

A small pocket camera uses a number of lenses, Figure 16-16. The viewfinder at the top of the camera allows you to see what is being photographed. Notice, however, that the image is being photographed using a

Thomas Russell

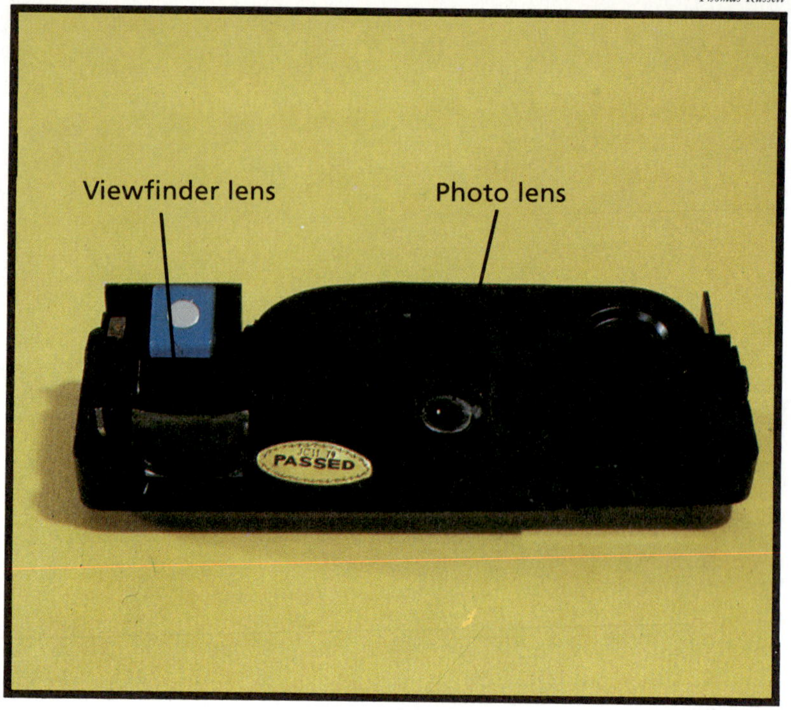

FIGURE 16-16. The image viewed through a small pocket camera is not the same as the image produced on the film. Note from the cross section that two lenses are used. One is for the viewfinder, and the other is used to produce the image on the film.

lens system other than that of the viewfinder. This is no problem in most photographs where the subject is some distance away. However, in taking a picture closeup, it could be a problem. The finished picture may be somewhat off-center from what you saw in the viewfinder.

Notice that the lens system of a camera may consist of a number of lenses. A single lens can have defects in the way it focuses light. To correct for the defects, other lenses are used. These lenses are designed to correct the defects in the convex lens.

FIGURE 16-17. A lens with a short focal length (a) produces a smaller image than a lens with a longer focal length (b).

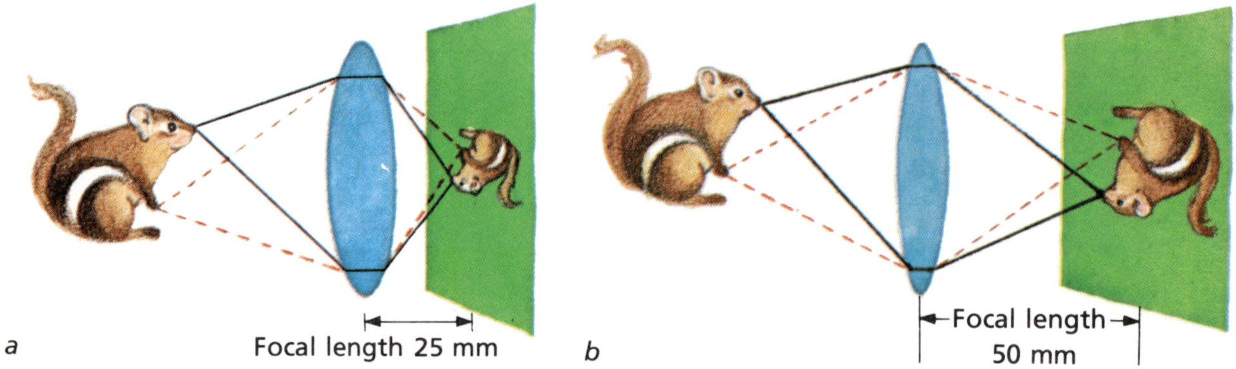

To achieve different effects, many cameras can use lenses with different focal lengths. The camera is made so a lens screws into an opening in the front. This way the lenses can be changed as needed. The focal length of a lens controls the size of the image produced. A lens with a short focal length produces a smaller image than other lenses, Figure 16-17. It is often used to take pictures of broad landscapes or pictures inside rooms where there is not much space. A lens with a long focal length produces a larger image. This kind of lens is often used to take pictures of things far away, Figure 16-18. With a lens of large focal length, the camera's field of view is reduced. This means less of the total scene is focused as an image on the film.

Why are some cameras made to use lenses with different focal lengths?

FIGURE 16-18. The photographs were taken from the same point using different lenses—(a) 35 mm, (b) 85 mm, (c) 205 mm, (d) 500 mm. What happens to the field of view as the focal length of the lens increases?

a b c d

Larry Hamill

Making Sure

9. What kind of lens would a photographer use to take a picture of several astronauts working together inside a spacecraft?

A lens with a short focal length.

10. What kind of lens would you use to take a picture of a kite flying high in the sky? Why?

A lens with a long focal length.

11. Why is a camera lens with a very long focal length often called a telephoto lens?

It is used in photographing distant objects.

16:6 Lasers

Someday many underground telephone lines in cities and towns will consist of fibers made of glass or clear plastic. Messages sent through these lines will be carried by light produced by lasers. The light will travel through the fibers in short bursts called pulses.

Telephone lines in use today are metal wires containing electric currents. What advantage is there in sending telephone calls by laser light? A laser beam can carry many more messages at the same time. Therefore, thinner lines can be used to carry the same number of phone calls. Also, the fibers made of glass or plastic are cheaper than metal wires.

Courtesy of Bell Laboratories

FIGURE 16-19. Plastic fibers can be used to carry messages by laser light.

What is laser light?

A laser produces a highly concentrated, powerful beam of light. Laser light is all of one frequency or color. All the waves in a beam of laser light vibrate together in a single plane, Figure 16-20. In this way, laser light is different from the light you know. Sunlight and lamplight is a mixture of light waves with many frequencies. These waves vibrate in an almost endless number of planes.

How does a laser work?

Lasers are made with different kinds of gases, plastics, and crystals. One kind of laser is a ruby rod with two flat ends. One end is completely covered with silver. The coating makes the surface a mirror. In the silver coating on the opposite end, a small uncovered space is left for light to escape. A bright light is then focused on the ruby rod. The light causes electrons in the chromium atoms of the rod to gain energy. All at once this energy is released inside the rod as red light waves. The red light is reflected back and forth between the mirrors at the ends of the rod. These rapid reflections cause the light to increase in intensity. All of the laser light waves are now vibrating in a single plane. They then burst out of the uncovered spot at the end of the rod as a narrow beam of red laser light.

FIGURE 16-20. The red light in the ruby rod bounces back and forth until all of the light waves are parallel.

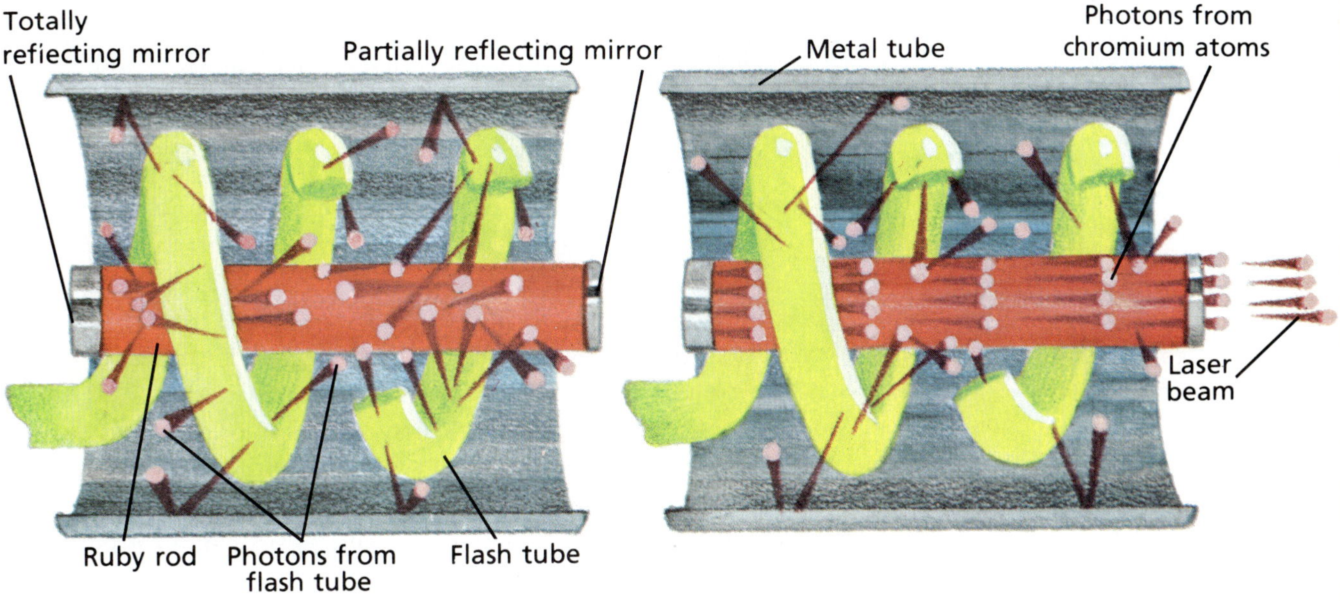

Larry Hamill

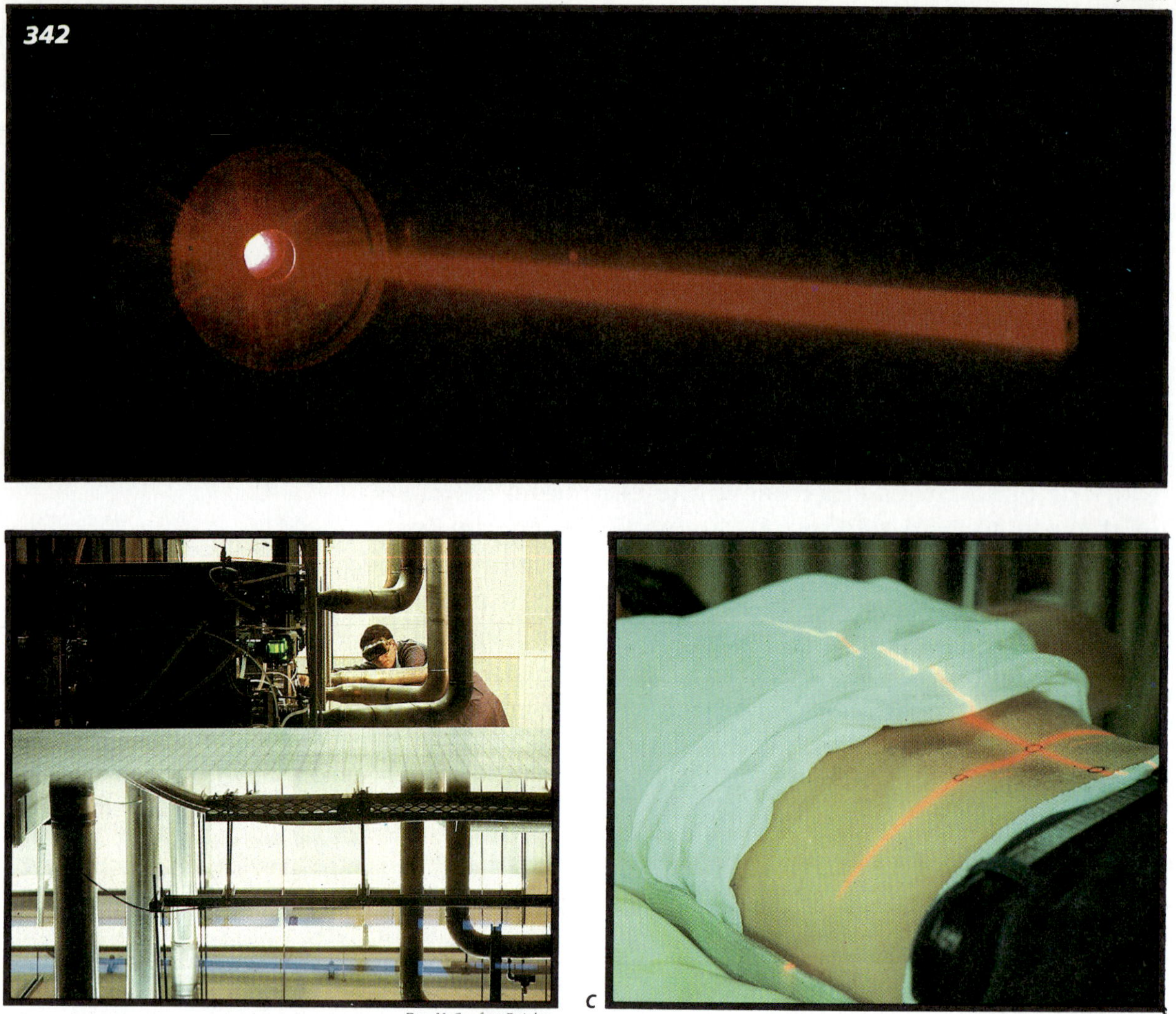

a b c

Dan McCoy from Rainbow

Dan McCoy from Rainbow

FIGURE 16-21. A ruby laser produces a narrow beam of red light (a). Lasers are used in the laboratory to separate mixtures of isotopes (b). A laser is used to mark the area being scanned to produce a picture of the patient's internal organs (c).

Light produced by a laser is not always visible light. Some kind of lasers produce ultraviolet light and others produce infrared light.

Lasers have an increasing number of uses. For example, pictures of swiftly moving objects have been made with beams of laser light. The light "stopped" the motion of the object while a camera snapped the picture. Lasers are used in surgery to mend torn retinas in people's eyes. Lasers are used to cut and weld certain materials. In experiments, TV pictures have been sent short distances by laser beams. Lasers are even used to produce unusual lighting effects for entertainment.

Points to Remember

1. Lenses are used to produce real and virtual images. *16:1*
2. A human eye has a convex lens which produces an image of what a person sees. *16:2*
3. A telescope and microscope contain lenses that produce enlarged images. *16:3 16:4*
4. A camera has a lens system that forms an image on film. *16:5*
5. The focal length of a lens controls the size of the image produced. *16:5*
6. Lasers are used in surgery, to send messages, to weld materials, and to make pictures. *16:6*

Words to Use

Write a sentence in which you correctly use each of the following words or terms.

concave lens	laser	real image
convex lens	microscope	telescope
focal length	principal focus	virtual image

Questions for Review

Do not write in this book.

A. True or False *Have the students rewrite the false statements to make them correct.*

Determine whether each of the following sentences is true or false.

F **1.** A convex lens and a concave lens have ~~the same~~ a different shape.

T **2.** A compound lens is in the eyepiece of a microscope.

T **3.** A virtual image cannot be projected on a screen.

T **4.** Changing the shape of a lens changes its focal length.

F **5.** A telescope contains two ~~concave~~ convex lenses.

T **6.** A real image is formed inside a camera.

T **7.** A lens with a short focal length produces a smaller image than other lenses.

T **8.** You can produce an enlarged image with a lens having a long focal length.

F 9. Laser beams are sent through ~~copper wires~~ glass fibers.

T 10. A laser beam is light of a single frequency.

B. Multiple Choice

Choose the word or phrase that correctly completes each of the following sentences.

1. A *(convex, concave)* lens is thicker in the middle than at the edges.
2. A movie projector produces a *(real, virtual)* image on a screen.
3. A *(convex, concave)* lens is sometimes called a reducing lens.
4. Farsightedness may be corrected with a *(convex, concave)* lens.
5. A refracting telescope uses *(convex lenses, concave lenses, prisms)* to magnify objects.
6. A reflecting telescope uses *(convex lenses, concave lenses, mirrors)* to magnify objects.
7. A pocket camera with a lens takes a picture in *(the same time, shorter time, longer time)* than a pinhole camera.
8. Light rays are *(reflected, refracted, absorbed)* as they pass through a camera lens.
9. *(Visible, Laser, Ultraviolet)* light consists of waves that vibrate in a single plane.
10. A beam of laser light has *(more, less, the same)* energy than / as a beam of white light.

C. Completion

Complete each of the following sentences with a word or phrase that will make the sentence correct.

1. A concave lens is thinner in the middle than at the edges.
2. Two triangular prisms held together are similar to a concave lens.
3. Nearsightedness can be corrected with concave lenses.
4. A parabolic mirror produces an enlarged image.
5. A stereo microscope is used to produce an enlarged 3-dimensional image.

6. The _film_ in a camera contains chemicals that are sensitive to light.
7. A _pinhole_ camera can take a picture without a lens.
8. A microscope produces an image that is _larger_ than the object being viewed.
9. _Laser_ light can be used to carry messages through glass fibers.
10. The _image_ formed on the film inside a camera is upside down.

Detailed answers to these questions are given in the Teacher's Guide at the front of this book.

D. How and Why

1. How is a virtual image different from a real image?
2. How is the focal length of the lens inside the eye changed?
3. How does a microscope form an image?
4. Why is light needed to take a picture with a camera?
5. What are some practical uses for lasers?

More Ideas to Explore

1. Obtain a book on color photography and find out how color pictures are made.
2. Do library research to find out how optometrists use lenses to correct different kinds of vision problems.
3. Make a poster that shows the difference between a telescope and a microscope. Label the main parts of the two instruments.

Readings to Discover

Branley, Franklyn M., *Color: From Rainbows to Lasers.* NY: Thomas Y. Crowell Co., 1978.

Garner, L., "On the Light Path." *Popular Electronics,* Vol. 14, August 1978, pp. 66-67.

Hand, A. J., "Zoom Lenses." *Popular Science,* Vol. 213, December 1978, pp. 74-78.

Wacker, Charles H., *Lasers: How They Work.* NY: G.P. Putnam's Sons, 1973.

Stop for one minute and listen. What sounds do you hear? Everyday you may hear thousands of sounds. How do these sounds reach your ears? Some people enjoy the sounds of a football game. Others think it is noisy? What is noise? Are some of the sounds you make considered noise?

Hank Morgan from Rainbow

Sound

17

Chapter 17 introduces the properties of compressional waves. This information is then applied to a study of sound. See the Teacher's Guide at the front of this book for additional teaching strategies for this chapter.

17:1 Compressional Waves

GOAL: *You will gain an understanding of sound waves and how they are produced and controlled.*

Waves can be produced in a coil spring by pinching together several coils and releasing them. Parts of the spring move to and fro in rhythm. At times, the particles of matter in the wave are compressed together. At other times, they are moved farther apart. This type of wave is called a **compressional wave.** In a compressional wave, matter vibrates in the same direction as the wave travels. A sound wave is one type of compressional wave.

How does matter move in a compressional wave?

As a wave goes through a coiled spring, each part is compressed and then spread apart. Where the coils are pushed together is an area of **compression.** Where the coils are spread apart is an area of **rarefaction.** Each part of the spring vibrates to and fro as the wave travels through it.

The blue curve in Figure 17-1 represents a transverse wave. It can also represent a compressional wave. The upward curve represents one complete compression. The downward curve shows one complete rarefaction. The wavelength of a compressional wave is the distance from the beginning of one compression to the next compression.

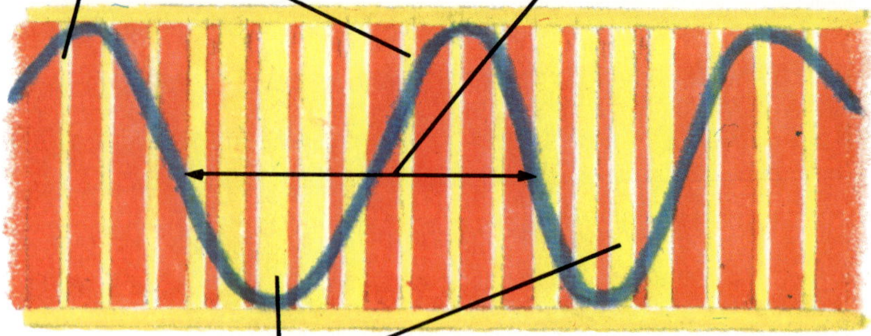

FIGURE 17-1. Matter contracts and expands as sound travels through it. A transverse wave can travel through a vaccuum. The parts of each type of wave are labeled.

How are sound waves produced?

Sound waves are produced when a bell or a tuning fork vibrates. When a person speaks, vibrations of their vocal cords produce sound waves. Sound waves are compressional waves produced by vibrations. Sound waves move through air or other matter. Sound waves cannot move through a vacuum. They may be detected by the ear and certain instruments. For example, a telephone mouthpiece can detect the sound waves of speech. The telephone converts these sound waves into electric waves which carry the spoken message over telephone lines.

Sound waves of different frequencies have different wavelengths. As frequency increases, wavelength decreases. When you strike the extreme right key of a piano, you produce sound waves of high frequency, Figure 17-3. Their wavelengths are about 7.7 centimeters long. Strike the extreme left key and you produce

FIGURE 17-2. The sound of a human voice (a) is made of many vibrations of different intensities (b).

a

Dan McCoy from Rainbow

b
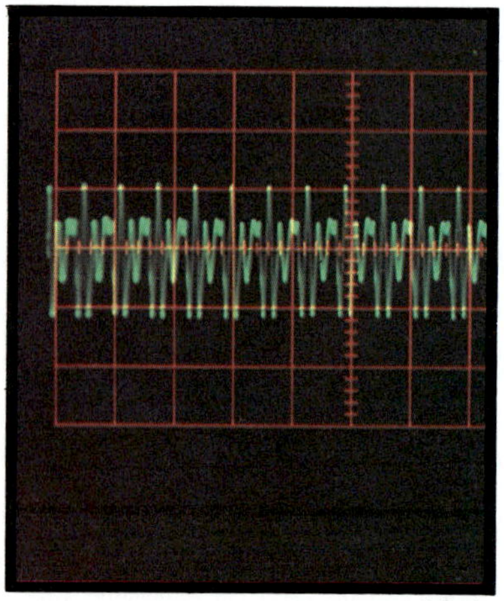

Kodansha

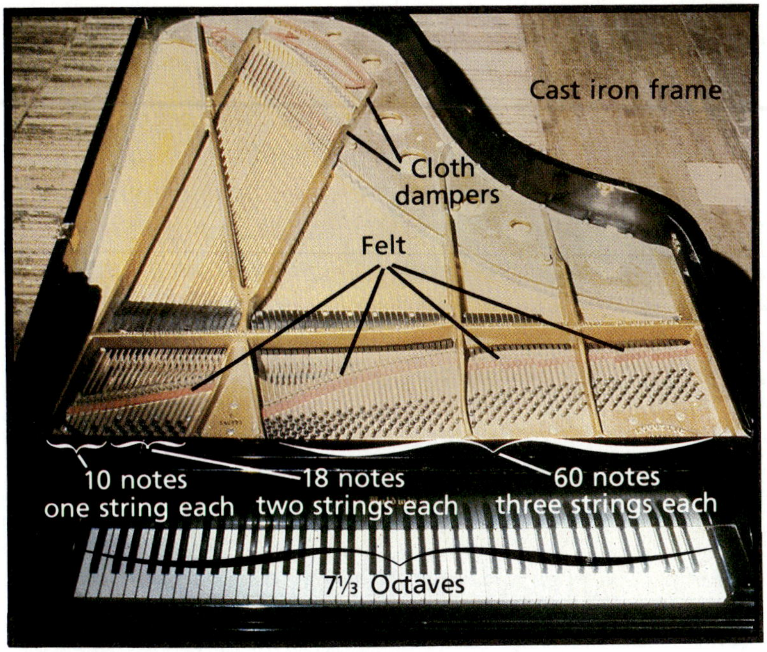

FIGURE 17-3. A piano contains strings of varying lengths to produce sounds of different frequencies.

waves of low frequency. Their wavelengths are about 12.2 meters.

Remind students that a hertz can mean cycles, waves, or vibrations per second.

There are many sound waves all around you. Some you cannot hear. Most people hear compressional waves if their frequency is between about 20 hertz and about 20 000 hertz. Sounds above this frequency range are said to be ultrasonic. Ultrasonic sounds cannot be heard by human beings. Some animals, however, can hear ultrasonic sounds. For example, a dog can hear sounds with frequencies up to 25 000 hertz.

What is ultrasonic sound?

FIGURE 17-4. The human ear can detect only those sounds in the red area of the graph. Sound intensities above the threshold zone cause pain.

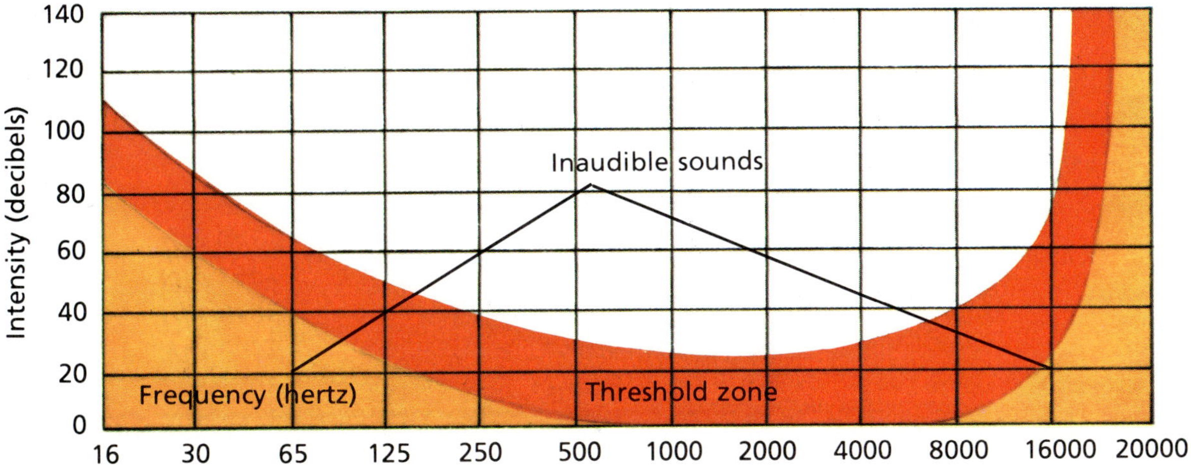

17-1 Detailed information concerning this Activity can be found in the Teacher's Guide at the front of this book.

ACTIVITY *Are compressional waves different than transverse waves?*

Obtain a "Slinky" toy or a large spring. Place the "Slinky" or spring on a level surface. Squeeze six or seven loops together. Release. Observe what happens. What type of wave results? Repeat. In what direction does the wave move? How is this wave different than a transverse wave?

The "Slinky" moves back and forth to form a compressional wave. The wave moves along the "Slinky." A compressional wave does not have a vertical displacement (amplitude); a transverse wave does.

Making Sure

1. How are sound waves different from electromagnetic waves?

Sound waves are compressional. There must be some substance for them to travel through. Electromagnetic waves are transverse. They can travel through a vacuum.

17:2 Speed of Sound

Sound cannot travel through empty space or a vacuum. It must have a substance to go through. Sound waves produced by vibrations are to-and-fro movements of particles of matter. Sound travels faster through solids than through liquids and gases.

How fast does sound travel in air?

The speed of sound in air is about 340 meters per second. Sound travels through warm air faster than through cold air. The speed of sound increases about 60 centimeters per second for each Celsius degree rise in temperature. At 20°C sound travels through air at 344 meters per second.

Table 17-1

Speed of Sound Through Various Substances	
air	340 m/s
water	1454 m/s
wood	3828 m/s
iron	5103 m/s
stone	5971 m/s

How can the speed of sound be used to calculate the wavelength of a sound wave?

The speed of sound can be used to calculate the wavelength of a sound wave. To find wavelength, divide the speed by the frequency. The equation is

$$wavelength = \frac{speed}{frequency}$$

Example

What is the wavelength of sound waves that have a frequency of 43 hertz in air at 20° C? The speed of sound in air is 344 m/s at 20° C.

Solution:

(a) Write the equation for the wavelength of a sound wave.

$$wavelength = \frac{speed}{frequency}$$

(b) Substitute the values given in the problem for frequency and speed.

$$wavelength = \frac{344 \text{ m/s}}{43 \text{ hertz}}$$

(c) Divide to find the answer. Recall that one hertz is one vibration per second. Therefore, the unit seconds will cancel out and the wavelength will be expressed in meters.

$$wavelength = \frac{344 \text{ m/s}}{43 \text{ hertz}} = 8 \text{ m or } 8 \text{ meters}$$

Making Sure

2. What is the wavelength of sound waves having a frequency of 256 hertz which are traveling through air at 20° C? *1.34 m*
3. What equation would you use to find the frequency of a sound wave when given the speed and wavelength? $frequency = \frac{speed}{wavelength}$
4. What is the frequency of sound waves which have wavelengths of 6 meters when the air temperature is 20° C? *57.3 hertz*

17:3 Volume

How is loudness related to amplitude?

Some sounds are so loud they hurt your ears. The loudness or volume of a sound is determined by the amplitude of the sound waves. As the amplitude of the sound waves increases, the loudness of the sound increases. Do you ever shout at a basketball or football game? When you yell, you produce sounds with amplitudes larger than those you make when you talk.

What unit is used to express the volume of sounds?

The volume of sounds are often measured in **decibels** (dB). Sounds that are loud enough to cause pain in the ear are about 120 decibels. A sound that can barely be heard has a volume of 0 decibels. Recall that the human ear can detect sounds in a frequency range of 20 to 20 000 hertz. However, any sounds having frequencies below 30 hertz or above 15 000 hertz are difficult to hear unless the volume or sound intensity is high.

FIGURE 17-5. The sound of a jet plane can reach 140 decibels (a). People working near loud sounds need ear protection. The sound of a whisper is only about 15 decibels (b).

a

Dept. of the Air Force

b

Hickson-Bender Photography

17:4 Pitch

You can recognize a sound by its pitch. For example, the pitch of the voice of a child is usually higher than that of an adult. Each note in a musical scale has a different pitch. The pitch of a sound depends upon the frequency of the sound waves. Sounds with high pitch have low frequencies. The higher the musical note on a scale, the higher its pitch.

On a guitar, all the strings are the same length. Thin strings produce high notes. Thick strings produce low notes. To make music, the strings of the guitar must be plucked so they vibrate. A musical sound is produced by matter that vibrates over and over at the same frequency. Sound produced by irregular vibrations with different frequencies are often unpleasant to hear. This kind of sound is called noise.

Making Sure

5. Explain why it takes more energy to make a loud sound than a low one. *The amplitude is greater. Thus, more energy is required to cause the greater displacement.*
6. How can a musician change the pitch made by a guitar string? *Tightening or loosening the string at the end of the guitar or using the fingers when playing will change the pitch.*

17:5 Musical Sounds

Many different kinds of instruments are used to play music. Some such as the clarinet have a thin piece of wood, called a reed, over which air is blown. When the clarinet player blows across the reed, it vibrates and makes sound. The sound is amplified by the long column of air inside the clarinet. Instruments like the clarinet are called woodwind instruments.

Hickson-Bender Photography

a

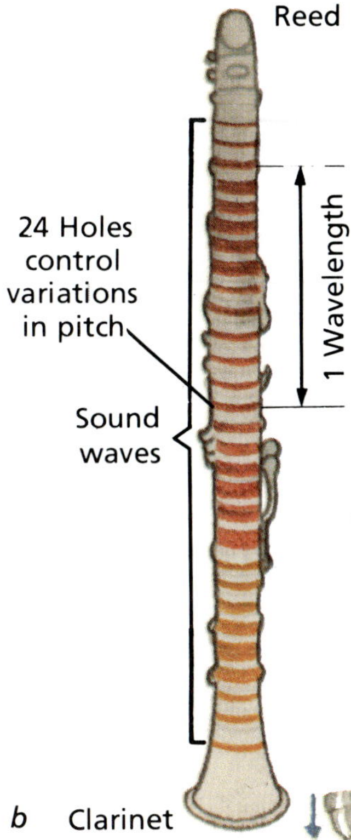

b Clarinet

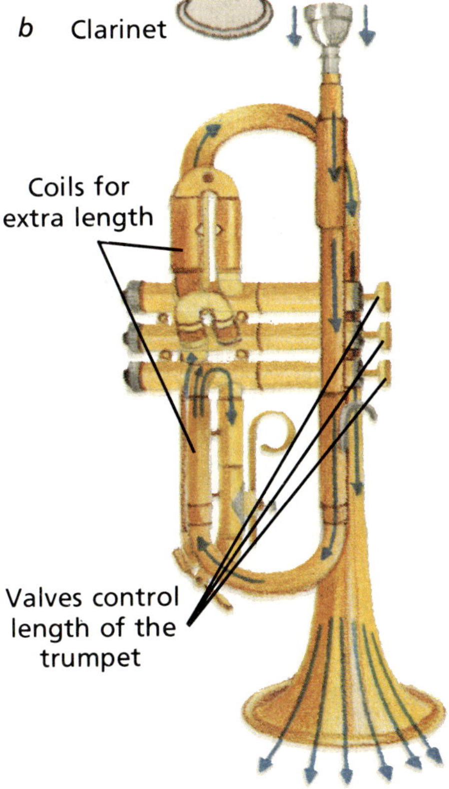

c Trumpet

FIGURE 17-6. A clarinet is a reed instrument (b). The sounds it produces can be controlled using the holes along the side. These holes control the length of the vibrating column of air. The sound of a trumpet is controlled by using the valves (c). These valves control the length of the trumpet.

Music from a trombone, flute, or trumpet is produced by vibrations in a tube of air. When the player blows into the instrument, a sound is made as the air inside vibrates. By changing the length of the column of air, different musical notes are produced. In a flute, changes are made by opening and closing holes in the instrument with one's fingers. A trumpet has tubes of different length and valves that control the air to these tubes. The instrument is played by blowing into it and pushing the valves to change the notes. How is the sound of a trombone controlled? *by sliding the tube*

What is a musical scale?

Each note in a musical scale has a different pitch. One kind of musical scale has eight notes which make up one **octave.** The last note in an octave always has a vibration rate twice as great as the first note. For example, a scale may have a low note of C with a frequency of 262 hertz. High C, the top note in the scale, has a frequency of 524 hertz. The notes in between have frequencies between the low and high notes. Most human voices have a range of one to two octaves.

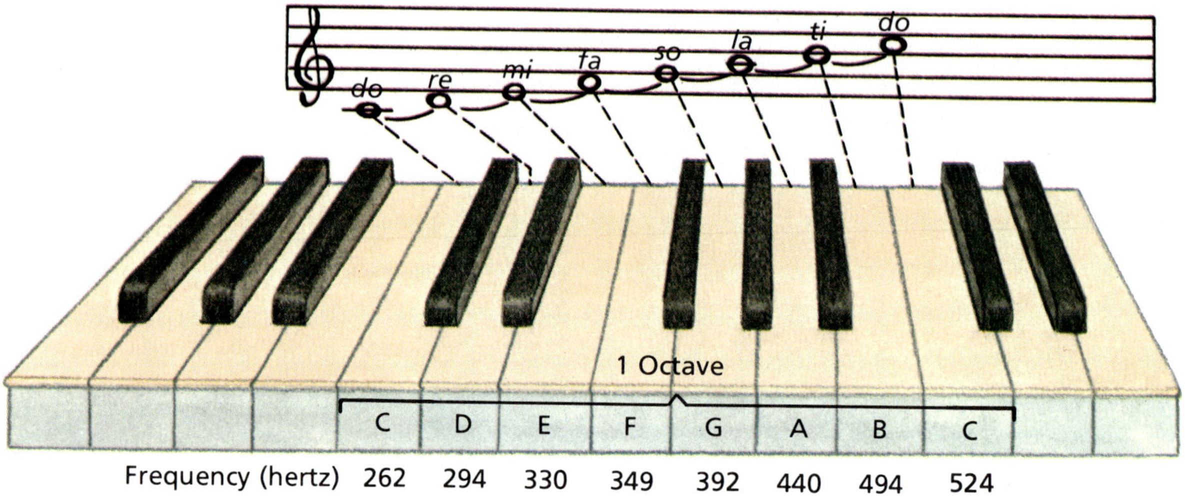

FIGURE 17-7. One octave contains eight notes of increasing frequency.

When musical notes are sounded in a certain order, a tune is produced. The songs you sing are combinations of different notes, each with a different pitch. Each note is a sound with a different frequency.

Explain what quality of sound means.

Every musical sound has a definite quality. Quality is what enables you to tell the difference between sounds of the same pitch and loudness. It is caused by overtones. In addition to its fundamental tone, every musical instrument and human voice also produces overtones. The overtones have a slightly higher frequency than the fundamental tone. Overtones cause a musical instrument and human voice to have a unique quality different from others. The quality is due to the number and strength of the overtones in the sound they produce.

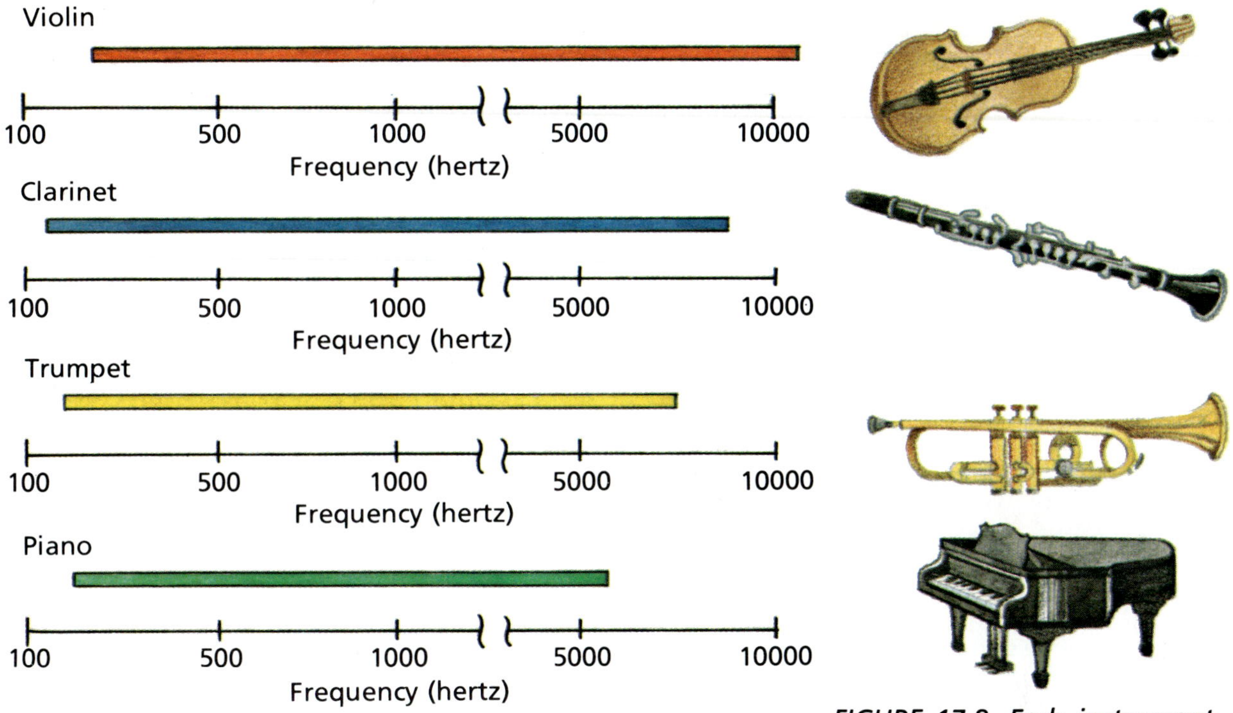

FIGURE 17-8. Each instrument produces sounds over a specific frequency range. The human ear can hear frequencies from 25 to 20 000 hertz.

Making Sure

7. How would you make a musical sound with each of the following? *a. blow across it b. hum through it*

a. soda pop bottle **b.** comb and wax paper
c. rubber band *c. stretch and pluck it*

8. What produces the vibration for each of the sounds in Question 7?

a. column of air vibrates
b. similar to a reed, paper vibrates
c. string vibrates

9. The wooden box of a violin makes the sound of the violin strings louder. Does the box increase or decrease the amplitude of the sound waves? *increases*

17:6 Interference

You may wish to refer students back to the section on interference for light, Section 15:7.

How does interference change sounds?

Interference between two or more sound waves can cause sound to increase or decrease in loudness. Recall that a sound wave is a series of compressions and rarefactions. When two waves interfere with each other, the compressions and rarefactions of each wave combine together. If the compressions and rarefactions match up, the interference is constructive. Constructive interference increases the amplitude. It makes the sound louder.

Destructive interference occurs when the compression of one wave combines with the rarefaction of the other wave. Destructive interference decreases the amplitude. It makes the sound lower in volume.

Interference can be heard when two tuning forks of slightly different frequency are sounded together. The interference causes the sound of the forks to alternately increase and decrease in loudness. As a result, the sound wavers in a series of steady beats.

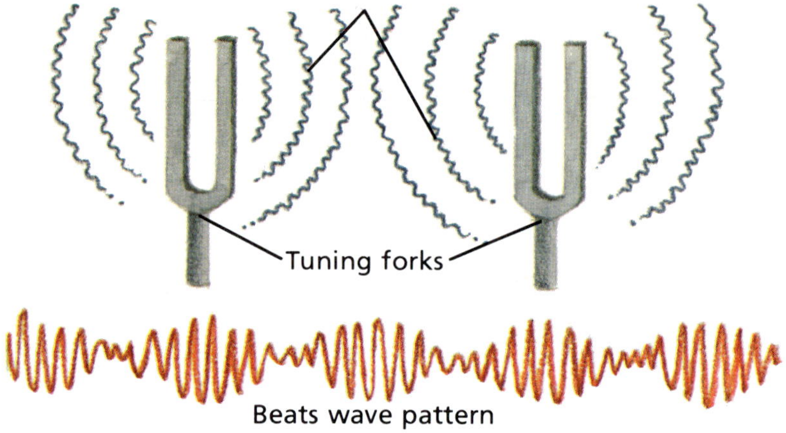

FIGURE 17-9. The interference of sound waves produces sound at regular intervals called beats. What points on the wave pattern show that the sound has faded?

Making Sure

Constructive interference increases the amplitude and the loudness of the sound.

10. Two tuning forks together make a louder sound than one tuning fork. Is this an example of constructive or destructive interference? Why?

17:7 Doppler Effect

You may wish to relate this effect to light in discussing the "red shift" as evidence of an expanding universe.

Pitch and frequency are related. The pitch of a sound is determined by its frequency. The higher the frequency, the higher the pitch. A change in pitch can be caused by the Doppler effect. The Doppler effect is a

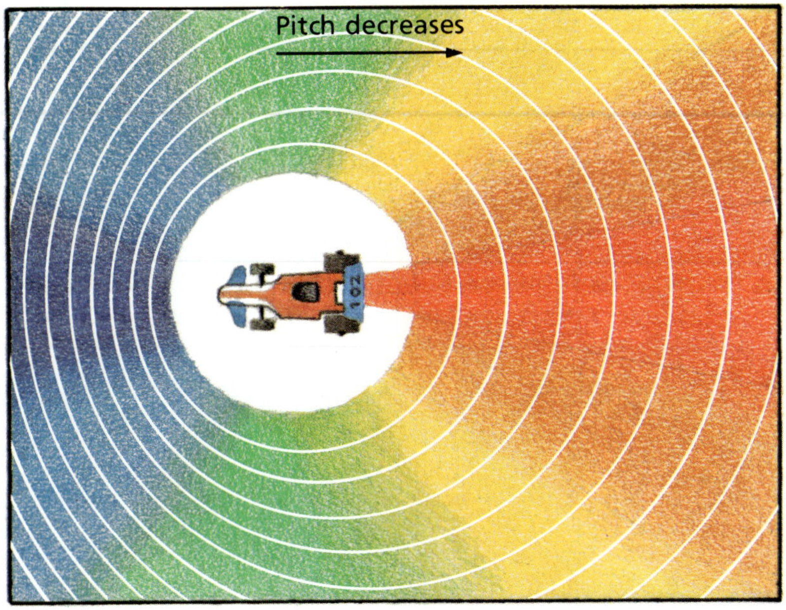

FIGURE 17-10. As the racing car moves past you, the sound of the motor decreases in pitch. The pitch is highest in front of the car and lowest to the rear of the car.

change in wave frequency caused by the motion of the wave source. For example, sound from the siren of an approaching police car increases in pitch. Why? As the car approaches, its movement crowds the siren sound waves together. This crowding causes a higher wave frequency and higher pitch. As the car passes by and moves away, the pitch of the sound you hear decreases. The sound waves are now farther apart. Both the frequency and pitch of the waves decreases.

What is the Doppler effect?

Describe one example of the Doppler effect.

The Doppler effect may also be produced if the observer moves toward the source of sound. If you ride on a train moving toward a warning bell at a crossing, the sound of the clanging bell rises in pitch. Increasing in pitch means that wave frequency is increasing and wavelength is decreasing.

By traveling in a small boat, you can see an effect similar to the Doppler effect. If you travel against the waves, they strike the boat with a relatively high frequency. The ride may be very choppy. If you travel with the waves, they catch up to the boat more slowly. The frequency with which the waves strike the boat is relatively low.

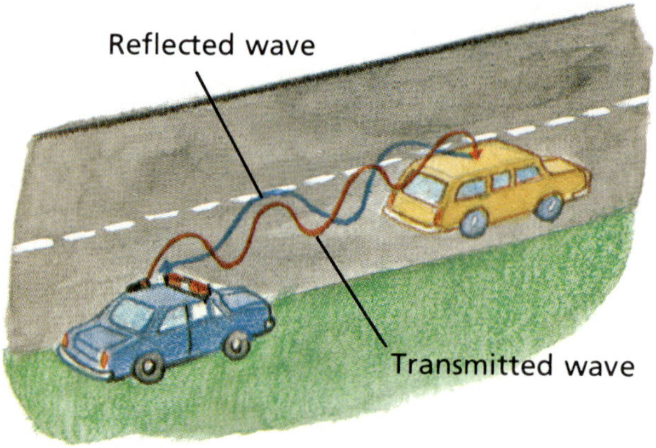

FIGURE 17-11. A radar speed detecting device sends out waves to a moving car. These waves are reflected back to the police car. The receiver notes the frequency and converts it to a rate of speed.

Larry Hamill

One practical use of the Doppler effect is in radar speed-detecting devices. Radar waves are sent out and reflected back from a moving car to a receiver. Changes in frequency of the radar waves are caused by the car moving toward the receiver. The change in frequency is converted to speed by the radar receiver. In this way, it is possible to detect vehicles traveling faster than legal speed limits.

17:8 Acoustics

Have you ever been in an auditorium where it was difficult to hear a speaker? Perhaps the speaker's voice didn't carry out to the audience. It could be that disturbing echoes made the speech unclear. Auditoriums are usually designed so that speakers, singers, and orchestras can be heard clearly. The room is made so noise can be controlled or eliminated. A noise is a sound of the wrong kind in the wrong place.

Acoustics is the study of sound and how it affects people. It includes the control of noise and vibrations that cause noise. Scientists and engineers who work in acoustics study sound and human hearing. They also

Michele Wigginton

FIGURE 17-12. An outdoor theater is designed to amplify sound in the direction of the audience.

study the ways in which different things are affected by sound. Engineers design buildings and communication systems for proper sound. They also figure out ways to protect people's hearing from harmful loud noises. The designs of the engineers are aimed toward ensuring that the sounds people hear are the kind they want or need.

One way to control noise is to make the source of the noise quieter. Have you ever been bothered by a noisy fan. A large fan that turns at a slow speed is much quieter than a small fan that turns at a fast speed. Noise can also be controlled by blocking its passage from one place to another. Have you ever closed a door to a noisy room? In doing so you shut off sound you did not want to hear. Porous materials such as carpets, drapes, and acoustical tiles absorb sound.

FIGURE 17-13. Acoustical tiles are porous to absorb sounds and prevent echoes.

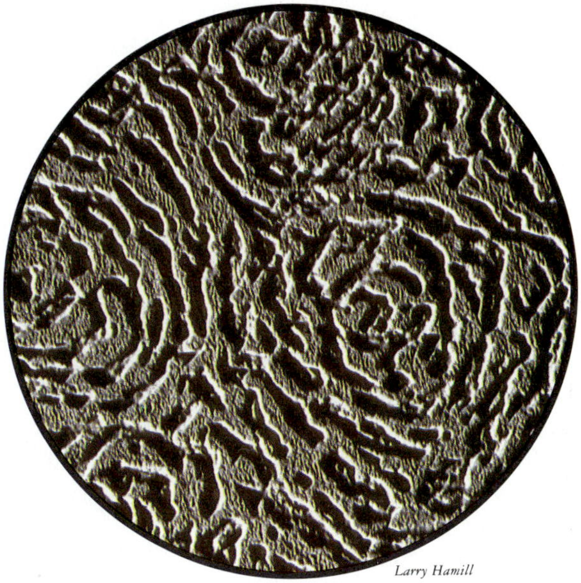

Larry Hamill

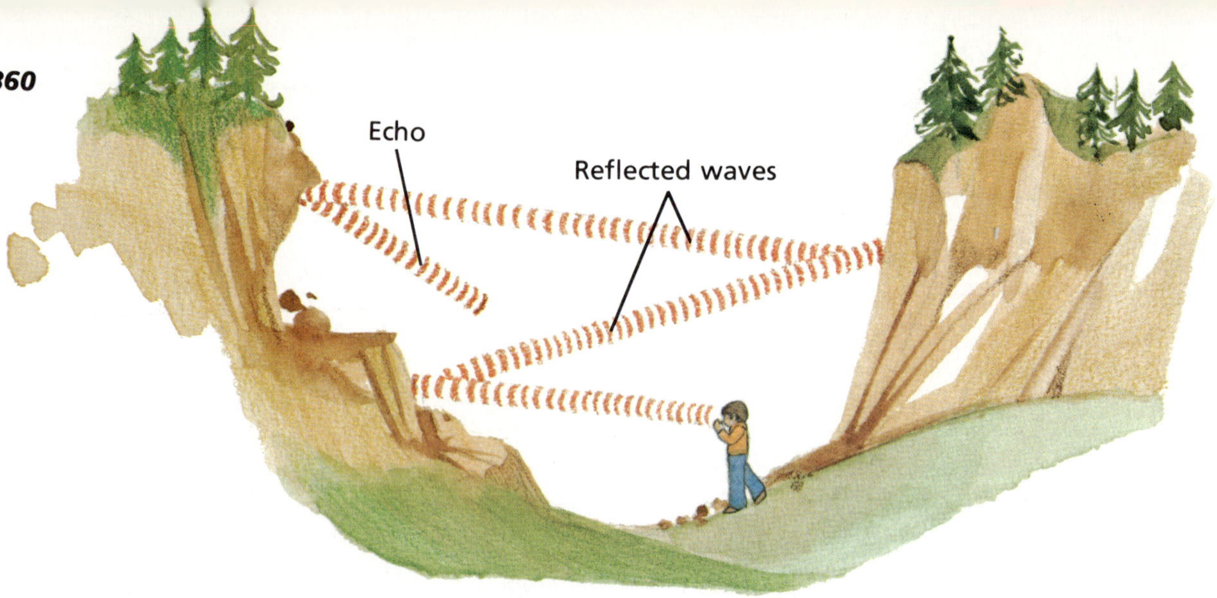

FIGURE 17-14. Echoes are formed from reflected sound waves.

Reflected sound you hear is called an echo. By properly shaping a large room echoes can be reduced. An echo that reaches your ear within 1/20 of a second after a sound is no problem. If the time interval is longer, the echo will be annoying. Another kind of disturbing sound is a reverberation. A **reverberation** is a mixture of many small reflected sounds that combine and die away slowly. In a music hall, they should last no longer than one second. Hanging long drapes and using upholstered seats in an auditorium reduces echoes and reverberations. Why?

What is an echo and a reverberation?

The sound is absorbed more quickly.

Larry Hamill

FIGURE 17-15. This concert hall was acoustically designed. Note the porous wall coverings and the varied shapes in the ceiling. These design elements control the time it takes for successive sound reflections to reach the audience.

Making Sure

11. How could a small room be made soundproof? *adding carpeting, heavy drapes, or acoustical tile may help*
12. Why are echoes less likely in a room filled with people than when the room is empty?
    The echoes are broken up and absorbed by the people in the room.

17:9 Noise Pollution

You probably know about different kinds of pollution such as smoke, litter, and harmful chemicals. But have you ever thought about noise pollution? In today's world, there are all sorts of sounds that people find annoying and unpleasant. What kinds of noise bother you the most?

Sound can cause damage to things. One example is the breaking of a champagne glass. The glass may be broken by the sound of a very high pitched musical note. Sound waves cause vibrations in the glass itself. When the push and pull of the vibrations is just right, enough stress is created to crack the glass.

FIGURE 17-16. The energy from sound waves can crack plaster (a) or glass (b).

a b

Larry Hamill

Sudden, sharp noises such as thunder, cannon shots, and sonic booms from jet planes can cause damage. Glass windows and weak sections of plaster in buildings have been cracked apart by loud sounds. Pressure changes caused by loud sounds can strain the inner parts of a person's ears. As a result, the ears may not operate properly. Usually the condition lasts only a short time. After some rest the ear heals and works as well as ever. However, if the loud noise lasts for a very long time, a loss of hearing may occur. Permanent damage may also result if the loud noise occurs often during a long period of time. In many jobs where people are around noisy machinery, they wear earmuffs to protect their ears.

Hearing sounds over 70 decibels can cause temporary hearing loss. Repeated exposure to levels around 100 decibels can cause permanent hearing loss. Noise can also cause other effects on the body. Changes in the breathing and heart rate, an increase in blood pressure, and changes in digestion are examples of these effects. Too much noise can make people irritable and tired and cause headaches and lack of appetite. Some doctors believe that the response of the body to our noisy world may cause problems such as heart disease, ulcers, and indigestion.

Dan McCoy from Rainbow

FIGURE 17-17. Frequent exposure to loud sounds can cause loss of hearing. Many rock stars are experiencing this problem.

Don Parsisson

FIGURE 17-18. Trees were planted along this highway to reduce the amount of noise in residential areas.

Many things are being done to reduce noise pollution. For instance, the powerful jet engines of new airplanes are designed to produce less noise than the old ones. When possible, takeoffs and landings are scheduled over water and other open spaces. Household appliances such as refrigerators and air conditioners are being designed to run more quietly. Keeping machines lubricated and replacing worn out parts cut down on noise. Sound absorbent material is put in noisy places to deaden noise. Better mufflers can be installed on cars and trucks to cut down the noise of their exhausts. Planting trees near busy highways helps cut down on noise because trees absorb sound.

What can be done to reduce noise pollution?

Making Sure

13. Which of the following noises annoy you? *answers will vary; you might ask students for reasons*

a. motorcycle **b.** heavy truck **c.** horn on a car

d. loud stereo music **e.** alarm clock

14. Why might your answers be different from someone else? *answers will vary*

15. What suggestions do you have for reducing noise pollution in your community? *Legislation can be used in helping reduce noise levels made by industry and private citizens.*

Focus On

Frontiers

Visible Speech

Dr. Ronald Cole, Carnegie Melon Institute

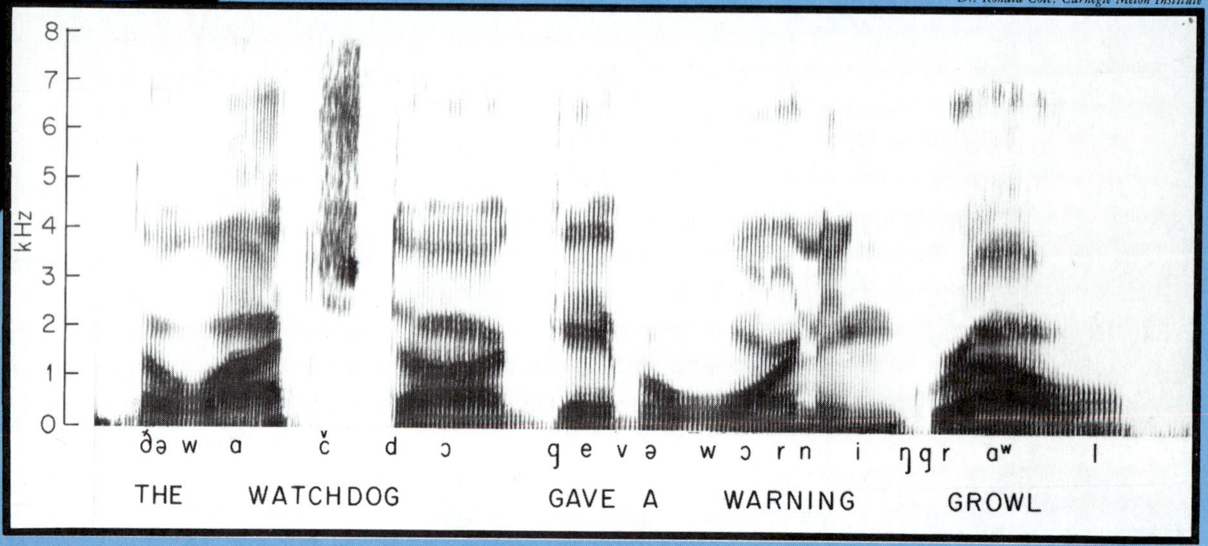

The average speaker of English can recognize between 10 000 and 50 000 different words. Each of these words can be represented using only 26 letters—the English alphabet. Spoken words are also composed of a small set of elements, called phonemes. To recognize spoken words, a person must hear the difference between each of the 40 phonemes of English.

Scientists are curious about the properties of phonemes. The best way to study phonemes is to use a picture of speech. The most useful picture is the speech spectrogram. A spectrogram shows the phonemes in a sentence in terms of their frequencies. Phonemes of low frequencies, like "m" or "n" appear at the bottom of a spectrogram. Phonemes of high frequencies, like "s", appear at the top.

Is it possible to read a spectrogram, just as you are reading this page? Research has shown that it is difficult to read a spectrogram. The reason is that phonemes do not look the same each time they occur. A phoneme's sound (and its appearance on a spectrogram) is often changed by neighboring phonemes. For example, on a spectrogram the phoneme "g" looks quite different in the words "goose" and "geese."

Dr. Victor Zue, a scientist at MIT, has learned to read spectrograms. He has spent more than 2000 hours studying spectrograms. In 1977 and 1978, scientists at Carnegie-Mellon University showed Dr. Zue spectrograms of sentences he did not know. His task was to read the sentences from the phonemes. The scientists found that Dr. Zue can identify almost ninety percent of the phonemes on a spectrogram of an unknown sentence.

This experiment raises the possibility of using spectrograms in teaching speech to people with hearing disabilities. A major problem for them in learning to speak is that they cannot hear what they say. Because they cannot hear, the hearing disabled cannot correct their speech. Using spectrograms, they can see the pattern of their words and compare it to the correct pattern. Comparing the spectrograms helps the speaker learn to say words correctly—without hearing them.

Written by Ronald Cole, Carnegie-Mellon University

Points to Remember

1. Sound waves are compressional waves produced by vibrations. 17:1
2. Sound does not travel through a vacuum. 17:2
3. The pitch of a sound depends on its frequency. 17:4
4. The loudness of a sound depends on the amplitude of the sound waves. 17:3
5. Interference between sound waves can cause sound to increase or decrease in volume. 17:6
6. When the source of a sound is moving the pitch of the sound changes. 17:7
7. Buildings and communication systems can be designed to reduce noise. 17:8

Words to Use

Write a sentence in which you correctly use each of the following words or terms.

acoustics	Doppler effect	overtone
amplitude	frequency	pitch
compressional wave	interference	ultrasonic
decibel		

Questions for Review

Do not write in this book.

A. True or False *Have the students rewrite the false statements to make them correct.*

Determine whether each of the following sentences is true or false.

T **1.** In a compressional wave, matter vibrates in the same direction as the wave travels.

F **2.** You ~~can~~ cannot hear ultrasonic sounds.

F **3.** Sound travels through ~~space.~~ matter

T **4.** The loudness of a sound is measured in decibels.

T **5.** A thin string on a guitar produces a higher pitch than a thick string.

T **6.** A sound can be caused by the vibration of air.

F 7. Every note in a musical scale has ~~the same~~ a different pitch.
F 8. The higher the frequency the ~~lower~~ higher the pitch.
F 9. The Doppler effect changes the ~~amplitude~~ pitch of a sound.
T 10. Carpets and drapes absorb sound.

B. Multiple Choice

Choose the word or phrase that correctly completes each of the following sentences.

1. A sound wave is a *(transverse, compressional)* wave.
2. As the frequency of a sound wave increases its wavelength *(increases, decreases, does not change)*.
3. Sound waves are *(the same as, different from)* electromagnetic waves.
4. The speed of sound in air is about 340 *(centimeters, meters, kilometers)* per second.
5. One hertz is one vibration per *(second, minute, hour)*.
6. You can hear sounds with a frequency range of about 20 to *(1000, 10 000, 20 000)* hertz.
7. The pitch of a sound depends on its *(volume, aplitude, frequency)*.
8. Destructive interference reduces the *(volume, frequency, pitch)* of a sound.
9. When the source of a sound is moving towards you the pitch *(increases, decreases, does not change)*.
10. The change in the sound of an approaching siren is due to *(echoes, reverberations, the Doppler effect)*.

C. Completion

Complete each of the following sentences with a word or phrase that will make the sentence correct.

1. Sound waves are produced when a bell or tuning fork vibrates.
2. A sound wave travels faster through glass than through air.
3. Sounds loud enough to cause pain in the ear are about 70 decibels.
4. Changing the length of a column of air controls the notes made by a flute.
5. Overtones give each musical sound a special quality.

6. Interference between sound waves causes beats.
7. Acoustics is the study of how sound affects people.
8. An echo is reflected sound.
9. Loud noise over a period of time can cause a loss of hearing.
10. A muffler on a car or motorcycle reduces noise pollution.

D. How and Why

Detailed answers to these questions are given in the Teacher's Guide the front of this book.

1. How is a compressional wave different from a transverse wave?
2. Give a reason why sound will not pass through a jar from which all the air is pumped out.
3. What features of sound make it possible for you to recognize another person's voice?
4. **a.** How can two tuning forks be used to produce beats?
   b. What causes beats?
5. How could the speed of sound be used to detect the distance to a nearby mountain?

More Ideas to Explore

1. The Doppler effect also occurs with light waves. Find out how this effect is used in astronomy.
2. Prepare a report on the use of sonar to locate fish and map the bottom of the ocean.
3. Learn about acoustics through library research and make suggestions for improving the acoustics of the room.
4. Prepare a report on the efforts of industry to protect workers from harmful noise.

Readings to Discover

Dennett, J.T., "Noisy Silence: Natural Infrasound Can Warn of Impending Disaster." *Science Digest,* May 1977, pp. 27-28.

Jones, Gadler, Engstrom, *Pollution: Noise We Hear.* Minneapolis, MN: Lerner Publishing Company, 1972.

Ortner, E.H., "Ultrasonic Polaroid SX-70 Camera Gets a Self-focusing System." *Popular Science,* Vol. 213, July 1978, p. 83.

Tannenbaum, Beulah, and Stillman, Myra, *Understanding Sound.* NY: McGraw-Hill, 1973.

Unit 6

The sun is a source of energy that we use directly. It warms us. Focusing the sun's energy in a solar cooker, we can cook food. Another source of energy is falling water. We use it to make electricity. How is heat energy related to electricity? How do we use them?

solar cooker © Sam Errico 1978/Tom Stack & Associates

Energy

hydroelectric plant Steve Lissau

Larry Hamill

Pictured here is a thermogram of a face. Thermograms show temperature differences. They are used to study the movement of heat in bodies. Scientists hope to use them in identifying diseases. How else might thermograms be used?

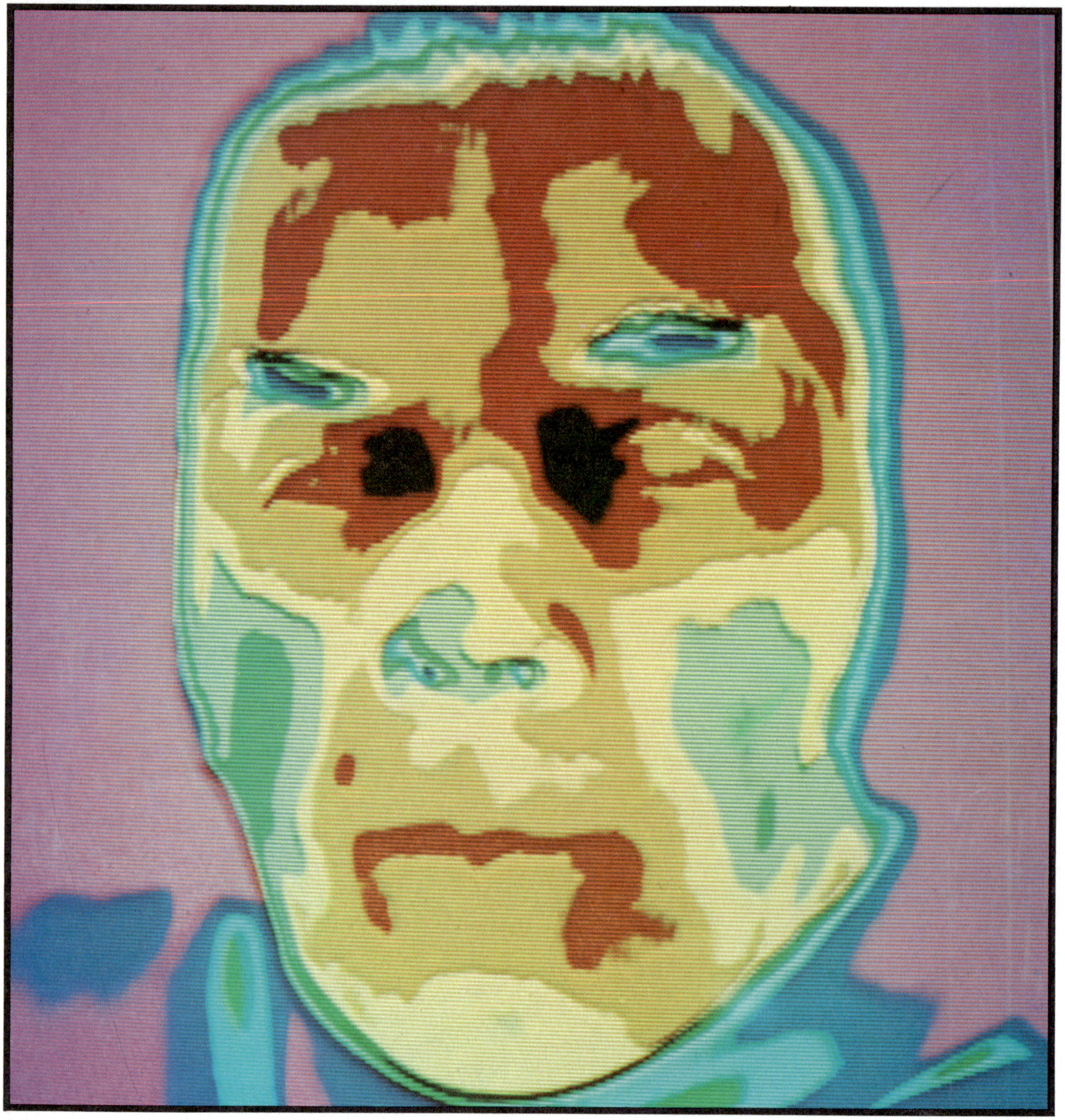

Dan McCoy from Rainbow

Heat

18

Chapter 18 covers the concept of energy as it applies to heat. The kinetic theory of matter is introduced. The effect of heat on the properties of matter is emphasized. See the Teacher's Guide at the front of this book for additional teaching strategies for this chapter.

18:1 Energy

GOAL: *You will learn the relationship between heat and kinetic energy.*

Energy is the capacity to do work. Recall that there are two basic types of energy, kinetic energy and potential energy, Section 3:6. Energy can be changed from one form to another. Potential energy can be changed to kinetic energy. As water falls over a dam, its potential energy becomes kinetic energy, Figure 18-1. Falling water has kinetic energy. As water hits the blades of the water wheel, the kinetic energy of the water is used to turn the wheel. Work is done by the falling water.

FIGURE 18-1.

Energy is never created or destroyed. What happens to the kinetic energy of a falling book? Some of it becomes the sound you hear when the book strikes the desk. The rest is changed to heat.

To raise a rubber ball to a height of five meters, work must be done to overcome the force of gravity. As the ball is raised, its potential energy with respect to the floor increases. The higher it is raised, the greater its potential energy. A rubber ball has more potential energy at a height of ten meters above the floor than at five meters. If the ball is dropped, it falls swiftly to the ground. Its potential energy decreases. When the ball is dropped, the potential energy is changed to kinetic energy. When the ball reaches the ground, all of the potential energy has been changed to kinetic energy.

18-1 Detailed information concerning this Activity can be found in the Teacher's Guide at the front of this book.

ACTIVITY *Can kinetic energy produce heat?*

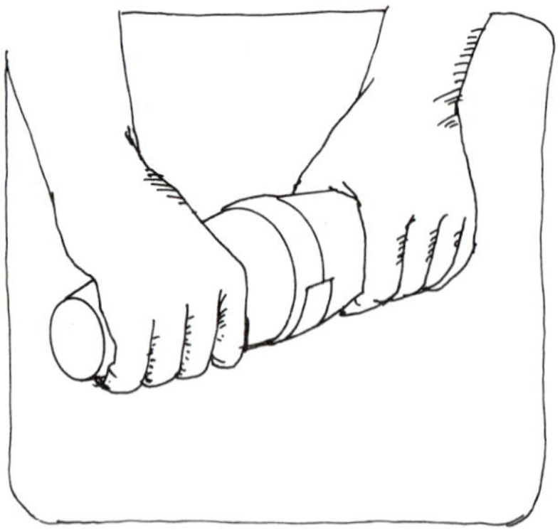

FIGURE 18-2.

(1) *Obtain two paper drinking cups. Fill one cup one third full of dry sand at room temperature.* ***(2)*** *Place the end of a thermometer in the sand and record the temperature.* ***(3)*** *Now invert the second cup over the first cup. Seal by wrapping a piece of tape around the seam between the two cups.* ***(4)*** *Shake the sand back and forth inside the cups for five minutes.* ***(5)*** *Punch a hole in the top of the cup.* ***(6)*** *Insert the thermometer. Record the temperature again. Is there a change in temperature? Why?* yes The kinetic energy is changed to heat.

Making Sure

It does work. It transfers to energy (work) in the nail.

1. What happens to the kinetic energy of a moving hammer when it hits a nail?

See the Teacher's Guide.

2. Explain how each of the following examples of potential energy changes to kinetic energy.
   - **a.** wound watch
   - **b.** stretched rubber band
   - **c.** diver on a diving board
   - **d.** a drawn archer's bow

18:2 Temperature and Heat

How is heat different from temperature?

All matter is made of particles. These particles are in constant motion. They have kinetic energy. Temperature is a measure of the average kinetic energy of the particles in a material. Two materials are at the same temperature when the average kinetic energy of the particles in each is the same. For example, an orange and a carton of milk are at the same temperature in a refrigerator. The average kinetic energy of the particles of the orange is the same as the average kinetic energy of the particles of the milk.

Temperature and heat are not the same. **Heat** is the total internal energy of the material. The total kinetic energy of the particles in a material is the **internal energy** or heat of the material. The internal energy of a material depends on its mass as well as its temperature. Imagine a swimming pool and a pan of water. The water

Hickson-Bender Photography

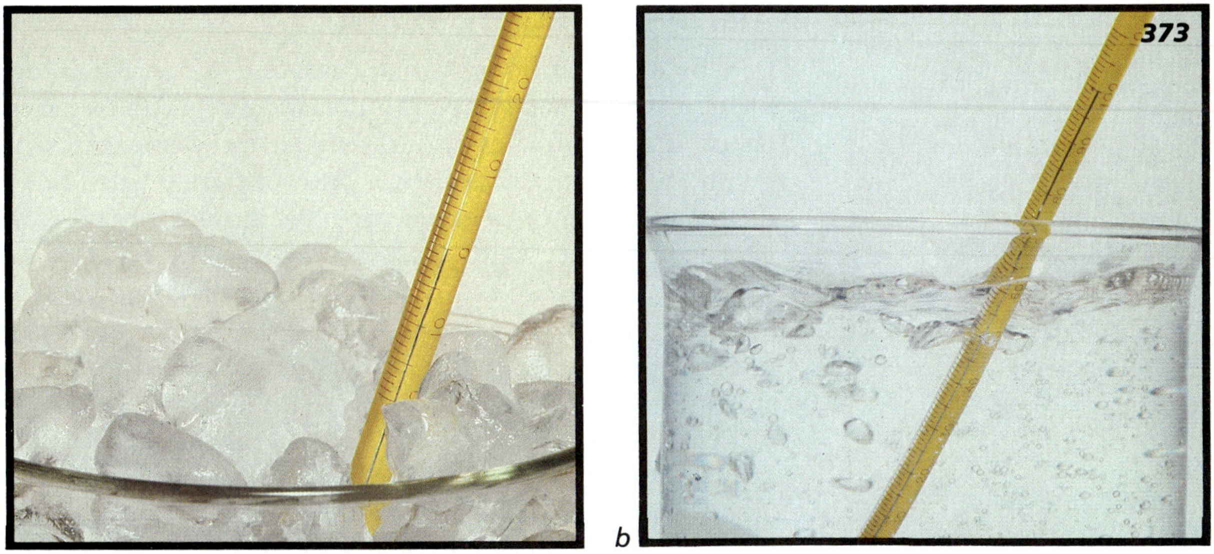

FIGURE 18-3. The thermometer shows 0°C in ice water (a). The mercury rises showing 100°C in boiling water (b).

in each is the same temperature. Which has more heat energy? The mass of water in the pool is greater than in the pan. A large mass of water has more particles than a small mass. A large number of particles has a higher total kinetic energy than a small number.

We will see in Section 18:4 that temperature is used to calculate heat energy. Recall that temperature is expressed in degrees Celsius (°C). An older unit for heat is the calorie. The modern unit is the joule (J). One calorie equals 4.18 joules.

Temperature also shows the tendency of a material to gain or lose heat. For example, when you put a thermometer in a glass of ice water, the column of mercury drops, Figure 18-3a. The thermometer lost heat to the ice water. If you put the thermometer in boiling water, the column of mercury rises, Figure 18-3b. The thermometer gained heat from the boiling water. Heat flows from regions of higher temperature to regions of lower temperature.

In what direction does heat flow?

Making Sure

3. What does temperature measure? *average kinetic energy*
4. Which will have more heat energy, a cup of boiling water or a pot of boiling water? *the pot*
5. What is the modern unit for heat energy? *joule (J)*

18:3 Specific Heat

Heat and temperature are related. When the internal energy of a substance is increased, its particles move faster. The kinetic energy of the particles increases as shown by a temperature rise. The substance gains heat. As a material loses heat, its particles move more slowly. The temperature of the material falls.

What units are used for specific heat?

Specific heat (C_p) is the ability of a material to absorb heat. It is measured using the units joule per gram Celsius degree (J/g · C°). For example, water has a specific heat of 4.18 J/g · C°. This value shows that 4.18 joules of heat energy are absorbed in raising the temperature of one gram of water one Celsius degree.

Different materials have different specific heats. Iron has a specific heat of 0.45 J/g · C°. It takes 0.45 joules to raise the temperature of one gram of iron one Celsius degree. Table 18-1 shows the specific heats of several substances.

Table 18-1

Specific Heat of Common Substances (in J/g · C°)

water	4.18	iron	0.45
aluminum	0.92	copper	0.38
carbon (graphite)	0.71	mercury	0.14

18-2 Detailed information concerning this Activity can be found in the Teacher's Guide at the front of this book.

ACTIVITY *Which metal holds more heat?*

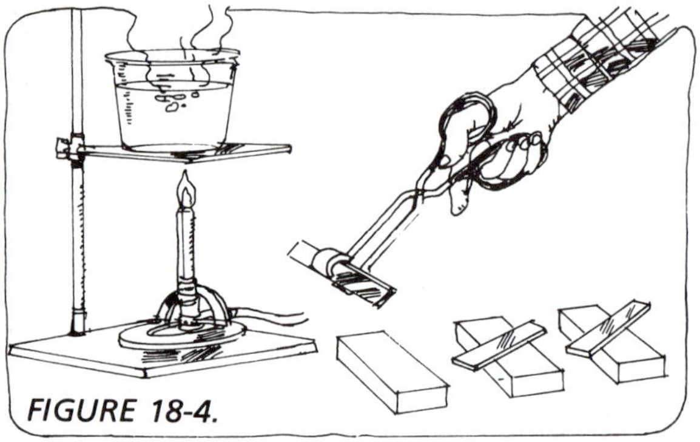

FIGURE 18-4.

***(1)** Obtain pieces of aluminum, copper, and iron. Each piece should be the same mass. **(2)** Place the metal pieces in boiling water for five minutes. **(3)** With metal tongs, remove each piece from the water and set it on a block of paraffin wax. Allow the pieces of metal to stand until they are cool. Which melts the most paraffin? Which metal has the most heat? Explain any differences.* aluminum aluminum

Making Sure

6. What is the effect of a gain in heat on the particles of a material? *increases kinetic energy*
7. What is specific heat? *ability of a material to absorb heat*

18:4 Measuring Heat

What measurements are made when calculating the gain or loss of heat?

Changes in the heat energy of a material can be measured. To find the change in heat energy, we measure the mass and temperature of the material. Then the material is heated or cooled. Another temperature reading is taken. Using the specific heat of the material, we can find the amount of heat energy absorbed or released by the material. This change in heat equals the temperature difference multiplied by the mass and the specific heat of the material.

$$\textit{Heat absorbed or released} = \textit{change in temperature} \times \textit{mass} \times \textit{specific heat}$$

$$\Delta H = (t_2 - t_1) \times m \times C_p$$
$$= \Delta t \times m \times C_p$$

Δ means change, so Δt means change in temperature.

Example

Ten grams of water are heated from 5°C to 20°C. How much heat energy is absorbed by the water?

Solution:

(a) Write the equation for the change in heat.

$$\Delta H = (t_2 - t_1) \times m \times C_p$$

(b) Substitute the values given in the problem.

$$\Delta H = (20°\text{C} - 5°\text{C}) \times 10\text{ g} \times 4.18\text{ J/g}\cdot\text{C}°$$
$$= 15\text{ C}° \times 10\text{ g} \times 4.18\text{ J/g}\cdot\text{C}°$$
$$= 627\text{ J}$$

Heat changes can be measured with a **calorimeter** (kal uh RIHM uht ur), Figure 18-5. For example, the heat energy of food may be found by burning it in the inner chamber of a calorimeter. Heat produced in the inner chamber is absorbed by the water in the outer chamber. This heat gain causes an increase in water temperature.

How is a calorimeter used to measure heat?

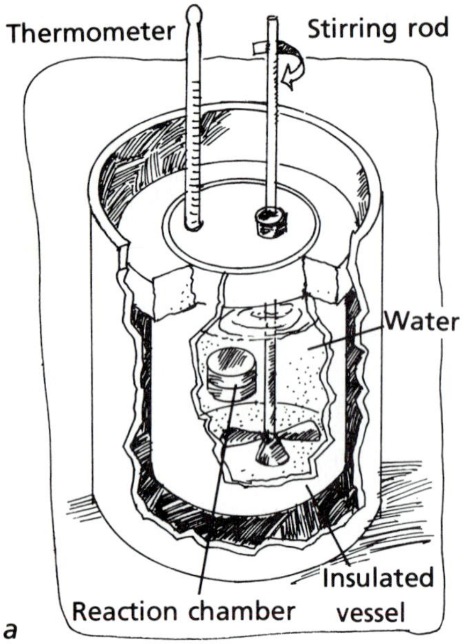

a

Hickson-Bender Photography/Ohio Wesleyan Univ.

b

FIGURE 18-5. The construction of a bomb calorimeter (a). An oxygen bomb calorimeter (b).

The temperature can be used to calculate the heat energy lost by the food. The amount of heat gained by the water is the amount of heat lost by the food.

18-3 Detailed information concerning this Activity can be found in the Teacher's Guide at the front of this book.

ACTIVITY *How does a calorimeter work?*

Setting Up

dowel rod 20 cm by 0.5 cm
50 grams of copper
glass wool
heavy cardboard
sheet of aluminum foil
thermometer
tongs
two cans of different sizes

Getting Started

1. *Cover the small can with glass wool and place it inside the larger can.*
2. *Make a cover by cutting the cardboard to fit over the cans. Tape the aluminum foil, shiny side out, to the cardboard.*
3. *Punch two holes in the cover; one for the thermometer and one for the dowel rod.*
4. *Place 100 milliliters of water in the small can and let it stand until it is at room temperature. Note that 100 milliliters of water is about 100 grams.*
5. *Heat the copper in boiling water for five minutes.*
6. *Record the temperature of the water in the calorimeter.*

Hickson-Bender Photography

FIGURE 18-6.

7. *Using the tongs, place the copper in the calorimeter.*
8. *Cover the calorimeter with the lid, aluminum foil down.*
9. *Gently stir the water and record the temperature every 30 seconds.*

Keeping Track

mass of water	
initial temperature of water	
final temperature of water	

Time	Temperature

Summing Up

1. *When the temperature stops rising, calculate the heat gained by the water. Note that the highest temperature is the final temperature of the water. Use the equation:*

$$H = (t_2 - t_1) \times \text{mass of water} \times \text{specific heat of water}$$

The specific heat of water is 4.18 J/g · C°.

2. *How much heat did the metal lose?*
3. *Why do you need to wait until the temperature has stopped rising to find the heat gained by the water?* As long as the temperature rises, the water is still gaining heat.

Making Sure

8. A 40-gram piece of carbon is cooled from 80° C to 15° C. How much heat is lost by the carbon? 1800
9. A 500-gram bar of aluminum is heated from 25° C to 100° C, then cooled in water to 40° C. How much heat is gained by the water? 28 000

18:5 Melting and Vaporization

Suppose you take the temperature of a beaker of ice. You find it is −20 degrees Celsius. Next you gently heat the ice taking its temperature every 30 seconds. You will use the data to plot a graph of the temperature versus the time, as in Figure 18-7.

Hickson-Bender Photography

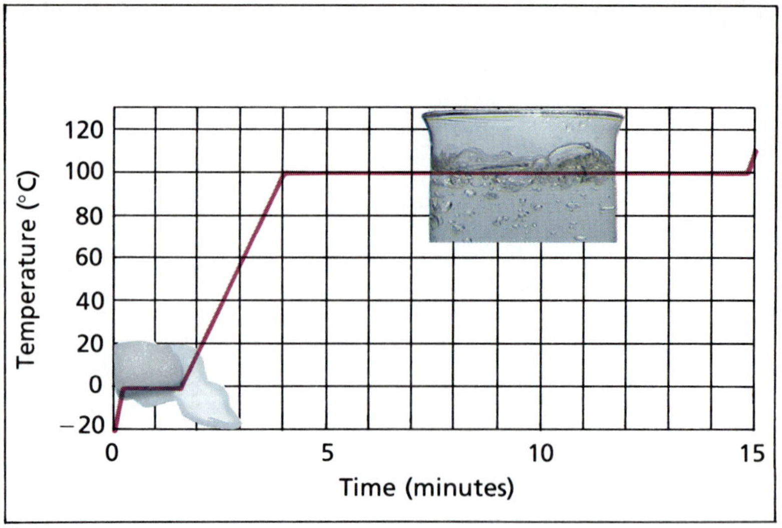

FIGURE 18-7. A graph showing the rise in temperature with time at a constant heat.

After a few minutes, the temperature stops rising. You notice that the ice is melting. Once the ice has melted, the temperature begins to rise again. While the ice was melting, all of the heat was being used to break the forces holding the water in the solid state. The melting point of ice is zero degrees Celsius. At zero degrees Celsius, one gram of water absorbs 334 joules of heat energy to change state or melt. The energy needed to change from the solid state to the liquid state is called the **heat of fusion.**

Define heat of fusion and heat of vaporization.

Suppose you continue to heat the water and plot the graph. Once the temperature reaches 100 degrees Celsius, it stops rising again. Now, suppose your beaker is covered. This time you wait longer for the temperature to begin to rise. During this time the water has turned to steam. More heat energy is needed for water to change from liquid to gas than to change from solid to liquid. One gram of water uses 2260 joules of heat energy to change from liquid to gas. This energy is called the **heat of vaporization** (vay puh ruh ZAY shun).

When a liquid changes to a gas, it gains heat energy. When a solid changes to a liquid, it gains heat energy. During the change of state the temperature remains constant. As a gas condenses to a liquid, it releases heat energy. A liquid changing to a solid releases heat energy. During each change of state, there is no temperature change.

Making Sure

10. Is there a temperature change when a material changes state? *no*
11. What is the effect of heat added during a change of state? *It breaks the bonds holding the substance in that state.*

18:6 Expansion

As heat is added to a material, the kinetic energy of the particles increases. Particles move faster as their energy increases. As the particles move faster, they collide with each other more violently. These more violent collisions push the particles farther apart. As the particles move farther apart in a material, the material's volume increases. The material expands.

Why does a substance expand when heated?

Many bridges are built with a space between the bridge and the roadbed, Figure 18-8. This space allows for the expansion of the bridge at different temperatures. At cool temperatures the space is wide. At warm temperatures the space is narrow.

Liquids expand and contract in the same manner as solids. For example, a gasoline can is filled to the top. Overnight the temperature drops. In the morning, the gasoline level is no longer at the top.

Hickson-Bender Photography

FIGURE 18-8. Space is left between a bridge and a road to allow it to expand.

Hickson Bender/Ohio State Univer., Marion Campus

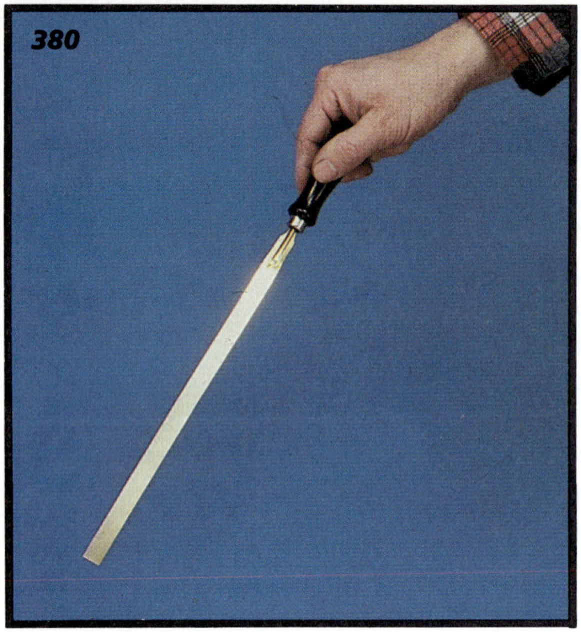

a

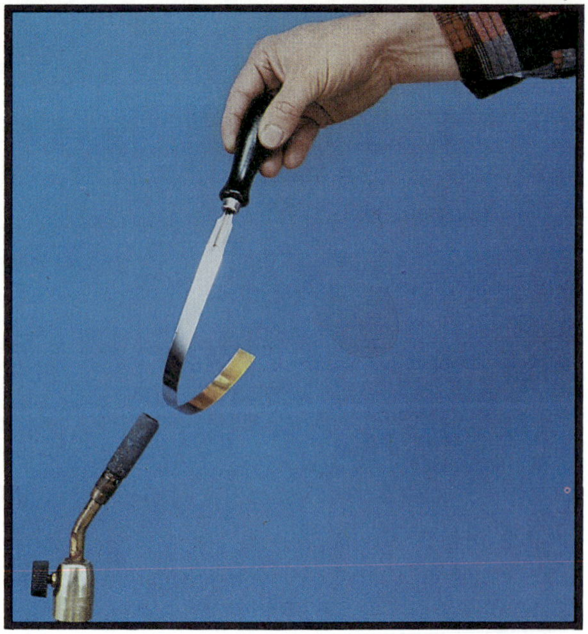

b

FIGURE 18-9. The iron side of a bimetallic strip (a). The strip bends toward the iron when heated (b).

Materials expand at different rates. A bimetallic strip can be made of iron and brass bonded together, Figure 18-9a. The strip will bend when heated. The brass expands faster than the iron. As a result, the strip bends toward the iron, Figure 18-9b.

18-4 Detailed information concerning this Activity can be found in the Teacher's Guide at the front of this book.

ACTIVITY *How does heat affect metal?*

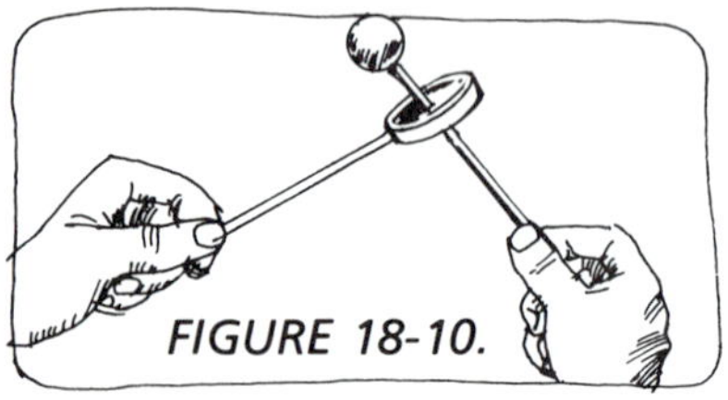

FIGURE 18-10.

***(1)** Obtain an iron ball and ring like those in Figure 18-10. Pass the ball through the ring. **(2)** Heat the ball over a flame for a few minutes. Try to pass the ball back through the ring. What do you observe? How did heating affect the ball? What happens if you allow the ball to cool completely? Explain what you observe.*

18-5 Detailed information concerning this Activity can be found in the Teacher's Guide at the front of this book.

ACTIVITY *How does a thermometer work?*

FIGURE 18-11.

***(1)** Fill a 250-milliliter flask with water. **(2)** Using a cloth, put a glass tube in a stopper. Be sure to wet the tube before putting it through. **(3)** Place the stopper in the flask, Figure 18-11. **(4)** Mark the level of the water in the tube. **(5)** Gently heat the flask in a pan of hot water, Figure 18-11. What happens to the water level in the tube? Explain your observations. The water level rises.*

18:7 Gases

A mechanic uses a gauge to check the pressure of an automobile tire. The pressure gauge shows 200 kilopascals. What causes this pressure in the tire? When air is pumped into a tire, the air is compressed. It is forced into a smaller space. The gas particles inside the tire have kinetic energy. They are in constant motion. As the particles move about, they strike each other and the walls of the tire. The force of the particles striking the walls of the tire produces the pressure.

Pressure is force per unit area. If the temperature of the gas is increased, the kinetic energy of the gas particles is increased and they move faster. Thus, the particles hit the walls of the tire more often and with greater force. As the overall force increases, the pressure increases. Another way to increase the pressure in a tire is to pump more air into it. With more particles hitting the walls of the tire, the pressure increases. The pressure of air inside a tire may be several times that of the air pressure outside. Suppose a car is driven many miles on a hot day. What can happen to the tire?

Hickson-Bender Photography

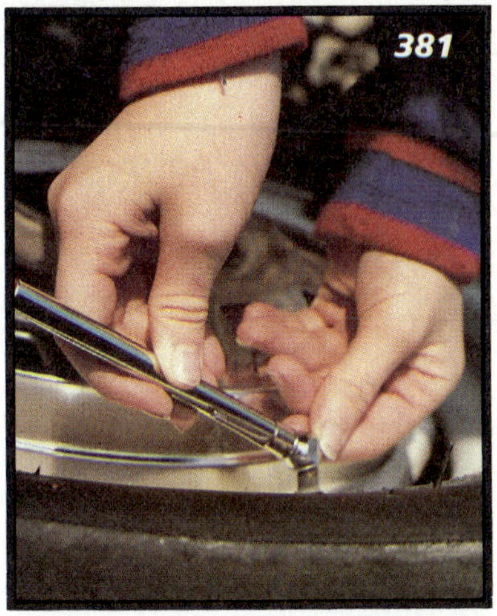

FIGURE 18-12. A person uses a pressure gauge to check tire pressure. Most tire gauges read pounds per square inch, instead of kilopascals.

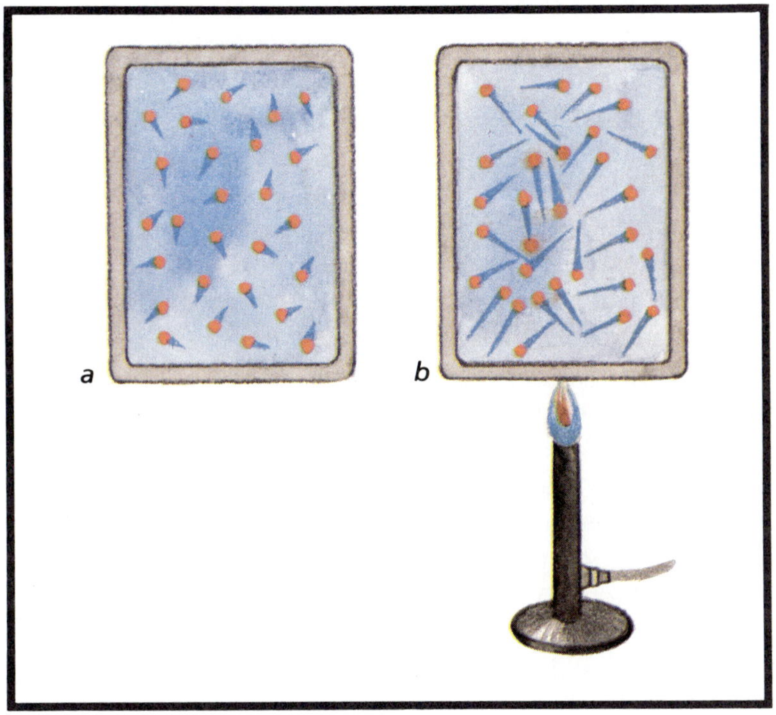

FIGURE 18-13. Gas particles moving in a container (a). When the gas is heated, the particles move faster (b).

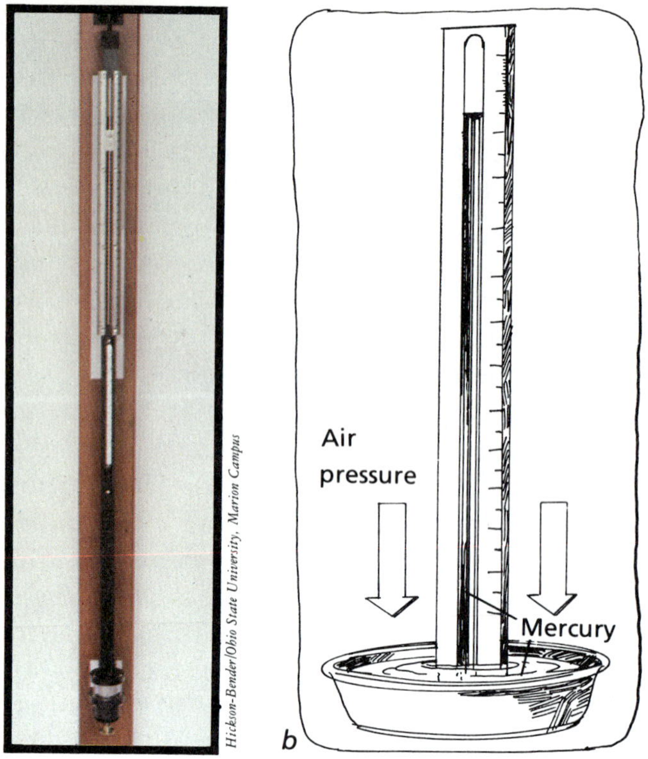

FIGURE 18-14. A mercury barometer (a). Air pressure supports the mercury in the column (b).

Barometers are used to measure air pressure, Figure 18-14. The unit of pressure is the **pascal (Pa).** Air pressure at sea level is 101 kilopascals. How many pascals are in a kilopascal? In a mercury barometer, a column of mercury 75 centimeters high gives a reading of 100 kilopascals.

1000

For a gas, there is a relationship between temperature, volume, and pressure. One statement of this relationship is called Boyle's law in honor of Robert Boyle, who discovered it. Boyle's law states that *the volume of a gas decreases as its pressure increases, if the temperature does not change.* Particles of a gas are pushed closer together when the pressure is increased. Thus, the volume decreases.

If the pressure on a gas decreases, the gas will expand. Remove the cap from a bottle of soda pop. Carbon dioxide gas comes out of solution. Opening the bottle reduces the pressure on the gas. A gas can be compressed into a smaller space or allowed to expand into a larger volume.

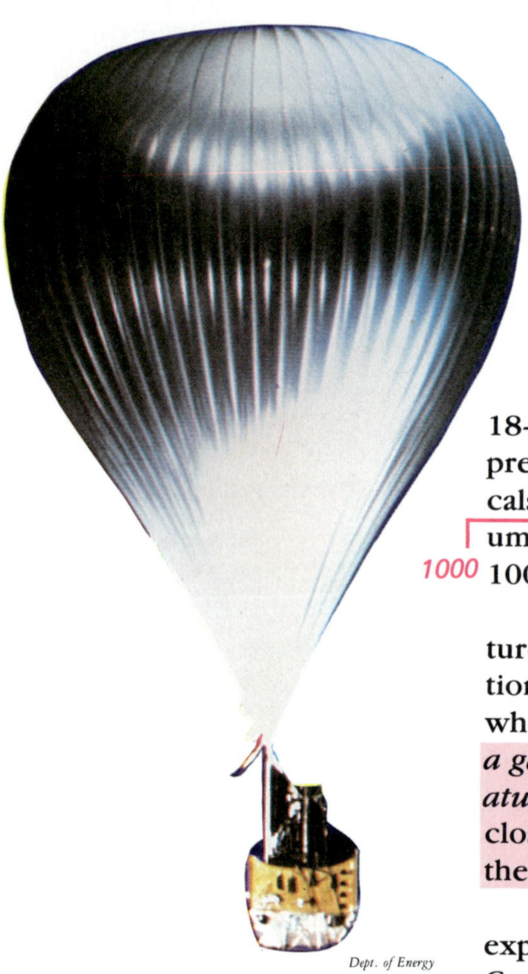

FIGURE 18-15. As a weather balloon rises, its volume increases. This is a demonstration of Boyle's law.

The volume of a gas increases as its temperature increases, if the pressure is not changed. This relationship is called Charles' law in honor of Jacques Charles, who discovered it. Heating a gas causes it to expand. Gas particles gain kinetic energy when they are heated. They move faster and strike the walls of the container more often. If the walls of the container are flexible, the gas pushes them out. There is an increase in volume. For example, if the air in a balloon is heated, the balloon expands.

How can the volume of a gas be decreased?

18-6 Detailed information concerning this Activity can be found in the Teacher's Guide at the front of this book.

ACTIVITY *How does heat affect a gas?*

(1) *Blow up a round balloon. Carefully measure its circumference.* **(2)** *Place it in a pan of hot water for ten minutes. Measure the circumference again. What happened to the balloon?* *The circumference increased.* **(3)** *Now place the balloon in a tray of ice for ten minutes. What is the result?* *The circumference decreased.*

Hickson-Bender Photography

FIGURE 18-16.

Making Sure

12. What is pressure? *force per unit area*
13. What happens to the pressure in a tire if the temperature increases? *The pressure increases.*
14. What happens to a gas if the pressure is decreased? *The volume increases.*

Focus On

Skills

Taking Notes in Outline Form

Outlining is another form of note taking. Outlining a chapter helps you sort information in order to see the relationships between main ideas and smaller details. A framework for an outline for this chapter is shown below. You are to add to this outline as you read the chapter, or make your own outline to organize the information.

I Energy
- A. Definition of: capacity to do work
- B. Types of:
  1. *kinetic*
  2. *potential*

II Temperature and Heat
- A. Temperature: a measure of the average kinetic energy of the particles in a material
  1. used to calculate heat energy
  2. expressed in degrees Celsius (°C)
- B. Heat: *the total internal energy of a substance*
  1. total heat energy of a system is dependent on temperature and mass
  2. heat units: *joules*

III Specific Heat (C_p)
- A. Definition of: *the ability of a substance to retain heat*
  1. expressed as joule per gram Celsius degree (J/g·C°)
  2. a physical property which is different for all materials

IV Measuring Heat
- A. To find changes in heat energy by experiment: measure the mass and temperature of the material. Change the temperature of the material, then measure the temperature again.
- B. Equation for calculating heat lost or gained: $H = \Delta t \times m \times C_p$

V Melting and Vaporization
- A. Heat of fusion: energy needed to change a substance from the solid state to the liquid state (gain in heat energy)
- B. Heat of vaporization: *energy needed to change a substance from the liquid state to the vapor (gaseous) state*

VI Expansion
- A. Description of: heat causes an increase in the kinetic energy of a substance. The particles move faster—they collide—they move further apart and the volume increases
- B. Materials expand at different rates

VII
- A. Pressure: force per unit area
- B. Barometers: *mercury columns used to measure pressure*
- C. Pressure units
  1. pascal (Pa)
  2. air pressure at sea level = 101 kilopascals
  3. 100 kilopascals = mercury barometer reading of 75 cm
- D. Boyle's Law: *the volume of a gas decreases as its pressure increases, if the temperature is to remain the same*
- E. Charles' Law: *the volume of a gas increases as its temperature increases, if the pressure is to remain the same*

Points to Remember

1. Energy can be changed from one form to another. *18:1*
2. Temperature is the average kinetic energy of the particles of a material. *18:2*
3. Heat energy is the total kinetic energy of the particles of a material. *18:2*
4. Specific heat is the ability of a substance to absorb heat energy. *18:3*
5. Changes in heat energy can be measured using temperature, mass, and specific heat. *18:4*
6. While a material changes state, heat energy is absorbed. *18:5*
7. Materials expand because particles move farther apart as their kinetic energy increases. *18:6*
8. For a gas, there is a relationship among temperature, volume, and pressure. *18:7*

Words to Use

Write a sentence in which you correctly use each of the following words.

calorimeter	heat of vaporization	pressure
expansion	internal energy	specific heat
heat	pascal	vaporization
heat of fusion	potential energy	

Questions for Review

Do not write in this book.

A. True or False *Have the students rewrite the false statements to make them correct.*

Determine whether each of the following sentences is true or false.

T **1.** Heat is a form of energy.

T **2.** Freezing water is an example of a change in physical state.

F **3.** When the temperature of a gas increases, its particles move ~~more slowly~~. *faster*

F **4.** The specific heat of iron is ~~greater~~ *less* than the specific heat of water.

F 5. A thermometer measures the ~~amount of heat an object contains~~. *temperature of an object*

T 6. Energy can be changed from one form to another.

T 7. The heat energy of a material can be measured.

F 8. The heat of fusion is the energy needed to change from ~~liquid to gas~~. *solid to liquid*

T 9. A bimetallic strip bends when heated.

F 10. Temperature and heat are *not* the same.

B. Multiple Choice

Choose the word or phrase that correctly completes each of the following sentences.

1. Kinetic energy is energy of *(position, motion)*.
2. Heat is measured in *(degrees Celsius, joules)*.
3. A temperature rise means there is an increase in the *(mass, size, kinetic energy)* of the particles.
4. Heat is measured with a *(thermometer, calorimeter)*.
5. If a bar of metal is heated, it *(expands, contracts, remains the same)*.
6. The energy of falling water is *(kinetic, potential)* energy.
7. Specific heat is the ability of a substance to *(absorb, generate)* heat energy.
8. Temperature is used to calculate *(heat, electric, potential)* energy.
9. The amount of heat needed to change from a solid to a liquid is the *(heat of vaporization, heat of fusion)*.
10. The heat absorbed by water as it changes to a gas is the heat of *(fusion, vaporization, condensation)*.

C. Completion

Complete each of the following sentences with a word or phrase that will make the sentence correct.

1. When water is heated, its internal kinetic energy *increases*.
2. Energy is the capacity to do *work*.
3. A book on a table one meter above the floor has more *potential energy* than a book resting on the floor.
4. Specific heat is measured in *joules* per gram Celsius degree.

5. Specific heat is the ability of a material to absorb heat.
6. A device for measuring heat changes is calorimeter.
7. Particles move at a faster rate as their energy increases.
8. Pressure is force per unit area.
9. According to Boyle's law, the pressure on a gas increases and the volume decreases, if the temperature remains the same.
10. In using a calorimeter, the amount of heat lost by a metal is the amount of heat gained by the water.

Detailed answers to these questions are given in the Teacher's Guide at the front of this book.

D. How and Why

1. How is heat different from temperature?
2. Why might the parts of an engine "freeze" if the engine overheats?
3. Why does the temperature of iron rise faster than water?
4. A piece of steel raises the temperature of 100 grams of water from 20°C to 60°C. How much heat does the water gain? How much heat does the metal lose?

More Ideas to Explore

1. Do some library research to find why fruit orchards are often located near large bodies of water.
2. Research and prepare a report on how the electric thermometers used in hospitals work. Compare them to mercury thermometers.
3. Many thermostats use bimetallic strips to control home heating systems. Obtain an old thermostat and take it apart. How is the bimetallic strip used? Compare this heat control with the heat control of an old electric iron.

Readings to Discover

Adler, Irving, *Energy.* NY: John Day, 1970.

Adler, Irving, *Hot and Cold: The Story of Temperature From Absolute Zero to the Heat of the Sun.* NY: John Day, 1975.

Balestrino, Philip, *Hot as an Ice Cube.* NY: Thomas Y. Crowell Company, 1972.

Cobb, Vicki, *Heat.* NY: F. Watts, 1973.

Hellman, Hal, *Energy and Inertia.* NY: Lippincott and Co., 1970.

Heat is used in preparing food to prevent disease. Our bodies use the food to produce energy to move. Heat energy is also produced, keeping us warm. What are some other ways to use heat to make life easier and more comfortable?

Hickson-Bender Photography

Heat and Its Uses

19

Chapter 19 relates heat energy to practical applications. Technological advances in heating and cooling systems are discussed. Causes and cures concerning thermal pollution are also presented. See the Teacher's Guide at the front of this book for additional teaching strategies for this chapter.

19:1 Movement of Heat

GOAL: *You will learn some of the practical uses of heat.*

Heat moves in three ways; conduction, convection, and radiation. If you leave a metal spoon in a bowl of hot soup, the spoon gets hot. The heat moves from one end of the spoon to the other. Recall that heat moves from areas of high temperature to areas of low temperature. The particles near the source have more kinetic energy. They move faster than the particles farther from the source. The movement of energy up the spoon occurs as kinetic energy is transferred. Kinetic energy is transferred as particles hit each other. Movement of heat in this manner is called **conduction.** In conduction, the energy is moved from particle to particle. Heat can be conducted through solids, liquids, and gases. Because the particles in liquids and gases are farther apart, they do not conduct heat as well as solids.

How is conduction different from convection?

Convection is the movement of heat in liquids and gases. When liquids and gases are heated, they expand. Their density decreases. The less dense material rises, causing currents that carry heat. For example, heat from a flame can warm the bottom of a pan of water. Water at

FIGURE 19-1. This thermometer uses temperature sensitive chemicals to show the temperature. As the temperature changes, the chemicals change color.

Don Parsisson

EROS Data Center

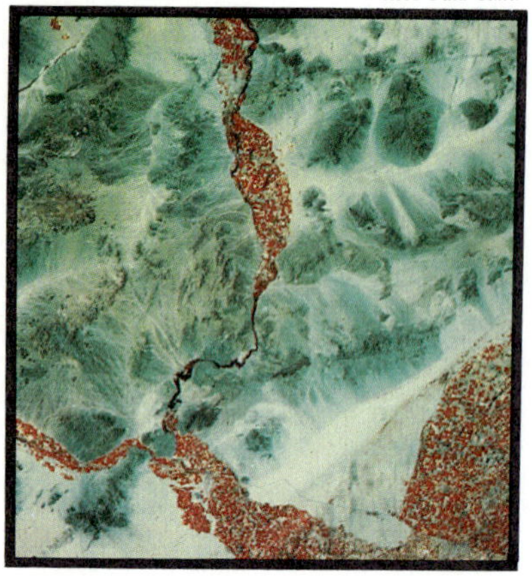

FIGURE 19-2. An infrared photo taken by a satellite.

the bottom of the pan becomes hot and decreases in density. This less dense water floats upward and carries heat with it. Winds and ocean currents are gases and liquids moving heat by convection.

Convection and conduction need the movement of particles to transfer heat. **Radiation** is a method of moving heat without moving particles. For example, radiant energy is released by the sun. This energy travels through space to the earth. Space is a vacuum. **Radiant energy** is electromagnetic radiation, Section 14:3. Light bulbs, hot skillets, and people release radiant energy. Often heat is released as infrared radiation. As a result, infrared cameras can be used to take pictures at night, Figure 19-3. Some satellites use infrared radiation to take heat pictures of the earth.

Heat usually moves by more than one method. Imagine you are in a cabin. Your only source of heat is the fireplace. Radiation from the fire heats the air in the room. The air starts to move forming convection currents.

Now suppose you are cooking a pot of stew over the fire. Radiant energy from the fire heats the bottom of the pot. Heat is conducted through the metal of the pot. Convection currents form carrying the heat through the stew.

FIGURE 19-3.

19-1 Detailed information concerning this Activity can be found in the Teacher's Guide at the front of this book.

ACTIVITY Can glass conduct heat as well as metal?

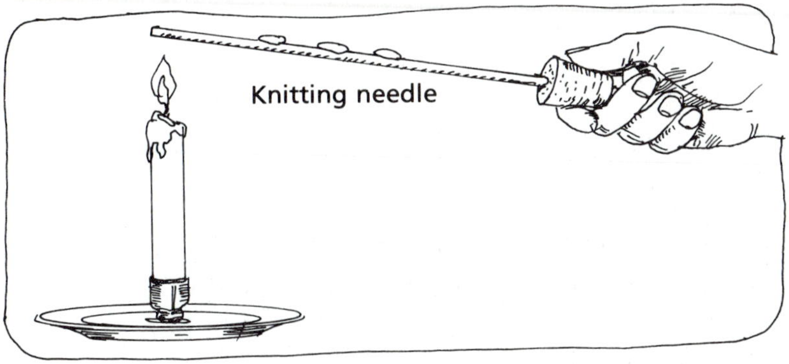

FIGURE 19-4.

Obtain a metal knitting needle and a glass rod. Both should have the same diameter and length. **(1)** *Push one end of the knitting needle into a cork. Use the cork as a handle.* **(2)** *Melt some wax from a candle onto the needle at three points two centimeters apart.* **(3)** *Light a candle and hold the free end of the needle in the flame. Continue heating the end of the needle until all the wax drops off. How long did it take for all the wax to melt?* **(4)** *Repeat this activity using the glass rod instead of the needle. Be sure to place the wax at about the points you did on the needle. Compare the conduction in the metal needle with that in the glass rod.*

19-2 Detailed information concerning this Activity can be found in the Teacher's Guide at the front of this book.

ACTIVITY What happens as water is heated?

FIGURE 19-5.

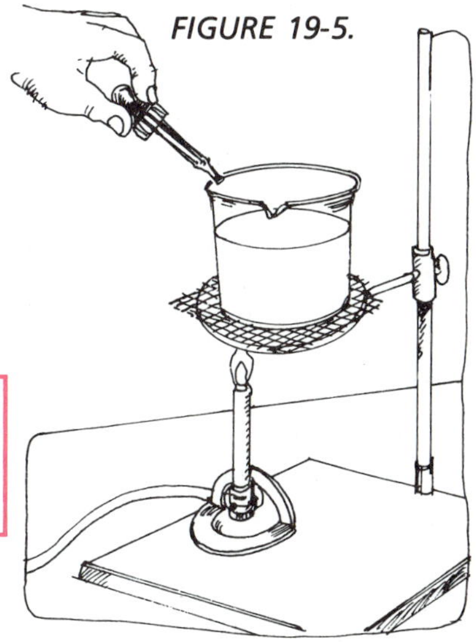

(1) *Fill a beaker about two-thirds full of water. Place it on a ring stand.* **(2)** *Add a drop of food coloring to the water at the side of the beaker. Do not stir. Be very careful not to disturb the water in the beaker.* **(3)** *Gently heat the water by heating the beaker on one side. What do you observe?*

convection current

Making Sure

1. What are three things in your room that give off heat as radiation? *Answers will vary. Radiator, light bulb, and people are examples.*
2. How does heat move in conduction? *The kinetic energy is transferred from one particle to another.*
3. What is the difference between convection and conduction? *In convection, groups of particles move transferring the energy.*

19:2 Insulation

Heat energy moves from areas with high temperatures to areas with low temperatures. Sometimes we want to stop or control heat movement. We control heat movement with insulation. **Insulation** does not allow heat to move easily.

How would you keep ice from melting on a picnic? You would insulate the ice from the heat. One way to insulate ice is to put it in an ice chest or cooler, Figure 19-6. The cooler is made of plastic foam. The foam does not conduct heat well. The foam is full of bubbles containing air. Air is a poor conductor of heat. The bubbles are so small that convection currents cannot form. You might want to insulate from the sun's radiant energy. To insulate from heat radiation, a metal, like aluminum, could be used inside and outside. The shiny surface of the metal reflects radiated energy. All of this insulation would keep the ice from melting for several hours.

Describe three uses for insulation.

Insulation is also used to keep things hot. We can use the cooler to keep a pot of soup warm for a winter day. In our homes, insulation is used to save energy. It helps keep the house from getting too cold or too hot.

One way to insulate a home is to put fiberglass insulation in the walls and roof. The insulation is made of many long thin fibers of glass packed close together. There are spaces of air between the fibers. Neither air

FIGURE 19-6. The cross section shows the insulation (a) of a picnic cooler (b).

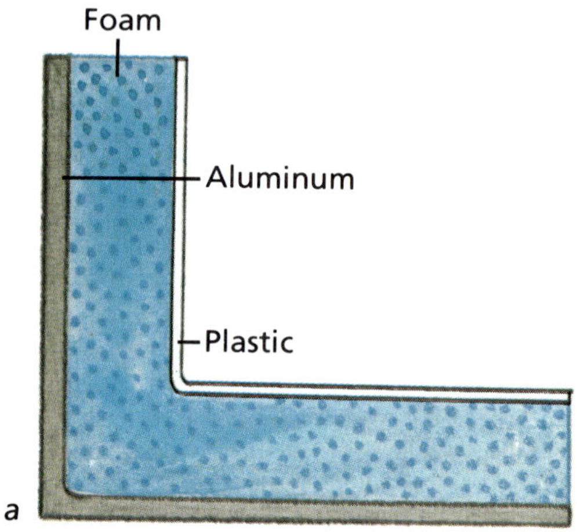

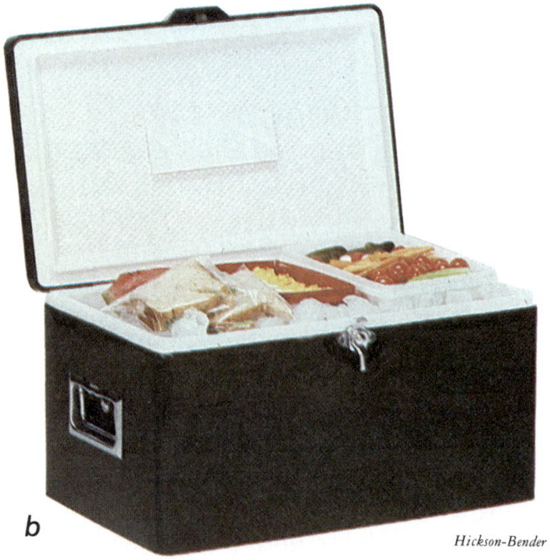

Hickson-Bender Photography

nor glass conducts heat well. The air spaces are too small for convection to occur. Insulating the walls and roof will reduce the heat loss in a house.

In addition to the walls and roof, doors and windows need to be insulated. One way to insulate them is to use weather stripping. Weather stripping closes gaps that allow convection with the air outside. Double paned windows also help by putting a space between the glass panes. Since the panes are not touching, conduction cannot occur. The space is small enough to prevent convection. Recall that heat can move in three ways. Insulation must be designed to control more than one of these ways.

Hickson-Bender Photography

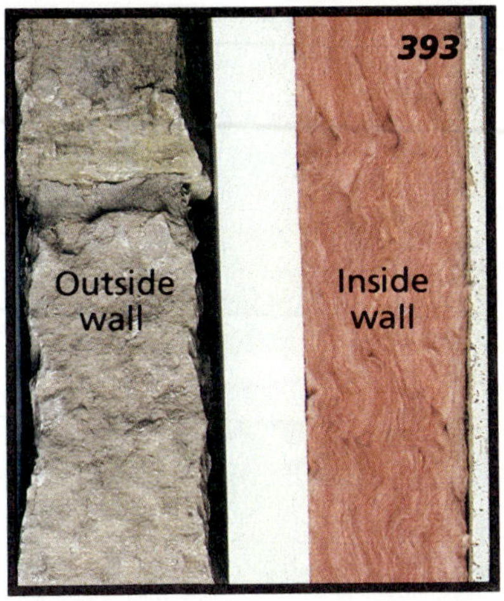

FIGURE 19-7. The cross section of this wall is stone, foam, fiberglass, and drywall.

19-3 *Detailed information concerning this Activity can be found in the Teacher's Guide at the front of this book.*

Activity *Which bottle has the best insulation?*

Setting Up

3 clear glass bottles
vacuum bottle
2 sheets of aluminum foil
sauce pan
hot plate
4 thermometers

FIGURE 19-8.

Getting Started

1. *Cover one bottle with aluminum foil, shiny side in, as in Figure 19-8.*
2. *Cover a second bottle with aluminum foil, shiny side out.*
3. *Leave the third bottle uncovered.*
4. *Using the sauce pan, heat water to boiling. Make sure you have enough to fill each bottle 2/3 full with hot water.*
5. *Carefully fill the vacuum bottle and each glass bottle 2/3 full with the hot water.*
6. *Place a thermometer in each bottle and record the temperatures.*
7. *Allow each to stand for 20 minutes. Observe and record the temperatures in the four bottles every five minutes.*

Keeping Track

bottle 1	bottle 2	bottle 3	vacuum bottle

Summing Up

1. *In which bottle does the water cool fastest?* uncovered
2. *Which way does heat travel in the bottles?* from inside to outside
3. *Which of the bottles is insulated the most?* vacuum bottle then shiny side in
4. *How does the aluminum foil affect the movement of heat?* slows the movement with the shiny side reflecting more than the other
5. *What could you do to improve the insulation of the bottles?* put the bottles inside other similarly covered bottles

Clothing can prevent both convection and radiation.

Making Sure

4. How is clothing used as insulation?
5. Name four ways insulation is used in your home.
   Some examples are walls, refrigerator, stove, windows.

19:3 Cooling Systems

Ice is used in cold drinks and picnic coolers. Ice is also used to preserve food. Ice cools things because it absorbs heat as it melts. When ice melts, each gram of ice absorbs 334 joules of heat. Recall that this value is the heat of fusion for ice, Section 18:5.

How does evaporation cool something?

The process of **evaporation** can be used as a cooling system. During evaporation, a liquid absorbs heat. The average kinetic energy of the particles in the liquid rises. At the surface of the liquid, some of the particles will have enough kinetic energy to escape. In leaving the liquid, the particles have removed heat from their surroundings. The surroundings are cooled.

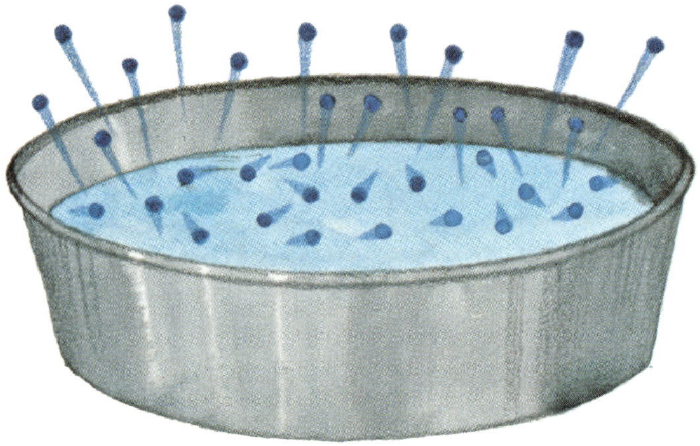

FIGURE 19-9. In evaporation, some of the particles at the surface of a liquid escape, cooling the liquid.

Refrigerators, freezers, and air conditioners work using evaporation. Many refrigerators use **freon** in their cooling systems. One gram of the freon compound CCl_2F_2 must absorb 167 joules of energy in order to evaporate.

Explain the use of freon in a refrigerator.

In a refrigerator system, the freon leaves a storage tank under high pressure, Figure 19-10. As the freon flows through the pipes, the pressure is reduced. At this lower pressure, the freon can evaporate inside the coils.

The freon absorbs heat from the surroundings as it evaporates. The surroundings are cooled as a result. The compressor raises the pressure of the vaporized freon. It is pumped to an area where the freon gas loses the heat it gained when it evaporated. The freon changes to a liquid. It is then pumped back to the storage tank.

The automatic defrost unit on a refrigerator also works using evaporation. In this system, hot gas from the compressor is used to melt the frost. The defrosted water is collected and carried to an area close to the compressor. The heat from the compressor evaporates the water.

Detailed information concerning this Activity can be found in the Teacher's Guide at the front of this book.

19-4 **ACTIVITY** *How does evaporation affect temperature?*

(1) *Wrap a small piece of absorbent cotton around the bulb of a thermometer. Tighten the cotton with a rubber band.* **(2)** *Set the thermometer in a beaker. Use a medicine dropper to moisten the cotton with water at room temperature.* **(3)** *Read and record the temperature.* **(4)** *Allow the thermometer to stand for five minutes, read the temperature again. Does the evaporation of water add or remove heat from the thermometer?* **(5)** *Repeat the activity using alcohol. What happens? How do the results with alcohol compare with the results using water?* *temperature goes lower*

remove

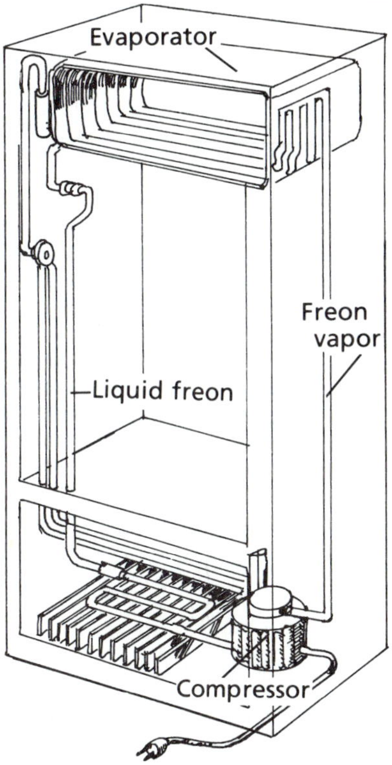

FIGURE 19-10. The construction of a refrigerator cooling system.

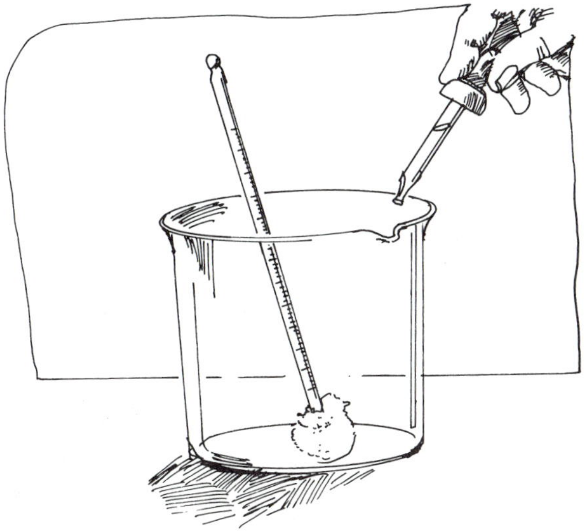

FIGURE 19-11.

The evaporating particles absorb heat and cool the remainder.

Making Sure

6. How can evaporation be a cooling process?
7. To cool food in a refrigerator, freon absorbs energy. Where does the energy come from? *inside the refrigerator*

19:4 Heating Systems

How does a hot water system heat a room?

There are a number of systems used to heat homes and other buildings. One kind is a hot water system, Figure 19-12. This system uses a furnace, a boiler, and radiators. The boiler and furnace are usually found in the basement. In the furnace, gas, coal, or oil is used to heat the water in the boiler. The water is heated to about 82 degrees Celsius.

Convection carries the water through pipes to radiators in the rooms. Heat flows from the hot water, through the metal radiator, to the cool air. Air near the radiator warms and rises. A convection current forms moving heat through the room, Figure 19-12. As the water cools in the radiator, it flows back to the boiler. Hot water replaces the cooled water. The circulation of water from boiler to radiator is repeated over and over.

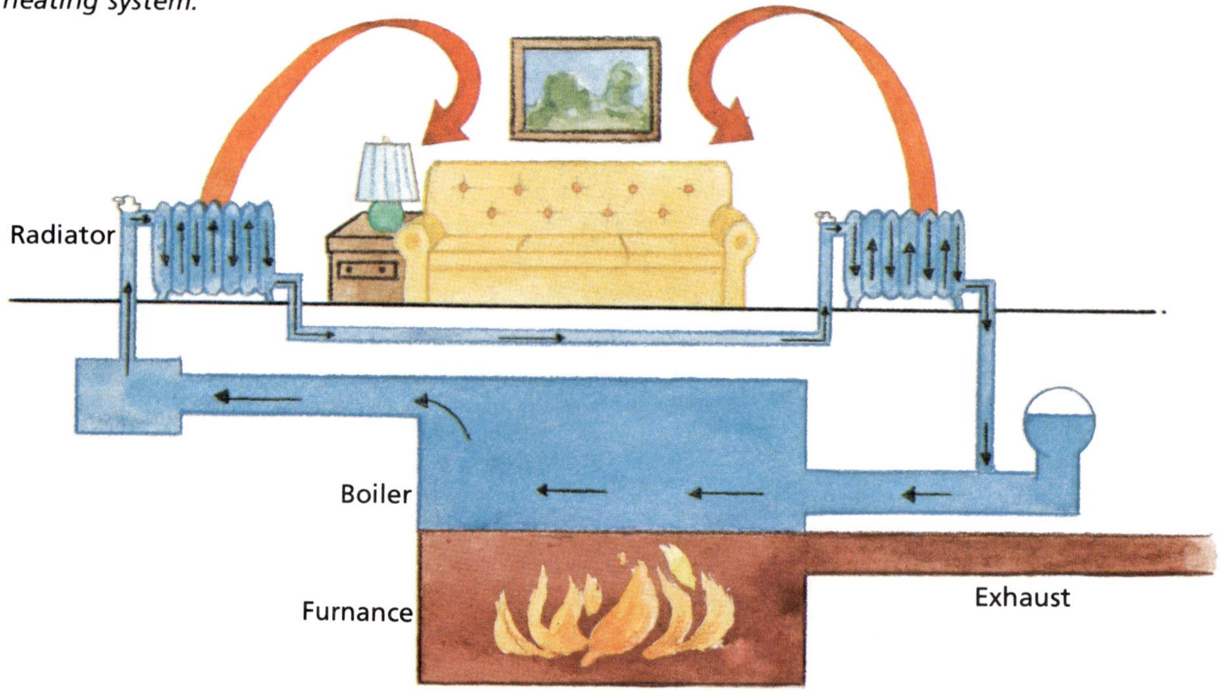

FIGURE 19-12. A hot water heating system.

In some systems, a pump forces the water through the pipes. A hot water heating system transfers heat from a furnace to air inside a room.

A steam heating system is an improvement over a hot water system. In a steam heating system, water is heated under pressure to boiling. Hot steam rather than water is circulated from the boiler to the radiators. Inside a steam radiator, steam condenses to water which runs back to the boiler.

Why is a steam system an improvement over a hot water heating system?

When one gram of steam condenses to water, it releases 2260 joules of heat. The heat of condensation of water is 2260 joules per gram. This value is also the heat of vaporization, Section 18:5. If 10 grams of steam condense, 22 600 joules of heat are released. Steam radiators release more energy than hot water radiators. It takes about 50 times as much hot water to give the same heat as steam.

Some heating systems use furnaces to heat air, Figure 19-13. The furnaces can burn a fuel, such as gas, or they can be electric. The heated air moves to other parts of the building by convection. Frequently a fan is attached to the furnace to move warm air faster. As the air cools, it returns to the furnace to be heated again.

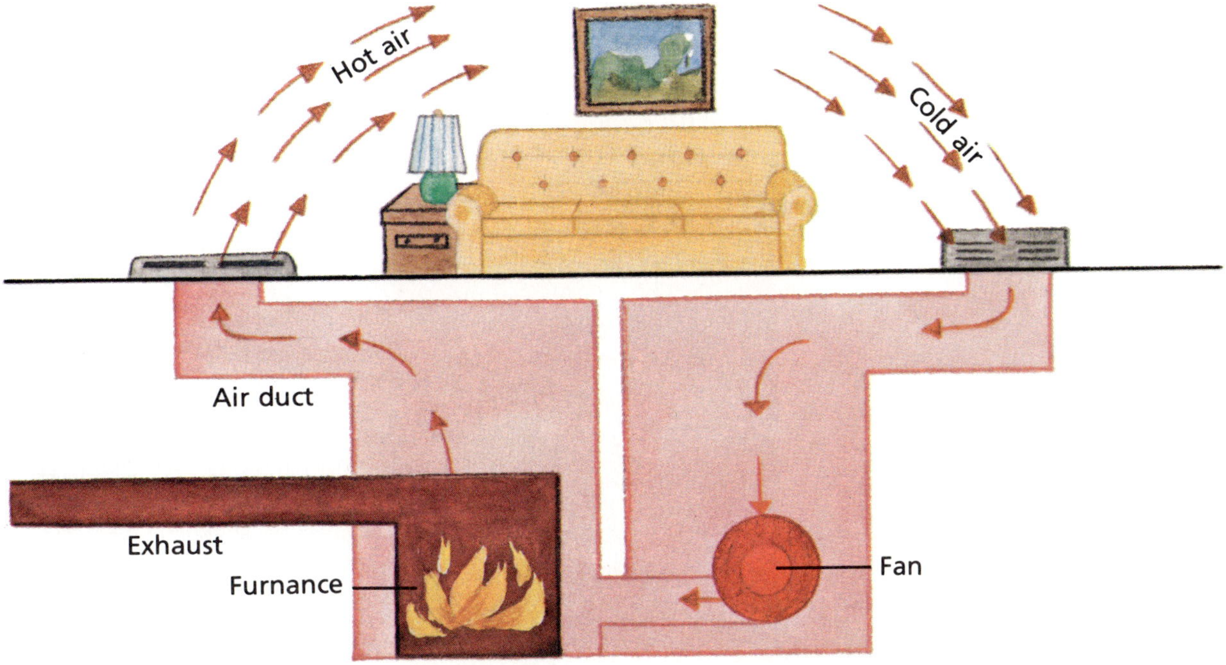

FIGURE 19-13. A hot air heating system.

Hickson-Bender Photography

FIGURE 19-14. One kind of solar panel for heating.

Other heating systems use solar energy. One solar heating system uses large black metal plates, Figure 19-14. Sunlight heats the plates. A plastic or glass covering over the plates reduces loss of heat into the air. Pipes containing water are attached in front of the plates. The hot plates heat the water in these pipes. An electric pump moves the water through pipes into the building where it is used in radiators.

Name four kinds of heating systems.

Another kind of solar heat uses water in large tanks to store heat. When the sun is out, radiant energy comes through the glass wall, Figure 19-15. The heat is absorbed by the water in the tanks. The tanks are black to increase their ability to absorb heat. At night or on a cloudy day, the glass is covered to prevent heat loss. The water in the tanks radiates heat into the air. As the air around the tanks becomes warmer, convection currents form, heating the rest of the house.

The heat pump is a method of heating by refrigeration, Figure 19-16. In winter, the heat pump takes heat from outside the house. A liquid is evaporated in the outdoor coil. The compressor pumps the gas to the coil

FIGURE 19-15. This system stores the energy from the sun in tanks of water.

Photo by Carl Doney/reprinted permission of "Rodale's New Shelter" magazine

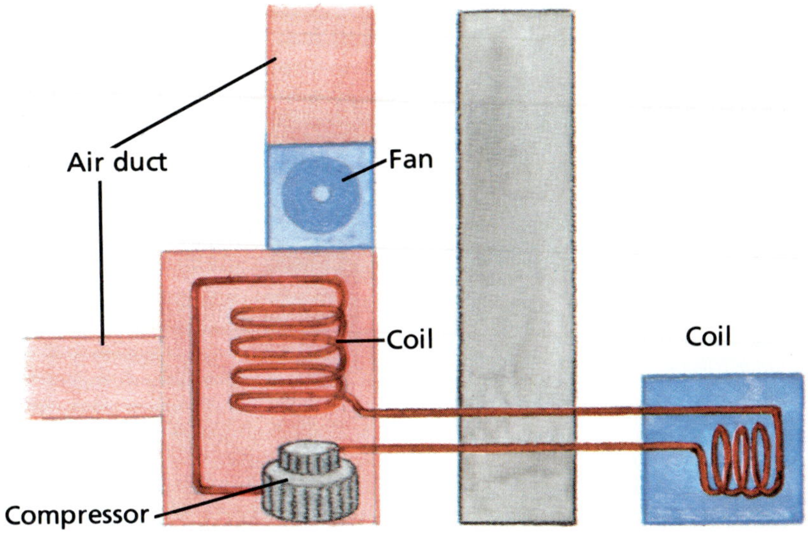

FIGURE 19-16. The basics of a heat pump system.

inside the house. Here the gas is compressed back to a liquid, releasing the heat it had gained. Fans move the air warmed by the hot coil to the rooms of the house. In the summer, the process is reversed. Heat is removed from inside the house and transferred outdoors. A heat pump transfers heat. Less energy is needed to transfer heat than to convert energy to heat from another form.

Making Sure

8. How is a heat pump different from the other heating systems? *The heat pump transfers heat instead of converting other energy to heat.*
9. What is the difference between the two solar heating methods discussed? *One uses moving water; the other uses stationary water.*
10. How are all of these heating systems similar? *They all use convection of air.*

19:5 Heat Engines

Engines change heat energy into mechanical energy. Mechanical energy can do work. Gasoline engines and diesel engines are examples of engines that do work. Each engine uses the heat from a burning fuel to increase the pressure of hot gases. Gasoline and diesel engines are called internal combustion engines. This name means the combustion or burning of fuel occurs inside the engine.

What is an internal combustion engine?

Hickson-Bender/Innskeep Oldsmobile, Buick, GMC Inc., Marion, Ohio

a

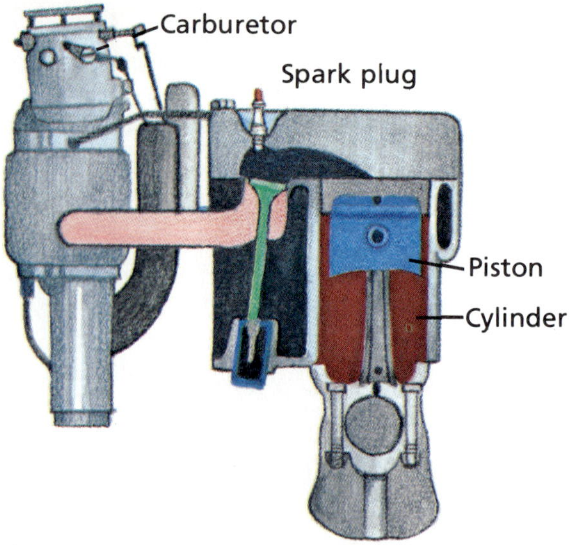

b

FIGURE 19-17. A gasoline engine for a car (a). The basic parts of a gasoline engine (b).

Most gasoline engines burn gasoline vapor and air inside cylinders, Figure 19-17. Gasoline is vaporized and mixed with air in the carburetor. From the carburetor, the gasoline and air mixture is sent to the cylinders. The mixture enters a cylinder through an intake valve.

How does a gasoline engine work?

Each cylinder has a piston. As the piston moves up the cylinder, it compresses the gasoline and air. When the piston reaches the top of the cylinder, the spark plug produces an electric spark. The spark ignites the fuel, producing an explosion of hot gases. The gases push against the piston, forcing it to move down.

As the piston moves up the cylinder again, it pushes the gases out through the exhaust valve. When the piston moves down again, more gasoline and air enter the cylinder. Each piston makes four strokes in a cycle, Figure 19-18. An engine that operates this way is called a four cycle engine.

FIGURE 19-18. The four strokes of a four cycle engine.

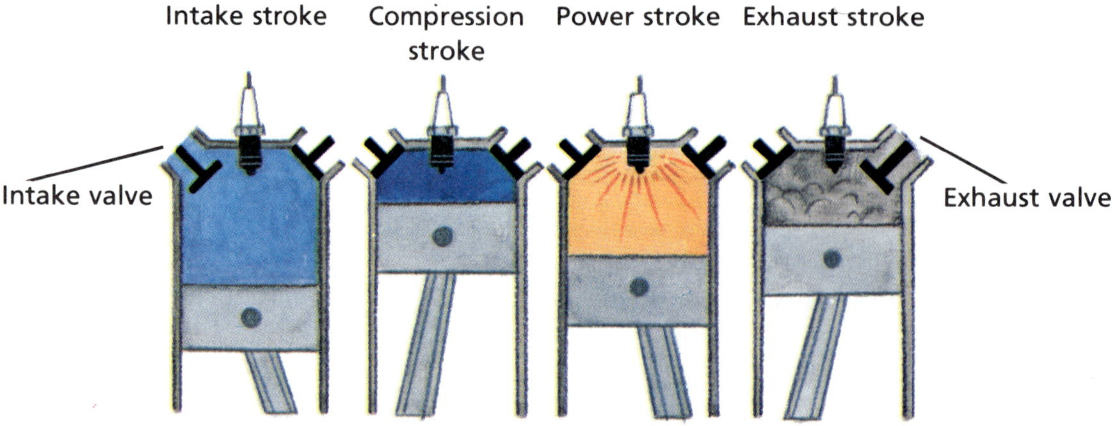

A four cycle diesel engine is similar to a gasoline engine, Figure 19-19. Like the gasoline engine, the first stroke is the intake stroke. However, a diesel only takes in air. In the compression stroke, the air is compressed to a higher pressure than in a gasoline engine. This pressure makes the air extremely hot. At the end of the compression stroke, the fuel is injected into the compressed air. A diesel engine does not use spark plugs. Instead the air is hot enough for the mixture to explode and push the piston out. This motion is the power stroke. The cycle is completed with the exhaust stroke.

In both the gasoline and diesel engines, the pistons are connected to a rotating rod called a crankshaft, Figure 19-20. The crankshaft is connected by gears to the driveshaft. At the end of the driveshaft is another set of gears which connects to the axle. As the pistons move up and down, they rotate the crankshaft which turns the gears. The gears turn the driveshaft. The gears at the end of the rotating driveshaft turn the axle. As the axle turns, the wheels push against the ground moving the car.

Both engines waste most of the fuel that they burn. Only about twelve percent of the energy in the fuel a gasoline engine burns is used for power. Although a diesel engine is heavier than a gasoline engine, it can get about twenty-five percent better mileage. Much of the heat value of the fuel goes out through the exhaust pipes of these engines. Some of the exhaust is in the form of unburned hydrocarbons. Other exhaust gases are carbon dioxide, CO_2, carbon monoxide, CO, and oxides of nitrogen, NO, NO_2. The wastes from gasoline and diesel engines make them sources of pollution. Most large cities have polluted air due partly to large numbers of automobiles on their streets.

Hickson-Bender/Innskeep Oldsmobile, Buick, GMC Inc., Marion, Ohio

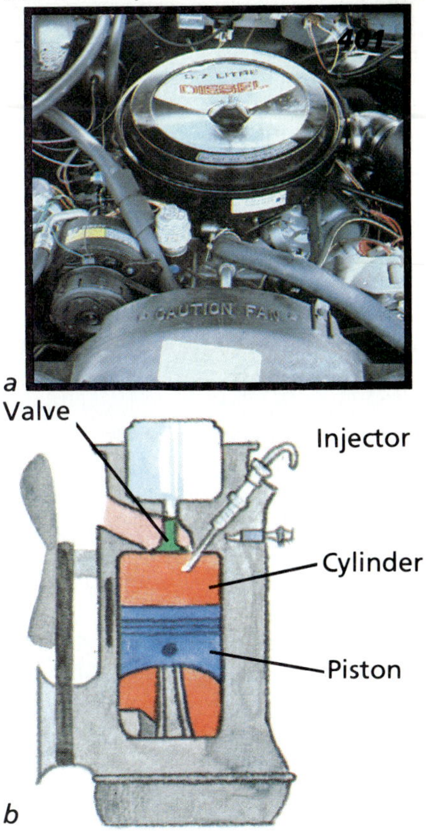

FIGURE 19-19. A diesel engine for a car (a). The basic parts of a diesel engine (b).

Water is another part of the exhaust of internal combustion engines.

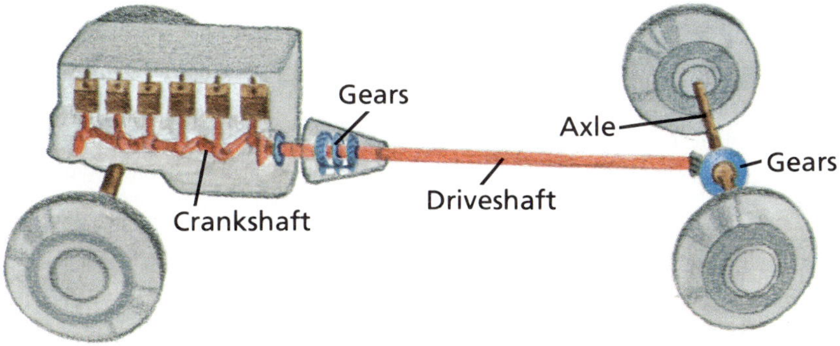

FIGURE 19-20. The power from the engine turns the driveshaft, which turns the axle.

Making Sure

11. Why is a diesel engine an internal combustion engine? *The fuel burns inside.*
12. What starts the fuel burning in a gasoline engine? a diesel engine? *gasoline—spark plug, diesel—heat of compression*
13. How does the energy from the fuel turn the wheels of a car? *through the crankshaft to the driveshaft to the axles*

Tom Stack/Tom Stack & Associates

FIGURE 19-21. The stream is filled with algae as a result of thermal pollution.

19:6 Waste Heat

What happens to the heat you use?

Engines, furnaces, electric lamps, and stoves give off heat. Much of the energy we use—light, electricity, chemical energy, mechanical energy—ends up as heat. Heat is the end product from the energy we use each day. Much of this heat is wasted. It goes off into the atmosphere and then into space. Waste heat in the air has changed the weather for some cities. They get less rain and snow and they do not get as cold as the nearby country in winter.

Electric power plants use water and heat to make steam and generate electricity. Many industries use water to cool machinery. The hot water from power plants is then dumped into a nearby river, lake, or ocean. More than 200 trillion liters of warm water are discharged from electric power plants each year. The warmer water may increase plant growth. The water may become clogged with green algae. It may become so hot that fish are killed. Most fish cannot survive high water temperatures. Brook trout, for example, can live

Lauren Freudmann from Rainbow

FIGURE 19-22. All of the energy used in a city will become heat energy.

only 30 minutes at 28°C and only 12 hours at an average 25°C. **Thermal pollution** occurs when waste heat damages the environment by raising the temperature. Dumping heated water into lakes, rivers, and oceans can cause thermal pollution.

How is thermal pollution harmful?

Cooling towers are one solution to thermal water pollution, Figure 19-23. Hot water from a power plant or factory is cooled to air temperature as it flows through pipes in the tower. After the water is air cooled, it is discharged into a nearby body of water. Because the water is cooled, it does not have a harmful effect on water life. There is no thermal pollution of the water. The excess heat is released into the air.

How can heat be used rather than wasted? One way waste heat can be used is to take salt out of seawater. The salt water is heated and evaporated. The evaporated water has no salt in it. This water vapor is cooled and condensed to form pure water. This water can be used for drinking, washing, and growing crops. Some of the heat can be used to heat buildings. Another use is heat for greenhouses.

Making Sure

damage to environment by waste heat

14. What is thermal pollution?
15. Name five things that produce heat. Where does the heat go? *Detailed answers to these questions are given in the Teacher's Guide at the front of this book.*

a

James N. Westwater

b

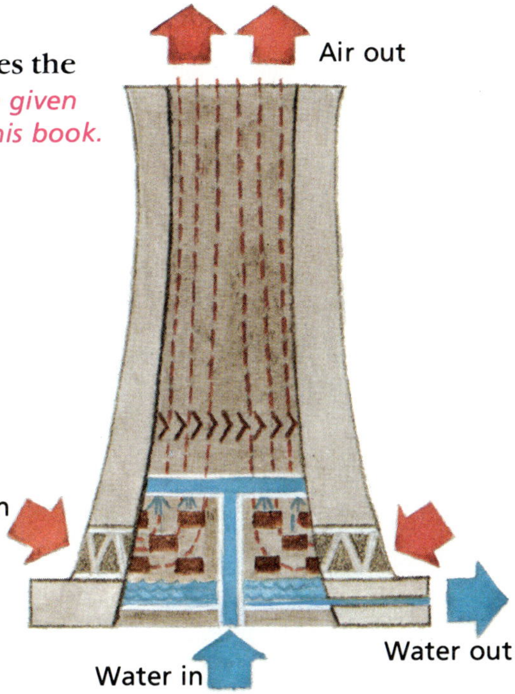

FIGURE 19-23. Cooling towers for a power station (a). Air flows through the tower from the bottom. The water is splashed down. As the air moves through the water, it removes the heat (b).

IN FOCUS

Science and Technology

Science and technology are related, but they are not the same. Science is an attempt to understand the universe and its laws. Technology uses the knowledge of science to make life easier. Keep these definitions in mind as we explore a little of our world.

We all like to relax and have a good time. We can go sailing or play with some toys. Perhaps our families go to an amusement park. Have you ever wondered how a sailboat works? This is a question for science. The force of the wind in the sails

Dept. of Energy

Steve Lissau

pushes the boat over the water. A keel and a rudder in the water keep the boat stable and help to steer it. By changing the shape and direction of the sails, the direction of the boat can be changed. Our toys and amusement park rides all use forces to work. Science tells us how these things work, but they are a part of technology. They use science to give pleasure.

One of the things found on many playgrounds is a set of monkey bars. To a small child they look like the frame for a building. The monkey bars are designed to support the weight of the children playing on them. They also withstand wind and rain. Buildings, too, must support a great deal of weight. They must stand up to wind and rain. In fact, science explains the structure of each in the same way. Thus, the frame of a building looks like a set of monkey bars. Technology uses scientific laws in many ways. But, it cannot do what the laws do not allow.

Our world is a world of technology. Technology builds on itself. Let us see how this works. Bridges are paths over open areas. They are supported at the ends and along the sides or in the middle. Bridges and houses are built using the same scientific laws. But, they do not look the same.

Steve Lissau

Larry Hamill

Dept. of Energy

Where in a house is a bridge? One place is a stairway. Another is a ceiling. They are supported by walls and are over open areas.

If we can build a one story house and bridges, why not add a second story? Or we can build a two level bridge. This process continues and before long we have a sky scraper. We have super highways and cities. Each step is a little bigger and a little more complex. The technology is building, but it still uses the same laws.

So far we have seen what technology does. We know how it relates to science. But, how does science become technology? The telephone is a good example.

Larry Hamill

Steve Lissau

Pennzoil

Dan McCoy from Rainbow

When Alexander Graham Bell made the telephone, electricity was being explored all over the world. Many people were interested in what it could do. The telegraph had already been invented. Thus, it was known that electricity could carry a message. Why not try to carry a voice? That was Bell's question. He applied what was known about electricity. And he learned more. In the end, the telephone was developed. Since then, more has been learned about electricity. Combining them with radio waves, telephone calls are carried around the world. Satellites, computers, televisions, cars, and planes were all developed from science's study of the world.

Experiments in laboratories around the world are exploring light and its uses. Others are exploring the atom. Still more are exploring the galaxy. Each experiment brings new knowledge that can be used in technology.

People
Solar Flight

Vince Streano

When Frederick Eshoo climbed into the gondola of his hot air balloon and floated aloft over Albuquerque, New Mexico, at dawn, the only sounds that could be heard were Eshoo's own cheers. For Eshoo, an Iranian paper manufacturer, was piloting a unique balloon; his own invention. He calls the balloon Sunstat. It uses the sun's energy to heat its air.

Sunstat operates like all hot air balloons for flight. The difference is in the source of heat. Most hot air balloons are equipped with propane burners. However, this limits the time aloft. As the weight of the propane tanks goes up the balloon tends not to. Fuel can be carried for two or three hours of flight at most. This problem prompted Eshoo's interest in the sun as a heat source.

"You come to just the right position when you're flying hot air," he says, "and you want to continue to fly the whole day. Then, pffft, the propane is finished and you land."

Sunstat combines a transparent surface with a black surface in the same balloon. One side of Sunstat is transparent and, because it is curved, acts like a lens to focus sunlight on the opposite, black side of the balloon. The black side absorbs the visible light of the sun. As the surface warms, it reradiates the absorbed energy as infrared radiation. As the air circulates inside the balloon, it is heated. The transparent side also acts as insulation because infrared will not pass through it.

To Eshoo, Sunstat is not just for sport. "Why cannot solar balloons by used commercially?" he asks. "Larger volume, larger lifts, larger loads." All the energy, he points out, is free. "Every flying machine needs some energy to fly. I am just getting it from nothing. Just some cloth and some air."

Vince Streano

Adapted from *The Sky's the Limit in a Solar Balloon* with permission © 1979 by Carol Haven.

Points to Remember

1. Heat moves by radiation, conduction, and convection. *19:1*
2. Insulation is used to control the movement of heat. *19:2*
3. Evaporation can be used as a cooling process. *19:3*
4. Heating systems use the three methods of moving heat energy to heat buildings. *19:1, 19:4*
5. Engines convert heat energy into mechanical energy to do work. *19:5*
6. Thermal pollution occurs when waste heat raises the temperature of the environment. *19:6*

Words to Use

Write a sentence in which you correctly use each of the following words.

conduction	freon	radiant energy
convection	engine	radiation
evaporation	insulation	thermal pollution

Questions for Review

Do not write in this book.

A. True or False *Have the students rewrite the false statements to make them correct.*

Determine whether each of the following sentences is true or false.

F **1.** Heat is transferred through water by ~~conduction~~ currents. convection

T **2.** Heat travels from the sun to the earth by radiation.

T **3.** Glass is not a good conductor of heat.

F **4.** Air is a ~~good~~ conductor of heat. poor

F **5.** ~~Convection~~ is a transfer of heat from one particle to the next. Conduction

F **6.** ~~Radiation~~ is a transfer of heat using moving particles. Convection

F **7.** Insulation ~~allows~~ heat to move easily. does not

T **8.** Refrigerators use evaporation for cooling.

T **9.** Heat engines use heat energy to do work.

F **10.** A diesel engine has spark plugs. no

B. Multiple Choice

Choose the word or phrase that correctly completes each of the following sentences.

1. Evaporation *(cools, warms, does not change the temperature of)* a material.
2. Heat travels through a spoon mostly by *(radiation, conduction, convection).*
3. Heat travels through a pot of soup by *(radiation, conduction, convection).*
4. Insulation is used to *(conduct, control)* heat.
5. Thermal pollution occurs when waste heat *(changes, does nothing to)* the temperature of the environment.
6. *(Convection, Conduction)* carries the water through pipes in a water heating system.
7. A diesel engine uses *(spark plugs, hot fuel, hot air)* to ignite the fuel.
8. A heat pump *(transfers, produces)* heat.
9. A carburetor supplies *(gasoline, air, gasoline and air)* to the cylinder of a gasoline engine.
10. The force to drive the wheels of a car comes from the *(intake, compression, power)* stroke.

C. Completion

Complete each of the following sentences with a word or phrase that will make the sentence correct.

1. Conduction ______ is the movement of heat through a substance from particle to particle.
2. Forces are produced in engines by expansion of hot gases ______.
3. Cooling towers are used to decrease thermal ______ pollution.
4. Waste heat can be used to take salt ______ out of seawater.
5. Fiberglass can be used as insulation ______.
6. Many refrigerators evaporate freon ______ in cooling.
7. Instead of a furnace, solar radiation ______ can be used to heat water.
8. One kind of solar heating system uses water ______ in large tanks to store heat.

9. All the energy we use ends up as heat.
10. The fuel is injected into the compressed air of a(n) diesel engine.

Detailed answers to these questions are given in the Teacher's Guide at the front of this book.

D. How and Why

1. The freon used to cool a refrigerator evaporates and condenses as it passes through coiled pipes. Explain the cooling action of the freon.
2. How is density involved in the process of convection? Give an example.
3. Explain how a gasoline engine produces power.
4. Compare the operation of a hot water system and a steam heating system.

More Ideas to Explore

1. Find information and report on groundwater heat pumps. Compare them to air heat pumps.
2. Write a report on how industries are reducing thermal pollution.
3. Make a collection of insulating materials such as aluminum foil, cork, and fiberglass. Obtain information on the insulating properties of each material. Find out the savings in fuel costs that result from proper insulation of a home.
4. Do library research and prepare a report on how waste heat can be used.

Readings to Discover

Haines, Gail Kay, *Super Cold/Super Hot: Cyrogenics and Controlled Thermonuclear Fusion.* NY: F. Watts, 1976.

Papallo, George, *What Makes It Work.* NY: Arco, 1976.

Urquhart, David I., *The Refrigerator and How It Works.* NY: Henry Z. Walck, Inc., 1972.

In 1800, Count Alessandro Volta of Italy made the first battery. Since then, the use of electricity has increased tremendously. Now electrical power is carried by wires from city to city. How is this power used? What would the world be like without electricity?

Dave Spier/Tom Stack & Associates

Electricity 20

Chapter 20 develops the concept of energy as it applies to electricity and its effects. Current and circuits are introduced using familiar examples. See the Teacher's Guide at the front of this book for additional teaching strategies for this chapter.

20:1 Electric Charge

GOAL: *You will gain an understanding of static electricity, electric current, and how each is produced.*

A glass rod and silk cloth are rubbed together. The glass rod and silk cloth attract each other. Each pulls on the other with a small force. Why? They attract each other because the rod and silk cloth have each gained an electric charge.

What causes an electric charge? All matter is made of atoms which contain charged particles. Two kinds of charged particles in atoms are the proton and the electron. A proton has a positive charge and an electron has a negative charge. Electrons can be moved. It is through their movements that objects become charged. When an object is rubbed, it may gain or lose electrons. As a result the object gains a charge. If the object has gained electrons, it has a negative charge. If it has lost electrons, the object has a positive charge.

How can you charge an object?

When a glass rod is rubbed with silk, the glass rod loses electrons to the silk. The silk takes on a negative charge and the rod a positive charge. The rod and silk attract each other. *Opposite charges attract.*

What kinds of charges attract each other?

Tom Stack/Tom Stack & Associates

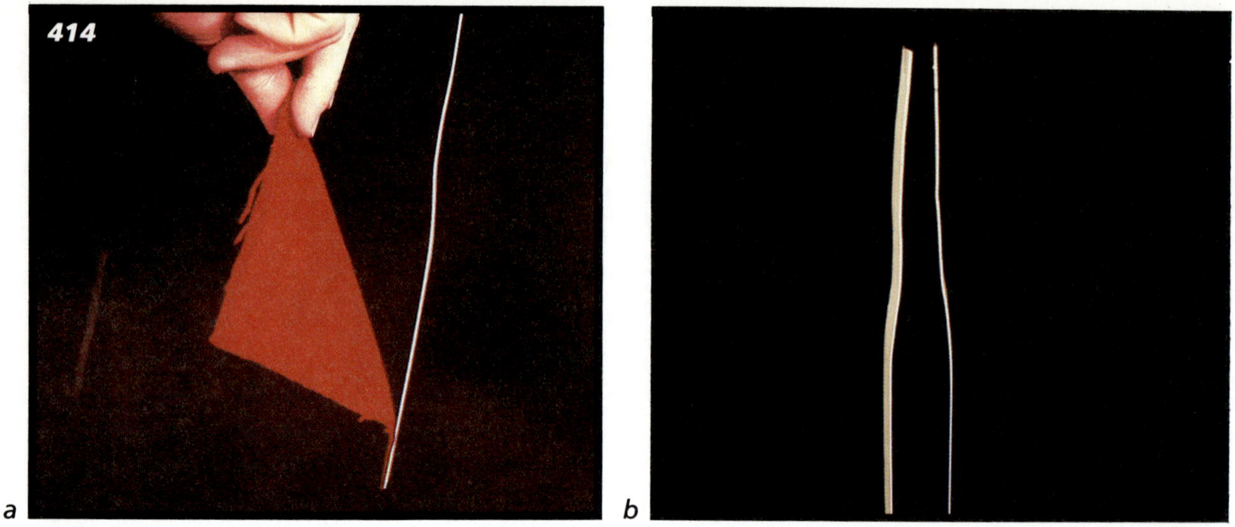

FIGURE 20-1. Plastic and wool attracting (a). Two plastic rods repelling (b).

If you rub a plastic rod with wool, the wool and plastic rod gain opposite electric charges. As a result, they attract each other. The plastic rod gains electrons from the wool. Thus, the rod becomes negatively charged. Because the wool loses electrons, it becomes positively charged.

What kinds of charges repel each other?

Like charges repel each other. Two charged glass rods repel each other because they both have a positive charge. Two charged plastic rods also repel each other.

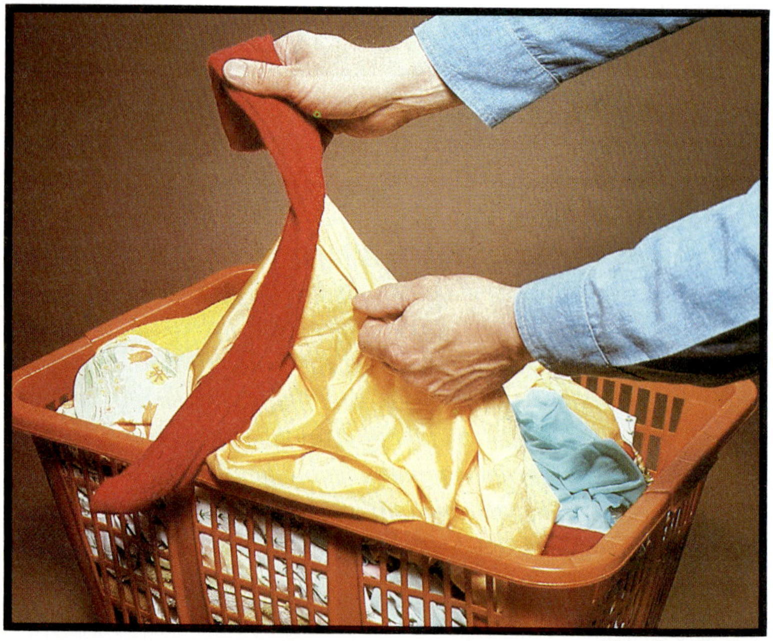

FIGURE 20-2. Clothing often gains a static charge in a dryer.

Hickson-Bender Photography

They both have a negative charge. However, a charged glass rod and charged plastic rod will attract each other. The charge on the glass rod is opposite the charge on the plastic rod. This charge, positive or negative, is called **static electricity.**

Static electricity is electric charge built up in one place. It is charge at rest, not moving. You may see examples of static electricity when you take clothes out of a dryer. For example, a wool sock or sweater may stick to clothes made of cotton. These pieces of clothing have gained electric charge by rubbing against each other in the dryer.

Detailed information concerning this Activity can be found in the Teacher's Guide at the front of this book.

20-1

ACTIVITY *How do electric charges behave?*

(1) *Run a comb through dry hair several times. Try to pick up bits of paper with the comb.* **(2)** *Hang a glass rod with thread as in Figure 20-3a. Rub the rod with a piece of silk. Rub another glass rod with silk. Bring it near the first rod. What happens?* **(3)** *Using thread, hang two plastic rods separately. Rub both rods with wool. Bring the rods together. What happens?* **(4)** *Bring a plastic rod rubbed with wool near a hanging glass rod rubbed with silk. What happens?* **(5)** *Use string to hang a glass rod and silk cloth as in Figure 20-3b. Rub the rod with the silk. Bring the silk cloth near the rod. What happens?*

Why did the comb attract the pieces of paper in Step 1? Why did the rods repel each other in Step 3? Why did the rod and cloth attract each other in Step 5?

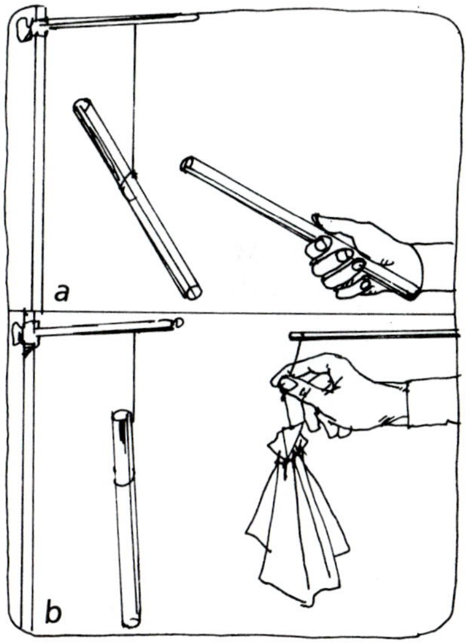

FIGURE 20-3.

Making Sure

1. A balloon gains a negative charge when rubbed against wool cloth. Why? *It takes on electrons from the cloth.*
2. Would the charged balloon attract or repel a glass rod rubbed with silk? *attracts rod*

20:2 Conduction

When you walk across a thick carpet, you may pick up an electric charge. If you then touch a metal doorknob, you see and feel an electric spark. The spark is

Describe what happens in a static discharge.

FIGURE 20-4. Conductors (a). Insulators (b).

Larry Hamill

a

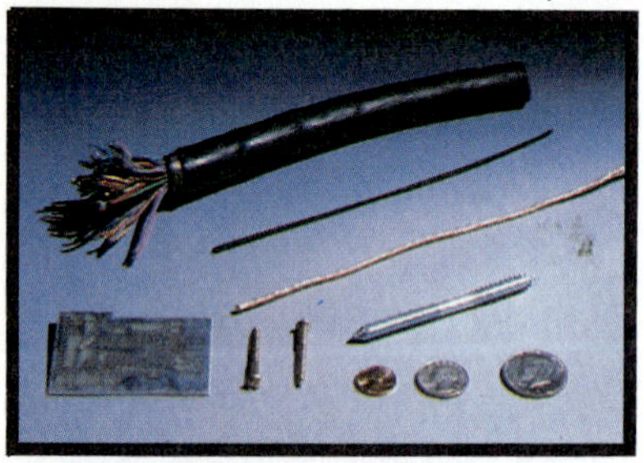

b

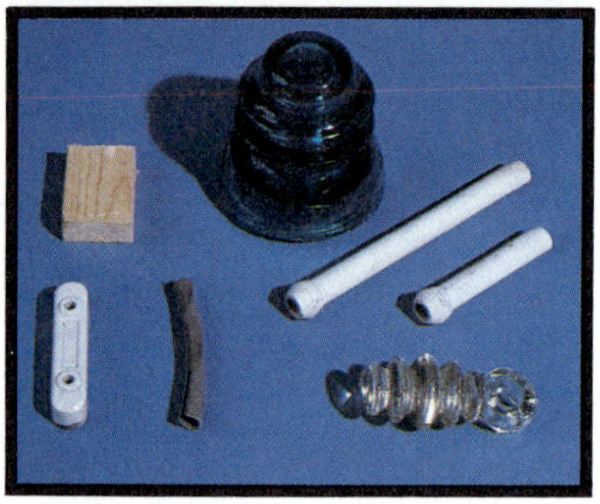

caused by electrons moving between your hand and the doorknob. It is called a static discharge. A **static discharge** is a loss of static electricity.

Suppose you walk across the carpet and become charged again. This time you touch the metal doorknob with a key. Now there is a spark between the tip of the key and the doorknob. Electrons move through the key and a static discharge occurs again. The movement of electrons through a material is called **conduction.** The material, or key in this case, is called a **conductor.** Metals are good conductors of electricity.

If you use a piece of wood instead of the key, nothing happens. There is no static discharge. Wood is not a conductor of electricity. A material that does not conduct is called an **insulator.** Plastic, rubber, and glass are three kinds of insulators.

A Van de Graaff generator is a device that produces a large static charge. The charge may be large enough to light a fluorescent bulb, Figure 20-6. Electrons are conducted from the generator through the person to the bulb. The bulb flashes when the generator discharges. The generator must build up another charge before the bulb can be lit again.

The person in Figure 20-6 is the conductor. A plastic stool is used to insulate the person from the ground. Without the stool, the electrons would be conducted to

FIGURE 20-5. Static discharge through a finger and through a key.

Craig Kramer

FIGURE 20-6. A Van de Graaff generator can light a fluorescent bulb.

the ground. None of the electrons would move to the light bulb. The earth is so large that it can absorb all of the electrons from the Van de Graaff and not show a charge. This process is called grounding. After grounding has occurred, both the earth and the Van de Graaff are neutral.

An **electroscope** (ih LEK truh skohp) is a device which detects a static electric charge. An electroscope has a metal rod inside a glass jar. At the bottom of the rod are two thin pieces of metal foil called leaves. When a charged object touches the electroscope, the leaves spread apart, Figure 20-7. Like charges in the leaves make them repel each other. When not charged, the leaves hang down.

20-2 Detailed information concerning this Activity can be found in the Teacher's Guide at the front of this book.

FIGURE 20-7. A charged electroscope.

Craig Kramer

ACTIVITY *How does an electroscope work?*

(1) *Use a curtain rod, cork, bottle, and two pieces of metal foil ($\frac{1}{2}$ cm x 2 cm) to construct an electroscope, Figure 20-8.* **(2)** *Cut the curtain rod to a length of 20 centimeters.* **(3)** *Make a hole in the cork, insert the rod.* **(4)** *Flatten 5 centimeters of the end of the rod. Attach the two pieces of foil with a rubber band.* **(5)** *Set the rod and cork in the jar with the leaves down.* **(6)** *Charge a plastic rod with wool. Touch the rod to the electroscope, Figure 20-8. What happens?* **(7)** *Now touch the electroscope*

FIGURE 20-8.

Craig Kramer

with your hand. What happens? *The leaves drop.* **(8)** *Repeat Step 6. Now touch the electroscope with a piece of pencil "lead" (graphite) instead of your hand. What happens?* *nothing* **(9)** *Repeat Step 6 with a glass rod and silk cloth. Now touch the electroscope with your hand. What happens?* *The leaves spread and drop.*

Why do the leaves spread apart when the electroscope is touched by the plastic or glass rods? *The leaves are charged the same and repel.* *Why do the leaves fall when you touch the electroscope with your hand?* *The hand allows electrons to leave or enter and discharge the leaves.*

20:3 Current

What is a wet cell?

Current is the movement of charge in a conductor. A Van de Graaff generator produces a current for a fraction of a second. The current is not constant. To keep a bulb lit, we need a constant source of current. One way to get a constant current is to use a wet cell.

A **wet cell** contains two different metals in a solution containing an acid, base, or salt. When acids, bases, or salts dissolve in water, ions are released, Section 13:3. Every ion is either positively or negatively charged. The solution has an equal number of positive and negative charges.

The wet cell in Figure 20-9 contains a strip of zinc in a zinc chloride, $ZnCl_2$, solution and a strip of copper in a copper(II) chloride, $CuCl_2$, solution. The solutions are separated by a porous cup. The cup keeps the solutions separated but allows the movement of ions

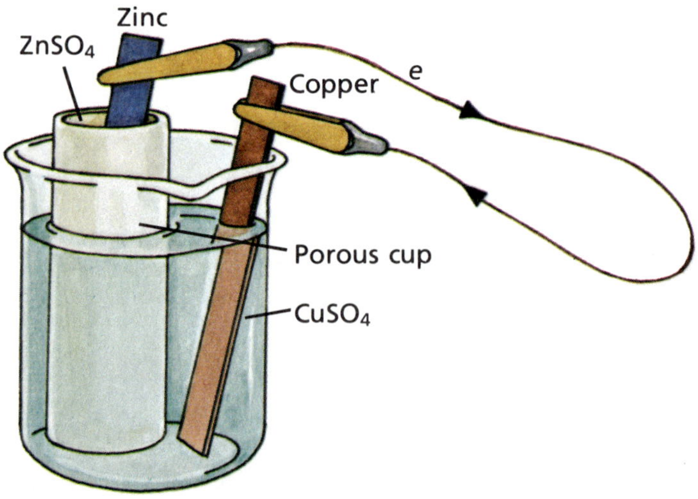

FIGURE 20-9. In the wet cell, electrons move from zinc to copper through wire.

between the solutions. The zinc and copper strips are connected by a wire. The zinc chloride solution contains zinc ions and chlorine ions. Zinc atoms in the strip of zinc enter the solution. Each zinc atom leaves behind two electrons as it leaves. The zinc atoms become zinc ions.

$$Zn(c) \longrightarrow Zn^{2+}(aq) + 2e^-$$

How does a wet cell produce an electric current?

A zinc atom is uncharged. A zinc ion has a charge of 2+. The two electrons left by each zinc atom move through the wire to the copper. As a result, the copper strip becomes negatively charged. The positive copper ions in the copper chloride solution move to the piece of copper. The copper ions gain electrons when they come in contact with the negatively charged copper strip. The copper ions react to form copper atoms.

$$Cu^{2+}(aq) + 2e^- \longrightarrow Cu(c)$$

In any wet cell, ions move through the solution. Electrons flow through the wire. The flow of electrons and the movement of ions are current. If the wire is removed from the zinc or copper, the electric current is stopped. An electric current differs from static electricity. Static electricity is a gathering or shortage of electrons in one place. A current is a flow of electrons.

A **dry cell** works in much the same way as a wet cell. It contains a carbon rod set in the middle of a zinc can, Figure 20-10. Chemicals in the form of a moist paste fill the can. The paste reacts with the zinc and releases electrons. These electrons flow through a conductor to the carbon rod.

FIGURE 20-10. The carbon rod in the center is positive. The zinc is negative.

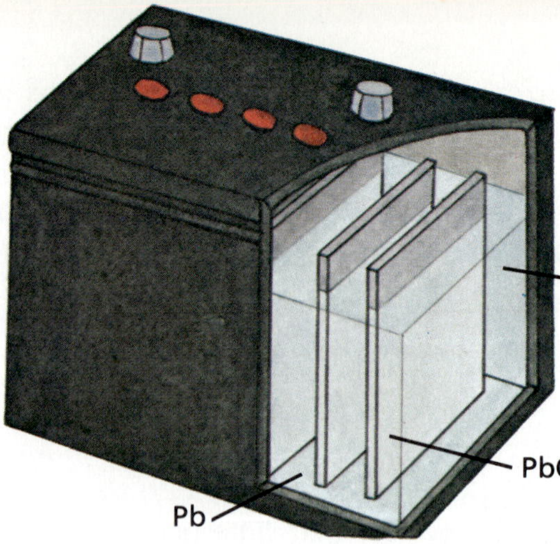

FIGURE 20-11. A lead, acid storage battery is often used in cars.

Two or more wet or dry cells which produce an electric current make up a battery. Electricity in a car is produced by a storage battery. Lead and lead dioxide plates act in the same manner as the copper and zinc strips in Figure 20-9. The lead battery also contains sulfuric acid. The chemical reactions are similar to the copper-zinc wet cell. Each lead atom loses two electrons as it reacts with the sulfuric acid.

$$Pb(c) + SO_4^{2-}(aq) \longrightarrow PbSO_4(c) + 2e^-$$

The lead dioxide plate gains two electrons as it changes to lead(II) sulfate.

$$PbO_2(c) + 4H^+(aq) + SO_4^{2-}(aq) + 2e^- \longrightarrow PbSO_4(c) + 2H_2O(l)$$

The electrons are moving in one direction. Electrons are charges. Electric current is defined as the movement of charges. Charge is measured in **coulombs (C)** (KOO lahmz). **Direct current** is the movement of charge in one direction. The unit of current is the **ampere (A)** (AM pihr). One ampere equals one coulomb of charge moving past a point in one second.

20:4 Potential Difference

What is the potential difference of a battery?

A battery maintains a difference of potential energy between the positive and negative plates or terminals. It is similar to the difference in potential energy between

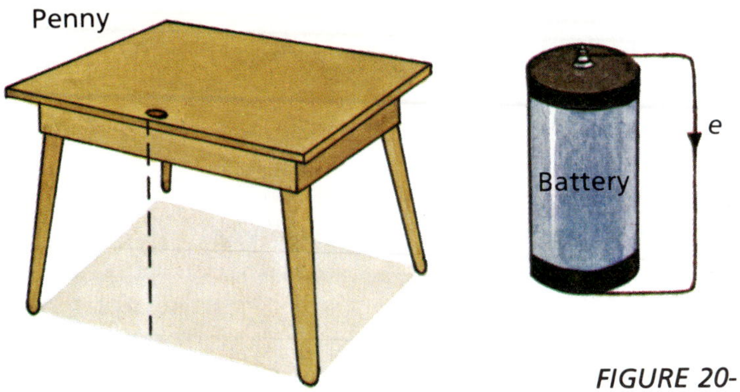

FIGURE 20-12.

the top of a table and the floor. This difference in potential energy is the electric force. The attraction of positive and negative charges produces this force. The **potential difference** is measured in **volts (V).** One volt is one joule of work per coulomb of charge. Potential difference is also called voltage.

If we move a penny off the edge of a table, it falls to the ground. Its path is the air. The path for an electron is the conductor. If the conductor is connected between the terminals of a battery, current will flow. For example, a flashlight bulb is connected to a $1\frac{1}{2}$ volt battery. The bulb lights. The path for the current is the bulb and the wire used to connect the bulb to the battery. The potential difference is $1\frac{1}{2}$ volts.

Craig Kramer

FIGURE 20-13. The path for the current is the wire and bulb. If the wire is broken, no current flows.

Making Sure

3. What is the unit of potential difference? *volt*
4. Why must there be a conductor to have a current? *Electrons must have a path to flow along.*

20:5 Resistance and Ohm's Law

The number of electrons moving through a conductor is determined by the resistance of the conductor. **Resistance** is a measure of how difficult it is to move electrons through a conductor. Resistance is measured in **ohms (Ω).**

What unit is used to measure resistance?

Different materials have different resistances. For example, one meter of aluminum wire has a resistance of

3.44 ohms. A similar piece of copper wire has a resistance of 2.09 ohms. A 100-watt light bulb has a resistance of 140 ohms.

Table 20-1

Resistance of Some Metals (Ω/m)

Metal	Resistance
silver	1.98
copper	2.09
gold	2.96
aluminum	3.44
brass	8.50
nickel	9.48
iron	12.1
tin	14.0
lead	26.7

What is a resistor?

A conductor that has a large resistance for its size is called a **resistor.** For example, a 1000-ohm carbon resistor is less than one centimeter long. By exerting different amounts of pressure on the carbon when making resistors, different resistances can be made. The size of the resistors remains the same, Figure 20-14. Carbon resistors are used in radios, televisions, and computers.

When current flows through a resistance, the electrons lose energy. As the electrons move through a resistance, they do work. This work is changed to heat. The

FIGURE 20-14. The colored bands on the resistors show their sizes.

Craig Kramer

relationship of potential difference, current, and resistance is know as **Ohm's law.** Ohm's law states: *current is equal to the potential difference divided by the resistance.*

$$\textit{current}\ (\text{amperes}) = \frac{\textit{voltage}\ (\text{volts})}{\textit{resistance}\ (\text{ohms})} \qquad I = \frac{V}{R}$$

Example

What is the current through a resistance of 100 ohms when a 12-volt battery is used?

Solution:

(a) Write the equation for Ohm's law. $I = \frac{V}{R}$

(b) Substitute the values for voltage and resistance given in the problem.

$$I = \frac{12\ \text{V}}{100\ \Omega} \qquad = 0.12\ \text{A}$$

20-3 Detailed information concerning this Activity can be found in the Teacher's Guide at the front of this book.

Activity *What is the relationship of current and resistance?*

Setting Up

ammeter *switch* *voltmeter*
battery *variable resistor* *wire*

Getting Started

1. *Connect the ammeter, resistor, and switch to the battery as shown in Figure 20-15. Be sure the switch is open.*
2. *Connect the voltmeter to the ends of the resistor as shown in Figure 20-15.*
3. *Have your teacher check your set up before closing the switch.*
4. *Close the switch and read the meters. Record the readings.*
5. *Vary the resistance by moving the slide to three or four different positions.*

Keeping Track

resistor position	potential difference	current	resistance
1. 2. 3.			

Calculate the resistance for each case using Ohm's law.

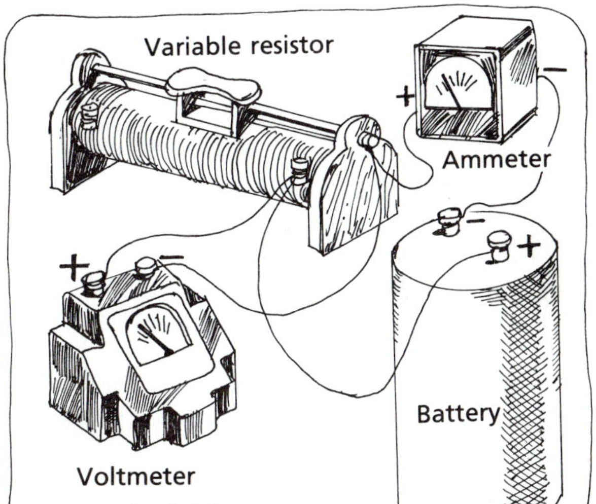

FIGURE 20-15.

Summing Up

1. *How does the length of the resistor affect the resistance?* greater length—greater resistance
2. *How does the change in resistance affect the current?* greater resistance—lesser current

Making Sure

5. Find the current when a 12-volt battery is connected through a resistance of 50 ohms. *0.24 A*
6. What would be the current in problem 5 if the potential difference were 6 volts? *0.12 A*
7. The potential difference is 120 volts and the resistance is 200 ohms. What is the current? *0.60 A*
8. The current is 10 amperes and the voltage is 120 volts. What is the resistance? *12 Ω*

20:6 Circuits

How is a series circuit different from a parallel circuit?

The path formed by the conductors for the electrons is called a **circuit.** There are two basic types of circuits. One is a **series circuit,** Figure 20-16a. In this circuit, the current is the same through each part. If the circuit is broken, the current in all parts is stopped. A switch is a device used to open and close circuits. When a circuit is open, there is no current. A switch in a series circuit can be used to turn the circuit on and off.

The other type of circuit is a **parallel circuit,** Figure 20-16b. In this circuit, there are two or more separate parts or branches. The voltage is the same in each branch. If one branch of the circuit is opened, current still flows through the rest of the circuit.

FIGURE 20-16. A series circuit has one current path (a). A parallel circuit has more than one current path (b).

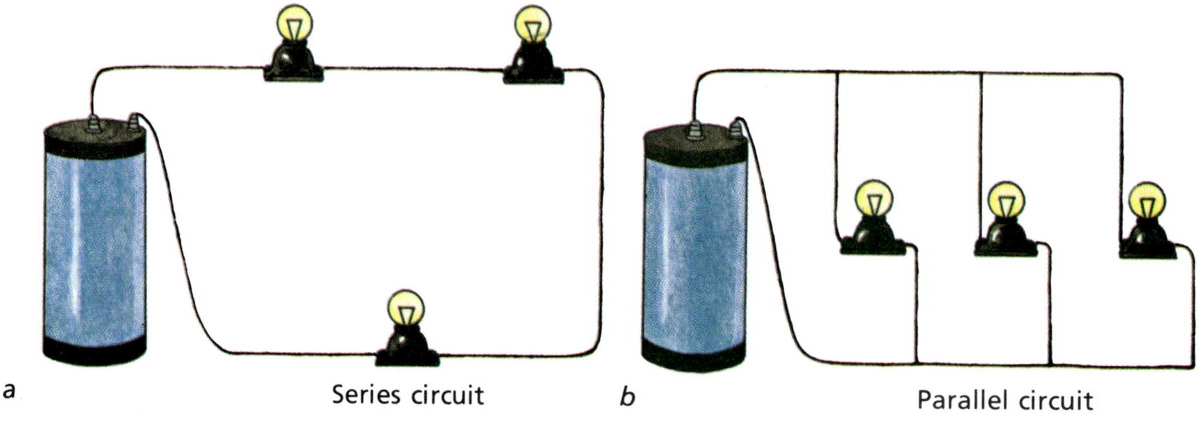

20-4 Detailed information concerning this Activity can be found in the Teacher's Guide at the front of this book.

ACTIVITY *How do series and parallel circuits work?*

Make sure the students do not connect the terminals together. This will result in a dead battery.

CAUTION: *If any of the wires become warm, disconnect the battery.* **(1)** *Cut pieces of wire 20 to 30 centimeters long. Strip 2 centimeters of insulation from each end.* **(2)** *Connect three light bulbs in series to a 6-volt battery as in Figure 20-16a. Unscrew one bulb. What happens?* **(3)** *Connect the bulbs in parallel as in Figure 20-16b. Is there any difference in the brightness of the lights? Unscrew one bulb. What happens?* **(4)** *Build the circuit in Step 2 again using a switch. Put the switch in different places in the circuit.* **CAUTION:** *Have your teacher check your circuits before closing the switch. What happens each time?* **(5)** *Build the circuit in Step 3 again using a switch. Put the switch in different places in this circuit. What happens each time?* **(6)** *Draw pictures of the circuits you made in Steps 4 and 5.*

All lights go out.

no difference, others stay on

All bulbs will light.

Depending on the position of the switch, one, two, or all bulbs will light.

The pictures will show series and parallel circuits with switches in various places.

20-5 Detailed information concerning this Activity can be found in the Teacher's Guide at the front of this book.

ACTIVITY *How are circuits drawn?*

A shorthand method can be used to draw circuits. Symbols are used to show the different parts of a circuit. Some common symbols for the parts of electrical circuits are listed below.

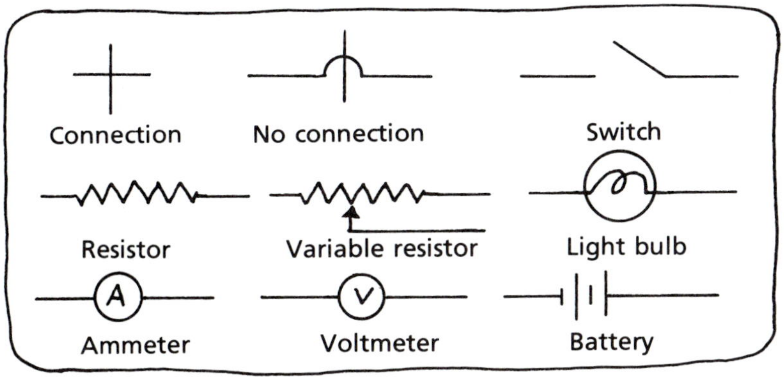

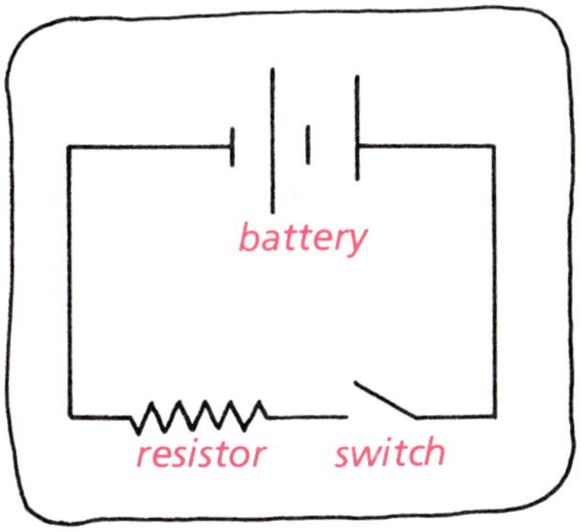

FIGURE 20-17.

(1) *Identify the parts of the circuit in Figure 20-17.* **(2)** *Draw a circuit diagram for the circuits you made in the Activities on pages 423 and 425.* **(3)** *Draw a circuit diagram for a circuit which contains the following: two light bulbs in parallel, a resistor in series with the light bulbs, a switch, and a battery.*

Hickson-Bender/W.D.I.F., Marion, Ohio Craig Kramer Craig Kramer

a b c

FIGURE 20-18. Power meters for a radio station (a), a short wave radio (b), and a stereo system (c).

20:7 Power

When an electric light is on, it uses power. Everything that operates on electricity uses power. Power is the amount of work done per unit time, Section 2:10. The power in a circuit is the voltage of the source multiplied by the current produced by the source.

$$power = voltage \times current \qquad P = VI$$

$$watts = \frac{joule}{coulomb} \times \frac{coulomb}{second} = \frac{joule}{second}$$

What unit is used for power?

Voltage is joules per coulomb. Current is coulombs per second. The result of the multiplication is joules per second, or watts (W).

Table 20-2

Power and Resistance of Some Light Bulbs

Light bulb size (watts)	Resistance (ohms)
100	140
75	190
60	240
40	330
20	740

Example

A battery has a potential difference of 12 volts. The current produced is 0.33 amperes. What is the power in the circuit?

Solution:

(a) Write the equation for power.

$$P = VI$$

(b) Substitute the values for voltage and current given in the problem.

$$P = 12\ \text{V} \times 0.33\ \text{A}$$
$$= 4\ \text{W}$$

Making Sure

9. A source of 120 volts delivers a current of 1.25 amperes to light an electric bulb. How much power is used to light the bulb? *150 W*

10. Another bulb uses 0.5 amperes from a source of 120 volts. How much power is used by the bulb? *60 W*

20:8 A Complex Circuit

What kind of circuits are in a house?

In Section 20:6 you studied simple circuits. The wiring in a house is really a connected set of simple circuits. Figure 20-19 shows the electrical wiring for a room. The room contains three ceiling lights, two table lamps, a stereo, and a television. The three ceiling lights are part of a parallel circuit. If one burns out, the others will still work. The switch is wired in series with the lights. All of the lights can be turned on or off at the same time.

FIGURE 20-19. The ceiling and wall circuits in a room are parallel.

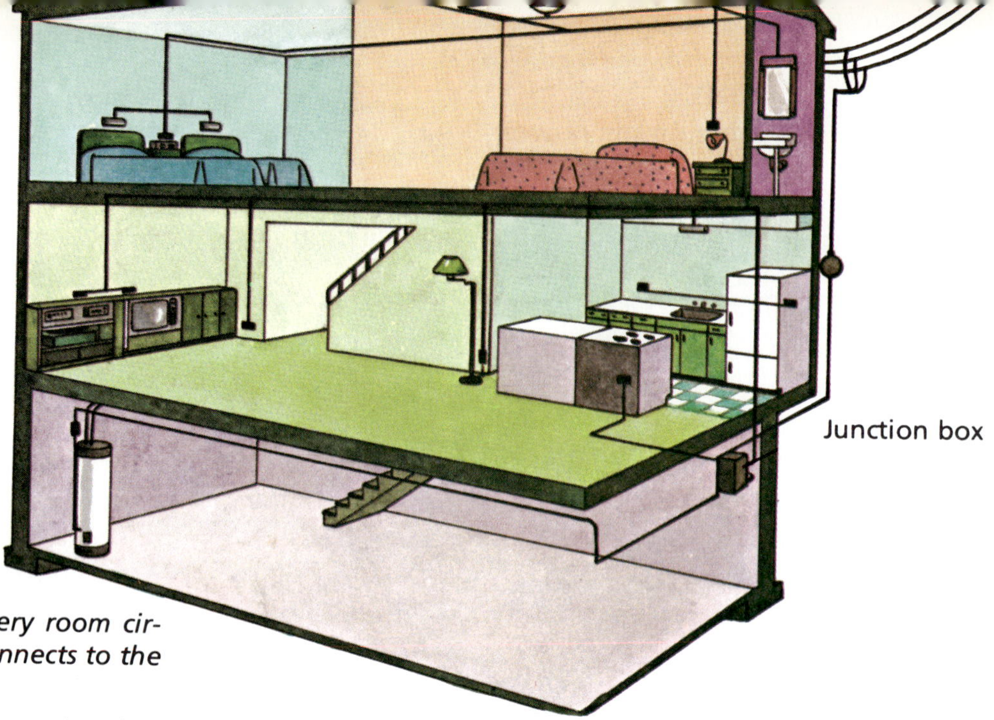

FIGURE 20-20. Every room circuit in a house connects to the junction box.

FIGURE 20-21. A circuit breaker (a). A junction box (b).

a

b

Tom Stack/Tom Stack & Associates

The table lamps, stereo, and television plug into wall sockets. Wall sockets are like the terminals of a battery. When you plug a lamp or television into the socket, a circuit is formed. The wall sockets are all parallel. Anything you plug in will get the same voltage. The lamp and television are parallel when plugged into the sockets.

The light circuit and wall socket circuit are wired in parallel at the **junction box.** Here, they are wired in series with a circuit breaker. A **circuit breaker** is a switch which will open automatically when too much current is being used.

Every room circuit in a house is connected to the junction box and a circuit breaker. The main circuit breaker is connected to each individual circuit breaker. After the main circuit breaker, the house is connected to the power line. The main breaker allows us to turn the power on and off. By opening the circuits when too much power is being used, the circuit breakers help prevent electrical fires.

The current in a house is not direct current. It is alternating current. The two types of current are different. In alternating current, the electrons reverse direction repeatedly. The electrons in direct current do not.

Points to Remember

1. Some objects can build up a static electric charge from friction. *20:1*
2. Current is charge moving in a conductor. *20:2, 20:3*
3. Potential difference or voltage provides the force to move the electrons. *20:4*
4. The movement of electrons must overcome resistance. *20:5*
5. Ohm's law shows the relationship of voltage, current, and resistance. *20:5*
6. Current flows through circuits. *20:6*
7. The two types of circuit are series and parallel. *20:6*
8. A house circuit is a combination of simple circuits. *20:8*

Words to Use

Write a sentence in which you correctly use each of the following words.

circuit breaker	electroscope	resistance
conduction	insulator	series circuit
coulomb	junction box	static discharge
current	ohm	static electricity
direct current	parallel circuit	voltage
dry cell	potential difference	wet cell

Questions for Review

Do not write in this book.

A. True or False *Have the students rewrite the false statements to make them correct.*

Determine whether each of the following sentences is true or false.

T **1.** A dry cell is a source of potential difference.
T **2.** An electroscope can be charged by conduction when it is touched with a charged rod.
F **3.** Like charges ~~attract~~ *repel* each other.
F **4.** Objects build up a static charge when ~~protons~~ *electrons* are lost due to friction.
F **5.** Current is charge ~~at rest~~. *in motion*
T **6.** A circuit is a path for current.
F **7.** Ohm's law shows the relationship of voltage, current, and ~~power~~. *resistance*

T 8. A Van de Graaff generator produces static charges.

F 9. Wet cells produce current when the plates are ~~not~~ connected.

F 10. There is no current in an open circuit.

B. Multiple Choice

Choose the word or phrase that correctly completes each of the following sentences.

1. Electrons are *(neutral, positive, negative)* particles.
2. A glass rod becomes *(positively, negatively)* charged when rubbed with silk.
3. When current flows through a resistance, electrons *(gain, lose)* energy.
4. Potential difference is measured in *(volts, ohms, amperes)*.
5. Ohm's law relates potential difference to *(current and power, power and resistance, resistance and current)*.
6. A circuit breaker is used to open circuits when there is *(too much, too little, normal)* current in the circuit.
7. Glass, plastic, and wood are *(insulators, conductors)*.
8. Copper, aluminum, and silver are *(insulators, conductors)*.
9. Current in a wet cell flows through *(the wire, the solution, both the wire and the solution)*.
10. Current is the movement of *(neutrons, atoms, charges)*.

C. Completion

Complete each of the following sentences with a word or phrase that will make the sentence correct.

1. An object gains a positive charge when it loses electrons.
2. Like charges repel.
3. The electroscope is used to detect static electricity.
4. Conductor is the opposite of insulator.
5. A wet cell produces electric current.
6. The power of an electric circuit is measured in watts.
7. A poor conductor has high resistance.
8. In a series circuit the current is the same in all parts.
9. Potential difference equals resistance times current.
10. Charge moving through a conductor is current.

Detailed answers to these questions are given in the Teacher's Guide at the front of this book.

D. How and Why

1. A 12-volt circuit has a resistance of 2 ohms. Calculate the current.
2. What is the power in the circuit for problem 1?
3. A source of 60 volts is used to light a 100-watt light bulb. Using Table 20-2, find the current in the circuit and the power.
4. How is static electricity produced?

More Ideas to Explore

1. Through library research, prepare a report on the nature of lightning.
2. Do some research to find out how and why static charges are prevented.
3. Do library research and prepare a report on nickel-cadmium batteries.
4. What can people do to reduce the use of electricity? Prepare a poster on this topic.

Readings to Discover

Clifford, Martin, *Basic Electricity and Beginning Electronics.* Blue Ridge Summit, PA: TAB Books, 1973.

DeWaard, E. John, and Klein, Aaron E., *Electric Cars.* NY: Doubleday and Co., 1977.

Martens, A.E., "Seeing Machines: Visual Labor Becomes Automated." *Science Digest,* Vol. 83, May 1978, pp. 24-28.

One way we use electricity is computers. Pictured here is a computer the size of a paper clip. It can be used to control the amount of fuel a car burns, making the car more efficient. What are some other ways this kind of computer could help save energy?

Bill Pierce from Rainbow

Electricity and Its Uses

21

Chapter 21 builds on the study of electricity through a discussion of the principles involved in electronic devices. See the Teacher's Guide at the front of this book for additional teaching strategies for this chapter.

21:1 Magnets

GOAL: *You will learn how magnets and electricity are used for practical purposes.*

An understanding of the way electricity is used requires an understanding of magnets and magnetic fields. Let us begin with a compass.

Describe the main features of a magnet.

A compass is a small thin magnet which has been mounted on a pivot. The pivot allows the magnet to turn freely, Figure 21-1. The magnet has two poles. The pole which always turns to point toward magnetic north is called the north seeking or north pole. The other pole is called the south seeking or the south pole. As with electric charges, like poles repel and unlike poles attract.

Every magnet exerts a force on other magnets or materials that can be magnetized. Around each magnet there is a field of force which runs from the north to the south pole. It is this magnetic force which attracts or repels other magnets.

What is a permanent magnet?

A magnet that holds its magnetic properties over a period of years is a **permanent magnet.** Permanent magnets are made of iron, cobalt, or nickel. These three metals are easily magnetized and will hold their magnetic properties. Magnets are also made of alloys containing at least one of these metals. A bar magnet and horseshoe magnet are permanent magnets.

FIGURE 21-1. The needle of a compass rests on a pivot.

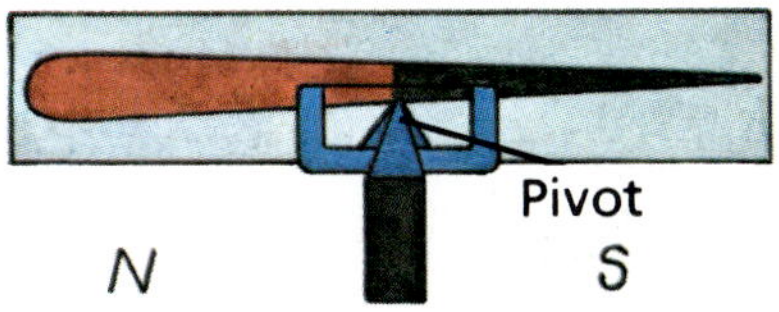

21-1 Detailed information concerning this Activity can be found in the Teacher's Guide at the front of this book.

ACTIVITY *How can you detect a magnetic field?*

Craig Kramer

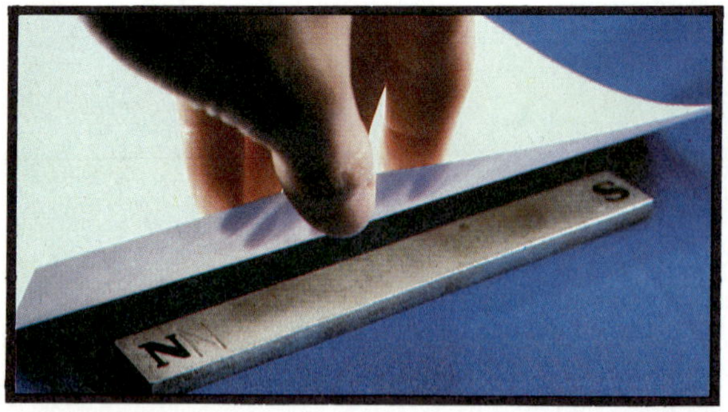

a

b

FIGURE 21-2.

Obtain a bar magnet, a piece of paper, and iron filings. **(1)** *Place the paper over the magnet on a table, Figure 21-2a.* **(2)** *Sprinkle iron filings on the paper.* **(3)** *Tap the paper to spread the filings around. Observe what happens to the filings.* **(4)** *Repeat the Activity using two bar magnets. Place them in different positions (parallel or right angles). Draw diagrams of the fields.* **(5)** *Now take a small compass and move it around the magnets, Figure 21-2b. What is the effect on the compass? Can you tell the direction of the field?* The compass needle always points north along the lines of force.

The filings arrange themselves along the lines of force.

You may also wish to use a horseshoe magnet.

21:2 Current and Magnetic Fields

FIGURE 21-3. All motors have these basic parts.

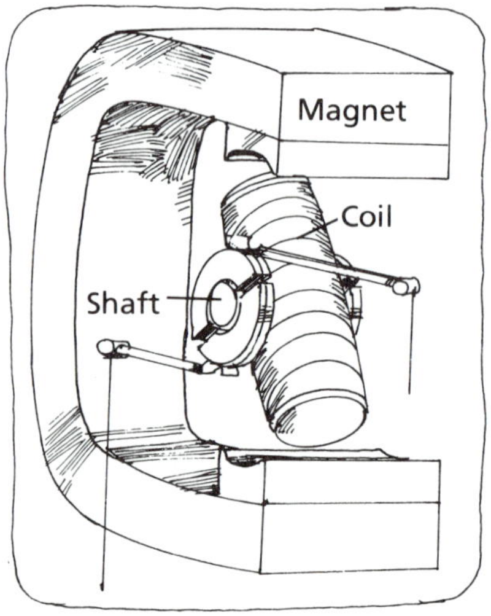

Magnetic fields are not limited to permanent magnets. A current in a wire creates a magnetic field around the wire. Like fields from permanent magnets, fields from electric currents are oriented from north to south. A coil with a magnetic field will attract and repel other magnets, just as permanent magnets do. It is the magnetic fields and their effects on magnets and coils that make magnets important in electronics.

An example of the effects of magnetic fields is an electric motor, Figure 21-3. In a motor, a coil of wire is wound around a shaft. The coil is in the magnetic field between the poles of a magnet. As current passes through the coil, a magnetic field is created in the coil. The effect of the two fields is to turn the shaft. The same result can be achieved by putting the magnet on the shaft and the coil around it. The two magnetic fields cause the rotation in each case because they repel.

Another device that uses a coil and a magnet is an electric meter, Figure 21-4. Again the coil is between the poles of a magnet. A needle is attached to the coil. When a current flows through the coil, the coil rotates. The amount of coil rotation depends on the amount of current flowing through it. As the current flowing through the coil increases, the amount of rotation increases. As the coil turns, the needle attached to it shows the amount of rotation. A meter that measures current is called an **ammeter.**

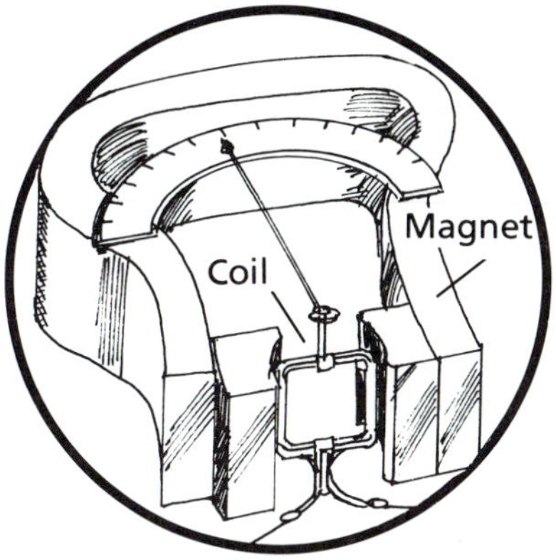

FIGURE 21-4. A meter has a needle on a coil that is between the poles of a magnet.

Making Sure

The two fields oppose each other and force the shaft to turn.

1. What is the effect of the two magnetic fields in a motor?
2. What causes the coil to rotate in a meter? *the opposing magnetic field set up in the coil because of the current*

21:3 Ammeter and Voltmeter

Electric meters are used to measure electricity. The amount of current, in amperes, is measured with an **ammeter.** A **voltmeter** is used to measure the potential difference in volts.

An ammeter and voltmeter have the same basic design. Each contains a coil of wire in a magnetic field. When an ammeter or voltmeter is connected to a circuit, current flows through the coil. As current passes through the coil, it turns and moves a needle on a scale.

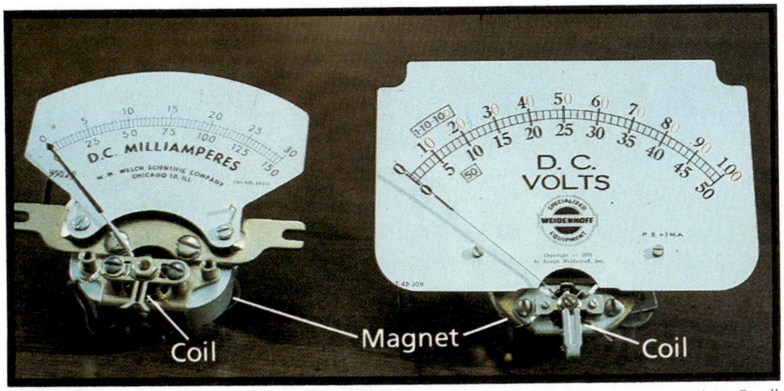

Thomas Russell

FIGURE 21-5. A voltmeter and ammeter have the same basic construction.

Printed on the scale are numbers of amperes or volts. The needle points to the number of amperes or volts in the circuit.

How is a voltmeter different from an ammeter?

An ammeter and voltmeter are different in one important way. The coil in an ammeter has low resistance. Thus, all the current in the circuit to which it is connected flows through the coil. The opposite is true for a voltmeter. A voltmeter has a very high resistance. When connected to a circuit, very little current flows through its coil. The amount of current that flows through the coil is proportional to the voltage. As the voltage increases, the current in the coil increases.

21-2 Detailed information concerning this Activity can be found in the Teacher's Guide at the front of this book.

ACTIVITY *How does a meter work?*

In this activity you will build a current meter. This meter will only show the presence of a current. It will not show the size of the current. **(1)** *Make a coil of wire about 5 centimeters in diameter and 15 to 20 turns long, Figure 21-6a.* **(2)** *Connect the ends of the wire to a six volt battery.* **(3)** *Move a small compass around and through the coil. What happens? Can you determine the direction of the field?* **(4)** *Disconnect one wire from the battery. Place the compass inside the coil, Figure 21-6a.* **(5)** *Connect the wire to the battery while watching the needle on the compass. What happens?* **(6)** *Repeat Steps 4 and 5 with the coil in a different position, Figure 21-6b. What happens? The compass and coil combination is a model of a current meter. Why does the compass needle move when the wire is connected to the battery?*

The needle deflects.

The compass needle reacts to the magnetic field.

Craig Kramer

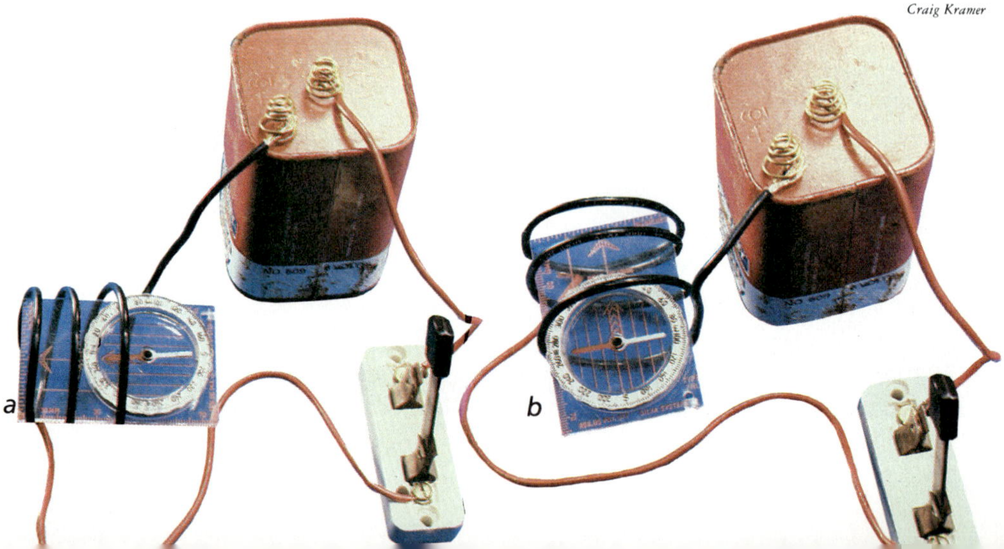

FIGURE 21-6. a b

a

Hickson-Bender/Ohio State University

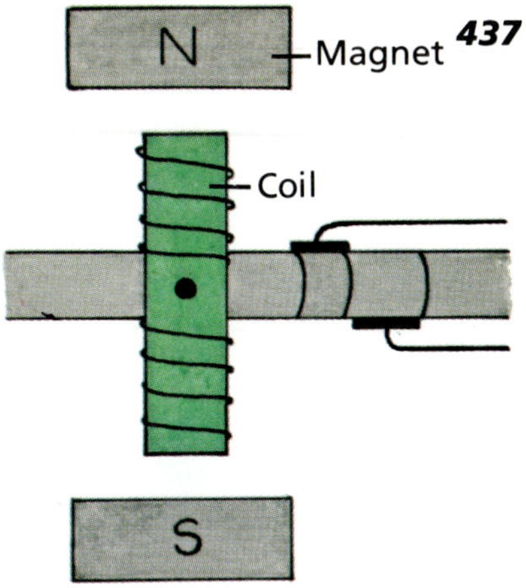

b

FIGURE 21-7. An electrical generator (a). The basic parts of a generator (b).

21:4 Generators and Alternating Current

We have seen how current can be used to produce a magnetic field. There is another use for magnets. If we turn a coil between the poles of a magnet, we get a current. The same thing happens when we turn a magnet inside a coil. Anytime a magnetic field moves across a wire, we get a current in the wire. A device that produces current this way is called a **generator**, Figure 21-7.

Explain how alternating current is generated.

When the coil or the magnet rotates, the magnetic field at a point in the wire changes direction. The changing direction of the field changes the direction of the current. Because the magnetic field constantly changes direction, the current also constantly changes direction. Current that changes or alternates in direction is called **alternating current (AC)**, Figure 21-8a. Alternating current is the kind of current in the circuits in your home and school.

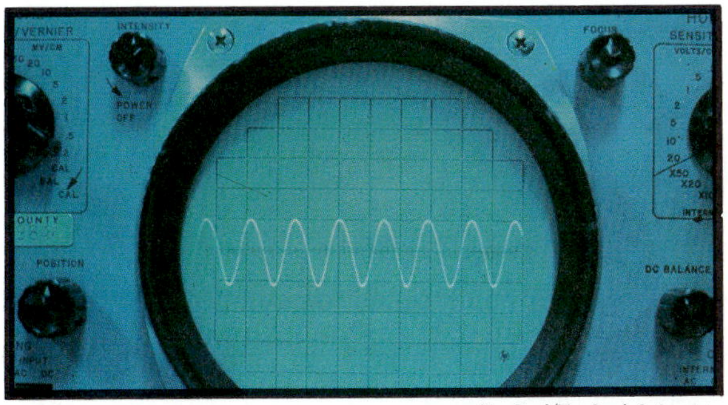

a

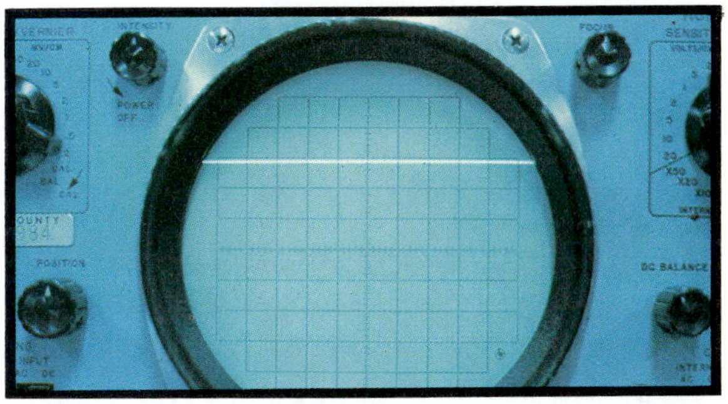

b

Tom Stack/Tom Stack & Associates

FIGURE 21-8. Alternating current (a). Direct current (b).

21-3 Detailed information concerning this Activity can be found in the Teacher's Guide at the front of this book.

ACTIVITY *How does a generator work?*

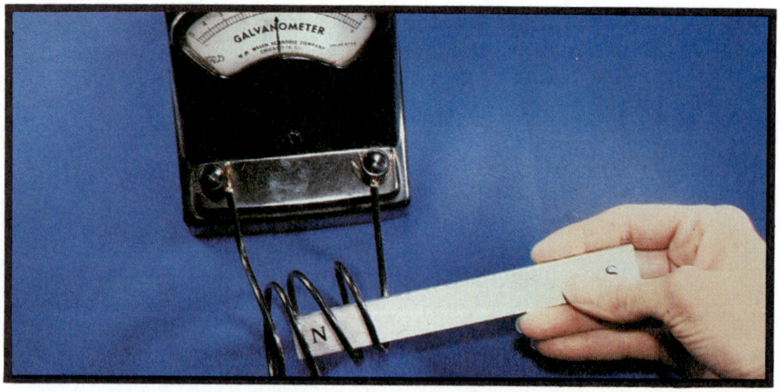

Craig Kramer

FIGURE 21-9.

(1) *Make a coil 5 centimeters in diameter and 20 turns long.* ***(2)*** *Connect it to a galvanometer, Figure 21-9. In a galvanometer, the needle can move in either direction.* ***(3)*** *Take a bar magnet and pass it through the coil in one direction. What happens to the meter?* ***(4)*** *Pass the magnet through the coil in the other direction. What happens to the meter?* ***(5)*** *Now move the magnet back and forth through the coil. What happens to the meter? What happens when you move the magnet faster?* ***(6)*** *Change the size of the coil. Repeat Step 5. What happens when you change the size of the coil? What kind of current did you make in Step 3? Step 4? Step 5?* DC, DC, AC

FIGURE 21-10. A rectifier circuit.

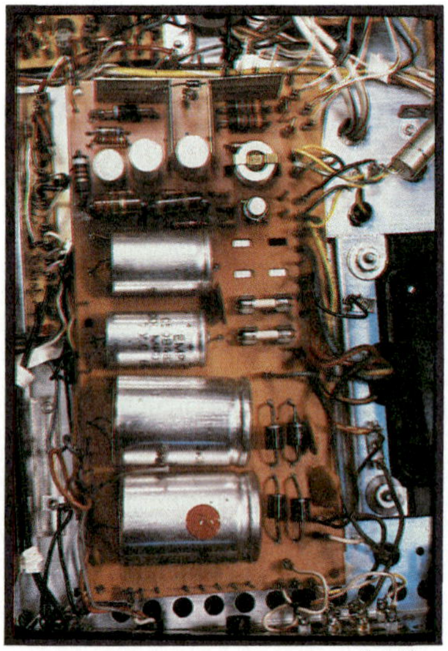

Craig Kramer

21:5 Rectifiers

Although most buildings have alternating current, some household appliances must have direct current to operate. Since stereos, televisions, and other appliances use direct current, there must be a way to change alternating current to direct current. A rectifier is used to make the change, Figure 21-10. A **rectifier** (REK tuh fire) is a device that conducts current in only one direction. Current moving in one direction is direct current, Section 20:3. The rectifier is connected to an alternating current circuit. As the current passes through the rectifier, it is changed to direct current. Rectifiers are part of the circuits in appliances like televisions that use direct current to operate.

Making Sure

3. How does a rectifier change alternating current to direct current? *It conducts a current in only one direction.*
4. Why are rectifiers used in stereos? *Stereos operate only on direct current.*

21:6 Amplifiers

Imagine you are at the back of an auditorium. A person on the stage whispers into a microphone. The sound you hear from the speakers is as loud as a shout. The sound became much louder. To see what happened to the sound, we will follow its path, Figure 21-11. The person whispers into the microphone. A microphone changes sound waves into small electrical signals. The microphone is connected to a device called an amplifier. The small signal, called the input signal, is made larger by the amplifier. The large signal is called the output signal. From the amplifier, the output signal goes to the speakers where it is changed into sound. The sound of the person's whisper has been amplified. An **amplifier** takes a small signal and amplifies or makes the signal larger.

Describe one use of an amplifier.

FIGURE 21-11.

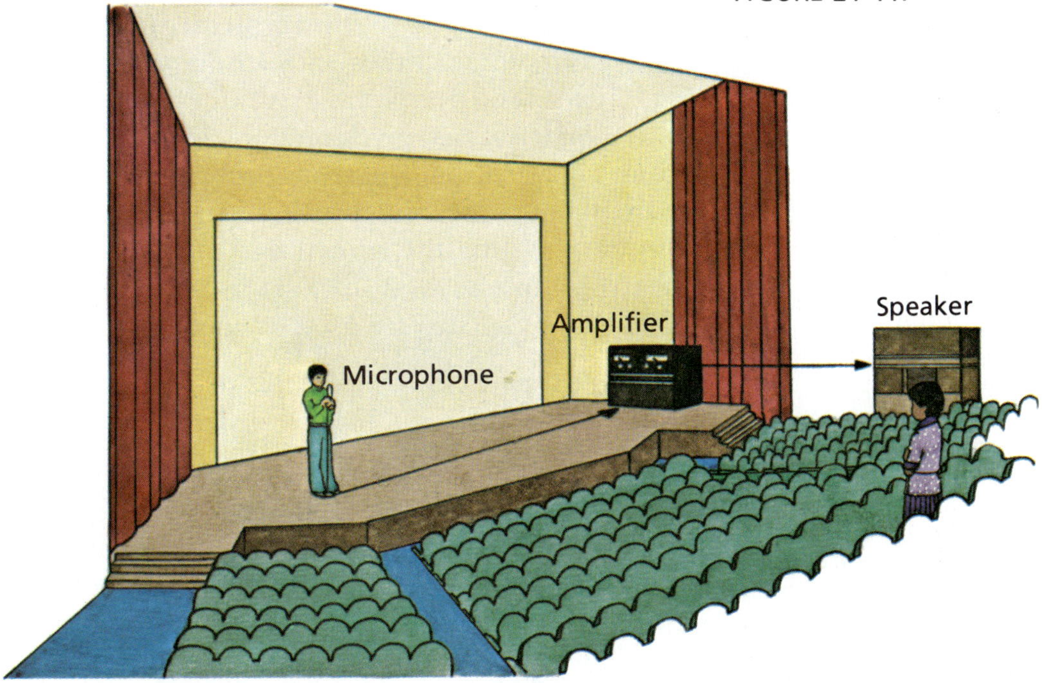

Tom Stack/Tom Stack & Associates

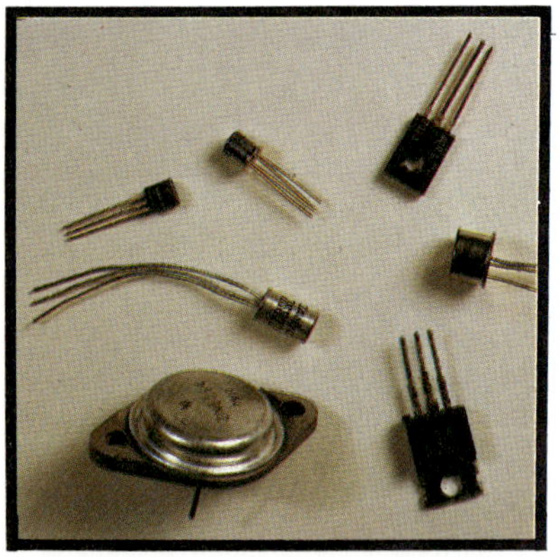

FIGURE 21-12. Transistors come in many sizes and shapes.

Amplifiers are made using **transistors,** Figure 21-12. When connected to a circuit, a transistor has a current flowing through it. The input signal is used to control the flow of the current. Small changes in the input signal create large changes in the flow of the current. These large changes are the input signal.

If the output signal of an amplifier is not large enough, it can be further amplified. The output of one amplifier is the input for the next amplifier. This process is continued until the signal is the desired size. Each individual amplifier is a stage of amplification. Amplifiers are used in many of the appliances that operate on direct current, such as radios, televisions, and stereos.

Making Sure

5. What does the input signal do in a transistor? *controls the flow of current*
6. What does a microphone do? *changes sound to electric current*
7. Why are amplifiers used? *to increase sound*

21:7 Cathode-ray Tube

A **cathode-ray tube,** Figure 21-13 is an electronic device which is used to show a picture of an input signal. Television picture tubes are cathode-ray tubes.

The screen portion of a cathode-ray tube is covered with a material that gives off light when it is hit by electrons, Figure 21-14. Electrons flow from an electron gun to the screen. The input signal determines the number of electrons hitting the screen by controlling the flow of electrons. In one kind of cathode-ray tube, four electrically charged plates are used to control the point on the

FIGURE 21-13. A cathode-ray tube used in a piece of electrical test equipment.

Tom Stack/Tom Stack & Associates

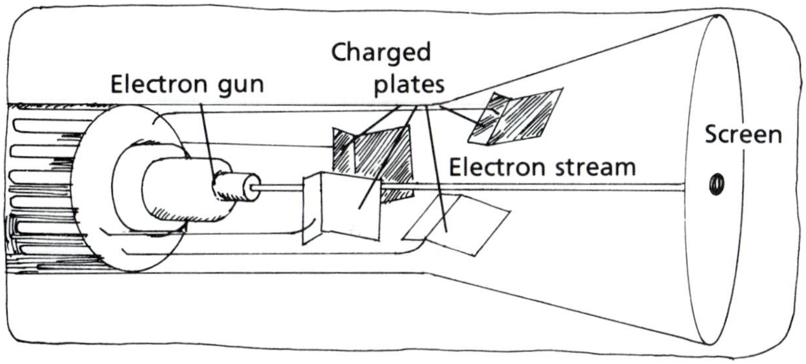

FIGURE 21-14. The basic parts of one kind of cathode-ray tube.

screen hit by electrons. Since the electron stream has a charge, it is affected by the fields of the plates. Changing the fields changes the direction of the electron stream. As the electron stream is moved rapidly across the screen, a picture is formed. Television picture tubes operate on a somewhat different principle.

A cathode-ray tube should be handled only by a qualified person. High voltages are needed to operate a cathode-ray tube. A potential difference of 20 000 volts is often used. This voltage can be fatal if misused.

Making Sure

8. How is the direction of the electron stream controlled? *electrical fields*
9. What determines the number of electrons hitting the screen? *the input signal*

21:8 Television Receivers

A television uses many of the devices we have discussed. The way the parts of a television work together can be seen by following two paths: the power supply and the signal. We will look first at the power supply, Figure 21-15. Alternating current is generated at the

FIGURE 21-15. The path of the power supply for a television.

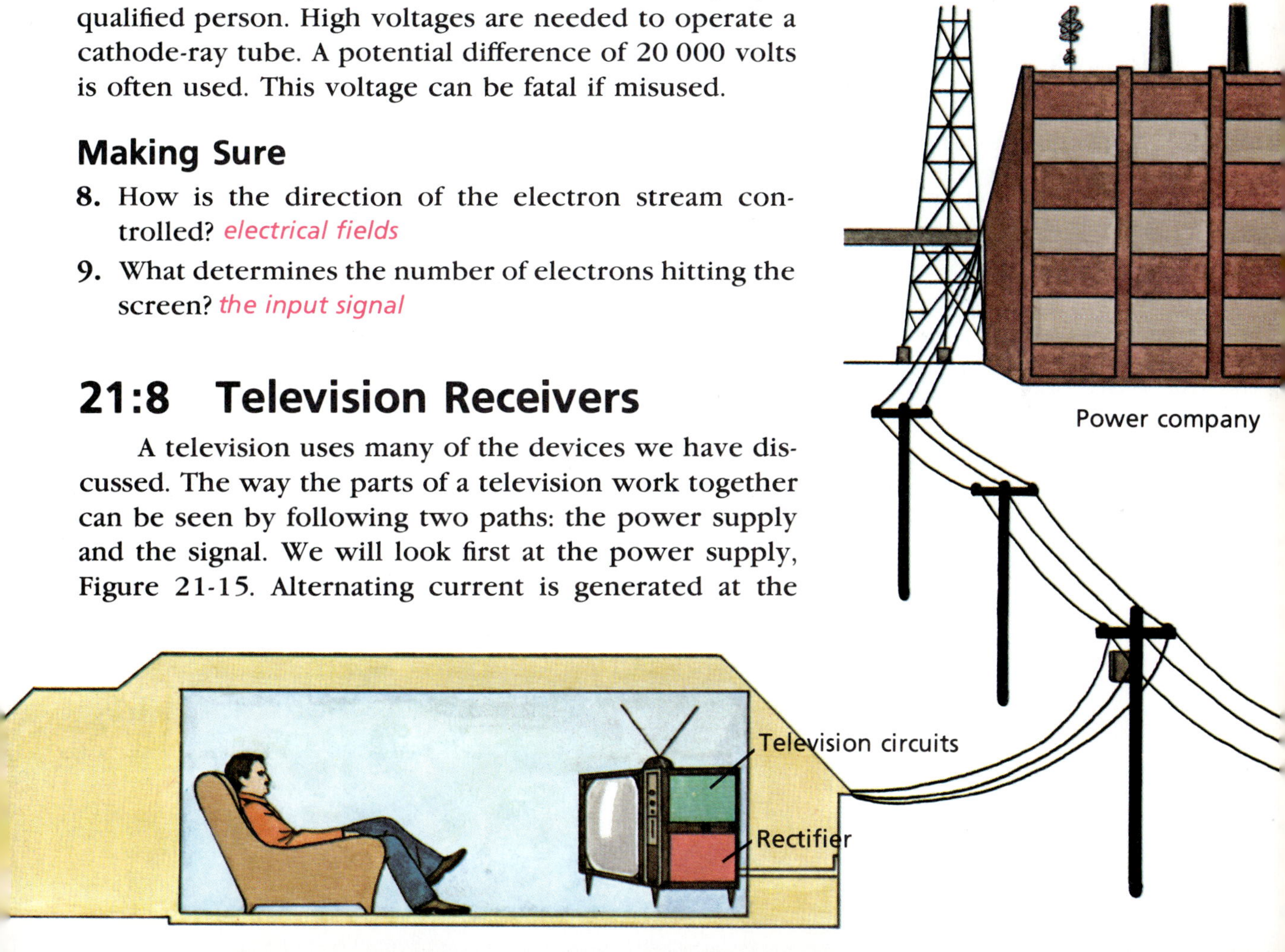

power plant. The current travels to the house. The television is plugged into the wall socket. A rectifier in the television changes alternating current to direct current. Direct current is used to operate the rest of the television's circuits.

A television signal travels a more complex path, Figure 21-16. The signal is received at the antenna and goes to the first amplifier section. There are two basic parts in the signal, the sound and the picture. After the first

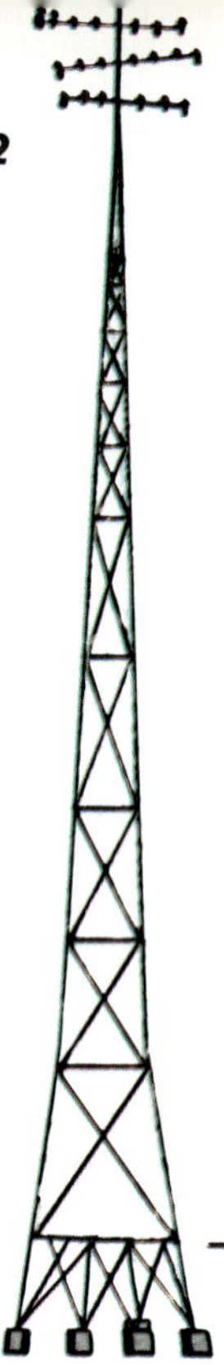

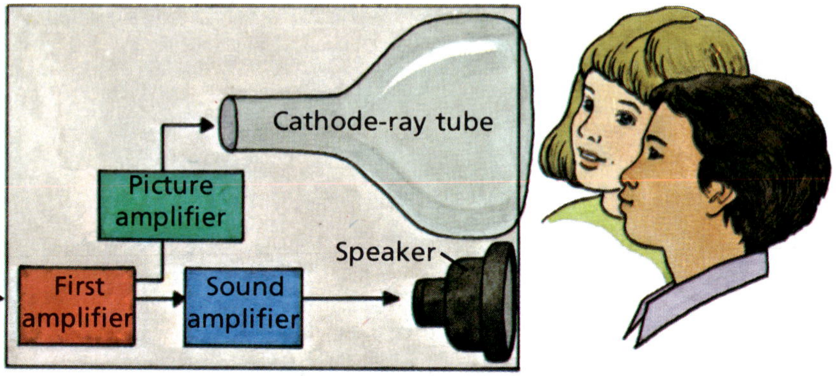

FIGURE 21-16. The path of the signal in a television set.

amplifier section, the sound and picture signals are separated. The sound signal is amplified and goes to the speaker. The picture signal is amplified and goes to the cathode-ray tube. The picture signal is the input signal for the cathode-ray tube.

In the picture tube of a color television there are three materials that give off light when struck by electrons. Each material gives off a different color—red, blue, and green. These materials are arranged in triangles of dots, Figure 21-17. Because the dots are small, the colors of light given off appear to blend. As a result, we see many different colors in addition to red, blue, and green.

FIGURE 21-17. The dot pattern of a color television screen.

Making Sure

10. What are the basic parts of the television signal? *sound, picture*
11. Where are the parts of the television signal separated? *after the first amplifier*
12. What is the input signal for the cathode-ray tube? *picture*

Alan Bagg/Tom Stack & Associates

a

Tom Stack/Tom Stack & Associates

b

FIGURE 21-18. A circuit board (a). An integrated circuit beside a transistor (b).

21:9 Integrated Circuits

In many appliances, a device called an **integrated circuit** is replacing transistor amplifiers, Figure 21-18b. One reason is that by using integrated circuits some appliances can be made smaller. For example, a television has many parts including resistors and transistors. These parts are attached to small plastic boards called circuit boards, Figure 21-18a. One circuit board might contain the first three amplifier sections. Each section has many parts. One integrated circuit can contain all three of the amplifier sections. All of the transistors and other parts are contained in the integrated circuit. The integrated circuit is about the size of the transistor for one amplifier stage. The advantages of the integrated circuit are the small size and one part instead of many.

Integrated circuits have made it possible to make calculators the size of credit cards. Radios are now the size of note pads. Electronic games use integrated circuits. Perhaps the most impressive result of the use of integrated circuits is in computers. A computer that once filled an entire room has been redesigned to sit on a desk.

Thomas Russell

FIGURE 21-19. Integrated circuits make small calculators possible.

Making Sure

13. What is a circuit board? *a small board containing many parts like transistors and resistors*

14. What are the advantages of integrated circuits? *small size, one part*

21:10 Computers

A computer is a device that can solve complex problems when it is given specific instructions. The instructions are called a **program.** The most common type of computer is the digital computer. A **digital computer** uses numbers to follow its instructions and perform calculations.

Figure 21-21 shows that a computer has five parts. Any computer, from a small calculator to the largest computer, has these five parts. In a small calculator, the keys are the input unit. By using the keys, you instruct the calculator to do arithmetic on the numbers you punch in. These instructions are a program. From the input unit, the program goes to the control unit. The control unit calls on the arithmetic unit to do the calculations. It also stores any information that must be remembered in the memory unit. When the instructions are complete, the control unit sends the answer to the output unit. Here the answer is displayed.

A large computer works the same way. Often the input unit has a keyboard like a typewriter. The program is typed into the unit and goes to the control unit. The control unit stores the program in the memory unit. When the computer has the whole program, the control unit begins to follow the instructions. It calls on the arithmetic unit to perform all the calculations. As each calculation is made, its answer is operated on again or

FIGURE 21-20. The Arizona Public Service computer center in Phoenix, Arizona.

Michael Collier

FIGURE 21-21. The five basic parts of a computer.

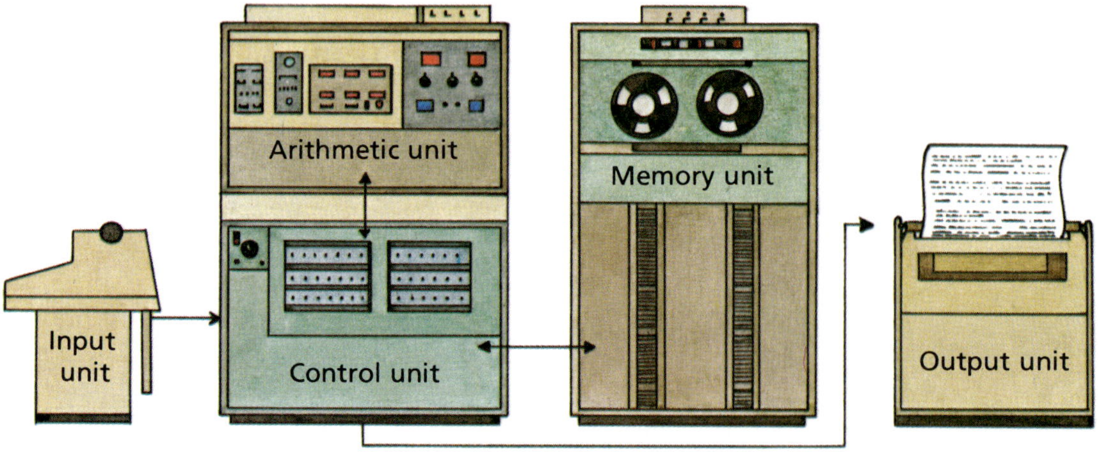

Alan Bagg/Tom Stack & Associates Alan Bagg/Tom Stack & Associates Tom Stack/Tom Stack & Associates

FIGURE 21-22. The input unit (a). The control, memory, and arithmetic units (b). The output unit (c).

stored in the memory unit. When the program is complete, the control unit takes the answer out of memory and sends it to the output unit. The output unit displays the results. The output unit might be a paper printer or a television screen.

What does the output unit do?

Another way to think of a computer is as a circuit, Figure 21-23. The person putting the program into the computer is called a programmer. The programmer is the source. The program is the current. The computer is the circuit for the program. When the results are displayed to the programmer, the circuit is complete. A computer can do only what it is programmed to do.

Making Sure

15. What are the basic parts of a computer? *input, control, arithmetic, memory, output*

16. What is a program? *a set of instructions*

17. What does the control unit do? *runs the program through the last three units*

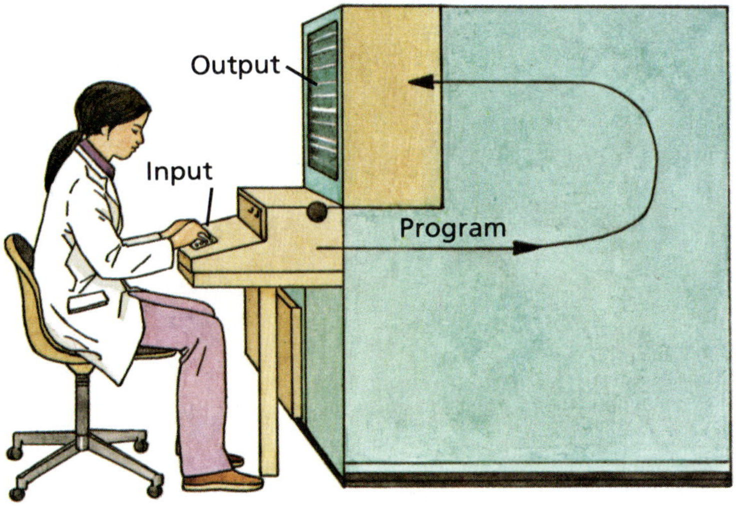

FIGURE 21-23. A computer is like a circuit.

Focus on

People

CHAOS

Mary E. Kroening

Computer systems can be found in many sizes. The smallest are microcomputer systems. In a microcomputer, the central processing or control unit fits on one integrated circuit. Central processing units for larger computers use many integrated circuits. Another difference between microcomputers and larger computers is cost. A complete microcomputer system costs as little as $500. Larger computer systems cost $10 000 and up.

Since microcomputers are inexpensive, many schools are purchasing them. They are used to teach students how to use computers. In 1975 Clairemont High School in San Diego purchased its first microcomputer. Over the next few years, Mary Kroening, along with Robert Haas and Jeff Levinsky, developed the basic computer into a very versatile machine. She called the system CHAOS. CHAOS stands for Clairemont High Advanced Operating System.

One of the reasons Mary developed CHAOS was to give more students time on the computer. With one keyboard, only one student could use the computer at a time. Using CHAOS, several students can use the computer at the same time. When several people use a computer at the same time, they are time sharing. In time sharing a computer divides its attention among several people's programs. The students use keyboards combined with television screens for the input and output.

Because CHAOS is a small computer, it has to store many programs outside its memory unit. Programs can be stored in two ways. One is a cassette tape. This is very convenient for students, since it fits in a pocket. Another way is to use a floppy disk, which is a flexible plastic disk that looks like a small record. The advantage of the disk is that it is much faster than the tape. When either the tape or the disk is in use, it becomes part of the memory unit.

Mary's development of CHAOS is unique. Although CHAOS uses a microcomputer, it can do almost everything larger computers can do. The experts thought a high school student could not develop a system like CHAOS, but Mary did. Since high school, Mary has continued to work with computers. She is the president of her own small business called, Computer Systems Design Group. Mary's company develops ideas for small computers used in education.

Points to Remember

1. Magnets exert a force on other magnets. *21:1*
2. A current creates a magnetic field. *21:2*
3. Magnets are important in electronics because of the effects of magnetic fields. *21:2*
4. Ammeters and voltmeters use the same basic design. *21:3*
5. Alternating current is current that changes direction. *21:4*
6. A rectifier changes alternating current to direct current. *21:5*
7. An amplifier takes a small electrical signal and amplifies it. *21:6*
8. A cathode-ray tube is used to show a picture of a signal. *21:7, 21:8*
9. Integrated circuits are more compact than transistors, allowing us to make many devices smaller. *21:9*
10. All computers have five basic parts: input, control, arithmetic, memory, output. *21:10*

Words to Use

Write a sentence in which you correctly use each of the following words.

alternating current	generator	output signal
ammeter	input signal	program
amplify	integrated circuit	rectifier
cathode-ray tube	magnetic field	transistor
digital computer	magnetic force	voltmeter

Questions for Review

Do not write in this book.

A. True or False *Have the students rewrite the false statements to make them correct.*

Determine whether each of the following sentences is true or false.

F 1. The north pole of a magnet attracts ~~north~~ poles. *south*

T 2. The magnetic field in a motor causes the shaft to turn.

F 3. An ammeter and voltmeter have ~~different~~ basic designs. *the same*

F 4. Rectifiers are used to change ~~DC to AC~~. *AC to DC*

T 5. An amplifier is used to make electrical signals larger.

T 6. Televisions contain cathode-ray tubes and amplifiers.

F 7. The three colors in a color television are red, ~~yellow~~, and blue. *green*

F 8. There are ~~four~~ five basic parts to a computer.

T 9. Computer programs are instructions for a computer.

F 10. The ~~arithmetic~~ control unit takes information from the memory unit.

B. Multiple Choice

Choose the word or phrase that correctly completes each of the following sentences.

1. *(Voltmeters, Ammeters)* give readings in amperes.
2. Permanent magnets can be made of *(carbon, lead, iron)*.
3. An amplifier amplifies *(light, electrical, sound)* signals.
4. In one kind of cathode-ray tube, charged plates control the *(direction, number)* of electrons.
5. Televisions use *(motors, generators, rectifiers)* to make direct current.
6. A television signal is split *(before, after, during)* the first amplifier stage.
7. The *(input, control, arithmetic)* unit puts instructions into memory.
8. The *(arithmetic, memory, output)* unit of a computer can be a paper printer.
9. Transistors are used as *(rectifiers, amplifiers, generators)*.
10. Cathode-ray tubes *(amplify, rectify, show pictures of)* an input signal.

C. Completion

Complete each of the following sentences with a word or phrase that will make the sentence correct.

1. The movement of the stream of electrons in one kind of cathode-ray tube is controlled by charged plates.
2. The five units of a computer are the input, control, memory, arithmetic, and output.
3. The arithmetic unit performs calculations.
4. North poles of magnets are attracted by south poles.
5. An ammeter has a(n) coil between the poles of a magnet.
6. The field of a magnet runs from the north pole to the south pole.
7. Alternating current is current that changes direction.

8. A television picture tube is a(n) *cathode-ray* ______ tube.
9. Rectifiers are used in devices that need *direct current* ______ to operate.
10. Ammeters and *voltmeters* ______ use the same basic design.

Detailed answers to these questions are given in the Teacher's Guide at the front of this book.

D. How and Why

1. Compare an electric generator and a meter. How are they alike and different?
2. Why would a Canadian nickel be attracted by a magnet when a recently minted American nickel is not?
3. Why is the development of the integrated circuit important?
4. Describe an experiment you could perform to show that a magnet deflects a stream of electrons.

More Ideas to Explore

1. Visit an electric power plant to learn how electricity is generated.
2. Take an old electric motor apart. Identify and make a diagram of the parts.
3. Through library research, prepare a report on the uses of computers.
4. Visit a television station or do library research and write a report explaining how a television signal is produced.

Readings to Discover

Buchsbaum, Walter H., and Mauro, Robert, "Electronic Games: Here's What Makes Them Work." *Science Digest,* July 1979, pp. 32-35.

Grosswirth, Marvin, *Beginner's Guide to Home Computers.* NY: Doubleday and Co., 1978.

O'Brien, Linda, *Computers.* NY: F. Watts, 1978.

Unit 7

Electricity is the life-giving force of today's cities. The energy fountain shown absorbs excess electric power. The use of solar cells will decrease our demand for fossil fuels. What other alternatives should we explore in order to conserve our resources?

Energy Resources for the Future

Dan McCoy from Rainbow

The nucleus of an atom is like a complex puzzle. Scientists are continually finding new pieces to add. The picture shows photographic tracks made by nuclear particles. These tracks prove the particles exist even though they cannot be seen.

Dan McCoy from Rainbow

Radioactivity and Nuclear Energy

22

Chapter 22 discusses the properties of radioactive substances, radiation detection, and nuclear reactions. See the Teacher's Guide at the front of this book for additional teaching strategies for this chapter.

22:1 Radioactive Elements

GOAL: *You will learn the properties and uses of radioactive substances.*

Certain atoms emit invisible radiation from their nuclei. These atoms are radioactive. As the radiation is released, the element many times becomes a different element. When a new element is formed decay occurs. **Decay** means the nucleus of an atom loses nuclear particles.

What is a radioactive element?

Radioactivity was discovered by a French scientist, Henry Becquerel, in 1896. He left some uranium salt lying on a photographic plate in a dark desk drawer. When he developed the plate, Becquerel was surprised to find an outline of the uranium salt. Uranium released invisible radiation that made the outline on the plate. Uranium is a radioactive element.

In 1898, Marie and Pierre Curie discovered two new radioactive elements. These elements were named polonium and radium. The Curies extracted these elements from uranium ore. Polonium and radium are more radioactive than uranium.

Most naturally radioactive elements are heavier than lead. These elements have an atomic number greater than 83. However, many natural isotopes of lighter elements are radioactive. Isotopes are atoms of the same element with different numbers of neutrons. For example, potassium and carbon each have radioactive isotopes.

Linda Young

a

Dan Guravich 1978/Photo Researchers, Inc.

b

FIGURE 22-1. The radioactive element uranium (a) is mined in deep and surface mines (b).

Name two synthetic elements.

Synthetic elements are those that have been produced in the laboratory or in nuclear reactors. They do not occur naturally. Elements with atomic numbers between 93 and 105 are synthetic elements. Einsteinium and nobelium are two examples of synthetic elements. All the synthetic elements are radioactive.

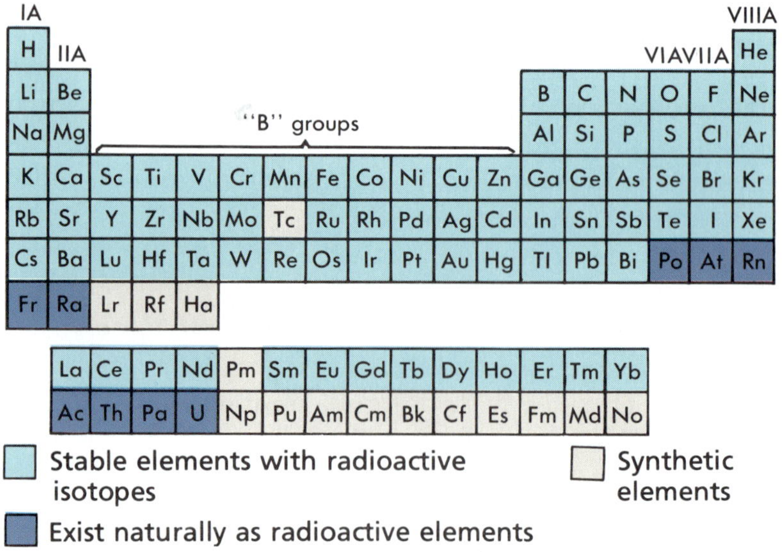

FIGURE 22-2. Most elements on the periodic table have at least one radioactive nuclide.

Table 22-1

Radioactive Elements

Element	Atomic number	Atomic mass number	Element	Atomic number	Atomic mass number
polonium	84	210	americium	95	243
astatine	85	210	curium	96	245
radon	86	222	berkelium	97	245
francium	87	223	californium	98	249
radium	88	226	einsteinium	99	254
actinium	89	227	fermium	100	252
thorium	90	232	mendelevium	101	256
proactinium	91	231	nobelium	102	251
uranium	92	238	lawrencium	103	257
neptunium	93	237	rutherfordium	104	257
plutonium	94	242	hahnium	105	260

Making Sure

1. What is a synthetic element? *One produced in the laboratory or in a nuclear reactor.*
2. Which elements in the periodic table are synthetic? *numbers 93-105*

22:2 Radioactive Nuclides

The radioactive nuclides of some elements occur in nature. A **nuclide** is a radioactive atom. Radioactive nuclides also may be produced in the laboratory by bombarding elements with neutrons or charged particles.

Why are certain nuclides radioactive? The stability of an atom of a light element depends upon the number of protons and neutrons in the nucleus. *When the ratio of protons to neutrons in an atom is nearly equal, the nucleus of the atom is stable.* Stable means that the nucleus is not radioactive. Carbon-12 is an example of a stable atom. It has six protons and six neutrons. The ratio of protons to neutrons in carbon-12 is 1:1.

You may wish to remind students that carbon-12 means the carbon isotope with an atomic mass of 12.

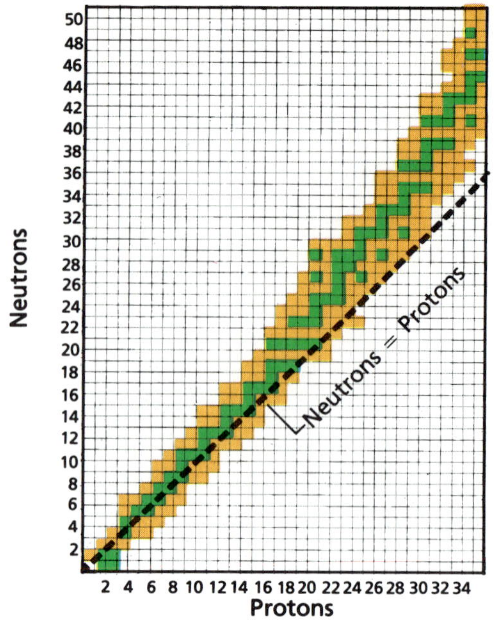

FIGURE 22-3. The graph shows the numbers of protons and neutrons for stable and radioactive elements. The line through the center of the graph shows the points where protons equal neutrons.

If there are too many neutrons for the number of protons in an atom, that element or isotope may be radioactive. Carbon-14 has six protons and eight neutrons. This isotope is radioactive. Many of the common elements have radioactive nuclides.

Table 22-2

Radioactive Nuclides of Some Common Elements

Nuclide	Atomic mass number	Protons	Neutrons
tritium (hydrogen)	*3*	*1*	*2*
helium	*5*	*2*	*3*
lithium	*8*	*3*	*5*
carbon	*14*	*6*	*8*
nitrogen	*16*	*7*	*9*
potassium	*40*	*19*	*21*

What are some uses for radioactive nuclides?

Synthetic radioactive nuclides have many practical uses. Radiation from nuclides such as cobalt-60 is used to treat cancer. High-energy radiation kills cancer cells. Radioactive nuclides are also used to trace an element in a plant or animal. By tracing the path of an element, a scientist may learn how it is used.

Phosphorus-32 placed in the soil around a plant will be absorbed into the plant. The movement of the phosphorus-32 through the plant can be followed with a Geiger counter. This instrument is used to detect radiation. Since a radioactive nuclide can be traced, it is called a "tagged atom." Its radiation is a tag which allows it to be detected.

Radioactive nuclides are also used to detect tumors and other diseases in organs. A small amount can be injected into the blood which carries it to the organ. Radiation emitted by the radioactive material can be compared with that in a healthy organ.

Dan McCoy from Rainbow

a

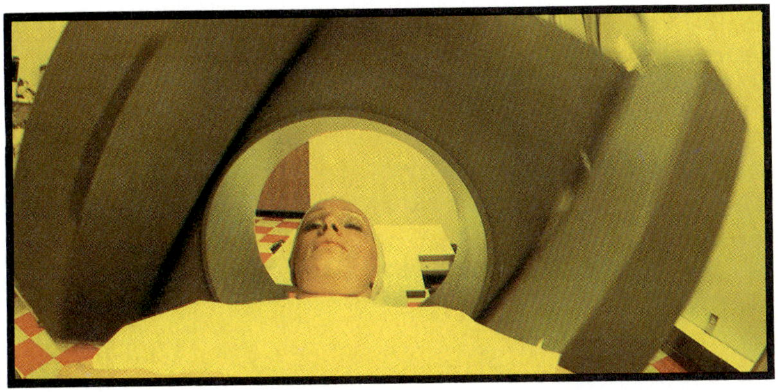

b

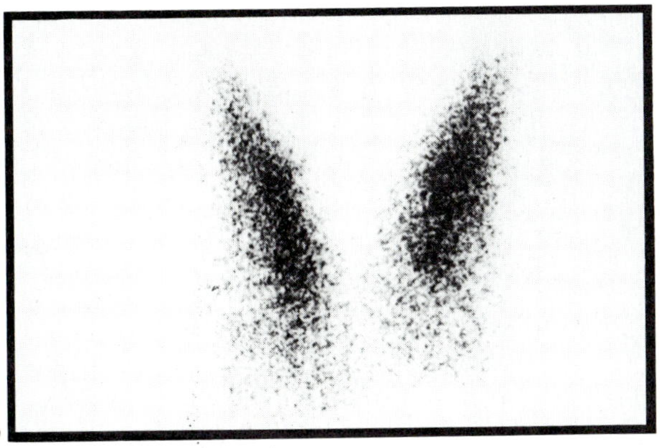

c

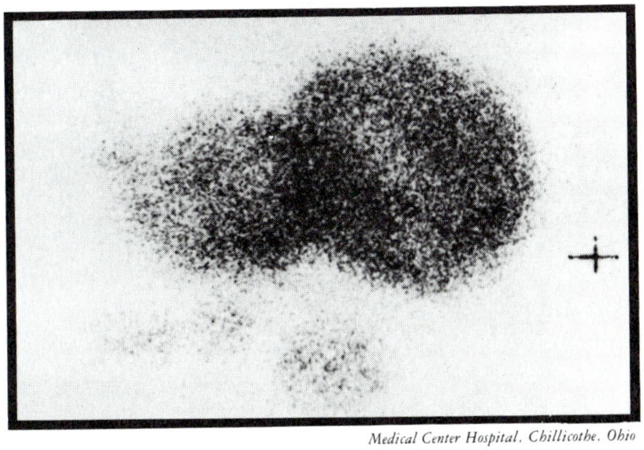

Medical Center Hospital, Chillicothe, Ohio

FIGURE 22-4. Radioactive iodine can be used to detect thyroid gland disorders. A photoscan (a) measures the amount of radiation absorbed by healthy (b) and diseased tissue (c). Note the size of the gland in (c).

Making Sure

3. What is the ratio of protons to neutrons for cobalt-60? 27:33

22:3 Nuclear Radiation

The nucleus of a radioactive element is unstable. When a change in the nucleus occurs, radiation is given off. There are three kinds of radiation which may be released from the nucleus. They are alpha particles, beta particles, and gamma rays.

What is an alpha particle?

Each **alpha particle** is a helium nucleus with two protons and two neutrons. It has a positive charge. However, it does not have much power to penetrate matter. An alpha particle can be stopped by a thin sheet of paper. Most alpha particles are stopped after traveling through a few centimeters of air.

List the characteristics of a beta particle.

Beta particles are positively or negatively charged electrons. Beta particles usually travel faster and farther than alpha particles. The penetrating power of beta particles is about 100 times greater than that of alpha particles. However, beta particles can be stopped by a sheet of aluminum one centimeter thick.

Every beta particle is a possible producer of X rays. X rays can be produced by slowed beta particles. The kinetic energy lost by an electron as it slows down becomes X-ray radiation and heat energy. When the moving negative charge is slowed, radiation is emitted.

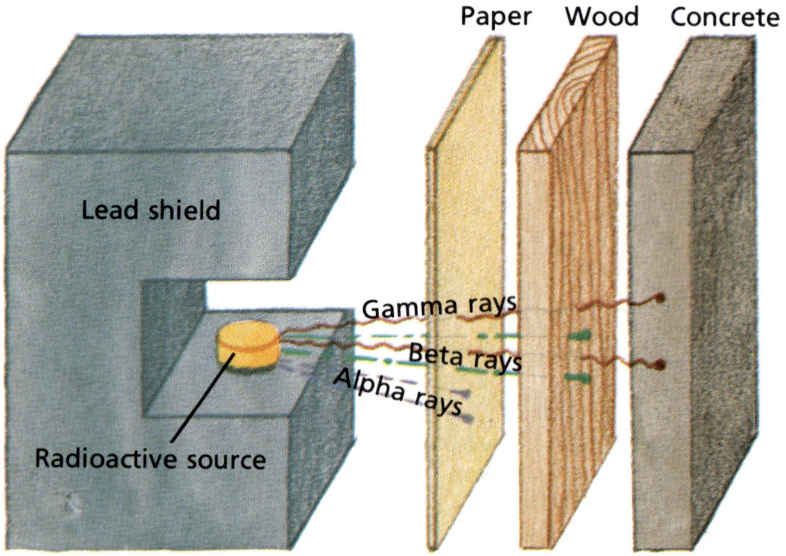

FIGURE 22-5. The energy and penetrating power of gamma rays is greater than that of alpha or beta rays.

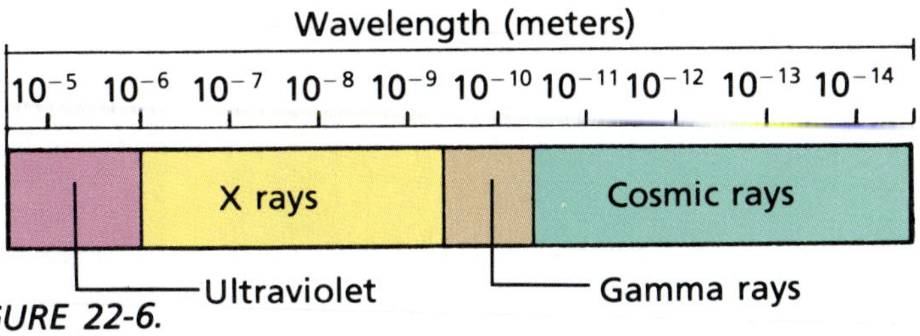

FIGURE 22-6.

Gamma rays are energy waves of short wavelength and high frequency. Gamma wavelengths are shorter than X-ray wavelengths. Most important, gamma rays are not charged particles. Gamma rays contain photons, or "bundles" of energy. They travel at the speed of light. Gamma rays are more penetrating than either alpha or beta rays. It takes dense materials such as lead or concrete to stop gamma rays.

Battelle, Columbus Laboratories

FIGURE 22-7. People working with radioactive materials must observe safety precautions. This clothing is designed to protect the wearer from the harmful effects of radiation.

Making Sure

4. Compare the penetrating power of gamma rays, alpha particles, and beta particles. *alpha—least; gamma—most*
5. Which has the shorter wavelength, X rays or gamma rays? Which has more energy? *Gamma rays have a shorter wavelength and therefore are more energetic.*

22:4 Decay and Half-Life

Define radioactive decay, half-life.

As a radioactive atom releases radiation from its nucleus, it can change into an atom of another element. Uranium-238 is a radioactive element that decays through a series of nuclear changes to form lead. Lead-206 is stable and is not radioactive. The nuclear reactions that change uranium into lead produce a number of radioactive elements.

Nuclear changes are completely different from chemical and physical changes. Temperature and pressure can affect chemical and physical changes. However, the rate of nuclear change is not affected by a change in temperature or pressure.

Half-life is the time it takes for half of the atoms in a radioactive material to decay. For one isotope, half-life may be a fraction of a second. For another isotope, it may be thousands of years or more. For example,

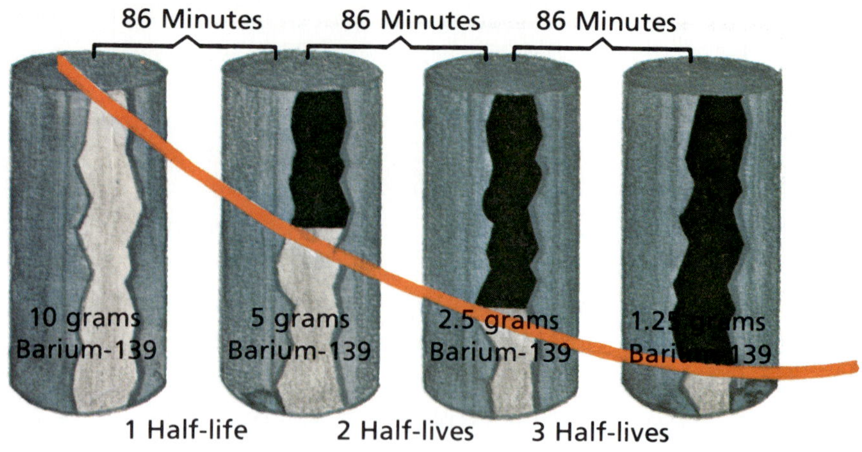

FIGURE 22-8. The mass of barium nuclide is reduced by half during each half-life.

barium-139 has a half-life of 86 minutes. Suppose you had ten grams of pure barium-139 in a lead container. After 86 minutes, one half of the atoms would have decayed. You would have only five grams of radioactive barium-139. After another 86 minutes, one half of the remaining barium-139 atoms would have decayed. You would then have 2.5 grams.

What happens to an element as it decays? When the number of protons changes, the element changes into another element. Figure 22-9 shows the changes of uranium-238 as it decays. The decay process continues

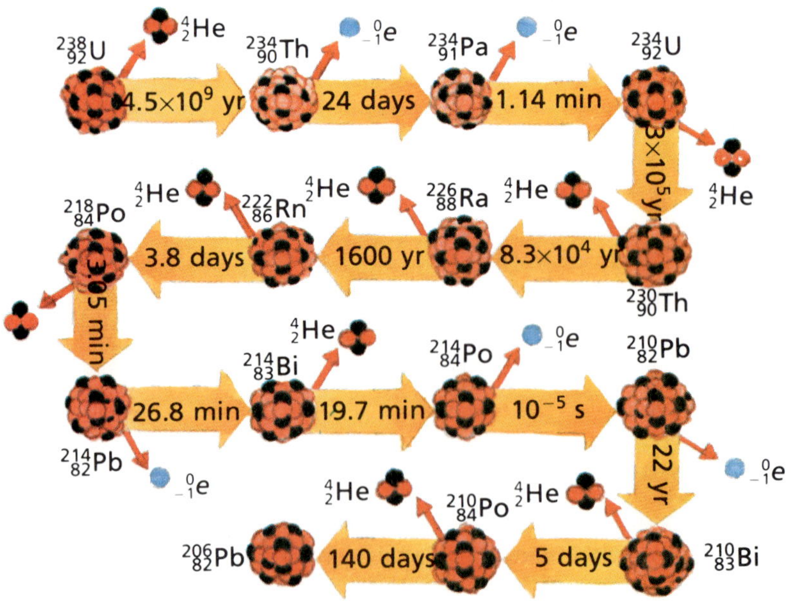

FIGURE 22-9. The natural decay process for uranium

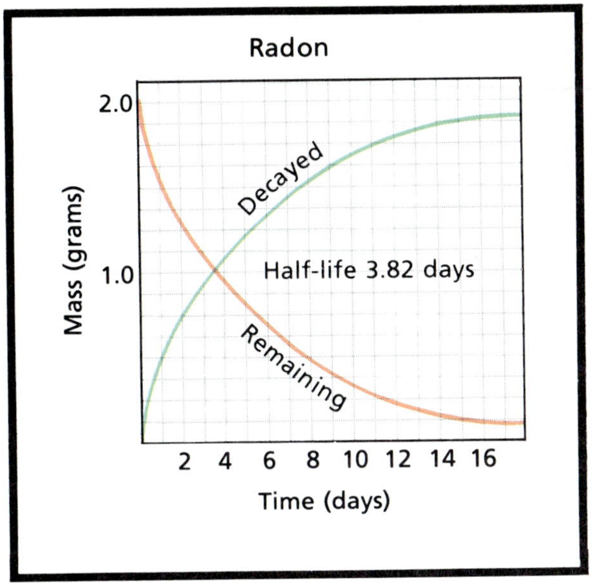

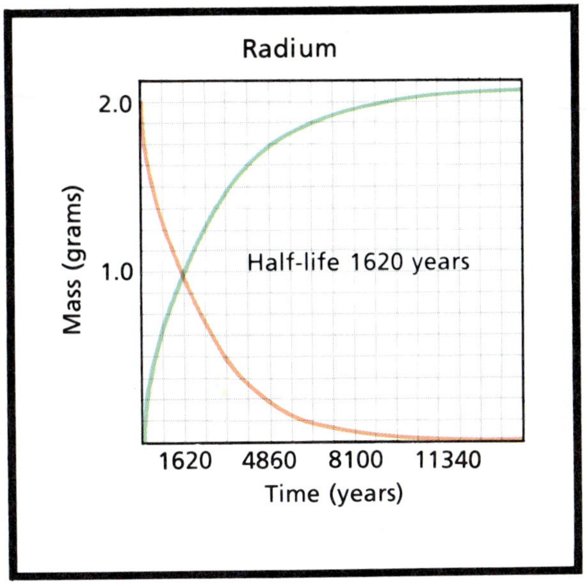

FIGURE 22-10. The shorter half-life of radon makes it less stable than radium.

until lead-206 is formed. This element is stable. Notice that each step in the decay process occurs at a different rate.

The half-life of some radioactive isotopes makes them useful in determining the age of very old objects. For example, carbon-14 with a half-life of 5730 years, is used to determine the age of some fossils. While an animal or plant is alive, it maintains a constant level of carbon-14. When the animal or plant dies the carbon-14 level decreases over time. The constant level can be maintained only while it is alive. In carbon dating,

How can a radioactive element be used to find the age of an object?

FIGURE 22-11. Carbon-14 can be used to determine the age of a fossil.

You may wish to inform students that some radioactive dating techniques have limitations in terms of the accuracy of the results.

a small sample of an object is used. The amount of carbon-14 is measured by counting the beta rays given off, Figure 22-11. Dating methods using other radioactive elements are also employed to find the age of objects.

Table 22-3

Half-Life of Some Radioactive Elements

Element	Half-Life
polonium-214	0.0001 second
radon-222	3.82 days
radium-226	1620 years
uranium-238	4 500 000 000 years

22-1 Detailed information concerning this Activity can be found in the Teacher's Guide at the front of this book.

ACTIVITY *Can you make a model to show radioactive decay?*

Obtain a square or rectangular box. Mark an X on one side of the box, Figure 22-12. Place exactly 100 kernels of corn in the box. Put the lid on the box, hold it level, and shake. Remove the lid. Pick out all the kernels that point toward the marked side of the box. Assume that these kernels are atoms that have decayed. Count these kernels and take them out of the box. How many undecayed kernels are still in the box? Record the number of decayed and undecayed kernels. Repeat the procedure and record the number of kernels after each shake.

Describe how your model shows what may occur during radioactive decay.

FIGURE 22-12.

Making Sure

6. You have a ten-gram sample of barium-139. How much would be left after 4 hours and 18 minutes? *1.25 grams*
7. How long does it take for polonium-210 to change into lead-206? *140 days*

22:5 Radiation Detection

Craig Kramer

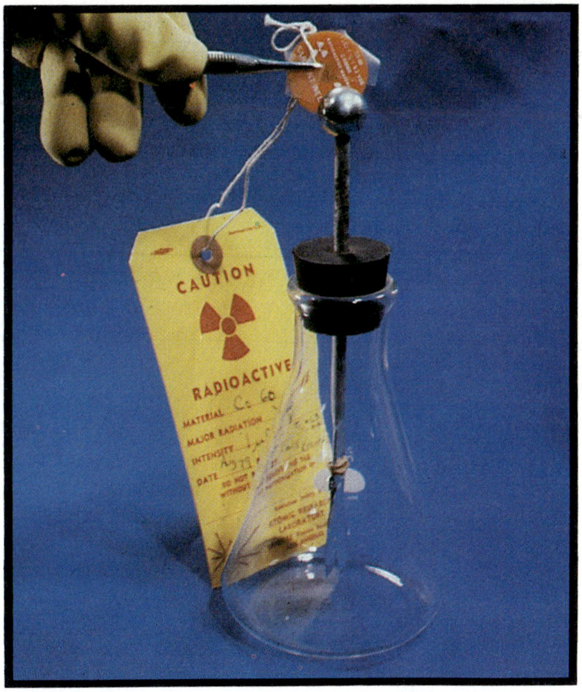

FIGURE 22-13. A radioactive source will discharge an electroscope.

Alpha, beta, and gamma rays cannot be seen, heard, tasted, smelled, or touched. However, it is possible to detect their presence.

One way to detect radioactivity is with an electroscope, Figure 22-13. Like X rays, radioactive radiation produces ions in matter. These ions will discharge a charged electroscope, Section 20:2. The loss of charge is due to the presence of ions produced by the radiation. Ions form in the air around the electroscope and are attracted to the knob of the electroscope.

A negatively-charged electroscope attracts positive ions. The electroscope, depending on its charge, either gains or loses electrons and becomes neutral. As the charge is lost, the leaves of the electroscope drop down. The greater the radiation, the more rapid is the discharge of the electroscope.

What is a cloud chamber?

Radioactivity also can be detected with a cloud chamber. A **cloud chamber** detects nuclear particles which leave tracks in the form of clouds. A cloud track is a line of condensed water vapor formed along a particle's path. It is similar to the vapor trail of a high flying jet.

One kind of cloud chamber contains air supersaturated with water vapor. Supersaturated means the air holds more moisture than normal. As the particle passes through the water vapor, the water condenses. The tiny condensed water drops produce the cloud track. A beta particle forms a long thin cloud track. The track of an alpha particle is shorter and thicker.

A diffusion cloud chamber can be made using a glass jar containing a liquid, Figure 22-14. Alcohol is often used because it vaporizes easily. The jar is set on a piece of dry ice. A bright beam of light is passed through it. The dry ice cools the bottom of the jar. Warmer vapor in the upper portion of the jar descends, cools, and becomes

Kodansha

Dan McCoy from Rainbow

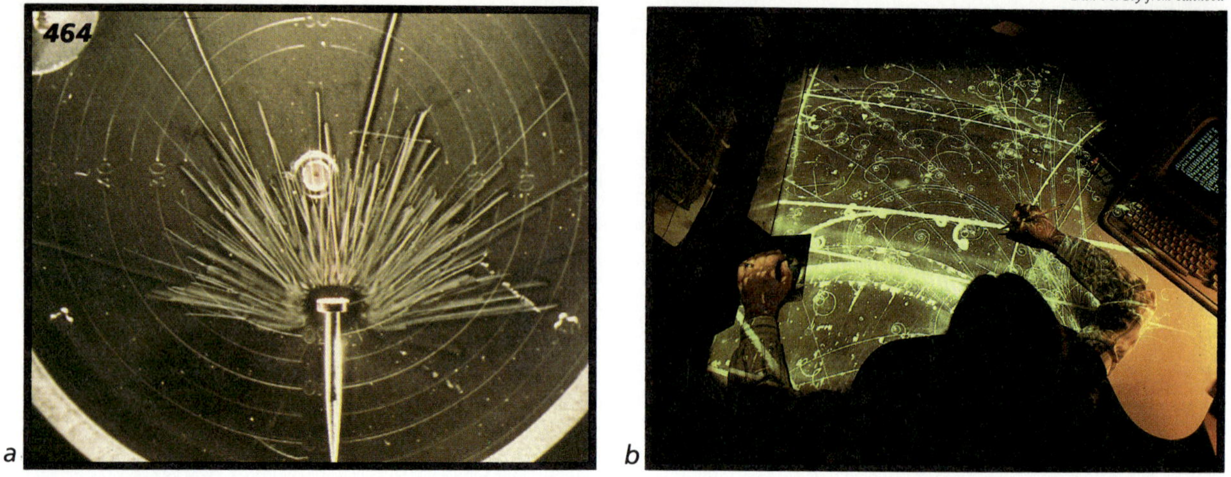

FIGURE 22-14. The tracks of alpha particles are shown in a cloud chamber (a). The tracks of neutrinos, smaller nuclear particles, are shown in (b).

supersaturated. Cloud tracks produced by radiation are visible in the lighted supersaturated vapor.

Charged particles can be detected by a photographic emulsion. An **emulsion** is a thick layer of the coating used in photographic film and print paper. The emulsion contains grains of silver bromide, AgBr, Figure 22-15. The thick layer forming a nuclear emulsion sometimes is called a "frozen cloud chamber." The emulsion is a solid rather than a gas or a liquid.

How is a photographic emulsion used to detect charged particles?

The charged particles change the grains of silver bromide in the emulsion. The effect is like the exposure of film with light when a picture is made. When the emulsion is developed, the path of the nuclear particle appears as a dark track. Nuclear particles travel relatively short distances. Because the emulsion is very dense, nuclear tracks are a few millimeters or less in length. Because they are short, the tracks are studied with a microscope.

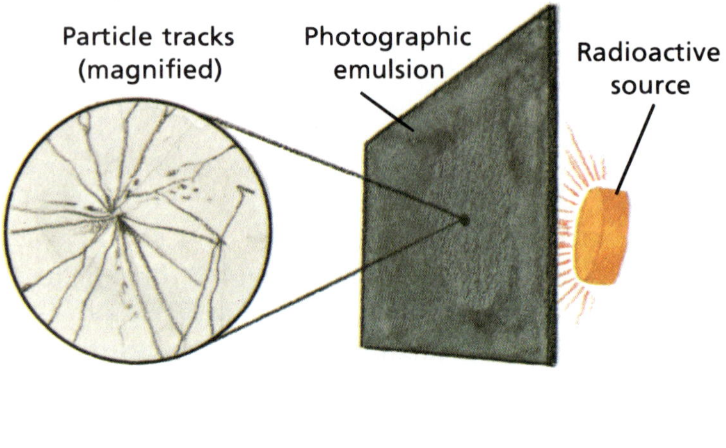

FIGURE 22-15. A photographic emulsion is used to study the tracks of nuclear particles.

Making Sure

8. Why might the track of an alpha particle be shorter than a beta particle? *It has less energy.*
9. Name three ways radiation can be detected.

electroscope, cloud chamber, photographic emulsion

22:6 Radiation Counters

A **Geiger counter** detects radiation through the formation of an electric current. The current is formed in a metal cylinder called a Geiger-Müller tube. The Geiger-Müller tube contains a gas, such as argon or helium, under reduced pressure, Figure 22-16. A thin sheet of mica in the tube forms a "window." Fine tungsten wire is stretched along the axis of the tube. The wire and the metal cylinder are connected to an electric circuit.

Explain how a Geiger counter works.

When radiation passes through the gas in the cylinder, ions are produced. The ions generate an electric current which forms a complete circuit. For example, when an alpha particle enters through the mica window, it frees a few electrons from the gas atoms. The gas atoms become positively charged ions. These positive ions are attracted to the negative wall of the tube (cathode). The free electrons are attracted to the positive wire in the center of the tube (anode). The flow of electrons to the wire produces a flash of current in the external circuit. This current is amplified and fed into recording or counting devices.

FIGURE 22-16. A Geiger counter (a) can determine the intensity of radiation. A highly radioactive source will cause more argon atoms to ionize. The needle on the counter will be deflected further (b).

a

Michael Collier

b

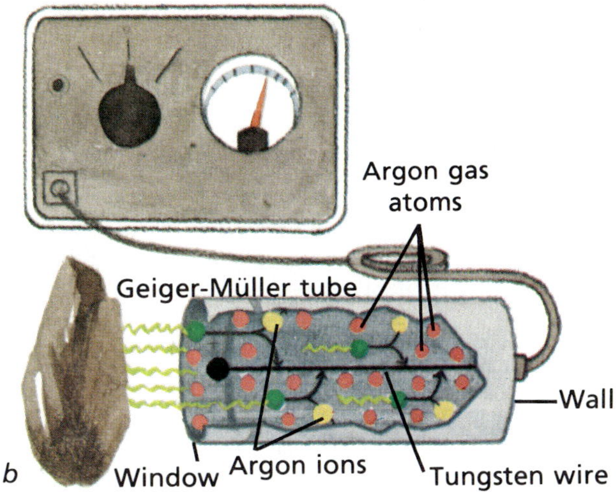

A small lamp or speaker is used as a counting device in a Geiger counter. A flash of the lamp or a click in the speaker occurs when a radioactive particle enters the Geiger-Müller tube. The number of clicks or flashes a Geiger counter makes per unit of time indicates the intensity of the radiation.

Making Sure

10. What are the advantages of using a Geiger counter over an electroscope for detecting radiation?

An electroscope indicates a radioactive material is present; the Geiger counter can show how intense the source of radiation is.

22:7 Fission

What change occurs in nuclear fission?

Radioactive elements can undergo a number of different reactions in the process of forming a stable element. Nuclear fission is one such reaction. **Fission** means to divide. Elements having atomic numbers greater than 90 can undergo fission. Uranium is one such element. In nuclear fission, the nucleus of an atom breaks up. If uranium-235 is bombarded with a beam of neutrons, its nucleus may split into two unequal nuclei. The nucleus will split if it gains a neutron forming uranium-236. The uranium-236 can divide to form many different fission products. In one reaction, barium-144 and krypton-90 are formed. Two neutrons are released.

$$^{235}_{92}\text{U} + ^{1}_{0}\text{n} \rightarrow ^{144}_{56}\text{Ba} + ^{90}_{36}\text{Kr} + 2\,^{1}_{0}\text{n}$$

Uranium-236 can also divide to produce other products. Note in each case different numbers of neutrons are produced.

$$^{235}_{92}\text{U} + ^{1}_{0}\text{n} \rightarrow ^{90}_{37}\text{Rb} + ^{144}_{55}\text{Cs} + 2\,^{1}_{0}\text{n}$$

$$^{235}_{92}\text{U} + ^{1}_{0}\text{n} \rightarrow ^{87}_{35}\text{Br} + ^{146}_{57}\text{La} + 3\,^{1}_{0}\text{n}$$

$$^{235}_{92}\text{U} + ^{1}_{0}\text{n} \rightarrow ^{72}_{30}\text{Zn} + ^{160}_{62}\text{Sm} + 4\,^{1}_{0}\text{n}$$

Fission in uranium atoms may result in a chain reaction. A nuclear chain reaction is a series of rapid nuclear fissions. A small sample of uranium contains billions of

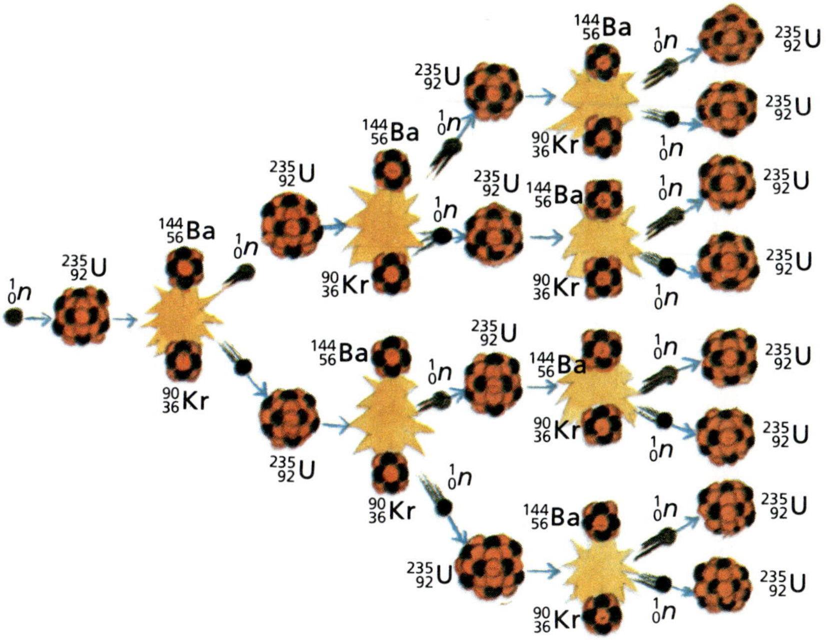

FIGURE 22-17. Each uranium fission releases two neutrons in the chain reaction.

atoms. When one uranium-235 nucleus is split by a neutron, it releases two neutrons. The two neutrons are used to split two more uranium nuclei. Each nucleus sends out two more neutrons. The neutrons are captured by four more nuclei, causing them to split. The fission of nuclei and release of neutrons becomes a chain reaction. In a chain reaction, billions of fission reactions may occur per second.

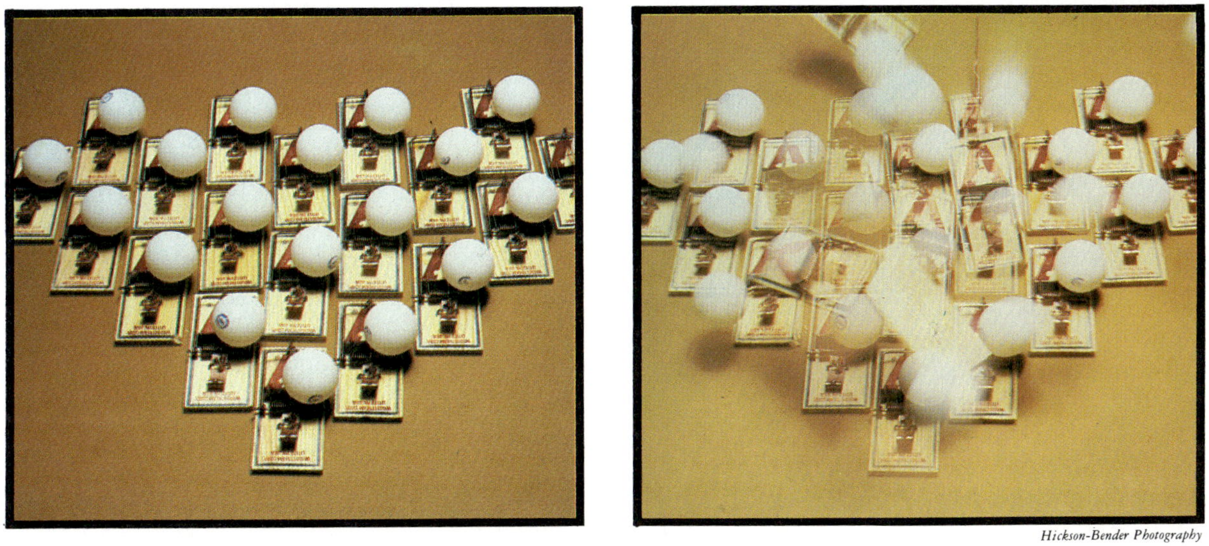

Hickson-Bender Photography

FIGURE 22-18. Mousetraps and table tennis balls can be used as a model to show what occurs during a chain reaction.

22:8 Fusion

How is nuclear fusion different from fission?

Another important reaction that radioactive elements can undergo is fusion. **Fusion** occurs when two nuclei are blended together to form one nucleus. A light element such as hydrogen can undergo fusion. Nuclear fusion is the opposite of nuclear fission. Elements with small masses combine to form elements with larger masses.

Ordinary hydrogen and its isotopes are the raw materials used for nuclear fusion. Deuterium is an isotope of hydrogen with one proton and one neutron in its nucleus. Tritium is an isotope of hydrogen with one proton and two neutrons in its nucleus. Tritium is expensive and scarce. However, the supply of deuterium is almost unlimited. It occurs naturally in water. It can be removed by electrolysis.

What conditions are needed for nuclear fusion?

For nuclear fusion to occur, temperatures close to one hundred million degrees Celsius must be reached. Nuclear fusion is called a thermonuclear reaction. *Thermo* means heat. At the tremendous temperatures of thermonuclear reactions, atoms as such no longer exist. The atoms lose their electrons and become plasma. Recall that plasma is the fourth state of matter. This state consists of nuclei and free electrons. The nuclei have enough energy to overcome forces of repulsion between them.

FIGURE 22-19. Burning stars are at temperatures high enough for fusion to occur.

California Institute of Technology, Carnegie Institute of Washington

The temperature conditions for fusion exist in the sun and stars. The sun has an internal temperature of about 20 million °C. In the sun, fusion occurs through a complex series of nuclear changes. For example, four hydrogen nuclei are fused into one helium nucleus in a series of steps.

FIGURE 22-20. The fusion of hydrogen is a stepwise process that releases a tremendous amount of energy.

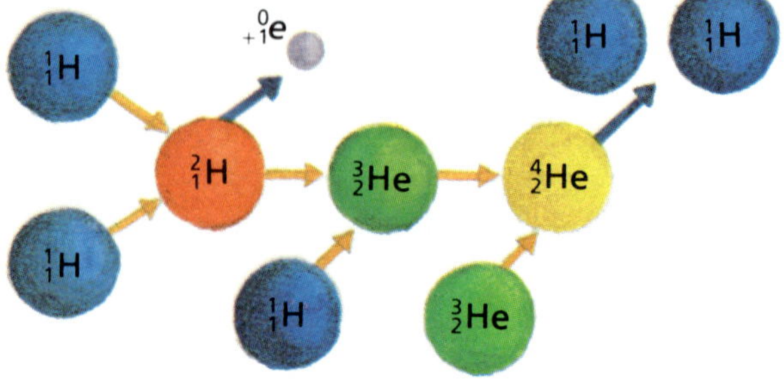

The sun is constantly losing hydrogen as it forms helium. A tremendous amount of energy is released during fusion. The energy comes from matter which is converted to energy. The helium that is formed has a mass almost one percent less than the mass of the four hydrogen atoms. This one percent mass is converted to energy.

Light and radiant energy from nuclear fusion travel 150 million kilometers from the sun to the earth. However, the total energy which reaches the earth is only about one–two billionth of the total energy released by the sun into space.

How do we know that fusion is occurring in the sun and stars? The light given off by the sun can be refracted to form a spectrum. Analysis of this spectrum shows the chemical composition of the sun. Recall that each element has its own characteristic spectrum. The chemical composition of a star can give us some indication of its age. A star which is composed of mostly hydrogen is a young star. As a star gets older its hydrogen is consumed. When some stars die, they produce heavy elements. It is believed that our sun is a second generation star. The sun contains many of the heavy elements present on earth, but in small quantities. Over ninety-nine percent of the sun's mass is hydrogen and helium. Through nuclear reactions, more helium and other heavier elements will be produced. Since these processes occur slowly, the sun is expected to keep burning for another five billion years.

FIGURE 22-21. The spectrum of the sun (a) is used to determine its composition. The spectrum of hydrogen (b) is shown for comparison.

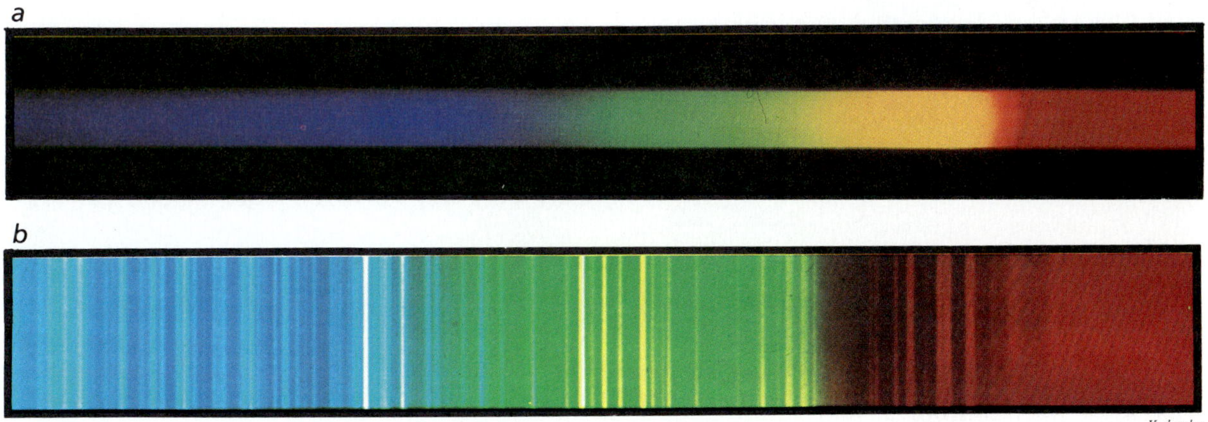

Kodansha

Focus On

Skills

Using Graphic Aids

A chart, table, or picture can provide useful information. The authors use these graphic aids to condense information and to help you visualize some of the ideas in the text. The following activities will help acquaint you with some of the graphic aids found in this chapter.

Use Table 22-1 to answer the following questions:

1. What type of elements are listed? *radioactive*
2. What is the atomic number of radium? *88*
3. Which elements have an atomic mass of 257? *lawrencium, rutherfordium*

Use Table 22-2 to answer the following questions:

1. Does the table list all radioactive isotopes? *no*
2. What particles determine the atomic mass number of an element? *protons and neutrons*
3. What is another name for the isotope tritium? *hydrogen*

Use Figure 22-3, the Sea of Instability, to answer the following questions:

1. For light elements, when is the nucleus stable? *when the ratio of protons to neutrons is 1:1*
2. What symbol is used in the picture to show the stable elements? the unstable elements? *orange green*
3. Do the unstable elements usually have more protons or neutrons? *neutrons*

Use Figure 22-8 to answer the following questions:

1. How many half-lives are shown for barium-139? *3*
2. What is the total time that has elapsed in the picture? *3 × 86 minutes*
3. How does the mass of barium-139 change during each half-life? *cut in half*

Use Figure 22-9 to answer the following questions:

1. What process is shown in the picture? *uranium decay*
2. How long does it take for thorium to change to proactinium? *24.1 days*
3. How many times does a lead isotope appear during the decay process? *three times*
4. What two radioactive particles are released during the decay process? *alpha and beta*

Use Figure 22-10 to answer the following questions:

1. What two elements are pictured in these graphs? *radon and radium*
2. What is the time unit for the first graph? *days*
3. Which of the two elements decays at a faster rate? *radon—shorter half-life*

Use Figure 22-17 to answer the following questions:

1. What is the process shown in the picture? *uranium fission*
2. What particle starts the reaction? *neutron*
3. What particle is split during fission? *uranium-236*
4. What are the products of the fission? *barium-144 and krypton-90*

Use Figure 22-20 to answer the following questions:

1. How many hydrogen nuclei ($^{1}_{1}H$) are required to make $^{3}_{2}He$? *3*
2. If two $^{3}_{2}He$ are needed for the final product, how many total hydrogen nuclei ($^{1}_{1}H$) are used? *6*
3. How many hydrogen nuclei ($^{1}_{1}H$) are produced? *2*
4. What is the net number of hydrogen nuclei that are needed to make one helium nucleus ($^{4}_{2}He$)? *4* (Subtract your answer to question 3 from your answer to question 2.)

Points to Remember

1. Nuclear radiation is released by nuclei of radioactive elements. *22:1*
2. Many radioactive nuclides occur in nature, others are made in the laboratory or in nuclear reactors. *22:2*
3. An alpha particle is a helium nucleus containing two protons and two neutrons. It has a positive charge. *22:3*
4. A beta particle is a high-speed electron emitted from a nucleus. It can have positive or negative charge. *22:3*
5. Gamma rays are high energy photons that pass through most substances. *22:3*
6. Half-life is a measure of the rate of decay for a radioactive element. *22:4*
7. Radiation can be detected with an electroscope, Geiger counter, cloud chamber, and nuclear emulsion. *22:5, 22:6*
8. X rays and nuclear radiation can produce ions in matter. *22:6*
9. Fission is the division of heavier atoms into two nuclei of unequal size. *22:7*
10. Fusion is the blending of two light nuclei to form one element. *22:8*

Words to Use

Write a sentence in which you correctly use each of the following words or terms.

alpha particle	gamma ray	nuclear fission
beta particle	Geiger counter	nuclear fusion
cloud chamber	half-life	nuclide
decay	nuclear emulsion	radioactive isotope
		radioactivity

Questions for Review

Do not write in this book.

A. True or False *Have the students rewrite the false statements to make them correct.*

Determine whether each of the following sentences is true or false.

F **1.** A uranium atom has an ~~equal~~ *unequal* number of protons and neutrons in its nucleus.

F **2.** The changing of uranium to lead is an example of atomic ~~fusion.~~ *decay*

F **3.** A beta particle is actually a ~~hydrogen nucleus~~ positive or negative electron.

F **4.** A beta ray has ~~no~~ positive or negative charge.

T **5.** The mass of a helium nucleus is the same as the total mass of two protons plus two neutrons.

F **6.** Carbon-14 has ~~a stable~~ an unstable nucleus.

T **7.** Fission is the splitting of the nucleus of an atom.

T **8.** Radiation can be detected with an electroscope.

T **9.** Uranium-238 is more stable than radium-226.

F **10.** The ~~longer~~ shorter the half-life, the more radioactive the isotope.

B. Multiple Choice

Choose the word or phrase that correctly completes each of the following sentences.

1. For light elements, as the proton-neutron ratio approaches one, the stability of a nucleus *(increases, decreases, remains the same).*
2. *(Lead, Aluminum, Copper)* is the best shield against radiation.
3. A fluorescent screen glows when it is exposed to *(heat, light, radiation).*
4. A particle containing two protons and two neutrons is a(n) *(alpha, beta, gamma)* particle.
5. A helium nucleus is a(n) *(alpha particle, beta particle, gamma ray).*
6. During nuclear fission, the mass of uranium *(increases, decreases, remains the same).*
7. An element found in the decay series of uranium is *(hydrogen, oxygen, carbon, lead).*
8. Two or more nuclei *(split, unite, decay)* in nuclear fusion.
9. The particles in a nucleus are held together by *(charge, gravity, nuclear forces).*
10. Lead-206 is a(n) *(stable, unstable)* isotope.

C. Completion

Complete each of the following sentences with a word or phrase that will make the sentence correct.

1. A nuclear chain reaction is produced when a uranium-235 nucleus is split by a(n) neutron.

2. Matter exists in the *plasma* state at millions of °C.
3. A(n) *chain reaction* is a series of rapid nuclear fissions.
4. Uranium finally becomes *lead* in the nuclear decay series.
5. Uranium must be bombarded by *neutrons* in order for a chain reaction to begin.
6. A beta particle can have a *positive or negative* charge.
7. The half-life of a radioactive element is the amount of *time* it takes for *one-half* of the atoms in a sample to decay.
8. The cloud tracks in a cloud chamber are produced in a(n) *supersaturated* mixture of liquid vapor in air.
9. Silver bromide is a chemical in the photographic *emulsion* used to detect radioactivity.
10. A(n) *Geiger counter* is a radiation detector in which an electric current is produced by alpha and beta particles.

D. How and Why *Detailed answers to these questions are given in the Teacher's Guide at the front of this book.*

1. Why does a Geiger counter click when it is near radioactive material?
2. What are the properties of alpha rays, beta rays, and gamma radiation?
3. What are some common uses of radioactive isotopes?
4. How can you tell if an element is stable or radioactive?
5. Explain how nuclear fission is different from nuclear fusion.

More Ideas to Explore

1. Find out how radiation is used to treat diseases. Make a report to your class.
2. Read a biography of Marie Curie which describes her discovery of radium.
3. Look up information about recent research on the plasma state of matter. Make a report to your class.

Readings to Discover

Ardley, Neil, *Atoms and Energy.* NY: F. Watts, 1976.

Grosswirth, Marvin, "What Is a Health Physicist?" *Science Digest,* July 1979, pp. 49-53.

Halacy, Dan, *Nuclear Energy.* NY: F. Watts, 1978.

As the price of fossil fuels increases, many people are turning to other sources of energy. The solar home in the picture makes use of energy from the sun. However, solar energy has some disadvantages. As you read the chapter, list the advantages and disadvantages of the energy sources discussed.

J. Webber/Tom Stack & Associates

Alternative Energy Resources

23

Chapter 23 contains descriptive material on some energy alternatives in use today. The advantages and disadvantages of each are presented with a concluding discussion on ways of conserving energy. See the Teacher's Guide at the front of this book for additional teaching strategies for this chapter.

23:1 Fossil Fuels

GOAL: *You will learn other ways energy can be produced to conserve fossil fuel resources.*

Name three fossil fuels.

About ninety-five percent of the total United States energy needs are met by fossil fuels. Coal, crude oil, and natural gas are **fossil fuels.** These materials are called fossil fuels because they are the remains of plants and animals that lived a long time ago. Gasoline and fuel oil are both obtained from crude oil. Fuel oil, natural gas, and coal are the main fuels used to heat buildings, generate electricity, and transport people and objects.

About ninety-three percent of the world's fuel reserve is coal. Coal is obtained from mines. Coal releases about two times as much energy as wood when burned, Table 10-4. Most of the matter in coal is carbon. Sulfur present in coal forms poisonous sulfur oxides when the coal is burned. These sulfur oxides and smoke cause air pollution.

Crude oil is another name for petroleum. This black, thick liquid is obtained from wells. Crude oil is a mixture of hydrocarbons. Much of our crude oil comes from wells in the United States. A large supply also comes from other countries that form the *Organization of Petroleum Exporting Countries* (OPEC). Crude oil provides about forty-two percent of all the energy used in the United States. Burning of gasoline and other fuels obtained from crude oil causes air pollution. The pollution results from the release of unburned hydrocarbons and carbon monoxide.

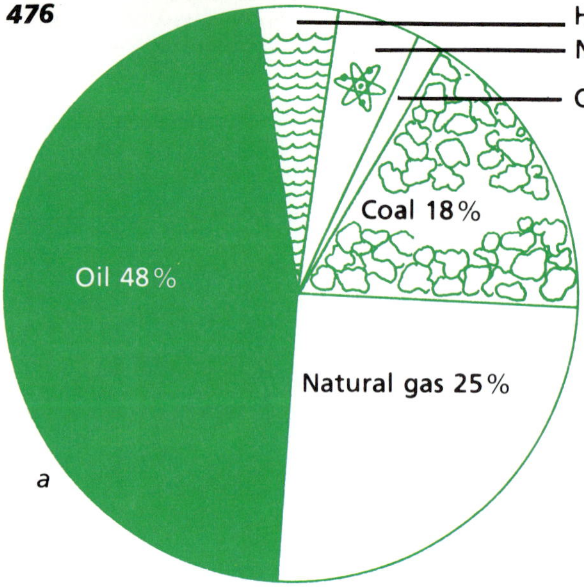

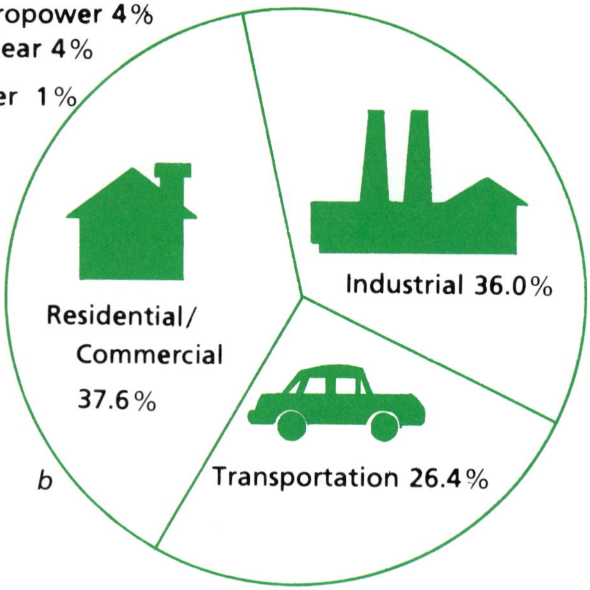

FIGURE 23-1. Graph (a) shows our major energy resources. Graph (b) shows how these resources are used.

What is natural gas and why is it a "clean" fuel?

Natural gas is methane, a hydrocarbon with the formula CH_4. Almost all the natural gas burned in the United States is used for cooking, heating, and producing electricity. One characteristic of natural gas is that it can be pumped through pipes from wells to places where it is used. Also, it is a "clean fuel," meaning it produces little air pollution. Natural gas can be shipped in liquid form, called LNG. LNG is short for liquefied natural gas. When cooled and compressed to form a liquid, the volume of the gas becomes 1/600 of its original size.

23-1 Detailed information concerning this Activity can be found in the Teacher's Guide at the front of this book.

ACTIVITY *What kind of energy is used in your home?*

Make a list of all the ways energy is used in your home. Next to each item on the list write down the kind of energy used. What kind of fuel is used to produce each kind of energy?

Making Sure

1. Fuels contain chemical energy. What is the chemical change that converts chemical energy to mechanical energy you can use to do work? *burning*
2. List the advantages and disadvantages to using coal, oil, and natural gas for fuel. *See the Teacher's Guide.*

23:2 Solar Energy

Solar energy is radiation from the sun. It has been used for centuries to dry foods and evaporate water. A greenhouse can be used to trap solar energy. Today, solar energy is used for heating water in many homes. Solar energy systems are also being used for heating and cooling the inside of buildings. Spacecraft use power from batteries that are charged with electricity produced by solar energy.

Tom Meyers/Tom Stack & Associates

FIGURE 23-2. Mirrors can be used to concentrate the energy from the sun.

Radiation from the sun is spread out. Under the best conditions, only about 1.2 watts per square meter of solar radiation hits the earth's surface. It takes about fifty times this amount of power to light fully a 60-watt lamp. Large curved mirrors are often used to collect the sunlight and focus it in a small area.

How can solar energy be collected?

Solar energy systems must have a means of storing energy for times when there is no sunlight. One storage method is to heat water, rocks, or gravel in a storage container. Another method is to use a photoelectric cell that converts the sun's rays into electricity. The electricity is then used to charge a storage battery. However, photoelectric cells are expensive to make. New discoveries may someday make the cost of the cells lower and thereby increase their use.

FIGURE 23-3. Passive solar homes are designed to collect sunshine through windows and heat absorbing materials such as water. Expensive heat exchangers and pumps are not necessary.

Dan McCoy from Rainbow

The plans for this house show overhangs which block the summer sun. The position of the sun in winter allows the rays to enter the windows to warm the house.

Large areas of glass, facing south, are used to collect sunshine to warm the living spaces. The walls of a passive solar home are usually made of concrete, or large drums filled with water. These materials absorb energy during the day and release it into the living spaces at night.

These large black columns absorb the sun's energy during the day. This energy is radiated throughout the room as the sun goes down.

John Webber/Tom Stack & Associates

Studio Ten

An earth berm at the back of this house protects it from severe winds in winter. Blowing snow is able to move up and over the house.

FIGURE 23-4. The movement of water through the water cycle provides the energy source for hydroelectric power.

23:3 Hydroelectricity

Hydroelectricity is produced from moving water. Usually the water is stored behind a dam on a river. As the water passes through a turbine, it spins the blades of the turbine. Rotation of the blades causes the turbine to turn an electric generator which produces electricity.

How is hydroelectricity produced?

The energy in hydroelectric power depends upon the sun. Sunlight warms water in the sea and evaporates it into the air. This water rises, forms clouds, and falls back to earth as rain or snow. Often the snow and rain fall on mountains. Water in rain or snow at high places has greater potential energy than at sea level. Over time this water will run back to the sea. Along the way it may pass through a hydroelectric power plant on a river or stream. As water flows through a turbine in the power plant, its potential energy is changed to kinetic energy. About one-half of the hydroelectric power in the United States is produced in the states of Washington, Oregon, and California. Here there are many mountains as well as heavy rain and snowfall.

Paul F. McCreary/National Park Service

FIGURE 23-5. A hydroelectric plant harnesses the kinetic energy of moving water.

An important characteristic of hydroelectric power is that it produces almost no pollution. Also, it is lower in cost than other forms of energy. Only about one-tenth of the world's hydroelectric potential has been developed and put to use. One drawback to hydroelectric power is that building a dam or changing the flow of a stream can harm the environment. It can kill fish and destroy plant life.

Making Sure

3. What kind of energy does a generator use to produce electricity? *the kinetic energy of the turbine*
4. Why does hydroelectric power depend on solar energy? *Solar energy evaporates the water which later falls as rain or snow. This water later passes through the power plant.*

23:4 Geothermal Energy

What is geothermal energy?

Inside the earth there is a huge amount of heat. The temperature increases as one goes deeper into a mine sunk into the earth. Also, volcanoes may release lava, a hot liquid rock. Heat within the earth is called geothermal energy.

Geothermal energy is obtained by drilling wells down into a "hot spot." A hot spot is a small rock area in which there is steam or very hot water. The steam or hot water is pumped out and used to generate electricity. Salts and hydrogen sulfide in water pumped up from the earth can cause pollution. However, geothermal power plants do have a good record. They have been in operation in Italy and California for many years without harming the environment.

Michael Collier

FIGURE 23-6. Geysers are a source of geothermal energy.

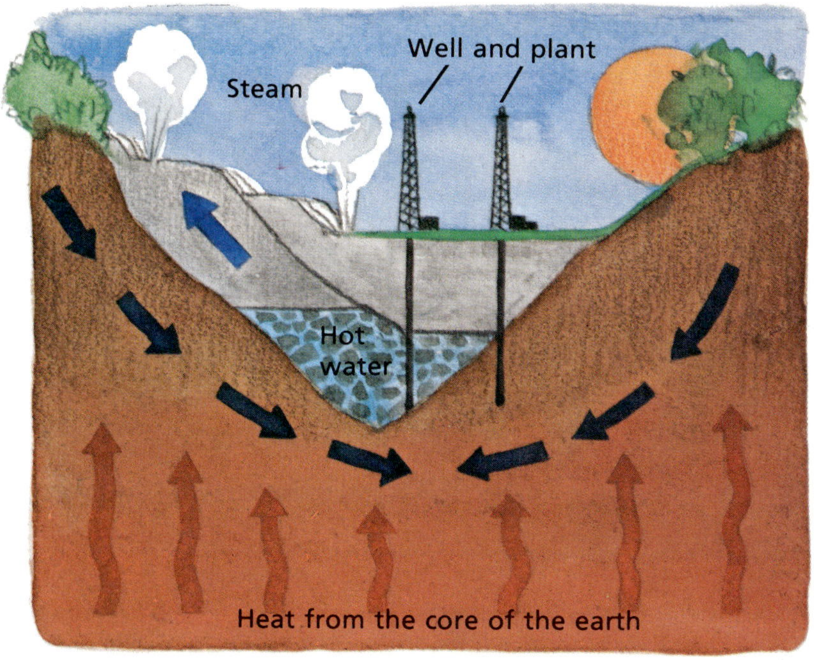

FIGURE 23-7. A geothermal power plant harnesses energy from heat deep inside the earth.

23:5 Nuclear Reactors

A nuclear reactor is a device for controlling and using the energy from a nuclear chain reaction. Inside the reactor is a controlled nuclear fission reaction. Controlled means the rate or speed of the fissions can be changed by the operator. It can be increased, decreased, or stopped completely. Most reactors are constructed in a similar manner. The six parts of a nuclear reactor are (1) fuel, (2) moderator, (3) control rods, (4) coolant, (5) heat exchanger, and (6) safety shields.

Name the six parts of a nuclear reactor.

FIGURE 23-8. Fission reactions release energy in a nuclear reactor (a). Nuclear fuel is being loaded into a fission reactor (b) and a fast breeder reactor (c).

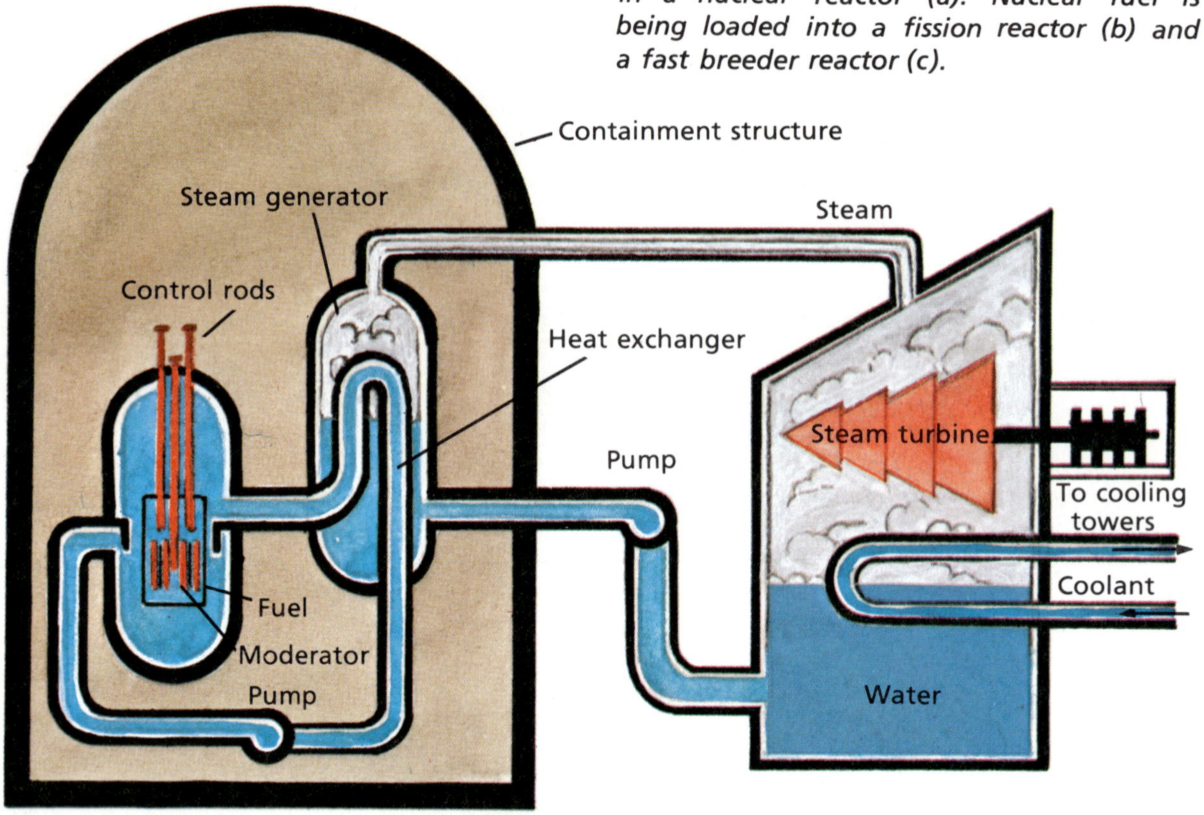

a

b

Dept. of Energy

c

Shostal Associates, Inc.

The fuel in a nuclear reactor is slightly enriched uranium oxide pellets. It is inserted into long rods. Nuclear energy is released from the fuel through a chain reaction.

The moderator is a material which slows the neutrons released during nuclear fission. To keep a chain reaction going, the speed of the neutrons must be reduced. The neutrons must be moving at a speed which allows them to be captured by other nuclei in the fuel. Graphite, a form of carbon, is one type of moderator. It surrounds the cans containing the fuel. Ordinary water, heavy water, and beryllium can also be used as moderators. Heavy water contains a heavier isotope of hydrogen rather than ordinary hydrogen.

Control rods regulate the rate of fission in the fuel. They absorb any excess neutrons not required to keep the chain reaction going. Control rods are made of boron or cadmium alloyed with aluminum or steel. These materials absorb neutrons. By pushing the rods into the reactor or pulling them out, the fission rate is controlled. Pushing the rods all the way in stops the fission reactions.

The coolant removes heat energy from the reactor. Examples of coolants are water, carbon dioxide, and liquid metals. Liquid sodium is one kind of metal used as a coolant. As coolant is pumped through spaces in the reactor, it absorbs heat released from fission. The coolant carries the heat to the heat exchanger.

In the heat exchanger, the reactor coolant is forced to flow around pipes containing water. The heat from the coolant changes the water in the pipes to steam. Steam carries the heat away from the reactor to a turbine. In the heat exchanger, the coolant and water which is changed to steam are in separate pipes. They do not mix together.

Safety shields are necessary to protect people from the nuclear radiation produced by a reactor. Nuclear radiation can produce burns, cancer, loss of hair, vomiting, and destruction of blood cells. An overdose can cause death. Strict safety regulations are enforced to protect workers and the general public from the dangers of

Don Parsisson

a

Camera M. D.

b

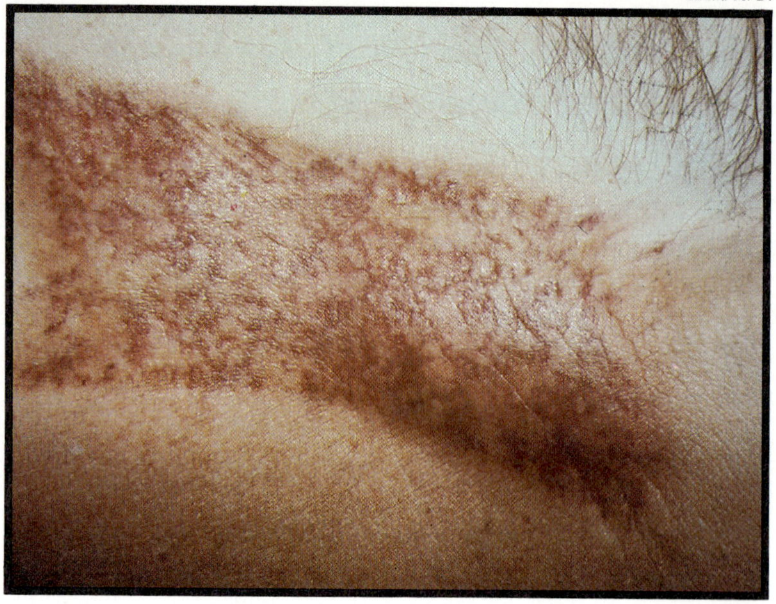

FIGURE 23-9. A radiation badge (a) is worn by these working with radioactive materials. The film inside blackens when exposed to gamma rays. The amount of blackening shows the level of radiation to which the wearer has been exposed. Overexposure to radiation results in radiation burns (b).

radiation. Lead and thick concrete walls are used as shields for reactors.

The steam produced by a nuclear reactor is used to do work. Steam is carried from the heat exchanger to turbines. A steam turbine is a machine with a central shaft connected to large blades. Steam under pressure passes over the blades causing the shaft to rotate. Steam turbines are used to turn electrical generators which produce electricity. A reactor generating one million watts of electric power per year fissions about one gram of fuel per day.

Making Sure

5. A nuclear reactor has a device which can drop the control rods into the reactor in less than a second. Why? *Any nuclear emergency requires people and equipme that can respond immediately to control a chain reactic*

23:6 Breeder Reactors

A **breeder reactor** produces both energy and nuclear fuel. It takes its name from the fact that it can produce more nuclear fuel than it uses. A breeder reactor can start with uranium and produce plutonium. The

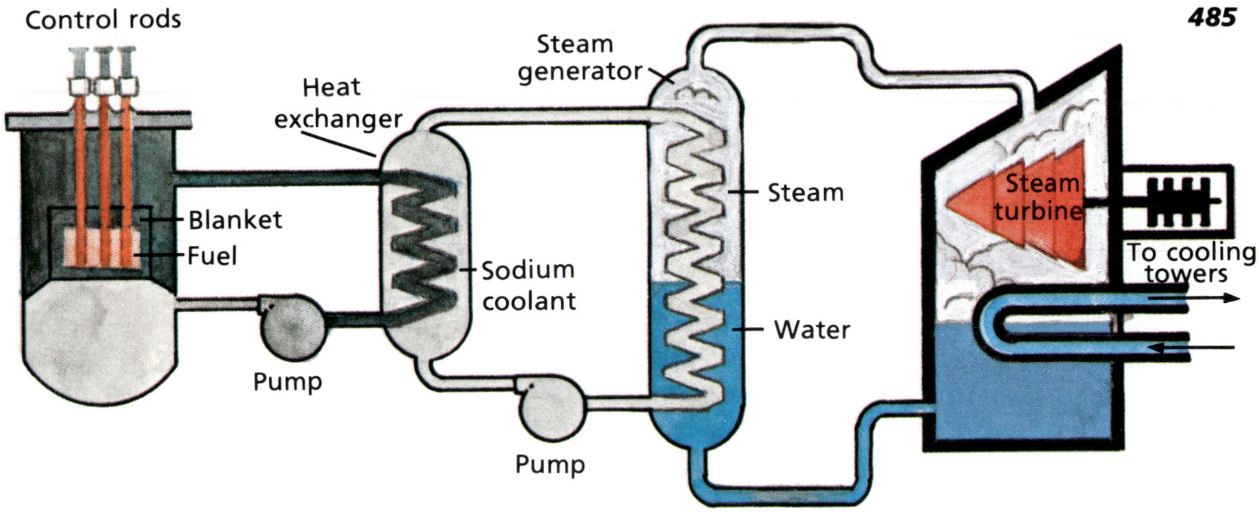

FIGURE 23-10. This breeder reactor uses sodium as a coolant.

plutonium can then be used as a nuclear fuel to generate more nuclear energy.

One kind of breeder reactor is like a standard nuclear reactor. It contains fuel, control rods, and coolant. However, it does not have a moderator. Lacking a moderator, the neutrons released in fission are not slowed down. These high speed neutrons are then used for the breeding reaction. Because it uses high speed neutrons, the reactor is called a "fast" reactor.

How is a breeder reactor different from a standard nuclear reactor?

Fission in a fast reactor releases a large number of neutrons. In a breeder reaction, the average number of neutrons released is greater than the amount absorbed by the fuel. The placement of fuel in the breeder reactor allows the greatest number of neutrons to be captured.

A series of nuclear changes occur as uranium produces or breeds plutonium. Uranium-238 captures a neutron and becomes uranium-239, a heavier isotope. The uranium-239 releases a beta particle and becomes neptunium-239. Neptunium-239 emits a beta particle and changes to plutonium-239.

$$^{238}_{92}U + ^{1}_{0}n \rightarrow ^{239}_{92}U$$
$$^{239}_{92}U \rightarrow ^{239}_{93}Np + ^{0}_{-1}\beta$$
$$^{239}_{93}Np \rightarrow ^{239}_{94}Pu + ^{0}_{-1}\beta$$

Making Sure

6. What part of the uranium atom changes when it becomes a plutonium atom? *the nucleus*
7. What advantage does a breeder reactor have over a standard reactor? *The breeder reactor produces both energy and fuel.*

23:7 Thermonuclear Power

The development of controlled nuclear fusion is being investigated by scientists and engineers in many countries. Since fusion requires such high temperatures, how can a controlled, tiny sun be made in the laboratory?

Experiments with nuclear fusion aim toward fusion of heavy hydrogen nuclei in magnetic bottles. A magnetic field is produced from an electromagnet wound around the tube containing the fusion fuel. High-voltage alternating current heats the fuel to a few million degrees in less than a second. The magnetic fields "pinch" the nuclei together inside the tube. Magnetic pinching keeps the nuclei from the walls of the tube.

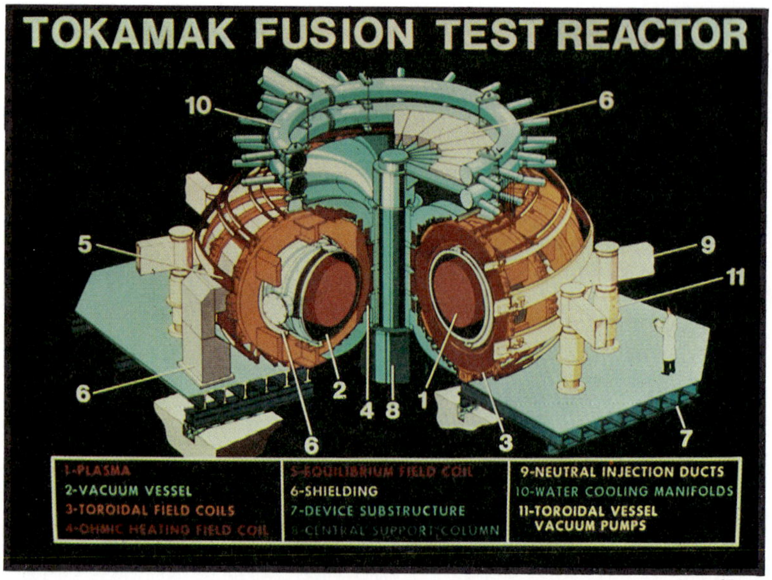

Dept. of Energy

FIGURE 23-11. Fusion reactors are still in the experimental stage. This drawing shows one proposed design.

To make a controlled thermonuclear reaction, scientists must discover how to maintain high temperatures for several seconds. Further, they must learn how to convert the heat energy produced through fusion into electricity. The solution of these problems is a challenge to science and technology. The possible rewards are certainly worth the effort. Fusion of the nuclei in one gram of heavy hydrogen would produce the power generated by burning eight metric tons of coal!

Why is it difficult to produce a controlled nuclear reaction?

FIGURE 23-12. Nuclear fuels yield much more energy per gram than fossil fuels.

23:8 Nuclear Energy and the Environment

What are the advantages in the use of nuclear energy?

Nuclear energy has some advantages over fossil fuels such as coal and oil. The burning of coal and oil can cause air pollution. Nuclear reactors are clean in that they do not add pollutants to the air. Also, a greater amount of energy can be produced from smaller amounts of nuclear fuels.

Nuclear power plants do require huge amounts of water to cool their reactors. If this hot water is dumped into rivers or oceans, thermal pollution may result. The heat can have a harmful effect on fish. To protect the environment, the water must be cooled before it is released. Large cooling towers are built for this purpose.

Dept. of Energy

FIGURE 23-13. Special containers are used in transporting nuclear fuel. These containers must be shock resistant in case an accident were to occur during shipment.

What wastes are produced by a nuclear reactor?

Nuclear reactors produce radioactive wastes. These wastes must be stored safely for thousands of years until the radiation decays. Strong safety measures are taken when storing this material underground. Accidental escape of radioactive wastes could kill plant and animal life. This is one major environmental problem in the use of nuclear energy. Overheating of the core containing the nuclear fuel could result in the release of wastes into the air. However, many mechanical safeguards are used to prevent overheating. Successful operation of nuclear reactors requires that many safeguards be in constant operation.

FIGURE 23-14. Spent nuclear fuel is processed and stored in underground facilities.

Dept. of Energy

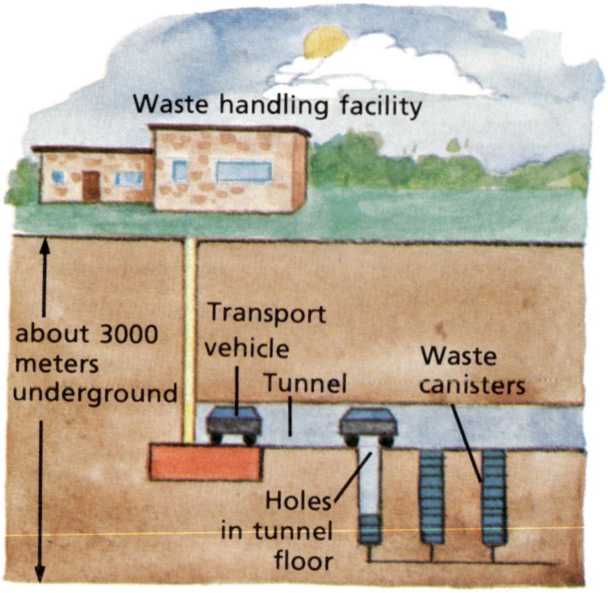

Some scientists believe nuclear fusion may be the best solution to the world's energy problems. Controlled nuclear fusion would provide an unlimited source of energy. The hydrogen used in fusion does not produce radioactive wastes that could pollute the atmosphere.

Making Sure

8. Why is nuclear energy sometimes called "clean energy"? *It does not pollute the atmosphere.*
9. Why do some people object to the building and operation of nuclear power plants?
10. What solutions do you see to the world's energy problems? *Answers will vary.*

The threat of a nuclear accident, problems of nuclear waste disposal, and thermal pollution of water are some reasons for the objections to nuclear energy.

23:9 Conserving Energy

Wise and careful use of a resource is called **conservation.** To conserve energy means not to waste it. Most of the energy we use is wasted and lost into the air as heat, Section 19:6. Fossil fuels are **nonrenewable resources.** When used up, they cannot be replaced. Fossil fuels will probably continue to be our main source of energy for the next 100 years. For this reason, it is important to use them wisely.

What is a nonrenewable resource? Give one example.

Most of the energy wasted in the United States is lost in the burning of gasoline in cars and through heating buildings. One way to save energy is to make cars more fuel efficient. Making engines that burn gasoline more completely with less waste aids conservation. People going to school and work in car pools and buses is an energy saver.

Describe two ways in which energy is wasted.

Another means of saving energy is to keep buildings cooler in the winter (20°C). Insulating homes and other buildings saves fuel by cutting down the heat loss in winter.

Solar and nuclear energy resources reduce our need for fossil fuels. The supply of fossil fuels will last longer if we can use other energy sources. However, until new sources of energy can be developed, our best source of new energy is conservation.

You may wish to show how conserved energy is "new" energy. Estimates are that we could conserve 25% of our new energy needs.

Refer students to Figure 23-15.

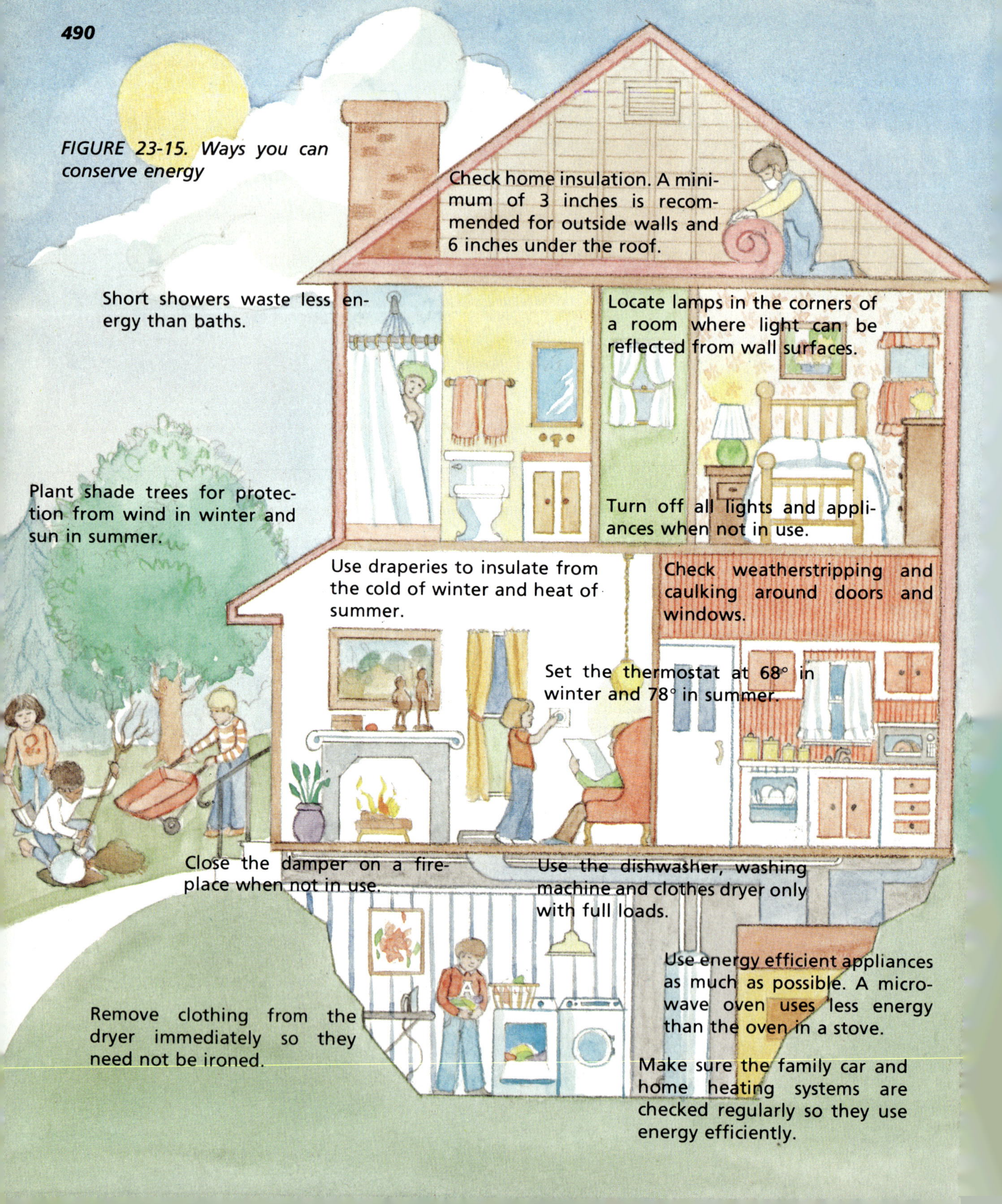

FIGURE 23-15. Ways you can conserve energy

Frontiers
Wind Power

In early times, muscle was the only source of power for people. Then they found that by using animals, more work could be done with less effort. Now we have electric power. Using electricity, we can do many things early humans could not. But, we face a problem. The fuel used to produce more of the electricity is running out. We are now searching for new ways to generate electric power. Wind is one way that is being explored.

As early as the sixth century, wind was used for power. At that time a windmill was used to grind grain into flour. The first windmills were horizontal. They had a vertical center pole that was attached to the grinding stone. Sails were attached to the pole. As the wind blew, the sails turned the center pole. This action turned the stone, grinding the grain.

With the passage of time, improvements were made in the windmill. It became a vertical device. The center pole was horizontal and connected by gears to the stone. The sails were improved, reducing the amount of wind needed to turn them. Vanes were added to the mills to keep them always pointing into the wind. As windmills developed, their power was used to do more than grind grain. One use was to pump water.

In 1890, a windmill was used to produce electricity. However, this idea had several problems. There had to be a fairly strong wind to operate the mill. This limited the choice of locations. Also, since the wind was not constant, the electricity was not constant. As a result other methods were used to produce electricity.

Although these problems still exist, scientists and engineers are learning to solve them. With new designs and lighter materials, windmills that will operate in light winds, can be built. Using large windmills increases the power produced by one mill. Another way to increase power is to use several windmills together. Even though windmills have improved, wind power alone is not enough. Used with other kinds, like solar and coal, wind power can help solve our energy problems.

Points to Remember

1. About ninety-five percent of the energy used in the United States comes from coal, crude oil, and natural gas. 23:1
2. Solar energy can be used to heat water, and to heat and cool buildings. 23:2
3. Moving water is used to generate hydroelectric power. 23:3
4. Geothermal energy is obtained from hot spots in the earth's crust. 23:4
5. Uranium is a major fuel used in nuclear reactors. 23:5
6. A breeder reactor can produce more fuel than it uses. 23:6
7. In a thermonuclear reaction, light elements are fused to form heavier elements. 23:7
8. Use of fuels causes pollution. 23:8
9. By conserving energy, our nonrenewable resources will last longer. 23:9

Words to Use

Write a sentence in which you correctly use each of the following words or terms.

breeder reactor	geothermal energy	nuclear reactor
conservation	hydroelectric power	solar energy
fossil fuel	nonrenewable resource	thermonuclear reaction

Questions for Review

Do not write in this book. Have the students rewrite the false statements to make them correct.

A. True or False

Determine whether each of the following sentences is true or false.

F 1. ~~Nitrogen~~ oxides in coal cause air pollution. Sulfur

T 2. Carbon monoxide is a pollutant.

T 3. Solar energy can be used to produce electricity.

F 4. Most of the hydroelectric power produced in the United States comes from the ~~east~~ coast. west

T 5. Geothermal energy comes from wells.

F **6.** A moderator ~~speeds up~~ a chain reaction. slows

T **7.** Heavy water contains an isotope of hydrogen.

T **8.** Liquid sodium is used as a reactor coolant.

T **9.** A breeder reactor produces radioactive fuel.

F **10.** Nuclear reactors add pollutants to the air. do not

B. Multiple Choice

Choose the word or phrase that correctly completes each of the following sentences.

1. The *(moderator, control rod, coolant)* regulates the fission rate of a reactor.
2. Hydrogen and its isotopes are raw materials for *(nuclear fission, transmutation, nuclear fusion).*
3. Uranium is changed to plutonium in a *(fission, fusion, breeder)* reactor.
4. Hydrogen is changed to helium in a *(fission, fusion, breeder)* reactor.
5. *(Coal, Oil, Natural gas)* forms the greatest part of the world's fuel reserves.
6. The temperature of the earth *(increases, decreases, remains the same)* as you approach its center.
7. A moderator slows *(protons, electrons, neutrons)* in a chain reaction.
8. Control rods absorb *(protons, electrons, neutrons)* in a chain reaction.
9. Nuclear reactors can cause *(thermal, air, noise)* pollution.
10. *(Coal, Oil, Natural gas)* is a clean fuel.

C. Completion

Complete each of the following sentences with a word or phrase that will make the sentence correct.

1. Natural gas is another name for methane.
2. Nuclear fusion occurs in a thermonuclear reaction.
3. The moderator in a nuclear reactor slows down neutrons.
4. A turbine is used to turn an electric generator.

5. A breeder reactor can change uranium to *plutonium*.
6. High speed *neutrons* are used in breeding reactions.
7. Thermonuclear reactions require high *temperatures*.
8. Fossil fuels are *nonrenewable* resources.
9. Most of the matter in coal is *carbon*.
10. Gasoline and fuel oil come from *crude oil (petroleum)*.

Detailed answers to these questions are given in the Teacher's Guide at the front of this book.

D. How and Why

1. Why are the fuel cans in a nuclear reactor made of a substance which is a poor neutron absorber?
2. How can nuclear energy be converted to kinetic energy?
3. What are the advantages of using nuclear power plants to produce energy? What are the disadvantages?
4. How could a nuclear power plant harm the environment?

More Ideas to Explore

1. Obtain information on a career in a field related to the development and use of energy resources. Find out the educational background needed and how to prepare for this field.
2. Obtain information on synthetic fuels, such as gas made from coal.
3. Many scientists oppose the building of breeder reactors. Through library research, find out reasons for their opinion. Make a list of reasons for and against breeder reactors.

Readings to Discover

Asimov, Isaac, "Hydrogen's Magic Wand—Fusion Power." *Science Digest,* September 1979, pp. 28-32.

Gadler, Steve J., and Adamson, Wendy Wriston, *Sun Power: Facts About Solar Energy.* Minneapolis, MN: Lerner, 1978.

Gwynne, Peter, "The Nuclear Power Dilemma: Yes or No?" *Science Digest,* August 1979, pp. 6-10.

Hoke, John, *Solar Energy.* rev. ed., NY: F. Watts, 1978.

Weaver, Kenneth F., "The Promise and Peril of Nuclear Energy." *National Geographic,* April 1979, pp. 459-493.

Appendices

Appendix A

Units of Measurement and the International System (SI)

You will make a great number of measurements in physical science and throughout your life. The common measurements made are those of mass, volume, length, time and temperature. The International System (SI) of measurement is accepted as the standard for measurement throughout most of the world. SI was selected for two reasons: (1) its simplicity; and (2) most countries of the world already use it as their standard. The International System consists of seven base units, Table A-1.

Table A-1

SI Base Units		
Measurement	**Unit**	**Symbol**
length	*meter*	*m*
mass	*kilogram*	*kg*
time	*second*	*s*
electric current	*ampere*	*A*
temperature	*kelvin*	*K*
amount of substance	*mole*	*mol*
intensity of light	*candela*	*cd*

Larger and smaller units of measurement in SI are obtained by multiplying or dividing the base unit by some multiple of ten. The new unit is named by adding a prefix to the name of the base unit. For example, 1/10 or .1 meter is a decimeter.

Table A-2

Common SI Prefixes					
Prefix	**Symbol**	**Multiplier**	**Prefix**	**Symbol**	**Multiplier**
	Greater than 1			*Less than 1*	
Mega-	*M*	*1 000 000*	*deci-*	*d*	*.1*
kilo-	*k*	*1 000*	*centi-*	*c*	*.01*
hecto-	*h*	*100*	*milli-*	*m*	*.001*
deka-	*da*	*10*	*micro-*	*μ*	*.000 001*

All other measurement units are combinations of the base units, or considered supplementary units. For example, Celsius temperature is a supplementary unit.

Table A-3

Units Derived from SI Base Units			
Measurement	**Unit**	**Symbol**	**Expressed in Base Units**
energy	joule	J	$kg \cdot m^2/s^2$
force	newton	N	$kg \cdot m/s^2$
frequency	hertz	Hz	$1/s$
potential difference	volt	V	$kg \cdot m^2/A \cdot s^3$ (W/A)
power	watt	W	$kg \cdot m^2/s^3$ (J/s)
pressure	pascal	Pa	$kg/m \cdot s^2$ ($N \cdot m$)
quantity of electric charge	coulomb	C	$A \cdot s$

Table A-4

Frequently Used Units	
Length	
1 centimeter (cm)	= 10 millimeters (mm)
1 meter (m)	= 100 centimeters (cm)
1 kilometer (km)	= 1000 meters (m)
Volume	
1 liter (L)	= 1000 milliliters (mL)
	= 1000 cubic centimeters (cm^3)
Mass	
1 gram (g)	= 1000 milligrams (mg)
1 kilogram (kg)	= 1000 grams (g)

The temperature scale used most in science class rooms is the Celsius scale (°C), which has 100 equal graduations between the freezing temperature (0°C) and the boiling temperature of water (100°C). The following relationship exists between the Celsius and kelvin temperature scales:

$$K = °C + 273$$

Appendix B
Laboratory Techniques

Hickson-Bender Photography/Ohio Wesleyan Univ.

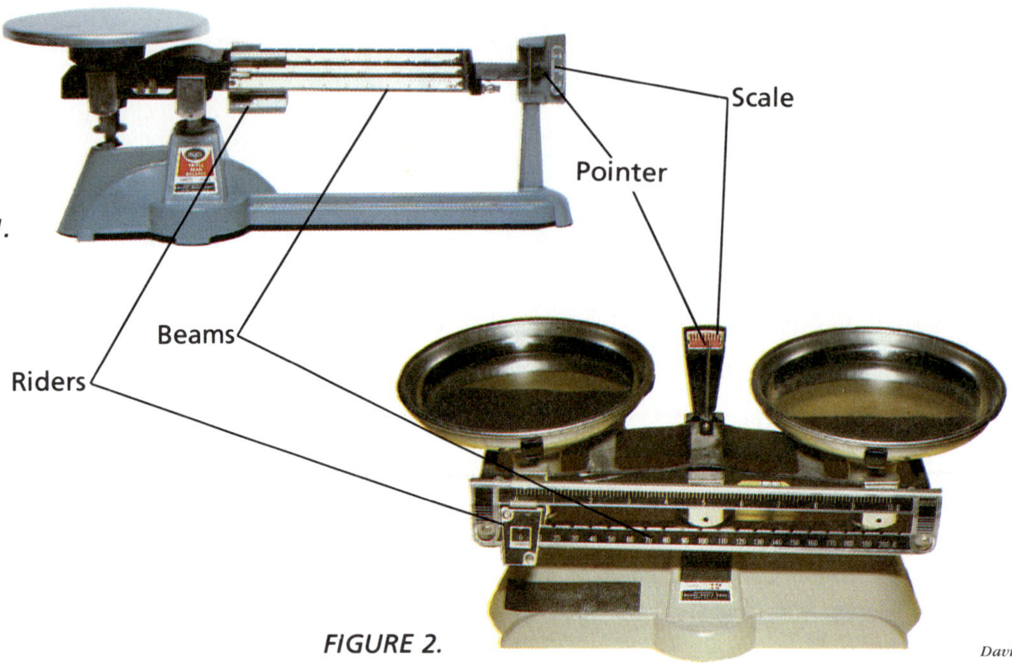

FIGURE 1.

FIGURE 2.

David M. Dennis

B:1 Using the Balance

There are various types of laboratory balances. The balance you use may look somewhat different from the ones in Figures 1 and 2; however all beam balances have some common features.

The following steps should be followed in using the balance.

1. Before determining the mass of any substance slide all of the riders back to the zero point. Check to see that the pointer swings freely along the scale. You do not have to wait for the pointer to stop at the zero point. The beam should swing an equal distance above and below the zero point. Use the adjustment screw to obtain an equal swing of the beams, if necessary. You should always repeat this procedure to "zero" the balance everytime you use it.

2. Never put a hot object directly on the balance pan. Any dry chemical which is to be massed should be placed on waxed paper or in a glass container. **Never pour chemicals directly on the balance pan.**

3. Once you have placed the object to be massed on the pan, move the riders along the beams beginning with the largest mass first. If the beams are notched, make sure all riders are in a notch before you take a reading. Remember the pointer does not have to stop swinging, but the swing should be an equal distance above and below the zero point on the scale.

4. The mass of the object wil be the sum of the masses indicated on the beams. For example

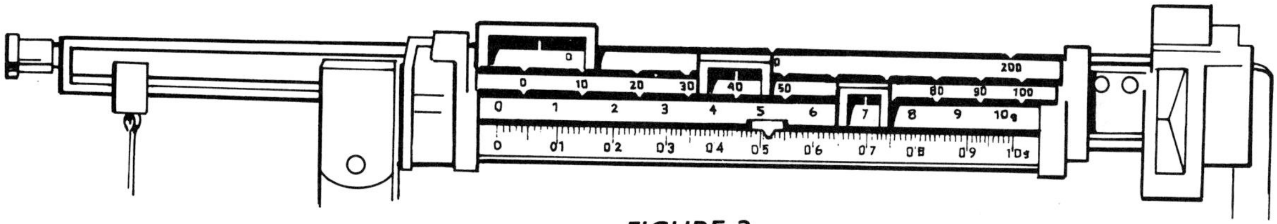

FIGURE 3.

The mass of the object would be read as 47.52 grams.

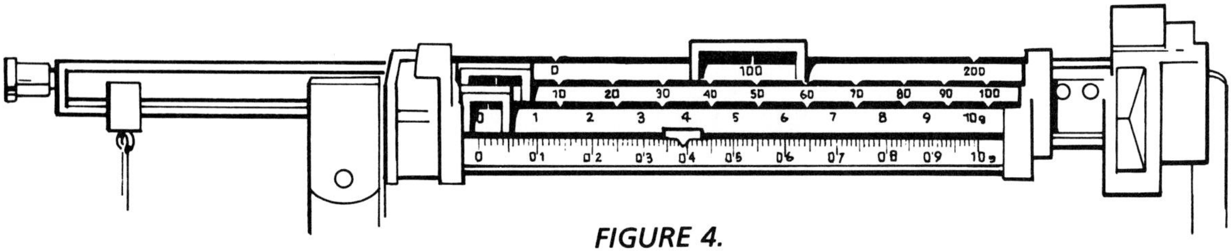

FIGURE 4.

The mass of the object would be read as 100.39 grams.

B:2 Adjusting the Flame on a Laboratory Burner

Most laboratory burners are made the same. There is an inlet for gas and a vent or valve for the adjustment of air which is mixed with the gas, Figure 5. For maximum heat the air-gas mixture must be correct, and the object to be heated should be placed just above the pale blue part of the flame, Figure 6.

To light the burner, hold a lighted match or a striker next to the barrel of the burner and turn on the gas. After lighting the burner, adjust the air vent until a light blue cone appears in the center of the flame. If the flame rises from the burner or appears to "blow out" after lighting, reduce the supply of gas.

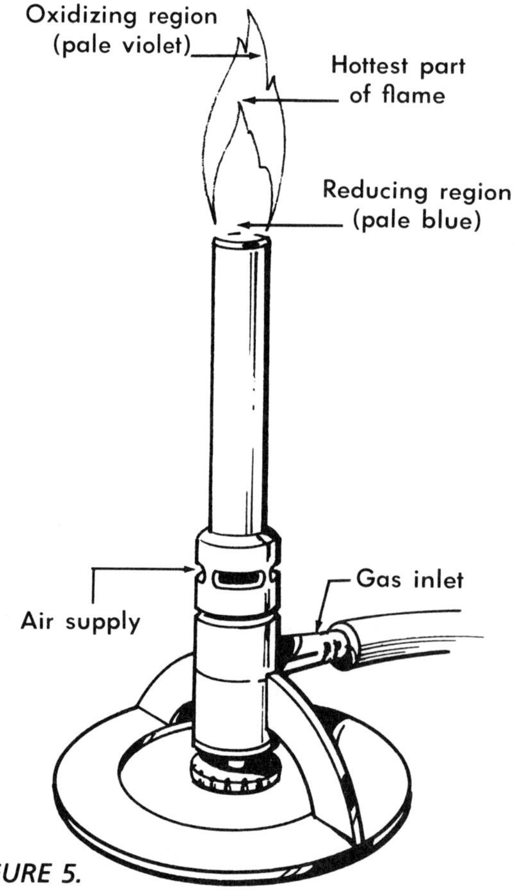

FIGURE 5.

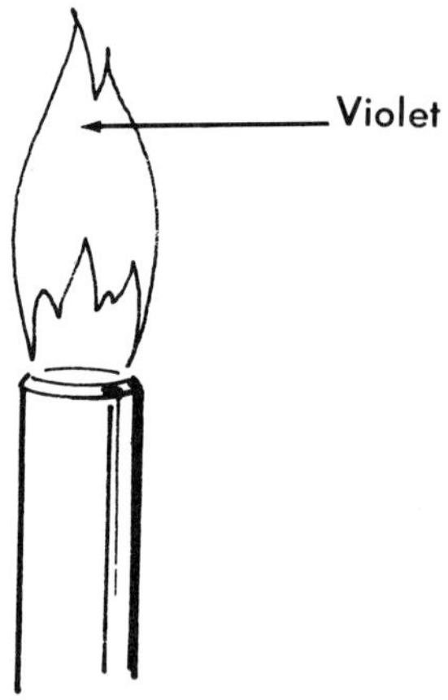

FIGURE 6.

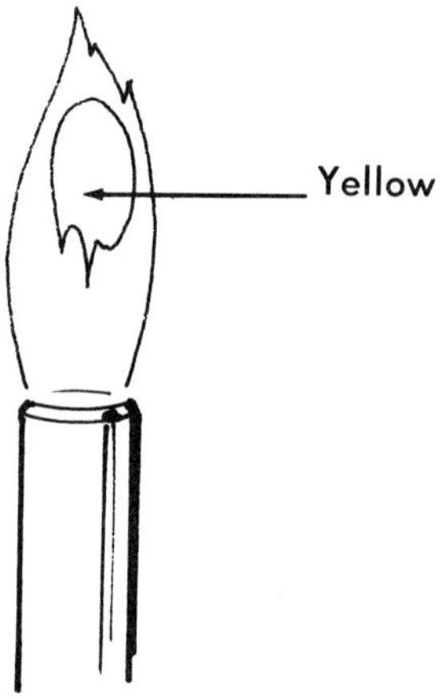

FIGURE 7.

B:3 Filtering Techniques

It is often necessary to separate a precipitate from a liquid. The most common process of separation used in most laboratories is filtration. The solution is filtered through folded filter paper to catch any precipitate that has not settled to the bottom of the beaker, Figure 8.

FIGURE 8.

Craig Kramer

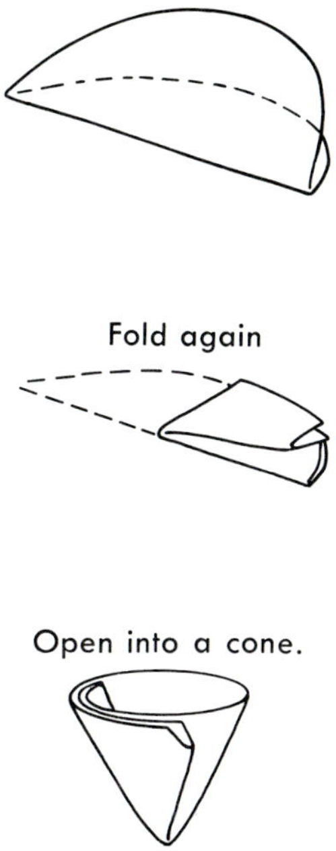

Folding a piece of filter paper.

FIGURE 9.

B:4 Working with Glass Tubing

When setting up apparatus for various activities, it is often necessary to use glass tubing. Figures 10-12 show the proper techniques to be used to cut, fire polish, and bend glass tubing. **CAUTION:** Glass cools slowly. Do not touch glass that has been heated unless sufficient time has been allowed for cooling.

Cutting Glass Tubing

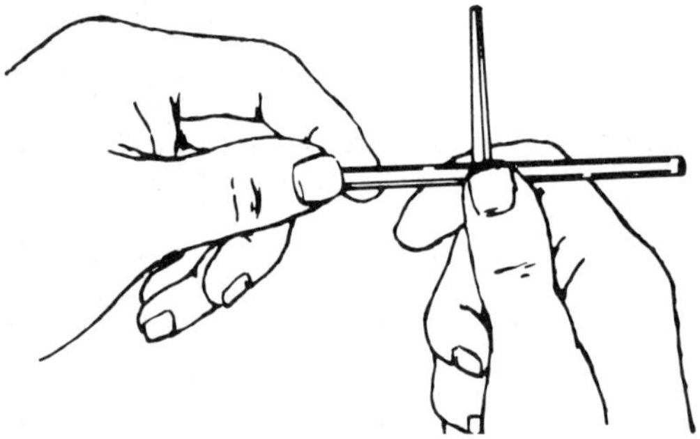

Score the tube once with a triangular file.

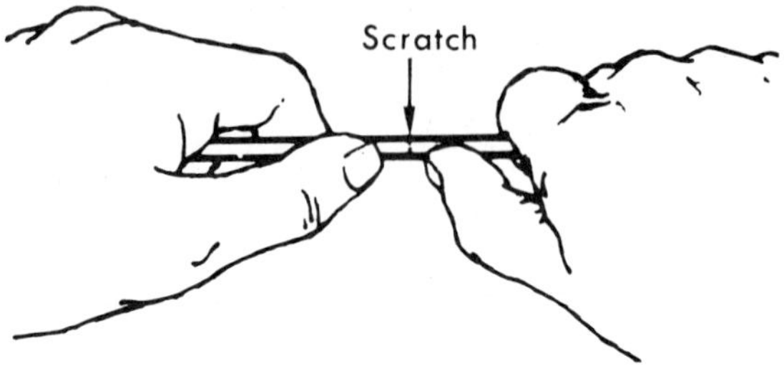

Place your thumbs opposite the scratch.

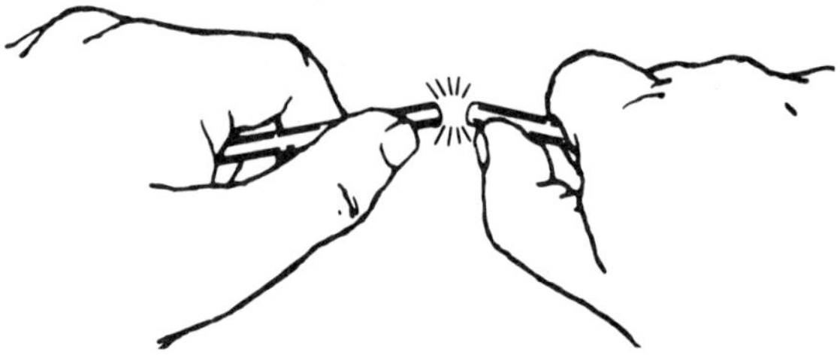

Apply pressure and bend the tubing with a quick motion.

FIGURE 10.

Fire Polishing Glass Tubing

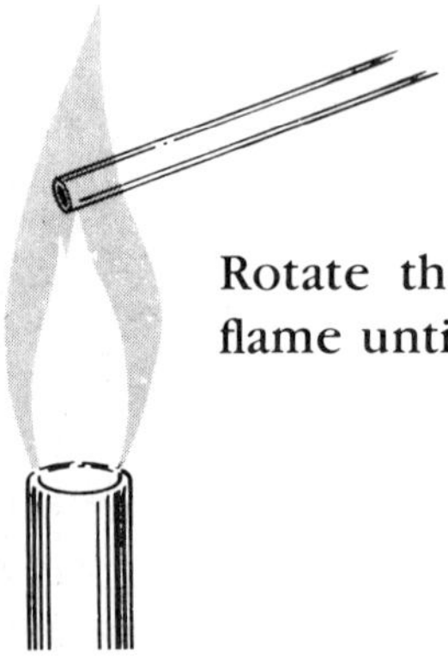

Rotate the tube in a laboratory burner flame until the edges are rounded.

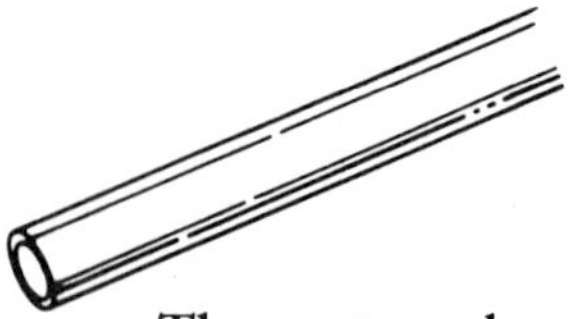

The cut end

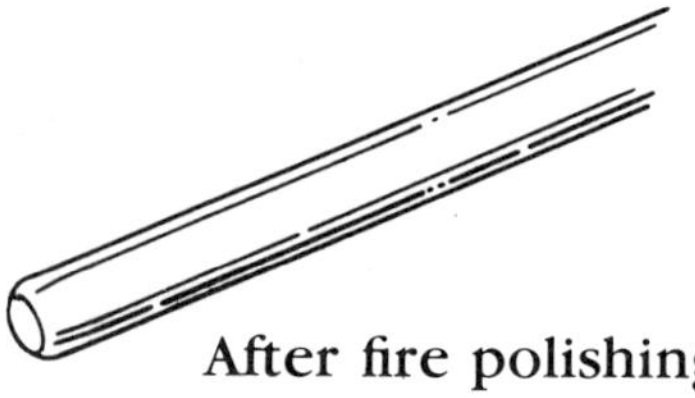

After fire polishing

FIGURE 11.

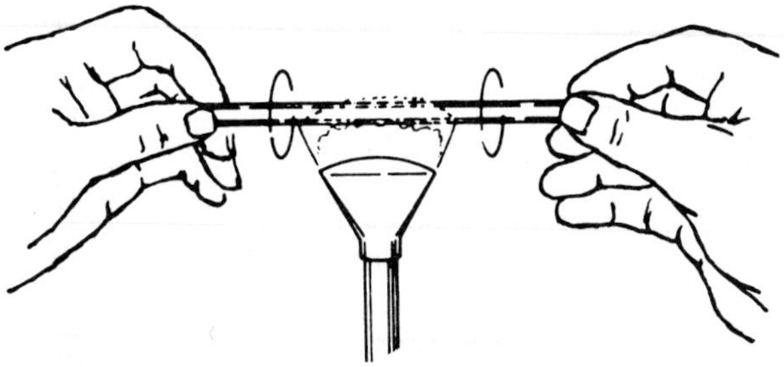

Use a wing tip on the laboratory burner. Roll the tube back and forth in the flame until the glass becomes soft.

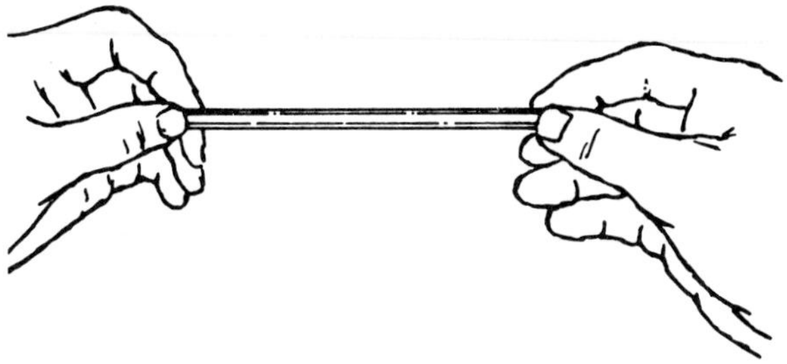

Remove from the flame and hold for a few seconds until the heat is evenly distributed.

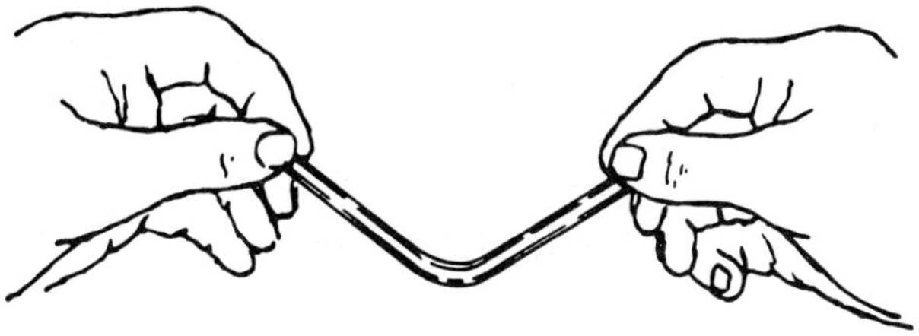

Bend quickly and hold until the glass hardens.

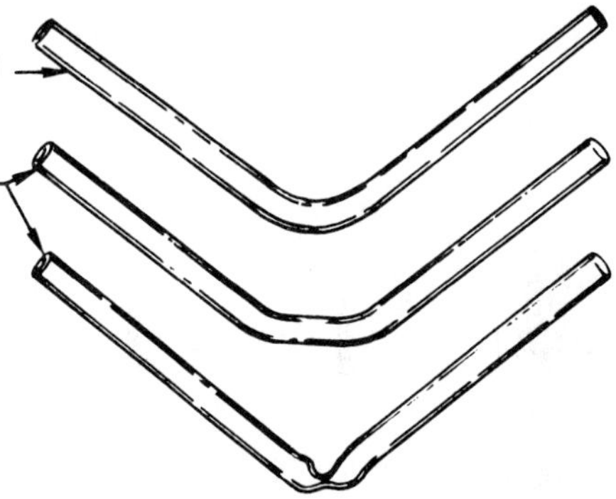

FIGURE 12.

Inserting Glass Tubing into a Rubber Stopper

FIGURE 13.

Begin by lubricating the tip of the glass tubing with water, glycerol, or some other suitable substance your teacher provides.

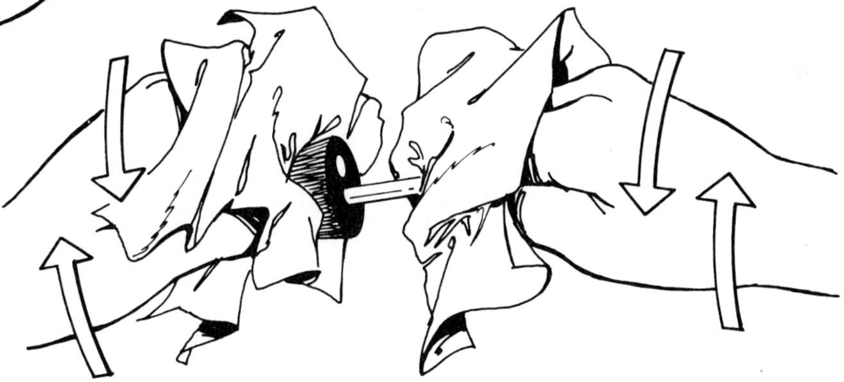

Protect your hands with a cloth or paper towels.

Never force the tubing into the stopper. Ease it in with a gentle twisting motion.

B:5 Using Chemicals and Reagents

Craig Kramer

FIGURE 15.
Use a spatula to remove solids from bottles. Always clean the spatula before inserting it into a bottle containing another chemical.

Craig Kramer

FIGURE 14.
When smelling a substance use a fanning motion to direct the vapor toward you. Never smell a substance in a test tube directly.

FIGURE 16.
Craig Kramer

A solid is easily transferred to a test tube using folded paper.

Craig Kramer

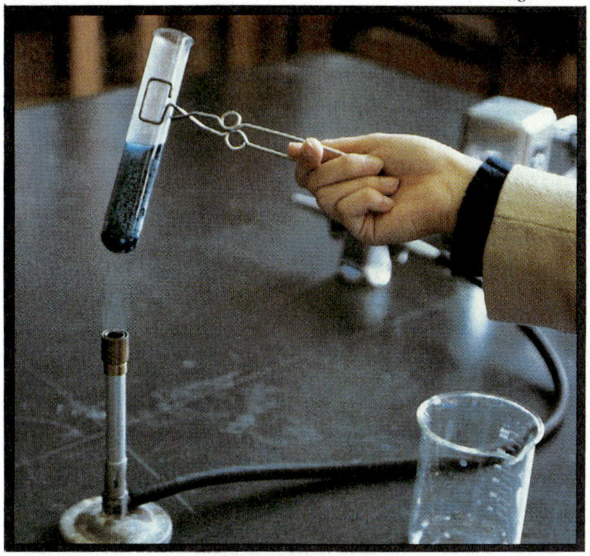

FIGURE 17.

When heating a test tube, always point the mouth of the tube away from yourself and others in the area.

FIGURE 18.

Craig Kramer

A beaker or paper can be used to catch the solid. Tilt and roll the bottle.

Craig Kramer

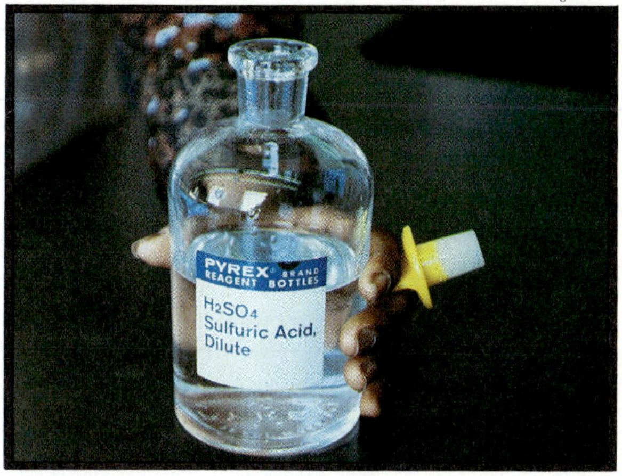

FIGURE 19.

Grip the top of a reagent bottle between your fingers. Hold it as you pour the liquid. In using a pipet always wash a dropping pipet before inserting it into another reagent.

FIGURE 20.

Craig Kramer

In preparing acid solutions slowly add concentrated acid to water; **never** the reverse.

B:6 Safety in the Science Classroom

The science classroom is a safe place in which to perform activities if you are careful. You must assume responsibility for the safety of yourself and your classmates. Here are some safety rules to help guide you in protecting yourself and others from injury.

1. Do not perform activities that are unauthorized. Always obtain your teacher's permission.
2. Study your assignment. If you are in doubt about any procedure, ask your teacher for help.
3. Use the safety equipment provided for you. Know the location of the fire extinguisher, safety shower, fire blanket, and first aid kit.
4. Safety glasses and safety apron should be worn when any activity calls for heating, pouring, or mixing of chemicals.
5. Report any accident, injury, or incorrect procedure to your teacher at once.
6. Smother fires with a towel. If clothing should catch fire, smother it with a blanket or coat or quench it under a safety shower. NEVER RUN.
7. Handle chemicals and bend glassware only under the direction of your teacher. If you spill acid or another corrosive chemical, wash it off immediately with water. Never taste any chemical substance or draw poisonous materials into a glass tube with your mouth. Never inhale chemicals. Keep combustible materials away from open flames.
8. Place broken glass and solid substances in designated containers. Keep insoluble waste material out of the sink.
9. When your activity is completed, be sure to turn off the water and gas and disconnect electrical connections. Clean your work area. Return all materials and apparatus to their proper places.

First Aid

1. Report all accidents or injuries to your teacher at once.
2. Know where and how to report an accident or injury. Know the location of the phone and fire alarm; and where to locate the nurse.
3. All cuts and bruises should be treated as directed by the instructions included in your first aid kit and should then be reported to a nurse or physician.
4. In case of severe bleeding, apply pressure or a compress directly to the wound. GET MEDICAL ATTENTION IMMEDIATELY.
5. If any substance is spilled on you or gets into your eyes, wash with plenty of water and notify your teacher for additional aid.
6. Minor burns should be immersed in cold water immediately. In case of severe burns, NOTIFY YOUR TEACHER AT ONCE.
7. In case of fainting or collapse, give the person fresh air and recline him/her so that the head is lower than the body. NOTIFY YOUR TEACHER AT ONCE. Mouth-to-mouth resuscitation may be necessary. Call a nurse or physican.
8. In case of poisoning, NOTIFY YOUR TEACHER WHO WILL CALL A PHYSICIAN AT ONCE. Note the suspected poisoning agent.
9. If any solution, acid, or base is spilled on you or your desk, wash the area with plenty of water at once. *Baking soda* (sodium bicarbonate) may be used on *acid burns* and *boric acid* on *base burns.* NOTIFY YOUR TEACHER AT ONCE.

Appendix C

International Atomic Masses

Element	Symbol	Atomic number	Atomic mass	Element	Symbol	Atomic number	Atomic mass
Actinium	Ac	89	227.02777*	Mercury	Hg	80	200.59
Aluminum	Al	13	26.98154	Molybdenum	Mo	42	95.94
Americium	Am	95	243.06139*	Neodymium	Nd	60	144.24
Antimony	Sb	51	121.75	Neon	Ne	10	20.179
Argon	Ar	18	39.948	Neptunium	Np	93	237.04819
Arsenic	As	33	74.9216	Nickel	Ni	28	58.70
Astatine	At	85	209.98704*	Niobium	Nb	41	92.9064
Barium	Ba	56	137.33	Nitrogen	N	7	14.0067
Berkelium	Bk	97	247.07032*	Nobelium	No	102	255.093*
Beryllium	Be	4	9.01218	Osmium	Os	76	190.2
Bismuth	Bi	83	208.9804	Oxygen	O	8	15.9994
Boron	B	5	10.81	Palladium	Pd	46	106.4
Bromine	Br	35	79.904	Phosphorus	P	15	30.97376
Cadmium	Cd	48	112.41	Platinum	Pt	78	195.09
Calcium	Ca	20	40.08	Plutonium	Pu	94	244.06424*
Californium	Cf	98	251.07961*	Polonium	Po	84	208.98244*
Carbon	C	6	12.011	Potassium	K	19	39.0983
Cerium	Ce	58	140.12	Praseodymium	Pr	59	140.9077
Cesium	Cs	55	132.9054	Promethium	Pm	61	144.91279*
Chlorine	Cl	17	35.453	Protactinium	Pa	91	231.03590*
Chromium	Cr	24	51.996	Radium	Ra	88	226.0254
Cobalt	Co	27	58.9332	Radon	Rn	86	222*
Copper	Cu	29	63.546	Rhenium	Re	75	186.207
Curium	Cm	96	247.07038*	Rhodium	Rh	45	102.9055
Dysprosium	Dy	66	162.50	Rubidium	Rb	37	85.4678
Einsteinium	Es	99	254.08805*	Ruthenium	Ru	44	101.07
Erbium	Er	68	167.26	Samarium	Sm	62	150.4
Europium	Eu	63	151.96	Scandium	Sc	21	44.9559
Fermium	Fm	100	257.09515*	Selenium	Se	34	78.96
Fluorine	F	9	18.998403	Silicon	Si	14	28.0855
Francium	Fr	87	223.01976*	Silver	Ag	47	107.868
Gadolinium	Gd	64	157.25	Sodium	Na	11	22.98977
Gallium	Ga	31	69.72	Strontium	Sr	38	87.62
Germanium	Ge	32	72.59	Sulfur	S	16	32.06
Gold	Au	79	196.9665	Tantalum	Ta	73	180.9479
Hafnium	Hf	72	178.49	Technetium	Tc	43	96.90639*
Helium	He	2	4.00260	Tellurium	Te	52	127.60
Holmium	Ho	67	164.9304	Terbium	Tb	65	158.9254
Hydrogen	H	1	1.0079	Thallium	Tl	81	204.37
Indium	In	49	114.82	Thorium	Th	90	232.0381
Iodine	I	53	126.9045	Thulium	Tm	69	168.9342
Iridium	Ir	77	192.22	Tin	Sn	50	118.69
Iron	Fe	26	55.847	Titanium	Ti	22	47.90
Krypton	Kr	36	83.80	Tungsten	W	74	183.85
Lanthanum	La	57	138.9055	Uranium	U	92	238.029
Lawrencium	Lr	103	256.099*	Vanadium	V	23	50.9414
Lead	Pb	82	207.2	Xenon	Xe	54	131.30
Lithium	Li	3	6.941	Ytterbium	Yb	70	173.04
Lutetium	Lu	71	174.97	Yttrium	Y	39	88.9059
Magnesium	Mg	12	24.305	Zinc	Zn	30	65.38
Manganese	Mn	25	54.9380	Zirconium	Zr	40	91.22
Mendelevium	Md	101	258*	Element 104†		104	257*
				Element 105†		105	260*

The mass of the isotope with the longest known half-life.

†Names for elements 104 and 105 have not yet been approved by the IUPAC. The USSR has proposed Kurchatovium (Ku) for element 104 and Bohrium (Bh) for element 105. The United States has proposed Rutherfordium (Rf) for element 104 and Hahnium (Ha) for element 105.

The Periodic Table

(Based on Carbon 12 = 12.0000)

	IA	IIA	IIIB	IVB	VB	VIB	VIIB	VIIIB	VIIIB	VIIIB	IB	IIB	IIIA	IVA	VA	VIA	VIIA	VIIIA (Noble Gases)
1	1 **H** Hydrogen 1.0079																	2 **He** Helium 4.00260
2	3 **Li** Lithium 6.941	4 **Be** Beryllium 9.01218											5 **B** Boron 10.82	6 **C** Carbon 12.011	7 **N** Nitrogen 14.0067	8 **O** Oxygen 15.9994	9 **F** Fluorine 18.998403	10 **Ne** Neon 20.179
3	11 **Na** Sodium 22.98977	12 **Mg** Magnesium 24.305											13 **Al** Aluminum 26.98154	14 **Si** Silicon 28.0855	15 **P** Phosphorus 30.97376	16 **S** Sulfur 32.06	17 **Cl** Chlorine 35.453	18 **Ar** Argon 39.948
4	19 **K** Potassium 39.0983	20 **Ca** Calcium 40.08	21 **Sc** Scandium 44.9559	22 **Ti** Titanium 47.90	23 **V** Vanadium 50.9414	24 **Cr** Chromium 51.996	25 **Mn** Manganese 54.9380	26 **Fe** Iron 55.847	27 **Co** Cobalt 58.9332	28 **Ni** Nickel 58.70	29 **Cu** Copper 63.546	30 **Zn** Zinc 65.38	31 **Ga** Gallium 69.72	32 **Ge** Germanium 72.59	33 **As** Arsenic 74.9216	34 **Se** Selenium 78.96	35 **Br** Bromine 79.904	36 **Kr** Krypton 83.80
5	37 **Rb** Rubidium 85.4678	38 **Sr** Strontium 87.62	39 **Y** Yttrium 88.9059	40 **Zr** Zirconium 91.22	41 **Nb** Niobium 92.9064	42 **Mo** Molybdenum 95.94	43 **Tc** Technetium 96.90639	44 **Ru** Ruthenium 101.07	45 **Rh** Rhodium 102.9055	46 **Pd** Palladium 106.4	47 **Ag** Silver 107.868	48 **Cd** Cadmium 112.41	49 **In** Indium 114.82	50 **Sn** Tin 118.69	51 **Sb** Antimony 121.75	52 **Te** Tellurium 127.60	53 **I** Iodine 126.9045	54 **Xe** Xenon 131.30
6	55 **Cs** Cesium 132.9054	56 **Ba** Barium 137.34	71 **Lu** Lutetium 174.97	72 **Hf** Hafnium 178.49	73 **Ta** Tantalum 180.9479	74 **W** Tungsten 183.85	75 **Re** Rhenium 186.207	76 **Os** Osmium 190.2	77 **Ir** Iridium 192.22	78 **Pt** Platinum 195.09	79 **Au** Gold 196.9665	80 **Hg** Mercury 200.59	81 **Tl** Thallium 204.37	82 **Pb** Lead 207.2	83 **Bi** Bismuth 208.9804	84 **Po** Polonium 208.98244	85 **At** Astatine 209.98704	86 **Rn** Radon 222
7	87 **Fr** Francium 223.09176	88 **Ra** Radium 226	103 **Lr** Lawrencium 256.099	104 257	105 260													

Metals; Transition Elements; Nonmetals

Rare Earth Elements

LANTHANIDE SERIES	57 **La** Lanthanum 138.9055	58 **Ce** Cerium 140.12	59 **Pr** Praseodymium 140.9077	60 **Nd** Neodymium 144.24	61 **Pm** Promethium 144.91279	62 **Sm** Samarium 150.4	63 **Eu** Europium 151.96	64 **Gd** Gadolinium 157.25	65 **Tb** Terbium 158.9254	66 **Dy** Dysprosium 162.50	67 **Ho** Holmium 164.9304	68 **Er** Erbium 167.26	69 **Tm** Thulium 168.9342	70 **Yb** Ytterbium 173.04
ACTINIDE SERIES	89 **Ac** Actinium 227.0274	90 **Th** Thorium 232.0381	91 **Pa** Protactinium 231.03590	92 **U** Uranium 238.029	93 **Np** Neptunium 237.04819	94 **Pu** Plutonium 244.06424	95 **Am** Americium 243.06139	96 **Cm** Curium 247.07038	97 **Bk** Berkelium 247.07032	98 **Cf** Californium 251.07961	99 **Es** Einsteinium 254.08805	100 **Fm** Fermium 257.09515	101 **Md** Mendelevium 258	102 **No** Nobelium 255.093

Key: Atomic number — 12; Element symbol — **Mg** (Magnesium); Average atomic mass — 24.305

Glossary

Glossary

The glossary contains all of the major science terms of the text and their definitions. Below is a pronunciation key to help you use these terms. The word or term will be given in boldface type. If necessary, the pronunciation will follow the term in parentheses.

a . . . back (bak)	ew . . . food (fewd)
ay . . . day (day)	yoo . . . pure (pyoor)
ah . . . father (fahth ur)	yew . . . few (fyew)
ow . . . flower (flow ar)	uh . . . comma (cahm uh)
ar . . . car (car)	u (+con) . . . flower (flow ur)
e . . . less (les)	sh . . . shelf (shelf)
ee . . . leaf (leef)	ch . . . nature (nay chur)
ih . . . trip (trihp)	g . . . gift (gihft)
i (i + con + e) . . . idea	
(i dee uh, life, life)	j . . . gem (jem)
oh . . . go (goh)	ing . . . sing (sing)
aw . . . soft (sawft)	zh . . . vision (vihzh un)
or . . . orbit (or but)	k . . . cake (kayk)
oy . . . coin (coyn)	s . . . seed, cent (seed, sent)
oo . . . foot (foot)	z . . . zone, raise (zohn, rayz)

A

absolute zero: zero on the Kelvin temperature scale

acceleration (ak sel uh RAY shun): rate of increase in speed

acid: a substance which increases the hydronium ion concentration when added to water

acid anhydride: compound which produces an acid when added to water

acoustics: study of sound and its effect on people

action force: a force exerted on an object

alcohol: a hydrocarbon in which a hydrogen atom has been replaced by an —OH group

alkali: a substance having the properties of a base

alkaline: having a pH above 7

alkane series (methane series): group of saturated hydrocarbons having the general formula C_nH_{2n+2}

alkene series: group of unsaturated hydrocarbons with one double bond

alkyne series: group of unsaturated hydrocarbons with one triple bond

allotropes (AL uh trohps): different molecular forms of the same element

alloy: a mixture of two or more metals

alpha particle (α): a positively charged helium nucleus with two protons and two neutrons

alpha ray: high speed alpha particles (helium nuclei) shot out from radioactive atomic nuclei

alternating current (A.C.): a continuous back and forth movement of electrons in a circuit

ammeter: instrument used to measure the amount of electric current in a circuit in amperes

amino acid: organic compound that contains nitrogen and is a building block in protein molecules

amorphous (uh MOR fus) **solid:** material such as glass or plastic which has no regular crystalline shape

ampere (AM pihr): the rate of electron flow in a circuit

amplify: to increase the amplitude of a wave; increase the volume of sound or strength of an electric current

amplitude: the distance a wave rises or falls as it travels

anesthetic: a substance used to produce a loss of sensation

angle of incidence: angle made between a wave striking a barrier and the normal to the surface

angle of reflection: angle between a reflected wave and the normal to the barrier from which it is reflected

anhydride (an HI dride): a compound formed from another by the removal of water; meaning "without water"

anode (+): positive electrode in an electrical circuit; gains electrons in a circuit

antacid: a base used to counteract the properties of an acid

aqueous: pertaining to water

armature (AR muh chur): an electromagnet that is the rotating part of a motor or generator

arithmetic unit: part of a computer that does the calculation

atom: smallest piece of an element which retains the properties of that element

atomic mass: mass of an atom compared to a standard mass, the carbon-12 atom

atomic mass number (A): average atomic mass rounded to the nearest whole number

atomic mass unit (a.m.u.): 1/12 the mass of the carbon-12 atom

atomic number (Z): number of protons in the nucleus of an atom

average atomic mass: average of the atomic masses of the naturally occurring isotopes which make up an element

B

barometer: instrument used to measure air pressure

base: a substance which increases the hydroxide ion concentration when added to water

basic anhydride: compound which produces a base when added to water

battery: two wet or dry cells that produce an electric current

beta particle (β): electron from a radioactive atom; negatively charged

beta ray: stream of fast moving electrons shot out from a radioactive atom

binary (BI nuh ree) **compound:** compound composed of only two elements

boiling point: the temperature at which a substance changes rapidly from a liquid to a gaseous state

Boyle's law: the volume of a gas decreases as the pressure on it increases if the temperature remains constant

C

calorimeter (kal uh RIHM ut ur): instrument used to measure heat energy

carbohydrate: compound composed solely of carbon, hydrogen, and oxygen that is a nutrient in food

catalyst: substance which increases or decreases the rate of a chemical reaction

cathode (−): negative electrode in an electric circuit; releases electrons in a circuit

cathode-ray tube: a vacuum tube which emits a beam of electrons from the cathode to a screen at the opposite end of the tube

Celsius (SEL see us) **temperature scale:** temperature scale on which 0° is the freezing point of water and 100° is the boiling point

centimeter (cm): metric unit of length; 1/100 of a meter

centripetal (sen TRIHP ut ul) **force:** a force acting toward the center around which an object travels in a circular path

Charles' law: the volume of a gas increases as its temperature increases if the pressure remains constant

chemical reactivity: ease with which an element reacts with other elements

chemical change: change in which a substance becomes another substance having different properties

chemical equation: shorthand description of a chemical reaction containing symbols and formulas

chemical property: characteristic of a material which depends on the material's reaction with other materials

chlorophyll: the green coloring pigment in plants

circuit: closed-loop path of conduction through which an electric current flows

cloud chamber: device which detects nuclear particles through the formation of cloud tracks

coefficient: number placed in front of a formula; used in balancing chemical equations

compound: a substance containing two or more elements chemically combined

compound machine: two or more simple machines working together

compression: most dense concentration of wave particles in a compressional wave

compressional wave: wave in which matter vibrates in the same direction as the wave moves

computer: complex electronic device used to solve problems through mathematical operations

concave lens: a lens which is thinner in the middle than at the edges; used to correct nearsightedness

concentration: amount of matter per unit volume

conclusion: a judgment or decision based on observation

condensation: change from the gaseous state to the liquid state

conduction: movement of heat or electricity through a substance; gain or loss of electrons through direct contact with a charged object

conductor: a substance through which heat or electricity can flow readily

conservation of momentum: principle which states that momentum cannot be created or destroyed

control: group or activity that serves as a standard of comparison for change in an experiment

control unit: part of the computer that regulates its operation

convection: transfer of heat energy by the actual movement of the heated matter; occurs in liquids and gases

convex lens: a lens which is thicker in the middle than at the edges; used to correct farsightedness

corrosion: destructive chemical change in a metal; e.g. rusting

cosmic rays: very high energy nuclear rays from outer space

coulomb (KEW lahm): unit of electric charge

covalent bond: bond between atoms produced by the sharing of electrons

covalent bonding: type of bonding in which electrons are shared

crest: high point of a wave

cryogenics (kri uh JEN ihks): scientific study of physical and chemical properties at very low temperatures

crystal: solid material having a regular, geometric form characteristic of a given compound or element

D

deceleration (dee sel uh RAY shun): rate of decrease in speed; negative acceleration

decomposition reaction: chemical change in which a compound breaks down or decomposes into other compounds and/or elements

density: mass of a substance per unit of volume; expressed in g/cm^3

deuterium (dew TIHR ee um): hydrogen isotope with one proton and one neutron in its nucleus

diatomic: a molecule composed of two atoms

diffraction grating: piece of transparent or reflecting material, contains many thousands of parallel lines per centimeter; used to produce a light spectrum by interference

digital computer: a device using numbers to solve mathematical problems; specifically, an electronic machine which uses stored instructions and information to perform complex computations at rapid speed

diode: electric vacuum tube containing a filament and a plate

Direct current (D.C.): flow of electrons in one direction through a conductor

discharge: loss of negative or positive electric charge

dissociation (dihs oh see AY shun): process in which an ionic compound forms ions when dissolved in water

distillation (dihs tuh LAY shun): physical separation of the parts of a mixture through vaporization and condensation

Doppler effect: change in wavelength caused by the motion of the wave source

double replacement reaction: chemical change in which two ions in two different compounds replace each other, forming a precipitate, gas, or water

dry cell: device for producing a current with moist chemicals

E

efficiency (ih FIHSH un see): the ratio of the work output of a machine to its work input

effort arm: the distance from the fulcrum to the effort force in a lever

electricity: a collection of electrons or movement of electrons

electrolysis (ih lek TRAHL uh sus): the decomposition of a compound into simpler substances by passing an electric current through the compound

electromagnet: soft iron core surrounded by a coil of wire through which an electric current is passed, thus magnetizing the core

electromagnetic spectrum: invisible, transverse energy waves, ranging from low frequency to very high frequency, which can travel at the speed of light in a vacuum

electron: negatively charged particle in an atom

electron cloud model: model of an atom showing a cloud of negative charge surrounding the nucleus

electronics: study of the release, behavior, and effects of electrons

electroscope (ih LEK truh skohp): instrument used for detecting positive and negative electrical charges

element: a substance which cannot be broken down into simpler substances by ordinary means

endothermic (en duh THUR mihk) **reaction:** a chemical change in which energy is taken on during the reaction

energy: ability to produce motion or change

energy level: average distance of an electron from the nucleus in an atom

equilibrium (ee kwuh LIHB ree um): the state of balance between equal opposing forces

evaporation (ih vap uh RAY shun): change from the liquid to the gaseous state

exothermic (ek soh THUR mihk) **reaction:** a chemical change in which the energy released is greater than the energy required to start the reaction

experiment: a process designed to yield observations under carefully controlled conditions

F

fat: compound composed of carbon, hydrogen, and oxygen that is a nutrient in food

flame test: procedure for identifying an element by heating it in a flame and observing the color given off

fluorescent: emitting light only when exposed to radiation such as cathode rays, X rays, and ultraviolet rays

focal length: distance between the principal focus of a lens or mirror and its optical center

force: any push or pull

formula: group of symbols used to represent a compound

formula mass: sum of mass numbers of the atoms present in a formula of an ionic compound

fractionation (frak shuh NAY shun): a type of distillation in which compounds in petroleum are separated

frequency: number of waves that pass a given point in a given unit of time

friction: a force that opposes motion

fulcrum (FUL krum): the point on which a lever rotates

G

galvanometer (gal vuh NAHM ut ur): a device consisting of a coil of wire rotating between the poles of a magnet; used to detect small electric currents

gamma ray (γ): high energy wave of high frequency and with a wavelength shorter than X rays

gas: state of matter which lacks definite shape or volume

Geiger counter: instrument used to detect radioactivity through the formation of an electric current

generator: a machine which changes mechanical energy into electrical energy

gram (g): unit of mass

gravity: mutual force of attraction which exists between all objects in the universe; force the earth exerts on all objects on or near it

ground: connection of an object to the earth by an electrical conductor to allow electrons to move freely into and out of the object

H

half-life: time required for one-half of the atoms in a radioactive material to decay

halogen: member of Group VIIA; reactive nonmetal

heat: a form of kinetic energy of molecules

heat of condensation: number of joules per gram given up when a vapor changes to a liquid without a change in temperature

heat of fusion: amount of heat required to melt 1 gram of a solid

heat of vaporization: amount of heat required to change 1 gram of a liquid to a gas

hemoglobin: red blood pigment containing iron

hertz: unit of wave frequency equivalent to 1 cycle per second

horizontal: level with the horizon or parallel to the ground

hydrated crystal: crystal that contains water molecules

hydrocarbon: compound containing only carbon and hydrogen

hydronium (hi DROH nee um) **ion:** H_3O^+; a positive ion containing a proton (hydrogen ion) bonded to a water molecule

hydroxide (hi DRAHK side) **ion:** OH^-; a negative ion containing one oxygen atom and one hydrogen atom

hypothesis (hi PAHTH uh sus): proposed answer to a question or tentative solution to a problem

I

image: reproduction of an object formed with lenses or mirrors

inclined plane: a slanted surface used to raise objects; a simple machine

index of refraction: amount that light is refracted when it enters a substance; ratio of speed of light in a vacuum to its speed in a given substance

indicator: chemical which changes color in an acid or a base

inertia (ihn UR shuh): tendency of matter to remain at rest or in uniform motion unless acted on by a force

input: information sent into the circuits of a computer

input signal: an electric current that becomes amplified

insulator (IHN suh layt ur): a substance through which heat or electricity cannot flow readily

integrated circuit: small electronic device which has replaced larger transistors and vacuum tubes in electronic equipment

interference: the addition of crossing wave patterns resulting in a loss of energy in certain areas and reinforcement of energy in other areas

ion: a charged particle formed from an atom or atoms that have gained or lost one or more electrons

ionic bond: a type of bonding in which ions are held together by the strong attraction of their opposite charges

ionization (i uh nuh ZAY shun): process in which a molecular compound dissolves in water to form ions

isomers (I suh murz): compounds having the same molecular formula but different structural formulas

isotopes (I suh tohps): atoms of the same element with different numbers of neutrons

insoluble: will not dissolve

J

joule: a unit of work or energy

junction box: place where circuits are connected together

K

kilometer (km): unit of length; 1000 m

kilowatt-hour (KWH): unit used to measure electrical energy; equal to 1000 watt-hours

kinetic (kuh NET ihk) **energy:** energy of motion

L

law of conservation of masses: mass is neither gained nor lost in a chemical change

law of multiple proportions: the same elements may unite in different ratios to form different compounds

law of reflection: angle of incidence equals the angle of reflection

lens: curved, transparent object; usually made of glass or clear plastic

lever: a bar free to rotate around a point; a simple machine

liquid: state of matter having a constant volume but no definite shape

litmus paper: an indicator used to test for an acid or base

liter (L): a unit of volume equivalent to 1000 cm^3

luminous (LOO muh nus): able to glow in the dark

M

machine: a device which makes work easier by changing the speed, direction, or amount of a force

magnetic field: area of magnetic lines of force

magnetism: a property of matter in which there is an attraction due to unlike poles

mass: quantity of matter in a body

matter: anything that has mass and takes up space

mechanical advantage (M.A.): the amount by which the applied force is multiplied by a machine

melting: change from solid state to liquid state

melting point: the temperature at which a substance changes from a solid to a liquid

metal: a substance that has a specific luster, is a good conductor of heat and electricity, and can be pounded or drawn into various shapes; usually has one, two, or three electrons in the outer energy level

metalloid (MET ul oyd): element, such as boron, having properties of both metals and nonmetals

meter (m): unit of length

milliliter (mL): unit of volume; 1/1000 of a liter

millimeter (mm): unit of length; 1/1000 of a meter

mixture: two or more elements or compounds which are blended without combining chemically

model: a representation of an idea in order to make it more understandable

molecular mass: sum of the atomic mass numbers for the atoms in a molecule

molecule: smallest particle of covalent compound

momentum: mass of an object multiplied by its velocity

N

neutralization (new truh luh ZAY shun): chemical reaction in which hydronium ions (acid) and hydroxide ions (base) combine to form water

neutron: neutral particle found in the atomic nucleus which has a mass about equal to a proton

newton (N): unit of force; force required to accelerate a 1-kg mass at the rate 1 m/s^2

Newton's first law of motion: an object remains in a state of rest unless a force causes it to move, and an object continues in motion along a straight line unless a force stops it or causes the object to change direction

Newton's law of gravitation: the gravitational attraction between two objects is proportional to the product of their masses divided by the square of the distance between them

Newton's second law of motion: the acceleration of an object is directly proportional to the size of the force producing the acceleration and inversely proportional to the mass of the body

Newton's third law of motion: for every force there is an equal and opposite force

noble gas: member of Group VIIIA; a stable gas that usually does not combine chemically

noise: sounds produced by irregular vibrations; sound at the wrong time and place

nonmetal: element with more than four electrons in the outer energy level, lacks the typical properties of a metal

normal: a line drawn perpendicular to a line or plane

nuclear chain reaction: series of continuous rapid nuclear fissions, beginning with the splitting of an atom

nuclear decay series: the nuclear reactions through which a radioactive element breaks down; in each reaction, a different radioactive element is formed

nuclear emulsion (ih MUL shun): a photographic emulsion, containing silver bromide dissolved in a gelatinlike solid, used to detect nuclear particles

nuclear fission: nuclear change in which a nucleus is divided into two nuclei

nuclear fusion: nuclear change in which two or more atomic nuclei unite to form a single heavier nucleus

nuclear reactor: device for producing energy from a nuclear fuel, such as uranium, through a controlled chain reaction

nucleus: the central portion of an atom containing neutrons and protons

nuclide: a radioactive atom

O

observation: act of taking notice and gathering data; scientific method basic to the process of science

ohm: unit for measuring electric resistance

Ohm's law: the relationship between volts and amperes in a circuit; $I = V/R$

organic compound: compound that contains carbon

organic chemistry: study of carbon and its compounds

output: information obtained from a computer's circuits

output signal: electric current after it is amplified

oxidation number: combining capacity of an element

P

parabola (puh RAB uh luh): a curved line representing the path of a projectile; the shape of the surface of a parabolic mirror

parabolic (par uh BAHL ihk) **mirror:** curved mirror

parallel circuit: a circuit in which two or more conductors are connected across two common points in the circuit to provide separate conducting paths for the current

pascal: unit of pressure

periodic law: when elements are arranged in order of increasing atomic number, there is a periodic repetition of similar properties

periodic table: an arrangement of the chemical elements, according to their atomic numbers, in vertical columns having similar properties and horizontal rows showing shifts in properties

permanent magnet: substance that remains magnetized for a long time after the magnetizing force has been removed

perpendicular: at right angles to

petroleum: liquid mixture of hydrocarbons that is obtained from wells drilled into the earth

pH: measure of hydronium ion concentration in a solution

phenolphthalein (feen ul THAYL een): an indicator which is colorless in an acid solution and pink in a basic solution

photochemical smog: substance that forms in the atmosphere as a result of the action of sunlight on airborne pollutants

photoconductor: a metal whose electric conductivity is controlled by light

photoelectric cell (photocell): a device containing a photoelectric metal which produces an electrical current when struck by light

photoelectric effect: electrons released from the atoms of certain metals when struck by light

photon: a packet or bundle of radiant wave energy

photosensitive: changed by the action of light or other radiant energy

physical change: change in size, shape, or state without a change in composition

physical property: characteristic of a substance which may be observed without changing the chemical composition of the substance

physical science: the study of matter and energy

physics: the study of how matter and energy are related

pitch: tone of a sound wave, determined by the frequency of the wave; the greater the frequency, the higher the pitch

plane mirror: mirror with a flat surface

plasma: state of matter in which atoms lose their electrons

polarized light: light in which all waves are vibrating in a single plane

pollution: unwanted or harmful matter or energy in the environment

polyatomic ion: ion containing two or more elements chemically combined; a group of atoms which act together as one ion or charged atom

polymer (PAHL uh mur): large molecule formed from the combination of molecules of many compounds

polymerization (pahl uh muh ruh ZAY shun): process in which a large molecule is formed from the combination of smaller units or molecules

potential difference: the difference between the potentials of two points in an electric field

potential (puh TEN chul) **energy:** energy of rest or position

power: amount of work done per unit of time

precipitate: a solid that separates from a solution by a physical change

pressure: force applied per unit of area

principal focus: common point to which rays parallel to the principal axis converge, or from which they diverge, after reflection or refraction

prism: transparent material with two straight faces at an angle to each other

product: substance formed as a result of a chemical change; substance to the right of a yield sign ($\rightarrow$) in an equation

program: set of instructions which enters a computer

projectile: object such as a stone, ball, bullet, or rocket, which is thrown or shot

protein: organic compound that contains nitrogen and is a nutrient in food

proton: positively charged particle in the nucleus of an atom

pulley: a form of a lever; a simple machine

R

radiation: process of emission and transmission of radiant heat from areas of high temperature to areas of low temperature; energy released from atoms and molecules as they undergo internal nuclear change

radioactive isotope: form of an element which emits high energy radiation from the nucleus

radioactivity: the emitting of high energy radiation from nuclei of radioactive atoms

rarefaction: least dense concentration of wave particles in a compressional wave

rate: ratio between two quantities

reactant: substance which undergoes a chemical change; substance to the left of a yield sign (→) in an equation

reaction force: a force equal to an action force but exerted in the opposite direction

real image: an image which can be projected onto a screen; formed by a parabolic mirror or convex lens

rectifier (REK tuh fire): device for changing alternating current to direct current

reflecting telescope: a telescope in which magnification is produced by a parabolic mirror

reflection: bouncing of a wave or ray off a surface

refracting telescope: a telescope in which magnification is produced by convex lenses

refraction: bending of a wave or light ray, caused by a decrease in speed as it passes from one substance into another

resistance: any opposition which slows down or prevents motion; opposition to the flow of electricity

resistance arm: the distance from the fulcrum to the resistance force in a lever

ring compound: organic compound in which carbon atoms are joined in the shape of a ring

ripple tank: shallow, transparent, waterproof box containing a layer of water about 1 cm deep; used to study waves

S

salt: solid substance produced by evaporation after a neutralization reaction; compound containing a positive ion from a base and a negative ion from an acid

saturated: solution in which the solvent has dissolved the maximum amount of solute at a given temperature

saturated hydrocarbon: hydrocarbon in which each carbon atom is bonded to four other atoms by single bonds

screw: a modified inclined plane; a simple machine

semiconductor: material with a resistance between that of a conductor and an insulator

series circuit: electric circuit in which the parts are connected so that the same current flows through all parts of the circuit

simple machine: device which makes work easier by changing the speed, direction, or amount of force

single displacement reaction: chemical change in which an uncombined or free element replaces an element which is combined in a compound

solid: state of matter having a definite volume and shape

solubility (sahl yuh BIHL ut ee): the amount of a substance (solute) that will dissolve in a specific amount of another substance (solvent)

solute: substance being dissolved in a solvent

solution: mixture in which a substance (solute) is dissolved in another substance (solvent)

solvent: substance in which a solute is dissolved

sound wave: compressional wave produced by vibrations

specific heat: the amount of heat needed to raise the temperature of 1 gram of a substance 1 C°

speed: distance traveled per unit time

stable: term given to a nucleus which is not radioactive; ratio of protons to neutrons is about 1:1

standard: a fixed quantity used for measuring

static electricity: electricity produced by charged bodies

steel: iron alloyed with one or more other metals

structural formula: a simple formula showing the symbols of atoms in a molecule of a compound and how they are bonded

sublimation (sub luh MAY shun): the direct change of state from a solid to a gas

subscript: small number which gives the ratio in which elements are combined in a compound

substituted hydrocarbon: organic compound in which one or more hydrogen atoms in a hydrocarbon have been replaced with another kind of atom

supersaturated solution: a solution containing more solute than the amount it would normally take to saturate it at a given temperature

synthesis reaction: chemical change in which two or more elements or compounds unite to form one compound

synthetic fuel: fuel made from some other substance

T

technology (tek NAHL uh jee): application of science for practical purposes

temperature: a measure of the internal kinetic energy of an object as measured by a thermometer

terminal speed: greatest speed reached by a falling body

tetrahedron (te truh HEE drun): four-sided shape of the molecule formed when a carbon atom shares electrons with four other atoms

theory (THEE uh ree): an explanation based on observations and experiments

thermal pollution: release of heated water into lakes, streams, and oceans

thermocouple: device with two different metals twisted or bonded together, used to produce an electric current

thermonuclear reaction: nuclear fusion reaction occurring at a temperature of millions of degrees

thermostat: device which regulates cooling and heating systems

transistor: semiconductor used as a replacement for vacuum tubes in electronic equipment

transition metals: elements located in the B columns of the periodic table; have two electrons located in the outer energy level

transverse wave: wave in which matter vibrates at right angles to the direction in which the wave travels

triatomic (try uh TAHM ik): molecules composed of three atoms

triode: electric vacuum tube containing a filament, a plate, and a grid

tritium (TRIHT ee um): hydrogen isotope with two neutrons and one proton in its nucleus

trough: valley of a wave

U

ultrasonic (ul truh SAHN ihk): sound waves with frequencies above 20 000 hertz

unsaturated hydrocarbon: hydrocarbon in which two or more carbon atoms are joined by double or triple bonds

unsaturated solution: solution containing less solute than the amount it would take to saturate it at a given temperature

V

vacuum tube: a gas-tight container, usually of glass, from which air is removed to form a vacuum; used in radios, televisions, and stereos

vaporization (vay pruh ZAY shun): change from liquid state to gaseous state

velocity (vuh LAHS ut ee): speed and direction of a moving object

vertical: extending up and down, or at right angles to the ground

vibration: rapid back and forth movement

virtual image: an image formed by a mirror or lens which cannot be projected onto a surface

visible light spectrum: band of colors produced by a prism when white light is passed through it

vitamin: complex organic compound present in tiny amounts as a nutrient in food

volt (V): unit of potential difference

voltmeter: an instrument used to measure the potential difference between two points in an electric circuit

volume: the amount of space matter occupies

W

watt (W): unit of power

watt-hour: unit used to measure electric power in a unit of time

wave: rhythmic disturbance which travels through space or matter

wavelength: total linear length of one wave crest and trough

wedge: a simple machine composed of two inclined planes put together

weight: the force with which an object is attracted toward the earth; measurement of gravity force

wet cell: device for producing electric current from two metals in a chemical solution

wheel and axle: a simple machine which is a variation of the lever

work: product of the force exerted on an object multiplied by the distance the object moved

work input: the effort force multiplied by the effort distance

work output: the resistance force multiplied by the resistance distance

X

X rays: invisible electromagnetic radiation of great penetrating power

Index

Index

A

B

J

K

L

M

N

O

P

R

1 2 3 4 5 6 7 8 9 10 11 12 13 14 15 — 85 84 83 82 81 80